1. "Help!" (1921 poster by Moor).

RUSSIA UNDER THE BOLSHEVIK REGIME
1919-1924

by the same author

THE FORMATION OF THE SOVIET UNION:
COMMUNISM AND NATIONALISM, 1917-23

STRUVE: LIBERAL ON THE LEFT, 1870-1905

RUSSIA UNDER THE OLD REGIME

STRUVE: LIBERAL ON THE RIGHT, 1905-44

SURVIVAL IS NOT ENOUGH

RUSSIA OBSERVED

THE RUSSIAN REVOLUTION, 1899-1919

RUSSIA UNDER THE BOLSHEVIK REGIME

1919-1924

RICHARD PIPES

HARVILL
An Imprint of HarperCollins*Publishers*

This edition published by arrangement with
Alfred A. Knopf Inc. 1994

First published in Great Britain in 1994 by
Harvill
an imprint of HarperCollins*Publishers*,
77/85 Fulham Palace Road,
Hammersmith, London W6 8JB

1 3 5 7 9 8 6 4 2

© 1994 by Richard Pipes
Maps for this edition made by Bernhard H. Wagner

The author asserts his moral right to
be identified as the author of this work.

A CIP catalogue record for this book
is available from the British Library.

ISBN 0 00 272088 4

Set in Times Roman

Manufactured in the United States of America

Truth *is* stranger than Fiction, but it is because Fiction is obliged to stick to possibilities; Truth is not.

—MARK TWAIN

CONTENTS

ILLUSTRATIONS

MAPS

ABBREVIATIONS

AfS	*Archiv für Sozialgeschichte*
AHR	*American Historical Review*
AiF	*Argumenty i fakty*
AfS	*Archiv für Sozialwissenschaft*
ARR	*Arkhiv Russkoi Revoliutsii*
BD	*Beloe delo*
BSE	*Bol'shaia sovetskaia entsiklopediia,* 65 vols.
Cahiers	*Cahiers du monde russe et soviétique*
Dekrety	*Dekrety sovetskoi vlasti,* 13 vols. (Moscow, 1957–)
Denikin, *Ocherki*	A. I. Denikin, *Ocherki russkoi smuty,* 5 vols. (Paris-Berlin, 1921–26)
EZh	*Ekonomicheskaia zhizn'*
FA	*Foreign Affairs*
IA	*Istoricheskii arkhiv*
ISSSR	*Istoriia SSSR*
IzvTsK	*Izvestiia TsK KPSS*
Jahrbücher	*Jahrbücher für Geschichte Osteuropas*
JCEA	*Journal of Central European Affairs*
JMH	*Journal of Modern History*
KA	*Krasnyi arkhiv*
KL	*Krasnaia letopis'*
KN	*Krasnaia nov'*
Lenin, *Khronika*	V. I. Lenin, *Biograficheskaia Khronika, 1870–1924,* 13 vols. (Moscow 1970–85)
Lenin, *PSS*	V. I. Lenin, *Polnoe sobranie sochinenii,* 5th ed., 55 vols. (Moscow, 1958–65)
Lenin, *Sochineniia*	V. I. Lenin, *Sochineniia,* 3rd ed., 30 vols. (Moscow-Leningrad, 1927–33)
LN	*Literaturnoe nasledstvo*
LR	*Literaturnaia Rossiia*
LS	*Leninskii sbornik*
MN	*Moscow News*
NP	*Narodnoe prosveshchenie*

NV	*Nash vek*
NYT	*New York Times*
NZh	*Novaia zhizn'*
PAN, Dokumenty	Polska Akademia Nauk, *Dokumenty i materialy do historii stosunkow Polsko-Radzieckich,* II (Warsaw, 1961)
PiR	*Pechat' i revoliutsiia*
PK	*Proletarskaia kul'tura*
PN	*Poslednie novosti* (Paris)
RiK	*Revoliutsiia i kul'tura*
RevR	*Revoliutsionnaia Rossiia*
RiTs	*Revoliutsiia i tserkov'*
RM	*Russkaia mysl'*
RTsKhIDNI	Russian Center for the Preservation and Study of Documents of Modern History (Moscow)
RR	Richard Pipes, *The Russian Revolution* (New York and London, 1990)
RuR	*Russian Review*
SR	*Slavic Review*
SS	*Soviet Studies*
SUiR	*Sobranie Uzakonenii i Rasporiazhenii Rabochego i Krest'ianskogo Pravitel'stva*
SV	*Sotsialisticheskii vestnik*
SZ	*Sovremennye zapiski*
TP	Jan M. Meijer, ed., *The Trotsky Papers, 1917–1922,* 2 vols. (The Hague, 1964–71)
VfZ	*Vierteljahreshefte für Zeitgeschichte*
VI	*Voprosy istorii*
VIKPSS	*Voprosy istorii KPSS*
ZhN	*Zhizn' natsionalnostei*

INTRODUCTION

*Russia under the Bolshevik Regime** continues and concludes *The Russian Revolution*; in a sense, it also completes the trilogy begun twenty years ago with the publication of *Russia under the Old Regime*. The present work, however, is meant to stand on its own. It deals with the attempts of the Bolsheviks to defend and expand their authority from the Great Russian base which they had conquered in the winter of 1917–18 to the borderlands of the defunct Russian Empire and beyond, to the rest of the world. By the fall of 1920 it had become apparent that these efforts would not succeed, and that the new regime had to concentrate on building a Communist state at home. The closing part of the book deals with the problems and crises this unexpected development caused Russia's new rulers. In addition, I discuss Communist cultural and religious policies. By treating these and other topics usually ignored in general histories, I seek to fulfill the promise given in the introduction to *The Russian Revolution* to provide a more comprehensive account of the subject than hitherto available: that is, to look beyond the struggle for power which is commonly seen as the quintessence of the Revolution to its makers' designs and uses of that power. The book concludes with the death of Lenin in January 1924, by which time all the institutions and nearly all the practices of the future Stalinism were in place.

The present work was virtually finished when the Soviet Union disintegrated and Russia's new government outlawed the Communist Party. This sudden turn of events provided something of a coda to my work. It must be an uncommon experience for a historian to find that his subject becomes history at the very time that he concludes writing an account of its origins.

The demise of the Communist Party ended its monopoly on archival sources. I was fortunate in the last stages of writing to be given access to what had been the Central Party Archive in Moscow, where are kept the most important documents bearing on the history of the CPSU since 1917. For this opportunity I would like to express gratitude to Mr. R. G.

---

*The title of this book was originally announced as "Russia under the *New* Regime." However, the changes which have occured in Russia during the past two years have invalidated this title, in that what was the "new regime" in 1917 became in 1991 an old regime.

Pikhoia, Director of the Russian Archival Committee, and to Mr. K. M. Anderson, Director of the Russian Center for the Preservation and Study of Documents of Contemporary History (RTsKhIDNI) and his staff. Acquaintance with this material (the personal archive of Lenin and that of his Secretariat, as well as the archives of Stalin, Dzerzhinskii, and others) enabled me to modify and amplify certain parts of my narrative, but in not a single instance did it compel me to revise views which I had formed on the basis of printed sources and archives located in the West. This gives me a certain degree of confidence that no new and startling information from other, still secret, archival repositories—notably the so-called Presidential Archive, which contains minutes of the Politburo, and the files of the Cheka/KGB—is likely to invalidate my account.

I wish to take this opportunity to express thanks to the John M. Olin Foundation for its generous financial support.

Richard Pipes

Russia under the Bolshevik Regime

1

The Civil War:
The First Battles (1918)

In the midst of World War I, in February–March 1917, the tsarist regime which had ruled Russia since the fourteenth century collapsed with startling speed and finality. The causes of its breakdown were many and reached deep into history, but the most immediate of them was public dissatisfaction with the conduct of the war. Russian armies did not acquit themselves well in the campaigns of 1914–16, being repeatedly beaten by the Germans and forced to abandon to them vast and rich territories, including Poland. There were widespread rumors of treason in high places which alienated conservative elements. The inhabitants of cities were angered by inflation and shortages of food and fuel. The spark that ignited the revolutionary conflagration was a mutiny of the Petrograd military garrison, manned by superannuated peasant conscripts. Once the mutiny erupted, public order broke down in no time, the process being encouraged by liberal and radical politicians eager to take over power. With the abdication of Nicholas II on March 2, the entire bureaucratic machinery of the state dissolved.

Into the vacuum stepped intellectuals whose ambitions far outstripped their administrative experience. The liberals, later joined by moderate socialists, staffed the Provisional Government, while the radicals joined the soviets, councils composed of worker and soldier deputies, but run by intellectuals from the socialist parties. The resultant dyarchy proved unworkable. By the summer of 1917, Russia was torn apart by growing social and ethnic conflicts, as communal peasants seized private land, workers took over factories, and the ethnic minorities claimed the right to self-government. Prime Minister Alexander Kerensky attempted to assert dictatorial powers but he was not temperamentally suited for the role, and in any event lacked an effective power base. In the fall, public opinion was severely polarized, with Kerensky trying to steer a middle course between liberals and radicals. The final blow to his authority was a quarrel toward the end of August with the Commander in Chief, General Lavr Kornilov, whom he accused of seeking to usurp his authority. The result was that the army, the only force capable of defending the Government, turned against it, leaving the field open to the Bolsheviks.

The Bolshevik Party was a unique institution. Organized as a conspiratorial group for the specific purpose of seizing power and making a revolution from above, first in Russia and then in the rest of the world, it was profoundly undemocratic in its philosophy and its methods of operation. The prototype for all subsequent totalitarian organizations, it resembled more a secret order than a party in the normally accepted sense. Its founder and undisputed leader, Vladimir Lenin, determined on the very day he learned of the outbreak of the February Revolution that the Bolsheviks would topple the Provisional Government by armed force. His strategy consisted of promising every disaffected group what it wanted: to the peasants, the land; to the soldiers, peace; to the workers, the factories; to the ethnic minorities, independence. None of these slogans were part of the Bolshevik program and all would be thrown overboard once the Bolsheviks were in power, but they served the purpose of alienating large groups of the population from the Government.

In the spring and summer the Bolsheviks made three attempts at taking power, but failed each time: the last, in July, was frustrated by Petrograd soldiers whom the government informed of Lenin's dealings with the German enemy. Following the third unsuccessful putsch, Lenin went into hiding in Finland, and operational command passed to Leon Trotsky. Trotsky and the other Bolshevik leaders decided to camouflage the next attempt at a power seizure as the passing of all power to the soviets, to which end they convened an illegal and unrepresentative Second All-Russian Congress of Soviets on October 25. The coup succeeded because this time the army, angered by Kerensky's treatment of Kornilov, refused to come to his assistance. From Petrograd, the Bolshevik coup spread to the other cities of Russia.

Although power was taken in the name of the soviets, in which all the socialist parties were represented, Lenin refused to admit other socialist parties into his government, staffing it exclusively with Bolsheviks. In the elections to the Constituent Assembly, which was to give Russia a new constitution and administration, the Bolsheviks were severely mauled, receiving less than one-quarter of the votes. Their dispersal of the Assembly in January 1918, after it had met but once, marked the onset of a one-party regime in Russia. Using politicized courts and the Cheka, the newly created secret police, the Bolsheviks unleashed a terror which in the first year of their power effectively silenced opposition on their territory. All organized activity was placed under the control of the Bolshevik Party, which itself was subject to no external controls.

But the Bolsheviks were masters only of central Russia, and even there they ruled only the cities and industrial centers. The borderlands of what had been the Russian Empire, inhabited by peoples of other nationalities and religions, as well as Siberia, had separated themselves and proclaimed independence, either because they wished to assert their national rights or (as in the case of Siberia and the Cossack regions) because they did not want to live under Bolshevik rule. The Bolsheviks, therefore, had literally to conquer by force of arms the separated borderlands as well as the villages in which lived four-fifths of Russia's population. Their own power base was not very secure, resting on at most 200,000 party members and an army then in the process of dissolution; but power is a relative concept and in a country in which no other organization disposed of comparable numbers, this was a formidable force.

The Bolsheviks took power for the express purpose of beginning widespread armed conflict, first in Russia and then in Europe and the rest of the world. Beyond the borders of what had been the Russian Empire, they failed. But inside them, they succeeded well enough.

The Civil War, which tore Russia apart for nearly three years, was the most devastating event in that country's history since the Mongol invasions in the thirteenth century. Unspeakable atrocities were committed from resentment and fear: millions lost their lives in combat as well as from cold, hunger, and disease. As soon as the fighting stopped, Russia was struck by a famine such as no European people had ever experienced, a famine Asian in magnitude, in which millions more perished.

As is true of many terms applied to the Russian Revolution, "Civil War" has more than one meaning. In customary usage it refers to the military conflict between the Red Army and various anti-Communist or "White" armies lasting from December 1917 to November 1920, when the remnant of White forces evacuated Russian territory. Originally, however, "civil war" had a broader meaning. To Lenin it meant the global class conflict between his party, the vanguard of the "proletariat," and the international "bourgeoisie": "class war" in the most comprehensive sense of the term, of which the military conflict was only one dimension. He not only expected civil war to break out immediately after his taking power, but took power in order to unleash it. For him, the October coup d'état would have been a futile adventure if it did not lead to a global class conflict. Ten years before the revolution, analyzing the lessons of the Paris Commune, Lenin agreed with Marx that its collapse was caused by the failure to launch a civil war.* From the moment the World War broke out, Lenin denounced pacifistic socialists who called for an end to the fighting. True revolutionaries did not want peace: "This is a slogan of philistines and priests. The proletarian slogan must be: civil war."[1] "Civil War is the expression of revolution. . . . To think that a revolution is possible without civil war is the same as to think it possible to have 'peaceful' revolution," wrote Bukharin and Preobrazhenskii in a widely read manual of Communism.[2] Trotsky put it even more bluntly: "Soviet authority is organized civil war."[3] From such pronouncements it should be evident that the Civil War was not forced on the Communist leaders by the foreign and domestic "bourgeoisie": it lay at the heart of their political program.

For the inhabitants of the former Russian Empire (except for those living under German occupation), the Civil War began in October 1917, when the Bolsheviks, having toppled the Provisional Government, moved to suppress rival political parties: at that time, before there were any "Red" or "White" armies, Russian newspapers already carried columns titled "*Grazhdanskaia voina*" (civil war), under which headings they reported on the clashes between the Bolsheviks and those who refused to acknowledge their authority. The "war on two fronts" of which the Bolsheviks liked to speak was a reality, and even seventy years later it is difficult to decide which cost them more effort: the struggle against civilian opponents, in which military force was frequently invoked, or the military conflict with the White armies. When on April 23, 1918, Lenin made what on its face sounds like an astonishingly foolish claim—"One can say with certainty that the Civil War, in the main, is over"[4]—he clearly meant the war against his civilian adversaries, not the one against the White armies, which had hardly begun.

This chapter and the next will deal mainly with the Civil War in the conventional, that is, military, meaning of the word. The subject is exceptionally confusing, because it involves many contestants dispersed over an immense territory: in addition to the principal armies, there were ephemeral partisan forces that frequently changed sides, and contingents of foreign troops. When an empire as vast and diverse as Russia disintegrates and its segments fly in all directions, no coherent structure remains; and where no coherence exists, the historian can pretend to provide it only at the risk of distorting reality.

The Russian Civil War was fought on three main fronts: the southern, eastern, and northwestern. It went through three major phases.

---

*Lenin, *PSS*, XVI, 454. In a letter of April 12, 1871, to Dr. Kugelmann, Marx wrote that the Communards were defeated because they "did not want to start a civil war." Karl Marx, *Pis'ma k L. Kugel'manu* (Petrograd, 1920), 115.

The first lasted one year, from the Bolshevik coup until the signing of the Armistice in France. It began in the winter of 1917–18 with the formation, in the Don Cossack region by generals Alekseev and Kornilov, of the Volunteer Army. Half a year later it was followed by the revolt of the Czechoslovak Legion on the mid-Volga and in Siberia, which resulted in the creation in that area of an Eastern front involving two anti-Bolshevik governments, each with its own armed force, one located in Samara (Komuch), the other in Omsk (the Siberian Government). This initial phase was distinguished by rapidly shifting front lines and sporadic engagements by small units. In Communist literature it is commonly referred to as the period of "partisan warfare" (*partizanshchina*). During this phase foreign troops—the Czechoslovaks on the anti-Bolshevik side, and the Latvians on the Bolshevik one—played a greater role than indigenous Russian forces. The Red Army was formed only at the end of this phase, in the fall of 1918.

The second and decisive stage of the Civil War extended over seven months, from March to November 1919. Initially, the armies of Admiral Kolchak in the east and those of General Denikin in the south advanced resolutely toward Moscow, mauling the Red Army and forcing it to retreat. In the northwest, General Iudenich penetrated the suburbs of Petrograd. But then the Red Army turned the tide of battle, defeating first Kolchak (June–November 1919) and then Denikin and Iudenich (October–November 1919). The fighting capacity of both the Kolchak and Denikin armies was broken concurrently, almost to the day, on November 14–15, 1919.

The concluding phase of the Civil War was the anticlimactic Wrangel episode of 1920, when the remnant of the Denikin army managed for a while to fortify itself on the Crimean peninsula. These forces would have been quickly routed by the vastly superior Red Army had it not been for the outbreak of a war with Poland (April 1920), which distracted its attention.* As soon as it was over, the Reds turned their full attention to Wrangel. In November 1920, the British and French navies evacuated what was left of the White army to Constantinople. This marked the close of the Russian Civil War in the military sense of the term; in the political and social senses, it would never really end.

Soviet historiography, especially under Stalin, went to great lengths to depict the Civil War as foreign intervention in which the anti-Bolshevik Russians played the part of mercenaries. While it is incontestable that there were foreign troops on Russian soil, the Civil War was throughout a fratri-

---

*Communist historians customarily treat the Soviet-Polish war of 1920 as part of the Russian Civil War; this view has also been accepted by some Western historians. This treatment, however, is difficult to justify, given that it was not a struggle among Russians for political control of their country but a conventional war between two sovereign states over territory. The misconception seems to date back to an article by Stalin in 1920, in which he labeled the Polish invasion of the Ukraine "the Third Campaign of the Entente" (*Tretii Pokhod Antanty*), the first two allegedly having been the campaigns of Denikin and Kolchak (*Pravda* No. 111 [May 25, 1920], 1, cited in Norman Davies, *White Eagle, Red Star,* London, 1972, 89).

cidal conflict. In late 1918 there was talk in Allied circles of a "crusade" against Bolshevism,[5] but such plans never came anywhere near realization. The casualty figures of the three-year war indicate that, except for a few thousand Czech volunteers (on the anti-Communist side) and several times that number of Latvians (on the Communist side), as well as up to 400 Britons, the combat fatalities were overwhelmingly Russian and Cossack. The French and their allies fought one skirmish with a pro-Bolshevik Ukrainian partisan detachment in April 1919, following which they withdrew. The Americans and the Japanese never engaged the Red Army. The Allied (essentially British) contribution consisted mainly of supplying the Whites with war matériel.

The anti-Bolshevik armies are commonly known as "White" (Belye), or even "White Guard" (Belogvardeitsy), adjectives coined by the Communists to discredit their opponents, who, in time, came to accept it. White, of course, was the standard of the Bourbons and nineteenth-century French monarchists. The Bolsheviks used it to create the impression that, as with the émigrés of the 1790s, their opponents' aim was to restore the monarchy. In reality, not one of the so-called White armies had the restoration of tsarism as its stated objective. All promised to give the people of Russia an opportunity to decide freely on their form of government. The most powerful force, the Volunteer Army, chose as its emblem not the Romanov black, orange, and white standard, but the national white, blue, and red,[6] and as its anthem the march of the Preobrazhenskii Guard Regiment, rather than "God Save the Tsar." Its founders and leaders—generals Alekseev, Kornilov, and Denikin, all of them descended from peasants—had never shown any partiality for Nicholas II: Alekseev had played a decisive role in persuading him to abdicate.[7] The White generals rejected the restoration of the monarchy not only as a matter of principle but for practical reasons: a restoration was not feasible given that every potential candidate for the throne either had been murdered or had withdrawn from politics.* In the somewhat romantic view of General Golovin, the movement was "White" only in the sense that white is the sum of all the colors of the spectrum: the spirit animating the Russian White armies, according to him, was not that of the counterrevolutionary force that invaded France in 1792, but of the revolutionary army from which emerged Napoleon.†

---

*Typical was the reaction of Grand Duke Nikolai Nikolaevich, the most popular member of the Imperial family, who in 1918 was living in retirement in the Crimea. When asked whether he would take charge of the White movement, he responded evasively: "I was born shortly after the death of Emperor Nicholas I and my entire upbringing was shaped in his traditions. I am a soldier accustomed to obeying and commanding. Now I have no one to obey. In certain circumstances, I have to decide on my own to subordinate myself to someone—for example, to the Patriarch if he told me to do such and such." "Otryvki iz dnevnika kn. Grigoriia Trubetskogo," Denikin Papers, Box 2, Bakhmeteff Archive, Rare Book and Manuscript Library, Columbia University, p. 52. Cf. Denikin, Ocherki, IV, 201–2.

†N. N. Golovin, Rossiiskaia kontr-revoliutsiia (Tallinn, 1937), Book 9, 93; Book 5, 65. At the same time it must be noted that the officers who fought in White ranks in the latter phases of

Fought on a terrain that, except for the modest heights of the Urals, was a boundless plain, the Russian Civil War had little in common with the campaigns waged in the West in 1914–18. Here there were no fixed fronts. Troops moved mainly along railroad lines, leaving large unoccupied spaces in between. Everything was in flux, to the extent that armies were often formed not in the rear but in the vicinity of the battlefield and thrown with little or no training into combat.[8] They emerged suddenly, and just as suddenly disintegrated and vanished. Units advancing with seemingly irresistible momentum would crumble and dissolve into a rabble upon encountering determined resistance. Front lines were thinly held: it was not uncommon for divisions manned by several thousand troops to defend a front of 200 kilometers, and for "brigades" to number a few hundred men.[9] Irregular units would desert to the enemy, fight for him for a while, and then change sides once again. Tens of thousands of Red soldiers on being captured would be inducted into the White forces and sent to fight yesterday's comrades. White prisoners captured after Wrangel's evacuation were fitted into Red Army uniforms and deployed against the Poles. Except for dedicated volunteers—a small minority—the troops on both sides usually had no idea what they were fighting for and frequently deserted at the first opportunity. The fluidity of the environment makes it next to impossible to depict the progress of the war in graphic terms, the more so that between and behind the principal combatant forces there operated independent bands of "Anarchists," "Greens," "Grigorevites," "Makhnovites," "Semënovites," and other partisans pursuing their own objectives. Some maps of the Civil War fronts resemble a Jackson Pollock painting, with white, red, green, and black lines running in all directions and intersecting at random.

Since the Red Army emerged victorious from the Civil War, it is tempting to ascribe its victory to better leadership and superior motivation. While subjective factors undeniably played a role in the outcome, scrutiny of the military balance indicates that the decisive factors were of an objective nature.* The situation was not unlike that in the American Civil War, in which the North enjoyed such overwhelming preponderance in population, industrial resources, and transport that it was certain of victory as long as

---

the Civil War became increasingly, and in some cases even fanatically, monarchist. This was observed by foreigners attached to the Whites, for example, Colonel John Ward, who spent 1919 at Kolchak's capital in Omsk. He says that "Russian officers are royalist almost to a man," with a "childlike adherence to the monarchist principle": John Ward, *With the "Die-Hards" in Siberia* (London, 1920), 160. In dealing with this issue, however, we must not assume that in 1919 the population of the country was as negatively disposed toward the monarchy as it had been two years earlier: when Lenin ordered the execution of Nicholas II and most of the members of the Romanov dynasty in the summer of 1918 he did so from fear of a resurgence of royalist sentiment in the country.

*By "objective" factors I mean those that were beyond the capacity of the protagonists to alter, for example, those determined by their respective geographic locations. "Subjective" factors flowed from their attitudes, values, abilities, and other personal traits.

it had the will to fight. From the strategic point of view, nearly all the advantages lay on the side of the Red Army. The ability of the Whites to carry on against such overwhelming odds and at one point even to seem near victory suggests that, contrary to conventional wisdom, it is they who had the superior generalship and morale. In the final analysis, they appear to have lost not because they represented a less popular cause or committed fatal political and military errors, but because they faced insuperable handicaps.

One critical advantage enjoyed by the Bolsheviks was that they were one whereas their enemies were many. The Red Army had a single, unified command taking orders from a tightly knit political oligarchy. Even if the Red leadership often disagreed, it could formulate and implement strategic plans. The White armies were fragmented and separated by large distances. They not only had no common strategy, but much of the time could not even communicate with each other to coordinate operations. Liaison between Kolchak and Denikin depended on brave officers willing to risk their lives to cross Red lines: messages could take as long as a month to reach the destination.* As a consequence, the southern, eastern, and northwestern armies operated independently, with minimal coordination. To make matters worse, the White armies were made up of an agglomeration of diverse components, each with its own command and interests: this held true of the most numerous contingent of the Southern Army, the Cossacks, who obeyed the commands of the White generals only if and when it suited them. Under these conditions, mistakes committed by the Red High Command could be corrected, whereas sound decisions by the Whites failed because they were not implemented.

The Reds enjoyed an immense, possibly decisive, advantage in the fact that they controlled the center of Russia, whereas their opponents operated on the country's circumference. This would be an overwhelming asset under any circumstances. "It seems to me," writes the historian Sergei Melgunov,

> that the movement from the periphery toward the center is almost always doomed to disaster. . . . It is the center that determines the success or failure of a revolution. (Civil War is Revolution.) Here one must take into account not only the important psychological factor. The center controls all the technical advantages, first and foremost in the form of an established administrative apparatus, which the periphery has to create virtually from scratch.[10]

Operating from the center, the Reds could shift forces from one front to another to defend endangered positions as well as to exploit enemy weaknesses. When forced to retreat, they gained the advantage of shortened lines of communication.

---

*Denikin, *Ocherki*, V, 85–90. This reality is often ignored by historians who, noting the lack of coordination among them, blame it on the ineptitude of White commanders: *e.g.*, George A. Brinkley, *The Volunteer Army and Allied Intervention in South Russia, 1917–1921* (Notre Dame, Indiana, 1966), 191.

Kolchak first and then Denikin advanced in what were called offensives over enormous territories. As they advanced they spread their lines ever wider and ever thinner. It seemed that they would go on till they had scarcely one man to the mile. When the moment came the Bolsheviks lying in the center, equally feeble but at any rate tending willy-nilly constantly towards compression, gave a prick or a punch at this point or that. Thereupon the balloon burst and all the flags moved back and the cities changed hands and found it convenient to change opinions, and horrible vengeances were wreaked on helpless people, vengeances perseveringly paid over months of fine-spun inquisition.[11]

Their geographic position gave the Reds not only strategic advantages but also incalculable material benefits.

To begin with, they had at their disposal far greater human resources. In the winter of 1918–19, when the Civil War got underway in earnest, the Bolsheviks ruled all of Great Russia, with a population of some 70 million. The territories controlled by Kolchak and Denikin had only 8 or 9 million inhabitants each.* This immense preponderance in population—4:1 and even 5:1 in the Bolsheviks' favor—gave the Red Army a much larger mobilization base. The Communists had within their borders all the manpower they needed: when in the critical engagements of 1919 they suffered heavy losses from casualties and desertions, they had only to call up more peasants, put them in uniforms, hand them rifles, and ship them to the front. By contrast Denikin and Kolchak, to increase their forces, had to conquer more and more territory, and, in the process, overextend themselves. In the fall of 1919, when the decisive battles of the Civil War took place, the Red Army had nearly 3 million men under arms: the combined effectives of the White armies never exceeded 250,000.† In every major engagement, the Reds enjoyed a substantial numerical advantage: I. I. Vatsetis, the Commander in Chief of the Red Army, advised Lenin in early January 1919 that the victories the Red Army had recently won were due to its numerical superiority.[12] In the Orel-Kursk battle of October 1919 that broke the back of the Southern (White) Army, the Red force was nearly twice as large.[13] The same was true of the battle for Petrograd.

Nor was a more-than-tenfold preponderance in numbers the Red Army's only manpower advantage. By controlling Great Russia, the Communists ruled an ethnically homogeneous population.‡ The Whites,

---

*Evan Mawdsley, *The Russian Civil War* (Boston, 1987), 146, 213–14. According to Denikin (*Ocherki*, V, 126), at the height of the summer 1919 offensive, the Southern Army's territory held 42 million people, but, as Mawdsley notes, such numbers were at Denikin's disposal for a few months only. The same applies to Kolchak, who at one point ruled an area inhabited by 20 million, but this, too, he controlled for only a brief time.

†Mawdsley, *Russian Civil War,* 181. Figures for the armed forces of both sides, especially of the Red Army, are notoriously unreliable: there always existed a vast discrepancy between the theoretical order of battle and the actual number of combatants. Some units reported more men than they actually had in their ranks in order to draw larger rations; some counted as present men who were AWOL or who had deserted. Still, the overwhelming numerical superiority of the Red Army in the second half of 1919 is not in dispute.

‡The population of Russia in 1917, exclusive of Finland, is estimated at 172 million:

by contrast, operated from territories inhabited largely by non-Russians who either took little interest in the outcome of the Civil War, or else, for their own national reasons, preferred a Red victory. A high proportion of White forces consisted of Cossacks more eager to gain independence for their homelands than to rebuild the Russian Empire. In the spring and summer of 1919, in his advance on Moscow, Denikin traversed territory inhabited by Ukrainians whose loyalty to Russia was even more questionable.

The Red Army enjoyed a great edge in weapons and munitions, and this for two reasons. Before the Revolution, most of the defense industries were located in Great Russia. In September 1916, Russia had over 5,200 enterprises engaged in war production, employing 1.94 million workers. They were geographically distributed as follows:[14]

Region	% of Enterprises	% of Workers
Moscow	23.6	40.4
Petrograd	12.7	15.6
Ukraine and Donbass	29.5	20.2
Urals	9.1	14.9
	74.9*	91.1

*The remaining factories were in Poland and other western regions occupied by the Germans.

Although in 1918 Russian defense industries had virtually stopped functioning, once they resumed production in the winter of 1918–19, their output went almost entirely to the Red Army.[15] The Whites had access only to secondary defense industries in the Urals and the Donbass region.

No less consequential was the fact that the Red Army inherited vast stores of war matériel. Communist historians agree that in the Civil War the Red Army "was almost fully and in all respects based on the stores left by the tsarist army. They were, on the whole, of incalculable quantity. Many items sufficed not only for the whole of the Civil War but until [1928]."[16] An inventory taken by the Communists in December 1917, said to be incomplete, showed that the warehouses of the old army held 2.5 million rifles, 1.2 billion rounds of small arms ammunition, nearly 12,000 field guns, and 28 million artillery shells.[17] Nearly all of this equipment fell into Communist hands. The Whites inherited from the old regime only the arsenals left behind in Romania, which they received from the Allies. Other-

S. I. Bruk and V. M. Kabuzan in *ISSSR*, No. 3 (1980), 86. Of this number, approximately 45 percent, or 77 million, were Great Russians.

wise, they had to rely on weapons captured from the enemy and on deliveries from abroad. Without the latter, the White armies, operating in areas with few defense industries or tsarist arsenals, would not have been able to carry on. By contrast the Red Army, combining what it had inherited with what Soviet war industries were turning out, toward the end of the Civil War attained a higher ratio of artillery and machine guns to manpower than had obtained in the tsarist army.[18]

The Reds benefited also from superior railway transport. The Russian rail network was designed on a radial pattern, the hub of which was Moscow. Lateral lines were poorly developed. Control of the center made it easier for the Communists to shift troops and supplies than for the Whites.

The only material advantage the Whites enjoyed over the Reds was an abundance of foodstuffs and coal. Shortages of food and fuel caused immense hardships to the Soviet government, but these bore more heavily on the civilian population than on the regime or its armed forces, for the authorities made certain that the bureaucracy and Red Army were provided for. Already in 1918, at least one-third and possibly as much as two-thirds of Soviet government outlays went for the military.[19] In 1919, the Red Army claimed 40 percent of the bread and 69 percent of the shoes produced in Soviet Russia. In 1920, it was a heavy consumer of the national product, absorbing, among other goods, 60 percent of the country's meat.[20]

The Red and White forces differed in a fundamental respect that redounded to the Communists' advantage as well. The Red Army was the military arm of a civilian government; the White armies were a military force that had also to act as a government. This double responsibility caused a multitude of problems with which the White generals were ill-prepared to cope.* They not only lacked administrative experience and personnel—and here subjective elements begin to blend with objective ones—they also had been conditioned by their whole upbringing to mistrust politics and politicians. Ex-tsarist officers found it more natural to obey than to command, and easier to serve the Bolshevik Government, much as most of them despised it, simply because it was *vlast'* (authority), than to assume the burdens of statehood. Politicians, even those eager to help them, spelled trouble, because they injected the spirit of partisanship and contentiousness into what should have been a united front. "Both [Alekseev] and I," writes Denikin,

> tried with all the power at our command to fence off ourselves and the army from the raging, struggling political passions and to base [the White move-

---

*This consideration influenced the French negatively toward the White movement from the beginning. Foch said in early 1919: "I do not attach great importance to the army of Denikin, because armies do not exist by themselves. . . . They must have behind them a government, legislation, and an organized country. It is better to have a government without an army than an army without a government." Cited in John M. Thompson, *Russia, Bolshevism, and the Versailles Peace* (Princeton, 1966), 201.

ment's] ideology on simple, incontestable national symbols. This proved
extraordinarily difficult. "Politics" burst into our work. It burst spontaneously also into the life of the army.[21]

This confession by the commander of the most important White army,
which Kolchak would have seconded, exemplifies a fundamental flaw in
the mentality of the anti-Bolshevik leaders, who liked to think in purely
military terms while struggling to restore the Russian state, which was by
its very nature a political task. The commanders of the Volunteer Army
required all who enlisted in its ranks to sign a pledge that while on active
service they would refrain from political activity.* The Red Army, by
contrast, was politicized from top to bottom: politicized not in the sense
of allowing free discussion, but in that it inculcated in the troops through
every propagandistic means the awareness that the Civil War was over
politics.

And, finally, while the Red Army was a revolutionary force, the White
armies remained tradition-bound. The difference was symbolized by their
appearance. Red troops in 1917–18 had no formal uniforms and wore
whatever they could lay their hands on: bits and pieces of tsarist uniforms,
leather jackets, civilian clothes. In 1919 they began to be outfitted with
uniforms of a new and original design. The Whites either wore tsarist
uniforms—if officers, with the traditional epaulets—or British ones. Their
mentalities were as different as their uniforms. Peter Struve was struck by
the "old regime" mentality of the generals of the Volunteer Army:

> Psychologically, the Whites conducted themselves as if nothing had hap-
> pened, whereas in reality the whole world around them had collapsed,
> and in order to vanquish the enemy they themselves had to undergo,
> in a certain sense, a rebirth. . . . Nothing so harmed the "White"
> movement as this very condition of *psychologically staying put in previ-*
> *ous circumstances,* circumstances which had ceased to exist—not its
> programmatic but its psychological "ancien-régimeness." . . . Men with this
> "old regime" psychology were immersed in the raging sea of revolutionary
> anarchy, and psychologically could not find their bearings in it. I deliber-
> ately stress that in this instance I mean "ancien-régimeness" not at all in the
> programmatic but in the psychological sense. In the revolutionary storm
> that struck Russia in 1917, even out-and-out restorationists had to turn
> revolutionaries in the psychological sense: because in a revolution, only
> revolutionaries can find their way.[22]

When one considers the enormous advantages of the Bolsheviks, mostly
the result of their early conquest of central Russia, the surprising thing is
not that they won the Civil War, but that it took them three years to do it.

---

*Alekseev, cited in S. Piontkovskii, ed., *Grazhdanskaia voina v Rossii (1918–21 gg.): Khre-*
stomatiia (Moscow, 1925), 497. Most lower-ranking officers and troops of the Volunteer Army
shared this attitude: "In the army nobody was interested in politics," recalled one White veteran.
"Our only thought was how to beat the Bolsheviks." N. V. Volkov-Muromtsev, *Iunost' ot*
Viaz'my do Feodosii (Paris, 1983), 347.

2. Alekseev.

The Civil War in the military sense of the term began when a small band of patriotic officers, humiliated by the destruction of the Russian army and the Bolshevik government's betrayal of commitments to the Allies, decided to continue the war against the Central Powers. Initially, their undertaking was not so much anti-Bolshevik as anti-German, because to them Lenin was nothing but an agent of the Kaiser. In the Southern Army, the anti-Bolshevik objectives emerged only later, after the Germans and Austrians had evacuated Russia and the Bolshevik regime, to everyone's surprise, remained in power. But the patriotic generals also pursued a domestic agenda. They hoped to stop the fratricidal class war that the Bolsheviks had let loose, by rallying the country on an anti-German platform: to reverse, as it were, Lenin's success in transforming a war between nations into a war between classes.[23]

On the Eastern front initially the situation was different. Here the early anti-Bolsheviks were either Socialists-Revolutionaries who raised the banner of the Constituent Assembly, or else Siberian separatists. By the end of 1918, however, when Admiral Kolchak assumed supreme command, nationalist slogans prevailed here as well.

The founder of the most effective White force, the Volunteer Army, was General M. V. Alekseev. Sixty years old when the Revolution broke out, he had had a distinguished military career that went back to the Turkish war of 1877–78. In 1915, after assuming personal command of the army, Nicholas II named him Chief of Staff: from then until the February Revolution, he was the de facto commander in chief of Russia's armed forces. Alekseev was deeply devoted to the army, which he viewed as the bearer of Russian statehood: in late 1916, to keep it intact in the face of serious reverses, he joined plots against the tsar. In February 1917, hoping to prevent the mutiny of the Petrograd garrison from spreading to the front, he helped persuade Nicholas to abdicate. During the Provisional Government he joined patriotic organizations committed to averting anarchy. Admired for his strategic ability and patriotism even by those who did not share his political views, Alekseev was a staff officer rather than a leader of men or a battlefield commander.

The Bolshevik coup found him in Moscow. Concluding that the new regime would neither honor Russia's wartime pledges nor arrest the deterioration of the armed forces, he made his way south, to the region of the Don Cossacks, with the intention of rallying what was left of the viable forces in the army and resuming the war against Germany. He was promised support by the Council of Civic Activists (Sovet Obschestvennykh Deiatelei), an informal association of prominent personalities dominated by the liberal Constitutional-Democrats (Kadets).* On arriving in the Don region, he succeeded in enlisting 400 or 500 officers in what was informally known as the "Alekseev Organization"—a disappointing number, given the hordes of demobilized officers in the area leading a life of idleness as they waited for something to happen.

At his headquarters in Novocherkassk, Alekseev was joined before long by other generals who had fled Bolshevik Russia. The most outstanding of them was Lavr Kornilov, who had escaped the prison at Bykhov to which Kerensky had confined him in August 1917, and in disguise had made his way across hostile territory. Impetuous, daring, adored by the troops, he was a perfect complement to the studious and reserved Alekseev. The latter, who admired Kornilov's generalship but mistrusted his political judgment, proposed an arrangement under which Kornilov would take charge of the troops and he, Alekseev, would assume responsibility for the army's politics and finances. Kornilov rejected this proposal, demanding undivided command; he threatened to leave for Siberia unless his condition was met.

The dispute between the two generals was resolved in January 1918 with the help of political figures who had come from Russia to Novocherkassk to advise the military leaders, among them Peter Struve and Paul Miliukov, the most powerful intellects, respectively, of Russia's conservative and liberal movements. They and their associates sided with Alekseev and warned Kornilov that unless he agreed to a dual command structure, no financial

---

*Alekseev in Piontkovskii, *Grazhdanskaia voina*, 496–99. Alekseev refers to a Union of National Salvation (Soiuz Spaseniia Rodiny), but his memory seems to have played him false.

3. Kornilov with young volunteers.

assistance would be forthcoming. Kornilov yielded and on January 7 an agreement was concluded by virtue of which Alekseev took over the new army's finances and its "external relations" (by which were meant mainly relations with the Don Cossacks on whose territory the new army was to be formed), and Kornilov became Commander in Chief. A "Political Council," made up partly of generals and partly of politicians, was created to guide the political affairs of the army and maintain contact with supporters living in Bolshevik Russia. Following this accord, the "Alekseev Organization" was renamed "Volunteer Army" (Dobrovol'cheskaia Armiia).

At the suggestion of Boris Savinkov, an old revolutionary turned patriot, the Volunteer Army released a vague programmatic statement that defined its mission as fighting "the German-Bolshevik yoke" and reconvening the Constituent Assembly.[24] The British and the French assigned liaison missions to the Army; the latter promised large sums of money (which never materialized).[25] This, for the time being, was the extent of Allied involvement. The Allies did not wish to side more openly with the Volunteer forces, out of fear of jeopardizing diplomatic efforts to dissuade the Bolsheviks from signing a separate peace with the Central Powers.

Eager to put the largest possible distance between himself and the politicians, Kornilov removed his headquarters to Rostov. As Chief of Staff he appointed General A. S. Lukomskii, an associate from the turbulent days of his conflict with Kerensky.[26] With volunteers signing up at a rate of 75 to 80 a day, toward the end of January 1918 the Army numbered 2,000 men, a high proportion of them junior officers, cadets, and secondary school students fired by patriotism and willing to serve in the ranks; hardly any ordinary soldiers enlisted.[27]

From the outset, the destiny of the Volunteer Army, and its successor, the Southern Army, was linked with that of the Don, Kuban, and Terek Cossacks, whose territories the generals chose as their base of operations and from whose ranks they drew most of their troops. And in this fact lay a source of serious weakness, for the Cossacks proved halfhearted and undependable allies.

The Don Cossack Host (Donskoe Kazach'e Voisko) had been the largest Cossack contingent in the Imperial army, providing it with the bulk of its cavalry; smaller contingents were supplied by the Kuban and Terek Cossacks. Formed in the early sixteenth century by runaway serfs in the no-man's-land between Muscovy, Persia, and the Ottoman Empire, the Don Cossacks at first made a living by hunting, fishing, and raiding Muslim settlements. In time, the Russian government restricted their independence and enrolled them, along with the other Cossack hosts, in its service. In return for bearing universal military duty, the Don Cossacks received generous allotments of land: on the eve of the Revolution, they held 13 of the 17 million hectares of arable land in the Don area, with an average household disposing of 12 hectares[28]—double the average allotment of peasant households in central Russia. They were one of the mainstays of the tsarist regime, frequently called upon to quell urban disturbances. During World War I they contributed 60 regiments of cavalry. When the Russian army dissolved in the second half of 1917, these units made their way back home in reasonably good order. In July, they elected as their *ataman*, or chief, General Alexis Kaledin, a Russian patriot who offered his services to the Volunteer Army.

The 2 million Don Cossacks, however, were an asset of uncertain value: Kaledin warned his friends that he could not guarantee their loyalty. While they refused to recognize the Soviet government, they did so less from objections to the Bolsheviks' legitimacy than from concern for their properties, which were threatened by the Soviet Land Decree nationalizing private land. They were much more interested in the affairs of the Don than in the fate of Russia—in Denikin's opinion, their attitude could be summed up as: "Russia is none of our business" (*"Do Rossii nam dela net"*).[29] As the Russian state dissolved, their attention turned to their own security, which essentially meant protecting their rich landholdings from external and internal enemies. To this end and only to this end were they prepared to cooperate with the anti-Bolshevik generals. Their main objective, at any rate until the Germans lost the war and evacuated Russia, was to establish an independent Don republic under German patronage. They joined the Whites only after losing their German mentors. Leon Trotsky correctly argued that if the Red Army respected their territories, the Don Cossacks would not stir.[30] When they did move out of their region, they invariably coupled fighting with looting, of which Jews were the principal victims. The situation was similar among the Kuban and Terek Cossacks, who throughout the Civil War considered themselves sovereign peoples, even if they had no control over the White armies operating on their territory: when they fought alongside the Volunteers, it was mainly to rob civilians.

The conflict between the Cossacks, who thought in local, regional terms, and the White generals, who had a national perspective, was by its very nature insoluble.[31] Denikin's frequent appeals not only to the (nonexistent) patriotism of the Don Cossacks but to their enlightened self-interest fell on deaf ears. Their behavior infuriated Kornilov:

> He was in the habit of assembling Cossacks in every Don settlement he was about to evacuate, in order to exhort them—always unsuccessfully—with a patriotic speech to follow him. These speeches invariably ended with the words: "You are scum (*svoloch*)."[32]

The Cossacks felt threatened by the Bolshevik Land Decree because in their midst lived peasants, not members of Cossack communities, much poorer than they, who could use it as a pretext for seizing their properties. These peasants were mostly immigrants, known as *inogorodnye,* or "outlanders," who had resettled to the Cossack regions from the overpopulated provinces of Great Russia. Here they either tilled marginal land or hired themselves out to the Cossacks as farm workers. In the Don area in 1917 they numbered 1.8 million: an estimated half a million had no land.[33] They constituted a very radical element: most of the Bolshevik supporters in the Don region came from their ranks. The outlanders were reinforced by deserters from the crumbling Caucasian and Black Sea fronts, as well as by some Cossack youths, whom the war had radicalized and who now turned against their elders.

By mid-February 1918 the Volunteer Army had 4,000 men—a highly motivated body, the nucleus of what in time would develop into the finest fighting force of the Civil War. Shortage of money seriously impeded the

Army's growth. Alekseev's friends in Moscow failed to make good on their pledges, claiming that the nationalization of banks and the seizure of bank safes had left them destitute.[34] According to Denikin, their total contribution to his army amounted to 800,000 rubles.[35] The Allies had promised 100 million rubles, but for the time being delivered only 500,000.* The Volunteer Army would have been stillborn had Alekseev not succeeded in withdrawing, with Kaledin's help, 9 million rubles from the Rostov branch of the State Bank.[36]

The news of the creation of a Volunteer Army on the Don in alliance with Kaledin's Cossacks set off alarm bells in Bolshevik headquarters at Smolnyi: well versed in the history of the French Revolution, the Bolsheviks immediately saw a parallel with the counterrevolutionary Vendée. The prospect was frightening not only for political and military reasons but also for economic ones, in that during the peace negotiations at Brest-Litovsk, then in progress, the Germans made it known that they intended to detach the Ukraine and make it a puppet state. The Bolsheviks thus faced the prospect of losing yet another major grain-producing area. To forestall the loss, Lenin instructed V. A. Antonov-Ovseenko to assemble such troops as he could and, together with Bolshevik sympathizers among the peasants and deserters on the Don, liquidate the incipient counterrevolution. His other mission was to occupy the Ukraine before the Germans could turn it into a protectorate. Antonov's army of 6,000–7,000 men advancing on the Don in December 1917 and January 1918 made good progress although undisciplined and plagued by desertions, because there was nothing to stand in its way. In the Don area, pro-Red peasants, workers, and deserters rose in its support.

Under assault from without and within, the Don Cossacks wavered in their loyalty to Kaledin and condemned him for siding with Alekseev and Kornilov. A Cossack elder expressed widespread sentiments: "Russia? Sure, it was a mighty power, but now it is gone. . . . Well, let it be. . . . We've got enough problems of our own."[37] Challenged in his authority, observing the spread of anarchy to his homeland without being able to arrest it, despairing of Russia's future, Kaledin committed suicide (January 29/February 11, 1918). For the next three months, until the election in May 1918 of General P. N. Krasnov as his successor, the Don Cossacks had no chief.

With the Don region in rebellion and a superior Red force drawing near, Kornilov faced the prospect of encirclement.[38] Before committing suicide, Kaledin had urged the White generals to move their small army into the region of the Kuban Cossacks, who he thought would be friendlier to them since there were fewer *inogorodnye* in their midst. Kornilov now followed

---

*In his *Russian Revolution* (p. 590), the author stated the French subsidy to Alekseev to have been 50 million rubles. This turns out to be incorrect.

this advice. On the night of February 21–22 (NS)* the Volunteer Army evacuated Novocherkassk and Rostov and headed south: in Denikin's words, "chasing a will-o'-the-wisp."[39] The exact number of those who participated in the Volunteer Army's legendary "Ice March" cannot be determined: the most likely figure is 6,000, of whom between 2,500 and 3,500 were combat troops and the rest civilian followers.† Following on its heels, the Red forces of Antonov-Ovseenko entered Novocherkassk and Rostov.

The small band of Volunteers traversed hostile territory, harassed by *inogorodnye* and pro-Bolshevik deserters, braving savage cold and freezing rain, short of food, clothing, and weapons. The men had to fight every step of the way. No facilities existed to care for the wounded; losses were made good by enrolling Kuban Cossacks. The army was cut off from the world at large: its friends in Moscow had no idea where it was or whether it still existed.

The most tragic episode of the Ice March occurred during the siege of the Kuban Cossack capital, Ekaterinodar. On April 13, Kornilov was directing operations from an isolated farmhouse: some 3,000 Volunteers, reinforced by 4,000 Cossack cavalry, with 8 field guns and 700 shells, assaulted a city held by 17,000 Bolsheviks armed with 30 guns and abundant ammunition.[40] Red artillery had targeted the farmhouse and Kornilov was urged to move, but was too preoccupied to heed the warning. He was bending over a map when a shell struck: the explosion threw him against a stove, cracking his skull and burying him under the collapsed ceiling.[41] He expired within a few minutes. His death dealt a severe blow to the army's morale, for General Anton Denikin, who instantly took over as Commander in Chief (he had narrowly escaped being killed by the same shell), had none of his magnetism and flair. Kornilov was interred in an unmarked grave, following which Denikin ordered the siege lifted and the Army to resume its march. After the Volunteers had departed, the Bolsheviks exhumed Kornilov's remains, bore them in triumph through the city, then tore them to shreds and burned what was left.[42]

Like any general who loses a war, Denikin has been severely judged by historians. Under the circumstances, however, he was not a bad choice, for although neither a forceful person nor an effective administrator, he had reasonably good strategic sense and combined personal integrity with utter devotion to the cause.[43] His intellectual quality is attested to by his memoirs

---

*"NS" or "New Style" refers to the Western or Gregorian calendar, which Soviet Russia adopted in February 1918. Until then, Russia had employed the so-called Julian calendar (OS), which in the twentieth century was thirteen days behind the Gregorian.

†Golovin, *Kontr-revoliutsiia*, Book 5, 72n. Denikin (*Ocherki*, II, 282) speaks of a total of 9,000, including civilians. General A. S. Lukomskii (*Vospominaniia*, II, Berlin, 1922, 7) lists 3,500 troops.

4. Denikin.

in five volumes, which display rare objectivity and an equally rare absence of rancor. One of his civilian associates, K. N. Sokolov, otherwise quite critical of Denikin, speaks of him personally in the highest terms, describing him as a "typical Russian *intelligent*."[44] The main impression he made was one of "irresistible charm." His external appearance

> was most ordinary. Nothing grand; nothing demonic. Simply a Russian army general with a tendency to stoutness, a large bald head bordered by trimmed graying hair, a pointed beard, and a twirled mustache. But he had a simply captivating, shy severity in his awkward, as it were, halting manners, and in the direct, stubborn glance, which dissolved in a good-natured smile and infectious laughter. . . . In General Denikin I saw no Napoleon, no hero, no leader, but simply an honest, steadfast, and valiant man, one of those "good" Russians who, if one is to believe Kliuchevskii, had led Russia out of the Time of Troubles.*

Although opponents on the left like to depict him as a reactionary monarchist, his politics are more aptly defined by a Communist historian as those of a "right Octobrist," that is, a liberal conservative:[45] from his recollections, we learn that he sympathized with the Liberation Movement which had ignited the 1905 Revolution. On the whole, however, he was true to the tradition of the Russian military, regarding political involvement as unbecoming a professional officer.[46]

*K. N. Sokolov, *Pravlenie Generala Denikina* (Sofia, 1921), 39–40. The "Time of Troubles" is the name given the interregnum at the beginning of the seventeenth century, during which Russia experienced prolonged civil strife and foreign intervention. Denikin, who like many anti-Communists saw a parallel between the turmoil of his own time and that three centuries earlier, called his memoirs *Outlines of Russia's Time of Troubles.*

The Ice March ended late in April when the Volunteer Army, having covered 1,100 kilometers in 80 days, half of them fighting, finally captured Ekaterinodar. The survivors were issued medals depicting a crown of thorns pierced by a sword.

Good news lay in store. Colonel M. G. Drozdovskii, commanding a brigade of 2,000 infantry and cavalry, had traversed the Ukraine from the Romanian front and reached the Don, where he placed himself and his troops at Denikin's disposal. It was the only instance of an entire unit of what had been the Russian army joining the Volunteers. Even such small numbers made a difference because in the Civil War one volunteer was worth a dozen conscripts. More encouraging still was the fact that after three months of life under Communist rule during which they had been subjected to food requisitions, the *inogorodnye* lost enthusiasm for Lenin's regime. Throughout April anti-Bolshevik risings broke out in the Don region which resulted in the expulsion of the Bolshevik forces from the area by the joint efforts of Drozdovskii, the Cossacks, and the Germans. In early May, the Volunteers recaptured Rostov and Novocherkassk.

While the Volunteer Army was forming in the northern Caucasus, other anti-Bolshevik groups were organizing along the mid-Volga and in Siberia. These movements were more political than military in character, their object being either to reconstitute a democratic all-Russian government or else to assert the region's independence from Moscow. The military forces here were an adjunct, at any rate until November 1918 when Admiral Alexander Kolchak took command of the Eastern front. The White forces in the east were in every respect inferior to the Volunteer Army, whether judged by the quality of leadership, organization, or morale. The only competent unit operating in the east—from May 1918 when they took to arms, until October when they withdrew from combat—was the Czechoslovak Legion.[47]

Socioeconomic conditions in Siberia differed in important respects from those prevailing in Great Russia. Siberia had not known peasant serfdom. The Russians here consisted of free peasants and traders, individualistic and enterprising, animated by a frontier spirit alien to the leveling ethos of the ex-serf. Living in their midst, however, were the same "outlanders" whom we have noted in the Cossack regions, peasant immigrants from central Russia, craving for the land of the old settlers (*starozhil'tsy*). They either cultivated marginal land or led a seminomadic existence employing the primitive slash-burn technique. In Siberia, as in the Northern Caucasus, social conflicts during the Revolution and Civil War pitted these newcomers against the prosperous old settlers and Cossacks. Bolshevik support in Siberia came either from this group or from the industrial workers of the Urals, both descended from serfs: as in Russia proper, there was a striking coincidence here between the heritage of serfdom and Bolshevism.*

Siberia had since the middle of the nineteenth century a vigorous regional movement that aspired to autonomy for the area on the grounds that its unique historical and social characteristics required special methods of administration. The movement gained momentum under the Provisional Government, when the Siberians created their own regional authority. After the Bolshevik coup in Petrograd, they became still more assertive: autonomy now served not only to give expression to Siberia's spirit but also to enable it to escape the looming civil war. In December 1917, the Socialists-Revolutionaries and Constitutional-Democrats joined forces to form in Tomsk a Siberian Regional Council (Sibirskaia Oblastnaia Duma), which assumed quasi-governmental functions.† The following month (January 27/February 9, 1918), the Council declared Siberia independent and announced a cabinet.[48] In early July, the new government, having moved to Omsk, issued a declaration in which it reconfirmed that it was the sole legitimate authority in Siberia.[49] The declaration left in abeyance the question of the region's ultimate relationship with Russia. Siberia, it stated, considered itself separated from Russia only temporarily and would do all in its power to restore national unity: its future relations with European Russia would be determined by the All-Russian Constituent Assembly. The Siberian government annulled Soviet laws, dissolved the soviets, and restored sequestered land to its owners. It adopted a white and green flag symbolic of Siberia's snows and forests.

While the Tomsk-Omsk government confined its claims to Siberia, the Committee of the Constituent Assembly formed in Samara on June 8, 1918, viewed itself as the only legitimate government in Russia. Its claim rested on the argument that the Constituent Assembly, elected in November 1917 by 44 million voters and then dispersed by the Bolsheviks, was the exclusive source of political legitimacy.

After the Bolsheviks had closed the Constituent Assembly, the Socialist-Revolutionary deputies from the mid-Volga area, a bastion of SR strength, returned home.[50] They attempted to reconvene the Assembly, but the effort collapsed.[51] Their opportunity came in June 1918 with the rebellion of the Czechoslovak Legion. These Czechs were prisoners of war of the tsarist army captured during World War I. After the Bolsheviks had made peace

---

*Speaking of Siberia, N. N. Golovin writes: "Bolshevism was supported only by one-time slaves": *Rossiiskaia kontr-revoliutsiia*, Book 7, 107. The industrial class here was divided in its loyalties: some workers turned anti-Bolshevik, supplying Kolchak with his best fighters: *Ibid.*, 113.

†V. Maksakov and A. Turunov, *Khronika grazhdanskoi voiny v Sibiri, 1917–1918* (Moscow, 1926), 52–55. The Kadets and Socialists-Revolutionaries traditionally dominated Siberian politics: in the elections to the Constituent Assembly, the two parties obtained here between one-third and three-quarters of the votes: A. M. Spirin, *Klassy i partii v grazhdanskii voine v Rossii* (Moscow, 1968), 420–23.

with the Central Powers, they arranged for their evacuation from Russia to France by way of Vladivostok. In May 1918 Trotsky ordered them to surrender their arms, whereupon they rebelled.[52] On June 8, the Czechs expelled the Bolsheviks from Samara. On the same day, five SR deputies to the Constituent Assembly, headed by V. K. Volskii, formed the Committee of Members of the Constituent Assembly (Komuch). The Committee grew to 92 members, all Socialists-Revolutionaries, most of them from the party's radical wing, headed by Victor Chernov.[53] Over its headquarters flew a red banner. On the day of its formation, Komuch declared Bolshevik authority in the province of Samara deposed, and all civil rights and freedoms restored. Existing soviets, handpicked by the Bolsheviks, were ordered dissolved and replaced by new ones, chosen in democratic elections with the participation of all the political parties.[54]

Nothing demonstrates better the irrelevance of political and social programs during the Civil War than the fate of Komuch. On July 24, Komuch issued a platform of unexceptional socialist and democratic credentials—the kind that the Western governments were forever urging on the White generals. It acknowledged as law the Bolshevik Land Decree and assured the peasants that they could enjoy in perpetuity the soil they had seized since February 1917. Soviet labor legislation also remained in force.[55] These pledges did nothing to gain the Komuch support among the population, which by now paid no attention to programs and promises. Since the elections to the Constituent Assembly the preceding November, the electorate had grown disenchanted with politics and to the extent that it cared to express political opinions, showed a trend toward the right. Thus, in the municipal elections held in Samara when Komuch was still riding high (August 1918), only one-third of the 120,000 eligible voters bothered to vote, and of that number, less than half cast ballots for the SR-Menshevik bloc. In Ufa and Simbirsk the socialists elected fewer than one-third of the municipal officials, and only in Orenburg did they win as much as one-half. In 1919, absenteeism in the municipal elections in some cities under non-Bolshevik control reached as high as 83 percent.[56]

Komuch formed a government composed of 14 SRs and a single Menshevik; under it served a military force called the People's Army (Narodnaia Armiia). It was initially hoped to man this army exclusively with volunteers, but as no more than 6,000 of these turned up, resort was had to conscription. Designed to bring in 50,000 soldiers, it actually realized fewer than 15,000. Commissioned officers were in very short supply because most of them disliked the left-wing orientation of Komuch, and if they enlisted, preferred to join the Siberian army or the Volunteers. The only effective anti-Bolshevik military force here were the 10,000 Czechs, the rear-guard of the Czechoslovak army still to the west of the Urals: in 1918 they made up 80 percent of the combat troops in the area and did most of the fighting.[57] In recognition of this fact, Komuch placed the People's Army under the command of a Czech officer. The only Russian fighting force in the area was a detachment of anti-Bolshevik workers from the Izhevsk and Votkino weapons factories.

During the summer of 1918, the Czechoslovak Legion was designated by the Supreme Allied Council in Paris an integral part of the Allied armed forces: its mission was to serve as the vanguard of an international contingent intended to reactivate the Eastern front against Germany. In pursuit of this objective, the Czechs expanded the area under their control. On August 7, they captured Kazan from its Latvian defenders: in this engagement, Russian troops, Red and White alike, fought without enthusiasm.[58] In Kazan the Czechs seized a hoard of bullion and securities that the Communist government had secretly evacuated the previous May when it feared the imminent fall of Petrograd and Moscow to the Germans. It consisted of nearly 500 tons of gold—half of the country's gold reserve— worth 650 million old rubles (the equivalent of $325 million), silver, foreign currency, and securities.[59] Representatives of Komuch followed on the heels of the Czechs.

Thanks to Czechoslovak intervention, in August 1918 Komuch exercised authority over the provinces of Samara, Simbirsk, Kazan, and Ufa as well as several districts of Saratov province. In administering this territory, the SRs, who routinely condemned the repressive policies of the Bolsheviks, proved themselves distinctly authoritarian, censoring critical newspapers, persecuting persons suspected of Bolshevik sympathies, and installing officials who quickly acquired the characteristics of tsarist bureaucrats, including a fondness for privileges and luxuries.[60] Although it depicted itself as a model democracy, Komuch has been called one of the most reactionary of the anti-Bolshevik regimes to emerge in the course of the Civil War.[61] Its personnel intrigued day and night against the Omsk government, hoping to subvert it and extend Komuch's authority over its territory.

The Siberian government in Omsk was also dominated by SRs, but of a more moderate and pragmatic orientation, willing to work together with non-socialist "bourgeois elements." To this end they established friendly relations with the liberals (Constitutional-Democrats or Kadets) and the powerful Siberian cooperatives. Owing to this spirit of compromise, the Siberian government succeeded in establishing a relatively efficient administrative apparatus.

The Omsk government also disposed of a superior military force. Officers preferred the Siberian army to the People's Army, since it was organized on traditional lines, retaining old titles and epaulets. Commanded by a young and energetic officer, Lieutenant Colonel A. N. Grishin (Almazov), it numbered 40,000 men, half of them Ural and Orenburg Cossacks.*

---

*S. P. Melgunov, *Tragediia Admirala Kolchaka*, I (Belgrade, 1930), 75. Grishin-Almazov was dismissed in early September as a result of political intrigues, following which he joined the Volunteer Army. In May 1919, while en route to Siberia carrying important messages from

5. A Latvian rifleman.

The Red Army was slow to form.[62] Delays were due not only to a shortage of volunteers and the near-universal disinclination of Russians to serve, but also to the Bolshevik aversion to a standing army. Revolutionary history taught them that a regular force commanded by professional officers was a breeding ground of the "counterrevolution." In Russia, this danger was enhanced by the fact that, given the country's demographic structure, a conscript army was bound to be an army of peasants, a class the Bolsheviks saw as hostile.

In the first few months in power the only military force on which the Bolsheviks could rely were three brigades of Latvian Rifles, 35,000 strong, the one contingent of the old army that they kept intact because of its Social-Democratic sympathies. The Latvians rendered the Bolsheviks invaluable services: dispersing the Constituent Assembly, putting down the Left SR uprising, defending the Volga from the Czechs, and guarding their persons from potential assassins.

But since this force was hardly adequate for the Civil War they intended to unleash, the Bolsheviks reluctantly reconciled themselves to the necessity

---

Denikin to Kolchak, he fell into Bolshevik hands and either was killed or committed suicide: Denikin, *Ocherki,* V, 88–89.

of forming a regular force. In March 1918, they created a Supreme Military Council (Vysshyi Voennyi Sovet) staffed by career officers of the old army, to serve as a skeletal general staff. Its head, Major General N. I. Rattel, had directed military communications in the Imperial army; its other members likewise were onetime imperial officers. This body was to coordinate and direct the Soviet war effort, but it accomplished little, since it had no troops to command.

Although formally the Red Army came into being in February 1918, for the next six months it led a merely paper existence. Apart from the Latvians, who were rushed from one endangered front to another, the forces fighting on the Bolshevik side consisted of scattered detachments of 700 to 1,000 men led by elected commanders; they had no formal military structure or chain of command, and therefore no coordinated strategy. By their very nature they had to conduct partisan warfare.[63] The Red Army became reality only in the fall of 1918, in the midst of concurrent campaigns against the Czechoslovaks and the Russian villages, when Moscow finally gambled on drafting masses of peasants and as many ex-tsarist officers as required to command them.

Although the White movements were military efforts par excellence, whose leaders scorned politics, they could not altogether dispense with political advice and support. This was supplied by two clandestine organizations with branches inside and outside Bolshevik Russia: the National Center (Natsional'nyi Tsentr) and the Union for the Regeneration of Russia (Soiuz Vozrozhdeniia Rossii). The former was liberal and dominated by Kadets; the latter was socialist and led by the SRs. Both, however, sought to transcend party loyalties and win a following on broad democratic platforms. The National Center, by far the more effective of the two, supplied the White leaders with political as well as military intelligence on conditions inside Soviet Russia. To some extent, it also influenced their conduct.

The origins of the National Center went back to the summer of 1917, when influential liberal and conservative politicians decided the time had come to set aside party rivalries and unite to stop the slide into anarchy. The Constitutional-Democratic Party, the driving force behind this effort, was, next to the Bolsheviks, the best organized political group in Russia: its centrist position enabled it to attract moderate socialists as well as moderate conservatives. The left-wing opposition, which gave rise to the Union for Regeneration, began to organize only in the spring of 1918. Because its socialist leadership could not quite make up its mind whom it disliked more, the Whites or the Reds, it never attained either the cohesion or the effectiveness of its rival.

The immediate forerunner of the National Center was the Council of

Civic Activists, formed in August 1917 by a number of outstanding parliamentary figures, generals, businessmen, Kadet politicians, and conservative intellectuals.* The Council's platform called for firm authority and the restoration of discipline in the armed forces. Kerensky suspected that the Council's hidden agenda was toppling him from power: his erratic behavior in August–September 1917, notably his provocative behavior toward Kornilov, was in good measure influenced by this perception.

In the winter of 1917–18, the Council backed Alekseev's efforts to create a new army on the Don and through a delegation sent to him in January, helped smooth his relations with Kornilov. In the spring of 1918, liberal and conservative groups in Moscow combined to form a "Right Center." The activities of this Center are shrouded in secrecy, for it left few documents, but it appears that its principal mission was organizing underground anti-Bolshevik military cells. It enrolled officers, some of whom it sent to Denikin, and others of whom it kept in readiness for a coup.[64]

The Right Center broke up in the spring of 1918 over foreign policy disagreements. Its more conservative members, having concluded that the principal threat to Russia came not from the Germans but from the Bolsheviks, requested the Germans to help them overthrow Lenin's regime. Negotiations to this end got underway after the arrival in Moscow of the German embassy, but they were terminated without issue on orders of Berlin, which decided to continue its pro-Bolshevik course.[65] The majority of the members of the Right Center, loyal to the Allies, broke away to form the National Center.

The socialist opposition coalesced after the ratification of the Brest-Litovsk Treaty (March 3, 1918), which it repudiated on the grounds that it opened the door to German political and economic domination of Russia. In April, after unsuccessful attempts to come to terms with the National Center, socialists and left liberals formed the Union for the Regeneration of Russia, whose program called for the restoration, with Allied help, of the territories surrendered at Brest-Litovsk, the formation of an effective national government, and the reconvocation of the Constituent Assembly.[66] The Union functioned separately from the National Center but maintained personal links with it through several left Kadets who belonged to both organizations.

The Union and the Center carried on intermittent negotiations to determine whether they could formulate a common platform. Convinced that the Bolshevik dictatorship could be defeated only by another dictatorship, the Center advocated a combined anti-Bolshevik military and political force

---

*See *NV* for August 9–11, 1917, and P. N. Miliukov, *Istoriia vtoroi russkoi revoliutsii*, I/2 (Sofia, 1921), Chapter 5. The membership included M. V. Rodzianko, generals M. V. Alekseev, A. A. Brusilov, N. N. Iudenich, and A. M. Kaledin, the businessmen P. P. Riabushinskii and S. N. Tretiakov, the intellectuals P. N. Miliukov, V. A. Maklakov, N. N. Shchepkin, P. B. Struve, N. A. Berdiaev, E. N. Trubetskoi, and V. V. Shulgin.

under a leader invested with broad discretionary powers. The Union preferred to fight the Bolsheviks without resort to a dictatorship. In May 1918 the two groups reached a compromise calling for a three-man Directory made up of one socialist, one non-socialist, and one military man without party affiliation. Conveyed to the Komuch and the Siberian government, the decision would bear fruit in August 1918.

The Allied leaders believed as late as September 1918 that the war would last at least another year: for this reason, the reconstitution of the Eastern front to divert German forces from the West remained for them a matter of high priority. They had sent token forces to Murmansk, Archangel, and Vladivostok; they had placed the Czechoslovak Legion under their command; and they had authorized Japanese landings in the Far East. But having hardly any troops of their own to spare, their main hope was to raise in Siberia a large Russian army.

Responsibility for organizing the new Eastern front was entrusted to the Allied missions in Siberia.* To fulfill this responsibility, they pressured the various governments that had sprung up east of the Volga—there may have been as many as thirteen—to unite into a single government and merge their armies. Allied officers were disgusted by the enmity between Omsk and Samara, which resulted in their refusing to supply each other with food, and each insisting that the other party's troops disarm before setting foot on their territory.[67] They urged the Siberian government and Komuch, as well as the Cossacks and the organizations representing the ethnic minorities of the Urals and Siberia (the Bashkirs, Kirgiz-Kazakhs, and so forth) to bury their differences and consolidate in one government that the Allies would recognize and supply. The Czechs, who were bearing the brunt of the fighting, were especially insistent on this.

In the summer of 1918, responding to the pressures, Russian politicians convened three conferences. The third and most productive of these meetings gathered from September 8 to 23 in Ufa. On hand were some 170 delegates representing most organizations and national groupings opposed to the Bolsheviks (but neither the Volunteer Army nor the Don or Kuban Cossacks).[68] Half were Socialists-Revolutionaries; the rest ranged from Mensheviks to monarchists. It was a mélange of politicians who had little in common except dislike of the Bolsheviks: noting the red carnations the SRs sported in their lapels, a Cossack general said that the mere sight of these flowers gave him a headache.[69] Badgered by the Czechs and sobered

---

*The principals were two High Commissioners, the Englishman Sir Charles Elliot, Chancellor of the University of Hong Kong, who spoke fluent Russian and was well versed in Russian affairs, and the French Ambassador to Japan, Eugène Regnault. They were assisted by the heads of military missions, Generals Alfred Knox (UK), Maurice Janin (France), and William Graves (U.S.A.). Japanese military and civilian officials were also on hand, but they kept to themselves. G. K. Gins, *Sibir', soiuzniki i Kolchak*, II (Kharbin, 1937), 60–61.

by bad news from the front—while the meeting was in progress Kazan fell to the Reds and Ufa itself was threatened—the delegates proved more conciliatory. A settlement was reached which resulted in the creation of an All-Russian Provisional Government. Its structure bore the earmarks of the resolution agreed upon in Moscow by the National Center and the Union for Regeneration. The executive, called the Directory, was a compromise between those who wanted a personal military dictatorship (the Siberians and the Cossacks) and the SRs, who preferred a government subject to the authority of the Constituent Assembly. The new Provisional Government was to function until January 1, 1919, when the Constituent Assembly would reconvene, provided there was a quorum of 201 deputies; if such was lacking, it would open in any event on February 1. This government was declared the only legitimate authority in all Russia. Komuch and the Siberian government, as well as the other regional governments present, agreed to subordinate themselves to it. Denikin, however, who was neither represented nor consulted, refused to follow suit.[70]

As ultimately constituted, the Directory, headquartered in Omsk, was composed of five men, under the chairmanship of the right SR, N. D. Avksentev.* Inordinately vain, according to one contemporary, Avksentev "immediately surrounded himself with adjutants, restored titles . . . [and] created buffoon pomp behind which lay nothing of substance."[71] General Boldyrev, who took command of the armed forces, although nominally partyless, had strong ties to the SRs. He had a distinguished war record but was not widely known and lacked Alekseev's prestige. Formally a coalition, it was for all practical purposes an SR government.

After much bickering, on November 4 the Directory formed a fourteen-man cabinet, chaired by Vologodskii. Admiral Alexander Kolchak, the onetime commander of the Black Sea Fleet, who happened to be passing through Omsk en route to the Volunteer Army, was pressed by Boldyrev into service as Minister of War. It was largely a ceremonial appointment. Kolchak was well known to the British and had in General Knox, the head of the British military mission, a warm admirer. Boldyrev is reported to have told him that he had been appointed for the express purpose of securing Allied support and was not to interfere with military matters.[72] The Directory's program called for the restoration of Russia's territorial integrity and the struggle against the Soviet government and Germany. Other questions were left for the Constituent Assembly.[73]

In October 1918, when the Directory assumed office, the international situation was rapidly changing. The German government had requested U.S. mediation and World War I was drawing to an end. This prospect

---

*The others were V. M. Zenzinov, also an SR, P. V. Vologodskii, representing the Siberian Government, General V. D. Boldyrev, a representative of the Union for Regeneration, who commanded the army, and V. A. Vinogradov, a Kadet.

6. Posters announcing the Red Army's capture of Kazan.

immediately affected the status of the Czech troops in Russia. On October 18, the Czechoslovak National Council in Paris proclaimed the independence of its country. As soon as the news reached them, the Czech troops resolved no longer to fight on Russian soil, since the cause for which they had been enlisted had triumphed: "The Allied victory had liberated Bohemia. The Czech troops were no longer mutineers nor traitors to the Hapsburg Empire. They were victorious soldiers and pioneers of Czechoslovakia. Home, which might have been forever barred and banned to them, now shone in the lights of freedom and of honor."[74] Soon soldiers' committees sprouted and politics took over. The combat capabilities of the Legion deteriorated to the point where the Russians were happy to see them go.[75] In the spring of 1919, yielding to French pleas, the Czechs agreed to delay evacuation home to guard the Transsiberian Railroad between Omsk and Irkutsk from pro-Communist partisans and bandits. But they did no more fighting. These were no longer the idealistic Czechs and Slovaks who had once placed themselves at the disposal of the Allied command: it was a remnant infected with the general corruption of the Civil War. While guarding the Transsiberian, they amassed much wealth in the form of industrial equipment and household goods, which they stored in 600 freight cars.[76]

After the Czechoslovaks had withdrawn from combat, the only military forces left to the Directory were the People's Army and the Siberian Cossacks. The People's Army was in pitiful shape. Having inspected his front-line troops, Boldyrev reported: "the men [are] barefoot, in rags, they sleep on bare planks, some go even without hot food since, lacking shoes, they cannot make it to the kitchen, and there is no one to bring it to them or to carry it."[77] There was no unified command: the most powerful entity, the Siberian Cossacks under Ataman Alexander Dutov, operated mostly on their own. Allied material help at this point was insignificant, consisting mainly of clothing. France and the United States held back; Japan minded her own business. Britain dispatched to Omsk the 25th Battalion of the Middlesex Regiment, commanded by Colonel John Ward, whose contingent of 800 soldiers had been declared unfit for duty on the Western front. Its mission was to maintain order in Omsk and give the Directory moral support. It did no fighting.* Omsk also had a contingent of 3,000 Czechs who sympathized with the SRs.[78]

The Directory, even more than the 1917 Provisional Government of which it viewed itself as the successor, was a paper government without administrative apparatus, financial resources, or even an official organ.[79] Such bureaucracy as it had consisted of functionaries of the Siberian government who continued to administer their area as they had done since 1917. Russian and foreign observers agree that the Directory never exercised effective authority, a fact that merits stressing in view of the legends circulated by Socialists-Revolutionaries after its fall. It was fatally hampered by irreconcilable differences between the SRs who headed both the government and the army, and the nonsocialists who ran the administration, controlled the money, and enjoyed the sympathy of the officers and Cossacks. Members of the Directory, according to Boldyrev, "were representatives and advocates of the groups that had sent them, groups which were deeply in conflict and even hostile in their political and social endeavors."[80] In the pithy phrase of Colonel Ward, it was "a combination that refused to mix."[81]

Unable to govern, the Directory and its cabinet spent much of their

---

*Richard Ullman claims that after reaching Omsk the British troops "had gone into combat against the Bolsheviks" (*Intervention and the War*, Princeton, 1961, 262). In fact, British units stationed in Omsk did no fighting. See Ward, *With the Die-Hards, passim.*

energy and most of their time on squabbles and intrigues. The socialists quarreled with the liberals, while the politicians who thought in all-Russian terms bickered with the Siberian separatists. The leaders of Komuch could not reconcile themselves to their loss of identity: although they had surrendered authority to the Directory, psychologically they still thought of themselves as a government within a government.

Chernov, the leading Socialist-Revolutionary, who had not been invited to join the Directory because he was considered too radical to work with the Siberians and Cossacks, was busy conspiring. In early August, the Central Committee of the Socialist-Revolutionary Party moved from Moscow to the Volga, leaving behind only a skeletal bureau.[82] Chernov arrived in Samara on September 19, as the Ufa meeting was concluding its deliberations. In his view, the Ufa accord was an act of surrender to the reaction, and he set about trying to subvert it. At his urging, the SRs adopted a resolution making the SRs serving in the government accountable to the Party's Central Committee. The result was to compromise Avksentev and Zenzinov in the eyes of the military and liberals.[83]

As putative successor to the Provisional Government of 1917, the Directory fully expected to receive Allied diplomatic recognition. This the British were prepared to grant, at any rate on a de facto basis, and the British cabinet made a decision to this effect on November 14, 1918. But because of the time required to draft an appropriate telegram, the decision had not been made public or even conveyed to Omsk by the time the Directory fell. Neither the French nor the Americans were willing to follow suit.

Throughout the Directory's eight-week existence rumors circulated that the SRs were plotting a coup.[84] It was not only ineffective but unpopular. Siberian peasants regarded it as "Bolshevik," and so did the officers in its service and local businessmen. The gulf between the right and the left was too great to bridge even in face of the common danger. The Directory lived in an unreal world and its demise was only a question of time.

By May 1918, the situation of the Volunteer Army had improved appreciably. The tide of pro-Bolshevism in the northern Caucasus had receded, partly from the reflux of deserters, partly from peasant anger over Communist food requisitions. In western Siberia, the Czechs had risen in revolt. The Allied troops that landed in Archangel and Murmansk were thought in Denikin's headquarters to be the advance party of a huge expeditionary force.

With the advent of spring, Denikin had to decide what to do next: on this decision, in his words, depended the fate of the Volunteer Army and even the entire White movement.[85] Alekseev wanted the Volunteer Army along with the Don Cossacks to be thrown against Tsaritsyn, the capture of which would make it possible to link up with the Czechs and the People's Army.

Once joined, the anti-Bolshevik armies of the east and the south could forge a single front from the Urals to the Black Sea. Capture of Tsaritsyn had the added attraction of disrupting Moscow's traffic on the Volga and cutting off access to Baku, its main source of petroleum. Alekseev feared that if the Volunteer Army remained much longer in the backwater of the northern Caucasus it would not only miss a unique strategic opportunity but lose its very raison d'être: unless it transformed itself into an all-Russian national army, he argued, it would disintegrate. But Denikin had other ideas.

In mid-May, the Don Cossacks elected, as successor to Kaledin, General P. N. Krasnov, an opportunist and adventurer to whom Russia meant little and the Don everything.*[86] On assuming office he entered into close relations with the German command in the Ukraine with a view to securing subsidies and weapons. Some of the weapons, drawn from the arsenals of the old Russian army, he bartered with the Volunteer Army for food,[87] but on the whole his relations with it were strained, for he looked on the Volunteers not as allies but as guests. His objective was a sovereign Don Cossack republic. To the extent that he was even willing to contemplate sending his Cossacks on Moscow it was as Commander in Chief of all the anti-Bolshevik forces, the Volunteer Army included. This was totally unacceptable to the White generals, for whom the Don was an inalienable part of Russia. Krasnov's ambitions and intrigues caused relations between the Volunteer Army and the Don Cossacks to sour in no time.† Throughout the Civil War, the Don Cossacks kept their units separate and on occasion ignored and frustrated plans drawn up by the Volunteer Army's command. In assessing the actions of what is loosely called the Volunteer Army it must never be left out of sight that it consisted of two discrete entities, the Volunteer Army proper and the Cossacks, whose interests coincided only in part. Until the summer of 1919, when Denikin entered the Ukraine and began to conscript the local population, the Cossacks considerably outnumbered the Volunteers.

Like Alekseev but for different reasons, Krasnov also wanted Denikin to concentrate on Tsaritsyn, so as to lift the threat to the Don region from Red forces operating in the northeast. So eager was he to capture the Volga city that he offered to place his Cossacks under Denikin's command if he would agree to assault it with the Volunteer Army. Identical advice came from the Army's friends in Moscow.[88]

Denikin, who had a considerable streak of stubbornness, rejected these counsels, resolving instead to march his Army south, into the Kuban steppe. He reasoned that before venturing outside the northern Caucasus,

---

*Although in October 1917 he had been the only commander willing to help restore Kerensky to power: *RR*, 493, 501.
†Archival sources indicate that Krasnov's intransigence after the armistice was encouraged by the French, who wanted to establish a protectorate over the Don, a region that, by agreement drawn up between the two powers in December 1917, lay in the British sphere of influence: Anne Hogenhuis-Seliverstoff, *Les Relations Franco-Soviétiques, 1917–1924* (Paris, 1981), 113.

he had to solidify his rear by liquidating the Red North Caucasian Army of 70,000 men, mostly made up of *inogorodnye,* which controlled the Kuban region. The Kuban Cossacks, who were both excellent soldiers and strongly anti-Communist, seemed likely to provide the kind of reliable support denied him by the Don host.[89] Denikin's strategic decision was subsequently much criticized: for by failing to unite with the armies forming in the east when it was still feasible, he made it possible for the Red Army to deal with him and the other Whites one by one. Denied Volunteer support, Krasnov attacked Tsaritsyn on his own. His Don Cossacks stormed it repeatedly during November and December 1918, but the city held.* It would fall to Denikin only in the summer of the following year, by which time the White armies in the east were in full retreat and the opportunity to create a unified anti-Bolshevik front had disappeared forever.

On June 23, the Volunteer Army set off on its second Kuban campaign. Taking part were 9,000 regular troops and 3,500 Cossacks. The artillery consisted of 29 field guns.[90] The months of July and August saw pitched battles that brought the Volunteer Army, outnumbered ten to one, many victories, culminating in the capture on August 15 of Ekaterinodar. On August 26 Denikin's men entered Novorossiisk, which would serve as the port of entry for English supplies. Thousands of Red Army soldiers were taken prisoner and immediately pressed into service; their commanders, considered Bolsheviks, were usually shot. Kuban Cossacks enlisted in large numbers. The Army's treasury was enriched by "contributions" exacted from villages known to have supported the Reds: these brought in 3 million rubles.[91] The second Kuban campaign was a great tactical success and the Volunteer Army emerged from it larger and stronger than ever: at its conclusion, in September 1918, it had 35,000–40,000 men (up to 60 percent of them Kuban Cossacks) and 86 field guns.[92] It was these victories that frightened the Bolshevik high command in August 1918 into requesting German military intervention against the Volunteer Army.[93]

---

*The fighting around Tsaritsyn in late 1918 marked the beginning of the conflict between Trotsky and Stalin. Lenin dispatched Stalin to Tsaritsyn to collect food. Stalin had himself appointed to the Revolutionary-Military Council of the Southern front and immediately began to interfere with military operations, which in the fall of 1918 were in the charge of a onetime tsarist officer, General P. P. Sytin, the Commander of the Southern front and an appointee of Trotsky's. He also communicated on military matters then and later directly with Lenin, bypassing Trotsky's Revolutionary-Military Council: D. V. Volkogonov, *Trotskii,* I (Moscow, 1992), 237. The record indicates that Stalin's main contribution to the defense of Tsaritsyn consisted of political intrigues and the imposition of a reign of terror, directed mainly at the ex-tsarist officers in Soviet service whom he mistrusted and some of whom he had arrested and shot: Boris Souvarine, *Staline* (Paris, 1977), 205; Dmitrii Volkogonov, *Triumf i tragediia,* I/1 (Moscow, 1989), 90–92; and Robert Argenbright in *Revolutionary Russia,* IV, No. 2 (December 1991), 157 –83. In early October 1918 Trotsky demanded Stalin's recall on the grounds of intolerable meddling with military decisions—advice which the Politburo accepted (L. Trotskii, *Stalinskaia shkola falsifikatsii,* Berlin, 1932, 205–6). Stalin and his associates paid Trotsky back with a whispering campaign of slander. Stalin later claimed credit for the successful defense of Tsaritsyn and had the city renamed Stalingrad in his own honor. Cf. Isaac Deutscher, *The Prophet Armed* (New York, 1954), 423–28.

The Volunteer Army's rear was secure. To Rostov and Novocherkassk streamed public figures escaping the Red Terror, including many Kadets and members of the National Center. But serious problems remained: perversely, their nature was such that they grew worse as the military situation improved. Although it by now controlled sizable territory, the Army had no effective administrative apparatus. Civil service personnel was in very short supply: when approached, persons with the requisite experience responded evasively, either from an unwillingness to assume responsibility, or from fear for their lives.[94] The administration, therefore, had to be improvised: Denikin placed military governors in charge of provinces and restored laws issued before October 25, 1917. By and large, the population was left to its own devices, which spelled not so much democracy as anarchy. Denikin later conceded that in territories ruled by his Army, justice served as a pretext for personal vendettas, the field-marshal courts which he had introduced being used by the Cossacks to settle scores with pro-Bolshevik "outlanders," and thus turning into "instruments of organized lynch law."[95] The more territory the Volunteer Army conquered, the more conspicuous was its inability to ensure elementary order and security for the population.

Alekseev died in October 1918. Shortly before, he had created a body to advise the high command, called the Special Conference of the Supreme Leader of the Volunteer Army (Osoboe Soveshchanie pri Verkhovnom Rukovoditele Dobrovol'cheskoi Armii). It was initially envisaged as a consultative body, but on the urging of the National Center, which argued that the Army could not function properly without a political arm, Denikin agreed in January 1919 to transform it into a shadow cabinet, under the chairmanship of General A. M. Dragomirov. Of the body's eighteen members, five were generals and the remainder civilians, ten of them representatives of the National Center. The resolutions of the conference were not binding on Denikin, who reserved for himself the right to legislate on his own authority.[96] According to the recollections of one of its members, the conference lacked a clear political coloration, but the generals who dominated the proceedings were of a rather liberal persuasion.[97] The discussions produced few disagreements, not so much from consensus as from lack of concern, from a sense that the conference's decisions made little difference:

> Our unity was distinguished by a certain passivity; our deliberations showed little vitality and our decisions had no willpower. Subsequently, the Special Conference was compared to a machine without belt drives. Such it always was. In theory, everything was based on the principle of unity of authority. In practice, there was the shapeless unity of passivity.[98]

There was a pervasive feeling, among the civilians as much as among the generals, that the only thing that mattered was military victory: hence, a certain sense of unreality hung over such deliberations. There was no sense of urgency about filling executive posts: months after the conference's formation, some of the most important posts remained vacant, among them, the directorship of the Department of the Interior.

The National Center was responsible for the political programs which Denikin and his generals reluctantly agreed to endorse in early 1919, largely under British pressure. The Center's agenda called for a combination of "firm authority," that is, military dictatorship, with liberal political and social pledges centered on the convocation of the Constituent Assembly, agrarian reform involving compulsory expropriation of large estates (the traditional Kadet platform), encouragement of small and medium-sized farms, and social security for industrial workers.[99] The generals doubted whether such promises mattered much one way or the other; but they yielded when told that the Allied governments, on whose assistance they depended, would not be able to offer it unless they could persuade their constituencies that the Whites were fighting for the same ideals of democracy and social justice for which the Allies had waged World War I.

The ultimate defeat of the Volunteer Army is often blamed on political ineptitude, but a more likely cause, apart from the objective factors mentioned earlier, was the inability of the command to control its military and civilian personnel. This failure manifested itself equally in the Southern and the Eastern White armies. All observers agree that the indiscipline among the Whites was extraordinary. Denikin conceded that much, and more, when he said in response to the complaints of General H. C. Holman, the head of the British mission, that pervasive corruption made it impossible properly to supply frontline troops: "I can do nothing with my army. I am glad when it carries out my combat orders."[100] Denikin either could not or would not enforce obedience or prevent marauding and looting. The problem was not so much with the original Volunteer Army as with the Cossacks and conscripts. The anti-Jewish pogroms by Cossacks serving under Denikin in the summer and fall of 1919 were only the most vicious manifestation of this indiscipline. Pilfering was all-pervasive except among the elite volunteer units. It not only alienated the population at large and demoralized the troops, but slowed the Army's movements, for the loot which it carried was bulky.

On January 8, 1919, Denikin assumed supreme command of all the anti-Bolshevik forces in the south: the Volunteer Army now became a part of the Armed Forces in the South of Russia and Denikin its Commander in Chief (Glavnokomanduiushchii Vooruzhënnymi Silami na Iuge Rossii). (He had refused the title "Supreme Leader"—Verkhovnyi Rukovoditel— held by Alekseev.)[101] The status of the Don Cossacks was partially resolved with Allied help. After the defeated Germans had withdrawn from the Ukraine and he had lost their patronage, Krasnov had no choice but to accommodate the Allies. They told him he would receive aid only through Denikin, and that to obtain it he had to subordinate himself to him.[102]

Krasnov had difficulty with this arrangement and in February 1919 made way for a Don Cossack of greater pro-Russian sympathies.* The Don Cossack army, however, was never fully integrated: it retained its distinct identity and was promised that it would be deployed only on the Don front.[103]

On the Eastern front—the Volga, Urals, and Siberia—where the politicians led and the military followed, there was growing dissatisfaction with the bickering and intrigues that marked the Directory's rule: to many it seemed a "repetition of Kerensky."[104] The Directory's impotence was indeed striking: it is said to have had "as much voice in affairs as a cuckoo-clock on the wall of a rowdy saloon."[105] Calls resounded for a "firm hand." How else, it was asked, could the most oppressive dictatorial regime in history be overcome, except by another dictatorship? A messenger dispatched from Moscow by the National Center brought to Omsk a recommendation to this effect; similar demands were made by Siberian politicians and even some Social-Democrats. "The idea of dictatorship hung in the air."[106]

The events that precipitated the November 17, 1918, Omsk coup that brought to power a dictator in the person of Admiral Alexander Kolchak were the subversive activities of the Socialist-Revolutionary Party. As noted, Chernov, the party's titular head and unchallenged leader of its left wing, had all along opposed the concessions his colleagues had made to the Right SRs and the liberals as a price of forming the Directory. On October 24 the Central Committee of the SR Party in Ufa passed on his motion a resolution that in effect repudiated the Ufa accords.[107] The "Chernov Manifesto," as it came to be known, stated that in the struggle between Bolshevism and democracy, "the latter is dangerously imperiled by counter-revolutionary elements that have allied themselves [with democracy] for the purpose of ruining it." While supporting the Directory in its struggle against "commissar autocracy,"

> in anticipation of possible political crises resulting from counter-revolu-
> tionary schemes, all the forces of the party must be immediately mobilized,
> given military training and armed, so as to be able to repel at any moment
> the attacks of the counter-revolutionaries who organize a civil war in the
> rear of the anti-Bolshevik front.

The document leaked, infuriating the military, whom it reminded of what the Petrograd Soviet had done to them in 1917. More sensible SRs were

---

*After leaving the Don, Krasnov served briefly in the army of General Iudenich: George Stewart, *The White Armies of Russia* (New York, 1933), 415. Later, in exile, he wrote novels about the Civil War which were quite popular in the West. During World War II he collaborated with the Nazis. Captured by the Red Army at the end of the war, he was executed at the age of 78.

appalled. General Boldyrev wrote in his diary that this "Manifesto" showed that the SR Central Committee was resuming its "treacherous work" by declaring the intention to form a new government and secretly gathering an armed force to put it in power: it was nothing less than a coup d'état directed from the left.[108] In the opinion of General Knox, had such a document been written in England, its authors would have been shot.[109] Avksentev and Zenzinov, members of the Central Committee as well as dominant figures in the Directory, were upset by the Manifesto, but out of party loyalty did not disown it, thereby reinforcing the prevalent impression that the SR members of the Directory were conniving in a looming putsch.

This belief provided the rationale for removing the SRs from the government—an act tantamount to liquidating the Directory. When Chernov's Manifesto became known in Omsk, Vologodskii, the Chairman of the Council of Ministers, and General Boldyrev called for the arrest of the SR Central Committee.[110] At the same time, judiciary proceedings were initiated against the document's authors.

While these events were taking place, Kolchak was on an inspection tour of the front; he returned to Omsk on November 16. The following day several officers and Cossacks approached him with the request that he take power. Among them was General D. A. Lebedev, Denikin's liaison officer in Omsk and once a close associate of Kornilov's, who hated the SRs for their role in the Kornilov affair. Kolchak refused for three reasons: he had no armed force at his disposal (this was in Boldyrev's charge); he did not know the attitude of the Siberian government; and he did not wish to act disloyally toward the Directory, which he served.[111] Rather than assume dictatorial powers, he said he was considering resigning his ministerial post, which was to him a source of endless frustration.

Rebuffed, the supporters of a dictatorship apparently decided to force his hand. At midnight of November 17–18, in a raging storm, a detachment of Siberian Cossacks, led by Ataman I. N. Krasilnikov, broke into a private meeting held at the residence of the Deputy Minister of the Interior. Present were several SRs, including Avksentev and Zenzinov. The latter two were arrested along with their host; Argunov, Avksentev's deputy, was taken in later that night. The coup, directed against the Socialists-Revolutionaries in the government and apparently masterminded by Lebedev, was a total surprise to everyone, including Kolchak.

Because of the myths spread about the circumstances that brought Kolchak to power—myths that had a very harmful effect on his relations with democratic circles in Russia and abroad—it is important to establish certain facts. For one, Kolchak did not engineer the coup: no evidence has been produced to show that he instigated it or even knew of it beforehand. There is no reason, therefore, to doubt his version of events, namely that he first learned of what had happened when he received a phone call in the middle of the night.[112] According to his biographer, Kolchak was "perhaps the only member of the Council of Ministers of whom it can be said with certainty that he was not privy to Krasilnikov's coup."[113] Nor is there any basis for the claim, originating with French generals, that the Omsk coup had been masterminded by the English mission.[114] The evidence, some of it made available only after World War II, corroborates General Knox's assertion that the coup "was carried out by the Siberian government without the previous knowledge, and without in any sense the connivance of Great Britain."[115] Archival materials indicate that ten days before the coup, when rumors of it were rife, Knox had warned Kolchak that such a step would be "fatal."[116]

The news of the arrests spread during the night and at six a.m. the cabinet of ministers held an emergency session. The demise of the Directory being accepted as a fait accompli, the cabinet temporarily assumed full authority.[117] The majority of the ministers felt that power should be entrusted to a military dictator. Kolchak suggested Boldyrev for the post, but the candidacy was rejected on the grounds that the general could not be spared from his responsibilities as Commander in Chief. The cabinet then chose Kolchak, with one dissenting vote. When he learned of this decision (he was at the front at the time) Boldyrev was so outraged that he advised Kolchak to resign, threatening that the army would not obey his orders.[118] Since Kolchak did not heed his advice, Boldyrev gave up his command and left for Japan.* Allied representatives in Omsk promptly gave Kolchak their support, as did the two members of the Directory not under arrest.[119] The Directory enjoyed so little popular support that no one rose to its defense: this much is conceded even by Argunov.[120] Maiskii, a Menshevik who later turned Bolshevik and ended up as Soviet ambassador to England, admits that the population of Omsk sympathized with Kolchak, from whom it expected the restoration of order: the people he encountered immediately after the coup wore the expression "if not of happiness then of something like relief." Local workers took the imposition of a military dictatorship in stride.[121]

Scrutiny of these events leads to the inescapable conclusion that what occurred was a coup by Cossacks and officers of the Siberian government, followed by a transfer of authority. After the arrest of the Directory's members, the Council of Ministers, which the Directory had appointed, took no steps to have them released and restored to power; instead, it claimed authority on its own behalf and immediately consigned it to Admiral Kolchak. There are thus no grounds whatever of speaking of "Kolchak's coup" or "Kolchak's seizure of power," as is commonly done in histories of these events. Kolchak did not take power: it was thrust on him.

Against his express wishes, he was given the title "Supreme Ruler" (Verkhovnyi Pravitel') rather than "Commander in Chief" (Verkhnovnyi Glavnokomanduiushchii), which he would have preferred. It was the intention

---

*Boldyrev was captured by the Reds in Vladivostok in 1922, at which time he acknowledged Soviet authority and asked for "forgiveness." He is said to have been given amnesty. V.G. Boldyrev, *Direktoria, Kolchak, Interventy* (Novonikolaevsk, 1925), 12–13.

of those who had appointed him to create a "steadfast supreme power, freed of executive functions, independent of any party influence, and endowed with equal authority over the civil and military personnel."[122] In a much more explicit sense than Denikin, Kolchak was not only a military but also a civilian commander in chief like Pilsudski in Poland. Serving under him was a Council of Ministers. But events soon forced Kolchak to assume full executive powers, and the cabinet—composed of the same ministers as under the Directory—was reduced to drafting legislative bills. Kolchak normally did not attend its meetings.

Kolchak was generous to his Socialist-Revolutionary opponents. The arrested SRs—who would probably have been murdered if Colonel Ward had not interceded for them[123]—were ordered released. Kolchak gave them a liberal allowance (between 50,000 and 75,000 rubles each), put them on a train, and had them escorted to the Chinese border, whence they made their way to Western Europe. There they immediately launched a bitter campaign of vilification against him, which was not without effect on Western attitudes toward intervention. The bitterness of the Socialists-Revolutionaries stemmed from the realization that the demise of the Directory marked the end of any hopes they might still have had of gaining power in Russia—power to which they felt entitled by their victory in the elections to the Constituent Assembly. They no longer could hope to play the role of a third force, but had to choose between the Reds and the Whites.

It did not take them long to make the choice. The SR Central Committee, pronouncing Kolchak an "enemy of the people" and a counterrevolutionary, appealed to the population to rise against him. To avoid inevitable retribution, it decided to go underground and revert to terror: with the approval of the Central Committee it pronounced a death sentence on Kolchak.[124] On November 30, Kolchak demanded of the members of the defunct Komuch that they cease inciting uprisings in the rear of the White armies and interfering with military communications, under threat of severe punishment.[125] To no avail. The SRs considered themselves in a state of war with the Omsk government, and given the size of their following in Siberia, it was not an idle threat.

On December 22, 1918, the SRs went from words to deeds and jointly with the Bolsheviks tried to stage a coup d'état in Omsk. It was quickly suppressed by the Czech garrison and the Cossacks: over 100 of the rebels—according to some accounts, as many as 400—were summarily executed. Kolchak was later personally blamed for this atrocity. But in fact when it was perpetrated he was seriously ill and had no knowledge of it.[126]

During the first year of the Bolshevik dictatorship, the Mensheviks and SRs living in Soviet Russia bided their time, convinced that the Bolsheviks would not be able to rule for long without their help. This conviction helped them patiently bear Bolshevik harassment. Their slogan was

"Neither Lenin nor Denikin (or Kolchak)." The Mensheviks were the more sanguine of the two. Although disenfranchised, throughout 1918 they refused to join any anti-Bolshevik organizations: their members were strictly forbidden to take part in activities directed against the Soviet regime. They felt confident that the people's democratic instincts would eventually triumph and force the Bolsheviks to share power: they saw their role as that of a loyal and legal opposition.[127] The SRs were divided. The Left SRs, after their abortive July 1918 coup, gradually melted away. The SR Party proper split into two factions, a more radical one under Chernov, which wanted to follow the Menshevik strategy, and a right one, which preferred to challenge the regime in the name of the Constituent Assembly. It was the latter that had organized Komuch and in September 1918 joined the Directory.

The establishment of a military dictatorship in Omsk frightened the Mensheviks and the Right Socialists-Revolutionaries alike and drove them into Bolshevik arms. They ignored the Red Terror, which was then in full swing, claiming thousands of lives, because, by and large, it did not affect them: for although the Cheka, the Bolshevik secret police, fulminated against the socialist "traitors," its victims were mainly officials of the old regime and well-to-do citizens. The terror the Mensheviks and SRs feared was the White one. They viewed Bolshevik policies with genuine distaste and missed no opportunity to make their opinions known, often at considerable risk to themselves. But in their view the Bolsheviks were definitely the lesser evil because they had only "half liquidated" the Revolution;[128] the Whites, if triumphant, would liquidate it completely. Faced with this prospect, in late 1918 the Mensheviks, followed by the SRs, moved toward reconciliation with Lenin's regime.

The Mensheviks, who had taken part neither in Komuch nor in the Directory, had been gravitating in this direction even before the Omsk coup. L. Martov, the leader of the Internationalist wing of the party, called for neutrality in the Civil War as early as July 1918 on the grounds that the defeat of the Whites would produce a democratic government in Russia.[129] Toward the end of October, excited by the prospect of a revolution in Germany, the Menshevik Central Committee declared the Bolshevik "revolution" to have been "historically inevitable."[130] On November 14—three days after the armistice on the Western front—the same Central Committee appealed to all the revolutionary elements to rise against "Anglo-American imperialism."[131] Prominent Mensheviks, among them Theodore Dan, called on workers and peasants to "form a single revolutionary front against the attacks of the counterrevolution and predatory international imperialism," warning "all enemies of the Russian Revolution . . . that when it is a question of defending the Revolution, our party, with all its power, stands shoulder to shoulder with [the Soviet] government."[132] In December 1919, the Social-Democrats Internationalists voted to join the Communist Party.[133]

As a reward for this about-face, the Bolshevik leadership reversed its decision of the previous June to expel the Mensheviks from the soviets.[134] In January 1919 the party received permission to bring out its organ, the newspaper *Vsegda vpered.* The paper published such scathing criticism of the government, especially of the Red Terror, however, that it was closed after several issues. It never reappeared.

The SRs were somewhat more reluctant to turn pro-Bolshevik, because, unlike the Mensheviks, who were a small remnant of the Social-Democratic Party without any political prospects, they, as the party with the greatest popular following, felt they had history's mandate to govern Russia. In December 1918, after the Directory had been overthrown, the Ufa Committee of the SR Party, the mainstay of Komuch, opened negotiations with Moscow. The talks were consummated in January with an accord calling on

> all soldiers of the People's Army to cease the civil war against Soviet authority, which, at the present historical moment, is the only revolutionary authority of the exploited classes for the suppression of exploiters, and to turn all their weapons against the dictatorship of Kolchak.[135]

Troops of the People's Army who obeyed this call were promised amnesty. Following this accord, nearly all units of the People's Army went over to the Reds.[136] In the course of these negotiations, the Bolsheviks compelled the Ufa delegation to renounce the idea of a Constituent Assembly.[137]

The main body of the SR Party felt it had no choice but to adopt the policy of accommodation as well. On February 6–9, 1919, its Central Committee Party and branch organizations on Soviet territory held a conference in Moscow to formulate a policy on the current situation. After voicing routine laments over the absence of democracy in Soviet Russia, the gathering accused the "bourgeoisie" and the "landlords" of seeking to reestablish the monarchy, and called on its members to "bend their efforts to overturn [reactionary] governments" created under Allied sponsorship. The conference placed itself on record as rejecting in

> an unequivocal manner attempts to overthrow the Soviet regime by means of an armed struggle, which, given the weakness and dispersion of labor democracy and the ever growing power of the counterrevolution, will only benefit the latter, enabling reactionary groups to exploit it for the purposes of a [monarchist] restoration.[138]

SRs were instructed to work for the overthrow of the governments of Denikin and Kolchak but to refrain from actively resisting the Communist regime. The policy was justified as a "tactical" concession that did not imply even a conditional recognition of Bolshevik authority.[139] This stipulation did not alter the fact that at the decisive phase of the Civil War, the Socialists-Revolutionaries placed themselves squarely on the side of the Bolsheviks. As reward, in February 1919 they were also allowed to rejoin the soviets.[140] On March 20, the SR Party was legalized and given permission to bring out its daily, *Delo naroda*. The paper, the first copy of which appeared on the same day, was suspended after six issues. Nevertheless, the SRs adhered to the new course, formalizing their pro-Communist orientation at the Ninth Council, held in Moscow in June 1919. The resolutions of this Council appealed to the party's members to discontinue the struggle against the Bolshevik regime. The SR Party should henceforth

> shift the center of its struggle against Kolchak, Denikin, and the others to their territories, subverting their work from within and fighting in the front ranks of the people who have risen against the political and social restoration, employing all the methods the Party had used against [tsarist] autocracy.[141]

Denikin could ignore such belligerent appeals, which called for a renewal of terrorism, because in the area where his troops operated in the first half of 1919 neither the SRs nor the Mensheviks had a significant following. But it was different in Siberia, where the SR appeals for subversion threatened the army's rear. Kolchak's officials now began to treat SRs as traitors and to arrest them along with Bolsheviks. Several members of Komuch were executed. The most savage persecutions were carried out by General S. N. Rozanov, who was appointed in March 1919 to suppress disorders in Enisei province. Emulating Bolshevik practices (according to a Soviet source, he had once served in the Red Army), he ordered imprisoned Bolsheviks and bandits to be treated as hostages and executed in reprisal for acts of violence committed against the regime.[142] Kolchak insisted that he had forbidden such practices;[143] no document bearing his signature ordering such executions has been found. But since they occurred under his rule, he shared the odium.

Mainly as a result of General Knox's sympathy, Kolchak received strong British support. Until his reverses in the summer of 1919, Britain pinned her hopes on Kolchak and made him, rather than Denikin, the main beneficiary of military aid. A second British battalion arrived in Omsk in January 1919, to bolster the impression of Allied backing, along with a small naval detachment that fought the Red Army on the Kama River—apart from Czechs, the only Allied unit to see combat in Siberia.[144] Knox assumed responsibility for the rear, that is, the lines of communication, and for the training in Vladivostok of 3,000 Russian officers.[145] The other powers were distinctly cool to the Supreme Ruler. General Maurice Janin, who arrived in Omsk in December in the double capacity of head of the French military mission and Commander of the Czechoslovak Legion (to which post he was appointed by the Czechoslovak National Council in Paris), regarded Kolchak as a creature of the British. He demanded to be placed at the head of all the Allied forces in Siberia, including Russian units. Kolchak rejected this request out of hand. Eventually, a compromise formula was devised by virtue of which Kolchak commanded Russian troops but coordinated military operations with Janin. The Czech National Council, which maintained close relations with the SRs and had taken a direct hand in creating the Directory, was from the outset inimical to Kolchak: after the overthrow of the Directory, it issued a statement denouncing the coup as a regrettable violation of the "principle of legality."[146]

The greatest trouble came from the Japanese, who opposed Kolchak from fear that he would prevent their annexing Russia's Far Eastern provinces. By late 1918, they had 70,000 troops in Eastern Siberia. Although these had been dispatched to help open a new front, Tokyo ignored British pleas in the summer to move them west and help the hard-pressed Czechs. Instead, they used them to establish a regular occupation regime of a very brutal nature, in which they were assisted by two Cossack warlords, G. M. Semenov and Ivan Kalmykov (the ataman of the Ussuri Cossacks), whom they gave military and financial assistance. The two thugs terrorized Siberia east of Lake Baikal, forming a buffer between Kolchak and the Japanese. As a consequence, Kolchak's authority never extended to the east of Baikal. Semenov, based in Chita, with bands controlling the territory between Khabarovsk and Baikal, refused even to recognize Kolchak. He was an ordinary brigand who hijacked trains and looted the civilian population, disposing of the proceeds in Japan and China. The commander of American troops in Siberia says that the bands of Semenov and Kalmykov, "under the protection of Japanese troops, were roaming the country like wild animals, killing and robbing the people. . . . If questions were asked about these brutal murders, the answer was that the people murdered were Bolsheviks."[147]

In August 1918 the United States dispatched from the Philippines to Siberia an expeditionary force that ultimately numbered 7,000 men, under the command of Major General William S. Graves. Graves's instructions were to help rebuild the anti-German front, but to refrain from any intervention in internal Russian affairs:

> It is the clear and fixed judgment of the Government of the United States . . . that military intervention there would add to the present sad confusion in Russia rather than cure it, injure her rather than help her, and that it would be of no advantage in the prosecution of our main design, to win the war against Germany. It cannot, therefore, take part in such intervention or sanction it in principle. Military intervention would, in its judgment, even supposing it to be efficacious in its immediate avowed object of delivering an attack upon Germany from the east, be merely a method of making use of Russia, not a method of serving her. Her people could not profit by it, if they profited by it at all, in time to save them from their present distresses, and their substance would be to maintain foreign armies, not to reconstitute their own. Military action is admissible in Russia . . . only to help the Czechoslovaks consolidate their forces . . . and to steady any efforts at self-government or self-defense in which the Russians themselves may be willing to accept assistance.[148]

These instructions suffered from an obvious contradiction inasmuch as the mere presence of U.S. troops in areas controlled by anti-Communist forces involved them in the Russian Civil War. Nevertheless, Graves would persevere in the effort to maintain the strictest neutrality and to function purely as a technical expert in a region where the contending parties were fighting for their very lives. He and his government received little gratitude for this behavior, the Bolsheviks treating the Americans as hostile interventionists and the Whites regarding them as Bolshevik sympathizers. Graves by his own admission knew nothing of Russia or Siberia, into which he writes he had been "pitch-forked," and he had scant idea what the Civil War was about: he felt "no prejudice against any Russian faction." After landing in Vladivostok, he was appalled to learn that the British and French actually sought to destroy the Bolsheviks, whom he understood to be Russians opposed to the restoration of autocracy.[149]

Until the spring of 1919, American troops in Siberia carried out ordinary garrison duties: subsequently, they assumed responsibility for the operations of the Transsiberian Railroad between Lake Baikal and the sea. U.S. transportation experts, originally invited by the Provisional Government, undertook, by the terms of an agreement concluded in March 1919, to maintain Siberia's railroads "for the Russians" regardless of whether they were Bolsheviks or anti-Bolsheviks. Graves announced publicly that no distinction would be drawn among the passengers (they would be carried "irrespective of persons . . . or politics") or the destinations of freight.[150] This sounded as if the Americans were prepared to transport Bolshevik partisans and their equipment, which astounded the British and infuriated the Whites. Whatever his professions of impartiality, Graves intensely disliked Kolchak's government, believing it to be made up of incorrigible reactionaries and monarchists. On the Bolsheviks, whom he had never encountered, he kept an open mind ("I was never able to determine who was a Bolshevik or why he was a Bolshevik"[151]).

Kolchak conceived his role in strictly military terms. He believed that Russia had been brought to her sorry state by the collapse of her army and would rise again only by the army's intercession: the army for him was the heart of Russia.[152] As he told the Bolshevik commission of inquiry after his arrest:

> I did not intend to make any sweeping, complicated reforms, because I regarded my power as temporary. . . . The country needed victory at any cost, and every effort had to be exerted to secure it. I had absolutely no definite political objectives; I should not side with any parties, should not aim at restoring anything old, but should try only to create an army of the regular type, since I believed that only such an army could gain victories.[153]

On assuming power, Kolchak issued a succinct declaration:

On November 18, 1918, the All-Russian Provisional Government fell
apart. The Council of Ministers assumed full authority and transferred it
to me, Alexander Kolchak, Admiral of the Russian Navy. Assuming the
cross of this authority in the exceptionally difficult condition of Civil War
and the complete disintegration of political life, I declare:
   I shall take neither the path of reaction nor the ruinous course of party
politics [*partiinost'*]. My principal objective is to create an army capable of
combat, victory over Bolshevism, and the introduction of legality and the
rule of law, which will make it possible for the nation to choose for itself,
unhindered, the kind of government it desires and to realize the great ideals
of freedom that have now been proclaimed throughout the world.
   I call you, citizens, to unity, to the struggle against Bolshevism, to work,
and to sacrifices.[154]

On November 28 Kolchak acknowledged Russia's obligation for her foreign debts and pledged repayment.[155] On another occasion he stated that he
considered himself bound by all the commitments and laws of the Provisional Government of 1917.[156] Beyond this he would not go. In common
with the other White leaders, he believed that political and social manifestos, especially in a country as contentious as Russia, unnecessarily complicated the task of fighting the Bolsheviks: "only the armed forces, only the
army, can save us," he told the officers on assuming command. "All else
should be subordinated to its interests and its mission."[157]

   The Supreme Ruler of Eastern Russia and Siberia was born in 1873 into
a military family.[158] He pursued a military career as well, enrolling in the
Naval Academy. He took part in three Arctic expeditions in the course of
which he displayed notable courage, earning the sobriquet "Kolchak-
Poliarnyi"—"Kolchak of the [North] Pole." He fought at Port Arthur
against the Japanese, following which he accepted appointment to the
Naval General Staff. During World War I he served in the Baltic until 1916,
when he was promoted to command the Black Sea Fleet: his mission was
to prepare and lead a naval expedition against Constantinople and the
Straits planned for the following year. In the summer of 1917 the Provisional Government sent him on a mission to the United States. His return
was disrupted by the Bolshevik coup. He tried to get back to Russia by way
of the Far East. In Japan he met General Knox, on whom he made a
powerful impression: the English general thought he had "more grit, pluck
and honest patriotism than any Russian in Siberia."[159] After the conclusion
of the Brest-Litovsk Treaty, which he viewed as the beginning of Russia's
subjugation by Germany, Kolchak offered his services to the British Army.
He was at first assigned to Mesopotamia and was en route there when his
English superiors changed their minds (almost certainly on the recommendation of Knox) and asked him to return to East Asia. He spent the early
months of 1918 in Manchuria in charge of security of the Chinese Eastern
Railway. In October 1918, traveling to the Don to join Denikin's forces, he
was passing through Omsk when General Boldyrev invited him to take over
the Directory's Ministry of War.

7. Kolchak.

Kolchak had admirable qualities: he was a man of great integrity, of proven courage, of selfless patriotism—in many ways, along with Wrangel, the most honorable White commander in the Civil War. Whether he had the traits required of a leader in such a war is another matter. For one, he was a complete stranger to politics: by his own admission, he had grown up in a military milieu and had "hardly interested himself in any political problems and questions." He saw himself simply as a "military technician."[160] As he stated in the declaration of November 18, he regarded his new duties as a "cross." To his wife, he complained of the "terrifying burden of Supreme Power" and confessed that as "a fighting man [he was] reluctant to face the problems of statecraft."[161] Politically untutored, he sought simplistic conspiratorial explanations for contemporary events: his favorite reading is said to have been the *Protocols of the Elders of Zion.**

Secondly, he was ill at ease among people: withdrawn, taciturn, and extremely moody, he was an outsider both in and out of power. Observing him in the midst of the Directory and its ministers, Colonel Ward saw "a small, vagrant, lonely troubled soul without a friend enter unbidden to a feast."[162] An associate wrote of him:

> The character and soul of the Admiral are so transparent that one needs no more than one week of contact to know all there is to know about him. He is a big, sick child, a pure idealist, a convinced slave of duty and service to

*Gins, *Sibir'*, II, 368. At the same time, unlike Denikin, he made it clear that he would tolerate no anti-Jewish excesses.

an idea and to Russia. An indubitable neurotic who quickly flares up, exceedingly impetuous and uncontrolled in expressions of displeasure and anger: in this respect he has assimilated the highly unattractive traditions of the naval service, which permit high naval ranks behavior that in our army has long ago passed into the realm of legends. He is utterly absorbed by the idea of serving Russia, of saving her from Red oppression and restoring her to full power and to the inviolability of her territory. For the sake of this idea he can be persuaded and moved to do anything whatever. He has no personal interests, no amour propre: in this respect, he is crystal pure. He passionately despises all lawlessness and arbitrariness, but because he is so uncontrolled and impulsive, he himself often unintentionally transgresses against the law, and this mainly when seeking to uphold the very same law, and always under the influence of some outsider. He does not know life in its severe, practical reality, and lives in a world of mirages and borrowed ideas. He has no plans, no system, no will: in this respect he is soft wax from which advisers and intimates can fashion whatever they want, exploiting the fact that it is enough to disguise something as necessary for the welfare of Russia and the good of the cause to be certain of his approval.[163]

Another associate wrote of Kolchak:

He is kind and at the same time severe, responsive and at the same time embarrassed to show human feelings, concealing his gentleness behind make-believe severity. He is impatient and stubborn, loses his temper, threatens, and then calms down, makes concessions, spreads his hands in a gesture of helplessness. He is bursting to be with the people, with the troops, but when he faces them, has no idea what to say.[164]

His photographs show a tortured expression: furrowed brows, compressed lips, eyes suggestive of a manic-depressive personality. Unable to understand people or to communicate with them, he proved an execrable administrator in whose name were committed unpardonable acts of corruption and brutality that he personally found utterly repugnant.

Except for integrity, courage, and patriotism, nothing qualified Kolchak for the responsibilities imposed on him by the Omsk politicians. A tragic quality attended his year-long dictatorship, which he did not seek and which, after fleeting triumphs, was to end in death before a Bolshevik firing squad.

2

The Civil War:
The Climax (1919–1920)

The campaigns that were to decide the outcome of the Civil War opened in the spring of 1919 and concluded seven months later, in November, with the crushing defeat of the principal White armies.

The Soviet government resolved in the fall of 1918 to proceed in earnest with the formation of a regular army. The initial plan called for a force of one million men: on October 1, 1918, however, Lenin ordered the creation by the next spring of an army of 3 million "to help the international workers' revolution."* General conscription followed, in the course of which hundreds of thousands of peasants were inducted.

The creation of an army of such size confronted the Soviet leadership with the problem of command. Clearly, an army of millions could not be led by elected commanders or party veterans, who alone were trusted, since few of them had any military experience at all, and fewer still had ever commanded units larger than a battalion. The regime therefore decided it had no choice but to draft tens of thousands of ex-Imperial officers consid-

---

*Lenin, *PSS*, L, 186. Early in 1919, the Red Commander in Chief, I. I. Vatsetis, reported to Lenin that the army numbered 1.8 million but that of this number only 383,000 were combat troops. *IA*, No. 1 (1958), 42–43, 45. Throughout the Civil War, the proportion of "fighters" to "eaters" in the Red Army averaged around 1 to 10. It is estimated that the number of its frontline troops at no time exceeded half a million: Orlando Figes in *Past and Present*, No. 129 (November 1990), 184.

ered irreconcilably hostile to Communism, officers whom it would keep in line through a combination of political controls and terror. This crucial decision made by Lenin and Trotsky, though controversial at the time, was undoubtedly a sound one. A few officers followed their consciences and, at the risk of their lives, collaborated with the Whites;* but by and large, the old officers, once they donned uniforms, performed as professionals, and it was they who won the Civil War for the Communists.

The first officers to fight for the Red Army were volunteers who enlisted in February and March 1918, during the breakdown of the Brest-Litovsk negotiations, when German troops were advancing into Russia. Responding to the government's call, over 8,000 ex-tsarist officers signed up, among them 28 generals and colonels.[1] They meant to defend Russia from the Germans; but the expected Soviet-German war never materialized, and before long they found themselves fighting fellow Russians.[2]

The drafting of commissioned personnel got underway in late July 1918 when ex-Imperial officers, military medical personnel, and civil servants between the ages of 21 and 26 were ordered to register or face trial by a Revolutionary Tribunal.[3] A decree of September 30, written by Trotsky, reinstituted the medieval Russian practice of collective responsibility by holding families of officers ("fathers, mothers, sisters, brothers, wives and children") personally liable for their loyalty.[4] Finally, on November 23, all officers under 50 and generals under 60 were ordered to register, again under the threat of severe penalties.[5]

Lenin's and Trotsky's orders to draft peasants along with ex-tsarist officers did not go unchallenged. The controversy over the hiring of "military specialists" paralleled the concurrent debate over "bourgeois specialists" in industry. It came to a head at the Eighth Party Congress in March 1919. Trotsky, who had had to dash off to the Eastern front, was absent, but his "Theses" served as the text of the secret debates.† In the "Theses," Trotsky called for strict centralization of the army command and the recruitment of ex-tsarist officers, both to work under the close supervision of the Central Committee. The opponents of the Lenin-Trotsky policy argued that such an army would be unreliable and that it was offensive for Bolshevik veterans to be ordered about by onetime tsarist officers. They preferred a collegial system of army management and greater authority being vested in commissars to intervene in military directives.[6] Lenin, however, supported Trotsky:

---

*One disloyal officer was a Colonel Makhin, a member of the SR Party, who is said to have been ordered by his Central Committee to enroll in the Red Army as a spy. He defected while Chief of Staff in Ufa, which led to its capture by the Czechs in the summer of 1918: I. Maiskii, *Demokraticheskaia kontr-revoliutsiia* (Moscow, 1923), 53. Another was P. E. Kniagnitskii, the commander of the Ninth Red Army in the Ukraine: Evan Mawdsley, *The Russian Civil War* (Boston, 1987), 179. There was also the case of Colonel V. A. Liundekvist, the Chief of Staff of the Seventh Army defending Petrograd. (See below, p. 124.)

†L. Trotskii, *Kak vooruzhalas' revoliutsiia* (Moscow, 1923), I, 186–95. The minutes of the closed session at which these matters were discussed were first made public seventy years later: *IzvTsK*, No. 9/296 (September 1989), 135–90; No. 10/297 (October 1989), 171–89; and No. 11/298 (November 1989), 144–78.

the time had come, he said, to end the "partisan" style of waging war. Under his prodding, the Eighth Congress approved Trotsky's "Theses."

The pool of officers available to the Communists was large (250,000) and socially diversified, since a high proportion consisted of commoners commissioned during World War I. The Russian officer corps on the eve of the Revolution was anything but an aristocratic preserve: of the 220,000 lieutenants commissioned during the war, 80 percent were peasants, and 50 percent had no secondary school diploma.[7] Officers differed from the rank and file not so much socially or economically as culturally: to peasant soldiers, any educated man—one who had attended, even if he had not finished, secondary school—was an *intelligent* and as such a *barin'*, or "master."[8] It was not the least of Russia's tragedies that for the population at large, the acquisition of an education above basic literacy made one an outsider and, as such, a potential enemy.

After the old army fell apart, officers living under Bolshevik rule led a miserable existence, persecuted by the regime as "counterrevolutionaries," shunned by civilians who feared the Cheka, and destitute, since their pensions had been cut off.[9] Other defeated countries neglected their returning war veterans, but only Bolshevik Russia dishonored and hunted down demobilized officers as if they were rabid dogs. The involvement of hundreds of officers in the Savinkov conspiracy and in his July 1918 uprisings on the upper Volga led to regular manhunts in which many perished.[10] By October 1918 no fewer than 8,000 officers sat in prison as hostages under the terms of the Red Terror.[11] But toward the end of the year the situation changed: the Communists needed the ex-officers to command their forces; the ex-officers needed jobs and status to shield them from persecution. In the winter of 1918–19 they began to enroll in the Red Army, some willingly, some under duress, to take command of newly created regiments, brigades, divisions, and armies.

The regime that was to prevail in the Red Army in the second, decisive phase of the Civil War represented an original blend of responsibilities under which the Communist Party exercised tight political supervision over the officers while conceding them wide discretion in the conduct of military operations. The system was put in place in early September 1918 after the Red Army had been severely mauled by the Czechs.

Following the decision on September 4 to transform Soviet Russia into a "military camp" (*voennyi lager'*), the government established a Revolutionary Military Council of the Republic (Revoliutsionnyi Voennyi Sovet Respubliki, or Revvoensovet);[12] it replaced the Vysshyi Voennyi Sovet and assumed full command of the country's war effort.* The new Council operated directly under the Central Committee of the Communist Party. Its

---

*Not to be confused with the Council of Workers' and Peasants' Defense, created on November 30, 1918, and presided over by Lenin, with Trotsky as deputy. This body coordinated military and civilian policies: Isaac Deutscher, *Prophet Armed* (London, 1954), 423n; N. I. Shatagin, *Organizatsiia i stroitel'stvo sovetskoi armii v 1918–1920 gg.* (Moscow, 1954), 98.

8. A demobilized officer of the Russian Army trying to make ends meet.

Chairman was the Commissar of War, Trotsky; during Trotsky's frequent visits to the front, it was run by his deputy, E. M. Sklianskii, an old Bolshevik and a physician by profession. Subordinated to it were Revolutionary Councils of the fourteen armies, made up of the army commander and his commissars. Members of the central Revvoensovet were regularly dispatched to the front to serve as "organs of communication, observation and instruction"; they were under strict orders not to interfere with the military decisions of the professional officers. The Revvoensovet included the Commander in Chief of All the Armed Forces of the Republic, a "military specialist" entrusted with broad authority in strategic and operational matters. For his directives to acquire force, however, they had to be countersigned by a civilian member of the Revolutionary Military Council.

He was empowered to recommend the appointment and removal of subordinate officers.[13] Under him served the Field Staff (Polevoi Shtab RVSR), which worked out the day-to-day operational directives. It was headed by four generals of the old army.[14] The Revvoensovet enjoyed immense powers not only over the entire military establishment but over all state institutions, which were required to assign its requests the highest priority.

At this time, emulating tsarist practice, the armies were organized into "fronts." Each was commanded by its own Revolutionary Military Council made up of one "military specialist," nearly always an ex-tsarist officer, and two political commissars, who countersigned his directives. A similar arrangement prevailed in the armies. Below the army level (division, brigade, regiment), political supervision of each unit was exercised by a single commissar. These traditional military units replaced the "detachments" (*otriady*) of 700 to 1,000 men under a commander and two assistants, as a rule elected by their troops, prevalent in the first year of Communist rule.[15]

In the course of the Civil War some 75,000 ex-Imperial officers served in the Red Army, in that number 775 generals and 1,726 other officers of the Imperial General Staff.[16] The preponderance of old officers in the command structure of the Red Army during the Civil War can be demonstrated statistically. They made up 85 percent of the commanders of fronts, 82 percent of the commanders of armies, and 70 percent of the commanders of divisions.[17] The extent to which the tsarist officer corps was integrated into the new, Soviet one, is illustrated by the fact that the two last tsarist Ministers of War (A. A. Polivanov and D. S. Shuvaev) and one Minister of War of the Provisional Government (A. I. Verkhovskii) also joined the Red Army. In addition, Moscow inducted many thousands of noncommissioned officers of the old army.

Although few of the old officers sympathized with the Bolshevik dictatorship or joined the Communist Party, most remained true to the Russian tradition that the military should stay out of politics. In photographs, with their indelibly old-regime faces, they look highly uncomfortable garbed in rough, ill-tailored revolutionary uniforms.

While maintaining tight political control over the military, the Bolshevik leadership did not, on the whole, interfere with the conduct of military operations. The Commander in Chief submitted recommendations to the Revvoensovet, which, after routine approval, forwarded them for implementation. S. S. Kamenev, an ex-colonel in the Imperial army who served as Commander in Chief from July of 1919 on, maintains that the High Command was "wholly responsible for military operations."[18]

Trotsky, often depicted as the man who "had founded a great army and had guided it to victory,"[19] made no such claims on his own behalf. The decision to build up a regular army staffed by ex-tsarist officers was taken not personally by him, but by the majority of the Central Committee,

9. Trotsky and Commander in Chief S. S. Kamenev.

although admittedly he pressed extremely hard for it; the conduct of military operations was in the hands of professional generals of the Imperial army. Trotsky had no military experience and his strategic sense left, in any event, a great deal to be desired.* A Soviet general turned historian, having studied the archival sources on Trotsky's activities during the Civil War, concluded that in military matters he was a "dilettante."[20]

Even so, he performed several important services. He would resolve disagreements among the Red generals, usually after consultation with Moscow, and ensure that they carried out the Center's decisions. Touring

---

*For example, in late 1918, expecting massive Allied landings in the Ukraine, he wanted the Red Army to concentrate its forces in the south rather than in the Urals, where Kolchak was making rapid advances. Fortunately for the Communist regime, he was overruled. A year later, he conceived a fantastic plan of creating a cavalry force in the Urals to invade India—this at a time when the Red Army was fighting for its life against Denikin: *TP*, I, 620–25. In a dispatch to Lenin from Kiev dated August 6, 1919, he insisted that the main thrust of Denikin's offensive was directed against the Ukraine, whereas in fact, it aimed at Moscow: *ibid.*, I, 629.

the front in his private train guarded by Latvians, equipped with telegraph, radio transmitter, printing press, and even a garage and an orchestra, accompanied by still and cinema photographers, Trotsky could assess the situation on the spot and, cutting through red tape, make rapid decisions on matters involving manpower and logistics. Thirdly, his appearances and speeches often produced an electrifying effect on dispirited troops:[21] in that respect he was, not unlike Kerensky, a "Persuader in Chief." His directives of the period are filled with exhortations, bearing edifying titles and often ending with exclamation marks: "Southern front, pull yourself together!"; "Round them up!"; "Proletarians, to horse!"; "For shame!"; "Don't waste time!"; "Once more, don't waste time!"; and the like.[22] He was also responsible for introducing draconian discipline into the Red Army, including capital punishment for desertion, panic-mongering, and even unjustified retreat: subject to such measures were commanding officers and Communist commissars as well as military soldiers. Essentially, he managed the armed forces by terror. He justified this with the argument that

> One cannot form an army without repression. One cannot lead human masses to their death without the commanding officers having in their arsenal the death penalty. As long as the evil tailless apes called human beings, proud of their technology, build armies and wage war, so long will those in command present soldiers with [the choice of] possible death in front and certain death in the rear.[23]

In reality, as we shall see, such discipline was only haphazardly enforced because it would have exterminated more than half of the Red Army.

As for Lenin, his wartime role was largely confined to sending alarmist messages to frontline commanders and commissars, demanding that they either hold the line at all costs, "to the last drop of blood,"[24] or advance and decisively smash the enemy, otherwise the "revolution" was lost. Typical was his communication to the commissar at the Southern front in August 1919 as the Red Army was falling back before Denikin's offensive:

> The delay in the advance in the direction of Voronezh (*from the first to the 10th of August!!!*) is monstrous. Denikin has had immense successes. What is the matter? Sokolnikov said that there (near Voronezh) we have 4 *times* superior forces. What is the matter? How could we sleep like that? Tell the Commander in Chief this *cannot* be. One must pay *serious* attention. Should we not send to the Revolutionary Military Council of the Southern front . . . the following telegram: (In code). It is entirely unacceptable to delay the offensive, because such a delay will deliver the entire Ukraine to Denikin and will cause us to perish. You are responsible for every lost day and even every hour of delaying the offensive. Let us immediately have explanations and the time when you will finally launch the decisive attack.
>
> Lenin
> Chairman, Council of Defense[25]

It is doubtful whether such exhortations had any influence on the course of operations. Lenin also never tired of urging his officers to terrorize the civilian population: "Try to punish Latvia and Estonia by military means," he suggested to Sklianskii, "(for instance . . . somewhere penetrate the border even for one verst and hang there 100–1,000 of their officials and rich people)."[26] In February 1920 he threatened to "slaughter" the entire population of Maikop and Groznyi if the local oil fields were sabotaged.[27]

As concerns the third major Communist figure, Stalin, who subsequently claimed the major credit for victory in the Civil War, a recent Russian publication has this to say:

> Careful study of the protocols of the meetings of the Central Committee of the Russian Communist Party and the Sovnarkom of the Russian Republic leads to the following definite conclusion: during all the years of the Civil War Stalin did not once advance in these bodies an independent constructive idea or suggestion on major problems of military organization and strategy.[28]

There were several occasions when the Bolshevik leaders as a group involved themselves in major strategic decisions. According to Trotsky, this was done because officers of the old school lacked appreciation of social and political issues.[29] In the spring of 1919 disagreement broke out among Bolshevik leaders over the question of whether to adopt a defensive stance against Kolchak in order to concentrate on the Southern front, where the danger seemed greatest, or to finish off Kolchak first. Trotsky and his protégé, I. I. Vatsetis, the Commander in Chief, favored the former course; Stalin and S. S. Kamenev, Commander of the Eastern front, the latter. Then another disagreement erupted, over the direction of the thrust against Denikin, which Trotsky wanted to focus on the Donbass, while Kamenev, supported by Stalin, preferred to invade the Don Cossack region. In the fall of 1919, a conflict arose over the defense of Petrograd, which Lenin wanted to abandon as a lost cause. Trotsky, for a change with Stalin's backing, persuaded the Politburo, the policy-making body of the Central Committee, that retaining Petrograd was essential. Finally, in the summer of 1920, during the war with Poland, the Central Committee settled the controversial question of whether to stop the advance of its armies at the ethnographic boundary known as the Curzon Line or to march on Warsaw.

In no time the new army came to resemble the old, even to the point of reintroducing the practice of saluting. In January 1919, the Red Army placed on the sleeves of uniforms "badges of rank" (*znaki razlichiia*): red stars with hammer and sickle plus red triangles for the lower ranks, squares for commanders up to the regimental level, and diamonds for those heading units of brigade size and larger. In April, the army received distinct uniforms; their most visible symbol was a peaked cap, popularly called *boga-*

10. Trotsky and Vatsetis.

tyrka, supposedly modeled on those worn by the heroes of medieval legends, but from a distance strikingly reminiscent of the dreaded German spiked helmet, or *Pickelhaube.* *

Because the Red Army won the Civil War, it is natural to assume that it had superior leadership and better-motivated troops. The evidence does not support this assumption. The Red Army suffered from the same problems as its adversary: mass desertions, a tendency on the part of commanders to ignore orders, difficulty of recruitment, inefficient logistics, inadequate medical services. What enabled the Red Army to cope better with these difficulties was its vast superiority in numbers.

Archival sources reveal a staggering rate of both refusals to obey induction orders and desertions.[30] Between October 1918 and April 1919, the government ordered the mobilization of 3.6 million men; of this number 917,000, or 25 percent, failed to report for induction. In the Ukrainian provinces in early 1919 only a fraction of those mobilized showed up at induction centers, for which reason mobilization orders sometimes had to be canceled.[31] The desertion statistics for 1919 were on a similar scale, as shown by the table on page 60. The number of deserters between June 1919 and June 1920 is estimated at 2.6 million.† In the second half of 1919, each

---

*O. V. Kharitonov, ed., *Illustrirovannoe opisanie obmundirovaniia i znakov razlichiia Sovetskoi Armii (1918–1958 gg.)* (Leningrad, 1960), *passim.* The distinctive epaulets (*pogoni*) of the tsarist army, which to revolutionaries symbolized black reaction and in 1917 often brought death to those caught wearing them, were restored by Stalin during World War II.

†Orlando Figes in *Past and Present,* No. 129 (November 1990), 200. The deserters, overwhelmingly peasants, gave as their main justification poor provisioning in the army and the need to help out with the farm work at home: S. Olikov, *Dezertirstvo v Krasnoi Armii i bor'ba s nim*

DESERTERS FROM THE RED ARMY IN 1919[32]

February	26,115
March	54,696
April	28,236
May	78,876
June	146,453
July	270,737
August	299,839
September	228,850
October	190,801
November	263,671
December	172,831
Total	1,761,105

month more soldiers fled from the Red Army than the Volunteer Army had
in its ranks. The vast majority of deserters returned within 14 days and were
classified as "weak-willed," which would correspond to Absent Without
Leave (AWOL). The punishments for desertion were very severe, but for
obvious reasons could not be strictly enforced. Most deserters were returned to their units; some were sentenced to hard labor. In the second half
of 1919, 612 were executed.[33] Desertions continued at the same rate during
1920. In February 1920, for example, a division deployed on the Western
front in anticipation of a war with Poland lost 50 percent of its men.[34] That
year, sweeping searches in the Ukraine yielded in five months half a million
deserters.[35] In view of this evidence, it is impossible to maintain that the Red
Army was made up of politically conscious masses fired with revolutionary
spirit. A Soviet philologist found that many Red Army soldiers had no idea
what the terms used by their government meant; included in that category
was "class enemy."[36]

A rare insight into the problems of the Red Army is provided by the records
of an investigation carried out in December 1918 at Lenin's request by Stalin
and Feliks Dzerzhinskii, head of the Cheka, to ascertain the causes of the
defeat of the Third Red Army at Perm. As a rule such information, damaging to the army's reputation, has been kept locked up in archives: in this

(Leningrad, 1926), 10, 13–14. Nearly a quarter indicated as the reason that their unit was about
to be sent to the front: Figes, loc. cit., 202. The Red Army definition of desertion included not
only men on active service who abandoned their units, but civilians who failed to report for
induction: G. F. Krivosheev, ed., Grif sekretnosti sniat (Moscow, 1993), 37n.

instance, Stalin ordered it published to discredit Trotsky. Stalin's and Dzerzhinskii's account of the "Perm catastrophe" could, with minor changes, have come from an inquest carried out in the White armies. "This was not, strictly speaking, a retreat," the two reported. "This was an ordinary disorderly flight of a routed and completely demoralized army whose staff had no idea what was going on." Artillery was surrendered without firing a shot. Soviet officials in Perm, said to be mostly holdovers from the tsarist era, abandoned their posts. Among the reasons for the wretched performance of the troops, Stalin and Dzerzhinskii cited the poor food supply, exhaustion, and hostility of the local inhabitants: in the Perm and Viatka provinces the population was ranged solidly against the Communists, they reported, partly from resentment of food requisitioning, and partly from the effects of White propaganda. As a result, the Red Army had to defend itself not only from the enemy in front of it but also from enemies in its rear.[37]

There are numerous corroborations of this analysis. In April 1919, after inspecting the front at Samara, Trotsky reported that wounded were left unattended because there were no physicians, medicines, or hospital trains.[38] The same month, G. Zinoviev, the boss of Petrograd, complained that while boots were piling up in his city, the troops defending it went barefoot.[39] Clothing and footwear sent to the front were routinely pilfered before reaching their destination. In August 1919, Trotsky reported that Red Army troops were going hungry, between one-half and one-third had no boots, and "everyone in the Ukraine has rifles and ammunition except the soldiers."[40]

An indication of the problems of loyalty and morale in the Red Army can be found in the extraordinary severity of its disciplinary provisions. Harsh punishments, including the death penalty, were decreed for military commanders not only for acts of treason but also for defeat. We have noted Trotsky's instructions making families of officers accountable for their loyalty. In a secret instruction Trotsky ordered registers to be compiled of the family status of every ex-tsarist officer and civil servant in Soviet service: only those were to be retained whose families resided in Soviet territory. Ex-tsarist officers were to be informed that the fate of their next of kin lay in their hands.[41] If an officer merely acted in a suspicious manner, he was to be treated as guilty and shot.[42] On August 14, 1918, *Izvestiia* published Trotsky's order mandating that in case of "unjustified" retreat, the commissar of the front was to be shot first, followed by its military commander.[43] In line with this instruction, the Military Revolutionary Council of the Thirteenth Army required commanders and commissars of units that retreated on their own authority to be turned over to a field Revolutionary Tribunal that was "mercilessly" to execute those found guilty:

> Units may and must perish in their entirety but not retreat, and this must be understood by the commanders and commissars; they must know that

there is no turning back, that in the rear there awaits them ignominious death, and in front, certain victory, because the enemy advances with small forces and acts only from impudence.[44]

The first known instance of mass execution of troops occurred on Trotsky's orders and with Lenin's approval at the end of August 1918 on the Eastern front, when the principle of "decimation" was applied and 20 men were shot, among them the regimental commander and commissar.[45]

Lenin, for whom execution by shooting was a favorite way of disposing of problems, was not averse to eliminating even his highest officers. On August 30, 1918—hours before he himself was shot and nearly killed—he wrote Trotsky, in connection with the poor performance of Red forces at Kazan, that it might not be a bad idea to execute Vatsetis, the Commander of the Eastern front, for further "delay or failure." This was the same Vatsetis who two months earlier had saved him and his government from the Left SR rebellion.[46]

Terror was applied also to the rank and file.[47] On entering active service, soldiers were required to acknowledge that their comrades had not only the right but the duty to shoot them on the spot if they fled from the field of battle, failed to carry out orders, or even complained of food shortages. In some Soviet units, the commanders and commissars were empowered to execute, without trial or any other formality, all "troublemakers" and "self-seekers." Documents show that on occasion reserve battalions deployed in the rear were ordered to open fire with machine guns to stop retreating Red Army units. In August 1919, Trotsky created on the Southern front "barring detachments" (zagraditel'nye otriady), composed of dependable and well-armed troops with a high proportion of Communists, to patrol the roads in the immediate rear of the combat zone. The number of Red Army soldiers executed during the Civil War is not known: but an idea can be obtained from statistics which indicate that in 1921, when the fighting stopped, 4,337 soldiers were shot.[48]

Such draconian measures exceeded in savagery anything known in the tsarist armies even under serfdom. They also had no counterpart in the White armies: Red Army deserters are said to have been astonished at the laxity of discipline on the White side.[49] They indicate that the Red Army experienced unusually serious problems of morale and discipline. Vatsetis thought the methods used to keep soldiers in line were counterproductive: "The discipline which has been and continues to be enforced in our Red Army, based on severe punishments, has led only to fear and the mechanical execution of orders, without any inspiration and sense of duty."[50]

Disciplinary provisions were implemented with intensive propaganda and agitation among frontline troops.[51] All armies and some divisions were equipped with printing presses that turned out posters and newspapers. Propaganda trains incessantly toured the front. The thrust of this effort was to instill in the troops the conviction that the Red Army was invincible and that a White victory would mean the restoration of the monarchy, the return of the landlords, and pogroms of workers. Whether it succeeded in creating the state of mass hypnosis which was its purpose is questionable, given the evidence of the extraordinary problems the Red Army had with discipline, desertions, and flight from the battlefield.

The Russian Civil War cannot be discussed without reference to the role of foreign powers, notably Great Britain. There never was anything resembling an "imperialist intervention" in the sense of a concerted, purposeful drive of the Western powers to crush the Communist regime. Western involvement in Russia, especially after November 1918, suffered from lack of clear purpose as well as from serious differences both within the Allied camp and among diverse groups in each Allied country. At the same time, without foreign intervention on the White side there would have been no Civil War (in the military sense of this word) because the immense superiority of the Bolsheviks in manpower and weaponry would have enabled them quickly to overcome all armed resistance.

Until the November 1918 Armistice, the objective of Allied intervention in Russia had been clear: to reactivate the Eastern front by helping Russians prepared to continue the war against Germany. After November 11, its purpose turned murky. This much was conceded by British Prime Minister David Lloyd George: "Our honorable obligations to the remnants of the Russian Army which, disregarding the Treaty of Brest-Litovsk, remained in the field to fight the Germans, put us in the embarrassing position of being under an obligation to help one of the parties in the Russian Civil War."[52] If the decision had been entirely up to him, the Prime Minister would have disengaged from Russia at once; his political instincts told him that the British people would not countenance involvement in another war, far from their shores, to settle a quarrel among foreigners. But the matter could not be resolved in such a simple manner. There were strong anti-Communist feelings among the Tories, of whom Winston Churchill was the most forceful spokesman. The elections of December 1918 returned a coalition government: his Liberal Party being both in a minority and divided within itself, Lloyd George became heavily dependent on Tory support. "Personally," Lloyd George wrote in his memoirs,

> I would have dealt with the Soviets as the *de facto* Government of Russia. So would President Wilson. But we both agreed that we could not carry to that extent our colleagues at the Congress, nor the public opinion of our own countries which was frightened by Bolshevik violence and feared its spread.[53]

As a result, he maneuvered and equivocated, intervening to please the Tories, but only in a halfhearted manner, to placate the trade unions and the Labour Party.

Dislike and dread of Bolshevism, on the one hand, and unwillingness to make a serious commitment to fight it, on the other, explain the vacillations of Allied policy toward Soviet Russia throughout the Civil War. Lloyd George justified his reluctance to render effective help to the Whites with various excuses: that the French Revolution had shown the futility of foreign powers trying to suppress revolution by force; that the Bolsheviks were certain to fall from power if they failed to win popular support; that their ability to beat off challenges indicated that they did enjoy such support; that the Whites were monarchists bent on restoring an expansionist empire that would hurt British interests more than Bolshevism. American President Woodrow Wilson largely shared these sentiments.

After the Armistice, the victorious Allies had one interest in common: to stabilize the situation in Russia in order to have a government there with which to agree on the frontiers of postwar Finland, the Baltic states, Poland, the Caucasus, and Transcaspia. Simply put, in the words of President Wilson, "Europe and the world cannot be at peace if Russia is not."[54] Lloyd George concurred: "There will be no peace until peace is established in Russia. It means that you have got war in half Europe and nearly half Asia as well. . . . Civilization cannot afford a distracted and desolate Russia."[55] The statesmen who gathered in Paris in early 1919 cared less who governed Russia than that Russia be governed. Ideally, they would have liked an accommodation between the warring parties that would make it unnecessary to choose between them; if this did not prove possible, they were prepared to come to terms with Moscow.

This one common interest apart, each Allied power had its own stake in the area. Britain, which throughout the nineteenth century had competed with Russia in the Middle East, wavered between the wish to see Bolshevism replaced by a traditional authority and the fear that such an authority would once again threaten India and encroach on the eastern Mediterranean. France wanted to recover the investments she had lost through Soviet expropriations and defaults, as well as to prevent a Russo-German rapprochement. The United States had no well-defined policy toward Russia, for she had no territorial and no significant financial claims on her: she wished the restoration of stability, preferably but not necessarily by democratic means. If this objective was not attainable, Washington was prepared to abandon Russia to her fate. Only Japan had a clear objective in mind and that was to annex Russia's Far Eastern provinces. To complicate matters still further, within each country there were rival groupings, some demanding the destruction of the Communist regime, others calling for accommodation with it: it was a conflict pitting Churchill against Lloyd George, and Secretary of State Robert Lansing against President Wilson and his adviser Colonel Edward House. Not surprisingly, intervention enjoyed greater support when the Whites were winning. In sum, foreign involvement in the Russian Civil War never approached the unity and purposefulness that Lenin had expected from it and Communist historians have attributed to it.

In the beginning, Britain and the United States sought to resolve the Russian problem by bringing the warring parties to the negotiating table.

Lenin never doubted that as soon as the fighting on the Western front stopped, victors and vanquished would join forces to launch a "capitalist crusade" against his regime. In early 1919, the Red Army command expected massive Allied military intervention on the side of the Whites. To avert this threat, Lenin had recourse to preemptive peace initiatives. Because he greatly overestimated the readiness of the Western allies to commit military forces in Russia, he was prepared to go as far as he had done a year earlier in accommodating the Germans at Brest-Litovsk. There is, therefore, good reason to believe that most of the proposals he made in the winter of 1918-19 were honestly meant.

On Christmas Eve 1918, Maxim Litvinov, an old Bolshevik and Deputy Commissar of Foreign Affairs, sent President Wilson a note from Stockholm phrased so as to appeal to the President's sentimental nature. In it he offered on behalf of his government to resolve by negotiation all outstanding problems with the West, including the matter of Russia's debts and Communist propaganda abroad.[56] In response, Washington sent an emissary to Stockholm to communicate with Litvinov. He reported that the offer appeared genuine, whereupon Lloyd George, with President Wilson's concurrence, proposed that the parties to the Russian Civil War meet in Paris. When it transpired that the French would not offer hospitality to such a conference, its location was shifted to the Turkish island of Prinkipo, off Constantinople.[57] Moscow promptly accepted the invitation, repeating its readiness to acknowledge Russia's foreign debts, make territorial adjustments, offer mining concessions, and suspend hostile propaganda.[58] The authors of an official Soviet history of diplomacy explain these concessions as a "diplomatic maneuver" designed not to satisfy the Western powers but to "unmask" their true aims.[59] The mercenary tone of the Soviet response produced an effect contrary to the one intended, offending the Western heads of state, who indignantly responded that they repudiated "the suggestion that such objects influenced their intervention in Russia. The supreme desire of the Allies is to see peace restored in Russia and the establishment of a Government based upon the will of the broad mass of the Russian people."[60]

The Prinkipo Conference never materialized because the White generals, appalled by the idea of negotiating with their mortal enemies, rejected it out of hand. The proposal seemed so preposterous that when Kolchak's advisers first heard it on the wireless, they believed a mistake had occurred in transmission and that the Allies were in fact proposing a conference of anti-Bolshevik parties.[61] It has been argued, however, that it is unfair to place the entire blame for the failure of the Prinkipo proposal on the White generals. They were so dependent on Allied assistance that if sufficient pressure had been brought to bear on them they would have had no choice but to acquiesce, especially if the alternative was a separate peace of the Western powers with Lenin.[62] If such pressure was not exerted the reason has to be sought in the attitude of France, which opposed the Prinkipo proposal and privately advised White representatives in Paris to ignore it. Churchill, who had just then taken over the War Office, gave similar counsel and promised the Whites military help whether they came or not.[63]

Determined to pursue the peace initiative, Wilson, with Lloyd George's tacit support (of which Lloyd George says that "our attitude was that of the Fox Whigs toward the French Revolution"[64]) initiated secret steps to determine whether it was possible to come to terms with Moscow without White participation.[65] To this end Wilson's principal foreign policy adviser, Colonel House, employed an American socialite, William Bullitt, an employee of U.S. intelligence services in Paris. Bullitt had expressed sympathy for the Soviet cause, which was probably the reason he was chosen for the mission, since he lacked any other qualifications: only 28 years old, he had no previous diplomatic experience. Formally, his assignment was to inquire into the actual state of affairs in Soviet Russia; but privately, Colonel House authorized him to ascertain the terms on which the Soviet government was prepared to make peace. In return for peace, he was to promise Lenin's government generous economic assistance.[66] Bullitt's mission was so secret that only four persons were privy to it: among those kept in the dark were the U.S. Secretary of State, the French government, and the British Foreign Office. Such extraordinary precautions were inspired by the fear that those who had aborted the Prinkipo proposal would also prevent direct contacts with Moscow. Bullitt took with him Captain Walter W. Pettit of Military Intelligence and Lincoln Steffens, a journalist known for his pro-Communist sympathies.

The three Americans arrived in Moscow in the middle of March 1919, shortly after the Communist International had concluded its first congress (see below, Chapter 4). Its proceedings and resolutions held for them no interest. Their Soviet hosts were friendly and eager for an accord. On March 14 the Central Committee handed Bullitt the terms on which it was prepared to make peace with the Whites.[67] The respective claimants to power in Russia were to retain the territories they actually controlled. Allied troops on Russian soil were to withdraw gradually, but assistance to the White armies was to cease at once. Russians who had taken up arms against the Soviet regime would be amnestied. The Russian parties would recognize joint responsibility for the country's debts. The issue of compensation for nationalized foreign properties was not addressed.

Bullitt's mission had an air of unreality about it. Only people ignorant of the causes of the conflict and the passions that it aroused could have conceived such a plan. Steffens, its author, treated the mission as high adventure: "I feel as I were going to see a good play at a good theater," he wrote.*

It is quite possible that had the Soviet offer been accepted, Eastern Europe would have gained a certain degree of stability. For a time, at any rate. The critical clause in the Soviet proposal called on the Allies immediately to suspend military assistance to the Whites. Had this been done, it would have been harmless enough for Moscow to leave the Whites in place. Cut off from their only available source of armaments, they would have inevitably succumbed to the combined pressures of the three-million-strong Red Army and internal subversion.

Bullitt sent back to Paris an enthusiastic report, in which he depicted Lenin, Georgii Chicherin, the Commissar of Foreign Affairs, and Litvinov as "full of a sense of Russia's need for peace" and unequivocally committed to paying off Russia's foreign debts.[68] The world had a unique opportunity to come to terms with Soviet Russia, where "a dull, inexperienced, a young people were trying rudely but conscientiously and at the cost of great suffering to themselves to find a better way to live for the common good than the old way."[69] On the basis of this report, Colonel House was ready to recommend a separate peace with Moscow.[70] But the Bullitt mission came to naught, aborted by French opposition and Lloyd George's fear of the Tories. Embittered, Bullitt retired to the Riviera to "lie on the sands and watch the world go to hell."† Further attempts to come to terms with Moscow were given up.

For the next six months, the Allies pursued a policy of half-hearted intervention on the side of the Whites. It was half-hearted because they did not quite know what they meant to achieve by it, had grave doubts about the viability of the White cause, and were divided among themselves as to the wisdom of intervening. Of the three powers most directly involved—Britain, France, and the United States—only Britain made a serious commitment to the Whites. France lost the taste for military intervention as soon as her troops in Russia had received a drubbing in the Ukraine from local partisans and mutinied, following which she turned her attention to constructing a *cordon sanitaire* to insulate Europe from Communist Russia. The United States withdrew most of her forces, leaving only those that were necessary to prevent the Japanese from seizing eastern Siberia. Essentially, the story of Allied intervention in the Russian Civil War is one of Britain's involvement, for it was she who bore virtually the entire cost of assistance

---

*Lincoln Steffens, *Letters* (New York, 1938), 460. According to Bullitt, Steffens coined the phrase that would bring him fame—"I have seen the future and it works!"—on the train in Sweden before setting foot in Soviet Russia: John M. Thompson, *Russia, Bolshevism, and the Versailles Peace* (Princeton, 1966), 176.

†George F. Kennan, *Russia and the West under Lenin and Stalin* (Boston, 1960–61), 134. In 1933, he was appointed the first U.S. Ambassador to the Soviet Union, an experience that turned him into a passionate anti-Communist. See Beatrice Farnsworth, *William C. Bullitt and the Soviet Union* (Bloomington, Ind., 1967).

to the Whites. And Britain's involvement was due primarily to Winston Churchill, who earlier than any other European statesmen understood the threat that Russian Communism posed to the West.

Although weakened, Britain remained after World War I the leading world power, with global interests directly affected by what happened in Russia. But her attitude toward Russia was anything but consistent. The records of British cabinet discussions reveal contrary pulls resulting in hesitations and confusion. These sources show that while reports of Bolshevik atrocities published in the British press (especially the details of the murder of the Imperial family) produced universal revulsion, they did not significantly affect Britain's policies.

Britain's policy toward Soviet Russia was primarily guided by two concerns: the fear of a rapprochement between Russia and Germany, and memory of Russia's historic threat to British Middle Eastern possessions. These twin concerns raised a fundamental question: what kind of Russian government better suited British interests—Lenin's or the one likely to be installed by the victorious Whites? A related question was whether it was preferable to encourage the dismemberment of the Russian Empire or to preserve her territorial integrity. Each position had its proponents.

Although the Bolshevik regime had no admirers in the British government, it had its advocates, who argued that from Britain's vantage point it was preferable to any realistic alternative. Between the battle of Waterloo and the emergence in the early twentieth century of an aggressive, militaristic Germany, the containment of Russia had been the foremost concern of British diplomacy. The weaker Russia was, the less of a threat she posed: and Bolshevik misrule seemed to ensure her permanent debility. The reasoning behind this position was analogous to that which in 1917–18 had prompted Germany to overcome her aversion for the Bolsheviks and offer them critical support: namely that they were ruining Russia and thereby lifting the threat to Germany's eastern frontier.[71] This view was held by Lloyd George, who throughout the Russian Civil War silently favored a Bolshevik victory even while, as minority premier of a coalition government, he had to yield to Tory pressures and intervene on the side of the Whites. On December 12, 1918, he told the War Cabinet that he did not think that a Bolshevik Russia "was by any means such a danger as the old Russian Empire was, with all its aggressive officials and millions of troops." In this assessment he was supported by the Tory Foreign Secretary, Arthur Balfour.* On another occasion, Lloyd George assured the cabinet that the "Bolsheviks would not wish to maintain an army, as their creed was funda-

---

*Minutes, Imperial War Cabinet, December 12, 1918, Cab. 23/42, in Richard Ullman, *Britain and the Russian Civil War* (Princeton, 1968), 75–76. A number of persons close to Lloyd George suspected that he harbored personal sympathies for Lenin and Trotsky (as he did later for Hitler). Lord Curzon, for example, observed that "the trouble with the P[rime] M[inister] is that he is a bit of a Bolshevik himself": Norman Davies, *White Eagle, Red Star* (London, 1972), 90.

mentally anti-militarist."[72] He made no secret of his desire to stay out of Russia: at a War Cabinet meeting on December 31, 1918, he said that he "was opposed to military intervention in any shape."[73] In expressing such opinions, based on intuition and wishful thinking rather than knowledge, the Prime Minister enjoyed the backing of the majority in the cabinet, which throughout 1919 opposed involvement in the Russian Civil War: according to Churchill's biographer, not one minister apart from Churchill favored supporting General Denikin.*

Such were the political realities behind the hesitations of Britain in the Russian Civil War. Like the Polish leader Marshal Jozef Pilsudski, who at a critical phase of the Civil War would leave the Whites in the lurch, Lloyd George and Balfour considered the threat posed by a restored national Russia to be greater than that posed by international Communism.

In addition, there were compelling domestic reasons for not pushing a pro-White policy too hard. British labor overwhelmingly opposed intervention, viewing it as an attempt to suppress the world's first workers' government. Since the Armistice had resulted in severe economic and social dislocations in Britain, continued involvement in Russia threatened domestic turmoil. In June 1919, the War Cabinet was advised that the growing labor unrest in the country was due mainly to the unpopular intervention in Russia.[74] As the year progressed, the hostility of the Labour Party and the Trades Union Congress to intervention intensified. This factor was probably decisive in Lloyd George's resolve to pull out of Russia by the end of 1919.

The most ardent advocate of military intervention was Churchill, who on taking charge of the War Office in January 1919 immediately adopted an anti-Communist rather than an anti-Russian stance. In this he enjoyed the support of Sir Henry Wilson, Chief of the Imperial General Staff, but of no one else who mattered. Churchill concluded that World War I had ushered in a new historical era in which narrowly national interests and conflicts would yield to supranational and ideological interests and conflicts. This conviction enabled him to grasp the meaning of both Communism and National Socialism sooner and better than other European statesmen, who tended to treat them as phenomena domestic in origin and scope. Churchill regarded Communism as unadulterated evil, a satanic force: he had no qualms about referring to the Bolsheviks as "animals," "butchers," "baboons." He was convinced that the White cause was also Britain's cause. In a memorandum written on September 15, 1919, when Britain was about to abandon the Whites, he warned:

> It is a delusion to suppose that all this year we have been fighting the battles of the anti-Bolshevik Russians. On the contrary, they have been fighting

*Martin Gilbert, *Winston S. Churchill,* IV (Boston, 1975), 309-10. Churchill received qualified support from Lord Curzon, who wanted Britain to intervene, but only in the Caucasus.

ours; and this truth will become painfully apparent from the moment that they are exterminated and the Bolshevik armies are supreme over the whole vast territories of the Russian Empire.[75]

Even though in a minority of one in the cabinet, he managed to play a leading role in Britain's policies toward Russia in part because he headed the War Office, and in part because he possessed formidable powers of persuasion.

The danger of an alliance between a reactionary or revolutionary Russia and a reactionary or revolutionary Germany worried the British cabinet even before Germany's surrender.[76] But no one except Churchill was haunted by this prospect and no one was prepared to draw from it the logical conclusions. Churchill foresaw a potential "combination of interest and policy" between the two pariah nations that would coalesce into a "mass against which the Western Powers will be quite unable to assert themselves and even, possibly in a few years to defend themselves."[77] "There will be no peace in Europe until Russia is restored," by which he meant "restored" under a non-Communist government. With prophetic insight he predicted the alliance of Soviet Russia, Germany, and Japan that would materialize twenty years later and nearly destroy England and her empire:

> If we abandon Russia, Germany and Japan will not. The new states which it is hoped to bring into being in the East of Europe will be crushed between Russian Bolshevism and Germany. Germany will regain by her influence over Russia far more than she has lost in colonies overseas or provinces in the West. Japan will no doubt arrive at a somewhat similar solution at the other end of the Trans-Siberian Railway. In five years, or even less, it will be apparent that the whole fruits of our victories have been lost at the Peace Conference, that the League of Nations is an impotent mockery, that Germany is stronger than ever, and that British interests in India are perilously affected. After all our victories we shall have quitted the field in humiliation and defeat.*

Churchill conceived the idea of containing Soviet Russia,[78] which his own country ignored but the United States would adopt after World War II. Had he had his way, the Western powers would have mounted an international crusade against Bolshevik Russia. The next best thing in his mind was enlisting Germany against the Bolsheviks. Fear of Bolshevism and of a

---

*Gilbert, *Churchill,* IV, 254. Churchill's anxiety about a prospective German-Soviet-Japanese rapprochement was influenced by the warnings of the founder of geopolitics, H. J. Mackinder, to the Peace Conference that the treaty it was drafting would engender a hostile military bloc. "[I]f we would take the long view," Mackinder asked, "must we still not reckon with the possibility that a large part of the Great Continent might some day be united under a single sway?" *Democratic Ideals and Reality* (New York, 1919), 89. According to Mackinder, Germany's control of Russia would assure her of world domination. The Nazi geopolitician Karl Haushofer adopted Mackinder's ideas to formulate the concept of an "invincible" alliance of Germany, Russia, and Japan.

Bolshevik-German alliance drove him after the Armistice to plead for a conciliatory policy toward Germany ("Feed Germany; fight Bolshevism; make Germany fight Bolshevism").[79] Whereas the majority of his colleagues eventually concluded that the ability of the Bolsheviks to defeat their adversaries reflected popular support, Churchill understood that it derived from unrestrained terror.

But while Churchill was a superb diagnostician, his remedies were quite unrealistic. His vision of an international crusade against Soviet Russia was sheer fantasy: there was not the slightest chance that the great powers, exhausted by four years of war, would dispatch hundreds of thousands of troops to the frozen wastes of Russia.* Lloyd George told Churchill—and in this he was probably right—that if Britain went to war against Russia there would be a revolution at home. The Germans not only would not fight the Russians, but would enter with them into secret military collaboration. In the end, Churchill had to settle for desultory intervention on behalf of the Whites—an involvement too small to affect the outcome of the Civil War, but large enough to enable the Communist regime to depict the struggle for its own survival as the defense of Russia from foreign invaders.

The British cabinet took the first steps toward intervention on November 14, 1918. Having rejected as impractical the idea of an anti-Bolshevik "crusade," it decided instead to support diplomatically and materially the anti-Bolshevik forces in Russia as well as those countries, once part of the Russian Empire, that had succeeded in separating themselves from it.[80] In early 1919 Lloyd George laid down the following guidelines for Britain's involvement:

"1. There must be no attempt to conquer Bolshevik Russia by force of arms.
2. Support would only be continued as long as it was clear that in the areas controlled by Kolchak and Denikin the population was anti-Bolshevik in sentiment.
3. The anti-Bolshevik armies must not be used to restore the old tsarist regime . . . [and] reimpos[e] on the peasants the old feudal conditions [!] under which they held their land."[81]

Once decided upon, British intervention took several forms: (1) the provisioning of the anti-Bolshevik forces with military matériel ranging from uniforms to airplanes and tanks, mostly drawn from surplus stores left over from World War I; (2) the maintenance on Russian soil and off the Russian coast of British military and naval contingents whose main mission was to perform guard duties and enforce the blockade, but which could, when

---

*The Allies had in Germany several million Russian prisoners of war whom they could have sent to Denikin, Iudenich, and Kolchak. In fact, they left their fate in the hands of the Germans, who exchanged them for their own war prisoners in Russia. A few took part in anti-Red operations in the Baltic; more sought refuge in Western Europe; but the majority were repatriated. Thompson, *Russia,* 328–30; Robert C. Williams in *Canadian Slavonic Papers,* IX, No. 2 (1967), 270–95.

threatened, defend themselves; (3) the training of White officers; (4) help with intelligence and communications; and (5), ultimately, evacuation of the remnant of the defeated White armies. The aid, although far below what Britain could have offered, was vital to the White cause.

On the question of the borderlands that had separated themselves from Russia, Britain could never quite make up her mind. On the one hand, she realized that the new states weakened Russia and her ability to commit aggression. On these grounds, Lord Curzon persuaded his government at the end of 1918 to recognize de facto the independence of Azerbaijan and Georgia, and to deploy small troop contingents in Transcaucasia and Transcaspia to protect India. In the winter of 1918–19, British naval forces would also help defend Estonia and Latvia from a Soviet invasion. On balance, however, the position of Britain was to support the territorial integrity of the Russian Empire, even under Communist rule, partly to avoid alienating the Russian population and partly to prevent the Germans from dominating the separated borderlands. While Britain pressured the White leaders to adopt democratic formulas, she did not object to the slogan "Russia One and Indivisible."

France's position on the Russian question was uncomplicated because, her colonial empire notwithstanding, she was primarily a continental power. Her overriding concern was preventing Germany's revival as a military power capable of launching a revanchist war. To this end, the friendship of a strong, stable, and friendly Russia was now, as before 1914, of paramount importance; barring that, France needed a chain of client states along Germany's eastern frontier. Secondly, France had lost the most from Lenin's nationalization degrees and defaults on state obligations: these losses she was determined to make good. Since, in spite of his occasional assurances that he was prepared to compensate foreign powers, Lenin seemed unlikely to do so, France was of all the great powers the most consistently anti-Communist. Her support of the White cause, however, was lukewarm. France's leaders did not give the Whites much chance and as early as March 1919 urged the other allies to abandon them to their fate and instead to transform Poland and Romania into a "barbed wire" to contain Communism.[82] Its pillar was to be independent Poland, whose function was to separate Russia from Germany. Not surprisingly, for nationalist Germans and Communist Russians, Poland, the product of Versailles, became the object of shared hatred and the basis for collaboration that began as early as 1919 and twenty years later found consummation in the fourth partition of that country.

American policy, as formulated by President Wilson, was that after the Armistice the Allies had no business keeping troops in Russia: they were to be withdrawn, leaving the Russians to settle their quarrel among themselves.[83] Wilson felt it was "always dangerous to meddle in foreign revolutions": "to try to stop a revolutionary movement by a line of armies is to employ a broom to stop a great flood. . . . The only way to act against Bolshevism is to make its causes disappear." Unfortunately, he confessed, "we do not even know exactly what its causes are."[84] In addition to noninterference, Wilson favored the nonrecognition of the Soviet government and the preservation of Russia's territorial integrity.[85]

Japanese policy toward Russia was the most consistent and the most transparent. The Japanese landed their first troops in the Russian Far East in the spring of 1918 on the initiative of the Allied Supreme Command, which had planned to deploy them against the Germans in a reactivated Eastern front. Nothing came of this idea, not only because it was impractical but also because the Japanese had no intention of fighting the Germans. Their interests were strictly predatory: they wished to take advantage of the Russian turmoil to seize and annex the maritime provinces. The United States, aware of these designs, deployed military forces in eastern Siberia, but American troops, whether in the Far East or the northwest, at no time engaged the Red Army in combat.*

On December 23, 1917, two weeks after the armistice between Russia and the Central Powers had gone into effect, the French and the British divided among themselves the spheres of responsibility for combat operations on Russian territory: France took charge of the German front and Britain of the Turkish. The British zone included the Cossack territories, the Caucasus, Armenia, Georgia, and Kurdistan. The areas to the west of the Don River—the Ukraine, the Crimea, and Bessarabia—fell in the French sector.[86] During the year that followed, the arrangement remained inoperative, because all these regions were under German or Turkish occupation.

As soon as the guns fell silent on the Western front, the Allies dispatched expeditionary forces to the Black Sea. On November 23, 1918, a small British-French naval detachment debarked at Novorossiisk.[87] A month later, the French landed troops in Odessa and the Crimea, recently evacuated by the Germans, while the British took over Baku from the Turks and assumed naval control of the Caspian Sea. British warships concurrently took up positions off the Russian coast in the eastern Baltic. This deployment was part of the post-Armistice blockade of Germany enacted to

---

*"The United States sent troops only to two areas of Russia: to the European north, in the neighborhood of Archangelsk on the White Sea, and to eastern Siberia. Both of these areas were far from the main theaters of the Russian civil war then in progress. In neither case was the decision to dispatch these troops taken gladly. . . . In neither case was it motivated by an intention that these forces should be employed with a view to unseating the Soviet government. In neither case would the decision have been taken except in conjunction with the World War then in progress, and for purposes related primarily to the prosecution of that war." George Kennan in *FA*, LIV, No. 4 (July 1976), 671. Cf. William S. Graves, *America's Siberian Adventure* (New York, 1931), 92.

prevent her from securing foreign economic assistance until she submitted to the Allied peace terms.* It was believed in the White and Red camps alike that these forces were the vanguard of a massive Allied army, deployed to protect Denikin's rear while he advanced on Moscow. The Soviet government took this threat very seriously: in drawing up campaign plans for the spring of 1919, the Red Army staff assumed that it would confront in the south a hostile Allied expeditionary force numbering between 150,000 and 200,000 troops.[88] In fact, no such massive military intervention was ever contemplated, since Great Britain could not afford, as Balfour put it, "to see its forces, after more than four years of strenuous fighting, dissipated over the huge expanse of Russia in order to carry out political reforms in a State which [was] no longer a belligerent Ally."[89] Nor, for that matter, could France.

France's small expeditionary force brought her little honor. In March 1919 France had on the Black Sea coast an ethnically mixed contingent of 65,000–70,000 men, a minority of them French, the remainder Greeks, Poles, Romanians, Senegalese, and other colonials. These units were sent not to fight but to occupy the areas evacuated by the Germans between Kherson, Nikolaev, Berezovka, and Tiraspol. But in the Civil War raging all around them, foreign troops could not act as a peaceful occupation army, and soon they were compelled to defend themselves. On March 10, a battalion of Greeks and two companies of French stationed in Kherson came under attack from a band of Ukrainian marauders led by a bandit named Nikifor Grigorev who had made common cause with the Red Army. After eight days of stiff fighting, in which they suffered heavy casualties, the defenders abandoned Kherson.[90] Grigorev moved on to Nikolaev and, following its capture, to Odessa. At this time, French sailors at Sebastopol, exposed to Communist antiwar propaganda, mutinied. The French had no appetite for combat: in the words of one of their officers, "Not one French soldier who saved his head at Verdun and the fields of the Marne will consent to losing it on the fields of Russia."[91] Having learned of these setbacks and the Sebastopol mutiny, and advised by the commander of the French contingent, General L. F. M. F. Franchet d'Esperey, that he could

---

*Ullman, *Britain,* 55–56. Britain also maintained a blockade of Soviet Russia after the Armistice, deploying naval units in the Gulf of Finland, cutting off her own shipments and exerting pressure on neutral countries to follow suit. The action was justified on the grounds that it prevented vital supplies from reaching Germany: it was a by-product of the German blockade (Thompson, *Russia,* 325). But even after a treaty had been signed with Germany and the blockade against her lifted, the Council of Four decided on May 9 to continue blockading Soviet Russia. Wilson declared on June 17 that this decision was unjustified, which it certainly was. It had only symbolic importance in any event, since Russia had neither much money nor commodities to engage in foreign trade. The principal breaches in the blockade occurred through Swedish collaboration: Ministerstvo Inostrannykh Del SSSR, *Dokumenty vneshnei politiki SSSR,* II (Moscow, 1958), 621–29. Subsequently, Soviet propaganda rather successfully blamed on the blockade everything that went wrong with the Soviet economy, from the lack of pencils for schoolchildren to the famine of 1921.

not supply Odessa with essentials, Paris ordered an immediate withdrawal of all French and French-led forces. Of this decision it did not even bother to inform Denikin.[92] On April 2, Franchet d'Esperey announced that the troops under his command—4,000 Frenchmen, 15,000 Greeks, and 3,000 Russian volunteers[93]—would evacuate Odessa in three days. They did so in two:

> The [French] evacuation was carried forward in such haste and confusion that it closely resembled a flight. Only a small number of the civilian population could procure passage. Thousands lined the docks, begging the French to take them anywhere. Not a few committed suicide. Pandemonium reigned in the city, for all knew that Red troops were ready to march in as soon as the guns of the French cruisers were out of range.[94]

In Sebastopol, arrangements for the withdrawal were coordinated with the Bolshevik soviet that had assumed control of the city while the French were still occupying it. The French navy evacuated 10,000 Russian military and 30,000 civilians;[95] among them were the Empress Dowager and Grand Duke Nikolai Nikolaevich.

This was the extent of French involvement in the Russian Civil War. And although the French remained the most ardent Red-baiters throughout, and sabotaged every Anglo-American effort at a rapprochement with Moscow until they themselves were ready for it, the brunt of the involvement henceforth was borne by Britain.

In the fall of 1918, after Latvians serving in the Red Army had recaptured from the Czechs several cities along the Volga, the situation on the Eastern front looked reasonably satisfactory from Moscow's point of view; it improved even more after November, when the Czechoslovak Legion withdrew from combat. Under these circumstances, the Red Army High Command began to shift forces from the east to the south. But it received a rude shock on Christmas Eve when Kolchak's troops unexpectedly routed the Third Red Army at Perm. The loss of Perm alarmed Moscow because it raised the possibility of Kolchak's troops linking up with the Allied contingent in Archangel.[96]

Kolchak knew little about land warfare. He entrusted strategic planning to D. A. Lebedev, a 36-year-old veteran of the Imperial General Staff, one of the leaders of the November 1918 coup against the Directory. Lebedev surrounded himself with an immense staff: at the height of his offensive, Kolchak had 2,000 officers to plan operations for 140,000 combat troops, whereas during World War I the Imperial headquarters made do with 350 officers to direct a field army of three million.[97] Most of these officers were youths commissioned during the war, few of whom had any staff experience.[98]

Kolchak proved to be a total disaster as an administrator. Omsk, his capital, teemed with malingerers, who speculated in all kinds of goods, especially British supplies: staff officers and their families are said to have enjoyed the right of first refusal on British uniforms and other goods that passed through Omsk en route to the front. Speculators bribed railway personnel to remove military equipment from trains and replace it with luxury goods destined for the civilian market.[99] Kolchak's army assumed responsibility for feeding 800,000 men, although its combat strength did not exceed 150,000. The staff of the Czech General Rudolf Gajda, the commander of Kolchak's Northern Army, which had fewer than 100,000 men, drew rations for 275,000. An investigation carried out on Gajda's orders revealed that of the meat, clothing, and shoes sent to his front from Ekaterinburg to Perm, only 35 to 65 percent reached their destination. Vegetables, canned and fresh, were pilfered in their entirety.[100] Many Russian officers, including those in the combat zone, lived with their wives and mistresses in well-furnished railroad cars that served as both command posts and billets.[101] The venality drove British liaison officers to exasperation. General Knox, head of the British military mission, was referred to by Omsk wits as the Quartermaster General of the Red Army: he even received a spurious letter from Trotsky, originating in the same circles, thanking him for the help he had rendered in equipping Red troops.[102]

A major handicap of the White Eastern Army was poor transport. Kolchak's troops were dependent for logistical support on the single-track Transsiberian linking Omsk with Vladivostok. The railroad, whose easternmost sectors were under the control of the Japanese and their protégés, atamans Semenov and Kalmykov, came under frequent attack from Bolshevik partisans and ordinary bandits. The situation improved in the spring of 1919, when the American army took charge of one major segment of the Transsiberian and the Czechs of another, but it remained far from satisfactory. Under even the best conditions, it took trains several weeks to deliver supplies from the Pacific port.

Much of the blame for the appalling state of the army's rear must be placed on Kolchak, who was so single-mindedly preoccupied with military matters that he regarded all else, civil administration included, as diversions undeserving of his attention. As late as October 1919, when his army was well on its way to extinction, he told a civilian associate:

> You know I view as hopeless all your civil laws and for this reason I am sometimes rude and you chide me for this. I have set myself a high goal: to crush the Red Army. I am Commander in Chief and do not trouble myself with reforms. Write only those laws which are necessary at present, and leave the rest to the Constituent Assembly.

When told that laws were necessary, if only to demonstrate that he was not a reactionary, he replied: "No, leave this alone, work only for the army.

Don't you understand that no matter what fine laws you write, if we lose, they will all the same shoot us!"[103]

Fighting on the Eastern front resumed after a two-month lull in March 1919, before the onset of the thaw, with a White offensive employing over 100,000 troops. The plan of operations envisaged the main thrust to be in the north: the largest and best-equipped White force was Gajda's Northern Army. Its objective was Archangel, to be reached by way of Viatka and Vologda; its purpose, to link up with Allied and Russian contingents deployed there under the command of Major General Edmund Ironside, and to make available another and much closer port through which to receive British supplies. The central front, aiming at Ufa and Kazan, was commanded by General M. V. Khanzhin. The Ural and Siberian Cossacks operated in the south along with Bashkir units, under Ataman Alexander Dutov. Their mission was the capture of Samara and Saratov for the double purpose of linking up with the Volunteer Army and isolating the Red forces in Central Asia.

The Red Army on the Eastern front underwent several reorganizations that ended in its division into two fronts: the northern under V. I. Shorin (Second and Third Armies) and the central under M. N. Tukhachevskii (First, Fourth, and Fifth Armies, and the Turkestan Army). Overall command of the Eastern front was entrusted to S. S. Kamenev. On March 1, according to the Red Army's estimate, its forces numbered 96,000 men and 377 field guns, while Kolchak had 112,000 men and 764 guns.[104] It was a rare instance of White numerical superiority, but it did not last, for before long Red reinforcements began to arrive in the east. According to confidential Red Army reports, the caliber of the two armies was roughly equal, with the Whites enjoying a considerable edge in the quality and numbers of officers.[105] The latter was of no small concern to the Red Army, because under the conditions of combat in Siberia, field commanders enjoyed a great deal of discretion:

> The tactical peculiarities of the Civil War, when relatively modest masses of troops operated on a broad front, when battles broke up into discrete nuclei and, for the major part, were conducted by regiments or, at best, brigades, the absence of proper communications and other technical means, the immense maneuverability of the units—all demanded of the commanders, commissars, and fighters great independence as well as boldness in making decisions and acting.[106]

Kolchak's forces made rapid progress, covering almost 600 kilometers in one month. Their advance was facilitated by anti-Soviet peasant uprisings in the rear of the Red Army in the provinces of Simbirsk, Samara, Kazan, and Viatka. The enemy retreated, offering little or no resistance: the Fifth Red Army proved to be especially loath to stand and fight.[107] By the middle of April, White troops reached a line extending from Glazov to Orenburg and Uralsk that was to mark their farthest advance. At this point they were less than 100 kilometers from the Volga, and in some places as close as 35 kilometers. They had occupied 300,000 square kilometers with over five million inhabitants.[108]

The Red command now realized how greatly it had underestimated the danger in the east. On April 11, the Central Committee decided to assign this front the highest priority.[109] Orders were given to mobilize the middle and poor peasantry, from 10 to 20 recruits per *volost'*, the smallest rural administrative unit. The order must have run into considerable resistance, given that in the end no more than 25,000 peasants were inducted.[110] The authorities were more successful in mobilizing party members and trade unionists. The Eastern front received all the new manpower and war matériel, and on June 12 the Red Army outnumbered Kolchak's by 20,000–30,000 men.[111] The advantage would grow prodigiously in the weeks that followed.

The strategic environment for Kolchak's army changed for the worse in May, with the advent of the spring thaw. In the late winter, combat operations had been conducted along well-defined roads, but now the front widened as "streams [turned] into rivers and rivers into seas."[112] In these conditions, the growing numerical superiority of the Red Army proved of decisive advantage. On paper, Kolchak's situation looked brilliant: but his troops were outnumbered as well as exhausted from the rapid advance, which had outrun supply trains.

To win domestic support, Kolchak needed Allied diplomatic recognition. This was important for psychological reasons, to bolster the authority of his ministers in the eyes of the population.[113] In 1918, the Bolshevik regime had drawn a great deal of strength from the popular perception that behind it stood the power of Germany. Inquiries by Soviet authorities into the causes of desertions from the Red Army revealed that one of the reasons given by the defectors was the feeling that it was useless to fight "the mighty power" of Russia's onetime allies.[114]

But the Allies procrastinated. On May 26, the Allied Supreme Council informed Kolchak that it no longer expected to come to terms with the Soviet government and was willing to provide him with munitions, supplies, and food—diplomatic recognition was not mentioned*—if he would accept the following conditions: (1) agree to convene, on victory, a democratically elected Constituent Assembly; (2) allow on territories then under his control free elections to organs of self-government; (3) renounce class privileges, refrain from restoring the "former land system," and "make no attempt to reintroduce the régime which the revolution had destroyed"; (4) recognize the independence of Poland and Finland; (5) accept assistance of

---

*This is important to stress, because it is not uncommon to read claims that the Allies "offered to recognize Kolchak's government": e.g., George Brinkley, *The Volunteer Army and Allied Intervention in South Russia, 1917–1921* (Notre Dame, 1966), 190.

the Peace Conference in settling Russia's territorial disputes with the Baltic, Caucasian, and Transcaspian republics; (6) join the League of Nations; (7) reaffirm Russia's responsibility for her debts.[115]

It was a strange set of conditions, intended to reassure the Allies' domestic constituencies about Kolchak, whom Bolshevik and socialist propaganda depicted as a reactionary monarchist. It served the additional purpose of ensuring that should Kolchak win, which in May seemed likely, he would follow policies agreeable to them.[116] Although the first of these conditions required Kolchak to convene a Constituent Assembly, presumably to decide on all issues in dispute, the Allies preordained that there would be no restoration of the monarchy as well as no return of the seized lands to their rightful owners, and that the borderlands that had separated themselves from Russia—Finland and Poland, and by implication, the Baltic as well as the Transcaucasian and Transcaspian republics—would be recognized as sovereign states. In other words, for all their democratic professions, they decided on their own the constitution and borders of the future Russia.

Kolchak was in no position to bargain, since nearly all his war matériel came from abroad: every round of rifle ammunition fired by his troops was of British manufacture. Between October 1918 and October 1919, Britain sent to Omsk 97,000 tons of supplies, including 600,000 rifles, 6,831 machine guns, and over 200,000 uniforms.[117] (The French provided Kolchak only with a few hundred machine guns that had originally been destined for the Czechs.)

Kolchak drafted his response with the help of General Knox and dispatched it on June 4. He accepted all the conditions posed to him, hedging only on the issue of Finnish independence, which he was prepared to recognize de facto but wanted the Constituent Assembly to settle de jure. He confirmed emphatically, however, "that there cannot be a return to the régime which existed in Russia before February 1917." He further affirmed that his government acknowledged "all the pledges and decrees" made by the Provisional Government of 1917.[118]

To enhance Kolchak's claim to foreign recognition, on June 12, Denikin acknowledged him as Supreme Ruler. This action is said to have antagonized the general's Cossack allies, who thought Kolchak and the Siberians were too liberal.[119]

Even though he had met their terms, the Allied leaders would not as yet grant Kolchak the diplomatic recognition that Churchill, Curzon, and the British General Staff were urging on them. The delay was largely due to the hostility of President Wilson, who mistrusted the Admiral and doubted that he would honor his pledges.[120] In Russian matters Wilson was strongly influenced by Alexander Kerensky, the former head of the Provisional Government that Lenin had overthrown, whom he regarded as the spokesman for Russian democracy. Kerensky, who worked assiduously to dis-

credit Kolchak in Western eyes, told American diplomats that if he succeeded in taking power, Kolchak would "inaugurate a regime hardly less
sanguinary and repressive than that of the Bolshevists."[121] Under the impression of Kolchak's battlefield victories, Lloyd George inclined toward
recognition, but at this critical moment Kolchak's armies were forced to
retreat and he promptly lost interest. In mid-June 1919, when the Supreme
Council met in Paris to decide what to do about him, Kolchak's armies were
losing. They never recovered. And recognition never came.

In March–May 1919, when Kolchak stood at the peak of his fortunes, Denikin's armies were mired in the Cossack hinterland. The British
thought that his was a secondary front and hence gave him much less
generous aid.

With the approach of spring, Denikin once again had to define his
operational objectives. In January, his staff had drawn up plans for a
campaign against Tsaritsyn and Astrakhan to effect a junction with Kolchak's left wing.[122] But these plans had to be abandoned because in March
and April the Red Army had mauled the Don Cossacks and was about to
invade the Don region. Moscow was determined to capture the Donbass
and its coal: in directives to the Red Army, Trotsky claimed that allowing
the Whites to control the Donbass would be a greater calamity than losing
Petrograd.[123] On March 12, the Southern front of the Red Army was
ordered to initiate operations against the Donbass to clear out the Whites.
But beyond this, as has become recently known, the Red Army was assigned the task of liquidating the Cossacks. A secret directive from Moscow
ordered

> the complete, rapid, decisive annihilation of Cossackdom as a separate
> economic group, the destruction of its economic foundations, the physical
> extermination of its officials and officers, and altogether the entire Cossack
> elite.[124]

When the Cossacks responded with rebellion, Trotsky, carrying out Lenin's
mandate, demanded that the "nests of the dishonorable traitors and turn-
coats be extirpated. . . . The Cains must be exterminated."[125]

Denikin was equally determined to keep the Reds out of the Donbass
region. Having gotten wind of this directive, on March 15 he attacked the
Eighth Red Army southeast of Lugansk.[126]

But the main strategic decision still had to be made. Denikin faced a
choice: either to send his main forces against Tsaritsyn and abandon the
Donbass, or save the Donbass and the Don Cossack army, forfeiting the
opportunity to forge a common front with Kolchak. In his memoirs he
writes: "Without hesitation, I chose the second course."[127] But it could not
have been that simple. Denikin's decision met with considerable opposition

from the generals, whose spokesman was Peter Wrangel, the commander of the Caucasian Army and possibly the ablest White officer. Wrangel subjected Denikin's strategic plan to fierce criticism. The Donbass was indefensible and should be given up, he argued. The Don Cossacks should protect the Volunteer Army's flank while it attacked Tsaritsyn: "Our principal and sole operational direction, I suggest, ought to be against Tsaritsyn, which will give us the opportunity to establish direct contact with the army of Admiral Kolchak. Given the immense superiority of enemy forces, simultaneous operations in several operational directions are impossible."[128] Indeed, at this time, Kolchak's left flank, made up of Ural Cossacks under Dutov, stood only 400 kilometers from Tsaritsyn, and half that distance from Astrakhan. Denikin rejected Wrangel's advice on the ground that the Don Cossacks, left to themselves, would not be able to hold on to the Donbass for one day; Rostov, as a result, would fall to the enemy.[129]

Denikin now divided his army in two: a smaller force, under Wrangel, was sent against Tsaritsyn, the major one into the Donbass. Some military historians consider this to have been the fatal decision that doomed the White cause. It deserves note that the Red Army general A. I. Egorov, who in the fall of 1919 would defeat Denikin, in his memoirs supports Denikin's strategic decision, saying that the main threat to the Soviet side came not from the prospect of a White capture of Tsaritsyn and a conjunction with Kolchak, but from an offensive against the Donbass and Orel.[130] But the immediate result of Denikin's ruling was a personal rift between him and his most outstanding officer, which in time would grow into open enmity and split the officer corps into contending pro-Denikin and pro-Wrangel factions.

In January 1919, Denikin had issued a decree stating that all laws issued by the Provisional Government remained in force.[131] In the spring, under British pressure, he went further and released a statement defining his political objectives. These called for the destruction of Bolshevism, reunification of Russia, convocation of a Constituent Assembly, decentralization of government, and civil liberty.[132] On the land issue he remained deliberately vague from fear of alienating the Cossacks. Denikin altogether hesitated to issue clear, specific programs because he felt that the anti-Bolsheviks, conservatives and liberals with differing aspirations, formed a coalition that could be held together not by divisive platforms but by the patriotic appeal to liberate Russia from Communism.[133]

Initially, the course of events vindicated Denikin's military decision. His forces made spectacular advances, in some measure because the Red Army command, having decided to concentrate on defeating Kolchak, had depleted the Southern front. He was also helped by the outbreak of Cossack uprisings in March in the rear of the Eighth and Ninth Red Armies; these the Communists suppressed with great difficulty with the help of Cheka units.[134]

Breaking out of the Rostov enclave in several directions, the Volunteer

Main Fronts of the Civil War

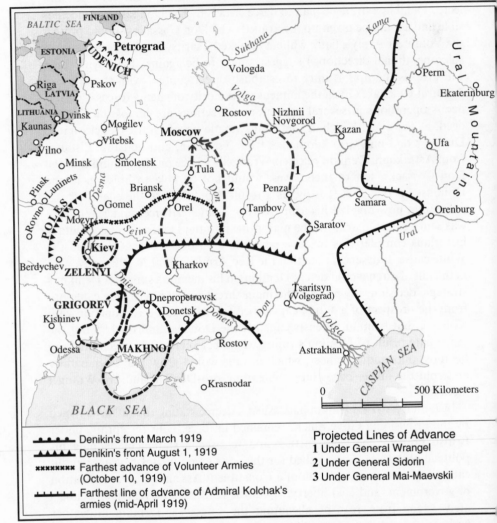

- ▬●▬●▬ Denikin's front March 1919
- ▲▲▲▲ Denikin's front August 1, 1919
- ✗✗✗✗✗✗ Farthest advance of Volunteer Armies
  (October 10, 1919)
- ⊥⊥⊥⊥⊥ Farthest line of advance of Admiral Kolchak's
  armies (mid-April 1919)

Projected Lines of Advance
1 Under General Wrangel
2 Under General Sidorin
3 Under General Mai-Maevskii

Army cleared out Bolshevik forces from the Donbass, following which it captured Kharkov (June 21) and Ekaterinoslav (June 30). The offensive culminated on June 30 with the fall of Tsaritsyn to Wrangel's Caucasian Army. This was a remarkable operation, in the course of which White cavalry and infantry traversed 300 kilometers of the Kalmyk steppe, where it had access neither to water nor to vegetation. Tsaritsyn was heavily defended by lines of trenches and barbed wire. Victory was achieved with the help of a few tanks, manned by British volunteers, which flattened barbed-wire entanglements and rolled over trenches, sending the defenders fleeing in panic. In Tsaritsyn, the Whites captured 40,000 prisoners of war along with immense booty, including thousands of trucks loaded with munitions.[135]

But by the time this spectacular victory had been won, the strategic importance of Tsaritsyn was lost because the Red Army, while yielding in the south, had advanced in the east. By the end of June, Kolchak's armies had been pushed back and a juncture of the two forces was no longer possible.

The Red counteroffensive in the east began on April 28 with a drive on the central front against Ufa.[136] At this point some White troops mutinied and went over to the enemy, but on the whole Kolchak's forces acquitted themselves well and gave the Red command anxious moments. At the end of May, the Whites counterattacked, but they were outnumbered and had to retreat. The fighting was fierce.

Ufa fell to the Reds on June 9; the Whites, however, retained their hold on Perm in the north, and Orenburg as well as Uralsk in south. According to reports submitted by S. S. Kamenev, his troops were adversely affected by anti-Soviet uprisings.[137] The Red Army enjoyed a slight advantage in manpower in the center and on the left flank, with 81,000 troops confronting 70,500 Whites; in the northern sector, it was outnumbered.[138] But the Whites had few reserves with which to compensate for battlefield losses.

The tide of battle took a decisive turn in late June, when the Fifth Army penetrated the Urals, the only natural defensive barrier in the area. The commander of the Fifth Army, the 27-year old Michael Tukhachevskii, was an aristocrat by origin, and his military record included wartime service in the elite Semenovskii Guard Regiment. He had joined the Bolsheviks in April 1918 and made a rapid career. Once the Red Army spread east of the Ural slopes—they captured Cheliabinsk on July 24-25—Kolchak's armies were unable to contain them. With the White forces in the center pushed back hundreds of kilometers, the northern and southern flanks had to be pulled back as well. To Gajda this was a bitter disappointment. Dismissed from command of the Siberian army, he broke with Kolchak and departed for Vladivostok, where in mid-November, in collaboration with the SRs, he staged an unsuccessful coup against him.*

The news of Kolchak's reverses had a decisive effect on Britain's attitude toward intervention. It led to a thorough reexamination of British policy in Russia, which in early August produced the decision to withhold from Kolchak all further assistance.[139]

Kolchak's troops, however, were far from beaten, and for the next two months (from mid-August to mid-October) they made a successful stand at

---

*On his subsequent fate, see *RR,* 628n.

the Tobol and Ishim rivers, 500 kilometers east of Omsk: fighting stubbornly, they stopped the Red advance.[140] Their cause was hopeless, but the sacrifice helped Denikin, who at this time was at the height of his offensive. It succeeded to the extent that it restricted the number of troops the Red command could transfer to the Southern front. The cost in human lives was great: between September 1 and October 15, Kolchak's army lost in wounded and dead 1,000 officers and 18,000 soldiers, more than one-quarter of its remaining combat force. Some White divisions lost up to one-half of their manpower.[141] These casualties could not be made good because Kolchak had in reserve no more than 1,500 troops. By contrast, the Red Army had a virtually inexhaustible pool of replacements. In September, Moscow dispatched tens of thousands of fresh recruits to the Eastern front: by mid-October, Soviet forces there had doubled in strength. On October 14, having replenished and rested their forces, the Reds resumed the offensive, crossing the Tobol River. The Whites continued to offer determined resistance: notable courage was displayed by a division of workers from the Izhevsk armaments plant. But by early November, the issue could no longer be in doubt and the Red command began to withdraw troops from the Eastern front to send them against Denikin.[142] The remnant of Kolchak's army retreated to Omsk.

Arriving in Tsaritsyn shortly after its capture, Denikin held a staff meeting to decide on the next strategic objective. At this time (July 1) the frontline ran from Tsaritsyn to Balashov–Belgorod–Ekaterinoslav–Kherson, with the flanks resting on the Volga and Dnieper rivers.[143] The generals agreed that the army had to advance on Moscow, but once again Denikin and Wrangel were at odds over the best way to attain this goal. It was typical of the lack of coordination between the disparate White armies that Denikin launched his drive on Moscow just as Kolchak was retreating.*

On July 3, Denikin issued order No. 08878, known as the "Moscow Directive."[144] It designated as the Army's next and presumably final mission the capture of the capital city. This was to be accomplished by means of a three-pronged attack:

1. Wrangel, in command of the Caucasian Army, was to advance on Saratov-Rtishchevo-Balashev, relieve the Don Cossack units there, then march on Penza, Arzamas, Nizhnii Novgorod, Vladimir, and Moscow;

2. V. I. Sidorin, leading the Don army, was to send some units to take Voronezh and Riazan, and the rest against Oskol, Elets, Volovo, and Kashira;

*In Denikin's defense it must be noted that he had only the sketchiest notion of what was happening on the Eastern front, there being no direct communication with Kolchak's headquarters except by occasional couriers who managed to slip through Soviet lines, or in a roundabout way, through Paris and London: Denikin, *Ocherki*, V, 88–90.

3. V. Z. Mai-Maevskii, at the head of the Volunteer Army, was to advance from Kharkov by way of Kursk, Orel, and Tula. This was to be the principal thrust since it was the shortest route to the capital. To protect his left flank, Mai-Maevskii was to detach some troops to capture Kiev. Other units were to secure Kherson and Nikolaev, which the French had abandoned three months earlier.

The offensive was to be carried out on a broad front extending from Samara in the east to Kursk in the west—a distance of 700 kilometers, which, after the projected advance into the Ukraine, would expand to 1,000 kilometers. Denikin committed nearly all his effectives, keeping next to nothing in reserve. As the front enlarged, so did the need for troops, and in the fall, the ranks of the Southern Army were filled with conscripts and prisoners of war.

Wrangel objected to Denikin's plans, warning of the danger of expanding the front without adequate reserves and a secure, well-administered rear. He outlined an alternative plan that concentrated the thrust on Saratov, in his own sector. According to Wrangel, after hearing him out Denikin exclaimed, "I see! You want to be the first man to set foot in Moscow!"[145] To Wrangel, Denikin's plan was "nothing more nor less than a death-sentence for the Armies of Southern Russia," since by failing to choose a single principal thrust of the offensive, it ignored all the principles of military strategy.[146]

It was, indeed, an "all-or-nothing" effort, a gamble necessitated by the realization that time was running out and that unless Moscow was captured before the winter, Britain would end all further support. The sense that British patience was wearing thin accounts in no small measure for Denikin's strategy, in which he who had previously been overly cautious now staked all his forces on a gamble. But behind the gamble also lay the awareness that the Red Army was growing by leaps and bounds, and that every day the disparity in forces increased to his disadvantage.

Denikin conceded that in overextending himself he was violating the principles of traditional strategy, but he felt that given the unconventional conditions under which he was forced to fight he had to act unconventionally:

> The strategy of external warfare has its laws: eternal, immutable. . . . It does not permit the dispersal of forces and demands that the front be of a size proportionate to them. . . . We occupied an immense expanse because only by following on the heels of the enemy, by denying him the opportunity to collect himself, had we the chance of breaking the resistance of his superior forces. We seized from the Soviet government its most fertile regions, depriving it of bread, of an immense quantity of military stores, and of inexhaustible reserves for replenishing the army. Our strength lay in the enthusiasm aroused by victories, in maneuverability and the momentum of the advance. . . . We extended the front hundreds of kilometers and by so doing we grew not weaker but stronger. . . . Only under this condition could

we continue the struggle. Otherwise we would have been smothered by our opponent's vastly superior strength, with his inexhaustible resources of manpower.[147]

General N. Kakurin, an ex-tsarist officer in the Red Army, in his authoritative history of the Civil War sides with Wrangel, agreeing that Denikin fought on too broad a front given the size of his army and that a concentrated thrust by way of Saratov would have been preferable. At the same time he concurs with Denikin that under the circumstances he had no alternative but to toss strategy to the winds and wager everything on one lucky throw of the dice.[148]

Although during the summer of 1919 Denikin's forces expanded by means of conscription, the Red Army increased its numerical superiority. By Soviet accounts, the Southern Red Army numbered 140,000 infantry, 20,600 cavalry, and 541 guns, as against 101,600 infantry, 50,750 cavalry, and 521 guns (inclusive of "deep reserves") for the Whites. According to Denikin, in mid-July the Reds had in the south 180,000 men, and the Whites 85,000.* Whichever figure is the more accurate, Communist superiority is an uncontested fact and it grew in the course of the campaign when the Red ranks received reinforcements of 60,000 fresh troops.

The fighting in the south during the next half year was exceedingly savage, accompanied by terrible brutalities, especially on the part of the Red Army. Trotsky forbade executions of prisoners of war, but this injunction was frequently ignored, especially in regard to captured White officers, sometimes on orders of the high command itself. Thus, in August, when White cavalry under the Don Cossack General K. K. Mamontov made a deep foray into Red territory, the Commander in Chief, S. S. Kamenev, ordered that "no prisoners be taken."[149]

> Wounded or captured [White] officers were not only finished off and shot, but tortured in every possible way. Officers had nails driven in their shoulders according to the number of stars on their epaulets; medals were carved on their chests and stripes on their legs. Genitals were cut off and stuffed in their mouths.[150]

The Whites also executed many captured Red officers, but they do not seem to have engaged in torture.

Denikin's offensive gained a striking success on August 10, with the raid of Mamontov's Don Cossacks on Tambov. The Cossack force of 8,000 men, breaking through a gap between the Eighth and Ninth Red Armies, penetrated nearly 200 kilometers into Soviet territory. It disrupted lines of communication, blew up ammunition dumps, and demolished railway

---

*N. Kakurin, *Kak srazhalas' revoliutsiia*, II (Moscow-Leningrad, 1925), 249–50; Denikin, *Ocherki*, V, 118–19. Trotsky in his letter to the Central Committee of October 1, 1919, confirmed that the Red Army in the south had 180,000 men: RTsKhIDNI, F. 2, op. 1, delo 24348.

facilities. At their appearance, peasants rose in rebellion against the Soviet regime. Red troops sent to intercept the raiders were so terrified that they refused to leave the railway cars that brought them to the front: Lenin ordered soldiers who refused to detrain shot.[151] Twenty thousand recruits about to be inducted into the Red Army were taken prisoner, and like so much cattle conscripted into the White Army. Mamontov's cavalry took Tambov almost without resistance, following which it captured Voronezh. The raid, had it been pursued, could have inflicted incalculable damage on the Red Army. But the Don Cossacks soon turned from fighting to looting, and their movement was slowed to a crawl by wagons filled with booty. Before long, many of the raiders left for home to store the spoils and help out with the harvest. By September 19, when the operation ended, the Cavalry Corps had fewer than 1,500 men left.[152] The main consequence of Mamontov's raid was to alert the Red commanders to the importance of cavalry, which they had previously neglected. Shortly afterwards, the Red Cavalry Corps was formed under Semen Budennyi, which would be used with devastating effect against Denikin in October and November.

Denikin's armies continued to advance in all directions throughout August and September. In the lead were Mai-Maevskii's Volunteers, who on September 20 captured Kursk. By then, the Red front between Kursk and Voronezh lay in tatters.[153] The general who won these victories was a most unlikely hero: according to Wrangel, "If he had not worn a uniform, you would have taken him for a comedian from a little provincial theater. He was as round as a barrel, and had a chubby face with a bulbous nose."[154] A good strategist, Mai-Maevskii had an unfortunate weakness for women and drink, in both of which he indulged at the height of combat.

Mai-Maevskii commanded three crack units of the Volunteer Army bearing the names Kornilov, Markov, and Drozdovskii. Their core consisted of volunteers who passionately hated the Bolsheviks. However, to compensate for combat losses, their ranks were diluted with draftees and POWs, and the units were enlarged from regiments to divisions, resulting in a decline of morale and fighting spirit.[155] The White front, 1,000 kilometers long, resembled a wedge, the base of which rested on Kiev in the west and Tsaritsyn in the east, with its tip on Kursk. It was not solid but porous: one historian describes it as "a series of patrols with occasional columns of slowly advancing troops without reserves."[156] Between them lay a spacious no-man's-land that an enemy counteroffensive could quickly fill:

> By virtue of the general strategic considerations and the peculiarities of the Civil War, which was conducted not with a solid front but along railroad lines and waterways, the occupation by the Volunteer Army, in its advance from the east to the west (and from the [south to the north]) of some railway station, especially a junction, meant that the Soviet army had to clear . . . a whole strip of territory to the east (or north) which thus fell to the victor without fighting. The mere fact of occupying a strategic railroad

point automatically led to the conquest of vast stretches of territory: there was no need to expel the enemy from most localities—these were peacefully occupied by constabularies and guards.[157]

This manner of campaigning made possible very rapid progress with small forces; by the same token, it made the advancing forces highly vulnerable to counterattack.

The only solid White sector was a short segment between Rzhava and Oboian. Here, on a front 12 kilometers wide, the Whites concentrated nearly 10,000 troops, or 800 per kilometer—a density previously not seen in the Civil War. They were to accomplish the decisive breakthrough and capture Moscow.[158]

A major problem confronting the White generals—one that the Bolsheviks resolved in a characteristically cynical manner—concerned the status of the non-Russian borderlands. The White leaders, who viewed themselves as trustees of Russian statehood, felt they had no authority to change the country's boundaries: that was a matter within the purview of the Constituent Assembly. They further reasoned that the nationalist platform on which they sought to rally their followers required the ideal of Russia one and indivisible: no one, wrote Denikin, would risk his life for a federated Russia.[159] On these grounds, the White leaders refused to recognize the independence of any of the secessionist states. It was a disastrous policy: Kolchak's refusal to acknowledge the independence of Finland and Denikin's unwillingness to accommodate Poland had a fatal effect on their cause, depriving them of help at critical moments in the war.

The White generals and their diplomatic representatives in Paris were reconciled to the ultimate independence of Poland, but they thought in terms of "Congress Poland," the diminutive kingdom created in 1815 by the Congress of Vienna. The Poles had much vaster ambitions. Resurrected after more than a century of foreign occupation, theirs was to be a Great Poland, ideally extending from the Baltic to the Black Sea, but even at its smallest including large areas inhabited by Belorussians and Ukrainians, once part of the Polish Commonwealth. Russians, both White and Red, regarded Belorussia and the Ukraine as inalienable parts of Russia. In the conflicts arising between Poles and Russians over these opposing territorial claims, the Whites proved intractable and the Reds very accommodating.

Of all the European leaders, Joseph Pilsudski, head of the independent Polish Republic, knew the Russians best, especially the Russian socialists, since he had been one of them: he had been arrested in 1887 for conspiring to assassinate Alexander III (in the same plot for which Lenin's brother, Alexander, was executed), and exiled for five years to Siberia. On taking office, he faced the problem of Poland's eastern frontier, which the Versailles conference had left open. A patriot with a deep sense of history, he wanted to ensure Poland's independence against the day when Russia and Germany, risen from the ashes, would again combine against her. His strategy was to exploit Russia's temporary weakness to detach from her the western and southern borderlands (Lithuania, Belorussia, and the Ukraine) and shape them into buffer states. The result would be a new balance of power in Eastern Europe capable of deterring Russian expansionism:

> Reduced to its frontiers of the sixteenth century, cut off from the Black and Baltic Seas, deprived of the agricultural and mineral wealth of the South and Southeast, Russia might easily sink to the status of a second-class power, incapable of seriously threatening the newly gained independence of Poland. And Poland, as the largest and strongest of the new states, might easily establish a sphere of influence which would range from Finland to the Caucasus Mountains.[160]

In pursuit of this objective, from February 1919 on, Polish forces in the east engaged Red Army troops in intermittent battles without a formal declaration of war, occupying disputed territories.

Pilsudski sounded out Denikin and the White diplomatic representatives in Paris on the issue of Poland's eastern frontiers and received what he considered entirely unsatisfactory answers. In late September 1919 he dispatched a mission under General Karnicki, a former tsarist officer, to Denikin's headquarters at Taganrog.* Karnicki quickly determined that Denikin was not prepared to satisfy Polish territorial demands.[161] Diplomatic sources independently confirmed this assessment. On the basis of this information, Pilsudski concluded that it was in Poland's interest to help the Red Army eliminate Denikin. The reasoning, as later explained by one of his generals, went as follows:

> The defeat of the Red Army would have resulted in the solidification of Denikin's regime and, in consequence, in the non-recognition in full of Poland's independence. It was a lesser evil to help Soviet Russia defeat Denikin, even though it was realized that we, in turn, would not escape a military conflict with the Soviets, should we desire to have a peace corresponding to our interests. Therefore, as long as there was an army of Denikin, Poland's war with the Soviets would be a struggle over Russia, whereas after the fall of Denikin it would be a struggle over Poland.[162]

Karnicki also sent an unfavorable assessment of Denikin's army, which led Pilsudski to predict that, their current successes notwithstanding, the Whites would fail to capture Moscow and end up being thrown back to the Black Sea.[163] In a conversation with the British ambassador on November 7, before the decisive battles between the Whites and Reds had been re-

---

*Denikin, *Ocherki*, V, 175. Tadeusz Kutrzeba, *Wyprawa kijowska 1920 roku* (Warsaw, 1937), 24, seems to err in dating it in July. See further Louis Fischer, *The Soviets in World Affairs*, I (Princeton, 1951), 239–41, and E. H. Carr, *The Bolshevik Revolution, 1917–1923*, III (New York, 1953), 154–55.

solved in the latter's favor, Pilsudski dismissed the White and Red forces as of equally low quality, and expressed the opinion that by the spring the Red Army would recover from its defeats.[164]

The issue of frontiers was not the only consideration behind Pilsudski's hostility toward the Whites. Some Polish diplomats calculated that once the Whites were out of the picture, Poland would be the main beneficiary of French and possibly British aid, and the young republic would become the fulcrum of Allied diplomacy in Eastern Europe.[165] This was a very flawed judgment, which both overrated Poland's international importance and underestimated the readiness of the Allies to come to terms with the Bolsheviks once the Civil War was over.

It was on these grounds, however, that Pilsudski decided in the fall of 1919 to deny the Whites all military assistance: he wanted Denikin crushed so as to be able to deal with a weak and isolated Bolshevik Russia. In late 1919, orders were issued to Polish forces in the east, deep inside contested territory and in a de facto state of war with Soviet Russia, to undertake no operations against the Red Army that could benefit Denikin.[166]

The shift in Polish policy was not lost on the Bolshevik leaders. They were prepared to pay a heavy price to prevent cooperation between Denikin and Pilsudski, offering the Poles not only unconditional independence but virtually any border arrangement that suited them. Such concessions were a tactical maneuver made in the conviction that before long not only the territories Poland claimed from Russia but Poland herself would become Communist. In the words of Julian Marchlewski, a Polish Communist who would serve as intermediary between Moscow and Warsaw, "The members of the Soviet government as well as other comrades whose opinion counted, myself included, were firmly convinced that in the near future all frontiers would lose significance because the revolutionary upheaval in Europe, therefore in Poland as well, was only a matter of time, a matter of a few years."[167]

Denikin, whose political perspicacity left much to be desired, seems to have been quite unaware of Pilsudski's calculations and the possibility of a Polish-Bolshevik rapprochement. In preparing the drive on Kiev, he believed he could count on combining forces with the Polish army, whose forward units were less than 200 kilometers from the Ukrainian capital, in the rear of the Red Twelfth Army.[168]

The groundwork for an understanding between Warsaw and Moscow against Denikin was laid in March 1919, during Marchlewski's secret talks with Jozef Beck, Sr., Vice-Minister of Internal Affairs and the father of the future Polish Foreign Minister. Marchlewski had spent the war years in Germany, where he helped found the extremely radical Spartacus League and in early 1919 participated in the Spartacist revolution there. Later on he would become an official of the Communist International. He impressed on Beck that the Whites represented a mortal danger not only to the

Bolsheviks but also to the Poles.[169] This encounter produced no immediate results. In May 1919 Marchlewski left for Moscow, where he suggested that the Soviet government enter into negotiations with Poland. In early July, when things were going badly for the Red Army, Moscow approved this proposal. Ostensibly, the negotiations that began later that month concerned the exchange of prisoners. When in the spring of 1919 the Poles had occupied Vilno, they arrested some local Communists. Moscow retaliated by taking hostage several hundred Poles residing in Russia.[170] Marchlewski proposed to the Central Committee that this dispute be used as a cover for diplomatic negotiations: the Poles, he maintained, could be bought off from intervening in the Civil War with territorial concessions. With the approval of the Soviet government, he initiated informal talks with Polish representatives in the middle of July in a hunting lodge in the Bialowierza Forest, in the course of which he indicated that the Soviet government was prepared to make to Poland the most generous territorial concessions.[171] The Poles responded cautiously out of fear of an adverse reaction from the Allies should they learn that Poland was negotiating behind their backs with Moscow. The talks were suspended in August and September when Polish troops continued to advance eastward.

They were resumed on October 11 and conducted intermittently until December 15 at Mikaszewicze, a small, out-of-the-way railroad station near Luck.[172] Confident that he held all the trump cards, Pilsudski instructed his diplomats to say that Poland would give up no territory that she had occupied and might even insist on the restoration of the 1772 borders. Marchlewski assured the Poles that Soviet Russia was willing to surrender to her Belorussia and Lithuania: "territorial questions do not exist, and Poland will receive what she wants."* Pilsudski's resolve to strike a deal with the Bolsheviks was strengthened by reports of Polish intelligence and diplomatic sources in the West that the Whites, feeling on the verge of victory, contemplated granting Poland independence only within the borders of "Congress Poland" and would insist on the evacuation of all other Russian territories occupied by Polish troops.[173] On October 26, Pilsudski's representative, Captain Ignacy Boerner, told Marchlewski, "We need you to defeat Denikin. Take your regiments, send them against Denikin or against Iudenich. We shall not touch you."[174] True to their word, at this very time when Red and White troops were fighting in the vicinity of Mozyrz (Mozyr) in Volhynia, Polish forces deployed in the rear of the Reds did not stir. This was an exposed area on the extreme right flank of the Red forces. Had the Poles advanced on Chernigov, they could have trapped a good part of the Twelfth Red Army. The inaction was deliberate. The

*Piotr S. Wandycz, *Soviet-Polish Relations* (Cambridge, Mass., 1969), 139. It is known from Karl Radek that Moscow offered Poland all of Belorussia up to the Berezina River, as well as Podolia and Volhynia: Karl Radek, *Die Auswärtige Politik Sowjet-Russlands* (Hamburg, 1921), 56.

Polish pledge of noninterference rendered an invaluable service to the Red Army, which had deployed its third largest contingent against the Poles. It enabled Moscow to withdraw 43,000 troops from the Western front and throw them against Denikin.[175]

On November 14, having heard Marchlewski's report, the Politburo agreed to Pilsudski's terms with one qualification, namely that Moscow would not promise to refrain from attacking Petlura, the commander of a Ukrainian national army.[176] Marchlewski returned to Mikaszewicze on November 22. On Polish insistence, the secret understanding produced no treaty, only an accord on the exchange of hostages: Pilsudski was displeased with Lenin's reservations about Petlura, on whom he had his own designs. He also did not want a formal treaty with the Bolsheviks, since that would compromise him in the eyes of the Allied powers. He mistrusted Bolshevik promises in any event and expected the frontier issue to be settled by force of arms the following spring.[177]

Pilsudski subsequently boasted through his emissary that the deliberate inaction of his troops at Mozyrz may well have decided the outcome of the Civil War.[178] Denikin and some other Whites came to see in this tacit Polish-Bolshevik collaboration the principal cause of their defeat.[179] Tukhachevskii and Radek agreed that if Pilsudski had cooperated with Denikin the tide of battle might well have turned the other way.[180]

On December 22, barely one week after the talks at Mikaszewicze had adjourned, by which time Denikin's forces were in full flight, the Polish Ministry of War was ordered to prepare the armed forces for a "definitive settlement of the Russian question" by early April 1920.[181]

So much for the Polish issue. Only marginally less detrimental to the White cause was the Whites' refusal to accommodate Finnish and Estonian nationalists. In early 1919, several Russian generals, supported by the National Center, began to assemble an army in Estonia with which to capture Petrograd. The troops were mostly prisoners of war released by the Germans in the Baltic. The founder of what was to become the Northern Corps was General Alexander Rodzianko, a well-known tsarist cavalry officer; in March N. N. Iudenich, a hero of World War I whom Kolchak had named his Commander in the Baltic area, took over. The force was small—16,000 men in May—and though it had the support of British naval units in the Baltic, it could accomplish its mission only with the help of the Estonians and Finns.

Here, however, the issue of Finnish and Estonian independence proved an insurmountable obstacle. Finland declared partial independence in July 1917, at which time the country's foreign affairs and military forces were still left in Russian hands. On November 4 (NS), the Finnish Diet proclaimed the country's full independence. Lenin's government formally recognized Finland's sovereignty on January 4, 1918 (NS), and immediately proceeded to subvert it. On the night of January 27–28 (NS), Finnish

Communists, assisted by the Russian army and navy garrison of 40,000, staged a putsch, which gave them control of Helsinki and much of southern Finland. The Communist government dissolved the Finnish Senate and Diet, and unleashed a civil war with the view of transforming Finland into a Soviet republic.

Finnish nationalists responded by creating a Defense Corps commanded by General Karl Mannerheim, a onetime tsarist officer. Mannerheim's volunteers had no difficulty clearing northern Finland of the Communists, but they were not strong enough to expel them from the south. The German units stationed in Finland that supplied and trained the Defense Corps doubted that the Finns could manage on their own. Fearing that the Allies would open a new Eastern front from Murmansk, they decided to help the Finns with German troops. Early in April, over Mannerheim's objections, German units under General R. von der Goltz landed in Finland. They made short shrift of the Bolsheviks, capturing Helsinki on April 12. By the end of the month, when the German-Finnish force captured Vyborg, Finland was rid of the Bolsheviks.

A year later, Iudenich's force, augmented by 20,000 Estonians, was deployed in Estonia. On May 13, 1919, it crossed into Soviet territory, launching an offensive against Petrograd from the south. With the help of intelligence supplied by agents of the National Center, Iudenich captured Pskov and threatened Petrograd, but his forces were not adequate to the task. He journeyed repeatedly to Helsinki to enlist Mannerheim's help.[182] The capture of Petrograd would have been immeasurably easier if attempted from Finnish territory, through the Karelian Isthmus, especially if the newly formed Finnish army were to join in the assault.

Iudenich urged Mannerheim to help him take Petrograd by launching a coordinated attack from Karelia. Kolchak seconded the request.[183] The Allies, however, were strangely ambivalent. On July 12, the Council of Four sent to the Finnish government a note advising it that if Finland desired "to accede to Admiral Kolchak's request for action against Petrograd, the Allied Governments . . . have no objection to raise to such an operation."[184] At the same time, they denied that they meant to exert any pressure on the Finns in this matter. Privately, the British warned Mannerheim *not* to attack Petrograd. Lord Curzon, the Foreign Secretary, told General Sir Hubert Gough, as he was departing to take charge of the Allied military mission in the Baltic, that "he was to be most careful not to encourage General Mannerheim . . . to march on Petrograd. I was to make it quite clear to him that he could not look for British support or approval if he undertook such an operation."[185] Curzon further advised Gough not to take the views of Churchill, his immediate superior, as his "sole guide."[186] Neither Britain nor France expressed a willingness to give the Finnish government the kind of financial guarantees it wanted as compensation for involvement in the Russian Civil War on the White side.[187] There is thus no shortage of evidence that the Allies did not desire the Whites to capture Petrograd. Their attitude seems to have been inspired by fear of Finnish-German cooperation, a fact emphasized by Britain's forbidding Iudenich to accept supplies offered him by the commander of the German force in the Baltic. A British Foreign Office official commented in October 1919 that it would be better if Petrograd were not captured than that it be captured by the Germans, by which he must have meant the German-backed Finns.[188] Evan Mawdsley rightly observes that if the Allies had been serious about overthrowing the Bolshevik regime, Petrograd would have been the ideal front from which to do it.[189]

This is a matter of considerable importance for the understanding of Allied ambivalence about intervention, even though the ability of Mannerheim to send troops into Russia was by no means certain. The socialists, who had a solid majority in the Finnish Diet, opposed involvement in Russian affairs; so did most members of Mannerheim's government.[190] There were fears that intervention would provoke social unrest in Finland.[191] But the quixotic position of the Whites on the issue of Finnish independence certainly wrecked such chances as there were of Finnish involvement.

Acknowledging Finland's independence would have been little more than a formality, given that Finland was now in fact fully sovereign and recognized as such by a number of countries, including France, Germany, and Soviet Russia. But Kolchak's political advisers in Paris, led by the onetime Minister of Foreign Affairs Sergei Sazonov, firmly opposed such recognition in advance of the Constituent Assembly.

Iudenich, realizing that his cause was doomed without Mannerheim's collaboration, and under strong pressure from the British military mission, agreed, on his own authority, to acknowledge Finland's independence; the boundary lines were to be settled by a plebiscite. A supplementary military accord entrusted Mannerheim with the command of Russian troops taking part in the projected assault on Petrograd, with the proviso that Russian officers would take charge of both Russian and Finnish troops once they had entered the city.[192] Iudenich's concession was repudiated by Kolchak, who cabled him on July 20 that he was not to enter into any agreements with Finland because her conditions were unacceptable and her willingness to help questionable.[193] Mannerheim cabled Kolchak that he was prepared to help but only if given "a certain guarantee," by which he meant formal recognition.[194] When this was not forthcoming, he washed his hands of the whole affair. He not only refused to commit Finnish troops, but, no less important, refused to permit the Whites to operate from Finnish territory.[195] Shortly afterwards (July 25), having lost the elections, he left for Paris to attend the Peace Conference.

After Mannerheim's retirement, Iudenich departed with his small staff for the Pskov-Iamburg area to assume command of the Russian troops. He wanted to bring in the Estonians, but they too kept aloof from fear that a non-Bolshevik Russia would refuse to grant them independence, whereas the Soviet government offered to do so on the sole condition that they cease cooperating with the Whites.[196]

As in the case of Poland, Moscow quickly seized the opportunity to sow disunity among its enemies. On August 31 it offered peace to Estonia, and on September 11 to Latvia, Lithuania, and Finland.[197] On September 14–15, representatives of the four countries meeting in Reval agreed to open negotiations with the Bolsheviks.[198] The three Baltic states informed Moscow they were ready to negotiate no later than October 25.[199] Britain protested this decision and, at the same time, urged Denikin and Kolchak to recognize these states, but received a firm refusal.[200]

For the next two months, the Northwestern front remained quiet. The operation against Petrograd resumed in late September, concurrently with Denikin's offensive in the Ukraine. Once again, the Whites would be compelled to assault the old capital from the south rather than the northwest.

Denikin had not only the Red Army to contend with, but also numerous bands of irregulars, popularly known as "Greens," who opposed both Reds and Whites alike. On his left flank emerged an anarchist movement led by Nestor Makhno, involving thousands of partisans who had no program other than abolishing all state authority and no objective other than looting. Born to a poor Ukrainian family, Makhno turned anarchist and spent many years doing hard labor in tsarist prisons.[201] If one is to believe his memoirs, in June 1918 he met in Moscow with Lenin and with Lenin's aide Iakov Sverdlov, and the latter helped to smuggle him into the Ukraine to work against the Germans.[202] Makhno, combining whimsical cruelty with a domineering personality, attracted deserters and adventurers as well as a scattering of anarchist intellectuals. After he captured Ekaterinoslav in December 1918, Trotsky appointed him commander of a Red Army detachment which in 1919 grew to some 10,000–15,000 troops. But his relations with Moscow were strained, for even while collaborating with it, he objected to food requisitions and to the activities of the Cheka. On August 1, 1919, he issued "Order No. 1," which called for the extermination of the rich bourgeoisie along with Communist commissars who "use force to uphold a bourgeois social order."[203] Operating in the Crimea and along the eastern shores of the Sea of Azov with as many as 40,000 followers, he had his men blow up bridges and ammunition dumps. In October, Denikin had to send six regiments against him which were desperately needed against the Red Army. The diversion had a very detrimental effect on the battle for Orel and Kursk, which decided the Civil War.[204]

The Whites also had to contend with the Ukrainian nationalist forces under Ataman Semen Petlura. Their troops and Petlura's entered Kiev at

11. Makhno.

almost the same time (August 30–31) and, to avoid a conflict, drew up a demarcation line that placed the city under White control.[205] But Petlura's forces were regarded by the White command as hostile, and troops had to be assigned to neutralize them. Eventually, Petlura retreated into Polish Galicia with the remnant of his army and entered into negotiations with Pilsudski that would bear fruit in the Soviet-Polish War the next year.

The Red Army faced similar problems with partisans in its rear, but in this case, too, its numerical preponderance was invaluable. In the summer of 1919, 180,000 Red Army men were assigned to combat internal resistance—a body of troops fully one-half the size of that engaged against the Whites.[206]

The collapse of Kolchak was a bitter pill for the few British statesmen not entirely averse to intervention. On July 27, having learned that the Red Army was in Cheliabinsk and thus east of the Urals, Curzon jotted down: "A lost cause."[207] The news led to a reassessment of the British commitment in Russia, at the very moment when Denikin stood poised for the final push on Moscow.

The War Cabinet scheduled a meeting for July 29 to discuss the Russian situation. The news of Kolchak's reverses emboldened those who had all along wanted an accommodation with Lenin. Their thinking was reflected in a memorandum submitted to the Cabinet by a Treasury official and banker named E. M. Harvey.[208] The document grossly distorted the internal situation in Russia to press the argument for abandoning the White cause. Its basic premise held that in civil war victory went to the side that enjoyed greater popular support, from which it followed that since Lenin's government had beaten off all challengers it had to have the population behind it:

> It is impossible to account for the stability of the Bolshevik Government by terrorism alone. . . . When the Bolshevik fortunes seemed to be at the lowest ebb, a most vigorous offensive was launched before which the Kolchak forces are still in retreat. No terrorism, not even long suffering acquiescence, but something approaching enthusiasm is necessary for this. We must admit then that the present Russian government is accepted by the bulk of the Russian people.

The pledge of the Whites immediately after victory to convene a Constituent Assembly meant little since there was no assurance that "Russia, summoned to the polls, will not again [!] return the Bolsheviks." The unsavory aspects of Lenin's rule were in good measure forced on him by his enemies:

> Necessity of state enables him to justify many acts of violence whereas in a state of peace his Government would have to be progressive or it would fall. It is respectfully contended that the surest way to get rid of Bolshevism, or at least to eradicate the vicious elements in it, is to withdraw our support of the Kolchak movement and thereby end the civil war.

Although the author did not explicitly say so, his line of argument led to the inescapable conclusion that support should also be withdrawn from Denikin and Iudenich.*

For the time being, the War Cabinet did not act on Harvey's recommendation. It decided to continue extending help to the Whites, but to shift the bulk of the aid to Denikin.[209] On this occasion, Lloyd George, echoing Harvey, said that "if Denikin really had the people behind him, the Bolsheviks could never overcome him"[210]—as if trial by battle were but a variant of balloting.

Opponents of intervention pressed the psychological advantage they had gained from Kolchak's reverses by demanding that the government release figures showing how much it was costing Britain. On August 14, the War Office published a White Paper itemizing direct British aid to the White Russians (including the Baltic states) during the year following the Armistice on the Western front. It came to 47.9 million pounds (239.5 million dollars).[211] A week later, Curzon advised Balfour that before the end of the year the sum would rise to 94 million pounds (470 million dollars, or 730 tons of gold).[212] Churchill described these figures as "an absurd exaggeration":

*In 1920, Harvey would be one of the influential voices urging Lloyd George to recognize Soviet Russia and enter into mutual trade relations as a means of "civilizing" her: Ullman, *Britain,* 344-45.

The actual expense, apart from munitions, was not a tithe as great. The munitions themselves, though they had been most costly to produce, were only an unmarketable surplus of the Great War, to which no money value can be assigned. Had they been kept in our hands till they mouldered, they would only have involved additional charges for storage, care and maintenance.[213]

On August 12, the War Cabinet adopted a motion of Austen Chamberlain, Chancellor of the Exchequer and an outspoken foe of intervention, that Denikin be offered a "final packet" of aid, nearly all of it to consist of "non-marketable" goods. The White general was to be told that he would receive no more.[214] The Prime Minister thus settled on a compromise: aid would continue, but the amount would be specified and when it ran out, nothing else would be forthcoming. Churchill was asked to assemble the relevant data.

The French, who had given very niggardly aid to the Whites, were also growing impatient: in September they made it known that no more supplies would be shipped on credit but only for cash or in exchange for goods. Negotiations were initiated with Denikin for the shipment of grain, coal, and other commodities from southern Russia, but before these could be delivered, Denikin's armies collapsed.[215]

These restrictions on aid, it must be stressed, were imposed at the moment when Denikin appeared closest to victory: like so much else of Allied behavior, they raise serious questions as to what the real intentions of London and Paris were.

The Whites' sense of being abandoned was reinforced by Allied evacuation of the northern ports: the decision was made in early March, but Kolchak was informed of it only in late April.[216] At the end of September, 23,000 Allied troops and 6,500 Russians were evacuated from Archangel; the Murmansk contingent departed on October 12. They were replaced by a force of 4,000 British volunteers, veterans of the World War. The evacuation was a complicated maneuver because the Bolshevik forces deployed on the perimeter of the Allied bases stood poised to attack. To protect his men, General Ironside ordered an offensive of British and Russian volunteers (August 10): the operation cost 120 British lives.[217] In all, Britain had suffered 327 fatalities in the course of her intervention in North Russia. American losses were 139 officers and soldiers, all victims of accident or injury.[218]

On October 7, as the Volunteer Army was approaching Orel, 300 kilometers from Moscow, and Iudenich was staging his second drive on Petrograd, the British cabinet agreed on a "Final Contribution to General Denikin," amounting to 11 million pounds (55 million dollars) in surplus matériel of no commercial value, 2.25 million pounds (11.25 million dollars) in surplus marketable stores, and an additional 750,000 pounds (3.15 million dollars) in cash, mostly to pay for transport.[219]

The seeds of betrayal were sown. After Kolchak had been forced to retreat, Britain's heart was no longer in intervention and her government was looking for ways to extricate itself from Russia. There could be no doubt that as soon as Denikin suffered the first serious reverses, and, in any event, before the end of the year, he, too, would be left in the lurch.* Thus, on top of all his other problems, Denikin had a time bomb ticking away.

In the Bolshevik camp, the strategic situation in the summer of 1919 provoked serious disagreements. After Ufa had been retaken and Kolchak's offensive contained, Trotsky and his protégé, the Commander in Chief Vatsetis, wanted to assume a defensive stance along the Urals and transfer all the troops that could be spared to the Southern front. Stalin preferred to finish off Kolchak first. He promoted as his candidate for Commander in Chief S. S. Kamenev, who had directed the operations against Kolchak. Since Kamenev sided with Stalin, Trotsky had him dismissed. But the Central Committee overruled Trotsky and appointed Kamenev to replace Vatsetis as Commander in Chief. This post he was to hold until 1924. The Committee further criticized Trotsky for his management of the Commissariat of War.[220] Piqued, Trotsky on July 5 offered to resign from both the Politburo and his post as Commissar of War on the ostensible grounds that his constant travel to the front prevented him from participating in the making of political and military decisions in the Center. He recommended that his place be taken by someone who could not be accused of "passion for bureaucratism and repressive methods."[221] The Politburo unanimously rejected this request, and to appease Trotsky, Lenin gave him a carte blanche endorsement over his signature, which Trotsky could use whenever his decisions were questioned.

The Civil War was accompanied by frightful pogroms in the Right-Bank Ukraine, the worst violence the Jews had suffered since the Cossack Hetman Bohdan Chmielnicki had ruled this region nearly three centuries earlier.

At the outbreak of World War I, almost two-thirds of the world's Jews lived in the Russian Empire. Their status was exceedingly precarious. Tsarist legislation compelled all but a handful of rich or educated Jews to reside in the Pale of Settlement, an area carved out of the western Ukraine, Belorussia, Lithuania, and Poland, where they had lived when Russia acquired those areas during the partitions of Poland. In this territory, as

---

*Ullman, *Britain,* 211–12. On October 1, 1919, the Polish ambassador in London cabled Warsaw that Denikin would be receiving aid only for a few more weeks: if he failed to take Moscow before winter, all assistance to him would cease and Russia would be "crossed off": PAN, *Dokumenty,* II, 388.

members of the burgher estate, they had to reside in the towns and make a living by trade and artisanship. There were quotas on Jewish admissions to secondary schools and universities. Jews were entirely excluded—the only ethnic group subject to this disability—from the civil service and officer ranks in the armed forces. They were treated as a pariah caste, a status that was increasingly anachronistic and contrary to the general trend of late Imperial Russia toward equal citizenship. Most seriously affected by these disabilities were secular Jews, who no longer fitted into traditional Jewish society and yet found most avenues of advancement in the dominant Christian society blocked.

In the early twentieth century, enlightened Russian bureaucrats urged that Jews be granted at least partial if not full equality.[222] They argued that Russia's medieval laws embarrassed her abroad and made it more difficult to secure loans from international banks, in which Jews played an important role. Furthermore, the artificial obstacles to their education and career opportunities drove Jewish youths into revolutionary activity. But this advice was not acted upon, in part because of the opposition of the Ministry of the Interior, which feared Jewish economic and political penetration into the villages, and in part because of the anti-Semitism of Nicholas II and his entourage.

The Pale of Settlement died a natural death during World War I, when several hundred thousand Jews moved into the interior of Russia, some expelled from their homes, others escaped from the front zone. Half a million Jews served in the Imperial army during World War I, but only as rank-and-file soldiers—the first Jewish officers, no more than a few dozen, were commissioned by the Provisional Government,[223] which formally abolished the Pale and eliminated the remaining Jewish disabilities. Jews kept on dispersing in the interior during and after the Civil War. In 1923, the Jewish population inhabiting Great Russia had grown to 533,000, from 153,000 in 1897. At the same time, in what had been the Pale, Jews moved from the small towns, where two-thirds of them had resided before the Revolution, to the larger cities.[224] After 1917, Jews, for the first time in Russian history, made an appearance as government officials. Thus it happened that with the Revolution Jews suddenly showed up in parts of the country where they had never been seen before, and in capacities they had never previously exercised.

It was a fatal conjunction: for most Russians the appearance of Jews coincided with the miseries of Communism and so was identified with them. In the words of a Jewish contemporary:

> Previously, Russians have never seen a Jew in a position of authority: neither as governor, nor as policeman, nor even as postal employee. Even then, there were, of course, better times and worse times, but the Russian people had lived, worked, and disposed of the fruits of their labor, the

Russian nation grew and enriched itself, the Russian name was grand and awe-inspiring. Now the Jew is on every corner and on all rungs of power. The Russian sees him as head of the ancient capital, Moscow, and in charge of the capital on the Neva, and in command of the Red Army, that most perfect mechanism of [national] self-destruction. He sees the Prospect of St. Vladimir bear the glorious name of Nakhimson, the historic Liteinyi Prospect renamed the Prospect of Volodarskii, and Pavlovsk become Slutsk. The Russian now sees the Jew as judge and executioner. He meets Jews at every step—not Communists, but people as hapless as himself, yet issuing orders, working for the Soviet regime; and this regime, after all, is everywhere, one cannot escape it. And this regime, had it emerged from the lowest depths of hell, could not be more malevolent or brazen. Is it any wonder, then, that the Russian, comparing the past with the present, concludes that the present regime is Jewish and therefore so diabolical?[225]

The consequence was the eruption of a virulent anti-Semitism, first in Russia, then abroad. Just as socialism was the ideology of the intelligentsia, and nationalism that of the old civil and military Establishment, so Judeophobia became the ideology of the masses. At the conclusion of the Civil War, a Russian publicist observed that "Hatred of Jews is one of the most prominent features of contemporary Russian life; possibly even the most prominent. Jews are hated everywhere, in the north, in the south, in the east and in the west. They are detested by all social orders, by all political parties, by all nationalities and by persons of all ages."* By late 1919, even the liberal Kadets were afflicted with the poison.[226]

The immediate cause of this psychotic hatred, symptomatic of a society in moral and psychic crisis, was the sense that whereas everybody else had lost from the Revolution, the Jews, and they alone, had benefited from it. This perception led to the conclusion that they had masterminded the Revolution. The view received spurious theoretical justification from the so-called *Protocols of the Elders of Zion,* a forgery fostered, and perhaps partly created, by the tsarist police; having attracted scant attention on publication in 1902, the *Protocols* now gained worldwide notoriety. Its argument that Jews were secretly conspiring to conquer and subjugate mankind appeared prophetic in the light of events in Russia. The connection between Jewry and Communism, drawn in the aftermath of the Revolution and exported from Russia to Weimar Germany, was instantly assimilated by Hitler and made into a cardinal tenet of the Nazi movement.

The Bolsheviks did not tolerate on their territory overt manifestations of anti-Semitism, least of all pogroms, for they well realized that anti-Semitism

*S. S. Masloff, *Russia after Four Years of Revolution* (London/Paris, 1923), 148. F. A. Mackenzie, in *The Russian Crucifixion* (London, n.d.), spoke of Jews as being hated in both Communist and non-Communist ranks "with a virulence difficult to describe": the population was only biding its time before carrying out a pogrom that would put all previous ones into the shade (p. 125).

had become a cover for anti-Communism.[227] But for the same reason they did not go out of their way to publicize anti-Semitic excesses on the White side, so as not to play into the hands of those who accused their government of serving "Jewish" interests. During the 1919 pogroms in the Ukraine, apart from a few perfunctory protests, Moscow maintained a prudent silence, apparently afraid to encourage pro-White sentiments among its population.*

The paradox inherent in this situation was that although they were widely perceived as working for the benefit of their own people, Bolsheviks of Jewish origin not only did not think of themselves as Jews but resented being regarded as such. When, under tsarism, for conspiratorial reasons they adopted aliases, they invariably chose Russian names, never Jewish ones. They subscribed to Marx's view that the Jews were not a nation but a social caste of a very pernicious and exploitative kind. They desired that Jews assimilate as rapidly as possible, and believed that this would happen as soon as they were compelled to engage in "productive" work. In the 1920s the Soviet regime would use Jewish Bolsheviks and members of the Jewish Socialist Bund to destroy organized Jewish life in Russia.

The reason for this apostasy lay in the fact that a Jew who, for whatever reason, wished to be rid of his Jewishness had only two choices open to him. One was to convert. But for a secular Jew, exchanging one religion for another was no solution. The alternative was to join the nation of the nationless, the radical intelligentsia, who constituted a cosmopolitan community indifferent to ethnic and religious origins and committed to the ideas of freedom and equality:

> Bolshevism attracted marginal Jews, poised between two worlds—the Jewish and the Gentile—who created a new homeland for themselves, a community of ideologists bent on remaking the world in their own image. These Jews quite deliberately and consciously broke with the restrictive social, religious, and cultural life of the Jews in the Pale of Settlement and attacked the secular culture of Jewish socialists and Zionists. Having abandoned their own origins and identity, yet not finding, or sharing, or being fully admitted to Russian life (except in the world of the party) the Jewish Bolsheviks found their ideological home in revolutionary universalism.[228]

Jews active in the ranks of Bolshevism and the other radical parties were for the major part semi-intellectuals who thanks to various "diplomas" won the right to live outside the Pale of Settlement: they broke with their own

*The myth was reinforced by some symbolic acts. For example, in the first years of the Communist regime public buildings were occasionally decorated with the six-pointed Magen David, the Star of David: see, e.g., *Krasnyi Petrograd: Vtoraia Godovshchina Velikoi Proletarskoi Revoliutsii* (Petrograd, 1920), 17. The five-pointed star or pentagram that the Red Army adopted in 1918 as its emblem was known to be a Masonic design, and for many Russians Freemasonry was synonymous with Jewry.

12. Anti-Trotsky White propaganda poster.

society without gaining acceptance to the Russian one,[229] except that segment of it made up of people like themselves.

Trotsky—the satanic "Bronstein" of Russian anti-Semites—was deeply offended whenever anyone presumed to call him a Jew. When a visiting Jewish delegation appealed to him to help fellow Jews, he flew into a rage: "I am not a Jew but an internationalist."[230] He reacted similarly when requested by Rabbi Eisenstadt of Petrograd to allow special flour for Passover matzos, adding on this occasion that "he wanted to know no Jews."[231] At another time he said that the Jews interested him no more than the Bulgarians.[232] According to one of his biographers, after 1917 Trotsky "shied away from Jewish matters" and "made light of the whole Jewish question."[233] Indeed, he made so light of it that when Jews were perishing by the thousands in pogroms, he seemed not to notice. He was in the Ukraine in August 1919, when it was the scene of some of the bloodiest massacres. A British scholar with access to the Soviet archives found that Trotsky had "received hundreds of reports about his own soldiers' violence and looting of Jewish-Ukrainian settlements."[234] And yet neither in his public pronouncements nor in his confidential dispatches to Moscow did he refer to these atrocities: in the collection of his speeches and directives for the year 1919, the word "pogrom" does not even figure in the index.[235] Indeed, at a meeting of the Politburo on April 18, 1919, he complained that there were too many Jews and Latvians in frontline Cheka units and in various office jobs, and recommended that they be more evenly distributed between the combat zone and the rear.[236] In sum, during that year of slaughters he never once intervened by either word or deed for the people on whose behalf he was said to have acted. Nor does one find greater concern among Lenin's other Jewish associates, or even among democratic socialists like Martov. In this respect the White generals, some of whom openly confessed to a dislike of Jews, have a better record than the Jewish Bolsheviks, in that, while they did next to nothing to prevent them, at least they condemned the pogroms and later expressed regrets over them.[237]

The desire of Jewish Bolsheviks to shed their Jewishness and disassociate themselves from their people sometimes attained grotesque dimensions, as in the case of Karl Radek, who, misquoting Heine to the effect that Jewishness was a "disease," told a German friend that he wanted to "exterminate" (ausrotten) the Jews.*

The White movement in the first year of its existence was free of anti-Semitism, at any rate, in its overt manifestations. Jews served in the Volunteer Army and took part in its Ice March.[238] In September 1918 Alekseev declared that anti-Semitism would not be tolerated in the Volunteer Army; the Jewish Kadet M. M. Vinaver affirmed in November 1918 that he had not encountered it in White ranks.[239]

All this changed in the winter of 1918–19. The hostility toward Jews that emerged in the Southern White Army at that time had three causes. One was the Red Terror, which it became customary to blame on Jews not only because of the conspicuous role they played in the Cheka, especially its provincial branches, but also because they were less victimized by it.† The

---

*Conversation of September 10, 1918, with Alfons Paquet: Winfried Baumgart, ed., *Von Brest-Litovsk zur deutschen Novemberrevolution* (Göttingen, 1971), 152. Heine actually said not that Judaism was a "disease," but that the Jewish religion was a "misfortune" *(ein Unglück):* ibid.

†On Dzerzhinskii's instructions, the Cheka took few Jewish hostages. This policy was not motivated by preference for Jews. Hostages were to serve as a guarantee against the Whites' executing captured Bolsheviks. Since it was felt that the Whites did not much care one way or the other what happened to Jews, taking them hostage would have served no purpose. See *RR*, 824n.

second had to do with the consequence of the evacuation by German forces of Russia, following the Armistice in the West. In 1917–18 Russian anti-Bolsheviks persuaded themselves that Lenin's regime was a German creation, without native roots, destined to fall the instant the Germans lost the war and withdrew from Russia. But the Germans withdrew and the Bolsheviks stayed on. This required a new scapegoat for the country's misfortunes, which role the Jews filled eminently well for the reasons stated above. Finally, there was the murder of the Imperial family, particulars of which emerged during the winter of 1918–19. The killing was immediately blamed on Jews, who in fact played a secondary role in it; the fate of the ex-tsar was identified with the martyrdom of Christ and interpreted in the light of the *Protocols* as yet another step in the Jewish march to world mastery.

According to Denikin, when the White army entered the Ukraine, the region was in the grip of rabid anti-Semitism that affected all groups of the population, the intelligentsia included. The Southern Army, he concedes, did not "escape the general disease" and "besmirched" itself with Jewish pogroms as it advanced westward.[240] Denikin now found himself under enormous pressure to purge the military and civil services of "traitorous" Jews. (This was not a problem for Kolchak, because few Jews lived in Siberia.) He tried but failed to stop the dismissals of Jewish officers demanded by Russians who refused to serve alongside them. His orders were ignored and he had to place Jews in reserve units. For the same reason Jews who either volunteered or were conscripted into the White Southern Army were formed into separate units.[241] In 1919 it became common practice in areas occupied by the White army to require the removal of "Jews and Communists" from all positions of authority. In August 1919 in occupied Kiev, the Whites installed a municipal government from which the single Jew was dismissed on orders of the White general Dragomirov.[242] Fearful of earning the reputation of a "Jew-lover," Denikin rejected every appeal (including one from Vassili Maklakov, the Russian ambassador in Paris) to appoint a token Jew to his civil administration.[243]

As it neared Moscow, Denikin's army became increasingly infected with hatred of Jews and lust for vengeance for the miseries they had allegedly inflicted on Russia. While it is absurd to depict the White movement as proto-Nazi, with anti-Semitism "a focal point of [its] world-view"[244]—that was provided by nationalism—it is indisputable that the White officer corps, not to speak of the Cossacks, was increasingly contaminated by it. Even so, it would be a mistake to draw any direct link between this emotional virulence and the anti-Jewish excesses during the Civil War. For one thing, as we shall note, most of the massacres were perpetrated not by Russian White troops but by Ukrainian irregulars and Cossacks. For another, the pogroms were inspired far less by religious and national passions than by ordinary greed: the worst atrocities on the White side were committed by the Terek Cossacks, who had never known Jews and regarded them merely as objects of extortion. Although the anti-Jewish pogroms had certain unique features, in a broader perspective they were part and parcel of the pogroms perpetrated at the time throughout Russia:

> Freedom was understood as liberation from restrictions imposed on people by the very fact of common existence and interdependence. For that reason the first to be destroyed were those who in every given locality embodied the idea of statehood, society, system, order. In the cities they were the policemen, administrators, judges; in the factories, the owner or manager, the very presence of whom served as a reminder that one must work to receive pay. . . . In the villages, it was the neighboring, nearest estate, the symbol of lordship, that is, simultaneously of authority and wealth.[245]

And in the small towns of the Pale, it was the Jews. Once pogroms and *razgromy* (destruction of property) became the order of the day, it was inevitable that Jews would be the principal victims: they were seen as aliens, they were defenseless, and were believed rich. The same instincts that led to the destruction of country estates and raids on kulaks led to violence against Jews and their properties. The Bolshevik slogan *"grab' nagra-blennoe"*—"loot the loot"—made Jews particularly vulnerable to violence because, having been compelled by tsarist legislation to engage in trade and artisanship, they handled money and thus automatically qualified as *burzhui.*

Anti-Jewish excesses began in 1918 under Hetman Skoropadski during the German occupation of the Ukraine.[246] They intensified after the German withdrawal in late 1918, when southern and southwestern Russia fell prey to anarchy. The worst year was 1919, with two peak periods of pogroms, the first in May and the second in August–October. The White Army was involved only in the last phase: until it made its appearance in the central Ukraine in August, the pogroms were perpetrated by the Cossack bands of Petlura, and by outlaws headed by various "fathers" or *bat'ko,* of whom Grigorev was the most notorious.

The pogroms followed a pattern.

As a rule, they were perpetrated not by the local population, which lived reasonably peacefully alongside the Jews, but by outsiders, either gangs of brigands and deserters formed to engage in plunder, or by Cossack units for whom looting was a diversion from fighting.* The local peasantry participated in the capacity of camp followers, scavengers of spoils that the robbers left behind because they were too bulky to carry.

The primary purpose of pogroms everywhere was plunder: physical violence against Jews was applied mainly to extort money, although mindless

---

*"The local non-Jewish population in the majority of cases took no part in the pogroms, treating them coldly and even with sharp hostility," writes a contemporary Jewish scholar. ". . . in the majority of cases the local Christian population took a lively part in the fate of Jews, hiding them in their homes, defending them, sending to this end delegations to the [military] command. . . . There can be no doubt that many Jews owed their survival to this circumstance, and without it the number of victims would have been immeasurably greater." N. I. Shtif, *Pogromy na Ukraine* (Berlin, 1922), 24.

sadism was not unknown: "In the overwhelming majority of cases, murder and torture took place only as instruments of plundering."[247] On breaking into a Jewish household, the bandits would demand money and valuables. If these were not forthcoming, they would resort to violence. Most killings were the result of the refusal or inability of the victims to pay up.[248] Furniture and other household goods were usually loaded onto military trains for shipment to the Don, Kuban, or Terek territories; sometimes they were smashed, or else distributed to the peasants who stood by with carts and bags. This process, carried out by armed men who moved back and forth with the fortunes of war across areas inhabited by Jews, entailed a methodical extraction from Jews of all their belongings: the first victims were the well-to-do; when they had nothing left, it was the turn of the poor.

Nearly everywhere, pogroms were accompanied by rape. The victims were often killed afterward.

Sometimes, the pogroms had a religious character, resulting in the desecration of Jewish houses of worship, the destruction of Torah scrolls and other religious articles; but on the whole religion played a much smaller role than economic and sexual motives.

The first major incident occurred in January 1919, in the Volhynian town of Ovruch, where an ataman by the name of Kozyr-Zyrka, affiliated with Petlura, flogged and killed Jews to extort money.[249] Next came pogroms at Proskurov (February 15) and Felshtin.[250] They were followed by massacres at Berdichev and Zhitomir.

Petlura, whose forces carried out most of these pogroms, did not himself encourage violence against Jews—indeed, in an order of July 1919 he prohibited anti-Semitic agitation.[251] But he had no control over his troops, which were loosely linked by an anti-Bolshevism that readily shaded into anti-Semitism. When the Red Army occupied the Ukraine following the German evacuation, its policies in no time turned the Ukrainian population against the Bolsheviks; and since among Bolsheviks active in the Ukraine were not a few Jews, the distinction between the two became blurred. Antonov-Ovseenko, who served as Lenin's proconsul in the Ukraine, in a confidential dispatch to Moscow identified among the various causes of Ukrainian hostility to the Soviet regime, "the complete disregard of the prejudices of the population in the matter of the attitude toward the Jews," by which he could only have meant the use of Jews as agents of the Soviet government.[252]

In early 1919 there appeared in the Ukraine gangs headed by Grigorev that laid waste the region of the lower Dnieper between Ekaterinoslav and the Black Sea. Grigorev, an army officer who had served in World War I, at first supported Petlura, but in February 1919 he switched to the Bolsheviks, who appointed him commander of a Red Army division. Heading a troop of up to 15,000 men, mostly peasants from the southern Ukraine, equipped with field guns and armored cars, he represented a considerable force: sufficiently strong, as we have seen, to defeat the French-led contingent in Kherson in March 1919. In early April, he captured Odessa.

Later that month, however, he began to turn against Communist commissars and Jews. He broke openly with the Communists on May 9, after refusing to obey an order to move into Bessarabia to reinforce the Communist government of Hungary: his rebellion frustrated Moscow's plans to link up with Communist Hungary and caused that government's fall.[253] After mutinying, Grigorev seized Elizavetgrad, where he issued a "Universal," appealing to peasants to march on Kiev and Kharkov to expel the Soviet government. It was in Elizavetgrad that his men carried out the worst Jewish pogrom up to that time, an orgy of looting, killing, and raping that went on for three days (May 15–17).[254] He denounced "hooknosed commissars" and encouraged his followers to rob Odessa, which had a sizable Jewish population, until it was "pulled to pieces."[255] Until their destruction later that month by the Red Army, Grigorev's bands carried out 148 pogroms. Grigorev lost his life in July at the hands of Makhno, who invited him for talks and then had him murdered.[256] Grigorev's followers, "impressed by this display of gangster technique, mostly joined Makhno."[257]

The wave of pogroms receded briefly after Grigorev's fall but rose again to attain unprecedented ferocity in August, when Denikin's Cossacks and Petlura's Ukrainians converged on Kiev, leaving behind a trail of devastation.[258]

In August and September, as the Volunteer Army was marching from victory to victory and the capture of Moscow seemed imminent, White troops threw caution to the winds: they no longer cared for the opinion of Europe. Moving into the western Ukraine and capturing Kiev, Poltava, and Chernigov, the Cossacks serving in White ranks carried out one vicious pogrom after another. The experience of these summer months, in the words of one historian, demonstrated that where Jews were concerned it was permissible to give free rein to bestial instincts with total impunity.[259] Little attempt was made to justify these atrocities: if justification was called for, Jews were accused of favoring Communists and treacherously sniping at White troops.

In Kiev a pogrom carried out by Terek Cossacks between October 17 and 20 claimed close to 300 lives. Night after night, gangs of armed men would break into Jewish apartments, stealing, beating, killing, and raping. V. V. Shulgin, the monarchist editor of the anti-Semitic daily *Kievlianin,* thus describes the scenes he had witnessed:

> At night, the streets of Kiev are in the grip of medieval terror. In the midst of deadly silence and deserted streets suddenly there begins a wail that breaks the heart. It is the "Yids" who cry. They cry from fear. In the darkness of the streets somewhere appear bands of "men with bayonets" who force their way, and, at their sight, huge multistoried houses begin to wail from top to bottom. Whole streets, seized with terrifying dread, howl

with an inhuman voice, trembling for their lives. It is terrible to hear these voices of the postrevolutionary night. . . . This is genuine fear, a true "torture by fear," to which the whole Jewish population is subjected.[260]

Shulgin felt that the Jews had brought these horrors upon themselves and worried lest the pogroms arouse sympathy for them.

The worst pogrom of all occurred in Fastov, a small and prosperous trading center southwest of Kiev, inhabited by 10,000 Jews, where on September 23–26 a Terek Cossack brigade commanded by a Colonel Belogortsev engaged in a Nazi-type *Aktion*: missing were only the vans with carbon monoxide outlets. An eyewitness described what happened:

> The Cossacks divided into numerous separate groups, each of three or four men, no more. They acted not casually . . . but according to a common plan. . . . A group of Cossacks would break into a Jewish home, and their first word would be "Money!" If it turned out that Cossacks had been there before and had taken all there was, they would immediately demand the head of the household. . . . They would place a rope around his neck. One Cossack took one end, another the other, and they would begin to choke him. If there was a beam on the ceiling, they might hang him. If one of those present burst into tears or begged for mercy, then—even if he were a child—they beat him to death. Of course, the family surrendered the last kopeck, wanting only to save their relative from torture and death. But if there was no money, the Cossacks choked their victim until he lost consciousness, whereupon they loosened the rope. The unfortunate would fall unconscious to the floor, after which, with blows of the rifle butt or even cold water, they brought him back to his senses. "Will you give money?" the tormentors demanded. The unfortunate swore that he had nothing left, that other visitors had taken everything away. "Never mind," the scoundrels told him, "you will give." Once again they would put the rope around his neck and again choke or hang him. This was repeated five or six times. . . .
>
> I know of many homeowners whom the Cossacks forced to set their houses on fire, and then compelled, with sabers or bayonets, along with those who ran out of the burning houses, to turn back into the fire, in this manner causing them to burn alive.[261]

In Fastov, the victims were mainly older people, women, and children, apparently because the able-bodied men had managed to flee. They were ordered stripped naked, sometimes tortured, required to shout, "Beat Yids, save Russia," and cut down with cavalry sabers; the corpses were left to be devoured by pigs and dogs. Sexual assaults were frequent, and second in frequency to looting: everywhere women were raped, sometimes in public. The Fastov massacre is said to have claimed 1,300–1,500 lives.*

While the Cossack detachments of the Southern Army committed numer-

---

*I. B. Shekhtman, *Pogromy Dobrovol'cheskoi Armii na Ukraine* (Berlin, 1932), 109–14; other eyewitness accounts, *ibid.*, 333–48. Following an inspection of Fastov, the White general Bredov, commander of the front southwest of Kiev, reported that nothing untoward had occurred there: *ibid.*, 347–48.

ous atrocities (none can be attributed to the Volunteer Army), a careful reckoning of the pogroms by Jewish organizations indicates that the worst crimes were the work of independent gangs of Ukrainians.* According to these analyses, during the Civil War there occurred 1,236 incidents of anti-Jewish violence, of which 887 are classified as pogroms and the rest as "excesses," that is, violence that did not assume mass proportions.²⁶² Of this total number, 493, or 40 percent, were committed by the Ukrainians of Petlura, 307 (25 percent) by independent warlords or atamans, notably Grigorev, Zelenyi, and Makhno, 213 (17 percent) by the troops of Denikin, and 106 (8½ percent) by Red Army units (on the last, historical studies are strangely silent).† The main element responsible for the atrocities committed by the Whites, the Cossacks, had been lured away from their settlements not by the vision of a restored and unified Russia but by the prospect of loot and rape: one Cossack commander said that after hard fighting his boys deserved four or five days of "rest" to inspire them for the next battle.²⁶³

While it is, therefore, incorrect to lay wholesale blame for the massacres of the Jews on the White Army, it is true that Denikin remained passive in the face of these atrocities, which not only stained the reputation of his army but also demoralized it. Denikin's propaganda bureau, Osvag, bore much responsibility for spreading anti-Semitic propaganda, and the harm was compounded by the tolerance shown to the anti-Semitic publications of Shulgin and others.

Personally, Denikin was not a typical anti-Semite of the time: at any rate, in his five-volume chronicle of the Civil War he does not blame Jews either for Communism or for his defeat. On the contrary: he expresses shame at their treatment in his army as well as the pogroms and shows awareness of the debilitating effect these had on the army's morale. But he was a weak, politically inexperienced man who had little control over the behavior of his troops. He yielded to the pressures of anti-Semites in his officer corps from fear of appearing pro-Jewish and from a sense of the futility of fighting against prevailing passions. In June 1919 he told a Jewish delegation that urged him to issue a declaration condemning the pogroms, that "words here were powerless, that any unnecessary clamor in regard to this question will only make the situation of Jews harder, irritating the masses and bringing out the customary accusations of 'selling out to the Yids.' "‡ Whatever the

---

*In the fall of 1919, when the pogroms often attributed to the Volunteer Army took place, the three Volunteer divisions operated in the regions of Briansk, Orel, and Elets—Great Russian areas with hardly any Jewish population. The largest number of pogroms occurred in Kiev province, followed by Podole and Ekaterinoslav. These provinces were the area of operations of the Terek and Kuban Cossacks. For this reason it is inappropriate to speak of pogroms by the "Volunteer Army."

†Gergel in *YIVO Annual of Jewish Social Science,* VI (1951), 244. An exception are the accounts of Red Army pogroms in Mogilev and other towns of southwestern Soviet Russia by the Menshevik David Dalin: *SV,* No. 11 (July 8, 1921), 11–12, and No. 13 (August 5, 1921), 13–15. See also the description of a Red Army pogrom in Odessa on May 2, 1919, in Ivan Bunin, *Okaiannye dni* (Moscow, 1990), 128.

‡Denikin, *Ocherki,* V, 150. This was a problem common to all parties involved in the Civil

justice of such excuses for passivity in the face of civilian massacres, they must have impressed the army as well as the population at large that the White Army command viewed Jews with suspicion and if it did not actively encourage pogroms, neither was it exercised about them.

The claim has been made that among "the thousands of documents in the White Army archives there is not one denunciation of pogroms."[264] The claim is demonstrably wrong. Denikin says, and the evidence supports him, that he and his generals issued orders condemning the pogroms and calling for the perpetrators to be severely punished.[265] On July 31, 1919, General Mai-Maevskii demanded that equal treatment be accorded all citizens: persons violating this principle were to be punished. He dismissed a Terek general implicated in pogroms.[266] On September 25, when the pogroms were at their height, Denikin instructed General Dragomirov to discipline severely military personnel guilty of them.[267] But anti-Jewish hysteria made it impossible to enforce such orders.* For instance, in obedience to Denikin's instructions, Dragomirov ordered court-martials for officers involved in the Kiev pogrom and had three of them sentenced to death, but he was forced to rescind the sentence after fellow officers threatened to avenge their execution by a pogrom against Kievan Jews in which hundreds would perish.[268]

The anti-Semitism of the Southern Army has been well documented and publicized. Little attention has been paid to Soviet reactions. The Sovnarkom is said on July 27, 1918, to have issued an appeal against anti-Semitism, threatening penalties for pogroms.[269] But the following year, when the wave of pogroms was rising, Moscow was conspicuously silent. Lenin issued on April 2, 1919, a condemnation of anti-Semitism in which he argued that not every Jew was a class enemy—the implication being that some were, but just how to distinguish between those who were and those who were not, he did not say.[270] In June, the Soviet government assigned funds to help certain victims of pogroms.[271] But Lenin no more condemned the Ukrainian pogroms than did Denikin, and probably for the same reasons. The Soviet press ignored the subject.[272] "Playing up" these atrocities, it turns out, was for the Communists "not good propaganda."[273] By the same token, neither was it good propaganda for the Whites.

The only prominent public figure to condemn the pogroms openly and unequivocally was the head of the Orthodox Church, Patriarch Tikhon. In an Epistle issued on July 21, 1919, he called violence against Jews "dishonor for the perpetrators, dishonor for the Holy Church."[274]

The number of fatalities suffered in the pogroms of 1918–21 cannot be ascertained with any precision, but it was high. Evidence exists that 31,071

War. Vinnichenko, a radical socialist in the Ukrainian Directory, whom no one has accused of anti-Semitism, told Jews who asked him to denounce the pogroms: "Don't make me fall out with the army." Arnold Margolin, *Ukraina i politika Antanty* (Berlin, n.d.), 325.

*Denikin, *Ocherki*, V, 149. Shekhtman confirms that in the prevailing atmosphere these orders and warnings produced no effect whatever: *Pogromy*, 188.

victims were given a burial.[275] This figure does not include those whose remains were burned or left unburied. Hence, it is commonly doubled and even tripled, to anywhere between 50,000 and 200,000.* Accompanying these massacres were immense losses of property: Ukrainian Jews were left impoverished, many of them destitute and homeless.

In every respect except for the absence of a central organization to direct the slaughter, the pogroms of 1919 were a prelude to and rehearsal for the Holocaust. The spontaneous lootings and killings left a legacy that two decades later was to lead to the systematic mass murder of Jews at the hands of the Nazis: the deadly identification of Communism with Jewry.

In view of the role this accusation had in paving the way for the mass destruction of European Jewry, the question of Jewish involvement in Bolshevism is of more than academic interest. For it was the allegation that "international Jewry" invented Communism as an instrument to destroy Christian (or "Aryan") civilization that provided the ideological and psychological foundation of the Nazi "final solution." In the 1920s the notion came to be widely accepted in the West and the *Protocols* became an international best-seller. Fantastic disinformation spread by Russian extremists alleged that all the leaders of the Soviet state were Jews.[276] Many foreigners involved in Russian affairs came to share this belief. Thus, Major General H. C. Holman, head of the British military mission to Denikin, told a Jewish delegation that of 36 Moscow "commissars" only Lenin was a Russian, the rest being Jews. An American general serving in Russia was convinced that the notorious Chekists M. I. Latsis and Ia. Kh. Peters, who happened to be Latvians, were Jewish as well.[277] Sir Eyre Crowe, a senior official in the British Foreign Office, responding to Chaim Weizmann's memorandum protesting the pogroms, observed "that what may appear to Mr. Weizmann to be outrages against Jews, may in the eyes of the Ukrainians be retaliation against the horrors committed by the Bolsheviks who are all organized and directed by the Jews."† For some Russian Whites, anyone who did not wholeheartedly support their cause, whether Russian or Western, including President Wilson and Lloyd George, was automatically presumed to be a Jew.

What are the facts? Jews undeniably played in the Bolshevik Party and the early Soviet apparatus a role disproportionate to their share of the population. The number of Jews active in Communism in Russia and abroad was striking: in Hungary, for example, they furnished 95 percent of

---

*Nora Levin, *Jews in the Soviet Union*, I, 43, speaks of 50,000–60,000 victims. S. Ettinger in H. H. Ben-Sasson, ed., *A History of the Jewish People* (Cambridge, Mass., 1976), 954, speaks of 75,000 fatalities. Gergel puts the casualties at 100,000 (*YIVO Annual*, VI, 1951, 251). S. Gusev-Orenburgskii, *Kniga o evreiskikh pogromakh na Ukraine v 1919g* (Petrograd, n.d.), 14, agrees, estimating the number as no less than 100,000. The 200,000 figure is given in Iu. Larin, *Evrei i antisemitizm v SSSR* (Moscow/Leningrad, 1929), 55.

†Ullman, *Britain*, 219n. This view was prevalent in British governmental circles, especially the Foreign Office: Among British statesmen, Winston Churchill alone seems to have understood the monstrous nature of the pogroms and to have urged Denikin to put a stop to them: Winston Churchill, *The Aftermath*, 255; Ullman, *Britain*, 218–19.

the leading figures in Bela Kun's dictatorship.[278] They also were disproportionately represented among Communists in Germany and Austria during
the revolutionary upheavals there in 1918–23, and in the apparatus of the
Communist International. But then Jews are a very active people, prominent in many fields of endeavor. If they were conspicuous in Communist
circles, they were no less so in capitalist ones (according to Werner Som-
bart, they invented capitalism), not to speak of the performing arts, literature, and science. Although they constitute less than 0.3 percent of the
world's population, in the first seventy years of the Nobel Prizes (1901–
70), Jews won 24 percent of the awards in physiology and medicine,
and 20 percent of those in physics. According to Mussolini, four of the
seven founders of the Fascist Party were Jews; Hitler said that they were
among the early financial supporters of the Nazi movement.[279]

Nor must it be deduced from the prominence of Jews in the Communist
government that Russian Jewry was pro-Communist. The Jews in Communist ranks—the Trotskys, Zinovievs, Kamenevs, Sverdlovs, Radeks—did
not speak for the Jews, because they had broken with them long before the
Revolution. They represented no one but themselves. It must never be
forgotten that during the Revolution and Civil War, the Bolshevik Party
was very much a minority party, a self-selected body whose membership did
not reflect the politics of the population: Lenin admitted that the Communists were a drop of water in the nation's sea.[280] In other words, while not
a few Communists were Jews, few Jews were Communists. When Russian
Jewry had the opportunity to express its political preferences, as it did in
1917, it voted not for the Bolsheviks, but either for the Zionists or for
parties of democratic socialism.* The results of the elections to the Constituent Assembly indicate that Bolshevik support came not from the region
of Jewish concentration, the old Pale of Settlement, but from the armed
forces and the cities of Great Russia, which had hardly any Jews.† The
census of the Communist Party conducted in 1922 showed that only 959
Jewish members had joined before 1917.‡ It was only half in jest that the
Chief Rabbi of Moscow, Jacob Mazeh, on hearing Trotsky deny he was a
Jew and refuse to help his people, commented that it was the Trotskys who
made the revolutions and the Bronsteins who paid the bills.[281]

In the course of the Civil War, the Jewish community, caught in the

---

*"When the Bolsheviks took power, Zionism was unquestionably the dominant movement
in Russian Jewish life," Levin, *Jews in the Soviet Union*, I, 87. At the All-Russian Jewish
Congress in 1917, Zionist candidates won 60 percent of the vote: Zvi Gitelman, *Jewish Nationality and Soviet Politics* (Princeton, 1972), 79.

†In the provinces in which the worst pogroms occurred, the pro-Bolshevik vote was minuscule: in Volhynia, 4.4 percent; in Kiev, 4.0 percent; in Poltava, 5.6 percent. Only in Ekaterinoslav
did the Bolsheviks gain 17.9 percent, but even this was quite below their national average of 24.0
percent, obtained mainly in the northern, Great Russian, areas. A. M. Spirin, *Klassy i partii v
grazhdanskoi voine v Rossii* (Moscow, 1968), 416–19.

‡I. P. Trainin, *SSSR i natsional'naia problema* (Moscow, 1924), 26–27. It may further be
noted that Jews were disproportionately represented among tsarist police spies: Jonathan Daly,
"The Watchful State," Ph.D. dissertation, Harvard University, 1992, 144.

Red-White conflict, increasingly sided with the Communist regime: this, however, it did not from preference but from the instinct of self-preservation. When the White armies entered the Ukraine in the summer of 1919, Jews welcomed them, for they had suffered grievously under the Bolshevik rule—if not as Jews then as "bourgeois."[282] They quickly became disenchanted with White policies that tolerated pogroms and excluded Jews from the administration. After experiencing White rule, Ukrainian Jewry turned anti-White and looked to the Red Army for protection. Thus a vicious circle was set in motion: Jews were accused of being pro-Bolshevik and persecuted, which had the effect of turning them pro-Bolshevik for the sake of survival; this shift of allegiance served to justify further persecutions.

For all practical purposes, Admiral Kolchak's army ceased to exist in November 1919, when it turned into a rabble guided by the principle *sauve qui peut*. Thousands of officers with their families and mistresses, as well as hordes of soldiers and civilians, rushed headlong eastward: those who could afford it, by train, the rest by horse and cart or on foot. The wounded and the ill were abandoned. In the no-man's-land between the advancing and retreating armies, marauders, mostly Cossacks, robbed, killed, and raped. All semblance of authority disappeared. Russians were accustomed to being told what to do: traditionally, political initiative took for them the form of defiance. But now when there was no one to give orders and therefore no one to defy, they foundered. Foreign observers were struck by the fatalism of Russians in face of disaster: one of them remarked that when in distress, the women would cry and the men take to drink.

All streamed to Omsk in the hope that it would be defended: the influx of refugees swelled the city from a population of 120,000 to over 500,000:

> When the main body of [Kolchak's] troops arrived at Omsk they found unspeakable conditions. Refugees overflowed the streets, the railroad station, the public buildings. The roads were hub-deep in mud. Soldiers and their families begged from house to house for bread. Officers' wives turned into prostitutes to stave off hunger. Thousands who had money spent it in drunken debauches in the cafés. Mothers and their babies froze to death upon the sidewalks. Children were separated from their parents and orphans died by the score in the vain search for food and warmth. Many of the stores were robbed and others closed through fear. Military bands attempted a sorry semblance of gaiety in the public houses but to no avail. Omsk was inundated in a sea of misery. . . . The condition of the wounded was beyond description. Suffering men often lay two in a bed and in some hospitals and public buildings they were placed on the floor. Bandages were improvised out of sheeting, tablecloths, and women's underclothing. Antiseptics and opiates were almost nonexistent.[283]

Kolchak wanted to defend Omsk, but he was dissuaded by General M. K. Diterikhs, whom he had appointed in place of Lebedev as Chief of Staff. Omsk was evacuated on November 14. The Reds took the city without a fight: by this time they enjoyed a twofold numerical preponderance, fielding 100,000 men against Kolchak's 55,000.[284] They captured a great deal of booty that was supposed to have been blown up but was not because they had arrived sooner than expected: three million rounds of ammunition and 4,000 railway cars; 45,000 recruits about to be inducted were taken prisoner, along with 10 generals.[285]

After the fall of Omsk, the flow of refugees streaming eastward turned into a flood. An English officer who had witnessed the rout recalled it as a nightmare:

> Tens of thousands of peaceful people had fled into Siberia during that space of time, rushing away from that Red Terror with nothing but the clothes they stood in, as people rush in their nightdresses out of a house on fire, as the farmer on the slopes of Vesuvius rushes away from the flaming river of lava. Peasants had deserted their fields, students their books, doctors their hospitals, scientists their laboratories, workmen their workshops, authors their completed manuscripts. . . . We were being swept along in the wreckage of a demoralized army.[286]

The misery was compounded by typhus, a disease communicated by body lice, which thrive in unsanitary conditions, especially in the winter. Infected Russians showed no concern for others, with the result that typhus spread unchecked among the troops and civilian refugees, claiming countless victims: "When I passed Novonikolaevsk on February 3, [1920]," writes the same eyewitness,

> there were 37,000 typhus cases in that town, and the rate of mortality, which had never been more than 8 percent, had risen to 25 percent. Fifty doctors had died in that town alone during the space of one month and a half and more than 20,000 corpses lay unburied outside the town. . . . Conditions in the hospitals were indescribable. In one . . . the head doctor had been fined for drunkenness, the other doctor only paid the place a short visit once a day, and the nurses only put in an appearance while the doctor was there. The linen and the clothes of the patients were never changed, and most of them lay in a most filthy condition in their everyday clothes on the floor. They were never washed, and the male attendants waited for the periodical attacks of unconsciousness which are characteristic of typhus in order to steal from the patients their rings, jewelry, watches and even their food.[287]

Entire trains, filled with the sick, dying, and dead, littered the Transsiberian Railroad. These ravages could have been avoided or at least contained by the observance of minimal sanitary precautions. Czechoslovak troops living in the midst of the epidemic managed to escape it, and so did U.S. soldiers in Siberia.

Kolchak left Omsk for Irkutsk, his new capital, on November 13, just ahead of the Red Army. He traveled in six trains, one of which, made up of 29 cars, carried the gold and other valuables which the Czechs had captured in Kazan and turned over to him. Accompanying him were 60 officers and 500 men. The Transsiberian between Omsk and Irkutsk was guarded by the Czechoslovak Legion. Billeted in tidy trains, the Czechs lived in relative luxury: exchanging the French francs they received in pay from Paris by way of Tokyo into rapidly depreciating rubles, they bought up (when they did not steal) everything of value.[288] On orders of their general, Jan Syrový, who worked closely with General Janin, they delayed Russian trains moving east, sidetracking Kolchak for over a month between Omsk and Irkutsk, to let through their own.[289] At the end of December, seven weeks after he had left Omsk, Kolchak was stranded at Nizhne-udinsk, 500 kilometers west of Irkutsk, forsaken by virtually everyone and kept incommunicado by his Czech guards.

On Christmas Eve 1919, a coalition of left-wing groups, dominated by Socialists-Revolutionaries but including Mensheviks, leaders of local self-government boards, and trade unionists, formed in Irkutsk a "Political Center." After two weeks of alternate fighting and negotiating with the pro-Kolchak elements, the Center took over the city. Declaring Kolchak deposed, it proclaimed itself the government of Siberia. Kolchak, "an enemy of the people," and other participants in his "reactionary policies" were to be brought to trial. Some of Kolchak's ministers took refuge in the trains of the Allied missions: most fled, disguised, in the direction of Vladivostok. On learning of these events on January 4, 1920, Kolchak announced his resignation in favor of Denikin and the appointment of Ataman Semenov as Commander in Chief of all the military forces and civilians in Irkutsk province and areas to the east of Lake Baikal. He then placed himself and the gold hoard under the protection of the Czechs and, at their request, dismissed his retinue. Having decked Kolchak's trains with the flags of England, the United States, France, Japan, and Czechoslovakia, the Czechs undertook to escort him to Irkutsk and there to turn him over to the Allied missions.[290] While this was happening, Semenov proceeded to massacre socialists and liberals in eastern Siberia, including the hostages whom pro-Kolchak elements had imprisoned following the Irkutsk coup.*

What happened subsequently has never been satisfactorily explained. As best as can be determined, Kolchak was betrayed by Generals Janin and Syrový, with the result that instead of receiving Allied protection he was handed over to the Bolsheviks.† Janin, who from the moment of his arrival

---

*Semenov later escaped to Japan. During World War II he seems to have collaborated with the Nazis. Captured at the war's end by the Soviet army, he was executed: Peter Fleming, *The Fate of Admiral Kolchak* (London, 1963), 234.

†Syrový's version of what occurred is reproduced in J. Rouquerol, *L'Aventure de l'Amiral Koltchak* (Paris, 1929), 184–86. He claims that he abandoned Kolchak to his fate after delivering him to Irkutsk because Kolchak had ordered Semenov to blast the tunnels and bridges leading

in Siberia had treated Kolchak as a British stooge whom he wished to be rid of, now had his chance. The Czechs wanted home. The French general, formally their commander, struck a deal with the Political Center on their behalf, arranging safe passage to Vladivostok for them and their loot in exchange for Kolchak and his gold. Having made these arrangements, he left Irkutsk.

On reaching Irkutsk in the evening of January 14, the Czechs informed Kolchak that on orders of General Janin he was to be turned over to the local authorities. The next morning, Kolchak, along with his mistress, the 26-year-old A. V. Kniper, and his Prime Minister, V. Pepelaev, were taken off the train and put in prison.

On January 20, Irkutsk learned that General Kappel, one of Kolchak's bravest and most loyal officers, was approaching at the head of an armed force to free Kolchak. On hearing this news, the Political Center, which had never exercised effective power anyway, dissolved and transferred authority to the Bolshevik Military-Revolutionary Committee. The Milrevkom agreed to allow the Czechs to proceed east, whereupon the Czechs turned over to it Kolchak's treasure.*

The new authority in Irkutsk formed a commission chaired by a Bolshevik and composed of another Bolshevik, two SRs, and a single Menshevik to "investigate" Kolchak and his rule. The commission sat from January 21 to February 6, 1920, interrogating Kolchak about his past and his activities as Supreme Ruler. Kolchak behaved with great dignity: the minutes of the testimony reveal a man in complete command of himself, aware that he was doomed but confident that he had nothing to hide and that history would vindicate him.[291]

The investigation, a cross between an inquest and a trial, was abruptly terminated on February 6, when the Irkutsk Revkom sentenced Kolchak to death. The official explanation given for the execution, when the news was made public several weeks later, was that Irkutsk had learned that General Voitsekhovskii, who had succeeded Kappel after the latter's death on January 20, was drawing near and there was danger of Kolchak being abducted.[292] But a document found in the Trotsky Archive at Harvard University raises serious doubts about this explanation and suggests that, as in the case of the murder of the Imperial family, it was an excuse to conceal that the execution had been ordered by Lenin. The order—scribbled by Lenin on the back of an envelope and addressed to I. N. Smirnov, Chairman of the Siberian Military-Revolutionary Council—reads as follows:

---

to Vladivostok, which would have prevented the Czechoslovak Legion from evacuating Russia. General Janin's memoirs are quite uninformative on this subject: *Ma Mission en Sibérie, 1918-1920* (Paris, 1933).
   *In April 1920, the gold was shipped to Moscow: *TP*, II, 144-47. Cf. A. Kladt and V. Kondratev, *Byl' o "zolotom eshelone"* (Moscow, 1962).

Cypher. Sklianskii: send to Smirnov
(Military-Revolutionary Council of the Fifth Army) the cypher text:
   Do not put out any information about Kolchak; print absolutely nothing but, after our occupation of Irkutsk, send a strictly official telegram
explaining that the local authorities, before our arrival, acted in such and
such a way under the influence of the threat from Kappel and the danger
of White Guard plots in Irkutsk.   Lenin
                                  [Signature also in cypher.]
   1. Do you undertake to do this with utmost reliability? . . . January
1920[293]

The editors of the *Trotsky Papers,* normally very cautious, who had first
made this document public, assumed that the date "January 1920" was in
error and that the document was actually written after February 7, the day
of Kolchak's execution.[294] There are no grounds for such an assumption.
The whole procedure ordered by Lenin closely recalls that employed to
camouflage the murder of the Imperial family—the killing allegedly done
on the initiative of local authorities from fear that the prisoner would be
abducted and the Center learning of it only after the fact. The explanations
offered were meant to remove from Lenin the onus for executing a defeated
military commander, and one, moreover, who was highly regarded in England, with which Soviet Russia was then initiating trade talks. Lenin's
instructions were almost certainly sent before Kolchak's execution, and
probably before Kappel's death on January 20.* The message must have
been received in Irkutsk on February 6, when the interrogation of Kolchak
was abruptly terminated.
   The incoherent verdict of the Irkutsk Revolutionary Committee read:

> The ex-Supreme Ruler, Admiral Kolchak, and the ex-Chairman of the
> Council of Ministers, Pepelaev, are to be shot. It is better to execute
> two criminals, who have long deserved death, than hundreds of innocent
> victims.[295]

When informed in the middle of the night, Kolchak asked: "This means
that there will be no trial?" For he had not been charged. A poison pill
concealed in a handkerchief was taken from him. He was denied a farewell
meeting with Kniper. As he was being led to his execution in the early hours
of the morning, Kolchak requested the Chekist commander to convey to his
wife in Paris a blessing for their son. "I will if I don't forget," the executioner replied.[296] Kolchak was shot at four a.m. on February 7, along with
Pepelaev and a Chinese criminal. He refused to have his eyes bound. The
bodies were pushed under the ice in the Ushakovka River, a branch of the
Angara.
   One month later (March 7), the Red Army took Irkutsk. Although the

*RTsKhIDNI, which has the original, dates it as sent "before January 9": F. 2, op. 1, ed. khr.
24362.

foreign press had already carried reports to this effect, it was only now that Smirnov, following Lenin's orders, informed Moscow of Kolchak's execution the previous month, allegedly on orders of the local authorities to prevent his capture by the Whites or Czechs(!).[297]

At Irkutsk the Red Army halted its advance, because it could not afford to become involved in hostilities with Japan and the Russian warlords under her protection.[298] For the time being, Siberia east of Lake Baikal was left to the Japanese. On April 6, 1920, the Soviet government created in eastern Siberia a fictitious "Far Eastern Republic" with a capital in Chita. When the Japanese withdrew from eastern Siberia two and a half years later (October 1922), Moscow incorporated this territory into Soviet Russia.

Astonishing as it seems, the Cheka was entirely oblivious of the pro-White underground organization the National Center and its intelligence activities until the summer of 1919, when a series of fortuitous accidents put it on the Center's trail.

The Cheka's suspicions were first aroused by the betrayal of Krasnaia Gorka, a strategic fortress protecting access to Petrograd, during Iudenich's May 1919 offensive.[299] At that time, documents were found on a man who was attempting to cross into Finland, containing passwords and codes by means of which Iudenich was to communicate with supporters in Petrograd.[300] Investigation revealed the existence of a National Center engaged in espionage and other intelligence activities.

In the third week of July a Soviet border patrol arrested two other men attempting to cross into Finland. During the interrogation, one of them tried to dispose of a packet that turned out to contain coded documents with information on deployments of the Red Army in the Petrograd region provided by a clandestine organization in that city.[301] Apparently the two prisoners cooperated, because a few days later the Cheka raided the apartment of the engineer Vilgelm Shteininger. The papers found in his possession indicated that he was the central figure of the Petrograd National Center.[302] On the Cheka's orders, Shteininger prepared memoranda on the National Center, the Union for the Regeneration of Russia, and other underground organizations. Although he was careful not to betray names, the Cheka succeeded in identifying and arresting several of his accomplices. They were brought to Moscow for interrogation by the "Special Department" of the Cheka, which revealed a clandestine organization far more extensive than the Soviet authorities had suspected. In view of Denikin's advance on Moscow, it was essential to uncover it fully: another Krasnaia Gorka could have fatal consequences. But the interrogations provided few specific clues.

Another stroke of good luck helped the Cheka solve the riddle. On July 27, a Soviet patrol in Viatka province in northern Russia detained a man who could not produce proper identity papers: on his person were found nearly one million rubles and two revolvers. He identified himself as Nikolai Pavlovich Krashennininkov; the money which he carried he said was given him by Kolchak's government and was to be turned over to a man, unknown to him, who would meet him at the Nikolaevskii railroad station in Moscow. Krashennininkov was sent to the Lubianka, but divulged nothing more. The Cheka then placed in his prison cell an agent provocateur, an officer who pretended to belong to the National Center. The latter offered, with the help of his wife, to convey messages to Krashennininkov's friends. Krashennininkov fell for the ruse. On August 20 and 28 he sent two messages, in the second of which, addressed to N. N. Shchepkin, he requested poison.[303]

The 65-year-old Shchepkin was the son of an emancipated serf who had acquired fame as a Gogolian actor. A Kadet and an attorney, he had served in the Third Duma. In 1918 he had joined both the Right Center and the Union for Regeneration, which made him one of the few persons to belong to both organizations. After most of his associates had fled Soviet Russia to escape the terror, he remained at his post, maintaining communications with Kolchak, Denikin, and Iudenich. A typical message from him sent to Omsk in May or June 1919 and signed "Diadia Koka" (Uncle Coca) described the mood of the population under Communist rule, criticized the socialist intelligentsia as well as Denikin, and urged Kolchak to release an unambiguous programmatic statement.[304] Shchepkin knew of the arrests in Petrograd and the danger he faced. At the end of August he told a friend: "I feel that the circle is progressively tightening. I feel we shall all die, but this is not important: I have long been prepared for death. Life holds no value for me: all that matters is that our cause not fail."[305]

At ten p.m. on August 28, following the lead provided by Krashennininkov's second letter, the Cheka arrested Shchepkin in his wooden lodge on the corner of Neopalimovskii and Trubnyi lanes, and took him to the Lubianka, leaving behind agents. Shchepkin and his fellow conspirators had foreseen such a contingency and taken precautions to limit the damage: if the house was safe, a pot with white flowers would stand in the window; if it was not there, the house was to be avoided. After Shchepkin's arrest, with Cheka agents inside, the pot could not be removed, and as a result many of the conspirators walked into a trap.[306] During his interrogation, Shchepkin, resisting threats, withheld information that could incriminate others.[307] But in a box found in his garden were secret messages with military and political intelligence, among them suggested texts of slogans for Denikin's use on approaching Moscow ("Down with the Civil War, Down with the Communists, Free trade and private property. On the soviets, maintain silence").[308]

On September 23, the Communist press published the names of 67 members of a "counterrevolutionary and espionage" organization who had

13. Shchepkin.

been executed. The list was headed by Shchepkin and included Shteininger and Krashennininkov: the majority were officers, members of the military branch of the Center. An editorial in *Izvestiia* labeled the victims "bloodthirsty leeches" responsible for the death of countless workers.* They had been interrogated around the clock. The executions were carried out to the sound of running truck engines in the Lubianka courtyard to muffle the shots. The corpses were driven to the Kalitnikov Cemetery and dumped into a common grave.

On September 12, 1919, Denikin ordered his troops "from the Volga to the Romanian border" to advance on Moscow.[309] On September 20 the Volunteer Army seized Kursk.

Alarmed by his progress, the Soviet leaders on September 24 designated a "final defense line" running from Moscow to Vitebsk, the Dnieper River, Chernigov, Voronezh, Tambov, Shatsk, and back to Moscow. This entire area, the capital city included, came under martial law.[310] In greatest secrecy, plans were laid for the evacuation of the Soviet government to Perm: lists of personnel and offices to be moved were drawn up; Dzerzhinskii instructed the Cheka to divide its 12,000 hostages into categories

---

*Izvestiia, No. 211/763 (September 23, 1919), 1. According to P. E. Melgunova-Stepanova (*Pamiati pogibshikh*, Paris, 1929, 74) the number of those executed in September 1919 in connection with the National Center exceeded the 67 names publicly announced.

in order to determine which to execute first to prevent their falling into White hands.[311]

The Whites soon pierced this defensive perimeter, capturing Voronezh on October 6 and Chernigov on October 12. On October 13–14, just as Iudenich's troops were fighting in Gatchina, not far from Petrograd, the Volunteer Army took Orel. It was the high-water mark of the Whites' advance: at this point, their forces stood 300 kilometers from Moscow and within sight of Petrograd. Their advance seemed unstoppable, the more so as masses of Red troops were deserting to them. The next objective of the Volunteers was Tula, the last major city on the road to the capital, and for the Reds a critical asset because it housed its most important defense industries.[312] The Red command was determined to prevent its fall at any price.

The Red Army kept on transferring to the south troops from the Eastern front, where the fighting was, for all practical purposes, over. But it also stripped the Western front: it was now that Pilsudski's pledge not to threaten the Red Army proved so valuable. In all, between September and November, the Southern front received an additional 270,000 men, which gave it an insuperable numerical advantage in the impending battles.[313]

On October 11, while the fighting in the south was reaching a climax, Iudenich launched his second offensive against Petrograd. The old capital had little strategic value, although it was a major center of war industry: but its capture was expected to have an incalculable effect on Communist morale. At the start of the campaign, Iudenich's force consisted of 17,800 infantry, 700 cavalry, 57 guns, 4 armored trains, 2 armored cars, and 6 tanks manned by Englishmen. Opposing it stood the Red Seventh Army with 22,500 infantry, 1,100 cavalry, 60 guns, 3 armored trains, and 4 armored cars. By the time the Whites drew near to Petrograd, however, the Red force had tripled in size.[314] The British military mission promised Iudenich to blockade Petrograd and to give naval support against Kronshtadt, the naval base located on an island in the Gulf of Finland, and against the batteries defending Petrograd.

On the eve of his offensive, Iudenich released a declaration stating that his government represented all the strata and classes of the population, that it rejected tsarism and would guarantee the rights of peasants to the land and workers to an eight-hour day.[315]

Iudenich's force made rapid progress against a demoralized Seventh Red Army. On October 16 it stood at Tsarskoe Selo, the old Imperial residence, a mere 25 kilometers from Petrograd. The Whites, among whom were many officers serving as ordinary soldiers, fought brilliantly, using night as a cover to disorient and frighten the enemy, creating the impression that he was greatly outnumbered. The appearance of tanks invariably threw the

Critical Battles

OCTOBER–NOVEMBER 1919

Moscow

Podolsk

Egorevsk

Vyazma

R　U　S　S　I　A

Serpukhov　*Oka*

Ryazan

Kaluga

Oka

Tula

RED ARMY'S
"STRIKING GROUP"

Briansk

Dankov

Efremov

Orel

Michurinsk

Elets

VOLUNTEER
ARMY

Lipetsk

Tambov

Kastornoe

"BUDENNYI'S
CAVALRY"

Kursk

Voronezh

Rylsk

Sudzha

Staryi Oskol

Sumy

Korocha

U　k　r　a　i　n　e

Belgorod

Lebedin

Kharkov

Poltava

Kupyansk

	Line of front beginning of October 1919
	Red Cavalry attack
	Volunteer Army's retreat

0   100   200

Kilometers

Reds into headlong flight. Iudenich was aided by Colonel V. A. Liunde-kvist, Chief of Staff of the Seventh Red Army, who conveyed to the Whites his army's dispositions and operational plans.[316] Participating were units of the RAF and the British navy, which provided artillery cover and bombed Kronshtadt, sinking, capturing, or severely damaging eleven Soviet ships, including two battleships.*

To Lenin, the situation in Petrograd seemed hopeless and he was prepared to sacrifice the former capital to hold the line against Denikin. But Trotsky thought otherwise; he managed to change Lenin's mind and persuaded him to issue orders to defend Petrograd "to the last drop of blood." At the same time, secret preparations were set in motion to evacuate the city.[317] Because Zinoviev had suffered something close to a nervous collapse, Trotsky was dispatched to Petrograd to take charge of the defense. Arriving on October 17, he found the army demoralized, retreating without giving battle in "shameful panic" followed by "senseless flight."[318] His first task was to boost morale and this he accomplished brilliantly. He replaced the com-mander of the Seventh Army with a general enjoying greater confidence among the troops. In addresses to the soldiers, he made light of their fears, assuring them that the enemy was outnumbered and attacked at night to conceal his weakness. He mocked the tank as "nothing but a metal wagon of special construction."[319] On his orders, the Putilov plant hastily modified a few vehicles to resemble tanks. It was the only engagement in the Civil War in which Trotsky's presence decisively affected the outcome. He did this largely on his own. Lenin's advice was useless: on October 22 he urged Trotsky to mobilize "10 thousand or so of the bourgeoisie, post machine guns in their rear, [have] a few hundred shot and assure a real mass assault on Iudenich."[320]

Once the Red force stopped panicking, the outcome could not be in doubt, because of its numerical superiority. The Whites with 14,400 men and 44 guns confronted a Seventh Red Army that now numbered 73,000 men supported by 581 guns.[321] To make matters worse for Iudenich, to the south stood another Red Army, the Fifteenth.

Iudenich's soldiers came nearest to Petrograd on October 20, when they occupied Pulkovo. Trotsky, mounted on a horse, rallied the fleeing troops and led them back into battle.[322] A critical factor in Iudenich's defeat was the failure of one of his officers, eager to be the first to enter liberated Petrograd, to obey orders to cut the railroad line to Moscow. This permit-ted the Red command to dispatch reinforcements, including 7,000 highly motivated Communists and military cadets who stiffened morale and turned the tide of battle.

On October 21, the Seventh Army counterattacked. It quickly pierced the White lines, behind which stood no reserves. Iudenich's men held out for a

---

*Geoffrey Bennett, *Cowan's War* (London, 1964), and Augustus Agar, *Baltic Episode* (Lon-don, 1963). In these operations, the British lost 128 men, 17 ships, and 37 aircraft: Bennett, *loc. cit.*, 228–29.

14. Barricades in Petrograd, October 1919.

while at Gatchina, but then the Fifteenth Red Army began to advance, capturing Luga (October 31) and threatening their rear. Iudenich's army had no choice but to retreat to Estonia, where it was disarmed.

On December 13, Estonia and Soviet Russia signed an armistice, which was followed on February 2, 1920, by a peace treaty. Lithuania, Latvia, and Finland made peace with Soviet Russia later that year.

To honor his role in the defense of the city, Gatchina was in 1923 renamed Trotsk, the first Soviet city to be named after a living Communist leader.

Toward the end of September 1919, the Red High Command assembled in great secrecy between Briansk and Orel a "Striking Group" (Udarnaia Gruppa) of shock troops. Its nucleus was the Latvian Rifle Division, dressed in its familiar leather jackets, which had been transferred from the Western front and was about, once again, to render the Communist regime an invaluable service.[323] Attached was a brigade of Red Cossacks, and several smaller units; it was later reinforced by an Estonian Rifle Brigade.[324] The group's overall strength was 10,000 infantry, 1,500 cavalry, and 80 guns.[325] Its command was entrusted to A. A. Martusevich, the head of the Latvian Rifle Division.

The order of battle on the eve of the decisive engagements is not easy to determine. According to Denikin, at the beginning of October the Red Army had on the Southern and Southeastern fronts 140,000 men. His own forces numbered 98,000.[326] According to the Red Army commander of the Southern front, the Reds had 186,000 troops.[327]

15. Latvian troops about to be dispatched to the Southern front, 1919.

On the very eve of the Red Army's decisive victories over the Southern Army, Trotsky addressed to the Central Committee a characteristically long and cantankerous letter. The entire planning of the campaign against Denikin, he wrote, had been faulty from the start in that instead of striking at Kharkov to cut him off from his Cossack supporters, the Red Army attacked the Cossacks, pushing them into Denikin's arms and enabling him to occupy the Ukraine. As a result, the situation in the south had deteriorated and Tula itself was endangered. Lenin jotted down on Trotsky's letter: "Received October 1. (Nothing but bad nerves.) This was not raised at the Plenum. It is strange to do so now."[328]

On October 11, A. I. Egorov was appointed commander of the Southern front. A career officer, he had in his youth belonged to the Socialists-Revolutionaries; wounded several times during World War I, he rose to the rank of lieutenant colonel. In July 1918 he joined the Communist Party. Together with the Commander in Chief, Kamenev, he was the architect of the Red victory.* Egorov reinforced the Striking Group by massing east of

*In the 1930s Egorov rose to be a marshal of the Red Army and in 1937 assumed Tukhachevskii's post after the latter's execution. Before long, he, too, lost his life in the Stalinist purge: *TP*, I, 97.

16. Budennyi and Egorov.

Voronezh a newly formed cavalry corps under Semen Budennyi, an "outlander" from the Don who passionately hated the Cossacks.* The Soviet High Command worked out a strategic plan whose main objective was to separate the Volunteer Army from the Don Cossacks, and pour into the breach Budennyi's cavalry. The Volunteers would then either have to retreat or find themselves in a trap.[329]† The Red counteroffensive was launched ahead of schedule because Egorov feared further retreats would demoralize his troops and cause their "complete disintegration."[330]

On October 18–19, as the Volunteer Army pushed toward Tula, the Second and Third Latvian Brigades launched a surprise attack against the left flank of the Drozdovskii and Kornilov divisions. In pitched battles, the Latvians defeated the exhausted Volunteers and on October 20 forced them to evacuate Orel by threatening to cut off their communications to the rear. In this decisive engagement of the Civil War the main force on the Communist side, the Latvians, lost in killed and wounded over 50 percent of the officers and up to 40 percent of the soldiers.[331]

*Kamenev gave Egorov credit for being the "creator" of the "Horse Army" (Konarmiia): *Direktivy glavnogo komandovaniia krasnoi armii* (Moscow, 1969), 675.

†Some Western historians suggest that much of what transpired in October–November 1919 on the Southern front was the result of improvisation (*e.g.*, Mawdsley, *Civil War*, 203–5). In fact the directives issued by the army's High Command in October (as reported in *Direktivy komandovaniia, passim*) do not envisage the kind of operation that was put into effect the next month. Cf. A. I. Egorov, *Razgrom Denikina, 1919* (Moscow, 1931), 148.

17. Budennyi's Red Cavalry.

The situation of the Volunteer Army was perilous, but far from cata-strophic, when suddenly from the east appeared another threat, Budennyi's Cavalry Corps, reinforced by 12,000–15,000 infantry. On October 19, Budennyi's horsemen defeated the Don Cossacks under Generals Mamon-tov and A. G. Shkuro, destroying the flower of the Don cavalry, following which, on October 24, they took Voronezh. According to Denikin, this disaster was brought about by the unwillingness of the Don Cossacks—who were more interested in defending their home territory than in defeating the Red Army—to deploy adequate forces at Voronezh.[332] From Voronezh, Budennyi continued westward, and on October 29 crossed the Don River. His orders were to seize Kastornoe, an important railroad junction linking Kursk with Voronezh, and Moscow with the Donbass. The assault on Kastornoe began on October 31. The fighting was fierce. The Red Cavalry finally captured the town on November 15, sealing the fate of the White advance on Moscow. Threatened with being cut off from the Don region, the three divisions of the Volunteer Army had to retreat. They did so in good order, falling back on Kursk. But their commander, General Mai-Maevskii, went completely to pieces, drinking, womanizing, and attending to his loot.[333] He was dismissed and replaced by Wrangel.

In the midst of these ordeals another heavy blow fell on the Whites. On November 8, Lloyd George in a speech at the Lord Mayor's Banquet in Guildhall, London, declared that Bolshevism could not be defeated by force of arms, that Denikin's drive against Moscow had stalled, and "other methods must be found" to restore peace. "We cannot . . . afford to continue so costly an intervention in an interminable civil war."[334] The speech had not been cleared with the cabinet and startled many Britons.[335] The Prime Minister explained the rationale for this turnabout in an address on November 17 to the House of Commons, from which it transpired that behind it lay fear not of White defeat but of White victory. Disraeli, the Prime Minister recalled, had warned against "a great, gigantic, colossal, growing Russia rolling onwards like a glacier towards Persia and the borders of Afghanistan and India as the greatest menace the British Empire could be confronted with." Kolchak's and Denikin's struggle for "a reunited Russia," therefore, was not in Britain's interest.

According to Denikin, these remarks had a devastating impact on his army, which felt abandoned at a critical time.[336] This assessment is confirmed by a British eyewitness:

> The effect of Mr. George's speeches was electrical. Until that moment, the Volunteers and their supporters had comforted themselves with the idea that they were fighting one of the final phases of the Great War, with England still the first of their Allies. Now they suddenly realized with horror that England considered the War as over and the fighting in Russia as merely a civil conflict. In a couple of days the whole atmosphere in South Russia was changed. Whatever firmness of purposes there had previously been, was now so undermined that the worst became possible. Mr. George's opinion that the Volunteer cause was doomed helped to make that doom almost certain. I read the Russian newspapers carefully every day, and saw how even the most pro-British of them shook at Mr. George's blows.[337]

On November 17 the Whites pulled out of Kursk. At this time they learned that three days earlier Kolchak had abandoned Omsk. In mid-December, after Kharkov and Kiev had fallen, their retreat turned into a rout. Territories that had taken months of hard struggle to conquer were given up without a fight. On December 9, in a letter in which he recalled how his warnings had been vindicated, Wrangel wrote Denikin that the "army has ceased to exist as a fighting force."[338]

In a reenactment of events in Siberia, mobs of soldiers and civilians, with the Red Cavalry in close pursuit, fled southward toward the Black Sea.

> Thousands upon thousands of unhappy people, some of whom had been fleeing for weeks before the advancing Bolshevists, set out again, without friends, without provisions or clothing. It would be senseless to brand these people as rich "bourgeois," fleeing from a revengeful populace; most of them had no longer a penny in the world, whatever their former fortunes had been, and many of them were working men and peasants who had sampled Bolshevist rule and wished only to escape its second coming.
>
> At one big town in South Russia terrible scenes took place when the town was evacuated. As the last Russian hospital train was preparing to leave one evening, in the dim light of the station lamps some strange figures were seen crawling along the platform. They were gray and shapeless, like big wolves. They came nearer, and with horror it was recognized that they were eight Russian officers ill with typhus, dressed in their grey hospital

dressing-gowns, who, rather than be left behind to be tortured and murdered by the Bolshevists, as was likely to be their fate, had crawled along on all fours through the snow from the hospital to the station, hoping to be taken away on a train. Inquiries were made, and it was found (so I was told) that, as usually happened, several hundred officers had been abandoned in the typhus hospitals. The moment the Volunteer Army doctors had left the hospitals, the orderlies had amused themselves by refusing the unhappy officers all attention. What would have happened to them when the mob discovered them is too horrible to be thought of.[339]

The fleeing masses converged on Novorossiisk, the principal Allied port on the Black Sea, hoping to evacuate on Allied ships. Here, in the midst of a raging typhus epidemic, with the Bolshevik cavalry waiting in the suburbs ready to enter the instant the Allies set sail, terrible scenes were enacted:

> The full weight of the human avalanche reached Novorossiisk at the end of March 1920. A non-descript mass of soldiers, deserters, and refugees flooded the city, engulfing the terror-stricken population in a common sea of misery. Typhus reaped a dreadful harvest among the hordes crowding the port. Every one knew that only escape to the Crimea or elsewhere could save this heap of humanity from bloody vengeance when Budenny and his horsemen should take the town; but the amount of shipping available was limited. For several days people fought for a place on the transports. It was a life-and-death struggle. . . .
>
> On the morning of March 27, Denikin stood on the bridge of the French war vessel, *Capitaine Saken,* lying in the harbor of Novorossiisk. About

18. Evacuation of White troops on British ships in Novorossiisk, early 1920.

19. Denikin in the Crimea on the day of his resignation.

him were the vague outlines of transports which were carrying the Russian soldiery to the Crimea. He could see men and women kneeling on the quay, praying to Allied naval officers to take them aboard. Some threw themselves into the sea. The British warship, *Empress of India,* and the French cruiser, *Waldeck-Rousseau,* bombarded the roads on which Red cavalry were waiting. Amid horses, camels, wagons, and supplies cluttering the dock were his soldiers and their families with hands raised toward the ships, their voices floating over the waters to nervous commanders, who knew that once their decks were full those who remained on shore must face death or flee where they could. Some fifty thousand were embarked. During the panic and confusion, criminals slunk abroad to prey like ghouls upon the defenseless. Refugees who could not secure passage were compelled to await the grim judgment of Red columns which were already raising dust along roads into the city.

The same day on which the evacuation occurred, Novorossiisk was occupied by the Bolsheviks and hundreds of White Russians, both civil and military, paid with their lives for resistance to the sickle and hammer of the new regime.[340]

On arriving at the Crimean port of Sebastopol on April 2, Denikin came under great pressure from disaffected officers to resign. He did so that very day. A poll of senior commanders unanimously elected Wrangel his successor. Wrangel, who had left the army and was living in Constantinople, immediately boarded a British ship bound for the Crimea.

By this time, the Red Army had swept into the Cossack regions, wreaking vengeance. Some Communists called for the wholesale "liquidation" of the Cossacks by "fire and sword." In anticipation, the Cossacks fled en masse, abandoning their settlements and ill-gotten loot to the outlanders: in some areas their population declined by one-half.[341] Ten years later, during collectivization, Cossackdom was abolished.

20. Wrangel.

Wrangel not only had a keen strategic sense, but understood the importance of politics: unlike his predecessors, he realized that in a civil war the combatants were not only armies but also governments, and that in order to win they had to mobilize the civilian population. He surrounded himself with able advisers, among them Peter Struve, whom he entrusted with the conduct of foreign relations, and A. V. Krivoshein, a onetime Minister of Agriculture, whom he placed in charge of domestic affairs, both conservative-liberals. Wrangel devoted much attention to civilian administration and to establishing friendly relations with the non-Russian minorities.[342] Even so, his task was hopeless. If he managed to maintain himself in the Crimea for five months it was only because shortly after he had assumed command, the Red Army was distracted by the Polish invasion. In his dual capacity as commander of 100,000–150,000 troops, and the civilian chief of 400,000 refugees who had crowded into the Crimean peninsula, he faced insurmountable difficulties whatever course he chose, evacuation or resumption of the armed struggle.

He could do neither without British help, and this help was denied him. On April 2, as he was leaving Constantinople, the British High Commissioner there handed him a note that called on the Whites to cease forthwith the "unequal struggle": in return, the British government offered to intercede with Moscow with the view of obtaining for them general amnesty. Their commanding officers were promised asylum in Great Britain. Should the Whites reject the offer, the note warned, the British government would "cease to furnish [them] . . . with any help or subvention of any kind from that time on."[343]

The British notion of Soviet amnesty for the Whites was frivolous and Wrangel gave it no serious thought. He was quite prepared to evacuate provided it did not entail abandoning half a million White soldiers and civilian sympathizers to the mercies of the Communists. The army's commanders agreed that evacuation was the only way out. To protect himself against possible future accusations that he acted dishonorably in abandoning the armed struggle, Wrangel requested and obtained from the generals their signatures to a document stating that in view of the British ultimatum, his task was to find a refuge for those who did not wish to rely on Soviet goodwill.[344] On April 4, in a response to the British ultimatum, he affirmed his willingness to accept a cease-fire and evacuate the Crimea, provided the Allies guaranteed asylum not only for himself and the commanding staff, but for "all those who prefer expatriation to the clemency of the enemy."[345]

Britain did not even reply to this request; and since he considered negotiations for an amnesty with Moscow futile, Wrangel had no choice but to prepare for a longer stay in the Crimea. At the end of April, after the Poles had captured Kiev, the possibility of maintaining a presence in the Crimea appeared reasonably realistic, especially as the French, eager to ease the pressure on the Poles by keeping units of the Red Army engaged in southern Russia, turned more friendly. Thus, by force of circumstances, arose the idea of transforming the Crimean peninsula into an enclave of democratic and national Russia. Wrangel and his advisers felt that if the Allies were to grant the government of Southern Russia diplomatic recognition, as they did to some of the other separated borderlands of Russia, it would be safe from Soviet invasion. At a press conference on April 11, he declared that "Russia can be liberated not by a triumphal march on Moscow but by the creation—even if only on a strip of Russian soil—of such order and such conditions of life that will attract all the thoughts and energies of the Russian people groaning under the Red yoke."[346] The concept was not unlike that which would be adopted by the Nationalist forces of China after they had evacuated in 1949 to Taiwan, with the significant difference that whereas the latter enjoyed firm U.S. diplomatic and military guarantees, Wrangel's government found itself virtually alone.

On assuming command, Wrangel promptly restored discipline in the army. It was thoroughly demoralized; the infantry had few weapons, most of which had been left behind in Novorossiisk, while the Cossacks had no horses. Harsh measures were applied, including the death penalty for officers and soldiers who disobeyed orders, drank on duty, or looted. The effect was immediate: Wrangel's force, renamed the Russian Army, is said to have resembled the original Volunteer Army of 1918 "before it had become diluted by forced mobilizations and corrupted by drink and pillage."[347]

Wrangel could not for long remain confined to the Crimea, because the peninsula did not grow enough food to feed its swollen population. Furthermore, the French made help conditional on very onerous terms, which required the Whites to supply them with foodstuffs and other commodities the Crimea lacked. Driven by these considerations, on June 6, in disregard of British warnings, Wrangel carried out surprise landings on the mainland along the coast of the Sea of Azov. The operation was a success, and the beachhead soon expanded into a sizable area rich in agricultural produce. To win the sympathies of the population, Wrangel issued an appeal in which he promised to protect religion, ensure the freedoms and rights of citizens, and make it possible for the population to choose its government. In a complicated land decree, he recognized as the peasants' property most of the land they had seized in 1917–18, with the proviso that the previous owners receive back minimal allotments as defined by law.[348]

In July and August, Wrangel sent a second expeditionary force to the Kuban, but this one was unable to gain a foothold.

Wrangel's ability to survive depended on the outcome of the Soviet-Polish war. When in September, following the Red Army's defeat at Warsaw, military operations in Poland were halted and the two countries opened peace negotiations, his fate was sealed. On October 20, the Red Army opened an offensive against the Crimea, charging White positions across the Perekop Isthmus: here, 37,220 Whites confronted 133,600 Red troops.[349] The attacking force included partisan units loyal to Makhno, which were sent to charge head-on the strongest White redoubt and accomplished the breakthrough at the cost of heavy losses. After the battle, Trotsky is said to have ordered the execution of the surviving 5,000 Makhno followers.*

While keeping the Red Army at bay, Wrangel made preparations to evacuate. The difficult withdrawal was carried out in exemplary fashion, the troops fighting and retreating in good order. On November 14, the Civil War formally ended as 83,000 military and civilian refugees boarded a fleet of 126 British, Russian, and French ships that carried them to Constantinople. Wrangel was the last to embark. About 300,000 anti-Bolsheviks were left behind: many of the officers among them were summarily shot by the Reds.[350]

Subsequently masses of White prisoners of war were incarcerated in

---

*I. Moroz in *AiF*, No. 37/518 (September 15–21, 1990), 7. In revenge, the next year Makhno murdered all the Communists he could lay his hands on in the Ukraine. He was defeated in August 1921 by the Red Army under Mikhail Frunze, following which he evacuated the remnant of his force to Romania. He died in France in 1934.

forced-labor camps. In November 1920 Lenin received from the Cheka, which was running them, alarming reports that in Ekaterinburg alone, 100,000 POWs, along with Cossacks expelled from their villages, were living in "incredible conditions." Camps in Kharkov held 37,000 prisoners from Wrangel's army. The Cheka asked that something be done to improve the lot of these people. Lenin's answer was: "To the archive."[351]

There were mass expulsions of Don Cossacks from their homesteads. To repopulate and reconstruct the desolated region, Moscow negotiated in 1922 with the German Krupp concern, offering to lease to it as much as 700,000 hectares of agricultural land in the Novorossisk region.[352] But even after the land offer had been reduced to 65,000 hectares, the Germans would not commit themselves and nothing came of the proposal.

For reasons adduced at the beginning of this volume, the victory of the Red Army was a foregone conclusion, given its immense superiority in manpower and war matériel and the advantages of its geopolitical situation. The relative weakness of the Whites was compounded by their inability to grasp the exigencies of Civil War and their stubborn refusal to acknowledge the separation of the non-Russian regions. Strategic mistakes were committed, of which the failure to link up with Kolchak was probably the costliest. Other grave errors were made as well, such as not providing proper civilian government and failing to keep a tight rein on the troops. This granted, it is doubtful that more intelligent politics or better strategic planning would have averted defeat. Had Wrangel rather than Denikin assumed command after the death of Kornilov, the agony would have been prolonged but the outcome would, very likely, have been the same. The "objective" elements were too unfavorable for the Whites.*

Among the factors that influenced the final outcome and that can be classified as "objective" even though they are not material but cultural, stress must be laid on the weakly developed sense of patriotism among the Russian population. The Whites took as their inspiration the Russian national uprising against foreign invaders in the early seventeenth century which ended the "Time of Troubles." They appealed not to class instincts, that is, not to the emotions of resentment and greed, but to the sense of national pride. And that evoked a response only from a small segment consisting mainly of the officer corps and the educated: on this Denikin and Kolchak concurred.[353] Neither the Russian peasantry nor the non-Russian minorities (among which, for this purpose, must be included the Cossacks) could be stirred with calls to liberate Russia. The tsarist government had failed to develop among its subjects a sense of national identity and common interest: the Bolshevik exhortations to looting, desertion, and separa-

---

*This also is the conclusion of Evan Mawdsley: *Civil War,* 272–90.

tism attracted them far more. Of course, once the Civil War was over and the Bolsheviks, anxious to begin the work of reconstruction, had, in turn, to invoke patriotism, they met with the same indifference. Their response was permanent terror.

It is common among historians of the Russian Revolution to attribute the White defeat to a failure to win mass support; this was allegedly due to their unwillingness to adopt progressive social and political platforms. In particular, it is said, the Whites lost the Russian peasantry because they failed to legitimize the land seizures carried out in 1917–18. This proposition can be neither demonstrated nor disproven because there were no elections, no referenda, and no opinion polls to put it to a test. It is not a conclusion arrived at from the evidence, but rather from an a priori assumption: in Allied (especially British and American) circles it was taken for granted that a regime that maintained itself in power had to enjoy popular support, and, conversely, one that failed to do so, lacked it. The premise, derived from the experience of democracies where power is acquired through the ballot, is entirely inapplicable to societies where it is secured and maintained by force. To "the question: 'How can the Bolsheviks rule unless they have a majority of people behind them'?" General Ward, the commander of British troops in Omsk under Kolchak, responded with a perfectly sensible question, "How did a one-man government exist in Russia from 'Ivan the Terrible' to Nicholas II?"[354]

A civil war is not a popularity contest. There exists no evidence that the Russian or Ukrainian peasants, given a free choice between Reds and Whites, would have opted for the former. For while it is true that the Reds had turned over to the communes the private holdings of the landlords and their fellow peasants, and that the Whites' attitude to that action was problematic, they nullified whatever popularity this policy had gained them with their brutal policy of food exactions and class war on the village. Such evidence as is available indicates that in the Civil War the peasantry stood to the side, cursing both parties to the conflict and wishing only to be left alone. Nearly all contemporary observers noted that when the Reds were in control of an area, its inhabitants longed for the Whites, but when subjected for any length of time to White rule, they wished the Reds to return. This "plague on both your houses" attitude is confirmed alike by Russian conservatives, liberals, and radicals, as well as by foreign observers: it was the legacy of centuries of patrimonialism, which treated the population as a mere object of authority and did not inculcate in it anything resembling a sense of citizenship. Peter Struve, who had spent 1918 under Bolshevik rule, wrote: "The population was always either an entirely passive element, or, in the shape of Green and other bands, an element equally hostile to both sides. The Civil War between the Reds and Whites was always conducted by relatively insignificant minorities, against the astounding passivity of the vast majority of the population."[355] Denikin found the peasant "without roots and confused. In him there were neither 'politics' nor 'the Constituent Assembly,' nor 'the republic,' nor the 'tsar.' "[356] The Menshevik Martov agreed that in the Civil War the masses were "indifferent and passive."[357]

The Bolsheviks, assisted by the Mensheviks and SRs, did manage to rally much of the industrial working class to their side, but it is questionable that there were enough workers (probably less than one million) to tip the scales in their favor.

Boris Savinkov, the terrorist turned patriot who had an opportunity to observe the Civil War at first hand on nearly all fronts, explained to Churchill and Lloyd George the situation in the Russian countryside. As recounted by Churchill:

> It was in some ways the story of the Indian villages over whose heads the waves of conquest swept and recoiled in bygone ages. They had the land. They had murdered or chased away its former owners. The village society had flowed over into new and well cultivated fields. They now had these long coveted domains for themselves. No more landlords: no more rent. The earth and its fullness—no more—no less. . . . Not for them the causes of men. Communism, Czarism; the World Revolution; Holy Russia; Empire or Proletariat; civilization or barbarism, tyranny or freedom—these were all the same to them in theory; but also—whoever won—much the same in fact. There they were and there they stayed; and with hard toil, they gained their daily bread. One morning arrives a Cossack patrol. "Christ is risen; the Allies are advancing; Russia is saved; you are free." "The Soviet is no more." And the peasants grunted, and duly elected their Council of Elders, and the Cossack patrol rode off, taking with it what it might require up to the limit of what it could carry. On an afternoon a few weeks later, or it may be a few days later, arrived a Bolshevik in a battered motor-car with half a dozen gunmen, also saying, "You are free; your chains are broken; Christ is a fraud; religion is the opiate of democracy; Brothers, Comrades, rejoice for the great days that have dawned." And the peasants grunted. And the Bolshevik said, "Away with this Council of Elders, exploiters of the poor, the base tools of reaction. Elect in their place your village Soviet, henceforward the sickle and hammer of your Proletarian rights." So the peasants swept away the Council of Elders and reelected with rude ceremony the village Soviet. But they chose exactly the same people who had hitherto formed the Council of Elders and the land also remained in their possession. And presently the Bolshevik and his gunmen got their motor-car to start and throbbed off into the distance, or perhaps into the Cossack patrol.[358]

"The mood of the peasants is indifferent," according to another contemporary.

> They just want to be left to themselves. The Bolsheviks were here—that's good, they say; the Bolsheviks went away—that's no shame, they say. As long as there is bread then let's pray to God, and who needs the [White] Guards?—let them fight it out by themselves, we will stand aside.[359]

The evidence to this effect is overwhelming and it indicates that the attitude of the "masses," especially those living in the countryside, had no effect on the outcome of the Civil War. Lenin was realist enough to know that his regime was not popular: neither in discussions with associates nor in conversations with foreign visitors did he pretend otherwise. He held both Russian workers and peasants in contempt. At any rate, he did not claim that the Bolsheviks won the war because they had the people behind them. It is for this reason that the Bolsheviks would hear nothing of convening a Constituent Assembly—something all White regimes were committed to do—and compelled the Socialists-Revolutionaries to abandon this slogan. It is not something they would have done had they any prospect of obtaining a majority in national elections.

The main base of Bolshevik support came not from the people at large, the "masses," but from the Communist Party apparatus, which grew by leaps and bounds during the Civil War: at its conclusion, the Party numbered between 600,000 and 700,000 members. People were enrolled without much scrutiny, to provide administrative cadres and to stiffen the ranks of the army: their loyalty was assured by the fact that if the Whites won, they faced retribution and possible death. They joined because membership offered privileges and security in a society in which extreme poverty and insecurity were the rule. Like all successful revolutionaries, the Bolsheviks brought into being a clientele with a vital interest in the preservation of the new regime: this they accomplished by distributing to their followers assets and jobs. The beneficiaries of this largesse (at someone else's expense) had an overriding stake in preventing a restoration of both the monarchy and democracy. Their numbers were relatively small—with their dependents perhaps 3 million—but in a country in which virtually no organized life above the village level had survived, such a cadre, subject to party discipline, represented an awesome force.

The human costs of the Russian Civil War are next to impossible to ascertain. Data recently released from Red Army archives indicate combat losses between 1918 and 1920 to have been 701,847 (exclusive of those who disappeared or did not return from captivity).[360] To this figure must be added the losses suffered in suppressing peasant risings, estimated at nearly a quarter of a million. (See below, page 373.) In all, the military fatalities of the Red Army in the Civil War were about three-quarters as great as those suffered by the Imperial Army in World War I (estimated at 1.3 million). White casualties are even less subject to precise accounting: one Russian demographer estimates them at 127,000.[361]

To the combat fatalities must be added the victims of epidemics, as well as those who died from malnutrition, the cold, and suicide: infectious diseases alone are estimated to have claimed over two million lives.[362]

It has been estimated that 91 percent of the victims of the Civil War were civilians.[363]

The combat and civilian losses affected mainly Great Russia, controlled during the Civil War by the Communists. The territories either mostly or wholly under White rule (the northern Caucasus, the Steppe region of Central Asia, and especially Siberia) showed a population increase.[364]

Finally, to the demographic declines Russia suffered from the Civil War must be added the loss of citizens who emigrated abroad: they numbered between one and a half and two million. The bulk of the émigrés initially went to Germany and France, each of which is estimated to have absorbed some 400,000. An estimated 100,000 sought refuge in China.[365]

The Russian emigration differed from that occasioned by the French Revolution. Fifty-one percent of the French émigrés belonged to the lower orders, 25 percent to the clergy, and 17 percent to the aristocracy.[366] The majority of the Russians, by contrast, were bureaucrats, professional people, businessmen, and intellectuals. They constituted a high proportion of the Establishment that had run pre-Revolutionary Russia and made up much of its Westernized elite. Furthermore, while most French émigrés eventually returned home, the Russians did not: with few exceptions, they ended their days abroad. Their children assimilated. Thus for Russia, the outflow represented a far more grievous loss.

The Russian émigrés carried with them their political beliefs and rivalries. The monarchists gravitated toward Germany, where they forged links with the nascent National Socialist movement and infused it with anti-Communism. In 1920, during the Russo-Polish war, some members of the right-wing emigration became pro-Soviet. For the leader of this trend, N. V. Ustrialov, reconstituting Russia as a "mighty and integral" state was the highest priority; inasmuch as the Bolsheviks, whatever their sins, had become the bearers of Russian statehood, they had earned the support of all Russians, and émigrés had a duty to go back to help them rebuild the country. Lenin regarded this movement, known as "Smena Vekh," or "Change of Landmarks," as useful and gave it financial support. Ustrialov and some of his "National Bolshevik" followers actually did return; tolerated for a while, they ultimately met violent deaths.

The SRs and the Mensheviks in emigration went their own way. Although critical of Communism, they opposed any armed resistance to it on the familiar grounds that it only served to rally the masses behind the regime, which, left alone, would in time give way to healthy democratic forces. Their hope rested on the natural evolution of Communism toward socialism and democracy.

The liberal movement in emigration split. Miliukov linked up with the socialists, while the bulk of the party wanted in some way to continue resistance to the Communist regime. Peter Struve, isolated from all political currents but a national liberal by conviction, called on the émigrés to concentrate on nurturing Russia's national culture until the day when the homeland was liberated. He denied that Communism was capable of evolution: because of the peculiar relationship between politics and economics in Soviet Russia, "The evolution of Bolshevism will be a condition and signal of a revolution against Bolshevism."[367]

The veterans of the Russian White Armies kept aloof from these controversies, although, given the hostility of the socialists and left-liberals to their struggle, they were attracted to the monarchist right. Wrangel settled in Yugoslavia, where he died in 1928. Denikin ended his days in New York.

Many Russians believed, with Struve, that the main national mission of the diaspora was to keep alive Russian culture. With financial support from the Czechoslovak and Yugoslav governments, they unfolded remarkable cultural activity, founding universities, schools, and learned institutes, and publishing books, periodicals, and newspapers. In 1920, 138 new Russian-language newspapers appeared abroad; Berlin alone had 58 Russian dailies and periodicals.[368] Russian writers, musicians, and artists, some with worldwide reputations, continued to create, often under the most difficult conditions. On the tenth anniversary of the Bolshevik coup, Vladimir Nabokov extolled the exile community as the custodian of the true Russia:

> We are the wave of Russia that has spilled over her shores; we have spread all over the world. But our wanderings are not always doleful . . . and although it sometimes seems to us that in the world roams not one but a thousand thousand Russias, sometimes poor and ill-tempered, sometimes quarrelling with each other—there is one thing that links us: some kind of common striving, a common spirit which the future historian will understand and value.
>
> It is for one reason that we celebrate ten years of freedom. The kind of freedom that we know perhaps no nation has known. In this special Russia which invisibly surrounds us, feeds and supports us, nourishes the soul, embellishes dreams—there is no law save the law of love for Russia, and there is no authority except our own conscience. We can say anything about her and write anything: we have nothing to hide, and no censorship places obstacles in front of us. We are the free citizens of our dream.[369]

3

The Red Empire*

The first nationwide census of the Russian Empire, conducted in 1897, indicated that its population (exclusive of the Grand Duchy of Finland) numbered 126 million.† The proportion of Russians depended on one's definition. The Imperial government included under this category three Slavic groups that in the twentieth century have come to be recognized as distinct nations: Russians proper, or "Great Russians" (56 million); Ukrainians, or "Little Russians" (22 million); and Belorussians (6 million). Counted as one, they made up two-thirds of the total.‡ If the Ukrainians and Belorussians were treated as nations in their own right, then the Russians (or, more exactly, Russian-speakers) were reduced to a minority (44.2 percent). It was in good measure to conceal this unpalatable fact that the

*This chapter summarizes the contents of my book *The Formation of the Soviet Union: Communism and Nationalism, 1917–1923*, originally published in 1954, and in a revised edition ten years later. The book provides ample documentation, which enables me to dispense with the usual scholarly apparatus, except where new materials, made available since 1964, have caused me to revise my earlier views.

†This figure and those that follow are taken from N. A. Troinitskii, ed., *Obshchii svod . . . pervoi vseobshchei perepisi naseleniia . . . 1897 goda,* 2 vols. (St. Petersburg, 1905).

‡The criterion used by the 1897 census-takers was not nationality but "native language," which inflated the number of Russians, since their language was the empire's lingua franca. According to the 1926 census, the number of citizens who considered Russian to be their native tongue exceeded those who claimed to be Russian by 8.2 percent.

tsarist regime persecuted Ukrainian nationalism with particular savagery, to the point of outlawing the publication of printed materials in the Ukrainian language.

The Belorussians and most Ukrainians shared with the Great Russians a common religion, and at a time when religious affiliation took precedence over national identity for the majority of the Empire's inhabitants, this was a significant bond. The tsarist authorities treated members of the three Slavic Orthodox groups as equals in terms of advancement in the civil and military service, which facilitated assimilation. Intermarriage further contributed to this end: in the 1926 census, which listed separately national status and linguistic preference, one in seven Ukrainians and Belorussians considered Russian to be their native tongue.

This said, the differences separating the three eastern Slavic groups were more significant than the similarities. Between the fourteenth and eighteenth centuries the Ukrainians and Belorussians had been subjects of the Polish-Lithuanian Commonwealth, a Catholic country, culturally close to Western Europe. As a consequence, until the second half of the eighteenth century, when they came under Russian rule, they had been exposed to a far greater extent than Muscovite Russians to Western influences. Specifically, the Ukrainians and Belorussians had much shorter experience with the three institutions that shaped the lives of Great Russians: patrimonial autocracy, serfdom, and communal landholding. At the turn of the century neither was as yet a fully formed modern nation, and such sense of national identity as they possessed was confined to a thin layer of native intelligentsia. As was the case with Great Russians, most Ukrainians and Belorussians thought of themselves as members not of a nation but of the Orthodox community, and as natives of the province in which they happened to live. The Ukrainian nationalist movement, encouraged and financed by the Austrians as a means of weakening Russia, acquired a broader constituency only during the Revolution and Civil War.

The 1897 census showed that the Empire had 85 distinct linguistic groups, the smallest of which numbered in the hundreds. Interesting as such communities may be to the anthropologist and ethnographer, for the historian most of them are of marginal importance.

Politically, the most active of Russia's ethnic groups were her 8 million Poles. They had been acquired by Russia in the partitions of the eighteenth century and at the Congress of Vienna in 1815. By 1900, as punishment for two rebellions (1830–31 and 1863), the Poles had lost the right to self-government: after 1863, all traces of Polish statehood were obliterated and the very name of Poland disappeared from Russian maps. Although the Poles were Slavs, their Catholicism caused them to be regarded by Russians as foreigners.* It is difficult to understand how the Russians hoped to keep

---

*Several million Ukrainians living in the western provinces joined the Catholic Church in the sixteenth century on terms that allowed them to continue practicing Orthodox rituals. The tsarist authorities and the Orthodox Establishment treated these so-called "Uniates" as apostates.

an ancient people, culturally much superior to the mass of their own people, in permanent subjugation. But Poland was geopolitically too important to St. Petersburg to relinquish: if the Ukrainians and Belorussians gave Russians a numerical preponderance in the Empire, Poland served them as an outpost from which to exert political and military influence on Europe. Some Polish intellectuals believed that only by holding on to Poland could Russia claim status as a European power.

Next, in terms of numbers, came various Turco-Tatar groups professing Islam and scattered from the Black Sea to the Pacific. For the most part, they were descendants of the nomadic tribes that in the thirteenth century had conquered the proto-Russian (Kievan) state, and later migrants who had moved from the Chinese border to the steppes south of the Russian homeland in the forest zone (taiga). Some of them pursued a nomadism or transhumance, while others settled down to engage in trade and artisanship. They were concentrated in three regions. The largest was Central Asia (the Steppe and Turkestan), inhabited by 7 million Muslims, most of them Turks but some of Iranian ancestry or a mixture of the two. Another major Muslim settlement, and the earliest to come under Russian rule, comprised Turkic groups living along the middle Volga and the Urals. Two million of them were Tatars, a partly commercial, partly agrarian people, and 1.3 million were largely nomadic Bashkirs. A third area of concentration was Muslim communities in the northern Caucasian mountains and to the south, in Transcaucasia (Azeri Turks, Daghestanis, Chechens, and so forth), as well as in the Crimean peninsula. Muslims totaled 14–15 million, or 11 percent of the Empire's population.

The Imperial government treated its Muslim subjects indulgently because it saw in them no political threat. In the early twentieth century a modernist cultural movement emerged among the Volga and Crimean Tatars; known as Jadidism, and, not unlike the Jewish *Haskalah,* its main objective was secularizing Muslim education. Potentially nationalistic, it did not assume political forms of expression until after the outbreak of the Revolution. The nomadic Turks enjoyed tribal autonomy and in the nineteenth century were protected by the government from Slav encroachments on their grazing lands. Most Muslims enjoyed exemption from military duty.

Russia acquired Finland from Sweden in 1809 as a present from Napoleon. Finland formed in the Russian Empire a semi-sovereign entity with her own legislature: the Russian tsar ruled there as Grand Duke, in which capacity he was subject to constitutional restraints. It was a satisfactory arrangement that began to fall apart toward the end of the nineteenth century owing to encroachments by the Russian bureaucracy on Finland's constitutional rights. The result was the emergence of a Finnish nationalist

---

Their church was abolished and its members forcibly integrated with the official church in the 1940s under Stalin.

movement. The inhabitants of Finland were exempt from Russian laws and service in the Russian army.

In the Baltic areas, then known as Livonia, Courland, and Estonia, the politically dominant element was Germans who controlled most of the land and dominated commerce. The Latvians and Estonians formed a lower class of peasants and industrial workers. No ethnic group in Russia showed greater loyalty to the tsarist regime than the Baltic Germans, and as a reward, St. Petersburg allowed them a free hand in running their provinces.

The Georgians (1.4 million) and Armenians (1.2 million) of Trans-caucasia were Orthodox Christians with their own "autocephalous" hierarchies. Surrounded by hostile Muslims, they tended to look to the Russians for security. In the late eighteenth century the Georgians requested Russia's protection and signed with her accords that the latter violated in 1801 by incorporating Georgia. Armenia was acquired in the early nineteenth century from the Ottoman Empire, in which the majority of Armenians continued to reside.

The 5 million Russian Jews were in a category all their own. Threatened in the early modern period by proto-Reformation movements known as the "Judaizing heresy," the Orthodox Church insisted that no Jew be allowed to set foot on Russian soil. This exclusionary policy received support from Russian merchants, whose primitive commercial culture placed them at a great disadvantage in competition with Jewish traders. Until the middle of the eighteenth century there were no Jews in Russia. This situation changed drastically in the second half of the eighteenth century, when, as a result of the partitions of Poland, Russia acquired over one million Jewish subjects. The Jews had an extremely high reproduction rate: despite the steady outflow of emigrants, at the turn of the century they constituted the single largest non-Slavic nationality in the Russian Empire. They were not only the largest Jewish community in the world but the center of rabbinical learning, Yiddish culture, and Zionism.

Catherine II tried to extend civil rights to Jews, but she had to abandon these efforts because of the hostility of the Russian merchant class and the Poles. In the early 1800s the principle was established that with minor exceptions Jews could reside only in the territories of what had been the Polish-Lithuanian Commonwealth (known as the Pale of Settlement). Furthermore, they were inscribed in the registers of the burgher estate *(mesh-chane)*, which entitled them to engage in trade and crafts, but barred them from agriculture as well as from the civil and military services. The economic situation of the Jews squeezed into the towns of the Pale of Settlement and rapidly multiplying was harsh and deteriorating: many sought to escape this hardship, as well as the pogroms that first broke out in 1881–82, by emigrating to Western Europe and the Americas. Some Jews managed to gain a foothold in the interior of Russia by qualifying for residential exemptions or bribing police officials; many others, especially youths, turned to revolutionary activity. The Imperial authorities regarded the Jews as the most dangerous ethnic group not only because of their involvement in radical movements, but also because of their resistance to assimilation, links to coreligionists abroad, and capitalist entrepreneurship, which—so the bureaucracy believed—threatened to destabilize the rural economy.

But the Jews encountered hostility not only from the Imperial authorities. In the Pale of Settlement they formed a socioeconomic group identified by its religious practices: a middle-class layer between a Catholic and Ortho-dox nobility and an Orthodox peasantry. Culturally superior to the popula-tion in the midst of which they lived by virtue of nearly universal male literacy, strong family bonds, and sobriety, they invited much envy, which created a propitious climate for the pogroms of the Civil War.

Apart from the Poles, who would be satisfied with nothing short of sovereignty within borders that extended deep into Russia, and possibly the Finns, the non-Russians did not give the Imperial authorities much trouble. What came to be known as the "nationalities problem" presented as yet more a potential than a tangible threat to the Empire's unity, in that the spread of mass education and literacy and the secularization of life had the effect of raising ethnic awareness. As a rule, the treatment of the minorities by the Imperial government stood in inverse ratio to their cultural level: the better educated they were and the higher their living standards, the more dangerous they seemed and the more carefully they were watched.

National identity among the non-Russians was stimulated by the 1905 Revolution and the constitutional regime that emerged from it. In 1905-06, the major ethnic groups convened congresses to air grievances and formu-late wants. In the electoral campaigns for parliament (Duma) many ran their own candidates. Most were affiliated with Russian parties, usually either the liberals (Constitutional-Democrats) or the socialists, but even so they had their own agendas and followed the practice of caucusing. A considerable number of Ukrainians cast ballots for the Ukrainian Socialist-Revolutionary Party (UPSR) or the Ukrainian Social-Democratic Party (USDP). Muslim Duma deputies formed a Muslim Union, which cooper-ated on legislative matters affecting their constituencies. There were na-tional parties to represent the Armenians (led by the nationalist party called Dashnaktsutiun), the Jews, and the Azeri Turks. These parties and group-ings (the Poles always excepted) confined themselves to expanding their nations' rights within the framework of a unitary Russian Empire: their leaders believed that the introduction of democracy and expanded self-government in the country at large would in and of itself satisfy their needs.

Considering the important role the nationality question was to play in the Revolution and Civil War, it may seem surprising how unaware Russians were of its existence, since even politically active intellectuals treated nation-alism and nationality as marginal matters. Behind this attitude lay a combination of historic and geographic factors. Unlike the European empires, which emerged only after national states had been put in place, the Russian Empire grew concurrently with the state: historically, the two processes were virtually indistinguishable. Furthermore, since Russia is not a maritime nation, her colonies were territorially contiguous, rather than—as was the case in Europe—separated by oceans: this geographic factor further blurred the distinction between metropolitan and Imperial possessions. To the extent that they gave the matter any thought, most educated Russians expected the minorities eventually to assimilate, and their country, like the United States, to form a single nation. The analogy had little in its favor, since unlike the United States, which, except for Native Americans and imported African slaves, consisted exclusively of voluntary migrants, the Russian Empire was made up of historic regions conquered by force of arms. But the attitude was deeply ingrained, as we have seen in the example of the White generals, who in this respect reflected public consensus.

Russian political parties treated this issue in a perfunctory manner: none was prepared even to contemplate the breakup of the Empire along ethnic lines. (The Bolshevik Party after 1913 formed an exception, but as will be indicated below, its advocacy of national self-determination was merely a tactical ploy: Lenin, too, wanted the Empire to remain intact.) The socialist parties viewed all expressions of nationalism as a legacy of capitalism, which the "ruling class" exploited to sow divisions among the masses. Liberals believed that democratization accompanied by regional autonomy would satisfy the minorities' legitimate grievances. The right-wing parties wanted "Russia One and Indivisible." The tsarist government, for its part, followed a policy of benign neglect: it dealt harshly with separatist trends, especially among the Poles, but believed that time was working in its favor and that eventually the minorities, succumbing to superior Russian political and economic power, would dissolve.

Such a policy worked as long as Russia remained relatively stable and her government exercised effective control over the country.

The nationality question arose in an acute form within days of the outbreak of the February Revolution. The collapse of tsarism gave the various ethnic groups the opportunity not only to articulate their demands, but to insist on their prompt satisfaction. Grievances that in the regions inhabited by Russian majorities assumed economic, social, or political forms, in the non-Russian regions combined in nationalism. Thus, for example, to the Kazakh-Kirghiz nomads, the Russian colonists who had taken over their grazing lands were not so much class enemies as ethnic enemies. To the Ukrainian peasants, the unwelcome prospect of having to share with Russians from the north the land acquired in 1917–18 similarly assumed ethnic forms.

The first to stir were the Ukrainians, who on March 4, 1917, formed in Kiev a regional soviet called Central Rada. Initially moderate in their demands, the Ukrainian nationalist leaders turned radical in proportion as central authority weakened. On June 10, the Rada issued a manifesto called, in remembrance of seventeenth-century proclamations of Cossack hetmans, a "Universal," in which it claimed to be the only institution entitled to speak on behalf of the Ukrainian nation: henceforth, it declared, the Ukraine would decide her own fate. The Universal presented the Provisional Government with the earliest overt challenge from an ethnic minority: for although the Rada stopped short of demanding independence, it soon set up a regional authority that for all practical purposes behaved like a sovereign body. In August 1917, the Provisional Government, by now fatally weakened, had no choice but to acknowledge the Rada's claims.

At this stage, Ukrainian separatism was largely a movement of the intelligentsia, encouraged and financially supported by the Austrians and Germans.* In the course of 1917 it acquired a mass following because of the peculiar nature of the region's land question. The southern regions of the Empire, the area of black earth, had more productive and therefore more valuable land than the Great Russian provinces. The inhabitants of the Ukraine and the Cossack Host had, therefore, no interest in participating in a nationwide distribution of privately held land, under which they would have to share the soil they obtained, or hoped to obtain, from the Revolution with the landless and land-poor communal peasants of the north. Ukrainian politicians accordingly insisted that the land distribution question be solved locally: the popular Ukrainian Socialist-Revolutionary Party advocated the creation of a Ukrainian Land Fund, which would take control of the soil in that region and distribute it for the exclusive benefit of the indigenous population.

The Muslims, too, began to organize. In March and April 1917 they held regional conferences, which culminated on May 1 in the First All-Russian Muslim Congress in Moscow. The movement was dominated by politicians close to the Russian liberals: their quarrel was not so much with the Russians as with the conservative mullahs. Inasmuch as their population was scattered, Muslim politicians advanced, as yet, no territorial claims. The Congress appointed a spiritual head to serve the Islamic population and granted women equal rights—an event without precedent in the history of Islam. On the nationality question, two trends emerged: one, dominated by the Volga Tatars, wanted cultural autonomy in a unitary Russian state; the other called for a federal solution. Submitted to a vote, the federal platform

---

*In *The Formation of the Soviet Union* I paid hardly any attention to the role of the Central Powers in the rise of nationalism among the Russian minorities during the Revolution because at the time of writing (1950–53), the German Foreign Ministry archives were unavailable to scholars. The information that has come to light since then indicates that encouraging and backing nationalism among the minorities, especially the Ukrainians and Georgians, was an essential element in the Central Powers' strategy aimed at dismembering Russia.

gained a decisive majority. The Congress established a National Central Council, or Shura, for Russia's Muslim inhabitants.

The national institutions of Muslim life soon weakened as a result of the disintegration of the state, and, in the latter part of 1917, the center of political activity shifted to the regions. In the Crimea and in Bashkiriia regional governments came into existence. The bitterest national conflict erupted in the Kazakh-Kirghiz steppe of Central Asia. Even before the Revolution, in July 1916, the Kazakh-Kirghiz revolted against the tsarist authorities in protest against orders mobilizing them for construction work in the rear—orders they saw as a violation of their traditional exemption from military service. In the ensuing violence, nearly 2,500 Russians and Cossacks lost their lives, and some 300,000 Kazakh-Kirghiz were dispossessed and forced to flee into the desert and neighboring China.[1]

A Kazakh-Kirghiz Congress met in Orenburg in April 1917. Three months later, its organizers formed a national party named Alash Orda, which called for Kazakh-Kirghiz autonomy. In reaction, local Russians and Cossacks demanded the expulsion of refugees of 1916 who had returned and claimed their lands. Semireche province, the scene of the most savage fighting between Slavs and Turks, was placed in September 1917 under martial law.

Farther to the south, in Turkestan, where Muslims outnumbered Russians, who were mostly officials and colonists, nearly 17 to 1, a Turkestan Muslim Central Committee came into being in April 1917. It lacked all authority, however, and soon dissolved, along with the nine-man Turkestan Committee, made up of five Russians and four natives, which the Provisional Government had appointed to administer the area. Here, as in Kazakhstan, Russians (along with Russified Ukrainians) of all political persuasions joined hands against their common enemy—the native Muslim population. The Congress of Soviets, which in early November carried out the Bolshevik coup in Tashkent, the capital of Turkestan, passed an extraordinary resolution that barred Muslims from serving in the soviets. In 1918–19, Central Asia would be the scene of violent clashes in which social ("class") conflicts expressed themselves mainly in national and even racial animosity.

In the Caucasus, the situation was complicated by an unusually intricate ethnic distribution, and aggravated by the intervention of the Germans and Ottoman Turks.

Politically, the Georgians were the most advanced nation in the area. Georgia was a stronghold of Social Democracy, especially Menshevism: in 1917, Georgian Marxists like Irakli Tsereteli and Nicholas Chkheidze played leading roles in the Petrograd Soviet. Georgia's national aspirations were closely linked to Russian democratic movements: the striving for independence emerged here only after the Bolshevik coup in Russia had crushed the prospect of democracy.

The majority of the estimated 3 million or more Armenians resided in the Ottoman Empire, mainly in eastern Anatolia, across the Russian frontier: about one-third lived under Russian rule. During World War I, the Turks, charging the Armenians with pro-Russian sympathies, ordered them deported from eastern Anatolia: the deportations, in 1915, assumed the form of massacres, in the course of which hundreds of thousands perished. Their situation in 1917–18 was extremely precarious, given that they were surrounded by hostile Muslims and could no longer count on Russian help. Ideally, they would have liked to come under the protection of a friendly European power; barring that, they were not averse to a Russian protectorate, even if it meant Bolshevization.

The Shiite Azeris resided partly in Iran and partly in the Russian Caucasus. They were in every respect—culturally, economically, and politically—the least developed of the Transcaucasian groups. And, finally, the Caucasian mountains were home to over one million Muslims of different ethnic and linguistic affiliations, living in villages separated by high ranges.

Compared to the rest of the Russian Empire, Transcaucasia remained relatively peaceful during 1917. As in other parts of the country, representatives of the various nationalities held discussions and issued proclamations, but there was less lawlessness. The Armenians and Georgians looked north, to Russia, for support against the Muslim majority, while the Azeri Turks, to the extent that they thought of independence, kept such ideas to themselves from fear of being charged with treasonous pro-Turkish sympathies.

As Russia dissolved, politicians representing the ethnic minorities became more assertive. The same held true of their constituencies. Returns from the elections to the Constituent Assembly, held in late November 1917, indicated that a high proportion, possibly the majority, of non-Russians voted for national tickets. Some of these continued their traditional partnership with Russian parties, but as the year drew to a close and Russian political organizations, under Bolshevik terror, disintegrated, they cut loose and turned into full-fledged nationalist parties. If early in the year the ethnic minorities wanted to assert their specific rights in a democratic Russia, later, after October, they sought to isolate themselves from the Russian dictatorship and the Civil War it unleashed.

Within days of assuming power, the Bolshevik government issued, over the signatures of Lenin and Stalin, a "Declaration of Rights" of the national minorities. It affirmed, without conditions or qualifications, that every nation had the right to self-determination up to and including separation. The Bolsheviks were the only party in Russia to advance such a drastic solution; and since it ran contrary to their centralist political philosophy, some explanation of its background is in order.[2]

In common with Marx and other socialists, Lenin favored large states over small ones, since bigger size promoted the development of capitalism, which had the effect of intensifying class conflicts. Once Communism triumphed, the greater its territory the easier would be the exercise of the "dictatorship of the proletariat." Lenin had no sympathy for nationalism in any form and was a complete stranger to the feelings of both patriotism and xenophobia. He desired the most rapid assimilation of the non-Russian nations, for which reason he rejected all solutions to the nationality problem that institutionalized ethnic differences. The programs most in vogue among Social-Democrats in the early years of the century were either "extraterritorial national-cultural autonomy" or federalism. The former, formulated by the Austrian socialists Karl Renner and Otto Bauer as a way of preserving the political integrity of the Hapsburg Empire, called for granting minority citizens the right to an education in their native languages and to other cultural activities regardless of where they happened to reside. This program appealed to many socialists because it satisfied what they considered the legitimate demands of the minorities, thus defusing national antagonisms, without causing the empire to disintegrate. Lenin, however, rejected this formula, because it perpetuated and even strengthened the cultural differences among the minorities. He liked no better the federalist solution and for the same reason. He wanted assimilation, but he realized that tactically it was an unacceptable slogan, since it was certain to alienate from the Bolsheviks one-half of Russia's population.

His solution, formulated in 1913, was to redefine the vague slogan of "national self-determination" of the Social-Democratic platform to mean one and one thing only: separation from Russia. Every ethnic group was entitled to independent statehood, if such was its desire. If it did not choose to avail itself of this right, it could claim no special privileges within the unitary Russian state. When his followers objected that his program would Balkanize Russia, Lenin responded with two counterarguments. First, capitalism had promoted the economic interdependence of the regions of the Russian Empire to such an extent that it was highly unlikely any of the borderlands would choose separation. Secondly, the right to national self-determination had to be understood as subordinated to that of "proletarian self-determination." By this he meant that even if, contrary to his expectations, in disregard of economic realities, some or even all of the borderland areas chose to leave Russia, a Bolshevik government would have the right to bring them back into the fold. Thus, an extremely liberal policy on the nationalities promised substantial advantages—the support of the ethnic groups—without carrying any risks.

Events disappointed Lenin's expectations and forced him to renege on the promise of self-determination. Some of the areas once part of the Russian Empire were in late 1917 under German occupation, and since it was German policy to dismember the Empire, Berlin encouraged them to proclaim sovereignty. On December 6, 1917 (NS), Finland, which had German military contingents on her soil, declared independence. Next came Lithuania (December 11, NS), followed by Latvia (January 12, 1918, NS). Estonia broke away in February 1918. At Brest-Litovsk in early 1918, the Central Powers recognized the Ukraine as a sovereign nation and signed a separate peace treaty with her. Under German pressure, Moscow was compelled to initiate negotiations leading to diplomatic recognition of the Ukraine. When, in January–February 1918, the Bolsheviks advanced on Kiev in disregard of their pledges, the Germans marched in and forced them to withdraw. From then until the end of the year, when the German army evacuated, the Ukraine was nominally a separate political entity under German occupation.

Elsewhere in what had been the Russian Empire the centrifugal tendencies were impelled mainly by the desire to escape the Bolshevik regime. How influential this consideration was may be seen on the example of Russian Siberia, which in the spring of 1918 declared independence while expressing the hope that someday she would reunite with the Russian homeland.[3]

Transcaucasia separated herself from Russia in early 1918, largely under the influence of the Germans and Turks. As the Russian front in the Caucasus crumbled and the Turkish armies advanced, the Georgians, Armenians, and Azerbaijanis agreed to create a regional authority. On November 11 (OS), two weeks after the Bolsheviks had taken power in Petrograd, they formed a Transcaucasian Commissariat, which served as a de facto government for the region without, as yet, claiming sovereignty. Urged by the Turks, who saw this area as their proper sphere of influence, and behind them, the Germans, on April 22, 1918, the Commissariat proclaimed an independent Transcaucasian federation. It was by its very nature a transient arrangement, given that the three principal nationalities here had little in common save territorial proximity.

In Central Asia, separatist movements were aborted by the Russian inhabitants, who established something akin to colonial ascendancy, which the Muslims were too weak to challenge. These Russians remained loyal to Moscow no matter who was in charge there.

In early 1918, Lenin confronted a situation he had neither desired nor foreseen. The empire had fallen apart. The slogan of "national self-determination" not only failed to persuade the nationalities to support his regime, but gave them a legitimate excuse to go their own way. On every occasion when able, he dispatched pro-Bolshevik armies to topple the newly formed nationalist regimes: in the Ukraine, Belorussia, Finland, and the Baltics. He did not always succeed in reconquering them, but when he failed it was not for want of trying.

What was he to do? Lenin, who had no difficulty changing tactics when necessary, decided now to abandon—in effect, though not in name—the principle of national self-determination in favor of federalism.

It was to be not genuine federalism, under which the member states are equal and endowed with powers over their territory, but a peculiar species of pseudo-federalism that provided neither equality nor power. Under the regime he had established in Russia, state (governmental) authority nominally derived from a hierarchy of democratically elected soviets. In reality, the soviets were only a facade to conceal the true sovereign, the Communist Party. This arrangement proved adaptable to dealing with the nationalities. Once they were reconquered and reincorporated into the new, Soviet empire, they could be granted the semblance of statehood, given that their governmental institutions, too, would be controlled ("paralyzed" was the word Lenin used) by the Russian Communist Party. And as for the Party, Lenin did not intend to divide it along ethnic lines. The result would be formal federalism, with all the trimmings of statehood, presumably able to satisfy the aspirations of the non-Russian peoples, concealing a rigidly centralized dictatorship centered in Moscow. It is this model that Lenin adopted and in 1922–24 incorporated in the constitution of the new state, the Union of Soviet Socialist Republics. He assumed that as other countries went Communist, they would join the U.S.S.R. on the same principles.

Once the Germans had lost the war and evacuated the Ukraine, the puppet government of Hetman Skoropadski, which they had installed, collapsed and vanished (December 1918). The Ukraine became the arena of bloody struggles involving Ukrainian nationalists, Cossack brigands under contending warlords, Communists, "Greens," and, eventually, the Volunteer Army. The year 1919 was a period of violent anarchy:

> The entire territory fell apart into innumerable regions isolated from each other and the rest of the world, dominated by armed bands of peasants or freebooters who looted and murdered with utter impunity. In Kiev itself governments came and went, edicts were issued, cabinet crises were resolved, diplomatic talks were carried on—but the rest of the country lived its own existence where the only effective regime was that of the gun. None of the authorities which claimed the Ukraine during the year following the deposition of Skoropadski ever exercised actual sovereignty.[4]

After briefly joining forces against Skoropadski, the Communists and Ukrainian nationalists turned enemies. The leading Ukrainian political-military force, the Directory under Semen Petlura, installed itself in Kiev. Moscow pitted against him the Communist Party of the Ukraine (KPbU), a branch of the Russian Communist Party, composed of a mixture of Ukrainians and Russians loyal to Moscow but in favor of a limited degree of self-government. Late in November 1918, on orders from Moscow, the KPbU proclaimed a rival government, headed by G. L. Piatakov. Its military arm, made up of units of the Red Army and brigand bands that joined the Communists, took to the field against the Directory: in January it occupied Kharkov, and in February, Kiev. Defeated, the Directory withdrew to the western part of the Ukraine.

The Communist government, whose base of support was exclusively urban, turned out to be no more able to administer than its predecessor. Soon its partisan allies (Makhno, Zelenyi, Grigorev) abandoned it in favor of brigandage and anti-Jewish pogroms.

When in the summer of 1919 the Volunteer Army and its Cossacks moved into the Ukraine, the Communists proved powerless to stop it. In August and September, the eastern and central regions of the Ukraine fell under the control of Denikin, while its western areas were in the hands of the Poles and Petlura. Ukrainian Communists fled to Moscow.

What ensued would be repeated time and again in the relations between the Communist leadership and its non-Russian followers. In principle, Communists active outside Russia acknowledged the need for centralized control and for following orders from the capital. In practice, they resented the wrongheaded orders that Moscow, unfamiliar with local conditions, often issued. They demanded to be heard. Moscow, convinced that its regional agents did not see the whole picture and scornful of their inability to hold on to power, ignored them. The result was conflict that invariably ended with Moscow removing such troublesome proxies on grounds of nationalism and replacing them with more pliable agents. The phenomenon that came to be known as "Titoism" after World War II appeared in the Communist movement inside Soviet Russia as early as 1919. It was inherent in the contradiction between the goals of a centralized movement with global aspirations and the infinitely complex reality that required adjustments to local conditions and therefore a measure of decentralization.

The deposed officials of the KPbU split between "centralists" and "federalists." The latter wanted a new party, allied with radical Ukrainian nationalists, which would have considerable discretion in making decisions affecting the Ukraine. Moscow treated this trend as a deviation and backed the "centralists." It dissolved the Central Committee of the KPbU and formed a new organ staffed with subservient personnel. It is this group that, in late 1919, after the defeat of Denikin, took charge of the Soviet Ukrainian Republic. The area was considered exceptionally hostile to Soviet authority and Moscow endowed the Cheka with extensive arbitrary powers to subdue local "kulaks" and "bandits."[5]

The Bolsheviks had virtually no following among the Muslim intelligentsia, which was minuscule to begin with and which, insofar as it inclined toward socialism, showed a preference for the Mensheviks and Socialists-Revolutionaries. For this reason Moscow made friendly approaches to the

21. Stalin in Tsaritsyn, 1918.

leaders of the all-Russian Muslim movement even though it knew them to be far from sympathetic to its objectives. In his capacity as Commissar of Nationalities, Stalin made generous offers to Muslim politicians to work with the Soviet government. When they refused to collaborate, their organization was dissolved. The new regime now concentrated on gaining the support of individual Muslim intellectuals. The few who did go over found employment in the Muslim Commissariat, a department of the Commissariat of Nationalities, with the mission of spreading Communism to Muslims in Russia and abroad.

When efforts to unite Russian Muslims had collapsed and the all-Russian Muslim organization was dissolved, the movement fell apart along territorial lines: unity yielded to regionalism. Attempts to create Islamic republics were made in Tatarstan and Bashkiriia, Kirghiziia (Kazakhstan), Turkestan, and Azerbaijan.*

The Bashkir region was inhabited by semi-nomadic herdsmen whose spokesman in 1917 was Zeki Validov, a 27-year-old teacher. Commanding a small army, Validov joined the Whites, but disappointed with Kolchak's treatment of the minorities, in February 1919 he defected with his troops to the Red Army. As a reward, he secured the pledge of an autonomous republic for his people. His partnership with the Communists also ran into trouble, in part because the Bashkirs interpreted it as giving them license to

*The Azerbaijani Republic will be discussed in connection with events in Transcaucasia.

expel Russian settlers, and in part because they mistakenly interpreted autonomy to mean independence. Both the Communist Party and the soviets on Bashkir territory were staffed by Russians, who sided with the settlers and opposed Bashkir autonomy as a matter of principle. In May 1920, after Moscow had made public a decree regulating Bashkir self-government that Validov saw as a violation of previous commitments, the entire Bashkir government fled to the Ural mountains. Russian workers and peasants eagerly joined punitive detachments to fight the Bashkir rebels. The new government of Baskiriia installed in the summer of 1920 had in it no natives.*

The neighboring Tatars, wealthier and better educated than the Bashkirs, had ambitious visions of a Volga-Ural (Idel-Ural) Republic embracing Bashkiriia. Moscow rejected these plans and after long and complicated intrigues, agreed to the establishment of a Tatar Autonomous Republic. Similar arrangements were made for the Chuvash, Mari, and Votiak peoples, who were accorded the status of autonomous "Regions" with even less authority.

Central (or Inner) Asia comprised two geographic zones, differing in economic conditions and demographic structure. The northern steppe zone was a grassy plain populated by Kazakh-Kirghiz whose principal occupation was raising sheep and cattle. The political party representing Kazakh-Kirghiz interests, Alash Orda, like the Bashkirs, initially cooperated with the Whites and then switched sides. Moscow promised it autonomy, but in this instance, too, its pledges were sabotaged by Russian settlers and urban inhabitants who refused to treat the natives as equals. Kazakh-Kirghiz protests to Moscow yielded few results and the Kirghiz Autonomous Republic, established in October 1920, was theirs only in name.† On the critical issue of land, Moscow promised to stop further colonization but to allow Slavic settlers to keep their possessions, including land they had seized from the natives in 1916 and 1917.

The southern region of Central Asia, Turkestan, was largely desert, interspersed with cities and fertile valleys. The indigenous population here was partly Persian, partly Turkic, and partly a mixture of the two. The Slavic inhabitants consisted mostly of government officials, merchants, and military personnel, nearly all living in cities. Tsarist Russia administered this region, in many respects similar to British Egypt, as a colony, principally valuable as a supplier of cotton and as an outpost for future incursions into Afghanistan and India. It tolerated two self-governing protectorates, the khanate of Khiva and the emirate of Bukhara, bastions of Muslim fundamentalism.

---

*Validov fled to Central Asia, where he joined anti-Communist partisans, and after the rebellion's suppression, to Europe. Turning scholar, he became professor of Turcology at the University of Istanbul under the name Zeki Velidi Togan.

†It was later renamed the Kazakh Republic. The modern Kirghiz Republic was formed in 1924 from parts of Turkestan.

Land here was not an issue. The potential conflict concerned foreign rule of a population that was much more committed to Islam than that of the Volga-Ural region or the steppe.

In the latter part of 1917, two governments emerged in Turkestan: a Soviet one in Tashkent, the region's capital; and a Muslim one in Kokand. The former had the support of virtually the entire Russian population, regardless of social or economic status. Here more than in any other part of the onetime Russian Empire, social conflicts assumed ethnic forms.

In mid-November 1917 the Bolsheviks and Left SRs convened in Tashkent a Regional Congress of Soviets that declared Turkestan to be under Soviet rule. In discussing the role of the native population, the Congress by substantial majorities not only rejected the idea of Turkestani autonomy, but barred Muslims, who constituted 97 percent of the area's population (1913),[6] from participating in Soviet institutions. The relevant resolution read as follows:

> At the present time one cannot permit the admission of Muslims into the higher organs of regional revolutionary authority, because the attitude of the local population toward the Soviet of Soldiers', Workers', and Peasant Deputies is quite uncertain, and because the native inhabitants lack the proletarian organizations that the [Bolshevik] faction could welcome into the organ of the higher regional government.[7]

The Communist historian G. Safarov has quite properly defined the course of events in Turkestan in 1917–18 a "colonial revolution."

To protest their treatment, Muslim political figures withdrew to Kokand in the Ferghana valley, populated almost exclusively by Muslims, where they felt secure from the pro-Bolshevik Russians. Here, at the end of November, they proclaimed Turkestan an autonomous region "united with the Russian democratic federative republic." The nature of this autonomy was left to the All-Russian Constituent Assembly to determine. A Provisional Government was created in which two-thirds of the seats were allocated to Muslims, and one-third to Russians.

These actions the Bolshevik and pro-Bolshevik elements in Tashkent would not tolerate. In mid-February, they dispatched a detachment of Russian soldiers accompanied by Austrian and German POWs to Kokand. The invading force made short shrift of the defenders, following which its troops were given license to loot and kill. Before withdrawing, they poured gasoline over the city and burned most of it to the ground.

Moscow, in receipt of disquieting reports from Turkestan, intervened. On its orders, in April 1918, local Communists proclaimed the region an autonomous republic. However, this was a mere formality, because being cut off from the Center by the White armies and therefore free of the Center, they continued to act as they had before. Tashkent next tried to conquer the emirate of Bukhara (March 1918), but its fanatical inhabitants beat off the invasion.

The colonial practices of the small Russian minority, which not only dominated the native population but excluded it from any voice in government, produced a regime described by a Communist eyewitness and historian as "feudal exploitation of the broad masses of the native population by the Russian Red Army man, colonist, and official."[8] It sparked a native revolt that began in the Ferghana valley and thence spread to the rest of Turkestan. The Turkic guerrillas, known as Basmachis, were independent bands, nearly always on horseback, not unlike those operating in the Ukraine at the same time, and like them combining brigandage with opposition to Russian rule.

It was only in 1919 that Moscow was able to impose its will on Turkestan. Yielding to its demands, local Russians allowed the natives to reopen their bazaars and invited them to join both the Communist Party and state institutions. These concessions in some measure mollified the natives and took some wind out of the Basmachi movement, but not for long. Once the Communists were firmly in the saddle, following the defeat of Kolchak, they introduced a regime of food expropriations and a variety of other measures that the native population resented, not so much on ethnic as on economic grounds. The Basmachi movement flared up anew, reaching its apogee in the years 1920–22. It was fully suppressed only at the end of the decade.

In February 1920 the Red Army captured Khiva. The fate of Bukhara was left to the discretion of Mikhail Frunze, the commander of the Turkestani Red Army.[9] He attacked in the fall and captured the city in fierce fighting. In both instances, the invaders availed themselves of the help of fifth columns made up of radical youths ("Young Khivans" and "Young Bukharans"). The emir of Bukhara fled to Afghanistan. The conquests gained new recruits for the Basmachis.

The treatment of Asians by pro-Bolshevik Russians led the most prominent Soviet Muslim Communist to revise the orthodox Marxist theory of class struggle. The Tatar Mirza Sultan-Galiev was in his youth a teacher in the reformed schools. In late 1917 he went over to the Communists and made a rapid career as Stalin's protégé in the Commissariat of Nationalities.[10] In articles published toward the end of 1919 in the official organ of his Commissariat, Sultan-Galiev argued that it was a fundamental mistake to rely on the West to bring about a global revolution because the weakest link in the chain of imperialism lay in Asia. This view was tolerable to the Kremlin since it did not contradict Lenin's theory of imperialism. But Sultan-Galiev did not stop there, and broadened his ideas into a full-fledged heresy in which some historians see an anticipation of Maoism.[11] He developed doubts whether even if the revolution in the industrialized countries were to succeed, it would improve the condition of colonial peoples. The

22. Sultan-Galiev.

Western working class was interested not in abolishing colonialism but in turning it to its own advantage. "We assert," he is quoted as saying,

> that the formula that offers the replacement of the worldwide dictatorship of one class of European society (the bourgeoisie) with another (the proletariat), that is, with another European class, will not bring about a major change in the social life of the oppressed element of mankind. At any rate, such a change, even if it were to occur, would be not for the better but for the worse. . . . In contradistinction to this we advance another thesis: that the material premises for the social transformation of mankind can be created only through the establishment of the dictatorship of the colonies and semi-colonies over the metropolitan areas.*

To implement his ideas, Sultan-Galiev called for the creation of a "Colonial International" to counterbalance the Communist International, dominated by Europeans; he also urged the establishment of a Muslim Communist Party. For these ideas, in April 1923 he was expelled from the Party and imprisoned on charges of forming an illegal nationalistic organization.[12] L. Kamenev called him the earliest victim of a Stalinist purge. Released after he had "repented," he was rearrested in 1928 and perished either in the 1930s or during World War II.

*Cited in A. Arsharuni and Kh. Gabidullin, *Ocherki panislamizma i pantiurkizma v Rossii* ([Moscow], 1931), 78–79. These quotations are known only from Stalinist histories and therefore cannot be taken entirely at face value.

In 1918, the Caucasus was under the influence of the Central Powers. The Germans were interested in Georgia with its rich manganese deposits, as well as Baku, the center of Russia's petroleum production. Some of them, notably General Ludendorff, entertained visions of Georgia serving as the nucleus of a German-dominated "Caucasus Bloc."[13] The Turks, too, had ambitions in this region, especially in Azerbaijan, whose population was ethnically and linguistically related to them. The Caucasus probably would have been occupied by the Turks, who advanced into it in the spring of 1918, had it not been for German involvement. Promised German protection, the Georgians seceded from the Transcaucasian Federation on May 26, 1918, and proclaimed independence. Two days later the Azerbaijanis and Armenians followed suit.

The Turks occupied Baku in September. They soon clashed with the Azerbaijan government, which was dominated by socialists of the Mussavat party advocating a radical land reform, and made themselves generally unpopular with the population. Following the Armistice in the West, the Turks evacuated Baku, which was occupied by a small British expeditionary force.

The Armenian Republic was in dire straits, crowded with refugees fleeing Turkish and Azeri pogroms, and diplomatically isolated: unlike the Azeris, who had the Turks, and the Georgians, who were on friendly terms with the Germans, the Armenians had no one to fall back on. General Denikin, who was at odds with Georgia and Azerbaijan, was their only friend, but he was in no position to help. Very unwisely, the Armenian government in May 1919 occupied and annexed territories in eastern Anatolia, which, prior to the massacres of 1915, had been inhabited by an Armenian majority. This action ensured the hostility of the new national government of Turkey led by Mustafa Kemal (Atatürk) and intensified Armenia's isolation.

Georgia was the most successful of the three successor states to the Transcaucasian Federation. From May to November 1918, the country lived under de facto German occupation, which provided a degree of stability. The government, headed by Noi Zhordaniia, was run by Mensheviks, better educated and with greater international connections than neighboring Azerbaijan and Armenia. Enforcing a land reform program, it expropriated properties in excess of forty acres: these it subdivided and either leased or sold to farmers. It also nationalized large industries and transport. In consequence of these socialist measures, in 1920, 90 percent of Georgia's workers were employed in state or cooperative enterprises. Tiflis had serious difficulties with several minorities, notably the Ossetians and Abkhazians, whose claims to self-government Tiflis refused to acknowledge. But, on balance, during her three years of independence, Georgia proved herself capable of statehood.

In the winter of 1919–20, as the White Army of the south was in headlong flight, the Allied Supreme Council in Paris granted the three Transcaucasian republics de facto recognition. It rejected, however, their petition for a League of Nations mandate; the United States Congress, for its part, rejected a bill submitted by President Wilson calling for an American mandate over Armenia. Following the withdrawal of British units from Baku (August 1919), therefore, Transcaucasia faced the prospect of a Communist invasion.

Moscow had never given up its claims to this region, which before the Revolution had provided Russia with two-thirds of her petroleum, three-quarters of her manganese, and one-fourth of her copper, as well as a high share of her subtropical produce (fruits, tobacco, tea, and wine). The reconquest was carried out in two stages—April 1920 and February 1921—accomplished by highly perfected tactics that combined external aggression with internal subversion. The critical factor that enabled Soviet Russia to reassert dominion over this region was diplomatic. Moscow secured the friendly neutrality of Kemal Atatürk, who depended on it for support against the Allied powers.* Kemal disavowed any pan-Turkic or pan-Islamic aspirations and, in exchange for Moscow's pledge to refrain from Communist agitation in his country, acquiesced to Russia's reconquest of the Caucasus. Russo-Turkish collaboration doomed the independent republics; Allied lack of interest sealed their fate.

Preparations for the Caucasian campaign got underway after March 17, 1920, when Lenin ordered the capture of Azerbaijan and Georgia.[14] The following month, the Central Committee of the Russian Communist Party created a Caucasian Bureau (the Kavbiuro), headed by a close friend of Stalin's, the Georgian Sergo Ordzhonikidze, to establish Soviet rule in the Caucasus and to extend assistance to "anti-imperialist" forces in the Middle East. The Kavbiuro worked closely with the staff of the Eleventh Red Army, which was to carry out the operation. It worked out a detailed plan of power seizure in the three republics involving regular military units, partisan detachments, and internal subversion.[15]

Azerbaijan was the first to fall. At noon on April 27, the Central Committee of the Azerbaijani Communist Party handed the Baku government an ultimatum to surrender power within twelve hours. Before the time was up, the Eleventh Red Army crossed the border and advanced on the Azerbaijani capital; other Communist units occupied strategic points in Baku. The next day, unopposed, the Eleventh Army entered the city. Ordzhonikidze, who arrived the next day with his deputy, Sergei Kirov, introduced a reign of terror that was to typify his methods of rule in the region. Defiance of Soviet occupation in the provinces was brutally suppressed. Ordzhonikidze arrested and executed a number of Azerbaijani leaders, including the Prime Minister and the Chief of Staff of the deposed government.

*See below, Chapter 4.

23. Ordzhonikidze.

Without stopping in Baku, the Eleventh Army continued the offensive, advancing on Erevan and Tiflis. On May 4, Ordzhonikidze cabled Lenin and Stalin that he expected to be in Tiflis no later than May 12.[16] But this was not to be, because at this very time a Polish-Ukrainian army, which on April 25 had invaded the Soviet Ukraine, was menacing Kiev. The situation was threatening and Moscow decided to suspend operations in Trans-caucasia. On May 4, Lenin sent Ordzhonikidze a cable instructing him to pull back the Red Army troops that had penetrated Georgia.[17] Thanks to the Russo-Polish war, Georgia and Armenia were given a temporary reprieve. On May 7, the Soviet government signed a treaty with Georgia in which it recognized Georgia's independence and pledged to refrain from interfering in her internal affairs. In a secret clause, Georgia consented to legalize the Communist Party.[18] Moscow appointed as its envoy to Tiflis Sergei Kirov, Ordzhonikidze's deputy, who calmly proceeded to lay the groundwork for the future conquest of Georgia. The following month, Moscow recognized the independence of Armenia within the boundaries of the pre-1914 Erevan province. Here, too, the Soviet mission, headed by Boris Legran, served as the headquarters of Communist subversion.

The campaign against the Caucasus resumed in December 1920, by which time the conflict with Poland was over and the last White forces had evacuated.

The Sovietization of Armenia occurred as a result of her unresolved territorial dispute with Turkey over eastern Anatolia, parts of which the Allied powers at Sèvres had assigned to her but the Armenians had occupied. In late September 1920 the Turks invaded. The tide of battle soon turned in the latter's favor and the Armenians had to sue for peace. In negotiations held in November, the Turks demanded that the Armenians surrender to them the seized territories.

Moscow lost no time in taking advantage of Armenia's predicament. On November 27, Lenin and Stalin communicated with Ordzhonikidze, instructing him to move into Armenia.[19] The move was intended to stop the Turkish advance. Two days later, the Soviet diplomatic mission in Erevan presented the Armenian government with an ultimatum calling for the immediate transfer of authority to a "Revolutionary Committee of the Soviet Socialist Republic of Armenia" located in Soviet Azerbaijan. Concurrently, the Red Eleventh Army marched into Armenia. The invasion was welcomed by the Armenian government and population alike as offering protection from the Turks. In December Armenia became a Soviet Republic; its first government was a coalition of Communists and representatives of Armenia's governing party, the Dashnaktsutiun.

Georgia was surrounded. Under the terms of the treaty signed with Moscow in May, Tiflis released from prison nearly one thousand Communists held on charges of armed rebellion. They promptly resumed preparations for a coup under the direction of Kirov, who maintained relentless pressure on the Georgian government with constant accusations that it was violating the terms of the treaty. The leading Georgian Communist Philip Makharadze admitted years later that the Party was fully preoccupied with preparing an armed uprising.[20] Ordzhonikidze was burning with impatience to enter his homeland as its conqueror: Georgian intelligence reported as early as December 9 that Soviet troops in Azerbaijan and Armenia were preparing, without Moscow's knowledge, to invade.[21] A meeting of local Communists and military commanders, convened in Baku on December 15 on the initiative of the Kavbiuro, decided on immediate action. As soon as he learned of this decision, Lenin ordered it canceled at once. Chicherin cabled Kirov on December 18 that the Politburo was determined to conduct a peaceful policy in the Caucasus, and that its decision was binding on all, Georgian Communists included.[22]

Moscow hesitated because it was in receipt of conflicting military assessments and inhibited by considerations of international diplomacy. The Commander of the Eleventh Army, Anatolii Gekker, sent Moscow an assessment, which the Georgians intercepted, stating that the invasion had every chance of success provided the Turks remained neutral.[23] This was not the view of his superior, S. S. Kamenev, the Commander in Chief of the Red Army, who submitted to Lenin three reports in which he raised troubling questions about the proposed operation. In the last of these, dated February 14, 1921, when the invasion of Georgia was already underway, he emphasized that the Eleventh Army was severely depleted by desertions and could not be reinforced any time soon because troops were needed to suppress revolts raging throughout Russia. He also pointed to the risk of both Allied and Turkish intervention on Georgia's side. On these grounds, he recommended against proceeding with the operation. He further expressed displeasure with the habit of the Caucasian army to take independent decisions capable of embroiling the country in unpredictable difficulties.[24]

Foreign policy considerations also mitigated against an invasion of Georgia. At the beginning of 1921, the Politburo, faced with a collapse of the economy and widespread peasant unrest, was contemplating a major shift in economic policy from "War Communism," or forced socialization, to a more liberal course. An essential element in economic reconstruction was foreign credits and investments. Lenin feared—unnecessarily as it turned out—that a military conflict in the Caucasus could jeopardize Russia's chances of receiving such assistance, especially since he could not be certain of Britain's reaction.

Faced with the threat of invasion, the Georgian government split between those who opposed any concessions to Moscow and wanted to seek a counterweight in Turkey, and those, headed by President Zhordaniia, who thought some kind of accommodation with Moscow possible.[25] In any event, in view of menacing concentrations of Red Army troops along Georgia's frontier with Azerbaijan and Armenia, Tiflis ordered a partial mobilization. It had little hope that foreign powers would come to Georgia's aid. The leaders of the Second (Socialist) International, who hailed Georgia as the only truly socialist country in the world, gave her much favorable publicity: in September 1920, a delegation of its luminaries, including Karl Kautsky, Emile Vandervelde, and Ramsay MacDonald, visited Georgia and returned very favorably impressed. But the Second International had neither a government nor an army. On January 27, 1921, the Supreme Allied Council accorded Georgia de jure recognition, but this step, too, had little concrete significance. Archival documents show that Britain, the only power able to prevent a Soviet invasion, was unwilling to commit herself and treated Georgia's fall as inevitable.[26]

Georgia might have survived but for the relentless pressure on Lenin by Stalin, Ordzhonikidze, and Kirov, the latter two of whom came to Moscow on January 2, 1921, to make a personal appeal in favor of immediate action. In a memorandum submitted on that day they argued for the immediate "sovietization" of Georgia on the grounds that the Menshevik republic served the cause of the counterrevolution, had an adverse influence on Soviet Armenia, helped strengthen Turkey's position in the Caucasus, and endangered the whole Soviet position in the area. "One cannot hope for an internal explosion. Without our help Georgia cannot be sovietized. . . . As a motive, one can raise an uprising in Abkhazia, Adzhariia, etc.," they wrote.[27] In a note of January 4, Stalin supported these arguments: Lenin jotted down on Stalin's letter, "Do not postpone."[28] A critical factor in overcoming his hesitation is said to have been a confidential assurance given by Lloyd George to Leonid Krasin, the head of the Soviet trade mission to England, that Britain considered the Caucasus to lie in the Soviet sphere of influence and had no plans to intervene militarily on its behalf.[29]

On January 26, the Plenum of the Central Committee of the Russian Communist Party adopted a complicated resolution drafted by Lenin that called for pressure on Georgia, and if that did not yield satisfactory results, for the Eleventh Army to march in.[30] This, the last Soviet territorial conquest until 1939, followed what by now had become a classic pattern. First came a "rebellion" of the disaffected masses. It was staged by the Kavbiuro on the night of February 11–12 in Borchalo, a region contested between Georgia and Armenia. Military "help," however, was delayed for nearly a week due to Lenin's continued hesitations. Finally, on February 14, Lenin agreed to the invasion but still in a rather qualified manner. On February 14, the Politburo approved Lenin's orders to Ordzhonikidze. Lenin wrote that the Central Committee was "inclined" to permit the Eleventh Army to march into Georgia provided its Revolutionary Military Committee guaranteed success.[31] S. S. Kamenev was not shown the dispatch and Trotsky, who was absent from Moscow, was not informed.[32]

On February 15, Ordzhonikidze sent Stalin a coded message in Georgian: "The situation demands we begin immediately. In the morning we cross [the frontier]. There is no other way out."[33] On February 16, units of the Eleventh Army penetrated the southeastern frontier of Georgia from Azerbaijan and headed directly for Tiflis, 80 kilometers away. They were assisted by cavalry of the Thirteenth Army under Budennyi. The invading force numbered over 100,000 professionally led and fully equipped troops, more than double the defending force, which lacked artillery. The Georgians fought bravely and managed for over a week to hold at bay a greatly superior enemy. In the end they succumbed, and on February 25, Red troops entered Tiflis. The Menshevik government intended to make a stand in western Georgia, but this was prevented by an invasion of Turkish troops, who on February 23 presented it with an ultimatum demanding the surrender of Batum. On March 18 the Georgians capitulated to the Red Army, signing an accord with it which ensured that Batum would remain Georgian. The same day the Georgian Government embarked on an Italian ship bound for Europe.

When asked about the invasion, Lenin on February 28 disclaimed any knowledge of it.[34] So did the Soviet envoy in Tiflis, who said that as far as he knew the conflict was one between Georgia and Armenia over Borchalo. In the West, some outrage was voiced, but the fall of Georgia was accepted as a fait accompli.

Even after the optimists had proven correct, Lenin worried about the consequences of Georgia's "sovietization." He had a high opinion of the popularity of the fallen Menshevik government, and correspondingly low esteem for Ordzhonikidze's diplomatic skills and tact. He urged Ordzhonikidze to be prepared to make far-reaching concessions to the Georgian intelligentsia and petty bourgeoisie, and to seek a political compromise with Zhordaniia and his fellow Mensheviks.[35] Lenin also impressed on him the necessity of displaying utmost discretion in dealings with Georgian Communists. This advice Ordzhonikidze and his Moscow patron, Stalin, chose to ignore, igniting conflicts with both the population at large and local Communists that before long would precipitate a major crisis in the Communist Party.

Soviet Russia had now acquired the boundaries that she would retain until 1939. Formally composed of six sovereign republics, she was a constitutional anomaly, since neither the relations among her constituent republics nor the role of the Russian Communist Party in the new multinational state were even approximately defined. The structure of the new state, from which emerged the Union of Soviet Socialist Republics, was conclusively formulated in 1922–23. It would become one of the subjects of violent disagreement between the dying Lenin and the rising Stalin.

4

Communism for Export

During the five years when Lenin was in charge, the foreign policy of Soviet Russia was an adjunct of the policies of the Russian Communist Party. As such, it was intended to serve, first and foremost, the interests of the global socialist revolution. It cannot be stressed strongly enough and often enough that the Bolsheviks seized power not to change Russia but to use Russia as a springboard for a world revolution, a fact that their foreign failures and subsequent concentration on building "socialism in one country" tend to obscure. "We assert," Lenin said in May 1918, "that the interests of socialism, the interests of world socialism are superior to national interests, to the interests of the state."[1] But inasmuch as Soviet Russia was the first, and, for a long time, the only Communist country in the world, the Bolsheviks came to regard the interests of Russia as identical with those of Communism. And once the expectations of an imminent global revolution receded, they assigned the interests of Soviet Russia the highest priority: for, after all, Communism in Russia was a reality, whereas everywhere else it was but a hope.

As the government of a country that had its own national interests and, at the same time, served as the headquarters of a supranational revolution, a cause that knew no boundaries, the Bolshevik regime developed a two-tiered foreign policy. The Commissariat of Foreign Relations, acting in the name of Soviet Russia, maintained formally correct relations with those foreign states that were prepared to have dealings with it. The task of promoting the global revolution was consigned to a new body, the Third or Communist International (Comintern), founded in March 1919. Formally, the Comintern was independent of both the Soviet government and the Russian Communist Party; in reality it was a department of the latter's Central Committee. The official separation of the two entities deceived few who cared to know, but it enabled Moscow to conduct a policy of concurrent détente and subversion.

The Bolsheviks insisted with a monotony suggestive of sincerity that if their revolution was to survive it had to spread abroad. This belief they reluctantly abandoned only around 1921, when repeated failures to export revolution persuaded them there would be no repetition of October 1917, at any rate for a long time to come. Until then they encouraged, incited, and organized revolutionary movements wherever the opportunity presented itself. To this end, they formed a network of foreign Communist parties by replicating the tactics Lenin had employed in the early 1900s to create the Bolshevik party, that is, by splitting Social-Democratic organizations and detaching from them the most radical elements. Simultaneously, Moscow negotiated with foreign governments for diplomatic recognition and economic aid.

The Bolsheviks had greater success in winning recognition than in exporting revolution. By the spring of 1921, the major European powers had established commercial ties with Soviet Russia, which were soon followed by diplomatic relations. Every attempt to spread revolution abroad, however, miscarried because of inadequate popular support and repression. On balance, therefore, Lenin's foreign policy failed. His inability to merge Russia with the economically and culturally more advanced countries of the West virtually ensured that she would eventually revert to her own autocratic and bureaucratic traditions. It made all but inevitable the triumph of Stalinism.

Lenin's one foreign policy success was to exploit for his own ends diverse groups abroad, ranging from Communists and fellow-travelers to conservatives and isolationists, which for one reason or another wanted to normalize relations with the Soviet regime and opposed intervention on behalf of the Whites. The "hands off Russia" slogan robbed the White armies of more effective aid from the West.

Lenin first tried to export revolution in the winter of 1918–19 to Finland and the Baltic republics: in Finland by means of a coup, in the Baltic countries, by means of an invasion. Strictly speaking, neither attempt was intervention, however, inasmuch as the four countries involved had been part of the Russian Empire.

In October–November 1918, when the Central Powers sued for peace, the Bolsheviks felt the hour they had been waiting for had arrived. The collapse of Germany and Austria had caused a political vacuum to emerge in the center of Europe: accompanied as it was by economic breakdown and social unrest, it seemed to provide an ideal breeding ground for revolution. The radical upheavals that shook Germany at the end of October and early November 1918—the mutiny of the fleet, the revolts in Berlin and other cities—while not directed from Soviet Russia were clearly inspired by her example. And yet, despite the role played by the proto-Communist Spartacus League and the importation of such Russian institutions as the soviets, the November revolution in Germany was not a Bolshevik one, since it was primarily directed against the monarchy and the war: "notwithstanding all the socialist appearance . . . it was a bourgeois revolution," that is, an analogue of the Russian February rather than October Revolution. The "Congress of Soviets" that convened in Berlin on November 10, 1918, and proclaimed the establishment of a "Soviet Government," was not even socialist in composition.[2]

In October 1918, just before collapsing, Germany had expelled from Berlin the Soviet embassy from which German radicals had carried out their subversive activities.[3] In its place, in January 1919 Lenin dispatched to Germany Karl Radek, an Austrian subject who had numerous contacts there and was well acquainted with her political situation. Radek was accompanied by Adolf Ioffe, Nicholas Bukharin, and Christian Rakovskii.[4] He lost no time taking charge of the newly formed German Communist Party directed by Paul Levi. But his main hope was the Spartacus League, formed out of the radical wing of the Independent Social-Democratic Party (USPD), led by Karl Liebknecht, Rosa Luxemburg, and her lover, Leo Jogiches.* Ignoring the hesitations of the Spartacists, Radek appealed to German soldiers and workers to boycott the elections to the National Assembly and overthrow the interim socialist government.[5]

The strategy, based on the experience of October 1917, misfired because the German authorities, avoiding the mistakes of the Russian Provisional Government, moved vigorously to crush the attempt by a small minority to defy the nation's will. On January 5, 1919, the Spartacists, joined by the Independent SDs, staged an uprising in Berlin. As the Bolsheviks had done in Russia, they timed the revolt to precede the elections to the National Assembly, scheduled for January 19, which they knew they could not win. Tens of thousands of excited workers and intellectuals filled the streets of the capital carrying red banners and awaiting the signal to attack. The

*According to Ruth Fischer, the most extreme radicals in the German socialist movement came from Eastern Europe: they brought with them a militancy and hatred of German imperialism that exceeded even that of native socialists. Among them, in addition to Luxemburg and Jogiches, was Julian Marchlewski, who would negotiate a Polish-Soviet truce in late 1919. See her *Stalin and German Communism* (Cambridge, Mass., 1948), 9.

24. Radek on the eve of World War I.

revolt had a reasonable chance of success, for the Socialist government had no regular forces at its disposal. Emulating the Bolsheviks, the Spartacists declared the government deposed and power transferred to a Military-Revolutionary Committee. Then they froze in inactivity. Unlike the Russian Provisional Government under similar circumstances, the German socialists turned for help to the military. They appealed to veterans to form volunteer detachments, the so-called Freikorps, staffed mainly by officers, many of a monarchist persuasion. On January 10, the Freikorps went into action and quickly suppressed the rebellion. Liebknecht and Luxemburg were arrested and murdered. Two weeks later Radek was taken into custody.[6] In a protest note to Moscow, the German government claimed it had "incontrovertible evidence" that Russian officials and Russian money were behind the rebellion.[7]

In elections to the National Assembly, which the Spartacists boycotted, the Independent Social-Democrats received only 7.6 percent of the vote: their one-time colleagues and now principal rivals, the Social Democrats (SPD), who had won 38.0 percent, formed a coalition government.[8] In February, in striking contrast to what had happened in Russia, the Executive Committee of the German Worker and Soldier Soviets, rather than claiming power, resigned in favor of the National Assembly.[9]

The German Communists ignored this setback and tried to seize power in several cities, including Berlin and Munich. Their rebellions were suppressed as well: in Berlin, over one thousand people lost their lives. The high point of these putsches was the proclamation in Munich on April 7 of a Bavarian Socialist Republic. The leaders of the Munich revolt, Dr. Eugen

Levine and Max Lieven, were veterans of the Russian revolutionary movement; Levine was a Russian Socialist-Revolutionary, and Lieven, the son of the German consul in Moscow, considered himself a Russian.[10] Their program, closely modeled on Russian precedents, called for arming the workers, expropriating banks, confiscating "kulak" lands, and creating a security police with authority to take hostages.[11] Lenin, who took a keen interest in these events, sent a personal emissary to Germany to urge the adoption of a broad program of socialist expropriations extending to factories, capitalist farms, and residential buildings, such as he had successfully carried out in Russia.[12] The strategy showed a remarkable ignorance of the German workers' and farmers' inbred respect for the state and private property.

During this brief revolutionary interlude, which ended in the summer of 1919, the Soviet government acted on the premise that in Germany, as in Russia in 1917, there existed "dual power" *(dvoevlastie)*, and addressed its official communications to both the German government and the Soviets of Worker and Soldier Deputies.[13]

Only in Hungary did the Communists achieve some success in exporting revolution, and this more for nationalist than socialist reasons.

Following the Armistice, Hungary was proclaimed a republic under a government headed by Count Michael Karolyi, a liberal aristocrat who cooperated with the Social Democrats. In January 1919 Karolyi became President. He resigned two months later in protest against the decision of the Allies to allocate Transylvania to the Romanians, a region with a predominantly Magyar population that the Allies had promised Romania in 1916 as a reward for entering the war on their side. The loss of this region aroused fierce nationalist passions in Hungary.

Hungary had few Communists: a high proportion were repatriated prisoners of war from Russia and urban intellectuals.[14] Their leader, Bela Kun, a onetime Social Democratic journalist, had commanded in Soviet Russia the Hungarian Internationalist detachment. Moscow sent him to Hungary ostensibly to arrange for the return of Russian POWs but in reality to act as its agent. At the time the Allies assigned Transylvania to Romania, he was serving time in a Hungarian jail for Communist agitation. There he was visited by a Social Democratic group who proposed to him forming a coalition government with the Communists: in this manner the SDs hoped to gain Soviet Russia's help against Romania. Kun agreed on several conditions: the Social Democrats were to merge with the Communists into a single "Hungarian Socialist Party," the country would be governed by a dictatorship, and there would be "the closest and most far-reaching alliance with the Russian Soviet government so as to preserve the rule of the proletariat and combat Entente imperialism."[15] The conditions were accepted and on March 21, 1919, a coalition government came into being. Lenin, who had always insisted on the Communists maintaining a separate organizational identity, expressed strong disapproval of the merger of Hungarian Communists with the Social Democrats, carried out on Kun's insistence, and ordered him to break up the coalition, but Kun ignored his wishes.[16] The Eighth Congress of the Russian Communist Party, held that month, hailed the Hungarian Soviet state as marking the dawn of the global triumph of Communism.* The new government hardly reflected Hungarian conditions, given that 18 of its 26 Commissars were Jews;[17] but then this was hardly surprising, given that in Hungary, as in the rest of Eastern Europe, Jews made up a large part of the urban intelligentsia and Communism was primarily a movement of urban intellectuals.

Regarded by Hungarians "as a government of national defense in alliance with Soviet Russia,"[18] the coalition initially enjoyed the support of nearly all strata of the population, the middle class included. Had it remained such, the Communists might have established themselves in Hungary for good. This did not happen because Kun, who was formally Commissar of Foreign Affairs but in reality head of state, was in a hurry to communize Hungary and from there penetrate Czechoslovakia and Austria. He rejected Allied compromise solutions of the Hungarian-Romanian territorial dispute, since his power depended on continued enmity between the two countries. He ordered the abolition of private property in the means of production, including land, but refused to distribute the nationalized estates to the farmers, forcing them into producers' cooperatives, which alienated the peasantry. The workers, too, soon turned against the Communists. As his authority eroded, Kun increasingly resorted to terror, the brutalities of which, together with inflation, estranged the population from the Communist dictatorship. When in April the Romanians invaded Hungary and the expected assistance from Soviet Russia failed to materialize,† Hungarian disenchantment was complete. On August 1, Kun fled to Vienna, his government resigned, and the Romanians occupied Budapest.‡ Communism was thoroughly discredited in Hungary and persecuted under the rule of Admiral Nicholas Horthy, who in March 1920 became Regent and head of state.

While still in power in June, Bela Kun tried to stage a putsch in Vienna, employing for the purpose a Budapest lawyer, Ernst Bettelheim, whom he

---

Vos'moi S''ezd RKP (b): Protokoly (Moscow, 1959), 444. The message of greetings contained the earliest hint of what later came to be known as the Brezhnev Doctrine, assuring the Hungarian Communists that "the workers of the entire world . . . will not permit the imperialists to raise a hand against the new Soviet Republic." In Communist vocabulary, "workers" was a synonym for Communist parties. A similar though less specific pledge was given by Chicherin to the short-lived Bavarian Soviet Republic: "Every blow aimed at you is aimed at us.": *Izvestiia,* No. 77/629 (April 10, 1919), 3.

†Lenin ordered the Red Army to send troops to link Hungary with the Soviet Ukraine: *PSS,* L, 286–87. The partisan leader Grigorev was to march into Bessarabia, but he refused to do so and revolted: his mutiny on May 7 doomed Bela Kun's government. *Direktivy glavnogo komandovaniia Krasnoi Armii* (Moscow, 1969), 234.

‡Kun, who later participated in revolutions in Germany, perished in Stalin's purges in 1939.

supplied generously with counterfeit banknotes. The only accomplishment
of the Viennese Communists was to set fire to the Austrian parliament.

Thus, the three efforts to stage revolution in Central Europe at a time
when the conditions for it were especially propitious went down in defeat.
Moscow, hailing each as the beginning of world conflagration, had stinted
neither on money nor on personnel. It gained nothing. European workers
and peasants turned out to be made of very different stuff from their
Russian counterparts. One could blame Communist failures on specific
tactical mistakes, but ultimately they were due to the futility of trying to
transfer the Russian experience to Europe:

> Lenin had completely misjudged the psychology of the working classes in
> Germany, Austria and Western Europe. He misunderstood the traditions
> of their Socialist movements and of their ideologies. He failed to grasp the
> real balance of power in these countries and thus deceived himself not only
> about the speed of revolutionary development there, but also about the
> very character of the revolutions when . . . they did break out in the
> countries of the Central Powers. He had assumed that they would evolve
> along the same lines as the Bolshevik Revolution in Russia; that the left
> wing in the labor movements would split away from the Social Demo-
> crat[ic] parties, and would form Communist parties, which then, in the
> course of the revolutionary processes, would capture the leadership of the
> working class from the Socialist parties, overthrow parliamentary democ-
> racy and set up a dictatorship of the proletariat.[19]

Indeed, these attempts at social revolution in Europe achieved the very
opposite result of that intended: they discredited Communism and played
into the hands of nationalist extremists who exploited the population's
xenophobia by stressing the role of foreigners, especially Jews, in inciting
civil unrest. In Hungary, the collapse of Bela Kun's regime led to bloody
anti-Jewish pogroms, and in Germany the Communist revolts gave credibility to the anti-Semitic propaganda of the nascent National-Socialist movement. It is difficult to conceive how right-wing radicalism, so conspicuous
in interwar Europe, could have flourished without the fear of Communism,
first aroused by the putsches of 1918–19: "The main results of that mistaken policy were to terrify the Western ruling classes and many of the
middle classes with the specter of revolution, and at the same time provide
them with a convenient model, in Bolshevism, for a counterrevolutionary
force, which was fascism."[20]

In the spring of 1919, Communist activities abroad were given a more
organized structure in the form of the Communist International (Komin-
tern or Comintern). The new International was designed as a militant
vanguard whose mission was to accomplish around the globe what the
Bolshevik Party had achieved in Russia. The task was spelled out in its

resolution: "The Communist International sets for itself the goal of fighting, by every means, even by force of arms, for the overthrow of the international bourgeoisie and the creation of an international Soviet republic."[21] A related assignment was defensive, namely preventing a capitalist "crusade" against Soviet Russia by arousing the "masses" abroad against intervention. The Comintern was to prove much more successful in its defensive than its offensive missions.

In the first year of its existence (1919–20), the Comintern assigned the highest priority to combatting Social Democracy. For Lenin, the assault on "bourgeois" regimes required disciplined cadres of workers and worker leaders, organized on the model of the Russian Bolshevik party. These cadres were in short supply in Europe because the socialist and trade union organizations there were dominated by "renegades" and "social chauvinists" who collaborated with the "bourgeoisie": hence the importance of splitting Social Democracy and detaching from it the truly revolutionary elements. This held especially true of Germany, a pivotal country in Lenin's strategy, as it had the world's strongest and best-organized socialist movement. As we shall see, to subvert the German Social-Democratic Party, Moscow was prepared to enter into partnership even with the most reactionary and nationalistic elements. It has been said that Lenin hated Karl Kautsky, the Nestor of German Social Democrats, more passionately than he did Winston Churchill.[22]

Lenin had decided to form a new International as early as July 1914, in response to the Second (Socialist) International's betrayal of pledges to oppose the war. The rudiments of what became the Comintern can be discerned in the so-called "Left opposition" at the Zimmerwald and Kiental conferences (1915–16), at which Lenin and his lieutenants sought, with only partial success, to deflect the antiwar socialists from pacifism to a program of civil war.[23]

Although the formation in Bolshevik Russia of a new International was a foregone conclusion, in the first year and a half in power Lenin had more pressing matters to attend to. During this time the sporadic efforts at foreign subversion were orchestrated by the Commissariat of Foreign Affairs, which formed special foreign branches for this purpose under Radek. Their personnel was assembled quite casually. According to Angelica Balabanoff, who in 1919 served as Secretary of the Comintern, they "were practically all war prisoners in Russia: most of them had joined the Party recently because of the favor and privileges which membership involved. Practically none of them had had any contact with the revolutionary or labor movement in their own countries, and knew nothing of Socialist principles."[24]

While World War I was on, these agents, supplied with abundant money, were sent, under cover of diplomatic immunity, to friendly Germany and Austria as well as to neutral Sweden, Switzerland, and Holland, to establish contacts and carry on propaganda. According to John Reed, in September 1918 the Commissariat of Foreign Affairs had on its payroll 68 agents in Austria-Hungary and "more than that" in Germany, as well as an indeterminate number in France, Switzerland, and Italy.[25] The Commissariat also employed for such purposes Red Cross personnel and the repatriation missions sent to Central Europe after the Brest-Litovsk Treaty to arrange for the return of Russian POWs.

In March 1919 responsibility for foreign subversion was transferred to the Communist International. The immediate stimulus for the creation of the new body was the decision of the Socialist International to convene in Berne its first postwar conference. To counter this move, Lenin hastily convened in the Kremlin on March 2 a founding Congress of his own International. Because difficulties of transport and communication prevented direct communication with potential supporters abroad, the gathering turned into something of a farce, in that the majority of the delegates were either Russian members of the Communist Party or foreigners living in Russia, hardly any of whom represented genuine foreign organizations. Of the 35 delegates, only five came from abroad and only one (the German Hugo Eberlein-Albrecht) carried a mandate.* Boris Reinstein, a Russian-born pharmacist who had returned to his place of birth from the United States to help the Revolution and posed as the "representative of the American proletariat," was accorded five mandates although he represented no one but himself. The affair in some respects recalled an amusing episode of the French Revolution when a group of foreigners living in France were garbed in native costumes and introduced to the National Assembly as "representatives of the universe."†

The expectations of the Comintern's founders knew no bounds: the All-Russian Congress of Soviets in December 1919 proclaimed its establishment "the greatest event in world history."[26] Zinoviev, whom Lenin appointed the Comintern's Chairman, wrote in the summer of 1919:

> The movement advances with such dizzying speed that one can confidently say: in a year we shall already forget that Europe had had to fight a war

---

*Angelica Balabanoff, *Impressions of Lenin* (Ann Arbor, Mich., 1964), 69–70. Like many of the founding members of the Comintern who had made their home in Soviet Russia, Eberlein perished in Stalin's purges.

†"On June 19 [1790] . . . there was arranged an unanticipated spectacle proper to attract the eyes of the multitude; sixty aliens were assembled, men without country living in Paris by swindling and intrigue. They are decorated with the pompous names of envoys of all the peoples of the universe; they are dressed up in borrowed clothes, and induced by the twelve francs promised them, they consent to play the role intended for them. . . . [The] troop of people were announced to be Prussians, Dutchmen, Englishmen, Spaniards, Germans, Turks, Arabs, Indians, Tartars, Persians, Chinese, Mongols, Tripolitans, Swiss, Italians, Americans, and Grisons. They wore the habiliments of these different peoples. The stock of the Opera had been exhausted. At the sight of this grotesque masquerade, every one stared open-eyed and waited in silence for an explanation. The initiated filled the hall with noisy acclamations. The galleries, overcome at seeing the universe in the midst of the National Assembly, clapped their hands and stamped their feet." *Mémoirs du Marquis de Ferrières,* II (Paris, 1822), 64–65, cited in E. L. Higgins, *The French Revolution* (Boston, 1938), 150–51.

25. The capitalist pig squirming: the sign reads "Third International."

for Communism, because in a year all Europe shall be Communist. And the struggle for Communism shall be transferred to America, and perhaps also to Asia and other parts of the world.[27]

Three months later, on the second anniversary of the October coup, Zinoviev expressed the hope that by the time of the third anniversary "the Communist International will triumph in the entire world."[28]

According to Zinoviev, during its first year his organization was no more than a "propaganda association."[29] But this statement cannot be taken at face value because a great deal of Comintern activity was clandestine. It happens to be known, for instance, that the head of the Soviet Red Cross Mission in Vienna gave local Communists 200,000 crowns with which to found their organ, *Weckruf*.[30] Since for the Bolsheviks newspapers were nuclei of political organizations, such action represented more than mere propaganda.

26. Lenin in May 1920.

Lenin addressed himself seriously to the Communist International only in the summer of 1920, when the Civil War was for all practical purposes over. His concept was simple: to make the Comintern into a branch of the Russian Communist Party, identically structured and, like it, subject to the directives of the Central Committee. In pursuit of this objective, he brooked no opposition: resistance to the principle of "democratic centralism" served Lenin as grounds for expulsion. Zinoviev defined this oxymoron to mean "the unconditional and requisite obligatory force of all instructions of the superior instance for the subordinate one."[31] Objections to it by foreign Communists Lenin discounted as Menshevik twaddle.

At the request of Zinoviev, who wished to placate the restless workers in his charge, the Second Congress of the Comintern opened on July 19, not in Moscow but in Petrograd. The decision to do so was kept secret to the last moment in order to avert potential assassination attempts against Lenin. Lenin traveled at night in an ordinary passenger train.* Four days later the Congress resumed in Moscow, where it sat until August 7. Foreign representation was far better this time. Present were 217 delegates from 36 countries, 169 of them eligible to vote. Next to the Russians, who had one-third (69) of the delegates, the largest foreign deputations came from Germany, Italy, and France. The casual way in which "national" represen-

*Balabanoff, *Impressions*, 110. This was to be Lenin's last visit to Petrograd.

tations were sometimes selected is evident in the fact that Radek, who in 1916 at the Kiental Conference had been listed as a spokesman of the Dutch proletariat, and in March 1919 had served as the envoy of the Soviet Ukraine to Germany, now appeared as the representative of the workers of Poland.[32] The Bolsheviks ran into considerable resistance to their program from foreigners, but in the end nearly always had their way. The mood of the Congress was euphoric, because while it was in session the Red Army was advancing on Warsaw: it seemed virtually certain that a Polish Soviet Republic would soon come into being, to be followed by revolutionary upheavals in the rest of Europe. In something close to revolutionary delirium, Lenin on July 23 cabled to Stalin, who was in Kharkov, a coded message:

> The situation in the Comintern is superb. Zinoviev, Bukharin and I, too, think that the revolution should be immediately exacerbated in Italy. My own view is that to this end one should sovietize Hungary and perhaps also Czechoslovakia and Romania. This has to be carefully thought out. Communicate your detailed conclusion.[33]

This extraordinary message can be understood only in the context of a decision taken in early July 1920, in the midst of a war with Poland, to carry the revolution to Western and Southern Europe. As has become known recently with the publication of a major speech by Lenin to a closed meeting of Communist leaders in September of that year, the Politburo resolved not merely to expel the Poles from Soviet territory and not merely to Sovietize Poland, but to use the conflict as a pretext for opening a general offensive against the West.

Poland declared her independence in November 1918. The Versailles Treaty recognized her sovereignty and defined her western borders. But the shape of Poland's frontier with Russia had to be held in abeyance until the Russian Civil War had been resolved one way or another and there was a recognized Russian government with which to negotiate the matter. In December 1919, the Supreme Allied Council drew up a provisional frontier between the two countries based on ethnographic criteria which came to be known as the "Curzon Line." The Poles rejected it since it deprived them of territories in Lithuania, Belorussia, and Galicia to which they felt entitled on historical grounds.* In fact, by the time the Curzon Line was drawn, Polish armies were already 300 kilometers to the east of it. Pilsudski was determined to seize as much territory from Russia as possible while that country was in the throes of Civil War and unable to resist. His armies occupied Galicia, dislodging from there a Ukrainian government, following

---

*The Curzon Line ran from Grodno south through Brest-Litovsk, assigning the Russians Vilno and Lwow and other territories that the Poles would conquer in 1919–1920 and hold until 1939. It resembled closely the border that Stalin imposed on Poland in 1945.

which they expelled Bolshevik forces from Vilno. In mid-February 1919, Polish and Soviet troops fought skirmishes which marked the onset of a de facto state of war. Pilsudski, however, did not immediately press his advantage because, for reasons previously stated, he wanted to give Moscow the opportunity to defeat Denikin, to which end in the fall of 1919 he ordered his troops to suspend operations against the Red Army. He only waited for Denikin to be out of the picture to resume the offensive.

Pilsudski probably could have secured at this time advantageous peace terms from Moscow. But he had very ambitious geopolitical plans, which, as events were to show, vastly exceeded the capabilities of the young Polish republic.

The outbreak of the Polish-Russian war is commonly blamed on the Poles and it is indisputable that their troops started it by invading, at the end of April 1920, the Soviet Ukraine. However, evidence from Soviet archives raises the possibility that if the Poles had not attacked when they did the Red Army might have anticipated them. The Soviet High Command began to plan offensive operations against Poland already at the end of January 1920.[34] The Red Army assembled a strong force north of the Pripiat marshes with the intention of sending them into action no later than April.[35] The principal front was to advance against Minsk, while a secondary, southern front was to aim at Rovno, Kovel, and Brest-Litovsk. The ultimate objective of the campaign was kept secret even from the front commanders: but from instructions issued by S. S. Kamenev that once inside Poland the two fronts were to link up, there can be little doubt that the next phase would have carried the offensive to Warsaw and farther west.[36] The hypothesis of Soviet plans for an invasion of Poland is reinforced by a recently declassified cable dated February 14, 1920, from Lenin to Stalin, who was with the Southern Army in Kharkov, requesting information on the steps being taken to "create a Galician striking force."[37]

The Polish assault disrupted these plans, which, as will be clear from Lenin's retrospective analysis discussed below, were meant to begin a general offensive on Western Europe.

In March 1920, Pilsudski proclaimed himself Marshal and took personal charge of the 300,000 troops deployed on the Eastern front. During March and April 1920, the Poles carried out negotiations with Petlura, which on April 21 resulted in a secret protocol. Poland recognized Petlura as head of an independent Ukraine and promised to restore Kiev to him. In exchange, Petlura acknowledged eastern Galicia as belonging to Poland.* The diplomatic agreement was supplemented on April 24 by an equally secret military convention providing for joint operations and the eventual withdrawal of Polish troops from the Ukraine.[38]

---

*P. Wandycz, *Soviet-Polish Relations, 1917–1921* (Cambridge, Mass., 1969), 191–92. The text of the accord is in John Reshetar, *The Ukrainian Revolution, 1917–1920* (Princeton, 1952), 301–2. See also Norman Davies, *White Eagle, Red Star* (London, 1972), 102–4. Its terms refute allegations that Poland intended to annex the Ukraine.

27. Brusilov during World War I.

The Polish army, made of troops that had fought on opposite sides in the World War, was high in spirits but low on equipment. The British refused help on the grounds that they had done their share by supporting the Whites, and Poland was France's responsibility. The French, as was their custom, gave nothing for nothing: instead of outright aid, they offered the Poles credit of 375 million francs with which to purchase, at current market prices, surplus war matériel, some of it captured from the Germans. The United States offered credit of 56 million dollars to buy stocks left behind by its army in France.[39]

On April 25, a numerically superior Polish army, assisted by two Ukrainian divisions, struck at Zhitomir in the direction of Kiev.* Although it had been preparing for action since January, the Twelfth Red Army fell back, weakened by mutinies and defections, especially among its Ukrainian units. The Red forces also had to contend with effective partisan activity in their rear. On May 7 the Poles occupied the Ukrainian capital: it is said to have been the fifteenth change of regime in Kiev in three years. The total Polish losses up to that point were 150 dead and twice that number wounded.

---

*Norman Davies in *White Eagle,* 105 and *passim,* maintains that the Polish offensive of April 1920 did not mark the beginning of the Soviet-Polish war but only "transformed the scale, the intensity, and the stakes of the war entirely." It is difficult to agree with this opinion, given that previous engagements between the two armies had been little more than skirmishes, lacking on either side a clear strategic objective.

Poland's triumph was short-lived. The expected rising of the Ukrainian population did not occur. Instead, the invasion ignited a patriotic frenzy in Russia that rallied socialists, liberals, and even conservatives behind the Communist regime that was defending the country from foreign aggressors. On May 30, the Soviet press carried an appeal by the ex-tsarist general Aleksei Brusilov, the commander of Russia's 1916 offensive, urging all ex-Imperial officers who had not yet done so to enroll in the Red Army.*

On June 5–6, Budennyi's cavalry broke through the Polish lines. The Poles abandoned Kiev on June 12 and retreated as rapidly as they had advanced. The Soviet counteroffensive proceeded on two fronts, separated by the impassable Pripiat marshes. The southern army advanced on Lwow; the northern one, under Tukhachevskii, crossed into Belorussia and Lithuania. On July 2, Tukhachevskii issued an order to his troops: "Over the corpse of White Poland lies the path to world conflagration. . . . On to Vilno, Minsk, Warsaw! Forward!"[40] Flushed with victory, on July 11 the Red Army took Minsk, the capital of Belorussia, and three days later Vilno. Grodno fell on July 19, and Brest-Litovsk on August 1. By then, Pilsudski's troops had lost all the territory they had conquered since 1918: the Red Army stood on the Bug River, the eastern boundary of the Polish population, poised to invade Poland proper. In all the occupied areas, Soviet methods of rule were introduced.

In Poland, the military reverses precipitated a political crisis. Under pressure from those who had all along opposed the Ukrainian adventure, and they were on both the right and the left of the political spectrum, the Polish government on July 9 advised the Allies that it was prepared to give up territorial claims against Soviet Russia and to negotiate a peace settlement.[41] Curzon immediately passed on to Moscow the Polish offer, suggesting a truce along the Bug as a provisional frontier, a permanent one to be worked out later. Britain offered her services as mediator. Curzon accompanied these proposals with a warning that if the Russians invaded ethnic Poland, Britain and France would intervene on her behalf.

Curzon's note produced disagreements in Bolshevik ranks. Lenin, supported by Stalin and Tukhachevskii, wanted to reject the Polish offer and to ignore the British warning: the Red Army should march on Warsaw. He was convinced that the appearance of Red soldiers and the proclamation of Bolshevik decrees favorable to workers and peasants would cause the Polish masses to rise against their "White" government and permit the installation of a Communist regime.

But behind Lenin's decision lay far weightier motives. What these were,

---

*Izvestiia, No. 116 (May 30, 1920), 1. In an unpublished diary written in 1925 during a visit abroad, Brusilov wrote that he had never offered his services to the Red Army and that the appeal had been obtained from him by subterfuge: "Moi vospominaniia," Aleksei Brusilov Collection, Bakhmeteff Archive, Rare Book and Manuscript Library, Columbia University, 59–67.

28. Tukhachevskii.

he explained to a closed meeting at the Ninth Conference of the Russian Communist Party on September 22, 1920, at which he sought to explain and justify what he called "the catastrophic defeat" which Soviet Russia had suffered in Poland. Lenin requested that his remarks be neither recorded nor published, but the stenographers kept on working: the text appeared in print seventy-two years later.* Although the formal objective of carrying the war into ethnic Poland had been Sovietizing that country, Lenin explained in his typically rambling fashion, the true objective was far more ambitious:

> We confronted the question: whether to accept [Curzon's] offer, which gave us convenient borders, and by so doing, assume a position, generally speaking, which was defensive, or to take advantage of the enthusiasm in our army and the advantage which we enjoyed to help Sovietize Poland. Here stood the fundamental question of defensive and offensive war, and we in the Central Committee realized that this is a new question of principle, that we stood at the turning point of the entire policy of the Soviet government.
>
> Until that time, waging war against the Entente, we realized—since we knew only too well that behind each partial offensive of Kolchak [or] Iudenich stood the Entente—that we were waging a defensive war and were defeating the Entente, but that we could not decisively defeat it since it was many times stronger. . . .
>
> And thus . . . we arrived at the conviction that the Entente's military

*The speech, deposited in RTsKhIDNI, F. 44, op. 1, delo 5, Listy 127–32, was first published in *IA*, No. 1 (1992), 14–29.

attack against us was over, that the defensive war against imperialism was over: we won it. . . . The assessment went thus: the defensive war was over (Please record less: this is not for publication). . . .

We faced a new task. . . . We could and should take advantage of the military situation to begin an offensive war. . . . This we formulated not in the official resolution recorded in the protocols of the Central Committee . . . but among ourselves we said that we should test with bayonets whether the socialist revolution of the proletariat had not ripened in Poland. . . .

[We learned] that somewhere near Warsaw lies not the center of the Polish bourgeois government and the republic of capital, but the center of the whole contemporary system of international imperialism, and that circumstances enabled us to shake that system, and to conduct politics not in Poland but in Germany and England. In this manner, in Germany and England we created a completely new zone of proletarian revolution against global imperialism. . . .

Lenin went on to explain that the advance of the Red Army into Poland set off revolutionary upheavals in Germany and England. On the approach of Soviet troops, German nationalists made common cause with Communists, and Communists formed volunteer armed units to help the Russians. In Great Britain, the emergence of a "Council of Action" (see next page) seemed to Lenin the beginning of a social revolution: he thought that in the summer of 1920, England was in the same situation as Russia in February 1917, and that the government had lost control of the situation.

Nor was this all, Lenin continued. The southern Red Army, by advancing into Galicia, established direct contact with Carpathian Rus', which opened up possibilities of carrying the revolution to Hungary and Czechoslovakia.

The overthrow of Poland offered a unique opportunity to liquidate the entire Versailles settlement. Both on this occasion and on others, Lenin justified the invasion of Poland as follows: "By destroying the Polish army we are destroying the Versailles Treaty on which nowadays the entire system of international relations is based. . . . Had Poland become Soviet . . . the Versailles Treaty, . . . and with it the whole international system arising from the victories over Germany, would have been destroyed."*

In short, Poland was but a stepping-stone from which to launch a general assault on western and southern Europe and to rob the Allies of the fruits of their victory in World War I. This goal, of course, had to be concealed: Lenin admitted that his government had to pretend it was interested only in Sovietizing Poland. The historian can but marvel at the utter lack of realism behind these assessments: as is often the case, fanaticism employs cunning means for quixotic purposes.

Trotsky took issue with Lenin's offensive strategy: he thought it advisable to accept the British mediation offer and urged that a pledge be given of respect for Poland's sovereignty.† In this, he enjoyed the backing of the Red

---

*Lenin, *PSS*, XLI, 324–25. Churchill, too, called Poland "the linch-pin of the Treaty of Versailles." Winston Churchill, *The World Crisis: The Aftermath* (London, 1929), 262.

†*TP*, II, 228–31. Several historians have questioned whether Trotsky really opposed the

High Command, which felt confident that it could crush the Polish army in two months, but only if assured that the Allies would not intervene militarily; in view of the British warning, however, and the possibility of Romanian, Finnish, and Latvian involvement, it recommended that offensive operations be suspended at the Curzon Line.[42] The party's leading experts on Poland, Radek and Marchlewski, cautioned against expectations that Polish workers and peasants would welcome the Russian invaders.

As was usually the case, Lenin's view prevailed. On July 17, the Central Committee resolved to carry the war into Poland, following which Trotsky and S. S. Kamenev instructed the commanders to ignore the Curzon Line and advance westward.[43] Britain was sent a polite note rejecting its offer of mediation.[44] On July 22, Kamenev ordered that Warsaw be taken no later than August 12. A five-man Polish Revolutionary Committee (Polrevkom) was formed under Dzerzhinskii and Marchlewski to administer Sovietized Poland. Moscow received a great deal of encouragement from the condemnation of the Polish government by Britain's Labour Party. On August 12, a conference of trade unions and the Labour Party voted to order a general strike should the government persist in its pro-Polish and anti-Soviet policy. To implement this decision, a Council of Action was formed under the chairmanship of Ernest Bevin. These developments made British intervention highly unlikely. At the same time, the Bureau of the International Federation of Trade Unions in Amsterdam, an affiliate of the Second (Socialist) International, instructed its members to enforce an embargo on ammunition destined for Poland.[45]

In the midst of these military and political engagements, the Second Congress of the Comintern opened its sessions. A large map of the combat zone was posted in the main hall, and the westward advance of the Red Army marked daily to the cheers of the delegates.

At the Second Congress of the Comintern, Lenin pursued three objectives: first, the creation in every foreign country of Communist parties: these were to be formed either from scratch or by splitting existing socialist parties. This, the most urgent task, was to be accompanied by the destruction of the Socialist International. In its resolutions, the Congress asserted that foreign Communist parties were to impose on their members "iron military discipline" and require "the fullest comradely confidence . . . in the party Center," that is, unquestioned obedience to Moscow.[46]

Second, Unlike the Socialist International, which was structured as a federation of independent and equal parties, the Comintern was to fol-

---

invasion of Poland as he later claimed. L. Trotskii, *Moia zhizn'*, II (Berlin, 1930), 193–94, and *Stalin* (New York, 1941), 327–28. But the documents cited against him date from August 1920, when the matter had long since been decided, and Trotsky, having fallen in line like a good Bolshevik, naturally desired a quick and decisive victory. See Titus Komarnicki, *The Rebirth of the Polish Republic* (London, 1957), 640–41, and Davies, *White Eagle*, 69.

29. Lenin and his secretary, Stasova, at the Second Congress of the Comintern.

low the principle of "iron proletarian centralism": it was to be the exclusive voice of the world's proletariat. In the words of Zinoviev: the International "must be a single Communist Party, with sections in different
countries."[47] Each foreign Communist Party was subordinate to the Comintern Executive (IKKI). The Comintern Executive, in turn, was a department of the Central Committee of the Russian Communist Party, whose
directives it was required to carry out.* To ensure absolute control, the
Russian Communist Party allocated to itself five seats on the Executive;

---

*Angelica Balabanoff, *My Life as a Rebel* (New York, 1938), 269. The relationship between
the Russian Communist Party and the Comintern was for a long time not understood abroad.
As well informed an observer as Alfred Dennis, who followed Soviet affairs for the U.S. State
Department, asserted in 1924 that the Russian Communist Party "belonged" to the Comintern,
whereas it was the other way around. Alfred L. P. Dennis, *The Foreign Policies of Soviet Russia*
(New York, 1924), 340.

no other party was assigned more than one. The principal criterion in selecting Comintern executives was obedience to Moscow. Parties and individual members, no matter how prominent, who disobeyed the Executive risked expulsion. To make certain that foreign Communist parties followed its orders, the Executive was authorized to establish abroad supervisory organs, independent of local Communist organizations.

Third, the immediate task of foreign Communist parties was to infiltrate and seize control of all mass worker organizations, including those committed to "reactionary" policies, along with all "progressive" organizations. According to Lenin's instructions, Communist cells were to be planted in every body of a mass character, openly where appropriate, secretly where not.[48]

The ultimate mission of the Comintern was "armed insurrection" against the existing governments[49] for the purpose of replacing them with Communist regimes, preparatory to the establishment of a worldwide Soviet Socialist Republic.

Lenin's exceedingly authoritarian proposals antagonized the foreign delegations, which admired Bolshevik achievements and objectives but knew little of Bolshevik ways. Lenin had to battle two groups: those who objected to his "opportunism" in seeking to work within the framework of parliaments and trade unions, and those who resented his undemocratic procedures in the Comintern.

Some foreign Communists, inspired by the Russian example, wanted to launch an immediate and direct assault on their governments: they saw no advantage to the tactic of gradual infiltration of the enemy's institutions advocated by Lenin. In a pamphlet distributed at the Second Congress, *Leftism, an Infantile Disease of Communism,* Lenin rejected this strategy on the grounds that the Communists abroad were too few and too weak to go on the offensive. The correlation of forces required them to follow a patient strategy of exploiting every disagreement in the enemy camp and entering into temporary alliances with every potential ally.[50] Foreign delegates who questioned this approach were rebuked by the Russians and on occasion prevented from speaking.

In line with Lenin's policy of infiltration, the Comintern Executive insisted that foreign Communist parties take part in parliamentary elections.[51] Some delegations, led by the Italians, opposed this demand on the grounds that by so doing they would only reveal the small size of their following, but Lenin stood his ground: he had not forgotten the mistake he had committed in 1906 when he ordered the Bolsheviks to boycott elections to the First Duma. As he saw it, winning elections was less important than using parliamentary immunity to discredit national governments and spread Communist propaganda. Emulating the tactics adopted by the Russian Social-Democrats and Socialists-Revolutionaries in 1907, he had Bukharin force through a resolution requiring Comintern affiliates to "make use of bourgeois governing institutions for the purpose of destroying them."[52] To ensure that foreign parties did not succumb to what Marx called "parliamentary cretinism," Communist legislators were required to combine parliamentary work with illegal activity. According to the resolutions of the Second Congress,

> Every Communist parliamentary deputy must bear in mind that he is not a legislator who seeks understanding with other legislators, but an agitator of the party, sent into the enemy camp to implement party decisions. The Communist deputy is accountable not to the amorphous body of voters but to his legal or illegal Communist party.[53]

There was much wrangling over policy toward trade unions. For Lenin, infiltrating and subverting unions was the second most important item on the Comintern's agenda, since the support of organized labor was a sine qua non of European revolution. This, however, would perforce be a formidable task, given that organized labor in the West was overwhelmingly reform-minded and affiliated with the Second International. European trade unionists present at the Second Congress argued in vain that their organizations were entirely unsuited for revolutionary work, since their members were interested in economic, not political, objectives. The strongest opposition came from the British and American delegations. The British resented being told to join the Labour Party since they knew it would not admit Communists and that an application for membership would only cause them embarrassment. John Reed, an American admirer of the Bolsheviks, was prevented from speaking when he tried to object to American Communists seeking affiliation with the American Federation of Labor. When he was finally allowed to make a motion, the vote on it was not even entered in the official record.[54] In protest against such undemocratic methods he later resigned from the Comintern.

A half-hearted attempt was made to move the headquarters of the Comintern. It had been the Bolsheviks' original intent to locate the Third International in Western Europe, but they abandoned the idea from fear of sharing the fate of Luxemburg and Liebknecht.[55] The Dutch delegate, who had suggested Norway as the Executive's permanent seat, said after his motion had been defeated that the Congress should not pretend that it had created a truly international body, because in fact it had vested "the executive authority of the International in the hands of the Russian Executive Committee."[56] The Comintern Executive established itself in Moscow in the luxurious residence of a German sugar magnate that in 1918 had been home to the German embassy.

Before adjourning, the Second Congress adopted its most important document, containing 21 "Conditions" or "Points" for admission to the Comintern. Lenin, its author, deliberately formulated the requirements for membership in an uncompromising manner in order to make them unacceptable to moderate socialists. The most important conditions were the following:

> Article 2. All organizations belonging to the Comintern were to expel from their ranks "reformists and centrists";
> Article 3. Communists had to create everywhere "parallel illegal organizations," which, at the decisive moment, would surface and assume direction of the revolution;
> Article 4. They were to carry out propaganda in the armed forces to prevent them from being used for purposes of the "counterrevolution";
> Article 9. They were to take over trade unions;
> Article 12. They were to be organized on the principle of "democratic centralism" and to follow strict party discipline;
> Article 14. They were to help Soviet Russia repel the "counterrevolution";
> Article 16. All decisions of Comintern Congresses and the Comintern Executive were binding on member-parties.*

Why did the delegates to the Second Congress of the Comintern, despite doubts and resentments, in the end vote with near-unanimity for rules that deprived them of all independence? They did so in part from admiration of the Bolsheviks, who, in their eyes, had carried out the first successful social revolution in history and, therefore, seemed to know what was best. But it has also been suggested that being only superficially acquainted with Bolshevik theory and practice, they did not realize what these requirements entailed.[57]

When the Second Congress of the Comintern adjourned, the fall of Warsaw and the establishment of a Polish Soviet Republic seemed a foregone conclusion. The Polish army was falling back at the rate of 15 kilometers a day: it was dispirited, disorganized, and lacking in basic supplies. It was also vastly outnumbered: by Pilsudski's estimates, the Red Army in Poland had 200,000 to 220,000 combat troops, while the Polish forces had been reduced to 120,000.[58] But the Poles enjoyed a geographic advantage when on the defensive, in that the invading Red Army had to divide itself in two, one north of the Pripiat marshes, the other south of it, whereas the Polish army could operate as one integrated body.[59]

German military circles rejoiced at the prospect of Poland's imminent destruction: like Lenin, they believed that its collapse spelled the doom of Versailles. The Weimar government, having declared neutrality in the Soviet-Polish war, on July 25 rejected a French request for permission to ship military supplies for Poland across Germany. Czechoslovakia and

---

*Jane Degras, *The Communist International, 1919–1943: Documents I* (London, 1956), 166–72. Hitler, who emulated many of Lenin's methods, imposed a "25-point program" for admission to the Nazi party: Karl D. Bracher, *Die deutsche Diktatur* (Franfurt a/M., 1979), 60.

Austria followed suit, which had the effect of virtually cutting Poland off from her Western allies.

On July 28, the Red Army occupied Bialystok, the first major Polish city west of the Curzon Line. Two days later the Polish Revolutionary Committee (Polrevkom) issued a proclamation informing the population that it was "laying the foundations of the future Polish Soviet Socialist Republic," to which end it has "removed the previous gentry-bourgeois government." All factories, land (except for peasant holdings), and forests were declared national property.[60] Revolutionary Committees and soviets were organized in all localities occupied by the Red Army. In communicating with his agents in Poland, Lenin urged the "merciless liquidation of landlords and kulaks . . . also real help to peasants [to seize] landlord land, landlord forest."[61] Lenin conceived what he called a "beautiful plan" of hanging "kulaks, priests, and landowners" and pinning the crime on the "Greens"; he further suggested paying a bounty of 100,000 rubles for each killed class enemy.[62] But the differences in political culture between Poland and Russia soon became apparent, as did the futility of appealing to primitive anarchist emotions in a different, more Western environment, for neither Polish workers nor Polish peasants responded to exhortations to loot and kill. On the contrary: faced with foreign assault, Poles of all classes closed ranks. To its surprise, the invading Red Army met with hostility from Polish workers and soon had to defend itself from partisan bands.

The invading force was organized in a Southwestern front under Egorov, composed of the Twelfth Army and Budennyi's cavalry, and a Western front under Tukhachevskii, made up of four armies—the Third, Fourth, Fifteenth, and Sixteenth—reinforced by the Third Cavalry Corps of General G. D. Gai Bzhiskian, a Persian-born Armenian veteran of the tsarist army. Stalin was attached to the Southwestern Army as political commissar. (He was originally assigned to Budennyi's cavalry by Trotsky.)[63] Stalin urged the Politburo to concentrate the main thrust of the offensive in the southern sector. He was overruled. On August 2, the Politburo ordered Egorov's infantry along with Budennyi's cavalry to pass under Tukhachevskii's command.[64] But, under circumstances which are far from clear, Kamenev, Stalin's protégé, delayed implementing this decision. It was only on August 11 that he ordered a temporary suspension of the operation against Lwow, and appointed Tukhachevskii Commander in Chief of both the Western and Southwestern fronts. The Twelfth Army and Budennyi's cavalry were to proceed toward Warsaw.[65] Stalin refused to follow these instructions.[66] According to Trotsky, his insubordination contributed materially to the Red Army's defeat in Poland.[67]

The hard-pressed Poles pleaded with the Allies for supplies. Lloyd George, who was in the midst of commercial negotiations with Soviet representatives Krasin and Lev Kamenev, lectured them on the aggression and even gave them an ultimatum, but Lenin, correctly sensing that the

British were not about to break relations with him over Poland, called his bluff.[68] The British Trade Union's Council of Action, subsidized by the Soviet authorities (it received the proceeds from the sale of jewels smuggled into England by Kamenev),[69] stopped shipments of war materiel to Poland by repeating its threat of a general strike. British dockers refused to load cargoes destined for Poland.

Such scanty assistance as the Poles received came from France. Some supplies were delivered by way of Danzig, then under British control, but French help consisted mainly of training and advice. Several hundred French officers who had arrived earlier in the year to instruct Polish troops were now joined by a military mission, headed by General Maxime Weygand, the Chief of Staff of Marshal Ferdinand Foch, the Commander in Chief of Allied Forces in France in 1918. Weygand expected to assume command of the Polish forces, but this was denied to him. Although he and his staff subsequently received much if not most of the credit for the "Miracle on the Vistula," in reality they contributed next to nothing to the victory for the simple reason that they were kept in isolation and their strategic plan, calling for a defensive stance, was rejected.[70] Weygand himself disclaimed credit for the defeat of the Red Army: "This is a purely Polish victory," he said after the event. "The preliminary operations were carried out in accordance with Polish plans made by Polish generals."[71] The French mission has been aptly described as "a symbolic substitute for [the] material aid that the Allies were unwilling or unable to supply."[72]

On August 14, Trotsky ordered the Red Army to take Warsaw without delay. Two days later, the Polrevkom moved to a location 50 kilometers from the Polish capital, expecting to enter it in a matter of hours. Warsaw was unperturbed: even as the sound of artillery could be heard in the capital, its inhabitants calmly went about their business. A British diplomat reported on August 2 that the *"insouciance* of the population here is beyond belief. One would imagine the country in no danger, and the Bolsheviks a thousand miles away."[73]

At this critical point in the war, Tukhachevskii committed fatal strategic blunders. Instead of concentrating forces on Warsaw, which he apparently considered to be his for the asking, he dispatched the Fourth Army, together with the Cavalry Corps, northwest of Warsaw—in Pilsudski's words, "into a void."[74] His apparent intention was to sever communications between Warsaw and Danzig in order to prevent Allied supplies from reaching the beleaguered city.* Later he would claim that he meant to encircle Warsaw from the north and west. But evidence from recently opened Russian archives suggests that he was acting on orders from above and that the purpose of the operation was political: to occupy the Polish Corridor and

---

*On August 14, the Revvoensovet ordered an assault on the Polish Corridor to seize war materiel believed to be stockpiled in Danzig: *Direktivy glavnogo komandovaniia*, 655.

Polish-Soviet War, 1920
POLISH OFFENSIVE (APRIL—MAY 1920)

turn it over to the Germans, reuniting East Prussia with the rest of Germany, thereby winning over nationalist circles there. "The approach of our troops to the borders of East Prussia, which is separated by the Polish corridor . . . showed that all Germany began to seethe," Lenin said in his September 19, 1920, speech. "We received information that tens and hundreds of thousands [!] of German Communists crossed the border. Telegrams came about the formation of German Communist regiments. It was necessary to pass resolutions to prevent the publication (of this information) and to continue declaring that we were waging war (with Poland)."*

No less disastrous was the gap which was allowed to develop between Tukhachevskii's main force, besieging Warsaw, and the Red Army's left wing (the Twelfth Army and Budennyi's cavalry) commanded by Egorov and politically supervised by Stalin. Here a front 100 kilometers long was defended by a mere 6,600 troops. In the historical literature, in no small

---

*IA, No. 1 (1992), 18. Victor Kopp, Lenin's agent in Germany, in a dispatch to Lenin of August 19, 1920, bluntly referred to the advance of the Red Army into the Polish Corridor as designed to restore to Germany territories of which she had been deprived by the Versailles Treaty: RTsKhIDNI, F. 5, op. 1, delo 2136.

Soviet Counteroffensive and Polish Breakthrough

(JULY — AUGUST 1920)

measure owing to the claims of Trotsky, the blame for this mistake is placed on Stalin, who, it is said, had ambitions of his own and wanted to occupy Lwow before Tukhachevskii took Warsaw, and hence failed to come to the latter's aid. But in view of Lenin's emphasis on the need to revolutionize South Central and Southern Europe, as stated both in his secret speech and in his cable to Stalin (above, p. 177), it seems more likely that this strategic blunder, too, was committed by Lenin, who apparently wanted Egorov's army to take Galicia as a base from which to invade Hungary, Romania, and Czechoslovakia, while Tukhachevskii marched on Germany.

Pilsudski quickly seized the opportunities presented to him by the Red Army's mistakes. He formulated his daring plan for a counterattack during the night of August 5–6.[75] On August 12, he left Warsaw to assume command of a secretly formed striking force of some 20,000 men, assembled south of the capital. On August 16, two days after the Russians had launched what was to have been the final assault on the Polish capital, he struck, sending this force through the gap, northward, to the rear of the main Red force. The counteroffensive caught the Red command by complete surprise. The Poles advanced for 36 hours without encountering resistance: Pilsudski, fearing an ambush, frantically toured the front in his car, looking for the enemy. To avoid having his armies trapped, Tukhachevskii ordered a general retreat. The Poles took 95,000 prisoners, including many soldiers who only recently had seen service with the Whites: a British diplomat who inspected them had the impression that nine-tenths of the captives were "good natured serfs," the rest "fanatical devils." Questioning revealed that the majority were indifferent toward the Soviet regime, respected Lenin, and despised and feared Trotsky.[76]

In the battles that followed the "Miracle on the Vistula," of the five Soviet armies that had invaded Poland, one was annihilated and the remainder were severely mauled: the remnants of the Fourth Army and Gai's Cavalry Corps crossed into East Prussia, where they were disarmed and interned. Estimates are that two-thirds of the invading force suffered destruction.[77] Stragglers were hunted down by Polish peasants. Budennyi's cavalry, retreating, assisted by two Red infantry divisions, distinguished itself by carrying out massive anti-Jewish pogroms. Lenin received a detailed account of these atrocities from Jewish Communists, describing the systematic annihilation of entire Jewish settlements and urgently requesting help. He noted on the margin: "Into the Archive."[78] After Trotsky had visited the collapsing front and reported to the Politburo, the latter with near-unanimity voted to seek peace.[79] An armistice went into effect on October 18.

Instead of installing a Soviet government in Poland and from there spreading Communism to the rest of Europe, Moscow now had to enter into negotiations from which it emerged much worse off than if it had accepted the terms proposed by the Poles in July. On February 21, 1921, the Central Committee, hard-pressed by domestic unrest, decided to make peace with Poland as soon as possible.[80] In the treaty concluded in Riga in March 1921, Soviet Russia had to surrender territories lying well to the east of the Curzon Line, including Vilno and Lwow.

The Soviet defeat in Poland profoundly affected Lenin's thinking: it was his first direct encounter with the forces of European nationalism and he had emerged the loser. He was dismayed that the Polish "masses" did not rise to aid his army. Instead of meeting resistance only from Polish "White Guards," the would-be Russian liberators confronted a united Polish nation. "In the Red Army the Poles saw enemies, not brothers and liberators," Lenin complained to Clara Zetkin.

> They felt, thought and acted not in a social, revolutionary way, but as nationalists, as imperialists. The revolution in Poland on which we counted did not take place. The workers and peasants, deceived by the adherents of Pilsudski and Daszynski, defended their class enemy, let our brave Red soldiers starve, ambushed them and beat them to death.*

*Clara Zetkin, *Reminiscences of Lenin* (London, 1929), 20. Ignacy Daszynski was a leader of Polish socialists and Poland's Vice Premier.

The experience cured him of the fallacy that incitement to class antagonism, so successful in Russia, would always and everywhere override nationalist sentiments. It dissuaded him from sending the Red Army to fight on foreign soil. Chiang Kai-shek, who visited Moscow in 1923 as a representative of the Kuomintang, then an ally of the Communists, was told by Trotsky:

> After the war with Poland in 1920 Lenin had issued a new directive regarding the policy of World Revolution. It ruled that Soviet Russia should give the utmost moral and material assistance to colonies and subcolonies in their revolutionary wars against capitalist imperialism, but should never again employ Soviet troops in direct participation so as to avoid complications for Soviet Russia during revolutions in various countries arising from questions of [nationalism].[81]

As soon as the Second Congress of the Comintern had adjourned, the Executive proceeded to implement its directives. Western Europe now witnessed a repetition of the events that twenty years earlier had destroyed the unity of Russian Social Democracy.

The Italian Socialist Party (PSI) was the only major socialist party in Europe to attend the Second Congress. The PSI was a genuine mass party and it was dominated by antireformists. In 1919 it had split into pro- and anti-Comintern factions. The majority, headed by G. M. Serrati, voted to affiliate with the Comintern: the PSI was the first foreign socialist party to join the new International. The minority, under Filippo Turati, opposed this decision, but for the sake of socialist unity submitted to it. As a result, the reformists were not ejected but remained in the PSI. Lenin found such tolerance unacceptable and insisted on the expulsion of the Turati faction. When Serrati refused, he became the object of a vicious slander campaign underwritten by the Comintern, including entirely baseless charges of bribery. It ended with his expulsion from the Comintern.[82] Subsequently, the ultraradical minority of the PSI, bowing to Moscow's wishes, broke away from the PSI to form the Italian Communist Party (PCI). In parliamentary elections a few months later, the PCI received only one-tenth of the votes cast for the Socialists. Despite their shabby treatment, the Italian socialists continued to consider themselves Communists and to profess solidarity with the Comintern. But the split in the PSI forced by Moscow weakened it appreciably and facilitated Mussolini's seizure of power in 1922.

The French Socialist Party voted in December 1920 by a three-to-one majority to join the Comintern. This triumph enabled the Communists to seize control of the party's organ, *L'Humanité*. The majority of 160,000 members now declared itself the Communist Party; the defeated minority retained the name of Socialist Party.

In Germany, the pro-Communist element was concentrated in the Independent Social-Democratic Party of Germany (USPD), founded in April 1917 by socialists opposed to the war. Its radical wing formed the Spartacus League. After the Armistice, the USPD gained considerable mass support. In March 1919, it came out in favor of introducing into Germany a Soviet-type government and the "dictatorship of the proletariat," which made it a Communist party in all but name. The leaders of the USPD were prepared to join the Comintern, but had difficulty persuading the rank and file to subscribe to Lenin's 21 Points. In the June 1920 elections, the USPD won 81 parliamentary seats, not markedly less than the Social-Democratic Party (SPD), which gained 113 seats and emerged as the second largest bloc in the Reichstag. The Communist Party (KPD), as the Spartacus League renamed itself, got only two parliamentary seats out of 462.[83] The USPD took a final vote on the Comintern's 21 Points in October 1920 at its Halle Congress, at which Zinoviev delivered an impassioned four-hour address. Ignoring the warnings of the Menshevik L. Martov, the delegates voted 236 to 156 to accept the 21 Points and join the Comintern. Of the 800,000 members in the USPD at the time, 300,000 enrolled in the German Communist Party, 300,000 remained in the USPD, and 200,000 left socialist ranks.[84] The consequence of the Halle Congress vote was a split in a party that seemed on the verge of becoming the largest in Germany. The USPD lay in ruins, but Lenin attained his objective. The VKPD (United Communist Party of Germany), which resulted from the fusion of the KPD and the breakaway faction of the USPD, became the Comintern's agency in Germany. It had approximately 350,000 members and constituted one of the largest Communist parties outside Soviet Russia.

When in March 1921 the Soviet government found itself in a crisis as a result of widespread peasant rebellions and the mutiny of the Kronshtadt naval base, it decided that a revolution in Germany could help it overcome domestic unrest. Disregarding the advice of the German Communist leaders, including Paul Levi and Clara Zetkin, it ordered a putsch. German workers did not stir and the uprising was readily crushed.[85] In the aftermath, the membership of the United German Communist Party declined by one-half, to 180,000 members.[86] Although they had been proven right in warning Moscow, Levi and Zetkin were forced out of both the Party and the Comintern.

The British Communist Party, formed in January 1921 of minuscule radical splinter groups, made up mostly of intellectuals and a small number of Scottish workers, in 1922 had only 2,300 members. Somewhat more numerous was the ILP (Independent Labour Party), with 45,000 members (1919), which, while in sympathy with the aims of the Comintern, refused to join. Lenin decided that British Communists could acquire greater influence by entering the Labour Party and subverting it from within. He persisted in this strategy despite Labour's hostility, as evidenced in 1920 by an overwhelming defeat—nearly 3 million votes against 225,000—of a motion calling on it to join the Third International.[87] He instructed British Communists to apply for admission, which they did, against their better judgment, only to meet with a humiliating rebuff: at the 1921 Labour Party Conference, the Communist Party's application was rejected by a vote of 4.1 million to 224,000. This was repeated in 1922 and the following years.[88] With their tiny membership, the British Communists had to live off subsidies secretly conveyed by the Comintern; and with financial dependence came servility.

The Czechoslovak Socialist Party, which had nearly half a million members, voted in March 1921 with virtual unanimity to join the Comintern.

The second objective of the Comintern in order of importance—penetrating and assuming control of the trade unions—proved more difficult to attain than creating Communist parties: it was easier to win the support of intellectuals dominant in political life than of workers in the trade unions. Lenin instructed his foreign followers to use any available means to gain controlling influence over organized labor. They must, he wrote, "in case of necessity . . . resort to every kind of trick, cunning, illegal expedient, concealment, suppression of truth, so as to penetrate into the trade unions, to stay in them, to conduct in them, at whatever cost, Communist work."[89] To promote this objective, Moscow founded in July 1921, at the Third Comintern Congress, a branch of the Communist International, subordinate to its Executive, called the Red International of Trade Unions, or "Profintern."* Its mission was to lure away organized labor from the International Federation of Trade Unions (IFTU), an affiliate of the Socialist International with headquarters in Amsterdam, representing over 23 million workers in Europe and the United States.[90] The Profintern experienced great difficulty in trying to make inroads into organized labor because Western trade unions were fully committed to ameliorating their members' economic conditions, and had no interest in making revolution. It had the greatest success in France, where syndicalist traditions were strong. The largest French trade union organization, Confédération Générale du Travail (CGT) split in 1921, following which the pro-Communist minority (CGTU) joined the Profintern.

In other countries, the Communists managed to win over from the socialist movement only splinter groups.[91] The latter typically came from declining or unstable sectors of the economy or "sunset industries," like the marginal coal-mining industry of Britain and the waterfronts of Australia and some United States ports. Indeed, these toeholds were often the only ones obtained in those countries, exactly as the First International found its major support in Britain in the dying crafts and seldom in the characteristi-

---

*According to Lewis L. Lorwin, *Labor and Internationalism* (New York, 1929), 229–31, a separate trade union organization was established in deference to the French syndicalists who did not want to be subordinated to the Comintern as a political organization. The Comintern created several other such front organizations, formally independent of it, including a Red Youth International (1919), a Sports International (1921), and a Peasants' International (1923).

cally capitalist large-scale industry of its day. On the Continent, in the 1930s at least, the Communist hold was in the smaller factories rather than in the bigger: "The bigger the factory, the smaller the communist influence; in the industrial giants it is altogether insignificant."[92]

The attempts of the Comintern to take over organized European labor, mandated by Article 9 of the 21 Points, ended in failure: "During the next fifteen years [1920–1935] the communists in the West were unable to conquer one single union."[93]

The fiasco, which both puzzled and frustrated Russian Communists, was principally due to cultural differences that they had difficulty grasping, for they had been weaned on an ideology that saw class conflict as the only social reality: warnings from foreign Communists that Europe was different they interpreted as lame excuses for inaction. But as experience was to demonstrate time and again, whatever their grievances, European workers and peasants were neither anarchists nor strangers to the sentiment of patriotism, attitudes that had greatly facilitated the task of revolutionaries in Russia. Even in relatively backward Italy, with its strong base of radical socialism, revolutionary ardor was missing. In August and September 1920, when Italy was seething with agrarian riots and factory seizures, the trade union leaders nearly to a man opposed revolution and failed to stir when the government forcibly restored order. Here, as in the rest of Europe, the decisive factor proved to be not the "objective" economic and social conditions, which were quite revolutionary in Italy, but that imponderable factor, political culture.[94]

An inquiry into the antirevolutionary spirit of Western labor must also take into account that workers in the advanced industrial countries enjoyed welfare benefits that gave them a stake in the status quo. In Germany, since the advent of Bismarck's "state socialism," they had been assured of compensation in case of sickness or accident, as well as support in old age and disability. In England they had had unemployment insurance since 1905 and old age pensions since 1908. The National Insurance Act of 1911 provided compulsory benefits for poorer workers from contributions by the government, the employers, and the workers, which guaranteed basic health and unemployment aid. Workers who had such protection from the state were not likely to want its overthrow, risking the benefits they had won from "capitalism" for the possibly more generous but much less certain rewards of socialism. The Bolsheviks did not account for this reality because prerevolutionary Russia had had nothing comparable.

A survey of Communist movements in Europe indicates that within a year of its Second Congress, the Comintern had achieved considerable success. By the end of 1920 it had won over, at least formally, most of what had been the Italian Socialist Party, and more than half of the French. It had a sizable following in Germany, as well as in Czechoslovakia, Romania, Bulgaria, and Poland.[95] All these parties had accepted the 21 Points, and by so doing placed themselves at the disposal of Moscow. Had Lenin showed greater respect for European traditions of political compromise and nationalism, the influence of the Communist International might have steadily grown. But he was accustomed to Russian conditions, where firm authority was all and patriotism counted for little. His tactless interference in the internal affairs of European Communist parties and his resort to slander and intrigue against anyone who dared to disagree with him soon alienated the most idealistic and committed followers. Their place was taken by opportunists and careerists—for who else would be willing to work under the rules set by Moscow, which treated independent thought and obeying one's conscience as treason?

Another factor that contributed to the degradation of Comintern personnel was money. Balabanoff was amazed by Lenin's willingness to spend whatever was necessary to buy followers and influence opinion. When she told him of her uneasiness, Lenin replied: "I beg you, don't economize. Spend millions, many, many millions."[96] The moneys realized from the sale abroad of Soviet gold and tsarist jewels reached Western Communist parties and fellow-travelers in devious ways, mostly by special couriers and Soviet diplomatic agents.* As will be seen (p. 233), in 1920 tens of thousands of pounds sterling were brought to England by two Soviet diplomats, Krasin and Kamenev, to finance a friendly left-wing newspaper and promote industrial strife there. But Moscow also utilized other channels, most of which remain concealed to this day. It is known, however, that in England one of the transfer agents was Theodore Rothstein, a Soviet citizen (later Soviet Minister to Iran) and the chief Comintern agent there, who transmitted Moscow's money to British Communists.[97] After 1921, when Moscow established commercial relations with Western countries, Soviet trade agencies served as additional conduits for funds. Little is known of these transactions, carried out in great secrecy, but it appears that nearly every Communist party and many pro-Communist groups benefited from Moscow's largesse: according to a French Communist, his was the only party that did not live off "Moscow's manna."[98] This claim is borne out by an internal financial statement of the Comintern which indicates that subsidies in currency (Russian and foreign) as well as "valuables" (mainly gold and platinum) were in 1919 and 1920 generously paid to Communist parties in Czechoslovakia, Hungary, the United States, Germany, Sweden, England, and Finland.† Subsidies ensured Moscow's control over Euro-

---

*A leading American Communist, Louis C. Fraina, admitted that he had received in Moscow $50,000, $20,000 or more of which he turned over to the English Communist John T. Murphy: Theodore Draper, *Roots of American Communism* (New York, 1957), 294. Fraina edited from 1919 *The Revolutionary Age,* the first publication in the U.S.A. to eulogize Lenin and Trotsky, and he possibly kept some of the money for that publication.

†This account can be seen on a two-page hand-written statement from late 1920 preserved in RTsKhIDNI, F. 495, op. 82, delo 1, list 10. The request of the Finnish Communists for 10 million Finnish marks in gold, platinum, and other precious objects, personally approved by Lenin, is *ibid.,* F. 2, op. 2, delo 1299.

pean Communist parties; at the same time they degraded the quality of these parties' leadership.

One reason for the ruthlessness with which Moscow treated its foreign adherents was the belief that revolution in Europe was imminent and that only the methods employed in Russia promised success. "The Bolsheviks simply reasoned that parties not wholly Communist would be prevented by vacillators from utilizing the revolutionary opportunities to seize power as the Bolsheviks had done in 1917, and to establish a Soviet dictatorship of the proletariat."[99] This is a generous explanation. It has been suggested by no less an authority than Angelica Balabanoff that behind it lay another motive, namely the desire to maintain power. Pondering the behavior of her Russian colleagues, she reluctantly concluded that it had less to do with the good of the cause than with the desire to dominate European socialism. Zinoviev's animus toward Serrati and insistence on his expulsion led her to believe "that the objective was not the elimination of right-wing elements but the removal of the most influential and important members, in order to make it easier to manipulate the others. To make such manipulation possible, it is necessary always to have two groups that can be played off against each other."[100] The vehemence with which Lenin insisted on dividing Western socialist movements and ejecting from the Comintern members with the greatest mass following in favor of docile flunkies, she declared, was primarily motivated by the desire to establish Moscow's—that is, Lenin's—hegemony over foreign socialist parties. The suspicion is bolstered by a 1924 letter of Stalin's to a German Communist editor that "the victory of the German proletariat will indubitably shift the center of the world revolution from Moscow to Berlin."[101]

Since all attempts by Communists to utilize revolutionary opportunities in Europe ended in disaster, the net legacy of Lenin's strategy was to splinter and thereby weaken the socialist movements. This made it possible in several countries, notably Italy and Germany, for radical nationalists to crush the socialists and establish totalitarian dictatorships that outlawed Communist parties and turned against the Soviet Union. In the end, therefore, Lenin's strategy promoted the very thing he most wanted to avoid.

Although it concentrated on the industrial countries, the Comintern did not ignore the colonies. Lenin had been persuaded long before the Revolution by J. A. Hobson's *Imperialism* (1902) that colonial possessions were of critical importance for advanced or "finance" capitalism. Capitalism had managed to survive because the colonies provided it with cheap raw materials and additional markets for manufactured goods. In *Imperialism, the Highest Stage of Capitalism* (1916), Lenin argued that the capitalist economy could not endure without colonies, profits from which capitalism used to "buy off" workers. "National liberation" movements in these areas would strike at the very lifeline of capitalism.

Immediately upon taking power, the Bolsheviks issued inflammatory appeals to the "Peoples of the East" urging them to rise against their foreign masters. Communist Muslims in Soviet Russia, a small body of secularized intelligentsia, were enlisted as intermediaries. Stalin told the Congress of Muslim Communists in Moscow in November 1918 that "no one could erect a bridge between the West and East as readily as you. This is because for you are open the doors to Persia, India, Afghanistan, and China."[102]

The problem with instigating a Marxist revolution in the East (by which term was meant both the Middle East and the Far East, and sometimes what later came to be known as the "Third World") was the absence there of an industrial working class. Adjusting to this reality, Lenin asked the Comintern to adopt a colonial program based on two premises: (1) the colonies could bypass the capitalist phase and proceed directly from "feudalism" to "socialism," and (2) in view of their numerical weakness, revolutionaries in the East had to form a common front with native "bourgeois nationalists" against the imperialists.

The latter proposition had little appeal to radical intellectuals from the colonial areas, because they considered native "bourgeois" as much of an enemy as the imperial conquerors. The issue caused acrimonious debates at the Second Congress of the Comintern.[103] Lenin's draft Theses called for the Comintern to "proceed in a temporary alliance with the bourgeoisie of the colonies and backward countries, but not to merge with it and unconditionally to safeguard the independence of the proletarian movement even in its most embryonic form."[104] Russian Social-Democrats had no difficulty adopting such a two-track policy, having followed it in regard to their own "bourgeoisie" since the 1890s. Asian delegates, however, found it objectionable. Their spokesman, the Indian M. N. Roy, wanted the Communists to wage the anti-imperialist struggle on their own, regarding the foreign imperialists and the native bourgeoisie as a common enemy. Asian Communists were so few in number that Lenin was willing to treat them with greater forbearance than those from the West, and he agreed, therefore, to some minor concessions in the wording of his Theses. But on the matter of principle he stood firm. While they were to accord principal attention to the peasantry, he insisted, colonial Communist parties had "actively to support liberation movements." They were to be "especially cautious and particularly attentive to national feelings, anachronistic as these were, in countries and among peoples that have long been enslaved," and "to collaborate provisionally with the revolutionary movement of the colonies and backward countries, and even form with it an alliance, but . . . not to amalgamate with it."[105]

To promote colonial revolution, Moscow convened in Baku in September 1920 a Congress of the Peoples of the East attended by 2,000 Communist and pro-Communist delegates from Soviet Asia and foreign Asian countries. When Zinoviev called for a *jihad* against "imperialism" and "capitalism" the frenzied participants raised high their swords, daggers, and revolvers. This Congress had no sequel and it is difficult to see what if anything it accomplished.[106]

The practical difficulties in implementing the Comintern tactic of collaboration with "bourgeois" nationalist movements became apparent in Soviet relations with Turkey. Following Turkey's capitulation in November 1918, Allied forces occupied her capital, Constantinople. Intervention inspired a movement of national resistance led by Kemal Pasha (Atatürk) who in September 1919 formed a rival government in Anatolia. Kemal was determined to expel foreign armies from Turkish soil, but because his forces were inadequate to the task, he made overtures to Soviet Russia. On April 26, 1920, three days after he had himself proclaimed President of the Turkish Republic, Kemal contacted Moscow, proposing concerted action against the "imperialists."[107] The initiative bore fruit in the form of Turkish neutrality when Soviet armies attacked, conquered, and annexed, one after another, Azerbaijan, Armenia, and Georgia; Turkey was rewarded by Moscow with bits of Armenian territory (Kars and Ardakhan). On March 16, 1921, the two countries signed a Treaty of Friendship that proclaimed their partnership in the struggle against "imperialism."[108]

The collaboration seemed to justify Lenin's colonial strategy. The trouble with it was that while Kemal was willing to go to great lengths to secure Soviet support against the West, he had no intention of tolerating Communists on his own territory. The small Turkish Communist Party was headed by Mustafa Subkhi, a member of the Comintern and Chairman of the Central Bureau of the Communist Organizations of the Peoples of the East. Moscow had sent him to Turkey in November 1920 to take charge of the Turkish party, founded earlier that year. Two months later he and 15 of his associates were found murdered under conditions that strongly suggested the responsibility of Kemal's government. The Soviet authorities and the Comintern Executive condemned these killings but did not allow them to affect relations between the two governments.[109] In this instance, as in all others, the interests of the Russian Communist Party and the state it governed took precedence over the interests of foreign Communist parties. Kemal introduced the one-party state, under which his Republican People's Party became the country's only legal political organization and the National Assembly was filled exclusively with his followers (1923–25). He was the first of many nationalist dictators to adopt the Communist model of the one-party state without embracing Communist ideology.[110]

On occasion, Moscow attempted to export Communism to the Third World by creating fictitious "Soviet republics" along its borders to serve as springboards into adjacent countries. Thus in Gilan, in northwestern

Persia, it supported a nationalistic but "progressive" movement headed by Mirza Kuchuk Khan, who had rebelled against Teheran. In May 1920, a Soviet military force under F. F. Raskolnikov, a onetime leader of Kronshtadt Bolsheviks, occupied Resht, the capital of the province, and proclaimed Gilan a Soviet Republic. Kuchuk Khan exchanged greetings with Lenin and Trotsky; the Soviet press waxed enthusiastic about Communism's new conquest in the East. But when, as soon happened, Moscow had to make a choice between a puppet regime in Gilan and the Persian government, it unhesitatingly sacrificed Kuchuk Khan. In February 1921, Moscow and Teheran signed a Treaty of Friendship that required Russia to withdraw troops from Persia. As soon as the Red Army had withdrawn from Gilan (September 1921), Persian forces reoccupied it, putting an end to the adventure. Kuchuk Khan was hanged.[111] This experience convinced Stalin, one of whose responsibilities was keeping an eye on the Middle East, that a Communist revolution in the ex-colonies was impossible. "In Persia," he wrote Lenin, "it is possible only to have a bourgeois revolution which leans on the middle class under the slogan 'Expel the English from Persia.' . . . Instructions to this effect have been given to the Iranian Communists."[112]

Moscow's single success was in the Far East. Taking advantage of the weakness of China and the indifference of the rest of the world to this primitive and remote area, it established in November 1921 a puppet republic in Outer Mongolia. This conquest placed it in an advantageous position to intervene in China.

While appropriating China's territory, Moscow also courted her government. In October 1920 a diplomatic mission from Peking arrived in Moscow. Lenin told its head, General Chang, that "the Chinese revolution . . . will finally cause the downfall of world imperialism." The general, in turn, told his hosts he was confident that the "principles of truth and justice proclaimed by the Soviet government will not perish but triumph sooner or later." He further expressed the hope to see Lenin installed as President of a World Republic.[113] Closer ties between the two countries, however, were impeded by China's objections to the Soviet occupation of Outer Mongolia and Soviet counterclaims that in Mongolia China was pursuing an "imperialist policy."[114]

If in her foreign operations Soviet Russia had to rely exclusively on Communists, her prospects would have been dismal, indeed: in the spring of 1919, when the Comintern came into existence, there must have been more vegetarians in England and more nudists in Sweden than there were Communists in either country. By 1920–21, the number of supporters abroad had grown considerably, but even so they were too few to influence the policies of foreign governments toward Soviet Russia. Such successes abroad, especially in the West, as Moscow could lay claim to in the early 1920s, it owed mainly to liberals and "fellow-travelers," people prepared to support the Soviet government without joining Communist ranks. Whereas liberals rejected both the theory and practice of Communism and yet found certain areas of agreement with it, fellow-travelers accepted Communism as a positive phenomenon, but were unwilling to submit to its discipline. Both groups rendered Soviet Russia invaluable services at a time when she was ostracized and isolated.

The affinities between liberalism and revolutionary socialism have been pointed out in the discussion of the Russian intelligentsia.[115] They derive from the fact that both ideologies believe that mankind, being entirely shaped by sensory perceptions (that is, devoid of inborn ideas and values), can attain moral perfection through the restructuring of its environment. Their disagreement is over the means toward that end, liberals preferring to reach it gradually and peacefully, through legislation and education, while radicals prefer a sudden and violent destruction of the existing order. Psychologically, liberals feel defensive toward genuine radicals, who are bolder and prepared to take greater risks: the liberal can never quite rid himself of the guilty feeling that while he talks the radical acts. Liberals, therefore, are predisposed to defend revolutionary radicalism and, if necessary, to help it, even as they reject its methods. The attitude of Western liberals toward Communist Russia did not much differ from that of Russian democratic socialists toward Bolshevism before and after 1917—an attitude distinguished by intellectual and psychological schizophrenia, which greatly contributed to Lenin's triumph. Russian socialists in emigration perpetuated it. While urging Western socialists to condemn the Communist "terroristic party dictatorship," they nevertheless insisted that it was the "duty of workers throughout the world to throw their full weight into the struggle against attempts by the imperialist powers to intervene in the internal affairs of Russia."[116]

The overwhelming majority of the spokesmen for Western liberals and fellow-travelers were intellectuals. The Bolshevik regime, for all its objectionable features, attracted them because it was the first government since the French Revolution to vest power in people of their own kind. In Soviet Russia intellectuals could expropriate capitalists, execute political opponents, and muzzle reactionary ideas. Because they have little if any experience with the exercise of power, intellectuals tend wildly to overestimate what it can do. Observing the Communists and fellow-travelers who flocked to Moscow in the 1920s and there put up with appalling living conditions and round-the-clock spying, the American journalist Eugene Lyons wrote:

> Fresh from cities where they were despised and persecuted, [they] had never been so close to the honeypots of power and found the taste heady. Not, mind you, the make-believe power of leadership in an oppressed or under-

ground revolutionary party, but the power that is spelled in armies, airplanes, police, unquestioned obedience from underlings, and a vision of
ultimate world dominion. Relieved of the risks and responsibilities under
which they labored at home, their yearning for position, career and privilege in many cases took on a jungle luxuriance. . . . No one who has not
been close to the revolutionary movement in his own country, can quite
understand the palpitant anxiety with which a foreign radical approaches
the realities of an established and functioning proletarian regime. Or the
exaltation with which he finally confronts the signs and symbols of that
regime. It is a species of self-fulfillment, a thrilling identification with
Power. Phrases and pictures and colors, tunes and turns of thoughts connected in my mind with years of ardent desire and even a measure of
sacrifice were now in evidence all around, in the places of honor, domi-
nance, unlimited power![117]

Confident of their ability to manage affairs better than politicians and
businessmen, they identified with the Soviet rulers even as they criticized
them, longing to duplicate (and improve on) their achievement. Whatever
mistakes they might have committed, Lenin, Trotsky, Zinoviev, Radek, and
the other commissars were people to whom they could relate as they could
not to a Clemenceau, Wilson, or Lloyd George. This sense of personal
affinity predisposed many Western intellectuals to sympathize with Russian
Communism, to ignore, minimize, or justify its failings, and to pressure
their governments to come to terms with it.

It took the Bolsheviks some time to realize the utility of liberals and
fellow-travelers. Friendly foreign visitors to Moscow had to overcome
Lenin's ignorance of conditions in postwar Europe and his deep-seated
suspicion of liberals to persuade him that in many countries, including
England, they could do more for Soviet Russia than could Communists.
They were right. While Communists staged futile putsches, liberals helped
prevent military intervention and economic embargoes against Soviet
Russia and paved the way for commercial and diplomatic accords with her.

A couple of examples will convey better than any generalizations the
attitude of Western liberals toward Soviet Russia.* We have noted the
overwhelming rejection by the British Labour Party and the Trades Union
Congress of Communists' applications for admission. In 1920, the Labour
Party and the TUC sent to Soviet Russia a fact-finding mission. To make
certain the foreign visitors obtained a favorable impression and yet did not
contaminate Russian workers with their trade-unionist ideas, Lenin asked
the Central Committee to issue appropriate instructions. The Soviet press
was to organize a systematic campaign to "unmask" *(razoblachat')* the
guests as "social-traitors, Mensheviks, accomplices in the English looting of
colonies," and workers were to be chosen to ask them embarrassing "questions." The "harassment" was to be carried out in an "ultra-polite man-

*For the purposes of this discussion, democratic socialists will be treated as liberals.

ner." The visiting Britons were, on the whole, treated well but they had no chance to find out the true sentiments of Russian workers, because, again on Lenin's orders, they were never left out of sight by a staff of "reliable" interpreters.[118]

Among the members of the delegation was Ethel Snowden, the wife of a leading Labourite and a member of the left-wing ILP. An intelligent woman with a sharp eye, she was determined to learn the truth. Like her husband and all but a small minority of British socialists and trade unionists, she felt no sympathy for Communist ideology, the October coup d'état, or the Bolshevik dictatorship. She saw the seamy sides of Communist life: the lawlessness and the terror, the social inequalities, the sham democracy. An audience with Lenin left her unimpressed: she thought him a cruel fanatic, a "dogmatic professor in politics." She departed from Russia with warm feelings for the people but without a good word for Communism. Moscow regarded the book she published on her return as hostile.[119] And still . . . in the midst of a devastating description of Communist misrule, there occurs an apologia that springs not from the mind but from the heart, since it has no connection with the accumulated evidence:

> Moscow is the Government's headquarters. It is the home of the Commissars. It is the seat of one of the most amazing experiments the modern world has seen. It is a place of great interest for the whole of the watching world. It is the pivot upon which earthshaking events will turn. And it deserves to be treated with respect, and not with the ignorant contempt which stupid people shower upon it. Mistakes have been made there, cruel things are being done there; but the mistakes are not bigger nor the cruel things more cruel than have recently been made and done in other capital cities by men who, for character and integrity, ability and personality are not fit to tie the shoe-strings of the best of the men and women of Moscow.[120]

She has somehow managed to convince herself—not without assistance from her hosts—that many if not most of the sordid aspects of Communist life were the fault of Western hostility. Once the West stopped intervening in Russia's affairs and helped her with food, clothing, medicines, machinery, and all else she so desperately needed, Russia would become "what she was destined from before the foundations of the world to become—a great leader in the humanitarian movements of the world."[121]

The official report of the British delegation on its visit showed similar equivocation. The authors saw less to criticize than Mrs. Snowden: what they disliked they attributed directly to the legacy of tsarism and Allied hostility. Russia, they explained, was simply not ready for democracy:

> Whether, under such conditions, Russia could be governed in a different way—whether, in particular, the ordinary processes of democracy could be expected to work—is a question upon which we do not feel ourselves competent to pronounce. All we know is that no practical alternative,

except a virtual return to autocracy, has been suggested to us; that a "strong" Government is the only type of Government which Russia has yet known; that the opponents of the Soviet Government when they were in power in 1917, exercised repression against the Communists. . . . The Russian Revolution has not yet had a fair chance. We cannot say whether, in normal conditions, this particular Socialist experiment would have been a success or failure. The conditions have been such as would have rendered the task of social transformation extraordinarily difficult, whoever had attempted it and whatever had been the means adopted. We cannot forget that the responsibility for these conditions resulting from foreign interference rests not upon the revolutionaries in Russia, but upon the Capitalist Governments of other countries, including our own.[122]

They concluded that Soviet Russia's domestic difficulties made her unlikely to pose a serious threat to the West.*

Not much different were the conclusions of H. G. Wells, the author of *The Time Machine* and an ardent believer in scientific utopia, who visited Soviet Russia in September 1920 at the invitation of Lev Kamenev. He was shocked by the sordid condition of Petersburg, which he remembered as a lively and elegant city. Under Communist rule, he thought, Russia had suffered "a vast irreparable breakdown."[123] Although he had nothing good to say about socialist doctrine—Marx was "a Bore of the extremest sort," and *Das Kapital* "a monument of pretentious pedantry"—he felt that what he termed "the greatest debacle in history" should not be blamed on Communism. Communism, he argued, was the result of ruination; its cause was imperialism and the decadence of tsarist Russia: "Russia fell into its present miseries through the world war and the moral and intellectual insufficiency of its ruling and wealthy people. . . . The Communist party, however one may criticize it, does embody an idea and can be relied upon to stand by its idea. So far it is a thing morally higher than anything that has yet come against it."[124] Russian anti-Bolshevik émigrés struck him as "politically contemptible" spreaders of "endless stories of 'Bolshevik outrages'" deserving no credence. Although acquaintances in Russia cautioned him to believe nothing that he was told, he returned convinced that the "better part of the educated people in Russia are . . . slowly drifting into a reluctant but honest cooperation with Bolshevik rule."[125] He recommended diplomatic recognition of the Communist government and the granting to it of economic assistance—"helpful intervention" that was certain to moderate

*During its visit to Soviet Russia, the British delegation demanded to meet with the socialist opposition. At a gathering arranged by the hosts, Victor Chernov made a dramatic appearance: he had been hiding from the Cheka and living on the verge of starvation. According to an eyewitness, he branded the Bolsheviks "corrupters of the Revolution and denounced their tyranny as worse than the Tsar's": Alexander Berkman, *The Bolshevik Myth* (London, 1925), 150, and Mrs. Philip Snowden, *Through Bolshevik Russia* (London, 1920), 160. The British delegates thought his appearance very sporting: his criticism of the Communists, however, made on them no impression. Chernov managed to elude the Cheka after this adventure, which led to the detention of his wife and 11-year-old child as hostages: Julius Braunthal, *History of the International*, II (New York, 1967), 223.

Communist excesses. As in the case of Mrs. Snowden, at a certain point objective observation was pushed aside to allow for assessments and recommendations that were pure acts of faith.

One of the earliest foreign visitors to Soviet Russia was William Bullitt, who came in March 1919 on a confidential mission for President Wilson (see above, pp. 66–67). Lacking knowledge of Russian and with his visit lasting only one week, Bullitt had to rely on information supplied by his Soviet hosts. And yet he felt no hesitation on his return in giving utterance to the most sweeping generalizations about Soviet Russia and her government.[126] As he summarized them later that year, "The destructive phase of the revolution is over and all the energy of the Government is turned to constructive work." The Cheka no longer engaged in terror: it only indicted suspected counterrevolutionaries. The people seemed generally to support the government and the Communist Party and to "lay the blame for distress wholly on the blockade and the governments which maintain it."[127] Russia should be left alone to allow internal forces to effect changes.

Such assessments—critical in specifics, sweepingly sympathetic in conclusions—were common among Western liberals of the 1920s. To European socialists in particular, no matter what the Bolsheviks did—whether violating the democratic precepts of Social Democracy or persecuting fellow socialists—they remained "comrades." This blindness was caused by the belief that any movement that professed to uphold socialist ideals was socialist: it placed slogans above reality. The October Revolution was for them a glorious event: for Karl Kautsky, Lenin's severest critic in socialist ranks and for Lenin an arch-"renegade," "it has made, for the first time in world history, a socialist party the ruler of a great power."[128] For the Austrian socialist Otto Bauer, "The dictatorship of the proletariat in Russia [was] not the subjugation of democracy but a phase in the development to democracy."[129] Like their Russian counterparts in 1917, democratic socialists in the West interpreted all anti-Bolshevism as a cover for anti-socialism, and hence saw it as ultimately directed against themselves. On this premise only they, the socialists, whose motives were pure, had the moral right to criticize the Communists.

The ambivalence of European socialists toward Communism found reflection in the confused explanation of the Labour Party's policy given in July 1919 by Ramsay MacDonald, who five years later would head Britain's first Labour cabinet:

> In supporting the Russian Revolution we are not necessarily taking sides either for or against the Soviets or Bolsheviks. We are recognizing that during a Revolution there must be Jacobinism, but that if Jacobinism be evil, the way to fight it is to help the country to settle down and assimilate the Revolution.[130]

Which statement, if it meant anything, had to mean that until and unless the people of Soviet Russia submitted to the Bolshevik dictatorship, Bolshevik terror was both inevitable and legitimate.

The pro-Communist policies of liberals and socialists were significantly and in some instances decisively influenced by considerations of internal politics, namely the desire to use Soviet Russia as an ally against domestic conservatives. Even as they refused to admit the Communists into their ranks, British Labourites entered into a tacit league with them against their common enemy, the Tories. They opposed intervention in Russia not only because they considered it directed against socialism but also because it enabled them to depict the British government as militantly antilabor. In the early 1920s the Labour Party consistently defended the foreign policies of Soviet Russia, even when, as in the case of the Rapallo Treaty with Germany, these policies harmed Britain's national interests. The underlying principle was simple: "The Labour's Party adversary was also Russia's enemy; how sensible, therefore, that the party should be Russia's friend."[131] Seen in this light, what actually was happening in Soviet Russia was of secondary importance.

The exploitation of Soviet Communism for internal political purposes was not confined to liberals. In the United States, isolationists like Senators Borah and La Follette turned into apologists for the Soviet Union for the same reason: "A group of Americans defended Soviet Russia not because of ideological commitment, but because of hostility toward American motives and actions. During the coming decade [of the 1920s], these isolationists were to remain in the seemingly anomalous position of advocating tolerance and diplomatic recognition of the Bolshevik regime."[132] In the words of *The New Republic,* "Anti-imperialists" (of both the right and left variety) "loved Russia for her enemies."[133] No American publication more insistently pressed for U.S. recognition of and help to the Soviet government than the conservative Hearst press: in its case, the rationale was not sympathy for Communist Russia, but dislike of Europe, especially Great Britain, and hostility to Washington.*

Non-Communist and even anti-Communist friends of this type were of inestimable value to Moscow. H. G. Wells was entirely correct when he told the Petrograd Soviet "it was not to a socialist revolution in the West that Russians should look for peace and help in their troubles, but to the liberal opinion of the moderate mass of Western people."[134]

---

*In a signed editorial in the New York *American* on March 1, 1918, William R. Hearst described Lenin's regime as "the truest democracy in Europe, the truest democracy in the world today." He maintained this position throughout the 1920s and early 1930s, when his sympathies shifted to Hitler's Germany: Joe Wershba in *The Antioch Review,* XV, No. 1 (Summer 1955), 131–147.

Fellow-travelers *(poputchiki)* acted from different motives from the liberal and socialist apologists. The term, adopted by Trotsky from the vocabulary of Russian socialism and applied to Russian writers who cooperated with but did not join the Communists, was extended to include foreign sympathizers. As the operating methods of the Comintern became better known and it was realized that all Communists were acting under orders of Moscow, they came to be perceived as Soviet agents. Once this happened, their credibility diminished and so did their ability to influence opinion. Fellow-travelers were free of this stigma because they acted, or, at any rate, seemed to act, in obedience not to a foreign power but to their own consciences. Such status was particularly important in the case of prominent Western intellectuals whose literary reputations appeared to provide a guarantee of integrity. Pro-Soviet statements by celebrated novelists like Romain Rolland, Anatole France, Arnold Zweig, and Lion Feuchtwanger, or scholars like Sidney and Beatrice Webb and Harold Laski, carried great weight with educated Westerners. Although the phenomenon of fellow-traveling assumed large proportions only in the 1930s, following the onset of the Depression and the Nazi takeover in Germany, it first emerged in the early 1920s after Soviet Russia had opened her borders to friendly visitors. Moscow assiduously cultivated sympathetic foreign intellectuals, treating them with a deference that exceeded anything to which they were accustomed at home.

In return, the fellow-travelers depicted Communist Russia to a curious but ignorant Western public as a country that endeavored, under the most difficult circumstances imaginable, to build the first truly democratic and egalitarian society in history. The role of the Party and the security police was passed over in silence, and Russia was portrayed as a society where political decisions were made democratically by the soviets, Russian equivalents of American town meetings.* Much was made of alleged social, racial, and sexual equality, as well as the unique cultural and educational opportunities offered the common man. To make these fantastic scenarios credible, shortcomings were conceded, but blame was attributed to the inevitable difficulties that attended the "striving to build the New Jerusalem."[135] Once the myth of a nearly perfect participatory democracy could no longer be

---

*According to M. Phillipps Price, the *Manchester Guardian* correspondent in Russia in the 1920s, "Nobody at the time saw . . . that the real seat of power in Russia was going to be no department of government but the Communist Party. Lenin was already quietly pushing the Party functionaries into all important organs of the State, thus making the Party the sole source of authority" (*Survey*, No. 41, April 1962, 22). A notable exception was Lydia Bach's *Le Droit et les Institutions de la Russie Soviétique,* published in Paris in 1923. In the United States, the role of the Communist Party in ruling Soviet Russia as well as the Comintern was first publicly revealed by Senator Henry C. Lodge in January 1924 on the basis of information provided by the Department of State: Christopher Lasch, *The American Liberals and the Russian Revolution* (New York and London, 1962), 216–17.

sustained—this happened as more came to be known abroad about Soviet conditions—all the failures of the regime to make good on its promises were attributed to tsarism. In the words of the *New York Times*'s Moscow correspondent, Walter Duranty, the prime supplier of arguments to American fellow-travelers, what perfection could be expected of a country that had just "emerged from the blackest of tyranny"?[136] Admittedly, Soviet Russia was a dictatorship, but then democracy was not learned in a day, which would have been a reasonable argument if Soviet Russia were, indeed, striving to become a democracy.

The motives of fellow-travelers varied as much as did the personalities of those who made the pilgrimage to Moscow: "anxiously heretical professors, atheists in search of a religion, old maids in search of revolutionary compensations, radicals in search of reinforcement for a wavering faith."[137] Angelica Balabanoff, who as Secretary of the Comintern was in a position to know, says that on their arrival in Soviet Russia all visitors were placed in one of four categories: "superficial, naïve, ambitious, or venal."[138] In practice, of course, few fitted neatly into any one of these categories. A "naïve" idealist found it easier to keep the faith if the reward was fame, while a "venal" visitor enjoyed his profits more if they could be justified in idealistic terms (as in, "Trade promotes peace" or "Trade civilizes"). The Hammers, *père* and *fils,* the most successful American entrepreneurs in Communist Russia in the 1920s, were said by Eugene Lyons to have "mixed the business of helping themselves with the pleasure of helping Russia."[139]

Material self-interest, and not only in the narrow commercial sense, was a powerful motive for turning into a Communist mouthpiece. The willingness faithfully to follow the Party line through all its zigzags ensured a writer or an artist of unstinting support by the Party's effective and well-financed propaganda machine: with its help many a mediocre writer became a celebrity and even a best-selling author. Examples include Romain Rolland, Lion Feuchtwanger, Upton Sinclair, Lincoln Steffens, and Howard Fast, whose productions have in due course sunk into well-deserved oblivion. English fellow-traveling authors had access to Victor Gollancz's Left Book Club, which at the height of its popularity in mid-1939 distributed pro-Soviet nonfiction to fifty thousand subscribers. Books of a similar orientation under the Penguin imprint sold in the six figures.[140] This happened at a time when *Darkness at Noon,* by the disenchanted Communist Arthur Koestler, a book that in time attained the status of a classic, had in England an initial printing of one thousand copies and total first-year sales of less than four thousand.[141] George Orwell's *Animal Farm* was rejected by fourteen publishers on the grounds of being too anti-Soviet.[142] Western journalists could make a name for themselves by being accredited to Moscow, and there enjoy a style of life quite beyond the reach of their colleagues at home, provided they wrote only what the Soviet authorities approved:

the alternative was disaccreditation and expulsion. And, of course, for venturesome and politically sympathetic businessmen there was money to be made from concessions and trade. From Moscow's point of view, sympathizers inspired by venal motives were the most dependable of all, because, having no ideals to begin with, they were immune to disillusionment.

Most fellow-travelers probably fitted in the category of "naïve." They believed what they heard and read because, desperately wishing for a world free of war and want, they ignored all unfavorable evidence about Soviet Russia. They believed that man and society could be made perfect: and since the world which they knew was far from perfect, they readily accepted Communist ideals for Communist reality. Capitalism disgusted them for the poverty it tolerated in the midst of affluence and for its inner contradictions that made for militarism and war. The aesthetes among them were revolted by the vulgarity of modern mass culture and correspondingly enchanted by the efforts of the Communists to bring "high" culture to the common man. Walter Gropius, the founder of the Bauhaus, in the non sequitur reasoning characteristic of the type, wrote: "Since at present we altogether have no culture but only civilization, I am certain that Bolshevism, notwithstanding all its evil byproducts, is the only way in the foreseeable future to create the premises of a new culture."*

Closing the mind to adverse evidence did not come easily to true idealists: they had to resort to all kinds of psychological stratagems to exclude from consciousness undesirable data. There exists much retrospective testimony from disenchanted Communists and fellow-travelers on how this process worked. Arthur Koestler, living in Soviet Russia in the early 1930s, at a time of mass starvation and total extinction of civil rights, developed the habit of rationalizing whatever he saw and heard by treating Soviet reality as something not quite real, "a quivering membrane stretched between the past and the future": "I learnt to classify automatically everything that shocked me as the 'heritage of the past' and everything I liked as 'seeds of the future.' By setting up this automatic sorting machine in his mind, it was still possible in 1932 for a European to live in Russia and yet to remain a Communist."[143]

Idealistic fellow-travelers found it especially difficult to cope with evidence that the leaders of Soviet Russia were not altruistic benefactors of mankind but self-seeking politicians of an unusually ruthless kind. They rarely talked, therefore, of Communist politics—of the Party's role in Soviet life, of the factional struggles within it, of the intrigues and slander which accompanied the purges that became a regular feature of Communist life once the Civil War was over. They preferred to treat Communism as exclusively a social and cultural phenomenon. Anna Louise Strong, one of the most faithful fellow-travelers, first of Moscow and then of Peking, could

---

*Cited in Heinrich von Gleichen, *Der Bolshewismus und die deutschen Intellektuellen* (Leipzig, 1920), 50. Loathing of the vulgarity of modern commercial culture could, of course, also assume other forms, such as Anglophilia (*e.g.,* Henry James and T. S. Eliot).

not acknowledge even to herself that her Communist idols struggled for personal power, as ordinary politicians do everywhere, so fixed were her eyes on the ultimate goals of Communism. To her, Stalin's expulsion of Trotsky from the Party made no sense: "I never quite saw why he was thrown out," she wrote. "I couldn't see so much difference between those theories. Everybody wanted to build this country, didn't they?"[144] Even after Stalin had become absolute master of the Soviet Union, such people would deny his dictatorship had a political dimension: "Oddly enough, the fellow-travellers were victims of their own intelligence and high education. Having learned in the best Enlightenment manner that there is a material or environmental cause of everything, they were not to be taken in by obscurantist hocus-pocus about one man's megalomania and paranoia."[145] In sum, the more intelligent and well-educated a person, the more difficult it was for him to grasp the true nature of a regime which observed no rational principles and which habitually resorted to violence to resolve differences that in a normal society are settled by compromises or appeals to the electorate. Coming to grips with such a regime came easier, for once, to the poor and uneducated, whom experience has always taught to accept irrationality and violence as facts of life.

Fellow-travelers were mesmerized by Stalin's tyranny: instead of seeing it as the crassest violation of Communist claims to democracy, they interpreted it as a guarantee of Communism's purity, since by eliminating politics and all the sordid infighting that went with it, it enabled the Communists to concentrate on what they assumed to be the movement's ultimate objective. Paradoxically, as soon as the Communist leaders themselves began to admit to failures and crimes, which happened after Stalin's death, fellow-travelers deserted them in droves. Soon the breed vanished. For the idealistic fellow-travelers, self-delusion was a necessity: they would ignore oppression and mass murder in the name of an ideal rather than subscribe to a more humane policy whose pragmatism robbed them of utopian dreams.

The soul of the idealistic fellow-traveler was an eternal battleground. For many, there was a limit to the negative evidence they were capable of rejecting: for them, sooner or later, came the moment of truth—for some, the expulsion of Trotsky, for others, the trials of the 1930s, the Nazi-Soviet Pact, or the suppression of Hungarian liberty. In every case it meant not only a painful admission of having been wrong, but a break with a community of believers of which one had been part, resulting in isolation as well as ostracism. Those who underwent this wrenching experience stress in their memoirs the misery of breaking with friends and finding themselves adrift in a hostile world in which not only Communists and fellow-travelers but liberals, too, treated them like despicable renegades.* For others, the limits

---

*Whittaker Chambers tells how after leaving the Communist Party and exposing Alger Hiss as a Soviet agent he became the victim of the animosity of "enlightened people": *Witness* (New York, 1952), 616 and *passim.* Cut off from the Party, he saw the world he was leaving as "the

of tolerance were infinitely expandable, and there was literally nothing that the Communists did for which they could not produce a satisfactory explanation.

The archetypal idealistic fellow-traveler was John Reed, the author of *Ten Days That Shook the World,* a book that more than any other contributed to making foreigners look at the Russian Revolution as a great romantic adventure. Reed's career combined the elements that, in varying proportions, went into the making of most fellow-travelers: middle-class origin, inordinate and unsatisfied intellectual ambition, genuine idealism. The son of a utility magnate from Oregon, he had spent his childhood in luxury, attended by liveried footmen, in a whirl of parties and balls.[146] At Harvard he found himself an outsider: his nouveau riche background did not impress schoolmates, and his un-"Aryan" appearance—he was short, with large eyes and dark hair—did not help. To his chagrin, he failed to make a "final" club. Walter Lippmann, who studied at Harvard with him, described Reed as someone for whom objects acquired reality only to the extent that they could be personalized: "Revolution, literature, poetry, they are things which hold him at times, incidents merely of his living."[147] He seems to have had cravings for intense experiences and for impressing others. A few days after arriving in Cambridge, he proposed to a fellow student collaboration on a book on Harvard. Asked how he proposed to write on a subject about which neither knew anything, Reed replied, "Hell, we'll find out doing the thing."[148]

It was in this spirit that he approached the Russian Revolution. He was as ignorant of Russia's past as he was of her language;[149] nor did he know anything about socialism. But this did not matter: revolutions were high adventure. Reed's first journalistic coup was an account of the Mexican Revolution. By the time he arrived in Petrograd in September 1917—it was his second visit, for he had spent a brief and unhappy time there as a war correspondent in the summer of 1915—he was one of America's most highly paid journalists. He was enchanted with the sights that greeted his eyes: "For color and terror and grandeur," he wrote on arrival, "this makes Mexico look pale." He observed the October coup rather like a spectator viewing a film in an unfamiliar foreign language, and in two months of feverish effort wrote down his impressions. *Ten Days* is structured as drama and could have served as a script for a colossal D. W. Griffith film. It has its stars—Lenin, Trotsky, and a few other leading Bolsheviks— backed by a supporting cast of thousands. The hero is the proletariat; the villain, the "propertied classes," in which category he places everyone, socialists included, who stands in the Bolsheviks' way. All complexities,

---

world of life and of the future. The world I was returning to seemed, by contrast, a graveyard" (*ibid.,* 25).

30. John Reed and Louise Bryant.

whether of character or narrative, are ignored for the sake of fast-paced, easily understood action pitting the "good guys" against the "bad."

Carried away by what he had seen, Reed turned fellow-traveler.* Like many sympathetic Western observers, he was captivated not by revolutionary ideas but by the Revolution's dynamism, in such sharp contrast with the despair of "bourgeois" Europe—by what a fellow journalist with similar political ideas described as "the creative effort of the Revolution . . . the living, vivifying expression of something hitherto hidden in the consciousness of humanity."† Reed's book, published in 1919 with Lenin's introduc-

---

*Reed would probably be best characterized as a "naïve" fellow-traveler; yet he, too, was not immune to the rewards normally reserved for the "greedy." It has become recently known that on January 22, 1920, he accepted from the Comintern treasury precious metals valued at 1,008,000 rubles: RTsKhIDNI, Fond 495, op. 82, delo 1, list 10. On the black market this sum would have fetched 1,000 dollars, the equivalent of 50 ounces of gold.

†Arthur Ransome, *Six Weeks in Russia in 1919* (London, 1919), p. viii. This was a common theme in Western reactions to Soviet Russia. In 1928, in an influential account of his trip to the

tion, made a great impression. Since its appearance it has been widely
regarded as a reliable account of October 1917, even though as a historical
record its only merit lies in conveying how the Russian Revolution struck
the imagination of an outsider in quest of excitement.*

Reed's disillusionment with Bolshevism began with his return to Soviet
Russia in October 1919, when he became aware of how Russian Communists manipulated the Comintern, which he had joined, and what misery
they had brought to Russia's rural population, as observed on a boat trip
on the Volga. He died of typhus in 1920, a thoroughly disenchanted man.
Angelica Balabanoff, who was with him during his last days, believes that
the "disillusionment and disgust which he experienced during the Second
Congress of the Communist International contributed to the causes of his
death. The moral and nervous shock deprived him of the wish to live."[150]
His break came quickly and early, because, being emotionally rather than
intellectually committed to Communism, he lacked the better-informed
fellow-traveler's repertoire of rationalizations with which to shield against
disappointment.

Others had an easier time of it. Reed's widow, Louise Bryant, managed
to accommodate herself to unpleasant experiences in Soviet Russia and
even to find a good word for the Red Terror. This terror, she insisted, was
a policy forced on such sensitive men as Lenin and Dzerzhinskii by circumstances beyond their control: "It was [Dzerzhinskii's] duty to see that the
prisoners were quickly and humanely disposed of. He performed this grim
task with a dispatch and an efficiency for which even the condemned must
have been grateful, in that nothing is more horrible than an executioner
whose hand trembles and whose heart wavers."[151]

One could shut one's eyes to Soviet reality even while living in Soviet
Russia, but it was obviously easier to do so from a distance. Louise Bryant
chose to eulogize Soviet Communism from the Côte d'Azur, where she had
settled with her millionaire husband, William Bullitt. After Hitler's advent
to power, Feuchtwanger and the circle of German fellow-travelers he
headed also found southern France a congenial refuge. Lincoln Steffens, an
ardent apologist first for Lenin and then for Stalin, similarly preferred to
make his home in the sunny regions and the spas of the capitalist West,
initially on the Riviera and ultimately in Carmel, California. "I am a patriot
for Russia," he wrote a friend in 1926, "the Future is there; Russia will win
out and it will save the world. That is my belief. But I don't want to live
there." The letter was postmarked Karlsbad.[152]

U.S.S.R., John Dewey defined the "essence of the revolution" to be the "release of courage,
energy and confidence in life": cited by Lewis S. Feuer in the *American Quarterly*, XIV, No. 2,
Part I (1962), 122.

*When told in Russia that "things didn't happen" the way he had described them, Reed
responded: "What the hell difference does it make?" The important thing was not "photographic
accuracy" but "over-all impression." B. D. Wolfe, *Strange Communists I Have Known* (New
York, 1965), 43.

The open hostility of Russia's Communist regime to "capitalism," and especially its denial of the right of private property, should have turned the Western business community into an uncompromising foe of Lenin's government. In fact, many of the pot-bellied, top-hatted capitalists of Soviet propaganda posters turned out to be remarkably friendly and cooperative. Western capitalists lost no sleep over the fate of their Russian brethren: they were quite prepared to make deals with the Soviet regime, leasing or buying at bargain prices the sequestered properties of Russian owners.* No group promoted collaboration with Soviet Russia more assiduously and more effectively than the European and American business communities. The Bolsheviks exploited their eagerness to do business by having them pressure Western governments for diplomatic recognition and economic assistance. When the first Soviet commercial missions arrived in Europe in the summer of 1920 in quest of credits and technology, they were shunned by organized labor, but welcomed by big business. Hugo Stinnes, the head of the Union of German Industrialists and an early backer of Hitler, while hosting the Soviet delegation, declared that he was "favorably disposed toward Russia and her experiments."[153] In France, the delegation was advised by a right-wing deputy not to rely on Communists and left-socialists: "Tell Lenin that the best way to win France over to doing business with Russia is through the businessmen of France. They are our only realists."†

Businessmen eager to exploit Russia's natural resources and sell to her manufactured goods justified trading with a regime that had violated, at home and abroad, all accepted norms of civilized behavior, with the following arguments: First, any country was entitled to the government of its choice. Hence, it would be not only unrealistic but undemocratic to ostracize Soviet Russia. As Bernard Baruch said in 1920: "The Russian people have a right, it seems to me, to set up any form of government they wish."[154] The unspoken premise behind this argument was that the Russian people had chosen the Communist government. Second, trade civilizes, because it teaches common sense and discredits abstract doctrines. This argument was frequently resorted to by Lloyd George, who in February 1920 called for the reopening of commercial relations with Soviet Russia: "We have failed to restore Russia to sanity by force. I believe we can do it and save her by trade. Commerce has a sobering effect in its operations. The simple sums in addition and subtraction which it inculcates soon dispose of wild theor-

---

*An honorable exception was Averell Harriman, who offered to turn over a percentage of the profits he expected to make from his manganese concession in Soviet Georgia to the mines' rightful proprietors.

†Simon Liberman, *Building Lenin's Russia* (Chicago, 1945), 133. The man who gave this advice, Anatole de Monzie, proved very helpful in establishing contacts between the Soviet government and France. He practiced similar "realism" during World War II when he promoted Franco-Nazi friendship, for which he was subsequently tried as a collaborator. *Ibid.*

ies."[155] Henry Ford, who managed to reconcile rabid anti-Communism and anti-Semitism with highly profitable commercial arrangements with the Soviet Union, also believed in the moral force of reality: "facts will control" ideas, he asserted, unwittingly paraphrasing Marx's dictum that being determines consciousness. The more the Communists industrialized, he argued, the more decently they would behave because "rightness in mechanics [and] rightness in morals are basically the same thing."[156]

Such rationalizations, frequently repeated and sometimes believed, received added strength from the unwillingness of businessmen to treat seriously Communist slogans about the coming world revolution. Businessmen tend to see in their own motives, in which material self-interest is the guiding force, the common aspirations of humanity. Ideas and ideologies not based on such interest they regard either as signs of immaturity or as camouflage: in the former case, they are curable by the actions of time, in the latter, they can be neutralized by attractive commercial propositions. The social and economic programs of the Bolsheviks appeared so fantastic to the average *homme d'affaires* that he refused to accept them at face value: as far as he was concerned, Russia's new rulers either did not mean what they said or else would quickly realize the absurdity of their ideas. In either event, they should be put to the test.

The Bolsheviks adroitly exploited this fallacy: already in 1918, Ioffe and Krasin had with some success advised German businessmen to ignore Moscow's "maximalism."[157] After the Civil War, when the economy had suffered a catastrophic collapse, Soviet representatives abroad used a similar tactic insinuating that, notwithstanding the Comintern, their country's supreme interest lay in peaceful commerce. While heading a trade mission to Britain in 1920–21, Krasin painted for English businessmen enticing prospects of trade with his country, which, in truth, had next to nothing to sell and little with which to buy. Moscow, which understood the weaknesses of the Western psyche far better than its strengths, exploited these illusions to the utmost. The New Economic Policy, a relaxation of economic restrictions introduced in 1921, which it depicted at home as a tactical and temporary retreat, was advertised abroad by no less an authority than Chicherin as intended to create "in Russia conditions that will favor the development of private initiative in the fields of industry, agriculture, transport, and commerce."[158] Such propaganda was readily believed by Western statesmen and businessmen since it fitted their preconceptions. The *New York Times* found a ready audience when it declared in 1921 in a dispatch of its Moscow correspondent that the Soviet government was "getting back to individualism" and personal initiative.[159]

A major reason why Western businessmen were so willing to ignore contrary evidence lay in the widespread conviction that Russia offered unlimited opportunities for the exploitation of natural resources and an outlet for manufactured goods; in the United States it was seen as the greatest "empty" market in the world, and in England as a "gold mine."[160] Given the immense expansion of productive capacity during World War I, especially in the United States, the Western business community had a very strong interest in the Russian market.

As it turned out, commercial arrangements paved the way for diplomatic recognition, which Western governments were reluctant to grant Soviet Russia because of her renunciation of debts and her subversive activities. Moscow had all along assumed, correctly as it turned out, that the way to diplomatic recognition lay through trade agreements, a premise Lloyd George confirmed when he told the House of Commons in March 1921 that the recent Anglo-Soviet trade accords were tantamount to de facto recognition of the Soviet state.*

The attitude of American labor could not have been more different. Samuel Gompers, the President of the American Federation of Labor (AFL), called the Bolsheviks "pirates." His successor, William Green, adopted a similar stance. American trade unions time and again turned down with large majorities pro-Communist resolutions sponsored by a small radical wing. The only organized labor groups to adopt a conciliatory attitude toward Soviet Russia were the Amalgamated Clothing Workers and the International Ladies' Garment Workers' Union, both organized by immigrants from Russia who harbored romantic illusions about the Communist experiment.

The posture of Western governments toward Soviet Russia was affected by a variety of factors, some of them of a contradictory nature. As had been the case with revolutionary France, the great powers were not unhappy to see a traditional rival weakened by internal turmoil. This fact was noted with dismay by Peter Struve, Wrangel's Foreign Minister, when in the summer of 1920 he met with Allied diplomats to seek help for his government.[161] The Germans in 1918, and Lloyd George as well as Joseph Pilsudski in 1919, acted on the assumption that Bolshevik Russia presented less of a threat than would a restored national Russia. This consideration helped them suppress their loathing of Communism and fear of its subversive activities.

The Western powers could not immediately grant recognition to the Soviet government even after victory in the Civil War had given it undisputed control of the country, because of its reputation as an outlaw regime: a regime that not only treated its citizens in a barbarous manner, but

---

*E. H. Carr, *The Bolshevik Revolution,* III (New York, 1953), 287n. Recognition was a matter of considerable importance for Soviet foreign trade, because Soviet purchases abroad were paid for in gold: as long as Soviet Russia lacked diplomatic recognition, the gold was liable to be seized on behalf of foreign creditors. On May 12, 1921, a British court ruled that Soviet bullion was not subject to such seizures: I. Maiskii, *Vneshniaia politika RSFSR* (Moscow, 1923), 102.

violated accepted norms of international conduct. In the latter category, its worst offense was repudiating the country's debts and nationalizing foreign properties.

Defaulting on debt was not a Soviet invention: it was a practice frequently resorted to by capitalist governments.* Even so, there was a fundamental and very troubling innovation in the Soviet move. Traditionally, defaulting countries pleaded inability to pay without denying responsibility for their debts. The Soviet decree of January 21, 1918, was the first instance in history of a government repudiating its country's obligations on principle. The Soviet action could not be accepted without imperiling the entire structure of international finance. No less important was its size, which dwarfed every previous default. As of January 1, 1918, the Russian state debt, domestic and foreign, was estimated at 60 billion rubles (nominally, 30 billion dollars), of which 13 billion rubles (6.5 billion dollars) was owed to foreign creditors.[162] In addition, Soviet nationalization decrees inflicted heavy losses on foreign owners of Russian enterprises and securities: French investors alone lost 2.8 billion dollars.

Moscow realized that this issue presented the greatest single obstacle to normalizing foreign relations and securing economic assistance abroad. In 1919, 1920, and 1921, Chicherin and other Soviet officials hinted more than once that their government was prepared, under certain conditions, both to repay its foreign debts and to compensate foreign investors. Thus, in July 1920, in response to the terms submitted by Britain for a trade accord, Moscow acknowledged "in principle" its obligation to repay moneys owed foreign citizens.[163] This total Russian foreign debt (to foreign governments and individuals) was estimated by officials in the Commissariat of Finance to amount to 4.4 billion gold rubles (2.2 billion dollars) of debt incurred before the outbreak of the World War, more than half of it owed to France, and the wartime debt of 8 billion gold rubles (4 billion dollars), mostly owed to Great Britain.[164] That the offer of repayment was not serious became apparent when the Soviet government made known its conditions: it would honor foreign debts provided that it received, in return, compensation for losses suffered from foreign assistance to its enemies. These, in its estimate, considerably exceeded the sums due to foreigners. Just by how much may be gathered from an internal report prepared for Lenin by an official in the Commissariat of Finance, S. Piliavskii, in September 1921. Combining the direct expenses for the Civil War, entirely charged to the Allies, with compensation for deaths and wounds suffered by the Red Army, also charged to them, Piliavskii arrived at the figure of 16.5

*See David Suratgar, ed., *Default and Rescheduling* (Washington, D.C., 1984), and F. Borchard and W. Wynne, *State Insolvency and Foreign Bondholders* (New Haven, Conn., 1951). According to Clifford Dammers (in Suratgar, *Default,* 77), in 1880, 54 percent of foreign government obligations were in default. Mr. Dammers in his survey inexplicably ignores the Soviet default of 1918, the greatest in history.

billion gold rubles (8.25 billion dollars). To this sum he added 30 billion gold rubles owed for "losses caused by pogroms and the moral injury inflicted on the population by torture," which he fixed at 30 billion gold rubles. He then added the cost of epidemics, decline of education, and all else that afflicted Russia since October 1917, to arrive at the global sum of 185.8 billion gold rubles or 92.9 billion dollars, which Soviet Russia could demand from the Allies. Piliavskii further thought, without attaching a figure, that Russia had the right to compensation for failing to obtain Constantinople and having to accept an unsatisfactory border with Poland.[165] These absurd claims were never released: Lenin recommended that they be seriously studied, but that the relevant documentation be destroyed.[166]*

Because of such factors, any rapprochement with Soviet Russia had to be accomplished gradually and obliquely: the way chosen was commerce. Lloyd George had unbounded faith in its efficacy: "The moment trade is established with Russia," he predicted, "Communism will go."[167] British "experts" saw great economic advantages accruing to the West from such trade, on the grounds that imports of Russian cereals, timber, and flax would lower world costs of these commodities and compel the United States to reduce grain prices.[168] In December 1919 and January 1920, the Allies agreed in Paris to terminate military intervention in Soviet Russia and to resume normal commercial relations with her.[169] But trade, too, was difficult to initiate as long as the issue of Russian debts remained unresolved, since Soviet assets were liable to be seized abroad by creditors. Hence, the Allies decided to open commercial relations not with the Soviet government but with Russian cooperatives.† From talks with Soviet cooperative leaders, including the head of Russian cooperatives abroad, Alexander Berkenheim, they learned that these organizations were "apolitical." The Paris bureau of the Russian cooperative movement claimed to have 25 million members and to hold vast stocks of grain for export. On January 16, 1920, the Allies agreed to enter into trade relations with the Russian cooperative organization, stipulating that this step did not imply diplomatic recognition.

In truth, Soviet cooperatives were not independent agents, having been nationalized in the spring of 1919 and integrated into the state economic machinery: their directing organ, Tsentrsoiuz, was a government department. The little independence they had managed to preserve they lost on

---

*In his confidential report to the Ninth Party Conference (September 1920), Lenin mocked "the strange people" in England and France "who still hoped to retrieve" the billions they had lost in Russia: *IA*, No. 1 (1992), 15.

†The notion that Soviet cooperatives were free agents and good potential trade partners is said to have been popularized by the historian Bernard Pares and by E. F. Wise, the top British representative on the Supreme Economic Council in Paris. See Bernard Pares, *My Russian Memoirs* (London, 1931), 562, and Richard H. Ullman, *The Anglo-Soviet Accord* (Princeton, 1972), 11.

January 27, 1920, when, anticipating their use in dealings with the West, Lenin drafted a decree placing them under complete Communist control.[170] The following month, Krasin departed for Western Europe to negotiate as head of Tsentrsoiuz. In reality, he represented the Soviet foreign trade organization (Vneshtorg): Radek described him as traveling in a "Trojan horse."[171] The charade made it possible for Western enterprises, eager for trade with Russia, to resume commerce without settling the thorny issue of Russian debts.

Fiction paved the way for reality. In the spring of 1920, Britain initiated commercial discussions with Moscow. The war with Poland and other impediments delayed the signing of a trade accord until April 1921. In the meantime, in May 1920, Sweden and Germany had concluded their own trade agreements with Moscow. These were the first commercial treaties between Soviet Russia and Western governments. The United States lifted the ban on private trade with Russia in July 1920. Soon the major European countries followed suit.

To the architects of Soviet Russia's foreign policy four countries were of special concern: Great Britain, the United States, France, and Germany. The highest priority they assigned to relations with Germany.

France remained the most implacable foe of the Bolshevik regime, for economic as well as political reasons. She had the greatest investments in Russia, and, therefore, suffered the greatest losses from Bolshevik defaults and nationalizations. She wanted a government there that would make good these losses. France also desired a friendly Russia to counterbalance Germany, whose revanchist aspirations she greatly feared. The U.S. refusal to join the League of Nations and to honor the pledge, given jointly with Britain, to defend France from foreign aggression, left her exposed and insecure. France sought to compensate for her weakness by conducting an intransigent policy toward the Weimar Republic and creating a *cordon sanitaire* separating Germany from Soviet Russia. The policy was exceedingly short-sighted, for it had the effect of undermining Germany's pro-Western government and pushing the Bolsheviks and German nationalists into each other's arms. Moscow had nothing to expect from France.

The United States, which had been relatively uninvolved in continental rivalries and lost relatively little from Soviet economic actions* regarded Communist Russia as an outlaw state and refused to have official dealings with her. In August 1920, the U.S. Secretary of State, Bainbridge Colby, explained why the United States could not recognize the "present rulers of Russia as a government with which the relations common to friendly gov-

---

*Total U.S. losses in Soviet Russia have been estimated at 223 million dollars: Dennis, *Foreign Policies,* 457.

ernments can be maintained." This stemmed not from objections to her political or social system, but from the Soviet regime's violations of "every usage and convention underlying the whole structure of international law." Its leaders "have frequently and openly boasted that they are willing to sign agreements and undertakings with foreign Powers while not having the slightest intention of observing such undertakings or carrying out such agreements." They have furthermore declared:

> The very existence of Bolshevism in Russia, the maintenance of their own rule, depends, and must continue to depend, upon the occurrence of revolutions in all other great civilized nations, including the United States, which will overthrow and destroy their governments and set up Bolshevist rule in their stead. They have made it quite plain that they intend to use every means, including, of course, diplomatic agencies, to promote such revolutionary movements in other countries.[172]

Washington, however, did not object to private commercial dealings with the Soviet government, which in the 1920s were by no means negligible.

From the time Britain had disengaged from the Civil War, and until his resignation in October 1922, Britain's policy toward Soviet Russia was dominated by Lloyd George. The Prime Minister, unfortunately, knew very little about that country: how little, he revealed in a speech in which he informed the House of Commons that Britain was assisting not only General Denikin and Admiral Kolchak, but even "General Kharkoff."[173] With the troublesome Whites out of the way, he intended to repair relations with the Soviet government, starting with trade, which would bring economic benefits to Britain and, at the same time, help moderate Communism.

Public opinion in Britain was strongly anti-Communist for a variety of reasons, the most important of which was resentment over Russia's defection in 1917 from the war, for which England paid with many lives. The British press, led by the *Times,* gave great prominence to stories of Bolshevik atrocities. The Foreign Office and the War Ministry both opposed a rapprochement with Soviet Russia. Churchill, however, was discredited by now and without influence. His anti-Bolshevism was regarded as a personal obsession; the failed intervention was ridiculed as "Mr. Churchill's private war."[174] In the Commons in February 1920, Lloyd George made a plea for "peace and trade with the Bolsheviks." "Trade," he said, "will bring an end to the ferocity . . . of Bolshevism." Did Russia have anything to trade? Certainly, he told the skeptics: "the corn bins of Russia are bulging with grain."[175] In this case the Prime Minister was not so much ignorant as disingenuous: although for public consumption he depicted Soviet Russia as a cornucopia, he was in receipt of information from the Foreign Secretary, Lord Curzon, that the country faced "complete economic disaster" and was in desperate need of foreign economic aid.[176] Lloyd George resorted to deception because given the state of public opinion, the rapprochement with Bolshevik Russia that he ardently desired had to be disguised as economically beneficial to Britain.

British-Soviet negotiations began with the arrival in London in May 1920 of a Soviet trade mission headed by Krasin, the only prominent Bolshevik with business experience. Krasin came as the representative of Russian cooperatives, but from the outset his mission was treated as a diplomatic one, to the extent of Britain's allowing him to communicate with Moscow by code and to dispatch and receive mail under seal.[177]

Although less hurt than France, Britain had lost substantial sums from Soviet defaults: Russia owed her 629 million pounds, more than nine-tenths of it borrowed during the war.* Hoping to be repaid in due course, Britain was prepared for the time being to be satisfied with Moscow's acknowledgment of responsibility for this debt. Her main concern now lay elsewhere: in Communist agitation in British industrial centers and the Middle East. Lloyd George's cabinet apparently hoped that in return for de facto recognition, implied by a trade accord, Moscow would cease such hostile activities.

Churchill believed these expectations to be naïve:

> The Bolsheviks are fanatics. Nothing will turn a fanatic from his purpose. L[loyd] G[eorge] thinks he can talk them over and that they will see the error of their ways and the impracticability of their schemes. Nothing of the sort! Their view is that their system has not been successful because it has not been tried on a large enough scale, and that in order to secure success they must make it world-wide.[178]

But Churchill's warnings went unheeded, and the trade negotiations got underway on May 31, 1920, when Krasin met with Lloyd George and his staff. For the Soviet government this encounter represented a historic breakthrough: the first occasion when its emissary was received by the head of government of a great power.[179] Krasin turned out to be so charming, his appearance and behavior contrasted so sharply with the prevalent image of Bolsheviks as savages, that some Englishmen who met him expressed doubts whether he was the genuine article. He told his hosts that the issue of Russia's debts would be settled following the restoration of peace and full diplomatic relations between the two countries. He insisted, however, that Britain would have to refrain from giving aid to Poland during their war. In the matter of supreme concern to Britain, namely hostile Soviet propaganda, especially in the Middle East, he promised that if Britain committed herself to normalizing relations and ceased further assistance to Soviet Russia's enemies (including Wrangel, who was still holding out in the Crimea), "she, in turn, [was] prepared to furnish full guarantees from participation in or connivance at any kind of hostile action, not only in the

---

*Ullman, *Anglo-Soviet Accord,* 107. This was equivalent to 3.145 billion dollars or 4,900 tons of gold, worth in 1990 some 60 billion dollars.

East but elsewhere."[180] In giving this pledge, Krasin apparently exceeded his mandate, because British intelligence intercepted and decoded an angry rebuke from Chicherin protesting these concessions, and from Lenin the following advice: "That swine Lloyd George has no scruples or shame in the way he deceives. Don't believe a word he says and gull him three times as much."*

The negotiations were temporarily disrupted by the Red Army's invasion of Poland, which caused great consternation in London: the prospect of a Communist Poland and a common border between Soviet Russia and Germany alarmed even Lloyd George.[181] In July 1920 Krasin returned to Russia.

In Moscow's eyes, Germany held the key to world revolution: nowhere did the Comintern pursue more zealously its subversive activities. German was the official language of the first two Congresses of the Comintern, and German delegates to them were accorded special honors. Moscow sent its top officials, Zinoviev and Radek, to address conferences of German socialist parties and trade unions.

The main obstacle to the Comintern's designs on Germany was its Social-Democratic Party (SPD). It was a socialist government that suppressed Communist rebellions in the winter of 1918–19, and again in March 1921. The German socialists knew the Bolsheviks from long association in the Second International and treated them with unconcealed disdain. The Bolsheviks repaid them by slandering SPD leaders with particular vehemence.

The SPD stand on the Bolshevik regime was first formulated in the summer of 1918 by Karl Kautsky in *The Dictatorship of the Proletariat*. Kautsky, who had personally known Marx and Engels and served as their literary executor, spoke with unique authority. He had opposed World War I and helped found the party's radical wing, the USPD. He had welcomed the October coup. But the Bolsheviks' methods of government were to him entirely unacceptable. He reproached them for establishing a one-party dictatorship and for pretending that the soviets were a superior form of democracy while using them to destroy democracy. The Bolshevik regime had nothing in common with socialism. Kautsky rejected the Bolsheviks' favorite analogy with the Paris Commune: "[The Paris Commune] was the work of the whole proletariat. All socialist currents participated in it: none excluded itself or was excluded from it. By contrast, the socialist party that today rules Russia came to power in a struggle against the other socialist parties. It exercises power to the exclusion from its ruling organs of the other socialist parties."[182] In 1919, Kautsky published a second apprais-

---

*Christopher Andrew, *Her Majesty's Secret Service* (New York, 1986), 262. The British cryptographic service employed a Russian named E. C. Fetterlein, who cracked the Soviet diplomatic cipher: *Ibid.*, 261–62.

al of the Soviet experiment, *Terrorism and Communism*.[183] Here he described the Soviet Russian regime as *"Kasernensozialismus"* ("barracks socialism").

The Bolshevik leaders could not ignore this criticism, coming as it did from a man widely seen as the heir of Marx and Engels. Lenin, unable or unwilling to cope with Kautsky's arguments, resorted to abuse. In an essay written at the end of 1918 he castigated the German socialist as a "bourgeois lackey" and "base renegade."[184] Trotsky gave a more reasoned reply in his own *Terrorism and Communism*.* Conceding that Soviet Russia was a dictatorship, he pointed out that it was a dictatorship of the working class: in submitting to compulsion, the worker was in fact obeying himself.[185] Marx, he argued, had never made a shibboleth of democracy and had never placed it above the class struggle.

Especially damaging to the Bolshevik reputation in Germany was the censure of Rosa Luxemburg, who jointly with Karl Liebknecht headed the Spartacists, and whom no one, not even Lenin, dared to accuse of being a renegade, since she paid for her convictions with her life. Luxemburg actively worked for a socialist revolution in Germany during and after World War I and also approved of the Bolshevik coup. Nevertheless, she opposed Moscow's insistence on an immediate seizure of power in Germany on the grounds that German workers were not ready to take over. She also opposed the creation of the Comintern, fearing that it was bound to lead to the domination of international Communism by the Bolsheviks, whom she mistrusted.[186]

In the fall of 1918, while in prison for her antiwar activities, Luxemburg wrote a critique of Lenin's regime. German Communists judged it "inopportune" and delayed its publication until 1922: even then, they saw fit to bring it out only in a bowdlerized version.[187] Luxemburg lauded the Bolsheviks as the only committed socialists in Russia. She disapproved, however, of the Land Decree, because it strengthened the peasant's proprietary instincts and widened the gulf between city and countryside. She also denounced the Bolshevik policy of "national self-determination" as responsible for the disintegration of the Russian Empire, a regressive phenomenon from the socialist point of view.

But, like Kautsky, she reserved her harshest words for the Bolshevik suppression of democracy. (She did not refer to the Red Terror, formally introduced in September 1918, possibly because she did not know of it.) The critical event in the political degeneration of the Bolshevik regime was the dispersal of the Constituent Assembly. If, as the Bolsheviks claimed in self-justification, the Assembly elected in November 1917 no longer reflected the mood of the masses as of January 1918, then they should have

---

*Ann Arbor, Michigan, 1961. As a concession to American sensitivities, the book originally came out in the United States under the title *Dictatorship vs. Democracy*.

held fresh elections instead of liquidating it. Next in importance came the suppression of the press and the rights to assembly and association, "without which the rule of the broad masses is utterly inconceivable."[188]

> Freedom only for supporters of the Government, only for members of the Party, no matter how numerous they may be, is no freedom. Freedom is always the freedom for him who thinks differently. Not because of a fanatical commitment to "justice," but because everything enlightening, wholesome, and purifying in political liberty derives from its independence and loses effectiveness when "freedom" turns into a privilege.[189]

She criticized the Bolshevik practice of governing by decree, which had been a fine device for destroying the old order but was worse than useless in constructing a new one. Creativity demanded unfettered freedom. "The public life of states with restricted freedom turns out to be so inadequate, so poor, so schematic, so infertile, precisely because, by excluding democracy, it dams up all the living sources of prosperity and progress."[190] Without openness, Soviet officialdom was bound to fall prey to corruption. She predicted the thorough bureaucratization of Soviet life: its consequence will be a dictatorship not of the proletariat but of a "handful of politicians, *i.e.,* a dictatorship in the bourgeois sense, in the sense of Jacobin rule."[191]

These astute analyses, which anticipated the theories of the "Eurocommunists" of the 1960s, Luxemburg went on to weaken with the absurd claim that, properly understood, "dictatorship" was not an alternative to "democracy" but its complement: "Dictatorship is the art of using democracy, not of eliminating it."[192] As she defined it, the dictatorship of the proletariat presumed mass participation. When leading the German Revolution in November 1918, she would indeed insist that the "Spartacus League will never take power except in accordance with the clearly expressed will of the great majority of the proletariat masses of Germany"[193] —which was as good as saying never. In practice she exhorted the minuscule minority of revolutionaries affiliated with the Spartacists to topple the government of Philipp Scheidemann and Friedrich Ebert, although the government had taken office with the consent of the All-German Council Congress, which represented the great majority of German labor.[194]

These polemics revealed once again the cultural chasm separating Russian and European radicals. Kautsky and Rosa Luxemburg spoke of democracy and civil freedom as indispensable preconditions of socialism. For Lenin and Trotsky, who had acquired their political education under tsarism, politics was warfare and victory required unquestioned obedience: in Trotsky's phrase, "intimidation" was as indispensable to revolution as to war[195]—a truism that by a sleight of tongue was made to apply not to enemies but to one's own people. Both Lenin and Trotsky argued in the terms, sometimes in the actual language, of the most reactionary defenders of tsarist autocracy. But whatever their argument lacked in theoretical substance, it gained from the incontrovertible fact that they had acquired power and their German critics had not.

Controversies of this kind exacerbated the animosity between the Bolsheviks and German Social Democrats. Although the SPD opposed Allied intervention in Russia and in 1920 prevented Allied military supplies from reaching Poland, Moscow never forgot that it was their government that had suppressed Communist uprisings in Germany. To add to its sins, the SPD favored a pro-Western policy. In 1923, Zinoviev publicly accused German Social Democrats of paving the way for the "Fascists."[196] This charge became official policy of the Comintern after its Fifth Congress had designated the German Social-Democratic Party the "left-wing of Fascism."[197]

Moscow, however, was not without potential allies in Germany, and of these the most promising were the reactionary political and military circles, the future supporters of Hitler. It was a marriage of convenience based on a shared hatred of the SPD and the Versailles Treaty.

Recent scholarship has demonstrated the remarkable continuity of German *Russlandpolitik* from its birth in Imperial Germany, through the Weimar Republic to the Nazi era. From the February Revolution until the Nazi invasion of Soviet Russia, German conservatives and militarists viewed an alliance with Russia, in which Germany would play the role of senior partner, as an indispensable precondition first of retaining and then, after November 1918, of recapturing for their country the status of a world power.[198] During the Weimar period this trend was intensified by the desire to abrogate the Versailles Treaty, in which Germans could only rely on the help of Moscow. As soon as the terms of the treaty had been made public (May 1919), the Soviet Commissariat of Foreign Affairs denounced it and appealed to German workers to follow suit.[199] The Comintern released on May 13 a proclamation, "Down with the Versailles Treaty!" which set the tone of its policy.[200] This reaction paved the way for an understanding between Moscow and the German right. Standing alone against France and the "Anglo-Saxons," Germany was powerless; with Soviet Russia at her side, she was a power to be reckoned with.[201] The issue was starkly formulated by the German Prime Minister, Joseph Wirth: "The only chance I see for us to rise again as a great power is for the German and Russian people to work together as neighbors in friendship and understanding."[202]

The attraction of nationalistic Germans for Soviet Russia became evident as early as 1919, when a German academic of extreme right-wing views urged the adoption of Bolshevism as a means of escaping Allied "enslavement."[203] Such ideas produced a curious movement, labeled by Karl Radek "National Bolshevism," which gained a following in the left wing of the Nazi Party. Its philosophy called for an alliance between Communists and nationalists in a united front against democracy and the Western powers. Although Moscow initially rejected this heresy, which won some adherents also in the German Communist Party (KPD), it soon changed its mind. In March 1920, during the so-called Kapp putsch organized by right-wing politicians and generals to place the country under a military dictatorship, the leadership of the German Communist Party, almost certainly on orders from Moscow, assumed a neutral stance, announcing that "the proletariat will not lift a finger for the democratic republic."* If Moscow could not have a Communist Germany, it preferred a right-wing military dictatorship there to a democracy governed by the Social Democrats.

The link between Moscow and the German right was provided by Radek, who had spent many years before the war in Germany working as a Social Democratic journalist and knew well German conditions. Incarcerated in February 1919 for his role in the Spartacist revolt, he was at first kept in strict isolation. After the publication of the Versailles Treaty his treatment greatly improved and henceforth he lived in comfortable quarters, treated more like a guest than a prisoner. In August 1919, when he was allowed visitors, he established what he called a "prison salon," receiving Communists as well as prominent military and political figures, including Walter Rathenau, then President of the giant AEG concern and later Minister of Foreign Affairs, a strong advocate of economic ties with Soviet Russia.[204] Radek owed such preferential treatment to German generals eager to inaugurate military cooperation with Moscow. The Spartacist Ruth Fischer was astonished to have her meeting with Radek arranged by officers who provided her with false identity papers for the occasion.[205]

Radek had been sent to Germany to organize a revolution. The experience of the Spartacist revolts, however, disillusioned him: he reluctantly concluded that Germany was not ripe for revolution and would be of greater use to Soviet Russia as a military and economic partner. Under his influence, Rathenau founded a commission to study the prospects of trade with Russia.[206] In October 1919 Germany rejected the Allied demand that she join in the blockade of Russia: it was her first act of defiance since Versailles.[207] The action received full backing from the nationalist right. In November Germany welcomed Victor Kopp, an official of the Commissariat of Foreign Affairs. Kopp's ostensible task was to arrange for the exchange of civilian and military prisoners of war, but he was treated as a de facto Soviet envoy and permitted to communicate with Moscow in cipher.[208] He sent Lenin frequent and elaborate letters on the internal situation in Germany and on Russo-German relations. In January 1920 Gustav Hilger went to Moscow as his counterpart.[209]

Collaboration with Soviet Russia had support among various strata of German opinion, the Social Democrats excepted, but its most zealous champions were the military, and among them no one supported it more

*Ossip Flechtheim, *Die Kommunistische Partei in der Weimarer Republik* (Offenbach a.M., 1948), 62. This tactic was later abandoned under the pressure of the Communist rank and file: Gerald Freund, *Unholy Alliance* (New York, 1957), 59–60.

31. Von Seeckt.

enthusiastically than General Hans von Seeckt, a political general who
viewed the army as the "purest reflection of the State."[210] The provisions of
the Versailles Treaty requiring the virtual demilitarization of Germany were
for him tantamount to a death sentence on the nation. In March 1920 he
refused to join the generals who under Wolfgang Kapp tried to seize power.
His reward was appointment as Chief of the Army Command (Chef der
Heeresleitung), the highest military post in the country, which he held until
1926.[211] He immediately began to draw up plans for building an army of
21 modern divisions: once that force was in place, Germany would present
the Allies with a fait accompli and renounce the Versailles Treaty.[212] This
objective, however, could be attained only with Soviet help.

Seeckt, who cultivated Radek, initiated in 1919 secret military negotiations with Soviet Russia with the view to circumventing those provisions of
the Versailles Treaty that denied the German army, or Reichswehr, the
sinews of modern warfare: aviation, heavy artillery, tanks, and poison gas.
The collaboration, which he initiated and which continued in greatest secrecy until 1933, was to prove of immense importance to both the German
and Soviet armies in preparing them for World War II. Unfortunately,
since the Germans systematically destroyed the documentary evidence[213]
and the bulk of the Soviet documentation has not yet been released, much
that concerns this episode remains obscure.[214]

In Seeckt's view, Germany's unchangeable objective was political and
economic understanding with "Great Russia." It lay in Germany's interest
to help reconstruct Russia economically: while Russia needed Germany as

a source of know-how and organization, Germany required Russian raw materials and foodstuffs.²¹⁵ Under postwar conditions this cooperation entailed the reestablishment, under Bolshevik rule, of the Russian state within its pre-1914 borders, which would restore a common border between the two countries; defeat of the White armies; and destruction of independent Poland, the bulwark of French influence:

> Only in firm cooperation with a Great Russia does Germany stand a chance of regaining her position as a world power. . . . It is quite immaterial whether we like or dislike the new Russia and her internal structure. Our policy would have been the same vis-à-vis Tsarist Russia or a state under Kolchak or Denikin. Now we have to come to terms with Soviet Russia— we have no alternative. . . . If we disregard earlier times, when it was wrongly held that our eastern neighbor could be rendered harmless through demolition, blasting, and partition, now everybody's eyes should be opened to the fact that the sole purpose of creating Poland, Lithuania, Latvia was to erect a wall to separate Germany from Russia.²¹⁶

To Seeckt and his followers, the very existence of independent Poland, a French "vassal" state, was an affront, since it provided the vital link in the French campaign to "encircle" Germany. Seeckt, Radek wrote Chicherin from Berlin, seemed perfectly calm and self-controlled except when the subject of Poland came up; then his eyes lit up like an animal's: "She must be partitioned," he said, "and will be partitioned as soon as Russia or Germany grows strong."²¹⁷ This view was widely shared. Many Germans believed that the destruction of independent Poland would in and of itself abrogate the Versailles Treaty—which, as we have seen, happened to be Lenin's view as well.* It would have the effect of allowing Germany to break out of the isolation imposed on her by the victors. A memorandum drafted by the staff of the German Ministry of War defined the issue as follows:

> The Allies realize clearly that only a German Reich that is surrounded on all sides by borderland states and in the West by the Allies cannot defend herself against the Versailles Treaty. Direct contact between Germany and Russia offers both countries fresh possibilities of development from which Germany must, without doubt, derive the greater advantage and greater utility in attaining the main objective: the revision of the Versailles Treaty.²¹⁸

To achieve this end, German nationalists were prepared to see the Red Army on the German frontier. They seem to have been unaware of Soviet strategy, for which the destruction of independent Poland was only a step to the German Revolution to be carried out with the help of the Red

---

*Germany also hoped to regain from Poland's destruction Danzig and Upper Silesia: *Sovetsko-Germanskie otnosheniia ot peregovorov v Brest-Litovske do podpisaniia Rapall'skogo dogovora,* II (Moscow, 1971), 167.

Army. In the summer of 1920 the majority of Germans, from the extreme left to the extreme right, cheered the Red Army as it advanced into Poland: in the Reichstag, all parties expressed sympathy for Russia's side in the war.[219]

On July 26, as the Red Army neared Warsaw, Seeckt sent the German President a memorandum outlining his political program.[220] Soviet victory over Poland was a foregone conclusion. Soon Soviet troops will approach the frontier of Germany, he predicted, and the two countries will once again stand in immediate proximity: a principal objective of Versailles—isolating Germany from Russia—will be foiled. It was in Germany's interest that Russia defeat Poland because Moscow was helping her fight "Anglo-Saxon capitalism and imperialism." "The future belongs to Russia": she was inexhaustible and unconquerable. "If Germany sides with Russia then she herself will become invincible": the Allies will have to reckon with Germany because in back of her will stand a mighty power. By contrast, a Germany aligned with the West would turn into a nation of "helots." Hence the government's policy of buying Allied goodwill with concessions was contrary to the national interest. Russia's intrusion in Germany's internal affairs need not be feared: she was certain to respect her sovereignty because she needed Germany. But even if Russia were to violate the frontiers of 1914, rather than turn for help to the Western democracies Germany should enter into an alliance with her. Seeckt believed that a pro-Soviet policy would have the additional advantage of enabling the government to appease the masses attracted to Bolshevism, in this manner helping to stabilize the home front. He advocated reforms that would bring together manufacturers and workers and thus neutralize Communist agitation. His program of combining nationalism with socialism directly anticipated the strategy adopted by Hitler.

Collaboration with Soviet Russia was also favored by German industrialists alarmed by the prospect of shrinking markets for their manufactures in a world dominated by the victorious "Anglo-Saxons." Already in the spring of 1919, a year before such commerce was officially legalized and in defiance of the Allied blockade, German enterprises began to export goods to Soviet Russia, accepting payment in worthless paper rubles. The Allied blockade and other obstacles to the illicit commerce were overcome by various devices, such as shipping merchandise by air from East Prussia or through neutral intermediaries.* Such activities were justified with the argument that Germany could not afford to lose her traditional markets in Eastern Europe. The German Ministry of Economics in June 1919 argued as follows:

> There is reason to fear that if in the future we should also refuse to have economic relations with Russia then other governments, notably

---

*Sovetsko-Germanskie otnosheniia, II, 107–09, 113–15, 116–18, 153–54. The German Ministry of Economics reported that a good part of the agricultural machinery that Germany exported to Denmark and Sweden these two countries resold to Soviet Russia at a high profit: Ibid., II, 119.

England and the United States of America, will take our place in the Russian economy. According to information reaching us, unofficial representatives of the Entente and America are active in this direction, working to ensure for themselves all kinds of economic connection with Russia.[221]

At a conference organized by the German Ministry of Foreign Affairs in February 1920, one of its officials said: "If in the past affairs connected with Russia were largely in German hands, then now our previous enemies are striving to take them into their own hands."[222]

The pro-Soviet orientation of Germany's politics and economics was vigorously supported by Ulrich von Brockdorff-Rantzau, the Minister of Foreign Affairs, who in 1917, as ambassador to Copenhagen, had been instrumental in arranging for Lenin's passage through Germany and would soon become Germany's ambassador to Moscow.[223] One of the few prominent dissenters from this consensus was Rathenau, who, favorable as he was to close relations with Soviet Russia, thought she was as yet in no position to become a serious trading partner: the idea that she had large surpluses for export he dismissed as "fables." Russia could revert to her traditional role as exporter and importer only after Germany had rebuilt her economy. Personally, he preferred to see Germany in the role of "intermediary" between Russia and the United States.[224]

After Germany had legalized private commerce with Soviet Russia (May 1920) the two countries experienced a rapid growth of economic relations: in the next five months, Germany sold to Russia merchandise in excess of 100 million marks in value, mostly agricultural implements, printing machinery, and office equipment.[225] Before long German firms entered into commercial agreements with Soviet Russia, from which they acquired concessions for the exploitation of natural resources. In January 1921, the Minister of Foreign Affairs told the Reichstag that his government had no objections to expanded commercial relations with Moscow: "Communism as such is no reason why a German republican and bourgeois government should not trade with the Soviet Government."[226] That summer, Krasin arrived in Germany. Following his visit, joint Soviet-German companies were set up to handle the sea and air traffic between the two countries. Concessions were granted to German firms, Krupp among them, to manufacture tractors. Ambitious plans were drawn up to lease the port and manufacturing facilities of Petrograd to the Krupp concern.[227] Communist subversion and repeated putsches did not alarm German businessmen; apparently they did not take those activities seriously, and, in any event, they felt confident that giving Soviet Russia a stake in capitalism would make her less eager to subvert Germany: "The Bolsheviks must save us from Bolshevism," was a slogan given currency by the Foreign Office.[228] The Communist putsch of March 1921, launched at the very time when the two countries were negotiating trade agreements, had no effect on the talks. Thus was put in place the groundwork for the German-Soviet rapprochement that the two powers were to spring on an unsuspecting world in 1922 at Rapallo.

Lenin made no secret of the importance he attached to propaganda: in a conversation with Bertrand Russell he identified it as one of the two factors that had enabled his government to survive against overwhelming odds (the other being the disunity of his opponents).[229] We shall treat the domestic propaganda campaigns of the Communist regime elsewhere[230] and here concentrate on their international dimension.

A major instrument of propaganda were the wire services, which the new regime nationalized. In September 1918, Moscow created the Russian Telegraphic Agency (Russkoe Telegrafnoe Agentstvo, or ROSTA) to serve "as the transmitter (*provodnik*) of the party line in the press."[231] ROSTA was not so much an information as a propaganda agency: it employed, for example, artists to design posters. In 1922 it received a monopoly on information services. In 1925 it was renamed the Telegraphic Agency of the Soviet Union, or TASS.

The West was immensely curious about Soviet Russia, and as soon as the Civil War was over, numerous travelers and journalists made their way there. Some published accounts: the market for such eyewitness literature was insatiable because Western readers, confused by contradictory information about the Communist experiment, trusted it more. In France alone between 1918 and 1924 there appeared 34 accounts by returning travelers.[232] By the time of Lenin's death, several hundred books and many more articles had been published in the West by foreign visitors to Soviet Russia.

Moscow could not, of course, control what foreigners wrote once they had returned home, but it could and did control whom to admit. Exit and entry visas were introduced early: two months after taking power, the new regime decreed that all who desired to leave or enter the country required permission and had to submit to frontier searches to ensure they were not carrying forbidden items, or documents that could "harm the political and economic interests of the Russian Republic."[233] The authorities made certain that foreigners who came to Soviet Russia were well disposed, or, at least, susceptible to manipulation.

In an age when the press served as the principal source of information, the best way to assure that Soviet Russia received favorable coverage abroad was to accredit only those newspapers and journalists who had given proof of a cooperative attitude. Whether they cooperated from conviction or self-interest was immaterial. Since every major newspaper and wire service wanted a bureau in Moscow, most complied with the demand to send friendly correspondents. Journalists in Moscow learned to minimize, rationalize, or, if necessary, ignore adverse information, blur the distinction between Soviet intentions and Soviet realities, and deride the regime's critics. Once they acquired the habit, they sooner or later turned into conveyors of Soviet propaganda. Much of the foreign press corps came to practice a form of self-censorship. Before cabling a dispatch, a correspondent had to secure approval of the Press Department of the Commissariat of Foreign Affairs. "One took them in," recalls Malcolm Muggeridge, "to be censored, like taking an essay to one's tutor at Cambridge; watching anxiously as they were read over for any frowns or hesitations, dreading to see a pencil picked to slash something out." One censor refused Muggeridge permission to cable some information, explaining: "You can't say that because it's true."[234]

Newspapers that refused to cooperate were penalized. The outstanding victim was *The Times* of London. During the Revolution and Civil War, *The Times* adopted an extremely hostile attitude toward the Bolsheviks. Its regular Russian correspondent, Robert Wilton, an unabashed monarchist and anti-Semite, left for England in September 1917; when he tried to return six months later, he was denied entry. *The Times* refused to replace him with a more compliant journalist, as a result of which, for the next twenty years, the most authoritative newspaper in the world had its Soviet correspondent based in Riga.[235] For direct reporting from Soviet Russia, the English public depended on journalists sympathetic to the Communist cause: Arthur Ransome of the *Manchester Guardian* and the *Daily News,* Michael Farbman and George Lansbury of the *Daily Herald,* and M. Phillipps Price, also of the *Guardian.**

Lansbury may serve as an example of an unscrupulous Western journalist who entered Soviet employ with open eyes. A self-designated "Christian pacifist," he was the editor from 1908 of the *Daily Herald,* the organ of the radical wing of the Labour Party. In early 1920 the paper fell on hard times. Facing insolvency, Lansbury journeyed to Moscow in search of financial assistance. As soon as his request for subsidies had been approved, the *Daily Herald* adopted an unambivalently pro-Soviet position: in a message from Copenhagen to Moscow intercepted by British intelligence, Maxim Litvinov, the Soviet Deputy Commissar of Foreign Affairs, reported, "In Russian questions [the *Daily Herald*] acts as if it were our organ."[236] One of the paper's directors, Francis Meynell, received in Copenhagen from Litvinov a packet of jewels that he smuggled into England. When in August 1920 Krasin and Kamenev arrived in London to resume the trade negotiations disrupted by the Polish war, they brought with them precious stones and platinum, which they sold through intermediaries. The proceeds,

---

*Forty-five years later, Price admitted that he had not behaved professionally when reporting from Soviet Russia. Referring to *My Reminiscences of the Russian Revolution* (London, 1921), a book based on his *Manchester Guardian* dispatches, he wrote: "I did not let the narrative speak for itself, but expounded my own views, as if I had been listening to the speeches of Lenin and Trotsky and were repeating something of what I had heard. Moreover, the book contains fairly extensive passages of communist jargon which I had picked up in those two years. I had become, in fact, a 'fellow-traveller.' " *Survey,* No. 41 (April 1962), 16.

amounting to 40,000 pounds, they gave to Lansbury; eventually, the subsidy reached the sum of 75,000 pounds. Unfortunately for the Russians, they were under surveillance by Scotland Yard, which kept a record of the banknotes realized from the sales. On August 19, the British government released to the press the intercepted messages between Litvinov and Chicherin concerning these handouts,[237] following which Lansbury had to return the money.* Kamenev was expelled from Britain for his role in the affair.[238] Lansbury remained loyal to Moscow: the services he had rendered to a foreign power did not disqualify him from being chosen in 1931 Chairman of the Labour Party.

The leading American daily, the *New York Times,* did not follow the example of its London namesake. In the early years of the Communist regime, it, too, was exceedingly hostile, contributing to the so-called "Red Scare." Much of its anti-Communism, however, was emotional and based on hearsay. In August 1920, Walter Lippmann and Charles Marz published a scathing critique of the *New York Times'*s coverage of Soviet Russia, showing that it had reported the demise of the Bolshevik government on no fewer than 91 occasions.[239] When in 1920 the *New York Times* requested Soviet permission to send a correspondent to Moscow, Litvinov replied that "while he would welcome conversations with sympathetic newspapers like the London *Daily Herald* or the *Manchester Guardian,* a hostile one like the *New York Times* would not be considered."[240] In other words, if the paper wanted a Soviet bureau, it would have to change its attitude toward Soviet Russia. The *New York Times* chose to comply.

One of the most outspoken anti-Communists on the *New York Times* staff was Walter Duranty. An Englishman by birth and upbringing, he had much in common with John Reed, in that like him he came from a socially undistinguished (although far less affluent) family and had suffered snubs from schoolmates.[241] Duranty, who in 1920 held a minor post with the *New York Times* Paris office, was eager to go to Russia as a full-fledged correspondent. Moscow cold-shouldered him, but he found ways to overcome its hostility by publishing some friendly remarks about Litvinov and assuring his readers that with the New Economic Policy (NEP) Lenin had "thrown Communism overboard."[242] A few days after these items had appeared in print, the *New York Times* was informed it could send a correspondent to Moscow. The assignment went to Duranty, who received a Soviet visa and accreditation, albeit on a "probationary" basis. Once in Moscow, he ingratiated himself with the Soviet authorities by cabling "on the spot" reports that played down, without denying, the sordid aspects of Soviet reality (such as the famine of 1921). He further stressed Lenin's alleged adoption of Western economic models, which was very important for Mos-

---

*The publication of these materials alerted the Commissariat of Foreign Affairs that its codes had been broken: RTsKhIDNI, F. 2, op. 2, ed. khr. 404.

cow to convey at a time when it actively sought foreign credits. To allay concerns about the revolutionary proclamations of the Communist International, Duranty drew a false distinction between the Comintern, which he portrayed as staffed by "fanatics," and the "realists" running the Soviet government, whom he depicted as "quite willing to let the communist fanatics blow off . . . steam."[243]

Duranty's "probation" was lifted, and as Moscow correspondent of the *New York Times* he became the most prestigious American journalist in Russia. The position not only brought him influence and fame, but also enabled him to enjoy Moscow's high life, which flourished under the NEP: nightclubbing at the Grand, poker at the Savoy, embassy parties, carousing in his imported Buick, the favors of a Russian mistress. His extravagant life-style led some to suspect that he was on the Soviet payroll.[244] Jay Lovestone, a leading figure in the American Communist Party and a frequent visitor to Moscow in the 1920s, believed Duranty to have worked for the security police.[245] To enjoy such perquisites, Duranty increasingly resorted to outright lies: he denied, for example, that Russia lived under police terror and assured his readers that a well-behaved Soviet citizen had no more to fear from the police than Americans from the Department of Justice.* His falsehoods gained credibility because he balanced them with minor concessions to the truth. He was neither a sympathizer of Communism nor a friend of the Russian people, but simply a corrupt individual who made a living by lying. Eugene Lyons, who saw him often, writes that Duranty "remained, after all his years in Russia, detached from its life and fate, curiously contemptuous of Russians. He spoke of Soviet triumphs and travail as he might of a murder mystery he had read, but with not half the passion or sense of personal involvement."[246]

Duranty had the good fortune to choose Stalin early as Lenin's most likely successor (he later boasted that he had picked "the right horse on which to bet in the Russian race"[247]), which greatly helped his career after Lenin's death. His eulogies of Stalin became ever more exorbitant and his mendaciousness ever more brazen. In the 1930s he praised collectivization and in 1932–34 denied the Ukrainian famine. To lure investments to Soviet Russia, he spread false stories about the great profits allegedly made by American businessmen there, especially his friend Armand Hammer.† These accomplishments earned him in 1932 the Pulitzer Prize for "scholarship, profundity, impartiality, sound judgment and exceptional clarity."[248]

---

*The analogy was also drawn by Louise Bryant, who wrote, "Even we ourselves have a Cheka, but we call it a Department of Justice": *Mirrors of Moscow* (New York, 1923), 54.
†Joseph Finder, *Red Carpet* (New York, 1983), 67. Julius Hammer, an American millionaire Communist, settled in Moscow and received a concession for the exploitation of asbestos mines in the Urals. His son, Armand, assisted him in this work and later manufactured pencils and office equipment. Lenin, *PSS*, LIV, 806. With his brother, Armand Hammer also sold abroad artworks the Communist regime had requisitioned from their owners and disposed of for badly needed hard currency.

It has been said that no individual had done more to promote in the United States a favorable image of the Soviet Union at a time when she was suffering under the most savage tyranny known to man. Radek said that his reporting had been most influential in paving the way for U.S. diplomatic recognition in 1933.[249]

Only slightly less harmful was the disinformation spread by Louis Fischer, the Russian correspondent of *The Nation,* who is said to have been under the influence of his wife, an employee of the Commissariat of Foreign Affairs.[250]

Russian émigres of every political persuasion tried to inform Europeans and Americans about the Soviet regime, but their influence was negligible because the outside world saw them as poor losers. The Mensheviks Martov and Rafael Abramovich appeared regularly at gatherings of European socialists to speak about Soviet realities. Their admonitions sometimes resulted in Western socialist and trade-union organizations passing perfunctory resolutions critical of the Soviet government. In practical terms, however, their exertions yielded nothing, since in typically schizophrenic Menshevik-SR fashion they neutralized such admonitions with exhortations to defend Soviet Russia from Western "imperialism."

Paul Miliukov, the titular leader of the Constitutional-Democratic Party, published in 1920 a warning to the West that Communism was not, as widely believed, a purely Russian affair.[251] Communism had two aspects, one internal, the other international. But it was primarily a doctrine for export and the driving force behind it was the idea of world revolution. Such counsel, too, found little acceptance in the West. Miliukov himself soon converted to the notion that Communism was a transitory illness and a prelude to the triumph of democracy in Russia.

Russian monarchists enjoyed much greater success abroad. In the 1920s Germany became a haven for Russian right-wing exiles, many of them uprooted Baltic Germans. These émigrés established connections with German nationalists and injected into their ideology the notion that Communism and Jewry were one and the same. It was they who popularized in the West the *Protocols of the Elders of Zion,* until then an obscure pamphlet available only in Russian.

The record of the Comintern, from its foundation in 1919 until its formal dissolution in 1943, is one of unrelieved failure. In the words of its historian, and onetime member, Franz Borkenau, "The history of the Comintern has many ups and downs. It contains no steady progress, not a single lasting success."[252] These failures have to be attributed first and foremost to the Bolsheviks' ignorance of foreign political cultures. Their leaders had spent long periods in the West: between 1900 and 1917, Lenin lived all but two years in Europe, Trotsky all but seven, and Zinoviev all but five. But even as they lived in their midst, they had little contact with Westerners, for they led isolated existences in émigré communities and communicated only with the more radical elements of European socialism. The Comintern's dismal record abroad emphasizes the extent to which Communism, its international trappings notwithstanding, was essentially a Great Russian phenomenon, unsuited for export. This cultural difference was seen by some observers already then as raising an insurmountable barrier between East and West: the expression "iron curtain" was in use as early as 1920.[253]

The failures of the Comintern can be also attributed to specific causes. In 1918–20, there were in Western Europe no revolutionary parties remotely like the Bolshevik Party in numbers and organization. When they emerged, first under Kemal in Turkey and then under Mussolini in Italy, they took the path of nationalism and employed Lenin's methods not to promote Communism but to fight it. European socialist parties were loosely organized on the Menshevik rather than the Bolshevik model, and although each had a radical wing, they were committed to reform: the closer their links to trade unions, the less appetite did they have for revolution. Moscow succeeded in forming European Communist parties only in the second half of 1920. In the critical period immediately following the Armistice, when the opportunities for spreading revolution were best, it had no dependable partners abroad.

But even when European Communist parties did emerge, the Bolsheviks were unable to use them effectively because they insisted on their adopting the strategy and tactics of coup d'état and civil war used in Russia. This was not feasible, if only because the anarchy the Bolsheviks had exploited in their own country did not exist in Western Europe: even in Germany, an effective government was in place three months after the Kaiser's abdication. Nor did the Russian leadership of the Comintern make allowance for European nationalism. When in April 1918 an anarchist pointed out that the Western worker would never have dared to make the October Revolution because he "feels himself the bearer of a fragment of power and a part of the same state which [he] is at present defending," whereas the Russian proletariat is "spiritually non-statist," Lenin dismissed such talk as "silly," "primitive," and "obtuse."[254] Much as he liked to remind the hotheads in his ranks that Europe was not Russia, that making revolution there was incomparably more difficult, in practice Lenin acted as if such differences did not matter. In July 1920, he ordered the Red Army to march on Warsaw, doing so in the conviction, based on the lessons of the Civil War, that the masses did not respond to patriotic appeals. He soon learned otherwise, but experience taught the Bolsheviks nothing in this respect: each failure abroad they blamed either on some tactical mistakes or the indecisiveness of foreign Communists. "We must teach, teach and teach the English Communists to work the way the Bolsheviks used to work," Lenin insisted.[255] This attitude exasperated foreign Communists. "Is there nothing more," a British Comintern delegate asked Zinoviev, "to learn from the struggles, movements and revolutions of other countries? Have [the Russians] come here not to learn, but only to teach?"[256] Another British delegate to the Second Congress of the Comintern wrote on his return:

> The utter incapacity of the Congress to legislate for the British movement was perhaps the most conspicuous fact there. Some of the tactics that were useful and successful in Russia would be grotesque failures if put into operation here. The difference between conditions in this highly-organized, industrially-centralised, politically compact and insular country, and medieval, semi-barbaric, loosely-organised (politically) and politically-infantile Russia is almost inconceivable to those who have not been there to see.[257]

In the end, foreign Communists almost always suppressed their doubts and yielded to Moscow's wishes because of its unique prestige earned by having staged the only successful revolution. Those who balked or protested too much, Lenin expelled from the Comintern. Thus the leading German Communist, Paul Levi, who had warned Moscow against staging putsches in his country, was in April 1921 declared a "traitor" and ousted from both the German Communist Party and the Comintern. He was penalized not for being wrong, since even Lenin conceded he had given him sound advice, but for being insubordinate.* Such methods succeeded in silencing the critics, but at the price of repeating the same mistakes.

Angelica Balabanoff assigns much of the blame for the Comintern's failures on Lenin's personnel policies. Because he insisted on unquestioned obedience, he purged from the movement true revolutionaries prone to independent judgment, in favor of careerists whose only qualification was submissiveness. The ranks of the Third International quickly filled with scoundrels and intriguers, beginning with its head, Zinoviev, of whom she wrote that after Mussolini he was "the most despicable individual I have ever met."[258] Referring to Lenin's "habit of selecting his collaborators and trusted men precisely because of their weaknesses and shortcomings and also because of their checkered past," she noted:

> Lenin was neither blind nor indifferent to the harm [that] personal dishonesty might do to the movement, yet he used individuals who were the scum of humanity. . . . The Bolsheviks . . . used any individual as long as he proved shrewd, unscrupulous, a jack-of-all-trades, able to obtain access anywhere, and a humble executor of his boss's orders. . . . Considering me a good revolutionist, though not a Bolshevik, [Lenin] and his collaborators believed I approved of their methods: corruption in order to undermine opposing organizations, slander of those capable or inclined to offer opposition by branding their actions as dishonest and dangerous.[259]

*Milorad M. Drachkovitch and Branko Lazitch, *The Comintern: Historical Highlights* (New York, 1966), 271–99. Levi committed suicide in 1930.

She did not approve, and resigned; the least worthy elements stayed on.

To these causes one may add a fourth, imponderable by its very nature and therefore difficult to demonstrate. This had to do with the "Russianness" of Bolshevism. The distinguishing quality of Russian radicalism had always been an uncompromising extremism, an "all or nothing" and "go for broke" attitude that scorned compromise. It derived from the fact that before seizing power Russian radicals, intellectuals with a small following and no influence on policy, had nothing but ideas to give them a sense of identity. Such people could be found in the West, too, especially among the anarchists, but there they constituted an insignificant minority. Western radicals wanted to reshape rather than destroy the existing order: the Russians, by contrast, saw little in their country worthy of preservation. Because of this profound difference in political philosophy, this Russian nihilism, the Bolsheviks had difficulty communicating with their Western sympathizers. In Russian eyes, they were not true Communists. "Bolshevism is a Russian word," wrote an anti-Communist émigré in 1919.

But not only a word. Because in that guise, in that form and in those manifestations which have crystallized in Russia during nearly two years, Bolshevism is a uniquely Russian phenomenon, with deep ties to the Russian soul. And when they speak of German Bolshevism or of Hungarian Bolshevism, I smile. Is that really Bolshevism? Outwardly. Perhaps politically. But without its peculiar soul. Without the Russian soul. It is pseudo-Bolshevism.[260]

5

Communism, Fascism, and National Socialism

What is fascism? It is socialism emancipated from democracy.

Charles Maurras[1]

The effect of the Communists' activities at home and abroad was not to unleash a global revolution, but, paradoxically, to give rise to movements that assimilated their spirit and copied their methods to fight Communism. For this reason, the so-called right-radical or "Fascist" movements that emerged in Europe in the wake of World War I are sometimes seen as antithetical to Communism. But as is often the case when ideologies, whether religious or secular, fight each other so fiercely, they do so not because they have contrary principles or aspirations but because they compete for the same constituencies.

The relationship between Communism and "Fascism" has long been a subject of controversy. The interpretation mandatory for Communist historians and favored by Western socialists and liberals holds that the two are irreconcilable phenomena. Conservative theorists, for their part, subsume both under the concept "totalitarianism." The issue is extremely sensitive because it raises the question whether "Fascism," and particularly Nazism, its most virulent expression, is related to Marxism-Leninism, and hence, ultimately, to socialism, or else derives from "capitalism."

The discussion which follows will not address itself directly to this controversy: on this subject there already exists a rich literature.[2] Instead, it will seek to throw light on the influence which Communism has exerted on

Western politics both as a model to emulate and a threat to exploit. Examination of the origins of right-radical movements in interwar Europe quickly reveals that they would have been inconceivable without the precedent set by Lenin and Stalin. The subject is strangely ignored by historians and political scientists who treat European totalitarian dictatorships as if they were self-generated: even Karl Bracher, in his standard account of Hitler's rise to power makes virtually no reference to Lenin, although his narrative at all stages reveals the analogies in the methods employed by the two men.[3]

Why is the Soviet experience largely ignored in the literature on Fascism and totalitarianism? For historians of the left even to raise the question of affinities between Soviet Communism and "Fascism" is tantamount to conceding the possibility of a causal relationship. Since "Fascism" for them is by definition the antithesis of socialism and Communism, no such affinities can be admitted and the sources of "Fascism" must be sought exclusively in conservative ideas and capitalist practices. In the Soviet Union this trend went so far that under Lenin, Stalin, and their immediate successors it was forbidden to use the term "National Socialist."

Secondly, in the 1920s, when the concepts "totalitarianism" and "Fascism" gained currency, Western scholars knew very little about the Bolsheviks and the one-party dictatorship that they invented. As we have noted,[4] the foundations of that regime were laid in 1917–18, when Europe, in the final year of World War I, had more urgent matters to claim its attention than internal developments in Russia. The true nature of the Communist regime was long concealed from foreign eyes by novel pseudo-democratic institutions, behind which stood the monopolistic Party. Strange as it may seem today, in the 1920s, "during which the the fascist movements developed, Communism had not yet revealed itself as a totalitarian system . . . but seemed the advocate of unrestricted freedom. . . ."[5] Between the wars, no study subjected the origins of the Communist regime to serious historical and theoretical analysis. The few systematic studies published on Soviet Russia, mostly in the 1930s, described the country under Stalin's rule, which created the false impression that it was he rather than Lenin who had fathered the one-party dictatorship. As late as 1951 Hannah Arendt could make the astonishing claim that Lenin had originally planned to concentrate power in the soviets and suffered his "greatest defeat" when on the outbreak of the Civil War "the supreme power . . . passed into the hands of the party bureaucracy."[6]

Early analyses of the totalitarian phenomenon were written almost exclusively by German scholars on the basis of their own national experience.[7] This explains the exaggerated importance attached by Hannah Arendt to anti-Semitism as an attribute of totalitarianism.[*] Other early writers (like

---

[*]In *The Origins of Totalitarianism* (New York, 1958), p. viii, she calls the Jewish question and anti-Semitism "the catalytic agent" first of the Nazi movement and then of World War II. The first four chapters of her book are devoted to this subject.

Sigmund Neumann) noted the similarities between the regimes of Joseph Stalin, Benito Mussolini, and Adolf Hitler but even they ignored the Russian influence on right-radical movements for the simple reason that they knew little about the operations of the Communist political system. The first systematic comparison of left-wing and right-wing dictatorships, published in 1956 by Carl Friedrich and Zbigniew Brzezinski, also provided a static rather than a historical analysis.[8]

The third factor inhibiting inquiries into the influence of Bolshevism on Fascism and National Socialism was the insistence of Moscow on banishing from the vocabulary of "progressive" thought the adjective "totalitarian" in favor of "Fascist" to describe all anti-Communist movements and regimes. The party line on this subject was laid down in the early 1920s and formalized in the resolutions of the Comintern. "Fascism," a term loosely applied to Mussolini's Italy and Hitler's Germany, as well as such relatively benign anti-Communist dictatorships as Antonio Salazar's in Portugal and Pilsudski's in Poland, was declared a product of "finance capitalism" and a tool of the bourgeoisie. In the 1920s official Soviet doctrine laid it down that all "capitalist" countries were bound to go through a "Fascist" phase before yielding to Communism (socialism). In the mid-1930s, when Moscow launched the policy of "Popular Fronts," it softened somewhat its stand on this issue to allow for collaboration with governments and movements that would fall within its definition of "Fascist." But the view that anti-Communism equals Fascism remained obligatory in countries subject to Communist censorship until the advent of Mikhail Gorbachev's *glasnost'*. It was prevalent also in foreign "progressive" circles. Western scholars who had the temerity to link Mussolini or Hitler with Communism in any way or to depict their regimes as genuine mass movements risked verbal or other forms of harassment.*

In the canonical left-wing version, formulated by the Comintern, "Fascism" is the antithesis of Communism, and attempts to bring the two under a common "totalitarian" umbrella are dismissed as by-products of the Cold War. In this view, "Fascism" is a facet of the imperialist stage of capitalism that precedes its final collapse. Beleaguered and frightened, "monopoly capitalism" resorts to the "Fascist dictatorship" in a desperate effort to keep the working class under control. The Executive Committee of the Communist International in 1933 defined Fascism as the "overt, terrorist dictatorship of the most reactionary, chauvinist and imperialist elements of finance capitalism."[9] For the committed Marxist, there is no essential difference between parliamentary democracy and "Fascism": they are merely different ways in which the bourgeoisie maintains itself in power against the wishes of the working masses. "Fascism" is conservative because it pre-

---

*See, for instance, the treatment meted out to Renzo de Felice by the Italian intelligentsia for stressing the popular, non-"bourgeois" roots of Fascism: Michael Ledeen in George Mosse, ed., *International Fascism* (London and Beverly Hills, 1979), 125–40.

serves existing property relationships: it is "not revolutionary but reactionary or even counterrevolutionary in that it seeks to prevent the natural development to a socialist society."[10] The revolutionary elements in Mussolini's and Hitler's regimes, so striking to contemporaries, are depicted as deceptive maneuvers.

The arguments against the concept of "totalitarianism," and against suggestions that Bolshevism influenced "Fascism," fall into two categories. On the lower polemical level, recourse is had to ad hominem methods. The concept of "totalitarianism" is said to have been devised as a weapon of the Cold War: linking Communism with Nazism helped turn public opinion against the Soviet Union. In reality, this concept antedates the Cold War by a good twenty years. The notions of "total" political power and "Totalitarianism" were formulated in 1923 by an opponent of Mussolini, Giovanni Amendola (later murdered by the Fascists), who, having observed Mussolini's systematic subversion of state institutions, concluded that his regime differed fundamentally from conventional dictatorships. In 1925, Mussolini adopted the term and assigned it a positive meaning. He defined Fascism as "totalitarian" in the sense that it politicized everything "human" as well as "spiritual": "Everything within the state, nothing outside the state, nothing against the state."* In the 1930s, with the rise of Hitler and the concurrent launching of the Stalinist terror, the term gained acceptance in academic circles. All this occurred long before the Cold War.

More serious theorists who reject "totalitarianism" do so on the following grounds: first, no regime has ever been able to enforce complete politicization and state control, and second, features attributed to so-called "totalitarian" regimes are not unique to them.

"Systems that in the strict sense of the word merit the appellation totalitarian do not exist," so runs the argument, "because there remain everywhere greater or lesser pluralistic residues." In other words, they fail to achieve that "monolithic unity" which is said to be their distinguishing characteristic.[11] To this it can be responded that if terms employed by the social sciences were consistently judged by the criterion of "strict" interpretation then none would pass the test. One could not speak of "capitalism," since even in the heyday of economic laissez-faire, governments were regulating and otherwise interfering with the operations of the market. Nor under such a standard could one speak of a "Communist economy," because even though in the Soviet Union it was, in theory, 99 percent state-owned and state-managed, it always had to tolerate a "second," free economic sector. Democracy means popular rule, yet political theory has no difficulty admitting the existence in the most democratic countries of

---

*The dictator of Ghana in the 1950s and 1960s, Kwame Nkrumah, an ally of the Soviet Union, had engraved on his monument the following paraphrase of the Gospels: "Seek ye first the political kingdom and all other things shall be added unto you."

special interest groups that influence policy. Such concepts are useful because they convey what a given system aspires to and what it achieves—not "strictly," in terms of its dictionary definition, as is done in the natural sciences, but broadly speaking, which is the maximum consistency attainable in human affairs. In practice, all political, economic and social systems are "mixed"; none is pure. The scholar's task is to identify those qualities that, in their aggregate, distinguish a given system and set it apart from the others. There are no valid intellectual grounds for holding "totalitarianism" to a more rigid standard. Indeed, totalitarian aspirations are so exorbitant that according to Hans Buchheim, they are by their very nature incapable of realization:

> Because totalitarian rule aims at the impossible—to control man's personality and fate completely—it can be realized only in part. It is of the totalitarian essence that the goal is never reached and actualized but must remain a trend, a *claim* to power. . . . Totalitarian rule is no uniformly rationalized apparatus, equally effective in all its parts. Such is the desired state, and in some areas actuality may approach the ideal; but seen as a whole, the totalitarian claim to power is realized only in a diffused way, with varying intensity at different times in the different areas of life—and in the process, totalitarian traits are always mingled with non-totalitarian ones. But it is for this very reason that the effects of the totalitarian claim to power are so dangerous and oppressive; they are vague, incalculable, and hard to prove. . . . Almost every observation made about a totalitarian measure has the fatal peculiarity of exaggerating the matter in some respects and underestimating it in others. This paradox follows from the unrealizable claim to control; it is characteristic for life under totalitarian governments and renders it so extraordinarily incomprehensible to all outsiders.[12]

A similar response can be given to those who argue that features attributed to totalitarianism (like commitment to ideology, mass appeal, and charismatic leadership) exist also in other political regimes:

> The argument of historical uniqueness of any configuration does not mean that it is "wholly" unique; for nothing is. All historical phenomena belong to broad classes of analytic objects. . . . History is primarily concerned with individualities, whether these be persons, things or events, and a sufficiently variegated pattern of distinctive elements therefore constitutes historical uniqueness.[13]

The study of Italian Fascism and German National Socialism is highly relevant for the understanding of the Russian Revolution for at least three reasons. First, Mussolini and Hitler used the specter of Communism to frighten their populations into surrendering to them dictatorial powers. Secondly, both men learned a great deal from Bolshevik techniques in building up a party personally loyal to them to seize power and establish a one-party dictatorship. In both these respects, Communism had a greater impact on "Fascism" than on socialism and the labor movement. And thirdly, the literature on Fascism and National Socialism is richer and more sophisticated than that on Communism: acquaintance with it sheds much light on the regime that emerged from the Russian Revolution.

Influences are treacherous terrain for the historian because of the risk of falling into the *post hoc ergo propter hoc* fallacy: "after it, therefore because of it." Communism cannot be said to have "caused" Fascism and National Socialism, since their sources were indigenous. What can be said is that once antidemocratic forces in postwar Italy and Germany gathered sufficient strength, their leaders had a ready model at hand to follow. All the attributes of totalitarianism had antecedents in Lenin's Russia: an official, all-embracing ideology; a single party of the elect headed by a "leader" and dominating the state; police terror; the ruling party's control of the means of communication and the armed forces; central command of the economy.* Since these institutions and procedures were in place in the Soviet Union in the early 1920s when Mussolini founded his regime and Hitler his party, and were to be found nowhere else, the burden of proving there was no connection between "Fascism" and Communism rests on those who hold this opinion.

No prominent European socialist before World War I resembled Lenin more closely than Benito Mussolini. Like Lenin, he headed the antirevisionist wing of the country's Socialist Party; like him, he believed that the worker was not by nature a revolutionary and had to be prodded to radical action by an intellectual elite. However, working in an environment more favorable to his ideas, he did not need to form a splinter party: whereas Lenin, leading a minority wing, had to break away, Mussolini gained a majority in the Italian Socialist Party (PSI) and ejected the reformists. Had it not been for his reversal, in 1914, of his stand on the war, coming out in favor of Italy's entry on the Allied side, which resulted in his expulsion from the PSI, he might well have turned into an Italian Lenin. Socialist historians, embarrassed by these facts of Mussolini's early biography, have either suppressed them or described them as a passing flirtation with socialism by a man whose true intellectual mentor was not Marx, but Nietzsche and Sorel.† Such claims, however, are difficult to reconcile with

---

*These criteria were established by Carl J. Friedrich and Zbigniew K. Brzezinski in *Totalitarian Dictatorship and Autocracy* (New York and London, 1964), 9–10. Economic planning was first realized in Soviet Russia in 1927, but its groundwork had been laid under Lenin with the creation in late 1917 of the Supreme Council of the National Economy (VSNKh). See *RR*, Chapter 15.

†It is one of the abiding myths of anti-Fascist literature that Sorel exerted a profound influence on Mussolini. The evidence suggests that such influence was small and transient. See Gaudens Megaro, *Mussolini in the Making* (Boston and New York, 1938), 228, and Ernst Nolte, *Der Faschismus in seiner Epoche* (Munich, 1963), 203. Mussolini's cult of violence derived not from Sorel but from Marx. Sorel, incidentally, wrote a eulogy to Lenin in September 1919

the fact that Italian socialists thought well enough of the future leader
of Fascism to name him in 1912 editor in chief of the Party's organ,
Avanti![14] Far from having a fleeting romance with socialism, Mussolini was
fanatically committed to it: until November 1914, and in some respects
until early 1920, his ideas on the nature of the working class, the structure
and function of the party, and the strategy of the socialist revolution were
remarkably like Lenin's.

Mussolini was born in Romagna, Italy's most radical province, the son
of an impoverished artisan of anarcho-syndicalist and Marxist beliefs. His
father taught him that mankind was divided into two classes, the exploited
and the exploiters. (This is a formula Mussolini used as socialist leader:
"There are only two fatherlands in the world: that of the exploited and that
of the exploiters"—*sfruttati* and *sfruttatori*.)[15] He was of much humbler
origins than the founder of Bolshevism, and his radicalism was of a more
proletarian nature. He was not a theoretician but a tactician, whose intellectual eclecticism, a blend of anarchism and Marxism, as well as his emphasis
on violence, resembled the ideology of the Russian Socialists-Revolutionaries. In 1902, at the age of 19, he moved to Switzerland, where he spent two
years in extreme poverty working as a casual laborer and studying in his
spare time.* During this time he mingled with radical intellectuals: it is
possible, though not certain, that he met with Lenin.† According to Angelica Balabanoff, who saw him frequently during this period, he was a vain
egocentric, with tendencies toward hysteria, whose radicalism was rooted in
poverty and hatred of the rich.[16] It was then that he developed an abiding
hostility to reformist, evolutionary socialism.

Like Lenin, he saw in conflict the distinguishing quality of politics. The
"class struggle" meant to him warfare in the literal sense of the word: it was
bound to assume violent forms because no ruling class ever peacefully
surrendered its wealth and power. He admired Marx, whom he called a
"father and teacher," not for his economics and sociology, but for being the
"grand philosopher of worker violence."[17] He despised "lawyer socialists"
who pretended to advance the cause by parliamentary maneuvers. Nor did

---

("Pour Lénine" in *Réflexions sur la violence,* 10th ed., Paris, 1946, 437–54), in which he said that
he would be immensely proud if it were true, as rumored, that he, Sorel, had contributed to the
intellectual development of a man who seemed to him "both the greatest theoretician of socialism after Marx, and a head of state whose genius recalls that of Peter the Great" (p. 442).

*His move is usually explained by the desire to evade the draft. But as A. James Gregor has
pointed out, this could not have been the cause since Mussolini returned to Italy in November
1904 and spent the next two years in military service: *Young Mussolini and the Intellectual
Origins of Fascism* (Berkeley, 1979), 37.

†Renzo de Felice, *Mussolini il rivoluzionario, 1883–1920* (Turin, 1965), 35n, believes such
meetings did occur. Mussolini, who never gave a clear answer to the question whether he had
encountered Lenin ("[the Russian émigrés] continually changed their names"), once cryptically
remarked: "Lenin knew me much better than I knew him." At any rate, during this period he
did read some of Lenin's writings in translation: he said they had "captivated him." Yvon de
Begnac, *Palazzo Venezia: Storia di un Regime* (Rome [1950]), 360.

he have faith in trade unionism, which he believed diverted labor from the class struggle. In 1912, in a passage that could have come from the pen of Lenin, he wrote: "A worker who is merely organized turns into a petty bourgeois who obeys only the voice of interest. Every appeal to ideals leaves him deaf."[18] He remained faithful to this view even after abandoning socialism: in 1921, as Fascist leader, he would describe workers as "by nature . . . piously and fundamentally pacifistic."[19] Thus, independently of Lenin, in both his socialist and his Fascist incarnation he repudiated what Russian radicals called "spontaneity": left to his own devices, the worker would not make a revolution but strike a deal with the capitalist, which was the quintessence of Lenin's social theory.*

These premises confronted Mussolini with the same problem that faced Lenin: how to make a revolution with a class said to be inherently unrevolutionary. He solved it, as did Lenin, by calling for the creation of an elite party to inject into labor the spirit of revolutionary violence. Whereas Lenin's concept of the vanguard party came from the experience of the People's Will, Mussolini's was shaped by the writings of Gaetano Mosca and Vilfredo Pareto, who in the 1890s and early 1900s popularized the view of politics as contests for power among elite groups. Mosca and Pareto were influenced by contemporary philosophical doctrines, notably those of Henri Bergson, which rejected positivist notions of "objective" factors as decisive in social behavior in favor of voluntarism. But the main impetus for such elite theories came from observation of democratic practices toward the end of the nineteenth century, which suggested that democracy did not work. Not only were continental democracies racked by continuous parliamentary crises and scandals—Italy had in the decade of the 1890s six different ministries—but evidence accumulated that democratic institutions served as a facade that concealed domination by oligarchic minorities. On the basis of these observations, Mosca and Pareto formulated theories that would have profound influence on European politics after World War I. The concept of "elitism" in politics has by now been sufficiently absorbed into the mainstream of Western thinking to seem commonplace: according to Carl Friedrich, the elite theory has been a "dominant theme in the history of Western thought in the last three generations."[20] But at the turn of the century it was a strikingly novel idea: in his *Ruling Class,* Mosca admitted that it was "rather difficult to grant, as a constant and natural fact, that minorities rule majorities, rather than majorities minorities":

> The dominion of an organized minority, obeying a single impulse, over the unorganized majority is inevitable. The power of any minority is irresistible as against each single individual in the majority, who stands alone before

*In Italian socialist circles the idea that class consciousness is the natural product of class status was refuted by various socialist theoreticians from 1900 onwards; among them, Antonio Labriola, A. O. Olivetti, and Sergio Panunzio. A. James Gregor, *The Fascist Persuasion in Politics* (Princeton, 1974), 107.

the totality of the organized minority. At the same time, the minority is organized for the very reason that it is a minority. A hundred men acting uniformly in concert, with a common understanding, will triumph over a thousand men who are not in accord and can therefore be dealt with one by one.*

Once he had decided that the working class was inherently reformist ("economic organizations [trade unions] are reformist because economic reality is reformist") and that under every political system it is a minority that rules, Mussolini concluded that if labor was to be revolutionized, it required "an aristocracy of intelligence and will" to lead it.[21] He espoused such ideas as early as 1904.[22]

On these premises Mussolini proceeded to remake the Italian Socialist Party. In *La Lotta di Classe* (The Class Struggle), which he founded in 1910, he hounded the reformist majority much as Lenin did the Mensheviks, although with less recourse to slander. Lenin would have had no hesitation in signing his name to Mussolini's editorial in the first issue of this newspaper:

> Socialism is coming, and the measure of socialism's realization in the bosom of the existing civil society is provided not by political conquests— the frequently illusory principles of the Socialist Party—but by the number, power, and consciousness of worker associations, which already today form the nuclei of the communist organization of the future. And the working class, as Karl Marx says in his *Misery of Philosophy,* will replace in the course of its development the old civil society with an association that will eliminate classes and their conflicts. . . . In the expectation of this, the conflict between the proletariat and the bourgeoisie is a *struggle of class against class,* a struggle that, carried to its highest expression, is total revolution. . . . The expropriation of the bourgeoisie will be the final result of this struggle and the working class will have no difficulty initiating production on a communist base inasmuch as already today, in its trade unions, it readies the weapons, the institutions, the men for this war and this conquest. . . . Socialist workers must form the vanguard, vigilant and combative, that spurs the mass never to forget the vision of the ideal goal. . . . Socialism is not an affair of merchants, not a game for politicians, not a dream of romantics: less still is it a sport. It as an effort at a moral and material uplifting, both individual and collective, and perhaps the mightiest drama that has agitated the human collective, and certainly the most cherished hope of millions of human beings who suffer and want no longer to vegetate but to live.[23]

Exploiting the frustrated radicalism of the rank-and-file, Mussolini succeeded at the Socialist Party's Congress of 1912 in ousting the moderates from the leadership. His followers, known as "Mussoliniani," included

*Gaetano Mosca, *The Ruling Class* (New York and London, 1939), 53. This theory explains why totalitarian regimes are so insistent on destroying or taking over not only rival political parties, but all organizations without exception. Atomization of society allows a minority to rule the majority far more effectively.

some of the luminaries of future Italian Communism, among them Antonio Gramsci.[24] He was appointed to the Party's Executive Committee and entrusted with the editorship of *Avanti!* Lenin welcomed on the pages of *Pravda* the victory of Mussolini's faction: "A split is a difficult, painful affair. But sometimes it is necessary, and in such circumstances every weakness, every 'sentimentality' . . . is a crime. . . . And the Party of the Italian socialist proletariat, by expelling from its midst the syndicalists and right reformists, took the correct path."[25]

In 1912, Mussolini, one year short of 30, seemed destined to head Italy's revolutionary socialists, or "intransigents," as they were called. In fact this did not happen, because of his reversal on the issue of Italy's participation in the war.

Like Lenin, Mussolini had threatened before 1914 that if the government declared war, the socialists would respond with civil violence. In 1911, after it had sent troops to Tripolitania (Libya), he warned that the socialists were prepared to transform the "war between nations into a war between classes."[26] The means to this end was to be the general strike. He repeated this warning on the eve of World War I: if Italy abandoned neutrality to join the Central Powers against the Allies, he wrote in August 1914, it would confront a proletarian uprising.[27] The historian of Fascism Ernst Nolte, for some reason ignoring Lenin, claims that Mussolini was the only prominent European socialist to threaten his government with rebellion if it went to war.[28]

The outbreak of hostilities and the wholly unexpected willingness of European socialists to vote for war credits shook Mussolini's self-assurance: in November 1914, to the astonishment of his associates, he came out in favor of Italy's participation on the Allied side. He matched words with deeds, joining the army as a foot soldier and fighting until February 1917, when he suffered serious wounds and was sent to the rear.

Various explanations have been advanced for this about-face, which resulted in Mussolini's expulsion from the Socialist Party. The least charitable holds that he was bribed—that he came under strong pressure from French socialists, who provided him with money to publish his own newspaper, *Il Popolo d'Italia*. The suggestion is that, in effect, Mussolini sold out. It is more likely, however, that his motives were political. After nearly all European socialist parties had violated their pacifist pledges and backed their governments' entry into the war, he seems to have concluded that nationalism was more potent fare than socialism. In December 1914, he wrote:

> The nation has not disappeared. We used to believe that it was annihilated. Instead, we see it rise, living, palpitating before us! And understandably so. The new reality does not suppress the truth: class cannot destroy the nation. Class is a collectivity of interests, but the nation is a history of

sentiments, traditions, language, culture, ancestry. You can insert the class into the nation, but they do not destroy each other.[29]

From this it followed that the Socialist Party must lead not only the proletariat, but the entire nation: it must create *"un socialismo nazionale."* Certainly, in 1914 the shift from international socialism to national socialism made good sense for an ambitious West European demagogue.[30] Mussolini remained loyal to the idea of violent revolution led by an elite party, but henceforth his was to be a national revolution.

One can also explain his reversal by strategic considerations, namely the conviction that a revolution required an international war. This opinion was common among Italian socialists-interventionists, as illustrated by the following reflections in *Avanti!* by the left-extremist Sergio Panunzio (later a prominent theoretician of Fascism) two months after the outbreak of hostilities:

> *I am firmly convinced that only the present war—and the more acute and prolonged it is—will unleash in Europe socialism of revolutionary action.*
> . . . External wars must be followed by internal wars, the former must prepare the latter, and jointly prepare the great, luminous day of socialism.
> . . . All of us are convinced that for socialism to happen it must be *wanted.*
> This is the moment of *wanting* and *having.* If socialism is inert and . . .
> *neutral,* tomorrow the historical situation may only reaffirm a state of affairs similar to the present one, but it may objectively turn in a sense more remote and contrary to socialism. . . . We are, all of us, certain that *all* the states—and *how much more so* the bourgeois states—*after* the war, victors and vanquished [alike], will lie prostrate, with broken bones. . . . All of them will be, in some measure, defeated. . . . Capitalism will be so profoundly damaged that a *coup de grâce* will suffice. . . . *He who supports the cause of peace, supports, unconsciously, the cause of preserving capitalism.*[*]

Such a positive attitude toward the war was not unknown to Russian socialists, especially those on the extreme left, although they rarely spoke so frankly. There is evidence that Lenin welcomed the outbreak of World War I and hoped that it would be long and devastating. While attacking the international "bourgeoisie" for the carnage, privately Lenin applauded its self-destruction. In January 1913, during a Balkan crisis, he wrote Maxim Gorky: "A war between Austria and Russia would be a very useful thing for the revolution (throughout Eastern Europe) but it is unlikely that Franz Joseph and Nikolashka [Nicholas II] will grant us this pleasure."[31] Throughout World War I Lenin rejected all manifestations of pacifism in the Russian and international socialist movements, insisting that the mis-

---

*Cited in de Felice, *Mussolini*, 245–46. The possibility has been raised that the actual author of this article was Mussolini himself. In 1919, Mussolini spoke of Italy's entry into the war as "the first episode of the revolution, its beginning. The revolution continued under the name of war for 40 months"; cited in A. Rossi, *The Rise of Italian Fascism, 1918–1922* (London, 1938), 11.

sion of socialists was not to stop the war but to transform it into a civil conflict, that is, revolution.

One must, therefore, agree with Domenico Settembrini that Mussolini's and Lenin's attitudes toward the war showed close affinities, even though the one favored his country's participation and the other opposed it, at any rate publicly:

> While [both Lenin and Mussolini] realized that the party could be instrumental in radicalizing the masses and shaping their responses, it could, on its own, not create the basic preconditions for revolution—the collapse of the capitalist social order. Whatever Marx said about the spirit of revolution automatically emerging from the impoverishment of the proletariat and the consequent inability of capitalism to sell its goods to a shrinking market, the fact was that the proletariat was not getting poorer, that the spirit of revolution was conspicuous by its absence, and the capitalist order was expanding rather than facing bankruptcy. A substitute had, therefore, to be found for Marx's supposed self-triggering mechanism, and that substitute was—war.*

Mussolini continued to think of himself as a socialist as late as 1919, the year he founded the Fascist Party. The country, teeming with veterans unable to find work, and suffering from inflation, faced serious social unrest. Hundreds of thousands of workers were on strike. Mussolini encouraged these disturbances. In January 1919, he incited an unlawful work stoppage of postal employees and urged workers to seize factories. According to one authority, in the summer of 1919, when social turbulence was at its height, he went to great lengths to outbid the ineffectual Socialist Party and General Federation of Labor with appeals to industrial violence: his *Popolo d'Italia* called for profiteers to be "strung up on lampposts."[32] The June 1919 program of the *fasci di combattimento,* which formed the nucleus of the Fascist Party, hardly deviated from that of the socialists: Constituent Assembly, eight-hour working day, worker participation in industrial management, national militia, partial expropriation of wealth by means of a "heavy tax on capital," and confiscation of church properties. The workers were exhorted to launch a "revolutionary war."[33] Experts in the Socialist Party regarded Mussolini as a *"socialisto rivoluzionario."*[34]

With these actions, the onetime socialist leader, discredited by his stand on the war, hoped to regain his position in the PSI. The socialists, however, would not forgive him: they were willing to enter into joint electoral blocs with the Fascists, but only on condition that they excluded Mussolini.[35] Isolated politically and backed mainly by socialists-interventionists, Mus-

---

*In G. R. Urban, ed., *Euro-communism* (London, 1978), 151. Settembrini raises the interesting question of "what Lenin would have done if the Tsar, like the Italian government in 1914, had remained neutral. Can one be sure that Lenin would not have become an ardent interventionist?": in George L. Mosse, ed., *International Fascism* (London and Beverly Hills, Cal., 1979), 107.

solini swung to the right. His evolution during the two postwar years indicates that it was not he who rejected the socialists, but the socialists who rejected him, and that he founded the Fascist movement as a vehicle for political ambitions that could not be accommodated in his old home, the Socialist Party. His break with socialism, in other words, was not ideological but personal.

Beginning in late 1920, armed Fascist rowdies moved into the countryside to beat up peasant squatters. Early the following year, they organized "punitive expeditions" to terrorize the smaller towns of northern Italy. In a manner reminiscent of Bolshevik practices, they disbanded socialist parties and trade unions by means of physical violence and threats. Like their Russian counterparts, the Italian socialists reacted passively to such strongarm methods, leaving their followers confused and demoralized. With these actions Mussolini earned the support of industrialists and landowners. He also exploited Italian resentment over the peace settlement: for although Italy had fought on the side of the victorious Allies, her territorial demands had gone largely unsatisfied. Mussolini played on popular anger by depicting Italy as a "proletarian nation": this tactic won him a following among embittered war veterans. By November 1921, the Fascist Party had 152,000 members, of whom 24 percent were agricultural laborers and 15 percent industrial workers.[36]

Even as the Fascist leader, Mussolini never concealed his sympathy and admiration for Communism: he thought highly of Lenin's "brutal energy," and saw nothing objectionable in Bolshevik massacres of hostages.[37] He proudly claimed Italian Communism as his child. In his maiden speech on June 21, 1921, in the Chamber of Deputies, he boasted: "I know [the Communists] very well, for some of them are of my making; I admit with a sincerity that may appear cynical that I was the first to infect these people when I introduced into Italian socialism a little Bergson diluted with plenty of Blanqui."[38] Of Bolshevism he had this to say in February 1921: "I reject all forms of Bolshevism, but if I had to choose one it would be that of Moscow and Lenin, if only because its proportions are gigantic, barbaric, universal."[39] It could hardly have been an oversight that he allowed the Communist Party to survive for a time the November 1926 decree banning independent political parties, associations, and organizations.[40] As late as 1932, Mussolini acknowledged Fascism's affinities with Communism: "In the whole negative part, we are alike. We and the Russians are against the liberals, against democrats, against parliament."[41] (Hitler would later agree, saying that there was more that connected than separated the Nazis from the Bolsheviks.[42]) In 1933, Mussolini publicly urged Stalin to follow the Fascist model, and in 1938, when the Soviet dictator had completed the most horrendous bloodbath in history, he bestowed on him the ultimate accolade: "In the face of the total collapse of the system of Lenin, Stalin has become a secret Fascist," with the difference that, being a Russian, "that is, a species of semi-barbarian," he did not emulate the Fascists' use of forced feeding of castor oil to punish their prisoners.[43]

The Russian Communists anxiously watched first Mussolini and then Hitler copy their political techniques. At the Twelfth Party Congress (1923), when such comparisons were still possible, Bukharin observed:

> It is characteristic of Fascist methods of combat that they, more than any other party, have adopted and applied in practice the experiences of the Russian Revolution. If one regards them from the *formal* point of view, that is, from the point of view of the technique of their political methods, then one discovers in them a complete application of Bolshevik tactics, and especially those of Russian Bolshevism, in the sense of the rapid concentration of forces [and] energetic action of a tightly structured military organization, in the sense of a particular system of committing one's forces, *uchraspredy,* mobilization, etc., and the pitiless destruction of the enemy, whenever this is necessary and demanded by the circumstances.*

The historical evidence thus indicates that Mussolini's Fascism did not emerge as a right-wing reaction to socialism or communism, even if, to promote his political interests, Mussolini did not hesitate to attack both movements.† Given the opportunity, Mussolini would have been glad as late as 1920–21 to take under his wing the Italian Communists, for whom he felt great affinities: greater, certainly, than for democratic socialists, liberals, and conservatives. Generically, Fascism issued from the "Bolshevik" wing of Italian socialism, not from any conservative ideology or movement.

Bolshevism and Fascism were heresies of socialism. National Socialism grew from different seeds. If Lenin came from the highest stratum of the Russian service nobility and Mussolini from the ranks of the impoverished artisan class, Hitler was of petty-bourgeois background and spent his youth in an atmosphere permeated with hostility toward socialism and hatred of Jews. Unlike Mussolini and Lenin, both avid readers familiar with contemporary political and social theories, Hitler was an ignoramus who picked up what he knew from observation, casual reading, and conversations: he had no theoretical grounding, but only opinions and prejudices. Even so, the political ideology he was to use with such deadly effect, first to eliminate

---

*XII S"ezd RKP (b): Stenografischeskii otchet (Moscow, 1968), 273–74. "Uchraspredy" were organs of the Secretariat of the Central Committee responsible for assigning party functionaries. The editors of the protocols of the Twelfth Party Congress dismissed Bukharin's analogy as "ridiculous," "baseless," and "unscientific": ibid., 865. See further Leonid Luks, Entstehung der kommunistischen Faschismustheorie (Stuttgart, 1984), 47.

†Renzo de Felice has drawn a distinction between Fascism as a movement and Fascism as a regime, stressing that the former was and remained revolutionary: Michael Ledeen in Mosse, International Fascism, 126–27. The same, of course, may be said of Bolshevism, which soon after coming to power turned conservative in order to maintain itself in power.

freedom in Germany and then to sow death and destruction across Europe, was deeply affected by the Russian Revolution, negatively as well as positively. Negatively, the triumph of Bolshevism in Russia and its attempts to revolutionize Europe provided Hitler with a justification for his visceral anti-Semitism, and the specter of a "Judeo-Communist" conspiracy with which to frighten the German people. Positively, it helped him in his quest for dictatorial power by teaching him the techniques of crowd manipulation and furnishing him with the model for a one-party, totalitarian state.

Anti-Semitism occupied in the ideology and psychology of National Socialism a unique place as a central and undeviating objective. Although the origins of Judeophobia go back to classical antiquity, the insanely destructive forms it assumed under Hitler had no historic precedent. To understand this, it is necessary to note the effect of the Russian Revolution on Russian and German nationalist movements.

Traditional, pre-twentieth-century anti-Semitism was primarily driven by religious hostility: the perception of Jews as the killers of Christ and a malevolent people who stubbornly rejected the Christian gospel. Propagated by the Catholic Church and some Protestant sects, this hostility was reinforced by economic competition and dislike of Jews as money-lenders and canny merchants. To the traditional anti-Semite, the Jew was the member neither of a "race" nor of a transnational community, but the follower of a false religion, doomed to suffer and wander homeless as a lesson to mankind. For the idea of Jews as an international menace to take hold, an international community had to come into existence. This happened in the course of the nineteenth century with the emergence of global commerce and global communications. Transcending regional and national boundaries, these developments directly affected the lives of communities and nations that until modern times had led fairly sheltered and self-contained existences. Suddenly and inexplicably, people began to feel they were losing control of their lives. When the harvest in Russia could affect the livelihood of farmers in the United States, or the discovery of gold in California, prices in Europe, when a political movement like international socialism could set as its goal overthrowing all existing regimes, no one could feel safe: and insecurity induced by international events quite naturally gave rise to the notion of international conspiracy. And who could better fill this role than the Jews, who not only belonged to the most visible international group, but occupied prominent positions in global finance and the media?

The vision of Jewry as a disciplined supranational community, commanded by a body of invisible superiors, first emerged in the wake of the French Revolution. For although Jews played no part in it, counterrevolutionary ideologists saw them as culprits, in part because they benefited from revolutionary legislation granting them civic equality, and in part because they were popularly linked with the Masonic movement, which French royalists blamed for 1789. By the 1870s, German extremists claimed that all Jews, whatever their citizenship, were governed by a secret international organization: this was usually identified with the Alliance Israélite Universelle, based in Paris, an institution whose actual mission was philanthropy. Such ideas became popular in France during the 1890s in connection with the Dreyfus affair. Prior to the Russian Revolution anti-Semitism gained widespread acceptance in Europe, mainly in reaction to the appearance of Jews as equals in societies that had been accustomed to treating them as a pariah caste, and from disappointment that even after being emancipated, they refused to assimilate. Jews were disliked for what was seen as their clannishness and secretiveness, their allegedly "parasitic" economic pursuits, and their Levantine manners. But they were not feared. The fear of the Jew came with the Russian Revolution, and turned out to be one of its most disastrous legacies.

The work that bears the greatest responsibility for this development is the so-called *Protocols of the Elders of Zion,* a forgery that, in the words of its historian, Norman Cohn, provided the "warrant" for Hitler's genocide.[44] The author of this fabrication has not been identified, but it apparently was compiled in the late 1890s in France from anti-Semitic tracts published during the Dreyfus affair under the stimulus of the first international Zionist Congress, held in Basel in 1897. The Paris branch of the tsarist Okhrana, the Russian secret police, seems to have had a hand in it. The book purports to reveal the secret resolutions of meetings held by the leaders of international Jewry at an unspecified time and place, allegedly obtained from a participant, to formulate a strategy for the subjugation of Christian nations and the establishment of Jewish dominion over the world. The means toward this supposed end was the fomenting of strife among Christians: sometimes by stirring worker unrest, sometimes by promoting the arms race and war, and always by encouraging moral depravity. The Jewish state that would emerge once this objective had been attained would be a despotism maintained with the help of a ubiquitous police: a society deprived of freedom but not lacking in social benefits, including full employment, to keep it docile.

The so-called "Protocols" were first published in 1902 in a St. Petersburg periodical. Three years later, during the 1905 Revolution, they came out in book form edited by Sergei Nilus under the title *The Great in the Small and Anti-Christ.* Other Russian editions followed, but there was as yet no foreign translation. Even in Russia it seems to have attracted little attention: Nilus, its most assiduous propagator, complained that no one took the book seriously.[45]

It was the Russian Revolution that launched the *Protocols* on its spectacular career. World War I left Europeans in a state of utter bewilderment, eager to find culprits to blame for the carnage. For the left, the conspirators responsible for World War I were the "capitalists," and especially the manufacturers of weapons: the charge that capitalism inevitably led to war won the Communists many adherents. Such was one version of the conspiracy notion.

The other, prevalent among conservatives, pointed to the Jew. Kaiser Wilhelm II, who bore greater responsibility for World War I than anyone else, blamed it on the Jews while the fighting was still in progress.[46] General Erich Ludendorff claimed that Jews had not only helped England and France to bring Germany to her knees, but "perhaps directed both":

> The leadership of the Jewish people . . . saw in the coming world war a means of realizing its political and economic objectives, to win for Jews in Palestine a state territory and recognition as a nation, and to win for themselves in Europe and America suprastatal and supracapitalist hegemony. On the road to realizing this goal, the Jews in Germany strove to attain the same position as in those countries [England and France] that had already surrendered to them. To this end, the Jewish people required the defeat of Germany.[47]

This "explanation" echoes the *Protocols* and was, without a doubt, inspired by them.

Bolshevik outrages, and the open incitement to world revolution by a regime in which Jews were highly visible, occurred at a time when Western opinion was looking for scapegoats. It became common after the war, especially among the middle classes and professional people, to identify Communism with a global Jewish conspiracy, and to interpret it as the realization of the program presented in the *Protocols*. While common sense might balk at the proposition that Jews were responsible for both "supracapitalism" and its enemy, Communism, the dialectic of the *Protocols* was flexible enough to accommodate such contradictions. Since the ultimate objective of the Jews was said to be subverting the gentile world, they could act, depending on the circumstances, now as capitalists, now as Communists. It was all a matter of tactics. Indeed, according to the author or authors of the *Protocols,* to bring their own "lesser brothers" into line, the Jews even had recourse to anti-Semitism and pogroms.*

After the Bolsheviks had seized power and unleashed their reign of terror, the *Protocols* acquired the status of prophecy. Once it became public knowledge that among prominent Bolsheviks were Jews hiding behind Slavic aliases, the whole thing seemed to become perfectly clear: the October Revolution and the Communist regime were decisive breakthroughs in the Jewish quest for world domination. The Spartacist putsches, the Communist "republics" in Hungary and Bavaria, in which many Jews were involved, were seen to mark the extension of Jewish power outside their

---

*The *Protocols* in *Luch Sveta,* I, Book 3 (May 1920), 238. It is almost certainly under this inspiration that the Soviet authorities tolerated, and by tolerating, gave credibility to, the thesis that Jews had helped Hitler organize the Holocaust in order to drive their reluctant brethren to Palestine: L. A. Korneev, *Klassovaia sushchnost' Sionizma* (Kiev, 1982).

Russian base. To prevent the prophecy of the *Protocols* from being fulfilled, Christians ("Aryans") had to realize the danger and unite against their common enemy.

The *Protocols* gained popularity in Russia during the terrors of 1918–19: among its readers was Nicholas II.* Its readership expanded after the murder of the Imperial family, which was widely blamed on Jews. When in the winter of 1919–20 thousands of defeated White officers sought refuge in Western Europe, some carried copies of the forgery. It served their interests to popularize the book to warn Europeans, on the whole rather indifferent to their fate, that Communism was not a Russian problem but the first phase of a world Communist revolution that would deliver them, too, into Jewish hands.

The most notorious of these émigrés was F. V. Vinberg, a Russian officer of German ancestry, whose obsession with Jews assumed manic proportions.[48] He saw the Russian Revolution as the handiwork of Jews and Jews alone: in one of his publications he supplied a spurious list of Soviet officials, virtually every one of whom was said to be a Jew.[49] Such views quickly gained acceptance in German right-wing circles, which were embittered by defeat and unnerved by Communist insurrections. It was Vinberg who, jointly with a notorious German Judeophobe, brought out the first translation of the *Protocols* in Germany. Published in January 1920, it was an instant success. In the next few years, Germany was flooded with hundreds of thousands of copies: Norman Cohn estimates that by the time Hitler took power, there were at least 28 editions in circulation in Germany.[50] Before long, translations appeared in Swedish, English, French, Polish; other foreign-language versions followed. In the 1920s, the *Protocols* became an international best-seller.

Especially receptive to its message was the fledgling German National Socialist Party, which from its inception in 1919 professed rabid anti-Semitism but lacked for it a theoretical foundation. The earliest Nazi platform, published in 1919, designated as Germany's enemies first the Jews, then the Versailles Treaty, and thirdly the "Marxists," by which were meant the Social-Democrats, not the Communists, with whom the Nazis maintained friendly contacts.[51] The connection between Jewry and Communism was established with the help of the *Protocols,* which are said to have been brought to Hitler's attention by Alfred Rosenberg. A Baltic German who had studied architecture in Russia, carried a Russian passport, and spoke Russian better than German, Rosenberg became converted to Vinberg's ideas and grafted them onto the Nazi movement, whose chief ideologist he became. Vinberg convinced him that the Russian Revolu-

---

*Empress Alexandra noted in her diary under the date April 7, 1918 (OS): "Nicholas read to us the protocols of the free masons" (*Chicago Daily News,* June 23, 1920, 2). The book was found among the effects of Alexandra in Ekaterinburg: N. Sokolov, *Ubiistvo tsarskoi sem'i* (Paris, 1925), 281. As previously noted, it was also Kolchak's favorite reading.

tion had been engineered by world Jewry to gain global dominion. The *Protocols* made on the future Führer an overwhelming impression. "I have read the 'Protocols of the Elders of Zion'—it simply appalled me," he told Hermann Rauschning, an early associate, "the stealthiness of the enemy, and his ubiquity! I saw at once that we must copy it—in our own way, of course."[52] According to Rauschning, the *Protocols* served Hitler as a major source of political inspiration.[53] Hitler thus used a spurious manual of Jewish strategy for world domination, not only to depict the Jews as the mortal enemy of Germany, but to carry out his own quest for world domination employing its methods. He so admired the alleged cunning of Jews in their drive to master the world that he decided to adopt fully their "ideology" and "program."[54]

It was only after he had read the *Protocols* that Hitler turned anti-Communist:

> Rosenberg left a permanent mark on Nazi ideology. The party was rabidly antisemitic from the moment of its foundation in 1919, but it became obsessed with Russian communism only in 1921–22; and this seems to have been largely Rosenberg's doing. He provided the link between Russian antisemitism of the Black Hundred type and the antisemitism of the German racists; more precisely, he took over Vinberg's view of Bolshevism as a Jewish conspiracy and reinterpreted it in *völkisch*-racist terms. The resulting fantasy, as expounded in innumerable articles and pamphlets, became an obsessive theme in Hitler's thinking and in the outlook and propaganda of the Nazi party.[55]

It has been said that Hitler had only two major political objectives: the destruction of Jewry and the expansion into the East European Lebensraum ("Living Space"), all other elements of his program, capitalist as well as socialist, being only means to these ends.[56] The right-wing Russian theory linking Jews with Communism allowed him to connect these two objectives.

Thus the ravings of extremist Russian monarchists, who sought and found a scapegoat for the catastrophe that had befallen their country in the "hidden hand" of world Jewry, injected themselves into the political ideology of a party destined before long to acquire total power in Germany. The rationale for the Nazi extermination of Jews came from Russian right-wing circles: it was Vinberg and his friends who first called publicly for the physical extermination of Jews.[57] The Jewish Holocaust thus turned out to be one of the many unanticipated and unintended consequences of the Russian Revolution.

As a political phenomenon, Nazism was two things: a technique of manipulating the masses to give the appearance of popular participation in the political process; and a system of government in which the German

National Socialist Labor Party monopolized power and transformed the institutions of the state into its instruments. In both instances the influence of Marxism in both its original and Bolshevik guises was unmistakable.

It is known that in his youth Hitler closely studied how Social Democrats managed crowds: "From the Social Democrats Hitler derived the idea of a mass party and mass propaganda. In *Mein Kampf* he describes the impression made on him when [he] 'gazed on the interminable ranks, four abreast, of Viennese workmen parading at a mass demonstration. I stood dumbfounded for almost two hours, watching this enormous human dragon which slowly uncoiled itself before me.' "* From such observations Hitler developed his theory of crowd psychology, which he later used with remarkable success. In a conversation with Rauschning, he conceded his debt to socialism:

> I have learned a great deal from Marxism as I do not hesitate to admit. I don't mean their tiresome social doctrine or the materialist conception of history, or their absurd "marginal utility" theories [!], and so on. But I have learned from their methods. The difference between them and myself is that I have really put into practice what these peddlers and penpushers have timidly begun. The whole of National Socialism is based on it. Look at the workers' sports clubs, the industrial cells, the mass demonstrations, the propaganda leaflets written specially for the comprehension of the masses; all these new methods of political struggle are essentially Marxist in origin. All I had to do is take over these methods and adapt them to our purpose. I only had to develop logically what Social Democracy repeatedly failed in because of its attempt to realize its evolution within the framework of democracy. National Socialism is what Marxism might have been if it could have broken its absurd and artificial ties with a democratic order.[58]

And, one may add, what Bolshevism did, and what it became.†

One channel for transmitting Communist models to the Nazi movement were right-wing intellectuals with a left-wing bent close to Hitler, known as "National Bolsheviks."‡ Their chief theoreticians, Joseph Goebbels and Otto Strasser, greatly impressed by Bolshevik successes in Russia, wanted Germany to help Soviet Russia build up her economy in return for her political support against France and England. To the argument of Rosenberg, adopted by Hitler, that Moscow was the headquarters

---

*Alan Bullock, *Hitler: A Study in Tyranny*, rev. ed. (New York, 1962), 44. A photograph of Hitler in a crowd listening to a Social Democratic speaker in the winter of 1919–20 is reproduced in Joachim Fest's *Hitler* (New York, 1974), between pages 144 and 145.

†In a speech delivered on February 24, 1941, Hitler bluntly stated that "basically National Socialism and Marxism are the same": *The Bulletin of International News* (London), XVIII, No. 5 (March 8, 1941), 269.

‡The term was coined in a pejorative sense in 1919 by Radek. The best study of this interesting if marginal movement is Otto-Ernst Schüddekopf's *Linke Leute von Rechts* (Stuttgart, 1960).

of an international Jewish conspiracy, they responded that Communism was a facade that concealed traditional Russian nationalism: "They
say world revolution and mean Russia."* But the "National Bolsheviks"
desired more than cooperation with Communist Russia: they wanted Germany to adopt her system of government by centralizing political power,
eliminating rival political parties, and restricting the operations of the free
market. In 1925, Goebbels and Strasser argued in the Nazi daily, *Völk-
ischer Beobachter,* that only the introduction of a "socialist dictatorship"
could save Germany from chaos. "Lenin sacrificed Marx," Goebbels
wrote, "and in return gave Russia freedom."[59] Of his own Nazi Party, he
wrote in 1929 that it was a party of "revolutionary socialists."[60]

Hitler rejected this ideology, but he followed it to the extent of using
socialist slogans to wean German workers away from the Social Democrats.
The adjectives "Socialist" and "Labor" in the title of the Nazi Party were
not simply fraudulent exploitations of popular words. The party grew from
a union of German workers in Bohemia formed in the early years of the
century to fight the competition of Czech migrants. The program of the
German Labor Party (Deutsche Arbeiter Partei), as this organization originally called itself, combined socialism, anticapitalism, and anticlericalism
with German nationalism. In 1918, it renamed itself the National Socialist
German Labor Party (NSDAP), adding anti-Semitism to its platform and
luring to its ranks demobilized war veterans, shopkeepers, and professional
personnel. (The word "Labor" in its name was meant to include "all who
work," not only industrial laborers.[61]) It was this organization that Hitler
took over in 1919. According to Bracher, the ideology of the party in its
early years "contained a thoroughly revolutionary kernel within an irrational, violence-oriented political ideology. It was in no sense a mere expression of reactionary tendencies: it derived from the world of workers and
trade unionists."[62] The Nazis appealed to the socialist traditions of German
labor, declaring the worker "a pillar of the community," and the "bourgeois"—along with the traditional aristocracy—a doomed class.[63] Hitler,
who told associates that he was a "socialist,"[64] had the party adopt the red
flag and, on coming to power, declared May 1 a national holiday; Nazi
Party members were ordered to address one another as "comrades"
(Genossen). His conception of the party was, like Lenin's, that of a militant
organization, a *Kampfbund,* or "Combat League." ("A supporter of a
movement is he who declares his agreement with its aims. A member is only
he who fights for it."[65]) His ultimate aim was a society in which traditional
classes would be abolished, and status earned by personal heroism.[66] In
typically radical fashion, he envisaged man re-creating himself: "Man is
becoming god," he told Rauschning. "Man is god in the making."[67]

---

*Schüddekopf, *Linke Leute,* 87. The idea that Communism really expressed Russian national
interests originated with N. Ustrialov and other theoreticians of the so-called "Smena Vekh"
movement in Russian emigration of the early 1920s. See above, p. 139.

The Nazis at first had little success in attracting workers, and their ranks were dominated by "petty bourgeois" elements. But toward the end of the 1920s, their socialist appeals began to have an effect. When unemployment struck in 1929–30, workers joined en masse. According to Nazi Party records, in 1930, 28 percent of the Party's membership consisted of industrial workers; in 1934, their proportion rose to 32 percent. In both years, they were the largest occupational group in the Nazi Party.* Given that membership in the Nazi Party did not carry the same responsibilities as that in the Russian Communist Party, it may well be that the proportion of bona fide industrial workers (as distinguished from ex-workers turned into full-time party functionaries) was actually higher in the NSDAP than in the Communist Party of the Soviet Union.

The evidence for Hitler's model of the totalitarian party being borrowed from Communist Russia is circumstantial: for while he was quite willing to admit his debt to the "Marxists," Hitler carefully avoided acknowledging any borrowing from Communist Russia. The notion of the one-party state apparently occurred to him in the mid-1920s, when, reflecting on the failure of the Kapp putsch of 1923, he decided to change tactics and take power legally. Hitler himself claimed that the concept of a disciplined, hierarchically organized political party was suggested to him by military organization. He was also willing to grant that he had learned from Mussolini.[68] But it would be most unusual if the Communist Party, whose activities were widely covered in the German press, did not influence him as well, although for obvious reasons he found this fact impossible to admit. In private conversation he was willing to concede that he had "studied the revolutionary technique in the works of Lenin and Trotsky and other Marxists."† According to him, he turned away from the socialists and started something "new" because they were "small men"[69]—incapable of bold action—which is not much different from the reason that caused Lenin to break with the Social Democrats and found the Bolshevik Party.

In the dispute between the adherents of Rosenberg and of Goebbels and Strasser, Hitler in the end sided with the former. There was to be no alliance with Soviet Russia because Hitler needed the specter of the Jewish-Communist threat to frighten the German voters. But this did not prevent him from adopting for his own purposes the central institutions and practices of Communist Russia.

*Karl Bracher, Die deutsche Diktatur, 2nd ed. (Cologne-Berlin, 1969), 256. David Schoenbaum, Hitler's Social Revolution (New York and London, 1980), 28, 36, gives slightly different figures. Some Marxist historians dispose of this embarrassing fact by excluding workers who joined the Nazi Party or voted for it from the ranks of the working class, on the grounds that the status of a worker is determined not by occupation but by the "struggle against the ruling classes": Timothy W. Mason, Sozialpolitik im Dritten Reich (Opladen, 1977), 9.

†Rauschning, Hitler Speaks (London, 1939), 236. In 1930 Hitler is said to have told his surprised associates that he had read and learned a great deal from Trotsky's recently published My Life, which he called "brilliant": Konrad Heiden, Der Fuehrer (New York, 1944), 308. Heiden provides, however, no source for this information.

The three totalitarian regimes differed in several respects: their differences will be discussed in due course. What joined them, however, was much more important than what separated them. First and foremost it was the common enemy: liberal democracy with its multiparty system, its respect for law and property, its ideal of peace and stability. Lenin's, Mussolini's, and Hitler's fulminations against "bourgeois democracy" and the Social Democrats are entirely interchangeable.

To analyze the relationship between Communism and "Fascism" one must disabuse oneself of the conventional ideal that a "revolution" is, by its very nature, egalitarian and internationalist, while nationalist upheavals are inherently counterrevolutionary. This was a mistake committed by those German conservatives who initially supported Hitler in the belief that an outspoken nationalist like him could not have revolutionary aspirations.[70] "Counterrevolution" can be properly applied only to movements that aspire to undo the revolution and restore the *status quo ante,* as held true of the French Royalists of the 1790s. If "revolution" is defined to mean a sudden overthrow of the existing political regime, followed by fundamental changes in the economy, social structure, and culture, then the term is equally applicable to antiegalitarian and xenophobic upheavals. The adjective "revolutionary" describes not the substance of change but the manner in which it is accomplished—namely, suddenly and violently. Hence it is as proper to speak of right-wing revolutions as of left-wing ones: the fact that the two confront each other as deadly enemies derives from competition over mass constituencies, not from disagreements over methods or objectives. Both Hitler and Mussolini regarded themselves as revolutionaries, and rightly so. Rauschning claimed that National Socialism was actually more revolutionary in its goals than either Communism or anarchism.[71]

But perhaps the most fundamental affinity among the three totalitarian movements lay in the realm of psychology: Communism, Fascism and National Socialism exacerbated and exploited popular resentments—class, racial, and ethnic—to win mass support and to reinforce the claim that they, not the democratically elected governments, expressed the true will of the people. All three appealed to the emotion of hate.

The French Jacobins were the first to realize the political potential of class resentment. Exploiting it, they conjured constant conspiracies by aristocrats and other enemies of the revolution: shortly before their fall they drafted legislation expropriating private wealth that had unmistakable communistic implications.[72] It was from the study of the French Revolution and its aftermath that Marx formulated the theory of class struggle as the dominant feature of history. In his theory, social antagonism was for the first time accorded moral legitimacy: hatred, which Judaism condemned as self-destructive, and Christianity (in the guise of anger) treated as one of the cardinal sins, was made into a virtue. But hatred is a double-edged sword, and before long the victims adopted it for self-protection. Toward the close of the nineteenth century doctrines emerged that exploited ethnic and racial resentments as a counter to the socialist slogan of class war. In a prophetic book of 1902, *Doctrines of Hate,* Anatole Leroy-Beaulieu called attention to the affinities between the left- and right-wing extremists of the day, and foresaw the kind of collusion between them that would become reality after 1917.[73]

It requires no elaboration that Lenin used resentment of the well-off, the *burzhui,* to rally the urban plebeians and the poorer peasants. Mussolini reformulated the class struggle as a conflict between "have" and "have-not" nations. Hitler adapted Mussolini's technique, by reinterpreting the class struggle as strife between races and nations, namely "Aryans" against Jews and the nations allegedly dominated by them.* An early pro-Nazi political theorist argued that the true conflict of the modern world pitted not labor against capital but states based on the sovereignty of the *Volk* against global Jewish "imperialism," which could be solved only if Jews were deprived of the possibility of surviving economically and in this manner exterminated.[74] Revolutionary movements, whether of the "right" or "left" variety, have to have an object of hatred because it is incomparably easier to rally the masses against a visible enemy than for an abstraction. The matter was theoretically explained and justified by Carl Schmitt, a theoretician close to the Nazis. Writing six years before Hitler's advent to power, he defined enmity as the defining quality of politics:

> The specifically political distinction underpinning political actions and motives is that between *friend* and *foe.* It corresponds in the realm of politics to the relatively independent contrasts in other realms: between good and evil in ethics, the beautiful and ugly in aesthetics, and so on. The [distinction between friend and foe] is self-sufficient—that is, it neither derives from one or more of these contrasts nor is reduced to them. . . . [It] can exist, both in theory and practice, without the concurrent application of other distinctions—moral, aesthetic, economic, and so on. The political enemy need not be morally evil or aesthetically ugly; he need not appear as an economic competitor, and it may even be very advantageous to do business with him. But he is the other, the stranger; and it is enough that he is, in an especially intensive existential sense, someone different and alien, so that, in the event of a conflict, he represents the negation of one's own being, and for that reason must be re-

---

*The possibility of the idea of class war being reinterpreted in a racial sense was raised as early as 1924 by a Russian Jewish émigré, I. M. Bikerman, as a warning to his pro-Bolshevik compatriots: "Why could not a free Cossack of Petlura or a Volunteer of Denikin follow a doctrine that reduced all history not to the struggle of classes but to the struggle of races, and, rectifying the sins of history, exterminate the race in which it sees the source of evil? Looting, killing, raping, excesses can be committed as conveniently under the one flag as under the other." *Rossiia i Evrei,* Sbornik I (Berlin, 1924), 59–60.

sisted and fought in order to protect one's self-like *(seinmässig)* life-style.[75]

The message behind this turgid prose is that the political process demands stress on the differences dividing groups, because this is the only way to conjure up the enemies whose existence is indispensable to politics. The "other" need not in fact be an enemy: it is enough that he be perceived as different.

It was the Communists' addiction to hatred that Hitler found so congenial, and the reason why he instructed the Nazi Party to welcome disenchanted Communists while barring Social Democrats: for hatred was easily redirected from one object to another.[76] So it happened that in the early 1920s, the largest number of adherents of the Italian Fascist Party were ex-Communists.[77]

We will consider the common features of the three totalitarian regimes under three rubrics: the structure, functions, and authority of the ruling Party; the relationship of the Party to the State; and the Party's relationship to the population at large.

1. *The Ruling Party*

Until the Bolshevik dictatorship, a state consisted of a government and the governed (subjects or citizens). Bolshevism introduced a third element, the monopolistic "party" that dominated both government and society while placing itself outside the control of either: a party that was not really a party, that governed without being a government, that ruled the people in their name but without their consent. "One-party state" is a misnomer both because the entity that runs the totalitarian state is not really a party in the accepted sense of the word and because it stands apart from the state. It is the truly distinguishing characteristic of the totalitarian regime, its quintessential attribute. It was the creation of Lenin. The Fascists and the Nazis faithfully copied this model.

A. THE PARTY AS THE ORDER OF THE ELECT

Unlike true political parties, which seek to enlarge their membership, the Communist, Fascist, and Nazi organizations were exclusive in nature. Admission was subject to close scrutiny, which employed such criteria as social origin, race, or age, and the ranks of members were periodically cleansed or "purged" of undesirables. For this reason they resembled "brotherhoods" or "oligarchical fraternities" of the elect, which perpetuated themselves by cooptation. Hitler told Rauschning that "party" was really a misnomer when applied to the NSDAP, which was better called an "order" *(Orden)*.[78]

A Fascist theorist referred to Mussolini's party as "a church, that is to say, a communion of faith, a union of wills and intentions loyal to a supreme and unique end."[79]

The three totalitarian organizations were led by outsiders, not members of the traditional ruling groups: loners who either destroyed the latter, as in Russia, or else established themselves as an alternate, parallel privileged estate and in time subordinated them. This quality further distinguishes totalitarian dictatorships from ordinary dictatorships, which do not create their own political machine but rely on the traditional instruments of rule, such as the bureaucracy, the church, and the armed forces.

The Italian Fascists enforced the most rigid standards of admission, restricting membership in the 1920s to fewer than one million. Preference was given to the young, who enrolled after an apprenticeship in youth affiliates, the Ballila and Avanguardia, copies of the Communist Pioneers and Komsomol. In the next decade its ranks expanded, and on the eve of Italy's defeat in World War II the Fascist Party numbered over 4 million. The Nazis had the loosest admission standards: after trying to keep out "opportunists," in 1933 they relaxed them and by the time the regime fell, nearly one out of four adult German men (23 percent) was a member.[80] The policy of the Russian Communist Party lay somewhere in between these two, now expanding ranks to meet administrative and military needs, now thinning them in massive and sometimes bloody purges. In all three cases, however, affiliation was deemed a privilege and enrollment was by invitation.

B. THE LEADER

Because they deny that objective norms should constrain their power, totalitarian regimes require a leader whose will takes the place of law. If that alone is "true" and "good" which serves the interests of a given class or nationality (or race), then there has to be an arbiter in the person of a *vozhd'*, Duce, or Führer to decide what these interests at any given time happen to be. Although in practice Lenin always had his way (at any rate, after 1918), he made no claims of infallibility. Both Mussolini and Hitler did. *"Il Duce a sempre ragione"* (The Duce is always right) was a slogan posted all over Italy in the 1930s. The first commandment in the Rules of the Nazi Party issued in July 1932 declared "Hitler's decision is final."[81] While a seasoned totalitarian regime may survive the death of its leader (as the Soviet Union did after the demise of both Lenin and Stalin), unless another leader takes over, it becomes a collective dictatorship that in time loses its totalitarian characteristics and turns into an oligarchy.

In Soviet Russia, the personal dictatorship of Lenin over his party was camouflaged by such formulas as "democratic centralism" and the custom of deemphasizing the role of individuals in favor of impersonal historic forces. It is nevertheless true that within a year after taking power, Lenin became the unchallenged boss of the Communist Party, around whom emerged a veritable personality cult. Lenin never tolerated a view that conflicted with his own, even if it happened to be that of the majority. By 1920 it was a violation of Party regulations, punishable by expulsion, to form "factions," a "faction" being any group that acted in concert against first Lenin's and then Stalin's will: Lenin and Stalin alone were immune to the charge of "factionalism."[82]

Mussolini and Hitler emulated this Communist model. The Fascist Party had an elaborate facade of institutions designed to give the impression that it was run collectively: but none of them, not even the "Gran Consiglio" and the Party's National Congresses, had effective authority.[83] Party officials, all of whom owed their appointments either to the Duce or to persons designated by him, swore an oath of loyalty to his person. Hitler did not even bother to camouflage his absolute control over the National Socialist Party. Long before he became dictator of Germany, he established complete domination over the Party, insisting, like Lenin, on strict discipline (that is, submission to his will) and, again like Lenin, rejecting coalitions with other political bodies since they would have diluted his authority.[84]

2. The Ruling Party and the State

Like Lenin, Mussolini and Hitler used their organizations to take over the state. In all three countries, the ruling party functioned as a private organization. In Italy, the fiction was maintained that the Fascist Party was merely a "civilian and voluntary force under the command of the state," although the truth was the opposite even if, for appearance's sake, government officials (prefects) formally took precedence over Fascist functionaries.[85]

The manner in which the Bolshevik, Fascist, and Nazi parties took charge of the administrations of their respective countries was, for all practical purposes, identical: once the Leninist principle had been assimilated, its implementation was a relatively straightforward matter. In each case the Party either absorbed or emasculated institutions that stood in the way of its aspiration to unlimited authority: in the first place, the nation's executive and legislative bodies, in the second, the organs of local self-government. These state institutions were not made to obey Party instructions directly: elaborate expedients were used to give the impression that the state acted independently. The Party ran the administration by placing its members in key executive positions. The explanation for this deception was that the totalitarian "movement," as its name implies, is dynamic and fluid, whereas administration, being static, requires solid structures and firm norms. The following observations about Nazi Germany apply equally to Communist Russia and Fascist Italy:

The movement itself makes the political decisions and leaves their mechanical implementation to the state. As phrased during the Third Reich, the movement assumed personnel management *(Menschenführung)* and left to the state the management of objects *(Sachverwaltung)*. In order as much as possible to avoid open breaks between political measures (which are not guided by any norms) and norms (which are unavoidable for technical reasons) the [Nazi] regime outwardly clothed its actions as nearly as possible in legal forms. This legality, however, had no decisive meaning; it served only to bridge the gap between two irreconcilable forms of rule.[86]

The "conquest of institutions," which one early student of Fascism regarded as "the most unusual conquest of the state known to modern history,"[87] was, of course, a mere copy of a similar process that had occurred in Soviet Russia after October 1917.

The Bolsheviks subjugated Russia's central executive and legislative institutions in a matter of ten weeks.[88] Their task was facilitated by the disappearance of the tsarist regime with its bureaucracy in early 1917, which left a power vacuum that the Provisional Government had been unable to fill. Unlike Mussolini and Hitler, Lenin confronted not a functioning state system but anarchy.

Mussolini proceeded at a much more leisurely pace: he became de facto and de jure dictator of Italy only in 1927–28, more than five years after capturing Rome. Hitler, by contrast, moved nearly at Lenin's speed, gaining control of the state in six months.

On November 16, 1922, Mussolini advised the Chamber of Deputies "in the name of the nation" that he had assumed power: the Chamber had the choice of either approving this fact or facing dissolution. It approved. But Mussolini pretended for the time being to govern constitutionally and introduced the one-party regime with deliberation, by stages. In the first year and a half, he included representatives of some independent parties in the cabinet dominated by Fascists. He ended the pretense at coalition government only in 1924 after coming under strong attack for the murder of Giacomo Matteotti, a Socialist deputy who had exposed the Fascists' illegal acts. Even so, he allowed rival political organizations to function a while longer. The Fascist Party was designated the sole legal political entity in December 1928, when the process of shaping the one-party state in Italy may be said to have been completed. Control over the provinces was secured by a device borrowed from the Bolsheviks of having local Fascist functionaries supervise the prefects and pass on to them the Duce's directives.

In Nazi Germany, the establishment of Party domination over the government and private bodies went by the name of *Gleichschaltung,* or "Synchronization."* In March 1933, two months after being appointed

---

*The term initially applied to the integration of Germany's federal entities into the centralized national state, but eventually it acquired a broader meaning, defining the subordination of all

Chancellor, Hitler extracted from the Reichstag an "Enabling Act," by virtue of which the parliament divested itself of the power to legislate for a period of four years—in fact, as it turned out, permanently. From then until his death twelve years later, Hitler ruled Germany by means of "emergency laws," issued without regard for the constitution. He promptly liquidated the powers enjoyed in both Imperial and Weimar Germany by the federal states, dissolving the administrations of Bavaria, Prussia, and the other historic entities, thus creating Germany's first unitary state. In the spring and summer of 1933, he outlawed independent political parties. On July 14, 1933, the NSDAP was declared the only lawful political organization: at that time Hitler asserted, quite incorrectly, that "the party has now become the state." In reality in Nazi Germany, as in Soviet Russia, the Party and the state remained distinct.[89]

Neither Mussolini nor Hitler dared to make a clean sweep of laws, courts, and civil rights of their citizens, as Lenin had done: legal traditions were too deeply rooted in their countries for the introduction of legalized lawlessness. Instead, the two Western dictators were content to limit the competence of the judiciary and remove from its purview "crimes against the state," which were turned over to the security police.

To deal with political opponents in an effective, extrajudiciary manner, the Fascists established two police organizations. One, known after 1926 as the Voluntary Enterprise for the Repression of Anti-Fascism (OVRA), differed from its Russian and German counterparts in that it functioned under the supervision not of the Party but of the state. In addition, the Fascist Party had its own secret police, which operated "Special Tribunals" to try political opponents and administered their places of confinement.[90] Despite Mussolini's frequently expressed fondness for the idea of violence, his regime, compared to the Soviet and Nazi ones, was quite moderate and never resorted to mass terror: between 1926 and 1943, it executed a total of 26 persons,[91] which was a fraction of the victims Lenin's Cheka claimed in a single day, not to speak of the millions who perished under Stalin and Hitler.

The Nazis also emulated the Communists in setting up the security police. It is from them that they adopted the practice (which in Russia originated in the early nineteenth century) of creating two distinct police establishments, one to protect the government, the other to maintain public order. These came to be known, respectively, as the "Security Police" (Sicherheitspolizei) and "Order Police" (Ordnungspolizei), corresponding to the Soviet Cheka and its heirs (OGPU, NKVD, and so forth), and the Militia. The Security Police, or Gestapo, as well as the SS, which jointly protected the Party, were not subject to state control, serving directly under the

previously independent organizations to the Nazi Party: Hans Buchheim, *Totalitarian Rule* (Middletown, Conn., 1968), 11.

Führer through his trusted associate Heinrich Himmler. This, too, followed the example set by Lenin in the case of the Cheka. Neither institution was restrained by judiciary institutions or procedures: like the Cheka and GPU, they could confine citizens to concentration camps, where they were deprived of all civil rights. Unlike their Russian counterparts, however, they did not have the authority to sentence German citizens to death.

These measures, which subordinated all public life to a private organization, the Party, produced a type of government that did not fit the standard categories of Western political thought. What Angelo Rossi says of Fascism could with equal if not greater measure be applied to Communism and National Socialism:

> Wherever fascism is established the most important consequence, on which all the others depend, is the elimination of the people from all share of political activity. "Constitutional reform," the suppression of parliament, and the totalitarian character of the regime cannot be judged by themselves, but only in relation to their aims and results. *Fascism is not merely the substitution of one political regime for another; it is the disappearance of political life itself, since this becomes a state function and monopoly.*[92]

On these grounds, Buchheim makes the interesting suggestion that it may be incorrect to speak of totalitarianism as endowing the state with excessive power. In fact, it is the negation of the state:

> In view of the different natures of state and totalitarian rule, it is a contradiction in terms to speak of a "totalitarian state," as is still quite generally done. . . . It is a dangerous error to see totalitarian rule as an excess of state power; in reality, the state as well as political life, properly understood, are among the most important prerequisites to protect us against totalitarian danger.[93]

The "elimination of the people from all share of political activity" and, its corollary, the liquidation of political life demand some kind of surrogate. Dictatorships that pretend to speak for the people cannot simply revert to predemocratic authoritarian models. Totalitarian regimes are "demotic" in the sense that they claim to reflect the will of the people, widely acknowledged since the American and French revolutions as the true source of sovereignty, without giving the people any voice in political decisions. The surrogates are of two kinds: sham "elections," in which the ruling party routinely wins nine-tenths or more of the votes; and grandiose spectacles that create the illusion of mass involvement.

The need for political drama was felt already by the Jacobins, who disguised their dictatorship with elaborate festivals, such as those honoring the "Supreme Being" and celebrating July 14th. By bringing together the all-powerful leaders and the powerless populace in secular rituals, the

Jacobins sought to convey a sense of being one with their subjects. The Bolsheviks used their sparse resources during the Civil War to hold parades, address thousands of the faithful from balconies, and stage open-air theatrical performances based on recent events. The producers of such spectacles went to great lengths to obliterate barriers separating actors from spectators and, thus, the leaders from the masses. The masses were managed in accord with the principles laid down in the late nineteenth century by French sociologist Gustave Le Bon, who ascribed to crowds a distinct collective personality that made them a willing object of psychic manipulation.* The Fascists first experimented with these methods during their occupation of Fiume in 1919–20, when the city was ruled by the poet-politician Gabriele d'Annunzio: "The succession of festivals in which d'Annunzio played a leading role were supposed to abolish the distance between the leader and the led, and the speeches from the balcony of the town hall to the crowd below (accompanied by trumpets) were to accomplish the same purpose."[94] Mussolini and other modern dictators found such methods indispensable—not as entertainment but as rituals designed to convey to opponents and skeptics alike the impression of an unbreakable bond between rulers and ruled.

No one excelled the Nazis in these productions. Using the latest techniques of the cinema and stage, they mesmerized Germans by rallies and pagan rituals that conveyed to participants and onlookers alike the impression of an elemental force which nothing could stop. The identity of the Führer and his people was symbolized by hordes of uniformed men lined up like lead soldiers, the rhythmic screams of the crowds, the illuminations, the flames and flags. Only the most independent spirits could retain enough presence of mind to realize the purpose of these displays. To many Germans, such live spectacles reflected the spirit of the nation far better than the mechanical computation of ballots. The Russian socialist émigré Ekaterina Kuskova, who had the opportunity to observe both Bolshevik and "Fascist" practices of crowd manipulation, noted the similarities: "Lenin's method," she wrote in 1925,

> is *to convince through compulsion*. The hypnotist, the demagogue subordinates the will of the object to his own will—herein lies compulsion. But the subject is convinced that he is acting out of his own free will. The tie between Lenin and the masses is literally of the same nature. . . . Exactly the same picture is provided by Italian Fascism.[95]

The masses subjected to such methods in effect brutalized themselves.

In this connection something needs to be said about totalitarian ideology.

*La Psychologie des foules (Paris, 1895). See *RR*, 398. It is known that Mussolini as well as Hitler had read Le Bon's book: A. James Gregor, *The Ideology of Fascism* (New York, 1969), 112–13, and George Mosse in *Journal of Contemporary History*, Vol. 24, No. 1 (1989), 14. Lenin is said to have always had it on his desk: Boris Bazhanov, *Vospominaniia byvshego sekretaria Stalina* (Paris and New York, 1983), 117.

Totalitarian regimes formulate and impose systems of ideas which purport to provide answers to all questions of private and public life. Secular ideologies of this kind, enforced by Party-controlled schools and media, are an historical innovation introduced by the Bolsheviks and emulated by the Fascists and Nazis. It is one of the principal legacies of the Bolshevik Revolution. Some contemporary observers, struck by its novelty, saw in it the most outstanding feature of totalitarianism and believed that it would transform people into robots.*

Experience has shown such fears to be groundless. The uniformity of the publicly spoken and printed word on any subject that mattered to the authorities was indeed virtually complete under the three regimes: none of them, however, succeeded in controlling thought. The function of ideology was similar to that of the mass spectacles, that is, to create the impression of the individual's total immersion in the community. The dictators themselves had no illusion and did not terribly much care that behind the facade of oneness their subjects thought their private thoughts. How seriously can one take Nazi "ideology," given that Hitler, by his own admission, never bothered to read Alfred Rosenberg's *Myth of the 20th Century,* officially proclaimed to be the theoretical basis of National Socialism? And how many Russians were really expected to master the abstruse and irrelevant economics of Marx and Engels? In Mao Zedong's China, indoctrination assumed the most extreme forms ever known, as one billion people lost access to education and to books other than collections of the tyrant's own sayings. Yet the instant Mussolini, Hitler, and Mao passed from the scene, their teachings dissolved into thin air. Ideology, in the end, proved to be but another spectacle, equally ephemeral.†

*Students of totalitarianism often stress the imposition of an ideology as a determining quality of such regimes. Ideology, however, has in these regimes a largely instrumental role, serving to manipulate the masses. (Speaking of Nazism, Rauschning wrote: "Program and official philosophy, allegiance and faith, are for the mass. Nothing commits the elite—no philosophy, no ethical standard. It has but one obligation, that of absolute loyalty to comrades, to fellow members of the initiated elite" [*Revolution of Nihilism,* 20].) The same may be said of Communist ideology, which in application proved itself infinitely flexible. In any event, democracies, too, have their ideologies: when the French revolutionaries in 1789 issued the "Declaration of the Rights of Man," conservative contemporaries such as Burke and du Pan thought this a dangerous experiment. Far from being "self-evident," the notion of inalienable rights was innovative and revolutionary for its time. Only a traditional ancien régime does not require an ideology.

†Intellectual historians like Hannah Arendt and Jacob Talmon trace the origin of totalitarianism to ideas. The totalitarian dictators, however, were not intellectuals eager to test ideas, but men craving power over fellow men. They exploited ideas to achieve their objectives: their criterion was that which worked. The impact of Bolshevism on them lay not in its programs, from which they borrowed what suited them, but in the fact that the Bolsheviks succeeded in establishing absolute authority using previously untried methods. These methods were just as adaptable to national revolutions as to the international one.

3. The Party and Society

For the people to become truly passive material in the hands of dictators it is not enough to deprive them of a voice in politics: it is necessary also to deprive them of their civil liberties—the protection of law, the rights of assembly and association, and guarantees of property. It is when a dictatorship ventures onto this path that it crosses the line separating "authoritarianism" from "totalitarianism." Although the distinction was first popularized in the United States by Jeane Kirkpatrick in 1980, and from her entered the vocabulary of the Reagan Administration, for which reason it has been rejected by some as Cold War rhetoric, its antecedents go back to the early 1930s. In 1932, on the eve of the Nazi takeover, a German political scientist wrote a book titled *Authoritarian or Totalitarian State?*, in which he made clear the distinction.[96] In 1957, a German émigré scholar, Karl Loewenstein, thus distinguished the two systems:

> The term "authoritarian" denotes a political organization in which the single power holder—an individual person or "dictator," an assembly, a committee, a junta, or a party—monopolizes political power. . . . However, the term "authoritarian" refers rather to the structure of government than to the structure of society. As a rule, the authoritarian regime confines itself to political control of the state without aspiring to the complete domination of the socioeconomic life of the community. . . . By contrast, the term "totalitarian" refers to the socioeconomic dynamism, the way of life, of a state society. The governmental techniques of a totalitarian regime are necessarily authoritarian. But the regime does much more than exclude the power addressees from their legitimate share in the formation of the will of the state. It attempts to mold the private life, the soul, the spirit, and the mores of the citizens to a dominant ideology. . . . The officially proclaimed ideology penetrates into every nook and cranny of the state society; its ambition is "total."*

The distinction between the two types of antidemocratic regimes is fundamental for the understanding of twentieth-century politics. Only someone hopelessly ensnared by the phraseology of Marxism-Leninism could fail to see the difference between Nazi Germany and, say, Salazar's Portugal or Pilsudski's Poland. Unlike totalitarian regimes, which strive radically to alter existing society and even to remake man himself, authoritarian regimes are defensive and in this sense conservative. They emerge when democratic institutions, buffeted by irreconcilable political and social interests, can no longer function properly. They are essentially devices to facilitate political decision-making. In governing, they rely on traditional sources of support and, far from trying to engage in social "engineering," attempt to preserve the status quo. In nearly every known case, whenever authori-

---

Political Power and the Governmental Process (Chicago, 1957), 55–56, 58. Loewenstein incorrectly claimed credit for having introduced the distinction in 1942 in a book on the pro-Fascist Brazilian dictator Getúlio Vargas (*ibid.*, 392, note 3).

tarian dictators died or were ousted, their countries experienced little difficulty restoring democracy.*

Judged by these criteria, only Bolshevik Russia at the height of Stalinism qualifies as a fully developed totalitarian state. For while Italy and Germany emulated Bolshevik measures intended to atomize society, even at their worst (Nazi Germany during the war) they fell short of what Lenin had intended and Stalin realized. Whereas the Bolshevik leaders relied almost exclusively on coercion, Mussolini and even Hitler followed Pareto's advice to combine coercion with consent. They were willing to leave society and its institutions intact as long as their orders were unquestioningly obeyed. In this case, historical traditions were decisive. The Bolsheviks, operating in a society accustomed by centuries of absolutism to identify government with arbitrary authority, not only could but virtually had to take over and manage society, engaging in more repression than strictly necessary in order to demonstrate they were in charge. Neither the Fascists nor the Nazis destroyed their respective social structures, for which reason, after they had suffered defeat in World War II, their countries could rapidly return to normalcy. In the USSR, all attempts between 1985 and 1991 to reform the Leninist-Stalinist regime led nowhere because every nongovernmental institution, whether social or economic, had to be built from scratch. The result was neither reform of Communism nor establishment of democracy, but a progressive breakdown of organized life.

In Russia, the destruction of independent, nonpolitical institutions was facilitated by the fact that social institutions, underdeveloped to being with, all but disintegrated in the anarchy of 1917. In some cases (for example, trade unions, universities, and the Orthodox Church), the Bolsheviks replaced existing management with their own personnel; other institutions they simply dissolved. By the time of Lenin's death, there remained in Russia virtually no institution that was not under direct Communist Party control. With the exception of the peasant commune, which was given a temporary lease on life, nothing stood between the individual citizen and the regime capable of interceding on his behalf.

In Fascist Italy and Nazi Germany, private associations fared much better: in particular, the trade unions, although placed under party control, continued to enjoy a degree of autonomy and influence that, insignificant as it may seem to citizens of democratic societies, was entirely out of reach of workers in the Soviet Union.

In asserting his personal authority over Italian society, Mussolini proceeded with the same caution he displayed in regard to political institutions. His revolution progressed in two phases. From 1922 until 1927, he was a typical authoritarian dictator. His move toward totalitarianism began in

---

*Examples are Franco's Spain, Salazar's Portugal, Greece following the removal of the military junta, Kemal Atatürk's Turkey, and Pinochet's Chile.

1927 with the assault on the independence of private associations. That year he required all such associations to submit to the government their statutes and membership lists. The measure served to bring them into line, since henceforth membership in organizations willing to defy the Fascist Party carried personal risk. The same year, Italian trade unions were deprived of their traditional rights and forbidden to strike. Even so, they retained some power because Mussolini used them as a counterweight to private enterprise: under Fascist legislation, business enterprises had to grant trade union representatives equal rights in decision-making under the overall guidance of the Party.

Hitler covered Germany with a network of Nazi-controlled associations embracing every professional and vocational group, including teachers, lawyers, physicians, and aviators.[97] Because of the strong Social Democratic influence, trade unions were dissolved (May 1933) and replaced with a "Labor Front," which, following the example of Mussolini, included not only workers and clerical help but also employers, the three groups being expected to settle their differences under Nazi Party supervision.[98] Membership in the Front being compulsory, the organization grew by leaps and bounds, eventually enrolling one-half of the country's population. Institutionally, the Labor Front was a branch of the National Socialist Party. In time, as in Stalin's Russia, German workers were forbidden to quit their jobs and managers could not discharge them without permission of the authorities. Emulating the Bolsheviks, in June 1935 Hitler introduced obligatory labor service.[99] The consequence of these policies was, as in Soviet Russia, the assumption by the Party of complete control of the country's organized life. "The organization of the community," Hitler boasted in 1938, "is a thing gigantic and unique. There is hardly a German at the present time who is not personally anchored and active in one or another of the formations of the National Socialist community. It reaches into every house, every workshop and every factory, into every town and village."[100]

As in Lenin's Russia, the Fascist and Nazi parties imposed governmental monopolies on information. In Russia all independent newspapers and periodicals were liquidated by August 1918. With the establishment in 1922 of the central censorship bureau, Glavlit, control of the printed word by the Communist Party became complete. Similar controls were established over the theater, cinema, and every other form of expression, including even the circus.*

Mussolini began his assault on the independent press within a year after coming to power, sending thugs to storm the editorial offices and printing presses of unfriendly newspapers. After the murder of Matteotti, papers that spread "false" news were subject to heavy fines. Finally, in 1925,

*See below, Chapter 6.

freedom of the press was officially abolished, and the government imposed uniformity of news coverage and editorial comment. Even so, ownership of publications remained in private hands, foreign publications were allowed in, and the church could circulate its own daily, *Osservatore Romano,* which by no means toed the Fascist line.

In Germany, press freedom was curtailed under emergency legislation within days of Hitler's assuming the chancellorship. In January 1934, a Reich "Press Leader" was appointed to ensure that the press followed Party directives, with authority to dismiss uncooperative editors and journalists.

The Nazi conception of law was identical with the Bolshevik and the Fascist: law was not the embodiment of justice but an instrument of domination. The existence of transcendental ethical standards was denied; morality was depicted as subjective and determined by political criteria. Lenin told Angelica Balabanoff when she criticized him for slandering as "traitors" socialists whose only sin was disagreeing with him: "Everything that is done in the interest of the proletarian cause is honest."[101] The Nazis translated this pseudomorality into racial terms according to which that was moral which served the interests of the Aryan race.* This convergence in the definition of ethics, one based on class, the other on race, resulted in similar conceptions of law and justice. Nazi theoreticians treated both in a utilitarian manner: "Law is that which benefits the people," the "people" being identified with the person of the Führer, who in July 1934 appointed himself the country's "Supreme Judge."† Although Hitler frequently spoke of the need eventually to abolish the entire judiciary system, for the time being he preferred to subvert it from within. To deal with "crimes against the people," as they chose to define them, the Nazis copied the Bolsheviks and introduced two types of tribunals: "Special Courts" (Sondergerichte), the counterpart of Lenin's Revolutionary Tribunals, and "People's Courts" (Volksgerichthofe), analogues of identically named institutions in Soviet Russia. In the former, customary legal procedures were set aside in favor of summary verdicts dictated by the Party. Throughout the Nazi period, whenever a crime was declared to be of a political nature, the need for legal proof was dispensed with.[102] "Healthy *Volk* perception" became the principal means of determining guilt or innocence.

On the face of it, a major difference between the practices of Communism on the one hand, and those of Fascism and National Socialism on the other, lay in their respective attitudes toward private property. It is this consideration that causes many historians to classify the regimes of Mussolini and

---

*Hitler defined justice as "a means of ruling." "Conscience," he said, "is a Jewish invention. It is a blemish, like circumcision." Rauschning, *Hitler Speaks,* 201, 220.

†Bracher, *Die deutsche Diktatur,* 235, 394. For further discussion of the Nazi conception and practice of law, see Ernst Fraenkel, *The Dual State* (New York, 1969), 107–149. The notion that morality is whatever benefits one's people is said to have been drawn from the *Protocols of the Elders of Zion,* which purported to state, "Everything that benefits the Jewish people is moral and holy." Arendt, *Origins,* 358.

Hitler as "bourgeois" and "capitalist." But a closer look at the way these regimes treated private property reveals that they regarded ownership not as an inalienable right but as a conditional privilege.

In Soviet Russia, by the time of Lenin's death all capital and all productive assets were state property. With the collectivization of agriculture in the late 1920s, which deprived the peasantry of the right to dispose of its product, the abolition of private property was completed. In 1938, according to Soviet statistical sources, the state owned 99.3 percent of the country's national income.[103]

Mussolini set the pattern that Hitler followed. He felt that private property had a place in the Fascist state, without acknowledging it as a "natural," and therefore inalienable, right: ownership of property was for him a qualified right, subordinate to the interests of the State, which had the authority to interfere with it, and, where the means of production were concerned, to abolish it by nationalization.[104] Fascist authorities incessantly meddled in private enterprises that did not live up to their expectations, whether because of poor management, bad labor relations, or some other cause. They had frequent altercations with industrialists, who resented having to treat trade unions as partners. They also intervened in the process of production and distribution, "adjusting" profits and replacing managers. Referring to these practices, one contemporary observed that it was inappropriate to regard Fascism as "triumphant capitalism," since under it private enterprise was as much controlled as was labor.[105]

The Nazis also saw no reason to abolish private enterprise, since it was cooperative and eager to help with the rearmament drive that Hitler designated his main economic objective. Tolerance of private business was an expedient, not a matter of conviction. Like the Fascists, the Nazis acknowledged the principle of private property but denied its sanctity on the grounds that productive wealth, like manpower, had to serve the needs of the "community." In the words of one Nazi theorist, "Property was . . . no longer a private affair but a kind of State concession, limited by the condition that it be put to 'correct' use."[106] Of course, "property" that is not a "private affair" is no longer private property. The Führer, as the personification of the national spirit, enjoyed the right to "limit or expropriate property at will where this limitation or expropriation was consonant with the 'tasks of the community.' "[107] On July 14, 1933, the day the NSDAP was declared the only legal party, a law authorized the confiscation of all property "hostile" to the interests of the Party and State.[108] The Nazi Four Year plans, directly borrowed from Communist practices and intended for the same end, namely rapid rearmament, greatly enhanced the ability of the State to interfere with economic activity.

A generation of Marxist and neo-Marxist mythology notwithstanding, probably never in peacetime has an ostensibly capitalist economy been directed as non- and even anti-capitalistically as the German economy between 1933 and 1939. . . . The status of business in the Third Reich was at best the product of a social contract between unequal partners, in which submission was the condition for success.[109]

The rights of farmers to dispose of their land was strictly regulated with a view to keeping it in the family.[110] Interference with business was constant, even to the point of limiting the amount of profits that corporations could pay out in dividends. Rauschning warned Western appeasers in 1939 that the expropriation by the Nazis of Jewish wealth was only a first step, a prelude to "the total and irrevocable destruction of the economic position" of Germany's capitalists and former ruling classes.[111]

The attribution to Nazism of a "bourgeois" character has traditionally rested on two arguments, both refuted by historical evidence. It has been widely believed that in his march to power Hitler benefited from financial support from industrial and banking circles. Studies of the documentary evidence, however, indicate that big business gave Hitler only negligible sums, much smaller than those it passed to conservative parties opposed to him, because it was suspicious of his socialist slogans:

> Only through gross distortion can big business be accorded a crucial, or even major, role in the downfall of the [Weimar] Republic. . . . If the role of big business in the disintegration of the Republic has been exaggerated, such is even more true of its role in the rise of Hitler. . . . The early growth of the NSDAP took place without any significant aid from the circles of large-scale enterprise.[112]

Secondly, it is not possible to show that at any time during the Nazi regime big business was able to resist the policies of the Nazis, let alone dictate policies to them. A German Marxist historian describes the place of the capitalist class under Hitler as follows: "In the self-perception of Fascism, the Fascist system of government is characterized by the primacy of politics. As long as the primacy of politics was safeguarded, it was a matter of indifference to the Fascists which groups profited from their regime. Since the economic order was, in the Fascist world outlook, of secondary importance, they also accepted the existing capitalist order."* The National Socialist movement, writes another scholar, "was from the beginning a government by a new and revolutionary elite which tolerated industrialists and aristocrats only so long as they were content with a status that gave them no real influence over the determination of politics."[113] And content they were with ample state orders and the profits they provided.

In this connection it should not be forgotten that Lenin had no qualms

---

*Axel Kuhn, *Das faschistische Hersschaftssystem* (Hamburg, 1973), 83. The author uses "Fascist" to mean Nazi. It has been noted that under the Weimar Republic the German business community "displayed . . . a surprising indifference to governmental forms": Henry A. Turner in *AHR*, Vol. 75, No. 1 (1969), 57.

about taking money from Russian millionaires as well as from the German Imperial government.[114] On coming to power he was quite willing to collaborate with Russian big business, initiating negotiations with capitalist cartels to have them work in partnership with the new regime. The plan came to naught because of the opposition of the Left Communists, eager to proceed to Communism.[115] But the intention was there; and if in 1921, when Lenin launched the New Economic Policy, anything had survived of Russian large-scale capitalist industry and commerce, he almost certainly would have struck a deal with it.

If we turn to the differences separating Communist, Fascist, and National Socialist regimes, we find that they can be accounted for by contrasting social, economic, and cultural conditions in which the three had to operate. In other words, they resulted from tactical adaptations of the same philosophy of government to local circumstances, not from different philosophies.

The outstanding difference between Communism on the one hand, and Fascism and National Socialism on the other, lies in their attitudes to nationalism: Communism is an international movement, whereas Fascism, in Mussolini's words, was not for "export." In a speech to the Chamber of Deputies in 1921, Mussolini addressed the Communists as follows: "Between us and the Communists there are no political affinities but there are intellectual ones. Like you, we consider necessary a centralized and unitary state which imposes iron discipline on all persons, with this difference, that you reach this conclusion by way of the concept of class, and we by way of the concept of nation."[116] Hitler's future Propaganda Minister, Joseph Goebbels, similarly believed that the one thing separating Communists from the Nazis was the former's internationalism.[117]

How fundamental was this difference? On closer investigation, it can be explained largely by the specific social and ethnic conditions of the three countries.

In Germany in 1933, 29 percent of the adult population worked on the land, 41 percent in industry and handicrafts, and 30 percent in the service sector.[118] Here, as in Italy, the distribution of urban and rural population, of wage earners, self-employed, and employers, of those who owned property and those who did not, was far more balanced than in Russia, which in this respect resembled Asia more than Europe. Given the complexity of social structure and the importance of groups that belonged neither to the "proletariat" nor to the "bourgeoisie," it would have been quite unrealistic in Western Europe to pit the one class against the other. Here, an aspiring dictator could not identify himself with a single class without seriously weakening his political base. The truth of this proposition was demonstrated by the repeated failure of the Communists to stir up social revolution in the West. In every case—Hungary, Germany, Italy—that part of the intelligentsia and working class they succeeded in inciting to rebellion was crushed by a coalition of the other social groups. After World War II, even in countries where they had the greatest following, Italy and France, the Communists could never break out of their isolation, because of their reliance on a single class.

In the West an aspiring dictator had to exploit national, rather than class, animosities. Mussolini and his Fascist theoreticians skillfully fused the two by claiming that in the case of Italy, the "class struggle" pitted not one class of citizens against another, but the entire "proletarian nation" against the "capitalist" world.[119] Hitler designated "international Jewry" as not only the "racial" but also the class enemy of Germans. While focusing resentment on outsiders—Carl Schmitt's "enemy"—he balanced the interests of the middle class, workers, and farmers, without overtly favoring any one of them. The nationalism of Mussolini and Hitler was a concession to the fact that the structure of their societies required resentment to be deflected outward, that the road to power lay through the cooperation of diverse classes against foreigners.* On a number of occasions—notably in Germany and Hungary—the Communists, too, had no hesitation in appealing to chauvinist emotions.

In the East, the situation was very different. Russia in 1917 was overwhelmingly a country of one class, the peasantry. Russian industrial labor was relatively small and, for the most part, still rooted in the village. This socially fairly homogeneous population of "toilers," which in the Great Russian provinces comprised 90 percent of the total, was distinguished from the remaining 10 percent not only socioeconomically but also culturally. It felt no sense of national identity with the largely Westernized landlords, officials, professional people, businessmen, and intelligentsia. To Russian peasants and workers, they could just as well have been foreigners. The class enemy in revolutionary Russia, the *burzhui,* was at least as much identified by his speech, manners, and appearance as by his economic status. The road to power in Russia lay, therefore, by way of civil war between the mass of peasants and workers and the Westernized elite.

But if Russia was less complex socially than Italy and Germany, she was considerably more complex in terms of ethnic composition. Italy and Germany were ethnically homogeneous; Russia was a multinational empire in which the dominant group accounted for less than one-half of the population. A politician who appealed openly to Russian nationalism risked alienating the non-Russian half, a fact realized by the tsarist government, which

---

*The more knowledgeable members of the Comintern realized this. At their June 1923 Plenum, Radek and Zinoviev insisted that to break out of their isolation, the German Communists had to link up with the nationalistically minded elements. This was to be justified on the grounds that the nationalist ideology of "oppressed" nations, of which Germany was one, bore a revolutionary character. "In Germany," Radek said on this occasion, "the heavy stress on the nation is a revolutionary act." Luks, *Entstehung der kommunistischen Faschismustheorie,* 62.

had avoided overt identification with Great Russian nationalism, relying instead on the ethnically neutral "imperial" idea. For this reason as well, Lenin had to take a different route from Mussolini and Hitler and promote an ideology devoid of ethnic coloration.

In sum, given Russia's fairly homogeneous social structure and heterogeneous ethnic structure, an aspiring Russian dictator could be expected to appeal to class antagonisms, whereas in the West, where the situation was reversed, the appeal would be to nationalism.

This said, it must be noted that in time, class-based and nation-based totalitarianisms tended to converge. Stalin from the outset of his political career discreetly encouraged Great Russian nationalism and anti-Semitism; during and after World War II, he did so openly, in brazen chauvinistic terms. Hitler, for his part, felt German nationalism to be too restricting. "I can attain my purpose only through world revolution," he told Rauschning, and predicted that he would dissolve German nationalism in the broader concept of "Aryanism":

> The conception of the nation has become meaningless. . . . We have to get rid of this false conception and set in its place the conception of race. . . . The new order cannot be conceived in terms of the national boundaries of the peoples with an historic past, but in terms of race that transcend those boundaries. . . . I know perfectly well, just as well as all these tremendously clever intellectuals, that in the scientific sense there is no such thing as race. But you, as a farmer and cattle-breeder, cannot get your breeding successfully achieved without the conception of race. And I as a politician need a conception which enables the order which has hitherto existed on historic bases to be abolished and an entirely and new anti-historic order enforced and given an intellectual basis. . . . And for this purpose the conception of race serves me well. . . . France carried her great Revolution beyond her borders with the conception of the nation. With the conception of race, National Socialism will carry the revolution abroad and re-cast the world. . . . There will not be much left then of the clichés of nationalism, and precious little among us Germans. Instead there will be an understanding between the various language elements of the one good ruling race.[120]

Communism and "Fascism" have different intellectual origins in that the one is rooted in the philosophy of the Enlightenment and the other in the anti-Enlightenment culture of the Romantic era. In theory, Communism is rational and constructive, "Fascism" irrational and destructive, which is why Communism has always had far greater appeal to intellectuals. In practice, however, this distinction, too, becomes blurred. Here, indeed, "being" determines "consciousness," in that totalitarian institutions subordinate ideology and reshape it at will. As we have noted, both movements treat ideas as infinitely flexible tools to be imposed on their subjects to enforce obedience and create the appearance of uniformity. In the end, the totalitarianism of the Leninist-Stalinist and Hitlerite regimes, however different their intellectual roots, proved equally nihilistic and equally destructive.

Most telling of all, perhaps, is the admiration that the totalitarian dictators felt for one another. We have mentioned Mussolini's high regard for Lenin and the praise he lavished on Stalin for turning into a "secret Fascist." Hitler admitted to intimates respect for Stalin's "genius": in the midst of World War II, as his troops were locked in savage combat with the Red Army, he mused about joining forces with him to attack and destroy the Western democracies. The one major obstacle to such collaboration, the presence of Jews in the Soviet government, seemed capable of resolution in light of the assurances that the Soviet leader had given Joachim von Ribbentrop, Hitler's Foreign Minister, that as soon as he had adequate cadres of gentiles he would remove all Jews from leading positions.[121] And, in turn, Mao Zedong, the most radical of Communists, admired Hitler and his methods. When reproached at the height of the Cultural Revolution for sacrificing the lives of so many of his comrades, he responded: "Look at World War II, at Hitler's cruelty. The more cruelty, the more enthusiasm for revolution."[122]

At bottom, the totalitarian regimes of the left and right varieties were united not only by similar political philosophies and practices, but by the common psychology of their founders: its driving motive was hatred and its expression violence. Mussolini, the frankest of them, referred to violence as a "moral therapeutic" because it forced people to make clear commitments.[123] In this, and in their determination to raze the existing world in which they felt themselves outcasts, at all costs and by all means, lay their kinship.

6

Culture as Propaganda

But then that was precisely the goal of the whole enterprise: to uproot the species spiritually to the point of no return; for how else can you build a genuinely new society? You start neither with the foundations, nor with the roof: you start by making new bricks.

Joseph Brodsky[1]

For the Bolsheviks, the social revolution meant also a revolution in culture. The subject has attracted considerable scholarly attention because it is more congenial than the somber record of repression and suffering that fills so much of the history of the time. In their first decade, the Communists displayed a tolerance for independent creativity that was quite absent from their politics and economics. This tolerance becomes even more striking when set against the rigidity and vulgarity of the Stalinist era. Scrutinized more closely, however, the innovations in literature, art, and education of the regime's early years appear as marginal aspects of a cultural policy that was from the beginning driven by political imperatives. The very concept of "cultural policy" is a contradiction in terms since true culture can only be unguided and spontaneous: it betrays the end to which the Communists intended to harness it.

That end was propaganda, that is, intellectual and emotional manipulation. Lenin as well as Anatolii Lunacharskii, his cultural commissar, defined the mission of all Soviet cultural and educational institutions as instilling Communist ideology for the purpose of raising a new and superior breed of human beings. The function of literature was to be propaganda; this was also the task of the visual and performing arts, and, above all, the educational system. No previous government had attempted to mold thought and feeling on such a comprehensive scale.

Propaganda was not a Bolshevik invention, of course. The concept originated in the early seventeenth century when the papacy established the Congregatio de Propaganda Fide to spread Catholicism. In its secularized form, it was frequently employed by eighteenth- and nineteenth-century governments: Catherine II of Russia made skillful use of it, as did the French revolutionaries and Napoleon. During World War I, the major belligerent powers carried out aggressive propaganda and set up special offices for this purpose. The novelty of what the Bolsheviks did lay in the centrality of propaganda in Soviet life: previously used to touch up or to distort reality, in Communist Russia it became a surrogate reality. Communist propaganda strove, and to a surprising extent succeeded, in creating a fictitious world side by side with that of everyday experience and in stark contradiction to it, which Soviet citizens were required to pretend to believe. This was made possible by the monopoly the Communist Party secured over sources of information and opinion. The effort was undertaken on so vast a scale, with such ingenuity and determination, that in time the imaginary world it projected eclipsed for many Soviet citizens the living reality.

Early Soviet cultural history reveals a striking dualism. On one level, bold experimentation and unrestrained creative freedom; on another, relentless harnessing of culture to serve the political interests of the new ruling class. While foreign contemporaries and historians focused on the whimsical creations of Bolshevik and "fellow-traveler" artists—the monochrome canvasses of Alexander Rodchenko, Vladimir Tatlin's fantastic skyscraper that was never built and his man-propelled glider that never left the ground, the *haute couture* workclothes designed by Rodchenko and Liubov Popova for starving workers and peasants—the more significant phenomenon was the silent rise of a "cultural" bureaucracy for whom culture was only a form of propaganda, and propaganda the highest form of culture. Years before Stalin took over and put an end to experimentation, the shackles on creativity were being set in place.[2]

Since, according to Marxist doctrine, culture is a by-product of economic relations, the Bolshevik leadership took it for granted that the revolutionary changes they had carried out in property relations would result in equally revolutionary transformations in culture: Trotsky merely affirmed a Marxist axiom when he stated that "every ruling class creates its own culture."[3] The "proletariat" was to be no exception. This said, the Bolsheviks far from agreed on the nature of the new culture and on the best ways of bringing it about. One disagreement concerned the freedom of the writer and artist. Some Bolsheviks believed that "cultural workers" should be subject to the same discipline as the other members of Communist society. Others argued that since creativity could not be regimented, they required greater freedom. Lenin was ambivalent on this issue. In 1905 he spoke of literature as an activity least subject to "mechanical leveling." To be sure, it had to be linked to the Party: in a socialist society, writers will have to be party members and publishing houses will have to come under party control. But since a socialist literature could not be created overnight, writers required freedom to be themselves.[4] Yet, in the same breath, Lenin broadened the concept of *partiinost*—an untranslatable term meaning total commitment to the Party—to cover literature. After the Revolution, he said, "Literature must be *partiinaia*": "Down with nonparty litterateurs!" "Down with litterateurs-supermen!"[5] And although Lenin showed much more tolerance for literature and art than for any other field of activity, when forced to choose he usually sided with those who saw culture as the handmaiden of politics.

The other issue dividing the leadership concerned the content of the new, proletarian culture: whether it was to assimilate the heritage of "bourgeois" culture and build on it, or to reject it and build from scratch. The latter thesis was upheld by the "Proletarian Culture" or Proletkult movement. Enjoying the patronage of Lunacharskii and the Commissariat of Enlightenment which he headed, its members dominated cultural activity during the first two years of the new regime, when Lenin was preoccupied with more urgent matters. But it was only a matter of time before they would be demoted, because for Lenin "culture" meant something very different: not so much literary and artistic creativity, which he doubted the Russian masses were capable of in any event, but a way of life guided by science and technology:

> Lenin's conception of the "socialist cultural revolution" emphasized the rational-planificatory tasks of the new revolutionary state power as well as the instrumental quality of knowledge and the pressing tasks of elementary mass education. Only when the foundations had been solidly laid, could the higher culture become accessible to the peasant and proletarian masses, cultured social relations be established, and the people, schooled in technology, experience a transformation of mentality. In this conception, the "cultural revolution" meant not the creation of a new "proletarian culture" but the acquisition of scientific, technical, and organizational means with which to overcome the socioeconomic backwardness of the country and its population.[6]

Even though he adhered to a less utilitarian notion of culture, Trotsky also rejected the philosophy of Proletkult. Since the historic mission of the "proletariat" was to abolish all classes, its culture could not bear the stamp of a single class: the workers' state would give birth to the first "truly human" culture.[7] In the end, Proletkult lost out. For reasons that will be spelled below, its ideas were declared heretical and its organizations, which at their height competed with the Communist Party, were dissolved. The regime chose a more eclectic path.

In matters of organization Lenin believed in bigness: his preference was for superinstitutions modeled on capitalist cartels to manage every major sphere of public activity. Thus, the Supreme Council of the National Economy was to direct all industry, the Cheka all that concerned security, and

32. Lunacharskii.

the Revolutionary Military Council every aspect of the Civil War effort. He similarly consolidated and bureaucratized the management of culture by subordinating it to a single institution, the Commissariat of Enlightenment (Narodnyi Kommissariat po Prosveshcheniiu, or Narkompros). Unlike the corresponding tsarist ministry, Narkompros assumed responsibility not only for education but for every facet of intellectual and aesthetic life, including entertainment: scholarship, literature, the press, painting, music, the theater, and the cinema. As defined in 1925, the function of the Narkompros of the Russian Republic was to "direct all scholarly, scientific, educational, and artistic activity of the Republic of a general as well as professional character."[8] Narkompros directed state publishing enterprises and enforced an increasingly rigorous censorship code. Because Lunacharskii was rather an indulgent person, as long as he was in charge (he was replaced in 1929) these functions were carried out in a relaxed manner, allowing to the Commissariat's personnel and to the recipients of its subsidies a degree of independence that was unthinkable in the other branches of government. Inefficiently managed, Narkompros failed to attract good talent, turning into a favorite haven for the wives and relatives of the Bolshevik bosses.[9]

But Lunacharskii's personality was not the only and not even the main reason for the regime's uncharacteristically benign treatment of the nation's intellectual elite. The conspicuous fact was that virtually the entire intelligentsia, both professional and "creative," rejected the Bolshevik dictatorship. The intelligentsia had been the first group in tsarist Russia to emancipate itself from the universal duty of service to the patrimonial state.[10] Whatever its sins, it genuinely believed in freedom, and having enjoyed more than a century of independence, it was unwilling to be reharnessed in state service. Most of Russia's writers, artists, and academics, individually and collectively, turned their backs on the new rulers, refusing to work for them, and either emigrated or withdrew into their private world. They did so not only for political reasons, but also from revulsion at the regime's vulgarity and its interference with their private lives. The young Vladimir Nabokov spoke not only for himself when on the tenth anniversary of the October coup he wrote in an émigré newspaper:

> I despise not the man, the worker Sidorov, an honest member of some Com-pom-pom, but the warped, stupid idea which transforms Russian simpletons into communist simplophiles, which turns people into ants of a new variety, *formica marxi, var. lenini.* . . . I despise the Communist faith as an idea of base equality, as a drab page in the festive history of mankind, as the rejection of terrestrial and nonterrestrial beauty, as something that stupidly encroaches on my unfettered *I,* as the encouragement of ignorance, obtuseness and smugness.[11]

How repugnant the new regime was to the "creative intelligentsia" may be judged from the fact that when in November 1917, a few days after the coup, the Bolshevik Central Executive Committee invited Petrograd's writers and artists to a meeting, only seven or eight turned up. The same fate befell Lunacharskii when in December 1917 he summoned 150 of its most prominent representatives: on this occasion, five came, among them two Communist sympathizers, the poet Vladimir Maiakovskii and the stage director Vsevolod Meyerhold, and the temporarily disoriented Alexander Blok.[12] Lunacharskii virtually had to beg students and teachers to end their boycott of the new regime.[13] Maxim Gorky was the only novelist with a national reputation who cooperated with the Bolsheviks, and even he subjected them to scathing criticisms that Lenin chose to ignore because he found his support so valuable. Trotsky's *Literature and Revolution,* written in 1924, poured scorn and hatred on Russia's intellectuals for spurning the Bolshevik regime. Infuriated by their refusal to join what he saw as the wave of the future, Trotsky ridiculed the "reactionary stupidity of the professional intelligentsia" and declared that the October Revolution had marked its "unqualified defeat."[14] In time, many intellectuals made their peace (or, rather, truce) with the regime, often to escape death from starvation, but even they proved grudging collaborators at best. The "creative intelligentsia" whom the regime succeeded in winning over were mostly hacks and daubers unable to make it on their own, who, like similar mediocrities in Nazi Germany, flocked to the party in power in quest of patronage. The policy of relative cultural tolerance at least neutralized the rest. Lenin, who held the Russian intelligentsia in no less contempt than had Nicholas II, believed that he could buy it off with a bit of freedom and some material rewards.

Writers and artists willing to collaborate found the conditions of work during Lenin's lifetime fairly decent. Even so, they produced little of lasting value because of the difficulty of working within the terms set by their Communist patrons. For the latter, human beings were not unique individuals with a free will and a personal conscience, but specimens of their class, that is, types who acted according to the dictates of their economic status. Communists intensely disliked individualism in all its manifestations: an influential theorist of Soviet culture of the 1920s, Aleksei Gastev, predicted the gradual disappearance of individual thinking and its replacement by "mechanized collectivism."[15] This outlook required writers to produce stock characters: it precluded a novel or play featuring a "good" businessman or a "bad" worker. As a result, the Soviet novel and drama presented two-dimensional, black-or-white personalities who talked in clichés and behaved like marionettes. They were permitted to lapse temporarily from the stereotype, to entertain doubts or commit mistakes, but in the end all had to work out as happily as in a Hollywood film. Since this made for predictable and therefore dull contents, the more imaginative Soviet writers and dramatists put their energy into experimenting with form. In the first decade of the Communist regime every traditional canon of literature, drama, and art was consciously violated: experimentation with form became an end in itself, pursued to conceal the poverty of the content.

The "Proletarian Culture" movement was founded in the early years of the century by Lunacharskii and his brother-in-law, Alexander Bogdanov (Malinovskii). Lenin appointed Lunacharskii, a dropout from the University of Zurich, Commissar of Enlightenment despite misgivings about this movement and suspicion of Bogdanov's political ambitions. Lunacharskii said that he owed his appointment to the fact that he was "the *intelligent* among the Bolsheviks and the Bolshevik among the intelligentsia."[16] For all his disagreements with Lenin about the nature of the new culture, he shared Lenin's conviction that the Soviet school had to be the "source of agitation and propaganda" and a weapon with which to destroy "all kinds of prejudices," religious as well as political.[17] He also defended censorship, which Lenin entrusted to his care.[18]

In the formative years of Bolshevism, Bogdanov was one of Lenin's closest and most dependable associates. In 1905, Lenin appointed him to the newly formed clandestine three-man Center that directed secret Bolshevik activities and managed its finances. Even then he displayed a keen interest in the sociology of culture.[19] His theory, not always clear or consistent, partly derived from Emile Durkheim and the neo-Kantians, can be summarized as follows: Culture is an aspect of labor, and since labor is a collective endeavor in man's perpetual struggle with nature, the creation of culture, too, is a collective process:

> All *creativity*—technological, socioeconomic, political, domestic, scientific, artistic—represents a variety of *labor* and is formed exactly the same way from the organizational (or disorganizational) efforts of man. . . . There is not and cannot be a strict delineation between creativity and ordinary labor; there not only exist transitional gradations, but often one cannot even say with certainty which of the two designations is more applicable. Human labor, always relying on collective experience and using means that have been collectively worked out, is in this sense always *collective,* no matter how, in individual cases, its objectives and its external, immediate form may be narrowly individualistic (that is, when such labor is performed by one person and only for himself). The same holds true of creativity. Creativity is the highest, most complex form of labor. For that reason, its methods derive from those of labor.[20]

Primitive, classless societies had a single, common culture, whose outstanding product was language. But poetry, music, and dance also helped organize communal work and warfare.

At a certain stage in human evolution, according to Bogdanov, came the division of labor and its corollary, social classes. The breakdown of social homogeneity led to a bifurcation of culture as the propertied elite monopolized thought and imposed its ideas and values on the inert masses. The result was a cleavage between intellectual and physical labor, which the owners of the means of production exploited to keep the laboring classes in thrall. In societies based on class distinctions, art and literature became highly individualized, their creators claiming to respond to personal "inspiration." But the individualism of feudal and capitalist cultures was more apparent than real. Adopting Durkheim's concept of *conscience collective,* Bogdanov argued that the roots of even the most individualistic creativity lay imbedded in values the writers and artists absorbed from their class.[21]

From these premises it followed that once the proletariat took power, a new culture would emerge, one reflecting its experience in the workplace. Shaped in the factory, where men worked as teams, it would be collective rather than individualistic, and in this respect closer to the culture of primitive society. The "I" of bourgeois culture would yield to "we." Under the new conditions, the heritage of the old, "bourgeois" culture would be of little if any value. Some of Bogdanov's more radical followers wanted not only to discard but physically to destroy the legacy of the past—museums along with libraries and even science—as irrelevant or positively harmful. Bogdanov himself adopted a more moderate stand. The worker, he wrote, would approach the culture of the bourgeois epoch much as an atheist approaches religion, that is, with detached curiosity. But he would not adopt it, because its authoritarian and individualistic spirit is alien to him. The new culture will emerge from the inexhaustible creative powers latent in the masses of industrial workers once they are given the opportunity to write, paint, compose, and to pursue every other intellectual and aesthetic activity from which the bourgeoisie has barred them.

In 1909, with the financial help of Maxim Gorky and Fedor Shaliapin, Bogdanov opened an experimental Bolshevik school in Capri to train cadres of worker intellectuals. A dozen or so students smuggled out of Russia prepared, together with their Social-Democratic instructors, curricula in philosophy and the social sciences which, upon graduation and return home, they were to disseminate among fellow-workers. The instructional system was organized so that the teachers not only taught their pupils but also learned from them. The focus of instruction was on propaganda and agitation. The following year a school based on similar principles was opened in Bologna.[22]

Lenin rejected the cultural philosophy of Bogdanov, for he believed that socialism, even as it destroyed capitalism, had to build on its foundations. He did not think that workers had the creative potential that Bogdanov ascribed to them. A technocrat, he viewed culture mainly in terms of science and engineering, of which the Russian masses were ignorant: he wanted to teach them, not to learn from them. Dismissing the theories of Proletkult as "utter nonsense," he insisted that "proletarian culture must be the logical *(zakonomernoe)* development of the accumulation of the knowledge that mankind had produced under the yoke of capitalist society. . . . One can become a Communist only by enriching one's memory with the knowledge of all the wealth that mankind has produced."[23] But what especially irritated Lenin about Bogdanov's theory was the notion that culture was an autonomous sphere of human endeavor, parallel to, and equal in importance to, politics and economics.[24] He suspected, not without reason, that the worker cadres trained at Capri and Bologna were intended to establish a separate Bolshevik apparatus, loyal to Bogdanov. Aware that some of his followers came to regard Bogdanov as his intellectual peer and a contender for leadership, Lenin had both him and Lunacharskii expelled from the Party (1909).

Bogdanov found a hospitable environment for his ideas after the Bolshevik coup owing to the friendship of Lunacharskii. In a decree issued shortly after assuming office as Commissar of Enlightenment, Lunacharskii (who had been readmitted to the Party in 1917) pledged to promote the "cultural-enlightenment organizations of workers, soldiers, [and] peasants" and their "full autonomy in relation to both the state center and the municipal centers."[25] This provision, which slipped through the loose nets of early Bolshevik legislation, ensured Proletkult a unique status in Lenin's dictatorship, exempting it from the supervision of party and party-directed state organs.

Drawing on generous subsidies from Lunacharskii's Commissariat, Bogdanov proceeded to cover Soviet Russia with a network of Proletkult organizations. Studios were opened where professional artists taught drawing and sculpting. There were poetry circles, folk theaters, extension courses, libraries, and exhibitions. Professional writers and artists involved in these activities taught the techniques of their craft, but they also sought to stimulate original creativity. They wanted everything done by teams, without resort either to individual "inspiration" or to past examples: one theorist of the movement extolled the newspaper as the model of collective creativity.[26] At "poetry workshops" poems were created in cooperative fashion, participants contributing individual lines. Poetry was to reflect the mechanization of modern industrial life: its rhythms had to change accordingly, replacing Pushkin's four-syllabic iamb that rendered "gentry leisure" with new, brisker rhythms. In the words of one Proletkult author, the world stood "on the eve of electrification of poetry in which the rhythm of the modern enterprise is provided by the central dynamo."[27]

Proletkult also attempted to reshape the culture of everyday life. The first Proletkult conference held in February 1918 earnestly debated a motion concerning "children's rights," which proposed to empower minors, regardless of age, to an education of their liking, and the right to leave their parents if dissatisfied with them.[28]

One of the more eccentric members of Proletkult was Aleksei Gastev, a metalworker turned poet and theorist. An early follower of Bogdanov, in the first years of the Bolshevik regime he wrote verse and came to be known as the "singer of steel and machines." After 1920 he concentrated on applying Frederick Taylor's "time-motion" methods of industrial productivity to improving efficiency of everyday life. Members of his "Time League," which had branches in every major city, were required to carry watches and to keep "chronocards," on which they recorded the exact use they made of every minute of the day. Ideally, he would have had everyone go to sleep and rise at the same hour. To economize on time he proposed to "mechanize speech" by replacing the long expressions customary in Russian with shorter ones, and by resorting to acronyms, for the widespread use of which in Soviet Russia he bore much responsibility.

In moments of visionary exaltation, Gastev proposed to mechanize man and his activities in accord with the time-motion experiments carried out at his Central Institute of Labor (Tsentralnyi Institut Truda). He had visions of a future in which people would be reduced to automatons known by ciphers instead of names, devoid of personal ideas and feelings, whose individuality would dissolve tracelessly in collective work:

> The psychology of the proletariat is strikingly standardized by the mechanization not only of motions, but also of everyday thinking. . . . This quality lends the proletarian psychology its striking anonymity, which makes it possible to designate the separate proletarian entity as A, B, C, or as 325, 075, and 0, et cetera. . . . This signifies that in the proletarian psychology, from one end of the world to the other, there flow powerful

psychological currents, for which, as it were, there exists no longer a million heads but a single global head. In the future this tendency will, imperceptibly, render impossible individual thinking.[29]

This nightmare, in which one Western historian perceives a "vision of hope,"[30] provided material for Evgenii Zamiatin's anti-utopian novel, *We*, and Karel Capek's *R.U.R.*, a play that popularized the word "robot."* By a strange inversion, a flaw Communism attributed to capitalism, namely the dehumanization of the worker, became for some Communists an ideal.

Proletkult expanded rapidly: at its height in 1920, it had 80,000 active members and 400,000 sympathizers.[31] In many factories it maintained cells, which functioned independently of regular Communist cells. Its leaders enjoyed a degree of autonomy from the Party granted no other group: they did not conceal that they regarded themselves as subject only to their own internal supervision. A Moscow conference of Proletkult organizations resolved that Proletkult "should become an independent class organization on an equal footing with other forms of the workers' movement—the political and the economic."[32] In a programmatic statement published in the first issue of its organ, the chairman of Proletkult argued that the cultural tasks of the regime required a division of labor: to the Commissariat of Enlightenment belonged responsibility for education, while Proletkult was to direct the creative energies of the proletariat. To accomplish its task, it had to be exempt from the restrictions imposed on other state organs.[33] Nadezhda Krupskaia, Lenin's wife, whom Lenin had asked to keep an eye on Narkompros, more than once objected to Proletkult's "separatism," but Lunacharskii, partly from sympathy for Bogdanov's ideas, and partly from an un-Bolshevik dislike of harsh measures, did nothing to correct the situation.

It was this political self-aggrandizement that proved the movement's undoing. Lenin turned his attention to Proletkult in August 1920, at which time he asked the historian M. M. Pokrovskii, one of its directors, for an explanation of the organization's "juridical" status.[34] As soon as he realized how much independence this organization had acquired and what claims it made to institutional sovereignty, he ordered Proletkult organizations to be integrated into the Commissariat of Enlightenment (October 1920). In the course of the next two years, the central and regional offices of Proletkult were shut down and most of its cultural activities curtailed.†

Proletkult managed to lead a desultory existence for a few more years but its philosophy was rejected. It was Lenin's view that prevailed. Soviet

---

*René Fülöp-Miller, *Geist und Gesicht des Bolschewismus* (Zurich, 1926), 274–87; also Richard Stites, *Revolutionary Dreams* (New York, 1989), 149–55. Gastev was arrested in 1938 and perished in 1941: Peter Gorsen and Eberhard Knoedler-Bunte, *Proletkult*, II (Stuttgart, 1974), 150.

†Bogdanov, a physician by training, subsequently turned his attention to medicine. In 1926 he founded an Institute of Blood Transfusions. He died in 1928 in consequence of an experiment he had performed on himself.

culture was to benefit from the entire heritage of humanity: the new order would raise culture to unprecedented heights, Lenin proclaimed, but it would do so step by step, without abrupt leaps. It was a significant decision and perhaps the only liberal measure that Lenin bequeathed to his successors. For it meant that even under the harshest restrictions on creativity imposed by Stalin, citizens of the Soviet Union had access to the cultural heritage of mankind. It helped them to retain their sanity under the most trying conditions.

The Communist regime controlled cultural activities by two devices: censorship and monopoly on cultural organizations. Censorship was a tradition in Russia, first institutionalized in 1826 and enforced until 1906, long after it had been abandoned in the rest of Europe. Until 1864, it was practiced in its most onerous "preventive" form: before publication or performance, every manuscript had to be submitted to the censors to obtain their license. This form of censorship was unique to tsarist Russia in modern times. In 1864, a new censorship code replaced "preventive" with "punitive" censorship, under which authors and editors were liable to prosecution after the offending material had been made public. Censorship was abolished in 1906, although in 1914, Russia, like the other belligerent nations, introduced military censorship. On April 27, 1917, the Provisional Government lifted the remaining restrictions on the press and exempted it from administrative penalties, except for disclosure of military secrets.[35]

It is indicative of the importance the Bolsheviks attached to controlling information and public opinion that the very first law they passed upon assuming power called for the suppression of newspapers that opposed their coup d'état. This was done by decree of the Council of People's Commissars of October 27, 1917, which ordered, as a "temporary and emergency measure," the closing of all "counterrevolutionary" newspapers.[36] Such haste at a time when the Bolsheviks had more urgent things to occupy their minds is explainable by Lenin's belief that "the press is the core and foundation of political organization"[37]—in other words, that freedom of the press was tantamount to the freedom to form political parties. The decree met with such resistance from all quarters, including the printers' union, which threatened to shut down all presses, Bolshevik ones included, that it had to be quietly dropped. It was replaced with another, milder censorship regulation in February 1918, according to which the right to publish was open to all citizens provided the names of the editors and addresses of the enterprise were made known to the authorities. Newspapers were required to publish government decrees and regulations on the front page.[38]

Even without a comprehensive censorship apparatus, the new regime adopted a variety of measures to restrict press freedom over the next five years, the net effect of which was to choke off independent publishing.[39] To begin with, it set up in the major cities "Commissariats of the Press," subordinated to the Sovnarkom, with discretionary powers to suspend hostile publications and impound their presses.[40] A decree of December 1917 entrusted similar authority to the soviets.[41] On January 28, 1918, a new repressive institution came into being, a Revolutionary Tribunal of the Press, attached to the Revolutionary Tribunal, to try editors and authors guilty of publishing "false or distorted" information.[42] In practice, most of the responsibility for censorship at this stage was assumed by the Cheka, which through its local branches collected information on hostile publications and turned over those responsible to the Revolutionary Tribunal. Papers that in its view worked for the overthrow of the Communist dictatorship the Cheka shut down. In the first seven months of Bolshevik rule (October–May) more than 130 "bourgeois" and socialist newspapers were closed in this manner.[43]

During the first half of 1918, as popular support for the new regime eroded, editors and publishers were frequently hauled before tribunals. Troublesome newspapers were subjected to stiff fines; many appeared with blank spaces where censors had removed offending articles. Some were shut down temporarily or permanently; as had been the practice under tsarism, those that survived had to print formal repudiations of the information that had gotten them into trouble. Drawing on experience acquired under pre-1906 tsarist censorship, the publishers of the suppressed papers often came out the very next day under a new editor and with a changed but similar-sounding name.[44] One frequently penalized daily, the Menshevik *Den'*, or "Day," managed to appear in the course of a single month (November 1917) under eight different names: after being forced to close, "Day" became "Midday" *(Polden')*, followed by "New Day" *(Novyi den')*, "Night" *(Noch')*, "Midnight" *(Polnoch')*, "The Coming Day" *(Griadu-iushchii den')*, "New Day" *(Novyi den')* (again), and "Dark Night" *(V temnuiu noch')*. Its last number was called "In the Dead of Night" *(V glukhuiu noch')*.[45]

To further limit press freedom, the Bolsheviks resorted to economic measures. On November 7, 1917, Lenin decreed advertising a state monopoly which deprived the press of its principal source of income. The authorities also nationalized many printing establishments, turning them over to Bolshevik organizations. Even so, an independent press managed to carry on. Between October 1917 and June 1918, some 300 non-Bolshevik newspapers continued to appear in the provincial towns, that is, outside Moscow and Petrograd. In Moscow alone, there were 150 independent dailies.[46]

The survival of independent dailies and periodicals, however, was only a temporary reprieve: Lenin made it no secret that he intended to liquidate them as soon as he was able to do so. When, in the course of an address to the Fourth Congress of Soviets in March 1918, he referred to newspapers and someone in the audience shouted "All are closed!" Lenin responded:

"Unfortunately, not all, but we will close them all."[47] The chief of the Petrograd police and Commissar of the Soviet Press, V. Volodarskii, said in May 1918: "We tolerate the bourgeois press only because we have not yet triumphed. But when we print in *Krasnaia gazeta,* 'We have triumphed,' from that moment on we shall not allow a single bourgeois paper."[48] The rationale for such threats was provided by a contemporary Communist writer, who explained that in the summer of 1918 "it became conclusively clear that the entire periodical press, except for that published by the government, very consistently [supported] the struggle for power of the parties and groups which stood behind them. The government had only one option: to close all the periodical anti-Soviet press."[49]

The independent press was finally liquidated in the summer of 1918, two years before the anticipated Bolshevik triumph in the Civil War. The process began in Moscow with the closing of all non-Bolshevik dailies on Sunday, July 7, the day the Latvian troops suppressed the Left SR uprising.[50] An emergency measure, it was formalized two days later when the government revoked permits to publish newspapers, journals, brochures, bulletins, and broadsides issued in Moscow prior to July 6: henceforth, such publications, with the exception of those produced and distributed by government institutions and those of the Russian Communist Party, were proscribed.[51] The ban initially applied only to the capital city and was to remain in force until the "final solidification and triumph of the Russian Soviet Socialist Federal Republic,"[52] but before long it was extended to all areas under Bolshevik control, and it was never rescinded. On July 19, 1918, *Izvestiia* published the text of the Constitution of the RSFSR, Article 14 of which provided that to guarantee the toilers "true" freedom of opinion, the government abolished "the printed word's [*pechat'*] defense of capital" and entrusted publishing to workers and poor peasants.[53] This stipulation provided the legal grounds for the methodical suppression of what remained of the non-Bolshevik press. Before the end of the year, 150 Moscow dailies with a combined circulation of 2 million were shut down.[54] The provincial press met the same fate. By September 1918, when the Red Terror was launched, Soviet Russia had no independent press left to report on the atrocities.

Along with daily newspapers, Lenin liquidated independent monthlies, Russia's celebrated "thick journals," some of which had been in existence since the eighteenth century: *Vestnik Evropy, Russkii vestnik, Russkaia mysl',* and dozens of others. In one fell swoop, Russia's leading organs of opinion and the main vehicle for the dissemination of belles-lettres vanished: the country was thrown back to conditions which had prevailed in pre-Petrine Russia, when news and opinion had been the exclusive preserve of the state.[55]

Like the tsarist regime, Lenin showed greater leniency toward books, since they reached a relatively small audience. But in this field, too, he

33. Krupskaia.

restricted freedom of expression by nationalizing publishing houses and printing presses. The State Publishing House (Gosizdat), which he founded in December 1917 and placed under Narkompros, was to enjoy a monopoly on book publishing: in this capacity it later was entrusted with book censorship.* The control of publishing was made effective by the introduction of a state monopoly on paper on May 27, 1919.[56] In 1920–21, the state monopolized the sale of books and other printed materials.[57] In 1919–23 some private publishing firms managed to carry on in Petrograd and Moscow, often by working on commission for Gosizdat. In the provinces, independent publishing ceased entirely: there, by 1919 virtually all books carried the imprint of the local branches of Gosizdat.[58]

In October 1921, the Cheka was given the authority to enforce preventive military censorship.[59] "Military secrets" were undefined: the effect of the measure was to extend the censor's power to publications that did not deal with military matters.

In 1920 an unusual attempt was made at retroactive censorship. Krup-

---

*On it, see A. I. Nazarov, *Oktiabr' i kniga* (Moscow, 1968), 135–88. Gosizdat actually began to function only in May 1919 and acquired responsibilities for censorship on December 12, 1921.

skaia, whom Lenin had appointed to a new propaganda bureau called Main Committee for Political Enlightenment (Glavpolitprosvet), decided that Soviet libraries should be "purged of obsolescent literature." She had the Commissariat of Enlightenment instruct Soviet libraries to remove from their shelves all copies, save two to be preserved in a "Special Depository" (Spetskhran), of the works of 94 authors, among them Plato, Descartes, Kant, Schopenhauer, Herbert Spencer, Ernst Mach, Vladimir Solovev, Nietzsche, William James, Leo Tolstoy, and Peter Kropotkin.*

The hitherto piecemeal subjection of information, ideas, and images to state control was consolidated on June 6, 1922, with the establishment in the Commissariat of Enlightenment of a central censorship office called Main Administration for Literary Affairs and Publishing (Glavnoe Upravlenie po delam Literatury i Izdatel'stva), or as it came to be popularly known, Glavlit.[60] Glavlit's charge was to carry out preliminary censorship of all publications and pictorial material and to make public lists of proscribed literature, in order to prevent the printing and distribution of works "containing agitation against Soviet authority." Except for publications of the Communist Party and its affiliates, the Communist International, and the Academy of Sciences, which were exempt from censorship, all works intended for publication in Soviet Russia henceforth required an official license (viza) from Glavlit or one of its provincial branches. Glavlit was further charged with fighting "underground" publications. Secret circulars of the Politburo and Orgburo (the Organizational Bureau of the Central Committee) forbade the importation of books of "an idealistic, religious, and antiscientific content," as well as foreign newspapers and "Russian White Guard literature."[61] Exempt from this proscription were high government officials, including Lenin, who regularly received foreign books and periodicals, including "White Guard" publications. The implementation of Glavlit's orders was entrusted to the GPU, the successor of the Cheka. In February 1923, Glavlit created a section called Glavrepertkom to make certain that the performing arts—the theater, cinema, musical and variety shows, and phonograph records—did not spread anti-Communist, religious, and similar material. In time, Glavlit and Glavrepertkom acquired a positive function: they not only prevented the publication or performance of works considered subversive, but released each year a "general orientation plan of publications," which set quotas for diverse subjects that the authorities believed required particular attention. It also appointed the editorial boards of periodical publications.[62] Glavlit was placed under the charge of an old Bolshevik, N. L. Meshcheriakov, an engineer by

---

*SV, No. 21/22 (1923), 8–9; R. Fülöp-Miller, Geist und Gesicht des Bolschewismus (Zurich, 1926), 75. The order apparently was not carried out, for it was reissued in 1923. S. A. Fediukin, Bor'ba s burzhuaziei v usloviiakh perekhoda k NEPU (Moscow, 1977), 170–71, claims that the list was not drawn up by Krupskaia and that she annulled it. See Pravda, No. 81 (April 9, 1924), 1.

training, and his deputy, P. I. Lebedev-Polianskii, a leading figure in Proletkult.

The rules guiding the work of Glavlit's censors were progressively tightened until every semblance of independent thought disappeared from public life.* They had a devastating effect on creativity, inasmuch as authors and artists, ever mindful of the censor peering over their shoulders, learned to practice self-censorship. The writer Panteleimon Romanov deplored this habit in 1928, before the more onerous Stalinist censorship went into effect:

> Russia happens to be such an unfortunate country it will never know real freedom. And how is it that they don't understand that by sealing off with a dead mark the sources of creativity, they retard and kill culture? Just think of it, nowhere but in the U.S.S.R. is there preventive censorship! When a writer has no assurance what tomorrow will bring, how can one expect him to speak honestly, openly? Everyone looks at the matter as follows: Never mind, I shall write *something,* only so it passes. . . .
>
> Once writers used to fight for their convictions, which they honored as sacred. Once, the writer viewed the government as something alien, something inimical to freedom. Now they make us treat it as our own. Now to shun the government is not liberalism, as before, but conservatism. And what are the convictions of today's writer? If he is told that his thrust is *unsuitable* he blushes like a schoolboy caught in a mistake, and is ready on the spot to change everything, to replace white with black. And all this because they have frightened us.[63]

Despite—perhaps because of—its unprecedented powers to control what was written or performed, information on Glavlit is exceedingly sparse: none of the three successive versions of the *Great Soviet Encyclopedia,* for example, even has an entry on this subject. The 1934 edition blandly informs the reader that the "October Revolution put an end to both tsarist and bourgeois censorship."†

When they took power, the Bolsheviks had no literary policy other than to make good books available to the mass reader. On December 29, 1917, in the decree setting up Gosizdat, the classics of Russian literature whose copyright had expired were nationalized: one consequence of this action was to deprive private publishers of an important source of income. A supplementary decree of November 26, 1918, declared cultural works, published or not, by persons living as well as dead, liable to be declared

---

*The number of books forbidden by Glavlit in 1921–22 was low: 3.8 percent in Moscow, and 5.3 percent in Petrograd: *PiR,* No. 6 (1922), 131. But these figures are meaningless, given that authors only submitted manuscripts they thought had a chance of being published.

†*BSE,* 1st ed. (Moscow, 1934), Vol. 60, 474. Less understandably, a standard Western monograph on its parent organization, the Commissariat of Enlightenment, by the American historian Sheila Fitzpatrick completely ignores Glavlit. A symposium called *Bolshevik Culture* (Bloomington, Ind., 1985) achieves the seemingly impossible feat of avoiding all mention of Glavlit even in the chapter devoted to "Lenin and the Freedom of the Press."

property of the state. Their creators were to be paid honoraria fixed by the authorities. A decree of July 29, 1919, exempted the government from restrictions placed by their owners on personal archives of deceased Russian writers, composers, musicians, and scholars on deposit in libraries and museums.[64] In the course of 1918, numerous private libraries were confiscated.[65] In this manner, step by step, the entire heritage of Russian culture became the property of the state, that is, the Communist Party.

As noted previously, Russia's literary establishment boycotted the new regime: the few willing to collaborate, such as Blok, Maiakovskii, and Valerii Briusov, found themselves ostracized by fellow writers. Many authors emigrated west, preferring to face the hardship and isolation of life abroad rather than the suffocating atmosphere at home—among them Ivan Bunin, Konstantin Balmont, Vladimir Khodasevich, Leonid Andreev, Marina Tsvetaeva, Ilia Ehrenburg, Zinaida Gippius, Maxim Gorky, Viacheslav Ivanov, Alexander Kuprin, Dmitrii Merezhkovskii, Aleksei Remizov, Alexis Tolstoy, and Boris Zaitsev.* Zamiatin, who obtained permission to emigrate in the late 1920s by special dispensation of Stalin, expressed the feeling of many of Russia's writers when he wrote in 1921 that if the country continued to treat its citizens like children, dreading every "heretical" word, "Russian literature [had] only one future: her past."[66] In a world in which nothing seemed to make sense, this paradox became a much-quoted platitude. Blok, who did not emigrate and soon drifted away from the Bolsheviks, groped for an explanation of the creative impotence that afflicted him under the new regime: "The Bolsheviks do not hinder the writing of verses, but they prevent one from feeling master of himself. . . . He is master who feels the pivot of all his creativeness and holds the rhythm within himself."[67]

Of those who stayed but refused to collaborate, many perished from hunger and cold. Many more would have done so if not for the intervention of Maxim Gorky, who helped them by capitalizing on his friendship with Lenin: Gorky thought Russia a barbarous country in which intellectuals, regardless of their politics, were a priceless asset. In the expropriated residence of a wealthy merchant, located in Petrograd on the corner of Nevsky and Bolshaia Morskaia, he set up a refuge for writers and artists: among the inhabitants of what came to be known as the "Crazy Ship" (from its resemblance, when lit up at night, to a boat) were the poets Osip Mandelshtam, Nicholas Gumilev, and Vladimir Khodasevich, and the painter Ilia

*Renato Poggioli, *The Poets of Russia* (Cambridge, Mass., 1960), 298; Anweiler and Ruffman, *Kulturpolitik der Sowjetunion*, 193. Of these émigrés, five eventually returned: Ehrenburg and Tolstoy in 1923, Gorky in 1931, Kuprin in 1937, and Tsvetaeva in 1938. Ehrenburg, Gorky, and Tolstoy went on to make careers under Stalin. Kuprin died the year after his return, and Tsvetaeva committed suicide in 1941. See further Marc Raeff, *Russia Abroad* (New York and Oxford, 1990), *passim*. By contrast, Mussolini, whose cultural policies were incomparably more liberal than Lenin's, managed to attract a number of prominent writers, including Luigi Pirandello, Curzio Malaparte, Giovanni Papini, and Gabriele d'Annunzio. Even writers and artists who rejected his regime found it possible to live in Fascist Italy and relatively few emigrated.

Repin. They lived far from luxuriously: one resident attempted to keep warm by writing about tropical Africa. But they did survive.

Prerevolutionary Russia had many literary circles grouped around programs and manifestos. Of these, the Futurists alone unreservedly collaborated with the Bolshevik regime. Futurism originated in Italy in 1909 and from there spread to Russia. As in postwar Italy, where the Futurists were the main literary allies of Fascism, and for much the same reason, the Russian Futurists made common cause with the Bolsheviks.[68] They despised as effete and ossified the existing cultures and yearned for a new culture attuned to modern technology and the rhythms of the machine age. The manifesto of Italian Futurism, written in 1909 by Filippo Marinetti, the movement's founder—which served also its Russian followers—called for the destruction of museums and libraries. It extolled rebellion, "aggressiveness," violence: racing cars were declared more beautiful than the statue of Victory of Samothrace.[69] The Futurists, who looked to "impulse" instead of reason as their guide, found Fascism and Communism attractive because of their hostility to the bourgeois life-style. They saw only the nihilism of these movements, not the constraints, which, once the old order was out of the way, would give way to totalitarianism.

The leading Russian Futurist, the poet and dramatist Vladimir Maiakovskii, joined the Bolsheviks the instant they took power and in mid-1918 went on Lunacharskii's payroll. Long before 1917 he had hailed the coming revolution as the "holy washer-woman [who] will wash away all filth from the face of the earth with her soap."[70] As poet laureate of the new regime, he placed his talents at the service of Communist agitation and propaganda. In his personal life, however, he was the very antithesis of the "collective man" favored by the new regime. A narcissistic self-promoter, from the beginning of his literary activity in 1913 he adopted himself as the hero: his first play he called *Vladimir Maiakovskii*, his first volume of verse *I!*, and his autobiography, *I Myself*. His enchantment with the masses stemmed not so much from interest in the common man as from a craving for the common man's adulation. He made certain always to be the center of attention, whether by staging scandalous plays, bellowing verse at public readings, painting propaganda posters, or carrying on an open affair with the wife of a colleague. Although no one claims that he was the greatest poet of his time, it has been said that no poet of the twentieth century has been accorded as much honor.[71]

This honor was lavished on him by the Communist establishment despite the fact that it was far from amused by the antics of Maiakovskii and his fellow Futurists. Lenin intensely disliked his poetry, calling his celebrated poem "150,000,000" "nonsense, stupid, arrant stupidity and pretentiousness."* He demanded that Futurist poetry be published at most twice a year

---

*LN, Vol. 65 (1958), 210. Trotsky was no kinder to this work, saying that the author meant it to be "titanic, but, as a matter of fact, it was at best only athletic": *Literatura i revoliutsiia* (Moscow, 1924), 114.

in small editions, and called for "reliable *anti*-futurists."[72] As a result of Lenin's disapproval, Maiakovskii and the Futurists became the object of harassment by the party establishment.[73] The movement survived thanks to the patronage of Lunacharskii and the willingness of its members to serve as propagandists. The Futurists were the only literary group on which the Bolsheviks could rely in the early years. In this position, they enjoyed access to state patronage, which they used to make life difficult for their literary rivals.[74] When Stalin took charge and bridled such displays of megalomania, Maiakovskii committed suicide (1930).

The favorite poet of the new regime, one of the few writers of peasant origin, was not Maiakovskii but Demian Bednyi ("Demian the Poor," whose actual name was Efim Pridvorov). An old Bolshevik, he wrote agitational-propagandistic poetry made up of political slogans set to rhyme, exhorting workers to hate and kill. To White soldiers he appealed to massacre their officers:

> *Death to the vermin! Kill them all, to the last!*
> *And having finished off the damned vermin,*
> *Liberated from the yoke of the lordly horde,*
> *One by one, by regiments, by squads,*
> *Join our brotherly ranks!*[75]

Such verses the regime published in the daily press, posted on walls, and scattered from airplanes. Trotsky extolled Bednyi on the grounds that there is "nothing of the dilettante in his anger and in his hatred. He hates with the well-grounded hatred of the most revolutionary party in the world." He thought it a virtue that Bednyi wrote not "only in those rare instances when Apollo calls," but "day in and day out, as the events demand . . . and the Central Committee."[76] During the siege of Petrograd in 1919, Red Army soldiers fleeing the battlefield are said to have been persuaded to turn around and face the enemy by the recitation of Bednyi's "Communist Marseillaise." Bednyi was ever ready to oblige with rhymed invective against the Communists' enemy of the hour—the Constituent Assembly, the Mensheviks and SRs, Clemenceau and Woodrow Wilson. He would perform similar services for Stalin during World War II. (Wits reported that after Petrograd had been renamed Leningrad, Bednyi demanded that the works of Pushkin be renamed after him.)[77]

Great poetry, lasting poetry, was written by poets who insulated themselves from the turmoil and the politics of their time. Anna Akhmatova and her husband, Gumilev, as well as Mandelshtam, members of the Acmeist circle, the Imagist Sergei Esenin, and Boris Pasternak, led quiet, private, unsubsidized, and unadvertised lives. Later generations would recognize the poetry they wrote as among the noblest achievements of Russian literature—long after the shrill voices of the hate-mongers had been silenced and forgotten. For this they paid a price, however. Gumilev was shot in 1921 for membership in a "counterrevolutionary" organization: he is said to be the first Russian writer of note whose place of burial is unknown. (He believed that the Huns who in the fourth century had crossed southern Russia and under Attila ravaged Europe, had been reincarnated in the twentieth century as Bolsheviks.[78]) Esenin killed himself in 1925. Mandelshtam perished in 1939 in a Stalinist camp where he had been sent for an anti-Stalin ditty.* Akhmatova and Pasternak survived, but had to bear humiliations that less stalwart souls would not have endured.

A special case was Alexander Blok, a refined writer whose "Twelve" and "Scythians" are generally acknowledged to be the greatest poems of the Bolshevik October. In his youth, Blok, a leading Symbolist, was entirely absorbed in aesthetics and religion and oblivious of politics. On the eve of and during World War I (in which he served) he developed broader interests, in part under the stimulus of patriotic emotions. He welcomed 1917, excited by the surge of elemental peasant and worker violence, which promised to burn to ashes not only "old" Russia but "old" Europe. In October 1917 he impulsively sided with the Bolsheviks (although politically he had greater affinity for the Left SRs). He wrote his two famous revolutionary poems in January 1918 in a spell of poetic delirium. "Twelve" depicts armed Red Guards—murderous, pitiless—marching behind an invisible Christ bearing a "bloody standard" to smash the bourgeois world. "Scythians" extols Russia's revolutionary masses as Asiatic hordes poised to ravage Europe: the Europeans are invited to become their brothers or die. The Bolsheviks never quite knew what to make of these poems, which depicted their leader as Christ and their followers as barbarian Mongols. Intellectuals ostracized Blok. His disenchantment set in almost at once, the instant he realized that the elemental forces whose praises he had sung were extinguished by the iron hand of the state. "What one cannot deny the Bolsheviks," he wrote in 1919, "is their unique ability to exterminate life *(byt)* and to destroy individuals."[79] He published no more poems after "Scythians," fell into depression, and died in 1921, thoroughly disillusioned.

For all practical purposes, no novels were written in Russia during the first years of the new regime: not only were the material conditions unfavorable to creativity, but the situation was so violent and fluid that novelists, whatever their politics, had difficulty finding their bearings. The first major novels written under Communist rule—Zamiatin's *We* (1920) and Boris Pilniak's *The Naked Year* (1922)—had in common an unconven-

---

*It has subsequently become known that Mandelshtam's attitude to Bolshevism was quite ambivalent and that in 1937, while in exile in Voronezh, he had written two panegyrics to Stalin: Gregory Freidin in *RuR*, XLI, No. 4 (October 1982), 400–26. The texts of the "odes" are reproduced by Bengt Jangfeldt in *Scando-Slavica*, XXII (1976), 35–41.

tional, fragmented form of narrative previously confined to avant-garde literature. *We,* first published in Czech translation and then in English in the United States, is the original anti-utopian novel and the inspiration for Orwell's *1984.* It depicts a future world of totally dehumanized beings, such as envisioned by Gastev, known collectively as "we," who bear numbers instead of names and whose every minute is regulated. Ruled by "the Benefactor," they build a spaceship to carry their civilization to other planets. Confining his subjects to a city walled off from the rest of the world, the habitat of the "hairy" survivors of mankind, the "Benefactor" disposes by "atomization" of those who, like the novel's hero, display such deviant behavior as falling in love. In *The Naked Year,* Pilniak describes, in a succession of scenes set during the Revolution and Civil War, the decline of an aristocratic family, sunk in alcoholism and disease, and the simultaneous rise of a coarse but robust new breed of "leather jackets." The novel stresses the peasant character of the Bolshevik Revolution and the reemergence of traditional Muscovite culture that had lain dormant in the village since Peter the Great.

Pilniak and Zamiatin were members of the "Serapion Brotherhood," a loose community of writers formed in 1920 under Gorky's patronage. They were not hostile to Bolshevism and some of them even sympathized with it. But they uncompromisingly defended the autonomy of literature and the freedom of the writer. The group dedicated itself to developing "a strategy for dealing with an unprecedented situation in which a tyrannical regime, basing its power on the illiterate, has proclaimed itself the sponsor and advocate of cultural enterprise."* It is in regard to them that Trotsky revived and popularized the socialist term "fellow-travelers." Writers associated with the Serapion Brotherhood (in addition to Zamiatin and Pilniak, they were Michael Zoshchenko, Vsevolod Ivanov, Isaac Babel, and Iurii Olesha) produced some of the best literature published in the Soviet Union in the 1920s.

From 1922 until the end of the decade, when Stalin's repressive measures eliminated virtually all creative freedom, Russian belles-lettres underwent something of a renascence. Efforts of the authorities to have writers abandon the central theme of the traditional novel—the struggle of the individual against passions, conscience, or social conventions—in favor of "collective" themes of class conflict, proved unenforceable. Even those writers most sympathetic to the new regime found that they had to focus on individuals because it was only by this device that they could inject into their narrative the element of drama. "Under all ideological regimentations, a writer, nonetheless, still worked alone. This means, at least hypothetically, that he remained susceptible to fits of extreme individualism known as

*Cited in Edward J. Brown, *Russian Literature Since the Revolution* (New York and London, 1963), 95. One circle of authors, who called themselves Nichevoki, or "Nothingers," responded to this situation by deciding not to write at all: *ibid.,* 29.

'inspiration.' He could be, and quite frequently was, a narcissist, nurturing his vain 'ego.' "[80] A dominant theme of much Soviet belles-lettres of the 1920s was the difficulty persons brought up on the values of the old world had in adjusting to the new, revolutionary order. Novels were often set in the Civil War, in which many of the writers had taken part. Emphasis was placed on violence, much of it mindless, not only because the Civil War happened to have been very violent, but because exposing the reader to it was certain to shock his sensibilities and give the impression that a new literature was being born.

In a country a high proportion of whose population was illiterate, the printed word reached relatively few. Since they were primarily interested in influencing the masses, the Bolsheviks devoted great attention to the theater and cinema as instruments of propaganda. There was much experimentation in both of these art forms. Alongside the traditional theater, the Communists developed new varieties ranging from political cabarets and street shows to reenactments of historical events employing thousands of extras. A decree of August 26, 1919, nationalized theaters and circuses, entrusting their management to Tsentroteatr, a department of the Commissariat of Enlightenment. The law authorized "autonomous" theaters (those not in receipt of state subsidies), but they had to submit annual reports of their activities and follow instructions of the central theater organization.[81] Actors became state employees, and as such, liable to be drafted for theatrical duty.

The revolutionary theater was supposed to generate support for the regime and simultaneously to instill hatred for its opponents. To this end Soviet directors borrowed from Germany and other countries the techniques of the experimental theater. Emulating the German theatrical innovator Max Reinhardt, they strove to abolish the barrier between spectators and actors by eliminating the formal stage and by performing in the streets, in factories, and at the front. Audiences were encouraged to converse with the actors. None of these techniques was new, but in Soviet Russia they were applied on a scale not seen previously.[82] The line separating reality from fantasy was all but obliterated, which also helped obliterate the distinction between reality and propaganda.

Agit-prop theater vulgarized drama by reducing the protagonists to cardboard symbols of perfect virtue and unalloyed evil, employing coarse ridicule and seeking to stir violent reactions in the audience. The leading innovator in the Russian revolutionary theater, Vsevolod Meyerhold, enjoyed in the early years of the new regime virtually dictatorial powers over the stage and cinema. An early convert to Communism, he was able to extract generous subsidies from Lunacharskii, with the help of which he sought to realize his ambition of carrying out an "October" in the theater.[83]

Meyerhold personally directed the earliest play by a Communist author for the Soviet stage, Maiakovskii's *Mystery-Bouffe,* which had its premiere on the first anniversary of the October coup. The leading characters were seven pairs each of "Clean" (rich) and "Unclean" (poor) who, having survived the Flood, find refuge at the North Pole. The Unclean manage to overthrow the Clean and leave them in hell. A Christ-like figure appears under the name "Simply Man" (the part was played by Maiakovskii) to bring a new gospel. "I do not preach the Christian paradise," he says:

> *My paradise is for all*
> *Save those poor in spirit. . . .*
> *Come unto me*
> *All who have calmly plunged a knife*
> *And turned from the enemy's corpse with a song!*
> *Ye are the first to enter*
> *My kingdom of heaven.*

The Unclean visit the paradise promised by religion, which they find as boring and corrupt as the earth. In their wanderings they finally reach the terrestrial paradise of Communism, a city that, judging by Maiakovskii's stage directions, is an idealized version of Henry Ford's Detroit: "The exposed mass of transparent factories and apartment houses strains to the sky. Enveloped by rainbows stand trains, streetcars, and automobiles. . . ."[84]

Despite complimentary tickets, workers and peasants stayed away from Maiakovskii's play, while professional actors boycotted it. Much more

34. Agitational or agit-prop theater.

popular with ordinary citizens were spectacles modeled on Punch and Judy shows. A favorite character was Petrushka, who would defend poor peasants and attack kulaks in improvised banter with the audience. There were also performances of *"agitki,"* brief productions on specific subjects, such as the vices of religion or the virtues of personal hygiene. These were performed with minimal decor in trains that traveled from town to town and from village to village, as well as from trucks and streetcars:

> The one-time enemy is constantly ridiculed and combatted in symbolic form on the open street, with the masses being encouraged to join in. A beloved genre is contrasting the past and the present in the form of radical images. First come tsarist soldiers in blue uniforms with fixed bayonets, leading through the streets a group of political prisoners, followed by red gendarmes escorting white police officers in chains. Next is produced a colorful company of priests, generals, and speculators, who are exposed to public mockery because, although garbed in the most elegant clothes, they wear thick ropes around their necks. During a demonstration against England a gesticulating doll was erected in the middle of the square to depict an English diplomat in the process of delivering a note. An immense worker fist puts an end to this political action with a punch to the nose of the foreign statesman. On a similar occasion the Englishman was also represented by a gigantic effigy in tails and top hat carried on the roof of a car. Whenever the speaker referred to England, he directly apostrophized the effigy. Soon the crowd, too, turned against it with threatening gestures. The "Englishman," in the meantime, walked up and down elegantly and arrogantly, a monocle casually inserted into his eye socket, until a Bolshevik worker swinging a hammer sprang onto the roof of the car. With one blow he forced the figure, which begged for pity, to its knees, at which point he turned to the crowd to ask whether the "Englishman" should be spared or not. As could be expected, the mob howled in unison: "Strike him down!" whereupon the worker raised his hammer and let it fall three times with full force on the effigy's head. A man in the crowd picked up the soiled and crushed top hat, collected the fragments of the monocle, and, displaying both to the assembled, proclaimed in triumph, "That's all that's left of our enemy!"[85]

The "worker" and "the man in the crowd," were, of course, professional actors, and the purpose of the production was neither to entertain nor to enlighten but to instill hatred.

A sensational example of such hate drama was the play *Do you hear, Moscow? (Slyshysh Moskva?)* by S. Tretiakov, staged in Moscow in 1924 under the direction of Sergei Eisenstein. Eisenstein, who before turning to the cinema was a leading light of the Proletkult theater, wanted to do away with the theater as an institution separated from everyday life. He constantly experimented with techniques that would permit him to manipulate the audiences' emotions to the highest degree of tension.[86] His greatest success in this was staging Tretiakov's play. According to the director's conception, the objective of the performance was "to collect into one strong-willed fist the diffuse emotions of the audience and to instill in the

35. Street theater.

spectator's psyche a purposeful directive, dictated by the current struggle of German workers for Communism."

> The second and third acts created in the audience sufficient tension which discharged itself in the fourth act in the scene showing [German] workers storming the Fascist platform. In the audience, spectators jumped from their seats. There were shouts: "Over there, over there! The count is escaping! Grab him!" A gigantic student from a worker's university, jumping to his feet, shouted in the direction of the cocotte: "Why are you fussing? Grab her," accompanying these words with a juicy curse. When the cocotte was killed on the stage and pushed down the stairs, he swore with satisfaction, adding, "She had it coming." This was said so forcefully that a lady in furs sitting next to him could no longer stand it. She jumped up and blurted out in fright: "My Lord! What is going on? They will begin here, too," and ran for the exit. Every killed Fascist was drowned with applause and shouts. It was reported that a military man, sitting in the rear, pulled out his revolver and aimed it at the cocotte, but his neighbors brought him to his senses. This enthusiasm affected even the stage. Members of the stage crowd, students . . . placed there for decoration, unable to hold back, joined in the assault on the installation. They had to be dragged back by their feet.[87]

Satirical theater of a more sophisticated kind was born in 1919, following the publication of an article by Lunacharskii which said that the prevailing harsh conditions of life made humor a necessity. Fulfilling his directive, *"Budem smeiatsia"*—"Let us laugh"—a satirical theater opened in Vitebsk;

from there it moved to Moscow. The "Theater of Revolutionary Satire," or "Terevsat," was modeled on prerevolutionary cabaret theaters. The Moscow Terevsat and its replicas in several cities enjoyed great popularity. The government began to cool toward the genre, however, when it became the target of its own satire. In 1922 the play *Russia 2* depicted in a half-mocking, half-nostalgic way the life of Russian émigrés in the West. Upset by the sympathy the audience expressed for the White émigrés and their anti-Communist sentiments, it ordered the satirical theater closed.[88]

A type of spectacle much favored in 1920 was *instsenirovki,* or "stagings," mass performances under the open sky, with innumerable extras, to reenact historic events in a manner favorable to the Communists.[89] Lavishly staged, such "docudramas" blended truth and fantasy, theater and circus. This genre, too, was not original, having been experimented with in Western Europe and the United States before World War I. But techniques that in the West served to entertain, in Soviet Russia were employed to persuade. Events were reduced to the starkest conflicts and the characters to symbols: mimicry and movement replaced words, burlesque concealed the complexity of human relations.

The most celebrated of these spectacles was staged on the third anniversary of the October coup in the heart of Petrograd under the title *The Capture of the Winter Palace.* The producers disclaimed any intention of "re-creating exactly the picture of events," and they were true to their word. The performers, of whom there were six thousand, were to be as "a single collective actor." A spectator left the following account:

> The discharge of an artillery gun announces the beginning of the show. The square is darkened. A few minutes pass in tense expectation, all eyes are

36. Scene from Tretiakov's *Do you hear, Moscow?*

focused on the stage, which is silent. . . . Music resounds. . . . The crowd of many thousands watches with bated breath as the action unfolds. Laughter and barbed quips greet the appearance of Kerensky, who pompously receives the homage of his admirers. "Now he got cut down to size pounding the doors of ministers and bankers abroad," one can hear from a group of workers. "Yeah, it's hard for him to make a buck," responds a young Red Army soldier, without taking his eyes off the stage.

The rapid change of events on the stage attracts the strained attention of the viewers. The July attempt to overthrow the detested Provisional Government of Kerensky, which ends in the temporary defeat of the proletariat, elicits a deep sigh of disappointment. . . . But now the choir, heralding the power of the soviets, resounds louder and louder and with growing confidence. The supporters of the Provisional Government, seized by panic, flee in all directions. Kerensky and his ministers save themselves in automobiles; their hasty flight delights the audience. The proletariat has triumphed! "Hurrah," shouts the choir from the stage. "Hurrah, hurrah!" respond the spectators.

There begins the impetuous assault on the Winter Palace. The viewers are electrified: an instant and it seems that the crowd will crush the barrier and together with the automobiles and mobs of soldiers and workers throw itself to storm the last bastion of despised Kerenskyism.

But now the cannonade stops. The Palace has been taken and above it unfurls the red flag. The orchestra strikes up the "Internationale," which tens of thousands of voices pick up.

The spectacle is over, rocket after rocket rises to the sky. Cones of golden rain burst and silently expire. Thousands of silver flames descend straight on the crowd. . . . For an instant it becomes as bright as in daytime.

It is only now that one can behold the multitude of people. The square is packed. Without any exaggeration it can be said that on Uritskii Square that evening there were no fewer than one hundred thousand people.*

Other such mass spectacles bore the titles *The Mystery of Liberated Labor* and *The Blockade of Russia,* the latter of which had a cast of 10,000 acting out a script by the poet Khodasevich. Such performances, also staged in provincial towns, had to be abandoned for reasons of cost. They were replaced by film productions.

Lenin is said to have been greatly impressed by the propagandistic possibilities of the cinema: he is quoted to the effect that for Bolsheviks it was the most important of the arts.[90] Its "main task," according to Lunacharskii, was propaganda.[91] During the Civil War, private as well as state-owned studios concentrated on the production of propagandistic shorts (*agitki*), usually less than 30 minutes long: of the 92 films turned out by Soviet studios in 1918–20, 63 were of this genre.[92] They were shown in

*A. Z. Iufit, ed., *Russkii sovetskii teatr 1917–1921* (Leningrad, 1968), 272–74; see further Frantizek Deak in *The Drama Review,* Vol. 19, No. 2 (T-66, June 1975), 15–21. In 1927, Sergei Eisenstein duplicated the spectacle of the "storming" of the Winter Palace in his film *October.* Since then, stills of this fictitious scene performed by cinematic extras have been frequently reproduced in the Soviet Union and the West as authentic documentary photographs: *RR,* 495.

37. Agitational train.

regular movie theaters and in agit-trains that crisscrossed the country. After
a period of cooperation with private industry, the regime nationalized
cinematic production and distribution, along with commercial photogra-
phy.[93] Goskino, a state agency, came into being in December 1922 to
manage cinema production.

Moving pictures appealed to Communist propagandists not only because
of cost considerations, but also because they were capable of a degree of
realism no other art form could duplicate. The propagandists noted that
Russian audiences displayed violent reactions to American movies, which
were widely shown in those years. Analyzing the reasons for these reactions,
one of the pioneers of Soviet cinema, Lev Kuleshov, concluded that they
were due to the application of two techniques: close-ups and "montage," a
rapid succession of short scenes depicting an event or an image from different vantage points.[94] Since a major purpose of Communist propaganda was
arousing violent political emotions against the regime's enemies, the cinema
seemed an ideal tool. The technical inspiration came from D. W. Griffith,
whose *Intolerance* was smuggled into Moscow in 1919. It is said that Lenin
was so impressed by it that he invited Griffith to take charge of the Soviet
movie industry. Whether the story is true or not, it is indisputable that all
Soviet movies produced in the first decade of the Communist regime bore
the stamp of Griffith's influence.*

*Jan Leyda, *Kino* (London, 1960), 142–43. "In 1923–24, the study of the American film was
the formal battle-cry of our cinematic innovators," wrote a Soviet film critic. "Griffith's formula

Artists, architects, and composers working for the Communists aspired to match the revolutionary changes in the country's political, economic, and social life. This meant dramatic innovation. The early years of Soviet Russia saw frenzied experimentation in the visual arts and musical composition. Painters and sculptors, for all the creative freedom they enjoyed, were supervised by a bureaucratic organization, the Department of Visual Arts (*Otdel izobrazitel'nykh iskusstv*, or IZO), formed in January 1918 as part of Narkompros and directed by the painter David Shterenberg. Musical activity was also supervised by Narkompros through a department known as Muzo. To break the hold on art of traditional institutions, the regime, on April 12, 1918, abolished the Academy of Arts.[95]

As in the performing arts, a major effort went into breaking down the walls separating art from everyday life. Professionalism was disparaged: in the paradoxical style then in fashion, the device of young architects working under N. A. Ladovskii proclaimed, "The future belongs to those who are extraordinarily untalented for art."[96] To bring "art into life," leading creative artists banded together in 1920–21 into a community of "Constructivists," who, following the example of the German Bauhaus, strove to eliminate the distinction between high and applied art. The Constructivists worked in all fields of aesthetic endeavor: painting and architecture, industrial design, couture, advertising, typography. Neither its adherents nor its historians have been able satisfactorily to define the aesthetic principles of Constructivism. Its programmatic declarations consisted of slogans, most of them negative. It is easier, therefore, to ascertain what the movement was against than what it was for. It was against "traditional art," which term presumably embraced everything from Neolithic artifacts to post-Impressionist paintings. It often assailed art: "We declare irreconcilable war on art!" was the epigraph of one of its manifestos. "Death to art!" "Art is finished! It has no place in the human labor apparatus. Labor, technology, organization!" and so on.[97] The original statement of the group called on the artist to abandon the atelier for the factory, the true source of modern inspiration. Art embodied in concrete objects was pronounced dead.[98]

Their declared intentions notwithstanding, artists of this school continued to turn out artistic objects—what else could they do?—and rather than mingle with factory workers, amused themselves, as artists have done since time immemorial, in studios and cafés in the company of fellow artists. Behind their creations it is difficult to discern any common principle except

---

for melodrama, based on the principle of the 'montage of attractions' and reinforced by the examples of [his] films . . . was decisive in shaping the first years of the Soviet cinema": A. Piotrovskii in *Zhizn' iskusstva*, June 30, 1929, 7.

38. Alexander Rodchenko in a worker's suit
of his own design, 1921, with a drawing of the suit.

the desire to be different and to shock. In his determination to kill painting, the Constructivist Alexander Rodchenko turned out three "canvases" covered with nothing but the three primary colors, red, blue, and yellow. "I affirmed: it's all over," he explained.[99] In typographic design, nothing was ever symmetrical or linear. Constructivist furniture aimed to please the eye without considering the user's comfort. Clothing designs imposed straight lines on the curves of the human body: futuristic costumes for an "illiterate population, shoeless and in rags."[100]

Museums were discouraged and stress was placed on street art. The government devoted much attention to the production of posters. During the Civil War, Soviet poster art was aimed at the Whites and their foreign backers. The enemy was represented as repulsive, bloated vermin while the Soviet hero had a clean-cut, trim, "Aryan" appearance. After the Civil War, posters were widely used for didactic purposes such as combatting religion, alcoholism, and illiteracy, and soliciting help for starving peasants. In 1918 and 1919, artists in Communist employ covered public buildings and residences, trains, and streetcars with graffiti bearing propagandistic slogans. In Moscow, the trees in front of the Bolshoi Theater were smeared with paint. In Petrograd, the Palace Square was given similar treatment. In Vitebsk, the cultural domain of Marc Chagall, the city center exploded in a riot of color and political slogans.[101]

Official architects and urban planners drew up fantastic schemes for the total reconstruction of Russian cities that called for wholesale demolition of existing structures to make room for monumental public and residential buildings. Little came of these projects, mainly for lack of money, but also from strong inhibitions against tearing down historic quarters. In the end, Petrograd was left virtually unaltered, a living historical museum. The center of Moscow was radically changed by the destruction of many old buildings, but this occurred later, under Stalin, and for reasons of security rather than aesthetics.

Avant-garde architects believed that Communist buildings had to be constructed of materials appropriate to the new civilization: declaring wood and stone "bourgeois," they chose iron, glass, and concrete.[102] The best-known example of early Communist architectural design was Vladimir Tatlin's 1920 projected monument to the Third International in Moscow. A leading Constructivist, Tatlin insisted that "proletarian" architecture had to be dynamic, its buildings as mobile as the modern industrial metropolis. The monument was designed on three levels. The lowest, in the shape of a cube that rotated around its axis once a year, was to provide facilities for the congresses of the Third International. Above it the second level, shaped like a pyramid, which turned once a month, was to house the Comintern's administrative offices. The edifice was to be crowned with a cylindrical structure, revolving daily, where the information and propaganda offices would be located. The outer casing gave the structure the shape of a gigantic cannon. Had it been built, Tatlin's monument, designed to rise 400 meters, would have been the tallest structure in the world. It was never erected. Tatlin also experimented with other forms of industrial design, such as a man-powered flying machine, called, in his honor, "Letatlin" (1929–31).

39. Agitational streetcar.

Pleasing as it was aesthetically, it was useless for the purpose for which it had been designed, namely flying, which was rather odd coming from an artist who launched the slogan "Not the Old, Not the New, but the Necessary."*

Musical activity depended on Muzo, whose license was required for all concert performances. It demanded strict accounting from musicians.[103] Russia's outstanding composers and performers, unwilling to submit to bureaucratic interference, left the country.[104] Those who remained split into two rival groups that competed fiercely for state subsidies: the "asmovites," who advocated modernism, and the "rapmovites," who championed musical primitivism. The gifted among them (such as Alexander Glazunov) ceased composing, while the hacks wrote "agit-music": "Much Soviet music composed during the 1920s is strangely barren and synthetic. . . . The 1920s are filled with the names of Russian composers, now dimly remembered, who copied external devices, modernistic tricks, sociological gimmicks."[105]

Such tricks and gimmicks involved dispensing with the conductor and performing with nonmusical instruments, for music, too, was to reflect modern life and relate to production. As in architecture, efforts were made to depart from reliance on traditional media. "Musical orgies" were staged in which the instruments were motors, turbines, and sirens, and the conductor served as "Noisemaster." "Symphonies of Factory Whistles" were performed in Moscow: the sounds are said to have been so confusing the audience was unable to recognize even the *Internationale*. The greatest triumph of the genre was the presentation in Baku in 1922, on the fifth anniversary of the October coup, of a "concert" performed by units of the Caspian Fleet, foghorns, factory sirens, two batteries of artillery, machine guns, and airplanes.[106]

The creations of writers and artists subsidized by Lenin's government had next to nothing in common with the tastes of the masses for whom they were intended. The culture of the masses was rooted in religion. Statistics on Russian reading habits indicate that both before and after the revolution, peasants and workers read mainly religious books; their tastes in secular reading ran to cheap escapist literature.[107] They were oblivious to the culture offered them by the Bolsheviks. The experiments in literature, painting, and music carried out in early Soviet Russia were manifestations of the European avant-garde, geared not to popular tastes but to those of the cultural elite. This was understood by Stalin, who on attaining absolute power put an end to experimentation and imposed literary and aesthetic

---

*"That *Letatlin* flew but a few yards in a test flight," write two Western historians of the movement, "is immaterial to its service as an extraordinary symbol of the desire to imbue the social realm of the practical with the spirit of an artist in touch with universal truths." Richard Andrews and Milena Kalinovska in The Henry Art Gallery, *Art into Life: Russian Constructivism, 1914–1932* (Seattle, Wash., 1990), 10. Whatever these "universal truths" may have been, they clearly were not those of aerodynamics.

standards that in crude realism and didacticism exceeded the worst of Victorian culture.

Lenin, as a rule, did not interfere in cultural affairs, leaving the matter to Lunacharskii. His one venture into art was a rather comical attempt to cover Russian cities with statues of the forerunners and heroes of socialism. Lenin borrowed the idea from the utopia of the seventeenth-century Dominican Tommaso Campanella, *The City of the Sun,* which had the walls of the ideal city covered with edifying frescoes. Allowing for Russia's harsh climate, Lenin proposed to erect busts and statues made of gypsum and concrete. In the spring of 1918 he told Lunacharskii of his idea of "monumental propaganda" and asked him to prepare a list of suitable candidates.[108] Lunacharskii and his staff, bewildered by this proposal and apparently hoping that Lenin would forget it, procrastinated. But Lenin did not forget, and after considerable delays, in July 1918 the pantheon was approved: it listed 63 persons, both Russian and foreign, among them some surprising names, the oddest being Dostoevsky, who hated socialism and socialists above all else in the world.[109] The monuments turned out to be either too futuristic to please the public or too traditional to satisfy the art critics. Some were rejected; the rest soon crumbled and had to be quietly removed. As with so much else of Communist legislation, the most enduring achievement of Lenin's endeavor was destructive in nature, namely the demolition of monuments to the tsars.

The Russian language has two words for education: *obrazovanie,* meaning instruction; and *vospitanie,* meaning upbringing. The first refers to the conveyance of knowledge; the second, to the molding of personality. The entire Soviet regime was dedicated to *vospitanie* in the sense that all institutions of the state, from trade unions to the Red Army, had as one of their principal missions inculcating in the citizenry the spirit of Commu-nism—so much so that in the 1920s some observers saw Soviet Russia as one gigantic school.[110] This was education in the sense in which Helvétius had used the word: a total environment designed to turn out perfectly virtuous beings.[111] The Bolsheviks, of course, also attached importance to education in the narrower sense, in part because they wished through the classroom to condition the mind and psyche of children, and in part because they wanted to promote science and technology. As with everything else in Communist Russia, classroom activities were to be conducted in a politi-cally correct manner: for Lenin there was no such thing as politically "neutral" education.[112] Accordingly, the Party program of 1919 defined schools as "an instrument for the Communist transformation of society."[113] This entailed "cleansing" pupils of "bourgeois" ideas, especially of religious

40. An example of "monumental sculpture": the novelist
Saltykov-Shchedrin by N. Zlatovratskii.

notions: propagation of atheism occupied a central place in the curriculum
of Soviet schools. It further meant imparting positive Communist values in
order to raise constructive members of society. Education was to begin the
instant the child came into the world. According to a Narkompros instruction of December 1917,

> The public free-of-charge education of children should begin the day they
> are born. The incorporation of preschool education into the general system
> of public education has as its purpose laying down the foundation work for
> the social upbringing of the child at the earliest stages of formation. The
> further development by the school of attitudes to work and society laid
> down in preschool age will turn out a physically and spiritually fully
> developed member of society, willing and able to work.[114]

The notion that upbringing was the responsibility of parents, because children "belonged" to them, was rejected. Evgenii Preobrazhenskii, a leading
economist and writer on ethical matters, put it bluntly:

> From the socialist point of view it is utterly senseless for the individual
> member of society to treat his body as his inalienable personal property,

because the individual is only one link in the transition of the species (*rod*) from the past to the present. But ten times more senseless is a similar view of "one's" offspring.[115]

Soviet educational policies went through two phases. The first, spanning the era of War Communism (1918–20), was relatively liberal, concentrating on the free development of the child's personality. It postulated that Communism was "natural" and that children liberated from traditional values and discipline would instinctively gravitate toward it. After the proclamation of the New Economic Policy in 1921, when the failure of progressive education became apparent and the authorities began to fear that the reintroduction of capitalist institutions would cool Communist ardor, emphasis was shifted to ideological indoctrination.

To realize its ambitious educational program, the regime nationalized educational institutions. A decree of May 30, 1918, placed all schools— elementary, secondary, and higher—whether belonging to the state, public institutions, or private bodies, under the authority of the Commissariat of Enlightenment. The declared purpose of this measure was to ensure that instruction was carried out in accord with "the principles of modern pedagogy and socialism."[116] The decree making education a state monopoly inadvertently realized the unfulfilled hope of tsarist bureaucrats of bringing all schools under their control.[117]

Shortly after taking power, the government ordered revolutionary changes in Soviet Russia's primary and secondary education.[118] A uniform network of Consolidated Labor Schools (Edinye Trudovye Shkoly) was introduced with standardized curricula on two levels: the lower for children 8 to 13, the higher for those 13 to 17. Whereas under the old system a student required a diploma from a certain kind of secondary school to qualify for admission to institutions of higher learning, henceforth there was to be but a single "staircase" leading from kindergarten to university. Attendance was obligatory for school-age children of both sexes, who were to be taught coeducationally.

In the new schools the authority of the teaching staff was severely curtailed, for they were known to be hostile to Lenin's dictatorship: in the Russian Republic as late as 1926 only 3.1 percent of the teachers in primary schools and 5.5 percent in secondary schools belonged to the Communist Party.[119] No longer called "teachers" (*uchiteliia*) but "school workers" (*shkolnye rabotniki,* or *shkraby* for short), they were forbidden to discipline pupils, to assign them homework, or to give them examinations and grades. The students' progress was to be judged by a collective. School administration was vested in committees in which "school workers" shared authority with the older pupils as well as with workers from nearby factories.

Lunacharskii, who admired John Dewey's educational philosophy, wanted pupils to "learn by doing." He believed that knowledge communicated through a combination of work and play would hold for youths an irresistible attraction. In essence, he sought to introduce on a mass scale the principles of progressive Western education, such as Dewey's "activity school," the English "Dalton system," and the Montessori method, which in the West were confined to experimental institutions. The most radical exponents of Soviet educational philosophy in the early 1920s went further still, calling for the abolition of schools and the shift of education to collective farms and factories.[120]

These educational theories remained largely on paper. The material condition of Soviet schools simply precluded experimentation: those that did not shut down for lack of fuel and light had no textbooks and were desperately short of notebooks and writing implements. The teachers, miserably paid, if paid at all, had no idea what was expected of them.* Krupskaia returned in the summer of 1919 from an inspection tour of the schools in the Volga-Kama region very discouraged. "Matters stand badly," she wrote a friend: "The Consolidated Labor School produces literally nothing but nonsense. . . . The entire initiative is left to the teachers, and this is the most miserable 'nation.' Only here and there do they begin to make some sense of it, but the majority understands nothing and asks such absurd questions that you stand astounded."[121] Lunacharskii himself had to concede in 1920–21 that the new school system had proven a utopian dream and that Russian schools were dying.[122] As a consequence, with the introduction of NEP, many of the innovations were abandoned or substantially modified: progressive education yielded to more traditional methods, with added stress on indoctrination.

Such indoctrination was not left exclusively to the mistrusted teaching staff. For this purpose the Communist Party relied heavily on two youth organizations, the "Pioneers" and the "Union of Communist Youth" or Komsomol. The Pioneers were founded in 1922 on the model of the Scouts, but with a strong political component added. Eligible to join were children under 15. The Pioneers were to inculcate Communist values: the first duty of members was to be faithful to the working class and to Communism.[123] The organization served as a recruiting ground for the Komsomol, which, in turn, furnished candidates for the Communist Party. In actuality, the Pioneers were not subjected to heavy ideological pressure, for which reason they were popular with children. The Komsomol was used to carry out various propagandistic assignments, especially against religious institutions and practices.[124]

Contemporary sources indicate that Soviet primary and secondary education approximated Lunacharskii's ideal only in a few model schools;

---

*In 1925, teachers received a fraction of workers' wages. From letters to the editor of a pedagogical journal it transpired that a well-qualified teacher of the second level in Kiev earned 45 rubles a month, whereas the school janitor received 70 and the parents of her pupils between 200 and 250 rubles. A. Radchenko in *NP*, No. 1 (1926), 110.

elsewhere things went on as before, only worse.[125] The contrast between intention and reality, characteristic of all Soviet life, was nowhere starker than in this field. According to one Communist historian, nine-tenths of the material published in Soviet pedagogical journals of the time consisted of abstract and irrelevant speculations.[126] From other materials one gains the impression the only innovations that struck root were those directed against academic standards and teachers' authority. The following excerpt from a contemporary literary work, written in the form of a 15-year-old boy's diary, conveys something of the atmosphere of the early Soviet schoolroom:

October 5

Our whole group was outraged today. This is what happened. A new *shkrabikha* ["school worker"] came to teach natural science, Elena Niki-tishna Kaurova, whom we named Elnikitka. She handed out our assignments and told the group:
"Children!"
Then I got up and said: "We are not children."
To which she: "Of course you are children, and I won't call you any other way."
I replied: "Please be more polite, or we may send you to the devil."
That was all. The whole group stood up for me.
Elnikitka turned red and said: "In that case be so good as to leave the classroom."
I answered: "In the first place, this is not a classroom but a laboratory, and we are not expelled from it."
So she: "You are a boor."

41. Moscow youths "pledge their allegiance to the
anti-imperialist world struggle," 1924.

And I: "You are more like a teacher of the old school. Only they had such rights."

That was all. The whole group stood up for me. Elnikitka ran off like she was scalded.[127]

The ideal of universal primary and secondary education came nowhere near realization—indeed, as the following table indicates, by the time of Lenin's death, compared to tsarist times, the number of both schools and pupils had regressed.

PRIMARY AND SECONDARY SCHOOLING IN RUSSIA[128]
(within boundaries of the USSR as of September 1, 1939)

	1914/15	1923/24
Schools	101,917	85,662
Pupils	7,030,257	6,327,739

The failure of the government to provide universal schooling was caused by fiscal constraints. Measured in terms of financial commitment to education, the Communist regime lagged behind its tsarist predecessor, which was not known to be lavish in this respect. Lunacharskii time and again complained that budgetary allocations to his commissariat fell far short of needs, given that it bore responsibility for all of the nation's schools, including those that before 1917 had been financed by the church and local authorities. In 1918–21, Narkompros's share of the national budget stayed under 3 percent: in Lunacharskii's estimation, this was between one-third and one-fourth of its requirements.[129] Under NEP this share fell further. According to Lunacharskii, Soviet per capita allocations for education in 1925–26, a time of relative prosperity, in real rubles were one-third lower than in 1913.* The ideal of free and universal education had to be abandoned. This was first done (1921) by local organs from necessity, and in early 1923 as a matter of national policy.[130] As had been the case in the final years of the tsarist regime, in 1923 only some 45 percent of eligible children attended school.[131]

Neither the new schools nor the Communist youth organizations succeeded in their primary mission, inculcating a Communist world-outlook. A survey conducted in 1927 among schoolchildren 11 to 15 years of age provided striking evidence of how little progress had been made in this regard. The pupils, all of them products of the Soviet educational system, displayed little ability to analyze current events in a Communist manner,

*NP, No. 2 (1926), 9. In 1928, he further said that the Soviet government spent on elementary school pupils 75 percent, and on those in secondary schools one-quarter of the sums allocated by the ancien régime: *RiK*, No. 11 (June 15, 1928), 21.

responding at best with memorized clichés. Forty-nine percent professed to
believe in God. Especially disturbing to the authorities was evidence that
with each year of schooling pupils developed more negative attitudes toward Soviet life.[132]

Surveying the results of Communist educational policies, Lunacharskii
had to concede failure. On the fourth anniversary of the October coup, he
wrote:

> War Communism seemed to many the shortest road to the kingdom of
> Communism. . . . For us, Communist pedagogues, the disappointment was
> especially keen. The difficulties of building a socialist system of popular
> education in an ignorant, illiterate country grew beyond all measure. We
> had no Communist teachers at all; the material means and the money were
> insufficient.[133]

The melancholy truth was that for all the boasting about advances in
the quality and accessibility of education, many children not only lacked the
benefit of formal schooling, but lost through the Revolution and its aftermath the most elemental educational right, available to all but the most
primitive animals, parental care. These were the *besprizornye*—orphans and
abandoned children—who in the 1920s roamed Russia like prehistoric
creatures.[134] Their number increased sharply during the famine of 1921,
when it was common practice for relatives to take over the properties of
orphans' parents and chase the children from the village.[135] It has never
been possible to determine how many homeless children there were in
postrevolutionary Russia because they had no stable home and evaded the
census takers. In 1922–23, Lunacharskii and Krupskaia estimated their
number at between 7 and 9 million.[136] Three-quarters were children of
peasants (54.5 percent) and workers (23.3 percent); 15 percent were aged
3 to 7, and 57.1 percent, 8 to 13.[137] They lived in gangs in abandoned
buildings, railroad terminals, lumberyards, coal depots, and wherever else
they could find a roof: "Going about in packs, barely articulate or recogniz-
ably human, with pinched animal faces, tangled hair and empty eyes,"
recalled Malcolm Muggeridge, "I saw them in Moscow and Leningrad,
clustered under bridges, lurking in railway stations, suddenly emerging like
a pack of wild monkeys, then scattering and disappearing."[138] They survived by begging, scrounging, and stealing; many, possibly most of these
children, both girls and boys, engaged in prostitution.[139]

In 1921, the security police turned its attention to the homeless waifs,
placing those it was able to catch in state-run colonies. Displayed to foreign
visitors as model self-governing communities ("children's republics"), they
are said to have rather resembled penal institutions. The *besprizornye*
proved psychically broken and socially unassimilable.

Initially, Soviet publicists blamed this phenomenon on the "capitalist

42. *Besprizornye.*

legacy," from which one observer deduced that tsarist Russia must have been the world's most developed capitalist country since Soviet Russia had the largest proportion of homeless children.[140] Only in 1925 did Krupskaia admit that it was "three-quarters" the product of "contemporary" conditions.[141]

Until the spring of 1918, the Bolsheviks did not interfere with institutions of higher learning.[142] Many of these suspended operations in any event, in part to protest the Bolshevik putsch, and in part because their students, forced to make ends meet, stayed away. The Bolsheviks left the universities alone for the time being even though they realized that the faculties, a high proportion of whom were Constitutional-Democrats, solidly opposed them. They knew that several university faculties had passed resolutions in October and November 1917 condemning their coup; in Petrograd, the new regime was denounced by the rectors of all the institutions of higher learning.[143] They chose to overlook such opposition because they needed the universities to raise the country's scientific and technological level. Lunacharskii recalled having been told more than once by Lenin: "A great scholar, a leading specialist in this or that field, must be spared to the most extreme limit, even if he is a reactionary."[144] The verb "spare" (*shchadit'*) in this context suggests that such tolerance was meant to be temporary.

The policies of the Bolshevik regime in regard to higher education had four objectives: (1) to eliminate faculty self-government; (2) to do away with those faculties, essentially the humanities and what came to be known as "social sciences," whose curricula could clash with Communist ideology; (3) to put an end to the "elitist" character of higher education; and (4) to develop on a massive scale vocational training.

The premier scholarly institution in Russia, the Academy of Sciences, fared tolerably well under Communism. Its hostility to the Bolshevik dictatorship was no secret: a conference of the Academy on November 21, 1917, passed a resolution condemning the Bolshevik power seizure and demanding that Russia remain in the war on the Allied side.[145] But Lenin chose to overlook its politics because he attached great value to the expertise of its 41 members and staff of 220, in whose ranks were some of the country's leading scholars and scientists. To enlist them in his service he was prepared to make far-reaching concessions in the matter that concerned the Academicians the most, institutional autonomy. Eventually, a compromise was struck. The Academicians agreed, although without much enthusiasm, to shelve fundamental research and concentrate instead on the applied sciences so as to help the government solve pressing economic and technical problems. In return, the Academy retained full discretion in choosing members (at any rate, during the 1920s). It was the only cultural institution exempt from control by the Commissariat of Enlightenment.[146]

Interference with universities started in the summer of 1918. The measures worked out by Lunacharskii's Commissariat far exceeded the curbs imposed on Russian academic institutions by the reactionary regimes of Nicholas I and Alexander III. Between 1918 and 1921 the Communists liquidated academic self-government, abolished, for all practical purposes, faculty tenure, and flooded the institutions of higher learning with unqualified but politically promising students.

A decree of October 1, 1918, did away with higher academic degrees (doctor, master) and dismissed professors who had taught at the same institution for ten or more years or had held professorial appointments anywhere for fifteen years or longer: their chairs were thrown open to nationwide competition among all who, in the words of the decree, had acquired a reputation as a scholar or teacher.[147] In early 1919, elections were held for the vacated positions: at Moscow University, the country's most defiant, the faculty reappointed every one of the ninety professors who had lost their chairs under the October 1 ruling, except for the single Communist in the group.[148] Elsewhere, the decree played havoc with university life. In many universities unqualified persons were appointed and lecturers were raised to the rank of professor by administrative order. This held especially true of the numerous new universities and scientific institutes. On January 21, 1919, it was decreed that four new universities would be founded and two institutions raised to university status.[149] In the summer of 1918, the Socialist Academy of Social Sciences came into being, and in 1920, the Sverdlov Communist University, the latter a propaganda school that enrolled exclusively party members, most with no more than an elementary education.[150] In the winter of 1918–19 the authorities closed university juridical faculties and the history departments of the historical-philological faculties, where the opposition to the new regime was strongest. They were replaced by faculties of social science,[151] a concept that embraced economics, history, and law. The curriculum stressed the antecedents of the October Revolution and the inevitable worldwide triumph of Communism.[152] An Institute of Red Professors (Institut Krasnoi Professury), composed mostly of Socialist Academy personnel, was set up in 1921 to train professors to teach history, economics, and philosophy in the Marxist manner.[153]

By 1925, the number of universities had increased from ten (1916) to thirty-four. The faculty, however, grew more rapidly than the student body: while the latter increased by one-third (from 38,853 in 1916 to 51,979 in 1925), the teaching staff more than tripled (from 1877 to 6174).[154] Many of the latter, however, had qualifications chiefly of a political nature. In 1921, on Lenin's instructions, all students at institutions of higher learning had to take obligatory indoctrination courses on historical materialism and the history of the Bolshevik Revolution. In 1924, the history of the Bolshevik Party was made a required subject.[155]

The status of Soviet institutions of higher education was definitively regulated by the university statute of September 2, 1921, which revived many provisions of the reactionary university statute of 1884.[156] Setting aside the liberal practices followed in Russia since 1906, it deprived faculties of the right to choose rectors and professors: the authority to do so was transferred to the Commissariat of Enlightenment.* The new statute also gave soviets supervisory powers over institutions of higher learning in their area. These measures aroused great hostility among professors and students. In November 1921, over one thousand Petrograd students marched in a protest demonstration.[157] The following spring, several hundred Moscow University professors took part in a protest strike.[158] As punishment, seven of the striking professors were expelled from the country. In 1921–22 party organs engaged in systematic surveillance of faculties teaching the social sciences, purging teachers who did not toe the official line.[159] The results were more dismissals and expulsions abroad.[160]

While eliminating university autonomy—the self-government of the faculties, especially in matters of appointment, and their right to set the curriculum—the new regime also interfered with student admissions. Its objective was to open access to higher education to youths of lower-class origin, especially children of workers and poor peasants, regardless of their academic qualifications.

The first and critical step in this direction was a sensational decree issued on August 2, 1918, which made it possible for all citizens over 16 years of

---

*According to the 1921 statute, Narkompros was to select rectors from lists drawn up by professors, students, trade unionists, and soviet officials. In 1922 a new provision empowered it to appoint to this post anyone it wanted: James McClelland, "Bolsheviks, Professors, and the Reform of Higher Education in Soviet Russia, 1917–1921" (Ph.D. dissertation, Princeton University, 1970), 398. In practice, rectors were nominated not by Narkompros but by the Party's Central Committee and local party cells: *ibid.,* 399.

age, male and female, to enroll at any institution of higher learning without having to submit proof of previous schooling, undergo entrance examinations, or pay tuition fees.[161] Masses of unqualified youths took advantage of this ruling. The professors, however, succeeded for the time being in neutralizing its effects by refusing to admit unqualified students to their seminars. Before long, many of those enrolled under the "open admission" policy dropped out.[162] Workers and poor peasants had neither the desire nor the leisure to pursue higher education: it proved unrealistic to expect them to attend university courses because the milieu was unfamiliar and most of them had no money for living expenses. Summarizing the results of the new admissions policy, an official Narkompros report declared:

> In this connection we must state with great bitterness that the vast majority of our students already have had a higher education, that the vast majority of the remainder have completed secondary schooling, and that only an insignificant number can, in terms of their status, approach the proletarian masses. . . . The proletarian masses did not come to us: who came was the intelligentsia.[163]

Women, in particular, stayed away: there were more female students in Russian universities in 1914 than in 1930.[164]

Once they became aware of these facts, the authorities took remedial steps, phasing out "open admission" and setting up special schools to prepare workers for the university. On September 15, 1919, institutions of higher learning were ordered to establish Workers' Faculties (Rabochie Fakultety or Rabfaki) to offer workers and poor peasants crash courses in secondary education. Most students who enrolled in Rabfaki belonged to the Party and its youth organizations, having gained admission on the recommendation of their party cells or trade unions; half studied part-time, the rest, full-time. In the middle of 1921, there were 64 Rabfaki with at least 25,000 students.[165] Despite deplorable living conditions, workers kept on enrolling, for completing a Rabfak opened opportunities to leave the factory for a white-collar job. By 1925, two-thirds of the students admitted to university faculties of science and technology, half of those in economics, a quarter in agriculture, and a fifth in medicine, were graduates of Rabfaki.[166] From their ranks came the Communist "cadres" Stalin would employ in the 1930s to replace the old intelligentsia.

In 1923, the government took further measures to rectify the social imbalance by introducing preferential admission quotas for students of the desired background. It also resorted to "purges" of students whose social origin was unacceptable: in 1924–25 some 18,000 students were expelled on such grounds.*

*James C. McClelland in *Past and Present*, No. 80 (August 1978), 130. This was in emulation of the policies of Nicholas I, who had sought to restrict admission to the institutions of higher learning to the gentry.

And still, the Bolsheviks never quite succeeded in transforming higher education from a preserve of the intelligentsia into mass institutions. Neither policies of discrimination against the intelligentsia nor those favoring workers and poor peasants significantly altered the social composition of the student body. The academy retained its "elitist" character for the rest of the decade. On the eve of World War I, 24.3 percent of the students at Russian universities had come from worker and artisan families; in the academic year 1923–24 workers accounted for only 15.3 percent of the student body. There was a significant rise in the proportion of peasants: 22.5 percent in 1923–24 as compared to 14.5 percent in 1914. The overall proportion of members of these two classes, then underprivileged and now favored, was thus actually lower after seven years of Bolshevik discriminatory policies: 37.8 percent in 1923–24 as against 38.8 percent in 1914.* More ruthless measures applied from the late 1920s onward did succeed in altering the balance of social groups at the institutions of higher learning, but as late as 1958, Khrushchev made the astonishing admission that in Moscow between 60 and 70 percent of the students came from families that were neither worker nor peasant.[167]

The reasons for the failure of the regime appreciably to alter the social composition of the student body are not hard to find. First, higher, specialized learning does not come either easily or naturally: respect for it has to be inculcated at home, in the family. Children from homes of the intelligentsia are more likely to aspire to it than those raised in illiterate or semiliterate homes. For this reason, no matter how much the regime encouraged them, children of workers and poor peasants either avoided the university or, if enrolled, tended to drop out. Secondly, those who did persevere automatically ceased to be workers and poor peasants. Students of lower-class origin at the universities and Rabfaki, upon completion of their studies, having joined the Party, hardly ever returned to the factory or to the field but took white-collar jobs.† Their sons and daughters, therefore, qualified as children of the "intelligentsia" (in the Communist sense of the word).

When they were not blaming hostile foreign powers, the Communist leaders liked to attribute their difficulties and failures to the low cultural standards of the population, of which illiteracy was the best indicator. Clara

---

*The 1914 figures are from Anweiler and Ruffman, *Kulturpolitik,* 10; those for 1923–24, from McClelland in *Past and Present,* No. 80 (1978), 131. It must be noted, however, that the pre- and postrevolutionary figures are not fully comparable because (1) those for 1914 refer to legal status rather than occupation, and (2) the category of "workers and artisans" before the Revolution included individuals whom the Soviet regime regarded as "petty bourgeois."

†"One may assume that more than half, if not two-thirds, of workers belonging to the party were compelled to abandon daily physical labor in factories and plants and go to work for the state and the party.": N. Solovev in *Pravda,* No. 190 (August 28, 1921), 4.

Zetkin once told Lenin that he should not complain of illiteracy in Russia, since it had helped the Communists to "sow seeds on virgin soil"—the minds of workers and peasants unpolluted by "bourgeois concepts and attitudes." Lenin agreed up to a point: "Yes, that's true. . . . Illiteracy tolerated our struggle for power and the need to destroy the old state apparatus," but, he felt, once the Communist state was in place, it became a hindrance.[168]

On December 26, 1919, Moscow decreed the "liquidation of illiteracy" among citizens aged 8 to 50.[169] All adults, male and female, were required to learn to read either Russian or their native tongue. Those unable to do so were to be taught by literate citizens whom the Commissariat of Enlightenment was authorized to draft for the purpose. The intention was to enable the entire population to take "a conscious part in the country's political life." Citizens who refused to learn were liable to criminal prosecution.

The Communist campaign has been described as "the most sustained and comprehensive attempt yet made to liquidate illiteracy."[170] Tens of thousands of "liquidation points" were set up in cities and villages, offering crash courses that usually lasted three months and required 120–144 hours of classroom attendance. Despite warnings of punishment, it proved difficult to attract peasants, who associated these courses with atheistic propaganda. In response to their complaints, this aspect of instruction was eventually attenuated. A rough estimate is that between 1920 and 1926 some 5 million persons went through the literacy schools in European Russia.[171]

The Communist government liked to convey the impression that the overwhelming majority of its citizens was illiterate: thus Trotsky spoke of the need to teach reading skills to "hundreds of millions."[172] In reality, illiteracy in prerevolutionary Russia was nowhere near that prevalent and, in any event, it steadily declined. As the following table indicates, at the time of the Revolution, 42.8 percent of the country's population was literate: among men, the proportion was 57.6 percent. In 1920, urban boys and girls aged 13 to 19 showed between 84.2 and 86.5 percent literacy.[173]

LITERACY IN RUSSIA/U.S.S.R.[174]

Year	Population as a whole	Male population
1867	19.1%	26.3%
1887	25.6	37.0
1907	35.3	49.2
1917	42.8	57.6
1926	51.1	66.5

These figures indicate that despite the publicity accompanying the anti-illiteracy drive, the results obtained showed no dramatic spurt but rather continued the progress achieved before the Revolution.

As with attempts to abandon admission standards for higher education, the drive against illiteracy suffered from shortcomings inherent in cultural crash programs. Soviet criteria of literacy were very low: to pass, a person had merely to be able to read large print, syllable by syllable. Ability to write was not required. According to one Soviet authority, many products of the campaign emerged semiliterate if not illiterate.[175] Allowance also had to be made for recidivism among the newly literate, which was not inconsiderable, since on completing the course they often lost contact with the printed word.

Especially disappointing was evidence that children 9 to 12 years old continued to show 45.2 percent illiteracy, which meant that as fast as adults were taught, young people without access to schooling filled the ranks of illiterates.[176] On the tenth anniversary of the decree of 1919, after the census of 1926 had revealed the realities behind the propaganda claims, Krupskaia conceded that not a single one of its provisions had been even approximately realized.[177] She pointed out that while every year one million adults acquired reading skills, a like number of school-age children entered society without the benefit of schooling. Hence, the actual achievement of the Communist regime was to "stabilize" illiteracy.[178]

The Russian language underwent interesting changes in the course of the Revolution and Civil War.[179] The most striking innovation was the widespread use of acronyms and telescoped words, such as Sovnarkom, NEP, and Proletkult. "Discredited" words of the old regime were replaced by more acceptable synonyms. Thus, the bureaucrat, *chinovnik,* became a "Soviet official" *(sovetskii sluzhashchii),* the tsarist policeman *(gorodovoi)* was relabeled militiaman *(militsioner),* and "sir" *(gospodin)* gave way to "comrade" *(tovarishch).* The attempt to replace the traditional expression for "thank you"—*spasibo,* derived from "God save you" *(Spasi Bog)*—with what were thought to be neutral words, such as *merci* ("May God have mercy on you"), never gained acceptance. Jocose euphemisms were coined for the business of killing: "to send to a meeting," "to dispatch to Dukhonin's headquarters" (with reference to General N. N. Dukhonin, lynched by soldiers in late 1917) "to put into an envelope and mail," the last signifying to arrest and then execute.

Such was the language of the Soviet city. Peasants in the village as well as those serving in the Red Army garbled and redefined the new words in ways that indicated they understood next to nothing of what was happening around them. They assimilated abstractions now no better than under tsarism, and translated the foreign-sounding vocabulary promoted by the Communists into concrete actions and objects. Thus, they interpreted "ultimatum" to mean "either you pay up, hand over the horse, or I will kill you." The following are other examples of peasant definitions as collected by contemporary linguists:

Civil marriage: Unmarried people living together
Kammunist (also *"kamunist"* or *"kamenist"*): One who does not believe in God
Commissariat: Where they register and send to war
Mars, Karlo-Mars: The same as Lenin
Billion *(milliard):* Paper money
Peners, pianers: Small children, like Bolsheviks, they walk with drums and sing

"Revolution," sometimes pronounced "levolution" *(levoliutsiia),* was understood to mean "doing what you like" *(samovol'shchina).*

In December 1917, the government institutionalized a new orthography which had long been advocated by some linguists and introduced by the Provisional Government. It simplified spelling by eliminating a number of redundant letters.[180] "God" was henceforth to be written with a small *g.*

Marxists regarded ethics as a branch of metaphysics and, as such, unworthy of serious attention. Marxist literature provided Soviet Russia's leaders with little guidance in this matter; but since every society requires norms of behavior, they had no choice but to address themselves to it. The principal Bolshevik ethical theoreticians were Eugene Preobrazhenskii and Nicholas Bukharin.

Preobrazhenskii's *Of Morals and Class Norms (O morali i klassovykh normakh),* published in 1923, sought to formulate a system of morals for Russia's victorious proletariat. The premises were familiar: in societies divided into classes morals serve the interests of the class in power; so-called eternal ethical "truths" are a fiction designed to conceal this reality. In dealing with its class enemy, the proletariat must not be inhibited by moral constraints: "every struggle has its rules of victory." Wherever the proletariat triumphs, individuals must submit to the dictates of the collective, and view themselves as "instruments of the working class." "Conscience" is replaced as the regulator of behavior by social approval and disapproval. All actions, including such seemingly private matters as sex relations and family life, are subordinate to the needs of society and the "race." "In the interest of safeguarding the race," society has the right to prevent syphilitics and other ill or deformed citizens from "poisoning" the blood by breeding. Society has the undeniable right to intervene in the sexual life of its citizens in order, through scientific "selection," to improve the race.[181]

Bukharin dismissed ethics as useless baggage. What philosophers call ethics is merely "fetishism" of class standards. As the carpenter performs whatever actions are necessary to make a bench,

43. Nicholas Bukharin.

exactly so does the proletariat in its social struggle. If the proletariat wishes to attain communism, then it must do such and such, as does the carpenter in building a bench. And whatever is expedient from this point of view, this must be done. "Ethics" transforms itself for the proletariat, step by step, into simple and comprehensible rules of conduct necessary for communism, and, in point of fact, *ceases to be ethics.*[182]

The obvious flaw in this ethical philosophy is that it assumes the abstraction called "proletariat" to be capable of acting. In point of fact, a communist society, like any other, is directed by individuals—in this case, the leaders of the Communist Party—and these individuals, with every action they undertake, make decisions. There is no scientific way of predetermining what is "necessary" for the cause of a class, since at every point there emerge choices: choices that are not only technical but also moral. Years later, Preobrazhenskii and Bukharin, having been subjected to torture and then executed for crimes they had not committed, by their own ethical standards had no grounds for complaint: "Communism" in this instance, too, acted as it deemed necessary.

The Revolution was intended to bring fundamental changes in the status of women and the relationship of the sexes. The classic Marxist statement on the subject, Engels's *Origin of the Family,* denied that the monogamous family was in any sense a natural institution. It was nothing

but the by-product of specific historical circumstances attending the triumph of private property over primitive, communal property, one result of
which was the subjugation of women. In the monogamous family, which
invests the ownership of property in men, woman is reduced to the status
of "head servant." To emancipate herself, she requires economic independence, which she can attain only by being relieved of domestic duties and
taking an outside job. This will spell the end of the "monogamous family
as the economic unit of society."[183] Society must assume full responsibility
for the traditional female tasks, child-rearing and cooking. The resulting
sexual liberation will be equally beneficial to men and women: adultery and
prostitution will disappear, yielding to love based on mutual inclination:

> The care and education of children becomes a public affair; society looks
> after all children alike, whether they are legitimate or not. This removes all
> the anxiety about the "consequences," which today is the most essential
> social—moral as well as economic—factor that prevents a girl from giving
> herself completely to the man she loves. Will not that suffice to bring about
> the gradual growth of unconstrained sexual intercourse?[184]

Engels's views greatly influenced socialist attitudes toward the so-called
"woman-question": once in power, the Bolsheviks promptly proceeded to
put them into practice. They passed laws designed to loosen traditional
family ties by facilitating divorce, abolishing discrimination against illegitimate offspring, and making society assume responsibility for the rearing of
children. But in this case, too, intentions were defeated by economic realities. As the Bolsheviks were to discover before long, the family was an
economic and social entity no less beneficial to them than to capitalist
society. After an initial outburst of legislation subverting the monogamous
family, they reversed themselves and restored it to its traditional role. And
since Communism led to a general lowering of living standards, the net
effect of Communist innovations was for the condition of married women
appreciably to deteriorate.

Soviet divorce legislation was the first in the world to allow either spouse
to terminate the marriage and to do so on the sole grounds of incompatibil-
ity. The rationale behind it was the idea of Engels's that insofar as marriage
presumed love, once either partner no longer felt love the bond lost meaning
and should be terminated. The decree of December 16, 1917, required
minimal formalities for the dissolution of marriage: it sufficed for one
partner to submit to the court a petition to this effect.[185]

Although it did not formally legalize abortion, in the first three years the
Soviet government treated it with forbearance. Because many abortions
were performed by unqualified individuals under unhygienic conditions
causing infections and death, a decree of November 18, 1920, legalized
them under strict medical supervision. Discouraged as a "moral survival of
the past," they were to be available free of charge at the mother's request

provided they were performed in hospitals by physicians.[186] This, too, was the first law of its kind.

In the best of all worlds Communist educators would have liked to take charge of children from the day they were born, removing them from their parents and placing them in communal nurseries. This was partly to free women for productive work, but also and mainly for purposes of conditioning and indoctrination. The wife of Zinoviev, Zlata Lilina, an official of the Commissariat of Enlightenment, insisted that it was best for children to be removed from their homes: "Is not parental love to a large extent love harmful to the child? . . . The family is individualistic and egoistic and the child raised by it is, for the most part, antisocial, filled with egoistic strivings. . . . Raising children is not the private task of parents, but the task of society."[187] In the Soviet Ukraine, which went furthest in this direction, it was actually planned to withdraw children at the age of four from parental care and place them in boarding schools where they would be "socialized."[188] Such proposals came to nought for lack of money and personnel. The social care of children proved unfeasible: for while mothers were prepared to devote countless hours of free labor to care for their offspring, hired caretakers had to be paid, and this required funds that were not available. The number of children in Soviet boarding schools never exceeded 540,000 (1922), declining to one-half that number under the NEP (1925).[189]

In Soviet Russia, as in the rest of Europe, World War I led to a loosening of sexual mores, which here was justified on moral grounds. The apostle of free love in Soviet Russia was Alexandra Kollontai, the most prominent woman Bolshevik.[190] Whether she practiced what she preached or preached what she practiced, is not for the historian to determine; but the evidence suggests that she had an uncontrollable sex drive coupled with an inability to form enduring relationships. Born the daughter of a wealthy general, terribly spoiled in childhood, she reacted to the love lavished on her with rebellion. To escape home, she married young, but left her husband after three years. In 1906 she joined the Mensheviks, then, in 1915, switched to Lenin, whose antiwar stand she admired. Subsequently, she performed for him valuable services as agent and courier.

In her writings, Kollontai argued that the modern family had lost its traditional economic function, which meant that women should be set free to choose their partners. In 1919 she published *The New Morality and the Working Class*,[191] a work based on the writings of the German feminist Grete Meisel-Hess. In it she maintained that women had to be emancipated not only economically but also psychologically. The ideal of *"grand amour"* was very difficult to realize, especially for men, because it clashed with their worldly ambitions. To be capable of it, individuals had to undergo an apprenticeship in the form of "love games" or "erotic friendships," which taught them to engage in sexual relations free of both emotional attachment

44. Alexandra Kollontai.

and personal domination. Casual sex alone conditioned women to safeguard their individuality in a society dominated by men. Every form of
sexual relationship was acceptable: Kollontai advocated what she called
"successive monogamy." In the capacity of Commissar of Guardianship
(Prizreniia) she promoted communal kitchens as a way of "separating the
kitchen from marriage." She, too, wanted the care of children to be assumed by the community. She predicted that in time the family would
disappear, and women would learn to treat all children as their own. She
popularized her theories in a novel, *Free Love: The Love of Drones* (*Svobod-
naia liubov': liubov' pchel trudovykh*) (1924), one part of which was called,
"The Love of Three Generations." Its heroine preached divorcing sex from
morality as well as from politics. Generous with her body, she said she loved
everybody, from Lenin down, and gave herself to any man who happened
to attract her.

Although often regarded as the authoritative theoretician of Communist
sex morals, Kollontai was very much the exception who scandalized her
colleagues. Lenin regarded "free love" as a "bourgeois" idea—by which he
meant not so much extramarital affairs (with which he himself had had
experience) as casual sex. What the Communist Establishment thought
about sex may be gathered from Lenin's ruminations, unmistakably di-

rected at Alexandra Kollontai and her followers, as reported by Clara Zetkin:

> I was told that questions of sex and marriage are the main subjects dealt with in the reading and discussion evenings of women comrades. They are the chief subject of interest, of political instruction and education. I could scarcely believe my ears when I heard it. The first country of proletarian dictatorship surrounded by the counterrevolutionaries of the whole world. The situation in Germany itself requires the greatest possible concentration of all proletarian, revolutionary forces to defeat the ever-growing and ever-increasing counter-revolution. And the women comrades discuss sexual problems. . . . Such misconceptions are particularly harmful, particularly dangerous in the youth movement. They can easily contribute to over-excitement and exaggeration in the sexual life of some, to the waste of youthful health and strength. . . .
>
> You must be aware of the famous theory that in Communist society the satisfaction of sexual desires, of love, will be as simple and unimportant as drinking a glass of water. This glass of water theory has made our young people mad, quite mad. . . . Young people, particularly, need the joy and force of life. Healthy sport, swimming, racing, walking, bodily exercises of every kind and many-sided intellectual interests. . . . Healthy bodies, healthy minds![192]

Studies of the sexual mores of Soviet youth conducted in the 1920s revealed considerable discrepancy between what young people said they believed and what they actually practiced: unusually, in this instance behavior was less promiscuous than theory. Russia's young people stated they considered love and marriage "bourgeois" relics and thought Communists should enjoy a sexual life unhampered by any inhibitions: the less affection and commitment entered into male-female relations, the more "communist" they were. According to opinion surveys, students looked on marriage as confining and, for women, degrading: the largest number of respondents—50.8 percent of the men and 67.3 percent of the women—expressed a preference for long-term relationships based on mutual affection but without the formality of marriage.[193]

Deeper probing of their attitudes, however, revealed that behind the facade of defiance of tradition, old attitudes survived intact. Relations based on love were the ideal of 82.6 percent of the men and 90.5 percent of the women: "This is what they secretly long for and dream about," according to the author of the survey. Few approved of the kind of casual sex advocated by Kollontai and widely associated with early Communism: a mere 13.3 percent of the men and 10.6 of the women.[194] Strong emotional and moral factors continued to inhibit casual sex: one Soviet survey revealed that over half of the female student respondents were virgins.[195]

The decisive influences on the sexual behavior of the postrevolutionary generation were economic: the unprecedented hardships of everyday life, especially the shortages of food and housing, and the stresses induced by relentless government demands. They forced the majority of Soviet youth, particularly women, to follow traditional norms of sexual behavior: the evidence gives "little support to the suggestion in the impressionistic literature of the time that promiscuity and an ideology of sexual liberation were widespread among women students."[196] Asked how the revolution had affected their sexual desires, 53.0 percent of the men reported these desires to have weakened; 41.0 percent of the men blamed hunger and other deprivations and pressures for complete or partial impotence; 59.0 percent of the female respondents saw no change in their desire for sex.[197] This was not what the authorities had expected. The author of one survey concluded that, regrettably, Soviet youth "still drew on the poisoned sources of the old sexual morality," with its preference for "hypocritical and spurious monogamy."[198] Another sociologist reported that of the seventy-nine women in his survey who admitted to having had sexual relations, "fifty-nine are married, and the rest dream of love and marriage."[199]

Unrestrained sexual license did not prevail, because it was not acceptable to most young people, nor, in the end, to the authorities: the trend was toward traditional values. The reaction culminated in 1936 with the promulgation of a new family code that outlawed abortion.[200] Under Stalin, the state sought to strengthen the family: "free love" was condemned as unsocialist. As in Nazi Germany, stress was placed on raising sturdy soldiers for the fatherland.[201]

Lenin's relative tolerance of the intelligentsia came to an abrupt end in the spring of 1922. He turned against them with a fury that can only be explained by the sense of failure that had haunted him since the spring of the preceding year, when the virtual collapse of the economy and nationwide rebellions forced him to adopt the New Economic Policy. He took a personal interest in the fate of hostile intellectuals, providing the GPU with names and indicating punishments he wished imposed.* His fanatical self-confidence now yielded to homicidal vindictiveness.

In March 1922 Lenin declared open war on "bourgeois ideology," which, in effect, meant war on the intelligentsia.[202] He was infuriated by the glee with which academics and writers criticized his regime and gloated over its reverses. Previously, when confident of victory, he had dismissed such talk as the rantings of has-beens. Now it touched a raw nerve and he reacted like a man obsessed. On March 5, in a confidential note, he declared a review of Spengler's *Decline of the West*, which he had read in a Soviet periodical, "a

---

*See, *e.g.*, his dispositions concerning eight Petrograd professors arrested in May 1921 in RTsKhIDNI, F. 2, op. 1, delo 24559. Lenin raised the case of the Menshevik historian N. A. Rozhkov at four separate Politburo meetings: *Rodina*, No. 3 (1992), 49. He was so obsessed with him that on December 13, 1922, when in a critical condition, he found the strength to send instructions that he be exiled: RTsKhIDNI, F. 2, op. 2, delo 1344.

literary cover for a White Guard organization."[203] Two months later he instructed Dzerzhinskii to have the GPU undertake a thorough study of literary and academic publications to determine which were "overt counter-revolutionaries, accomplices of the Entente, the organization of its servants and spies, and corrupters of student youth," and hence, "candidates for exile abroad." Such "military spies" were to be "regularly and systematically" apprehended and expelled from the country.[204] If Lenin seriously believed what he was saying—and the presumption is he did since he made these remarks in a confidential communication—one cannot help but suspect that he was suffering from some form of persecutory paranoia. For these "military spies" were some of Russia's most distinguished minds, who, hostile as they were to Communism, refrained from political activity, and certainly engaged in no espionage. Dzerzhinskii faithfully carried out Lenin's mandate, with the result that in the summer of 1922 scores of academics and writers were imprisoned.

On July 17, Lenin sent Stalin a note, which Stalin passed on to Dzerzhinskii, listing groups and individuals whom he wanted expelled from the country. He placed special emphasis on intellectuals connected with the SR Party, whose show-trial was then in progress. His orders were clear:

> Decisively "eradicate" *(iskorenit')* all SRs . . . all of them—get out of Russia. This must be done straight away—by the end of the SR trial, no later. Arrest a few hundred and *without explaining* the motives—"Out you go, gentlemen!"[205]

To give these instructions a legal form, the government issued, on August 10, a decree reintroducing administrative exile. It empowered the security services on their own authority to exile persons accused of "counterrevolutionary" activities either abroad or within the Russian Republic for a maximum term of three years.[206] The provisions on domestic exile revived the practices of late Imperial Russia: Lenin himself had been sent to Siberia in 1897 in this manner and for this term. The clauses authorizing exile abroad had no tsarist precedent.

In a report submitted to Lenin on September 18, G. G. Iagoda, the Chief of the Secret Operational Directorate of the GPU, wrote that in response to his instructions the GPU had arrested 120 anti-Soviet intellectuals (69 in Moscow and 51 in Petrograd). Taken into custody was the flower of Russia's academic intelligentsia, including the rectors of both Moscow and Petrograd universities, some of the country's leading agronomists, cooperative leaders, historians, sociologists, and philosophers.[207] The majority were subsequently placed on ships bound for Germany. Although officially the maximum term of administrative exile was three years, those deported abroad were banished for life: before departing, they had to sign documents acknowledging that if they either refused to leave or attempted to return they would be subject to execution. It would be difficult to find in recorded history a precedent for such mass expulsion of a country's intellectual elite.

Soviet cultural policies must be judged relatively more successful than the attempts to create a more democratic political system and a more efficient economy, but only relatively so. They did inhibit creativity, but they also made art, literature, and learning accessible to a mass public. If they did not accomplish the cultural revolution they had hoped for, the cause must be sought in their narrow conception of culture. For culture is not a by-product of economic and social relations, as they had convinced themselves, but a thing-in-itself, which influences the economy and society at least as much as it is influenced by them. Nor is it synonymous with books, paintings, or musical compositions. Least of all is it limited to science and technology. Broadly defined, culture is a way of coping with life under particular conditions as learned from experience and passed on from generation to generation: art and literature are only two of its expressions. By its very nature it cannot be regimented. Deprived of freedom or used for any purpose foreign to itself—especially politics—it turns sterile. Because the new regime ignored these precepts, the history of Communist literature and art is one of declining creativity: at first still driven by prerevolutionary impulses, it gradually dried up, ending in the barren conventions of "socialist realism." Worse still, the Communist regime methodically corrupted the "low" culture of ordinary people, with its customs acquired from ancestors and values rooted in religion, to make room for its own utilitarian and technological culture. The result was a spiritual vacuum that eviscerated Communism and contributed greatly to its ultimate demise.

7

The Assault on Religion

In histories of the Russian Revolution, religion receives little if any attention. W. H. Chamberlin devotes to this subject fewer than five pages in a book of nearly one thousand. Other scholars (for instance, Sheila Fitzpatrick and Leonard Schapiro) ignore it altogether. Such lack of interest can only be explained by the secularism of modern historians. And yet, even if historians are secular, the people with whom they deal were in the overwhelming majority religious: in this respect, the inhabitants of what became the Soviet Union—Christians, Jews, and Muslims alike—may be said to have lived in the Middle Ages. For them, culture meant religion—religious belief, but especially religious rituals and festivals: baptism, circumcision, confirmation, confession, burial, Christmas and Easter, Passover and Yom Kippur, Ramadan. Their lives revolved around the ceremonies of the religious calendar, because these not only glorified their hard and humdrum existences but gave even the humblest of them a sense of dignity in the eyes of God, for whom all human beings are equal. The Communists attacked religious beliefs and practices with a vehemence not seen since the days of the Roman Empire. Their aggressive atheism affected the mass of citizens far more painfully than the suppression of political dissent or the imposition of censorship. Next to the economic hardships, no action of Lenin's government brought greater suffering to the population at large, the so-called "masses," than the profanation of its religious beliefs, the closing of the houses of worship, and the mistreatment of the clergy. Although for reasons that will be spelled out below, Orthodox Christianity bore the brunt of Communist persecution, Judaism, Catholicism, and Islam were not spared.

Bolshevik policy toward religion had two aspects, one cultural, the other political. In common with all socialists, the Communists viewed religious belief as a relic of primitive times that stood in the way of modernization. They sought to uproot it with characteristic zeal by a combination of "scientific" education and ridicule. Socialists in Russia were particularly hostile to religious sentiments because of the Orthodox Church's intimate links to tsarism and its implacable anti-intellectualism. Already in the 1870s, Russian radicals had assigned high priority in their propaganda to combatting religious "superstition," because they saw it as a major impediment to their efforts at arousing the masses to rebellion: militant atheism has been called the element uniting the various groups of the intelligentsia under the tsarist regime.[1]

In their tactics for combatting religious belief, however, the Bolsheviks were divided. The cruder atheists among them wanted to attack it directly by every available means, especially mockery; the subtler ones, adapting the French proverb that one does not destroy except by replacing, wanted to raise socialism to the status of a surrogate religion.

To the latter, religion represented a genuine, if misplaced, yearning for spirituality that had to be satisfied in one way or another. Lunacharskii, the principal exponent of this viewpoint, acknowledged in *Religion and Socialism* (1908–1911) man's need for mystery and ardor. The quintessence of religion was to be found in man's relationship to nature. In the course of his historic evolution, man had gradually liberated himself from unthinking subjection to nature, seen as the plaything of gods or God, and with the help of science obtained mastery over it. Marxism marked the apogee of this evolution. In the early 1900s, Lunacharskii founded a movement called "God-building" *(Bogostroitel'stvo)*, which sought to replace traditional religion with human solidarity, with mankind itself as the object of worship. Proceeding from these premises, as Commissar of Enlightenment, Lunacharskii urged a sophisticated strategy:

> Religion is like a nail: if you hit it on the head, you only drive it deeper. ... Here one needs pliers. Religion must be *grabbed*, squeezed from below: you do not beat it, but pull it out, pull it with its roots. And this can be achieved *only by scientific propaganda, by the moral and artistic education of the masses.*[2]

Much Bolshevik antireligious activity in the 1920s followed this method, promoting science as the alternative to religion, and developing a Communist surrogate cult with its own divinities, saints, and rituals. In some official pronouncements, the function of Communism as a substitute for religion was explicitly affirmed, as, for instance, in a declaration that defined the aim of antireligious upbringing to be "the replacement of faith in God with faith in science and the machine."[3]

A cruder version of atheism was espoused by Emelian Iaroslavskii, who called for a frontal attack on religion on the grounds that it was nothing more than base superstition exploited by the ruling class. Trotsky, whom Lenin placed in charge of the antireligious campaign in 1922, seems to have shared Iaroslavskii's views.*

Lenin treated the theories of the "God-builders" with distaste, for he, too, felt that religion was a pillar of class society and an instrument of exploitation. He had little faith that scientific propaganda would be able by itself to eliminate it.[4] On these grounds he preferred the uncompromising atheism of Iaroslavskii. At the same time, keeping political considerations in mind, as always, as long as the Civil War was in progress he did not wish needlessly to antagonize the church with its one hundred million followers. Hence, he postponed an all-out assault on religion until 1922, when he was in unchallenged control of the country. It was then that he launched what he hoped would be the decisive offensive against the church.

Like the rest of the intelligentsia, the Bolsheviks felt confident that with the advance of the economy and the spread of education, religious *faith* would falter and ultimately disappear. Its eradication was only a matter of time.

Matters stood differently with *organized religion,* that is, the church, for in the one-party state, with its aspiration to a monopoly on all organized activity, the survival of an independent clergy, outside party control, was intolerable. This held especially true of the Orthodox Church, which ministered to the spiritual needs of three-quarters of the population and was "the last fragment of the political organization of the defeated classes still surviving as an organization."[5] Indeed, the symbiotic relationship between church and state in Russia before the Revolution resembled that prevalent in medieval Europe,

> in that the church and state were identical and the church provided the veritable ideal foundation of worldly rule. Hence if the Revolution really wanted fully to liquidate the old regime, it had to settle accounts with the church. It could not rest content with toppling the tsar, the supreme symbol of worldly authority: first and foremost, it had to seek to undermine the foundation on which the Russian world had hitherto reposed.[6]

The confrontation that got underway immediately after the October coup, attaining a climax in 1922, assumed a variety of forms. The clergy was made destitute by the abolition of state subsidies, confiscation of

---

*Both Trotsky and Iaroslavskii were Jews. The prominent role played by some Jews in the antireligious campaign of the Soviet regime has led to claims that it was part and parcel of a purported Jewish "war" on Christianity. The argument ignores the fact that Jewish religious institutions and observances were not exempt from abuse: indeed, Jewish Communists displayed particular zeal in persecuting fellow Jews.

church properties, and prohibition on the levying of dues. Churches and monasteries were despoiled and converted to utilitarian uses; so too, although less frequently, were synagogues and mosques. Clergymen of all faiths (except for Muslims) were deprived of civil rights and subjected to violent harassment and sham trials, which ended for many in imprisonment and for some in execution. Religious instruction for children was outlawed and replaced with atheistic propaganda in schools and youth organizations. Religious holidays gave way to Communist festivals.

Communist Party members were required to take an active part in atheistic activities and enjoined, under penalty of expulsion, from participating in all religious rites, including baptisms and church weddings.[7]

As the established Church, the Orthodox hierarchy had enjoyed unique privileges under tsarism. It alone had the right to proselytize and to prevent members from converting to other faiths. It received state subsidies. At the time of the Revolution, Russia had some 40,000 parish churches and over one thousand monasteries and cloisters. The clergy, "black" (monastic) and "white" (parish), numbered 145,000.[8]

So intimately was the Orthodox Church linked to the monarchy, and so isolated from political currents agitating the country, that the abdication of Nicholas II left it bewildered and perplexed. Its initial impulse was to ignore the February Revolution: many priests, from habit, continued to offer prayers for the tsar. Toward the Provisional Government, the Church hierarchy assumed an attitude of unfriendly neutrality, which had turned into outright hostility by the time the government fell. Such support as the Provisional Government received from this quarter came from reform-minded theologians and a minority of parish clergy who welcomed the loosening of the bonds joining the church to the state.[9]

While the Provisional Government paid little attention to ecclesiastical affairs, the drift of its legislation pointed to disestablishment. In June 1917, it abolished the post of Procurator of the Holy Synod, created by Peter the Great in place of the Patriarch, whose office he had done away with. This measure was welcomed by conservative as well as liberal churchmen who wanted to convene a Council to direct the reorganization of the Church. The clergy reacted less favorably to the government's other actions. In July, it proclaimed the equality of all religions, a measure which deprived the Orthodox priesthood of its privileged status. Next came a law that placed all schools that benefited from state subsidies, including those operated by the Church, under the Ministry of Education; subsequently, the subsidy paid the church was cut in half. The clergy was particularly angered by the government's edict eliminating the compulsory study of the Orthodox catechism from the school curriculum.[10] Churchmen interpreted these measures as steps toward secularization and blamed them for the decline of religious sentiment in the country.

Indeed, there were signs of hostility to the Church among the population at large. Immediately following the February Revolution, peasants in some villages assaulted and expelled priests. Known reactionaries, among them the notorious Archbishop Antonii Khrapovitskii of Kharkov, were evicted from their dioceses.[11] Here and there, clerical land was seized and distributed to the communes. It was reported that when Russian prisoners of war in German camps learned of the outbreak of the February Revolution, nine-tenths ceased to attend church services.[12] In addition, the February Revolution brought into the open smoldering conflicts within the Church between the parish and monastic clergy, the latter of whom had exclusive access to administrative posts.[13] These developments, against the background of spreading anarchy, had the effect of pushing the predominantly conservative Orthodox establishment still further to the right.

On August 15, 1917, the Orthodox Church convened in the Moscow Kremlin's Uspenskii Cathedral its first Council (Sobor) since 1666: it would sit, intermittently, for a year. Present at the opening session were Kerensky and two ministers. The 588 delegates, chosen by their dioceses, voiced alarm over the demoralization of the country, including the armed forces. They warned that Russia hovered on the brink of destruction, and appealed to the nation to bury its differences.[14] On this matter, the Council spoke with one voice. But when the proceedings turned to internal Church matters, it split into two factions, a conservative majority and a liberal minority. The most divisive issue was the proposal to reestablish the patriarchate. The conservatives favored such a course because they saw in the patriarch a leader who would defend the interests of the Church, now deprived of state patronage. Liberal clergymen, afraid that the patriarch would become a tool in the hands of conservatives, preferred to entrust the management of Church affairs to a council.

At the end of October, as pro-Bolshevik and anti-Bolshevik troops fought for control of the Kremlin, the Council voted to reinstitute the patriarchate. Three candidates were nominated, with the archconservative Khrapovitskii receiving the largest number of votes. As custom dictated, ballots with the three names were left overnight in an urn. In the morning, the oldest monk present drew from it one ballot: it bore the name of Tikhon, the Metropolitan of Moscow, who had received the fewest votes. Tikhon was a moderate whom one foreign observer described as "a pious unsophisticated monk . . . with more than a touch of Russian fatalism and apathy."[15] The installation ceremony took place on November 21 in the Uspenskii Cathedral. Following the ceremonies, the delegates adopted a new church constitution that represented something of a compromise between the conservatives and the reformers. Supreme authority was vested in the Church Council, which was to meet periodically: the Patriarch became the Church's chief executive, subordinate to the Council. One of his responsibilities was to represent the Church in dealings with the secular authorities.[16]

45. Patriarch Tikhon.

Tikhon was determined to keep the Church out of politics: who ruled Russia was none of its business, its true vocation being to minister to the nation's spiritual needs. His commitment to neutrality went so far that when early in 1918 Prince Grigorii Trubetskoi, about to depart for the Don to join the Volunteer Army, asked him to bestow a blessing on one of its leaders (apparently Denikin), Tikhon refused: he persisted in his refusal even after receiving assurances that the act would be kept in strictest confidence.[17] Such a policy of neutrality might have been feasible if the new regime governed in a conventional manner. But since it deliberately violated accepted norms of conduct, Tikhon, against his best intentions, soon found himself embroiled in a head-on conflict with it.

At the beginning of 1918, the Communist authorities had not as yet taken any measures overtly hostile to the Church, although their attitude toward it was difficult to mistake. The Land Decree of October 26, 1917, stipulated that church and monastic lands were subject to nationalization: in European Russia these properties amounted to 750,000 acres (300,000 hectares).[18] As of December 18 responsibility for the registration of births, marriages, and deaths, traditionally a prerogative of the Church, was transferred to the civil authorities. Henceforth only civil marriages had legal standing. Children born out of wedlock received the same rights as those born of married parents.[19] On December 11, all schools, including those not in receipt of government subsidies, were subjected to state control.[20] These blows to its prerogatives the Church could absorb. What worried it were reports that a government commission was at work drafting a law on the separation of church and state; after reading an account to this effect in the press in early January 1918, Metropolitan Benjamin of Petrograd warned the authorities to desist.[21] Nor could one ignore the mounting assaults on clergymen by soldiers and sailors, which the Bolshevik regime not only tolerated but encouraged. In many localities churches and monasteries were looted and priests abused. In late January 1918, drunken soldiers murdered the Metropolitan of Kiev, Vladimir.

On January 19/February 1 Tikhon signed an encyclical that deplored the hatred and cruelty let loose in Russia by those he called "the monsters of the human race . . . the open and concealed enemies of the Truth of Christ who have begun to persecute the [Orthodox Church] and are striving to destroy Christ's Cause by sowing everywhere, in place of Christian love, the seeds of malice, hatred, and fratricidal strife." Persons who engaged in such abominations were anathematized.*

The Bolsheviks responded the very next day with a decree that laid down the principles of their religious policy, terminating the relationship between the Orthodox Church and the state established when the Russian state first came into existence. Like most Soviet laws of the time, the decree was deliberately mistitled to conceal under the cover of liberal-sounding terminology its true totalitarian intent. The opening article of the "Decree on the Freedom of Conscience [and on] Church and Religious Associations" declared the Church separated from the state.† The articles that followed guaranteed every citizen the right to profess any religion or none. Foreign fellow-travelers and sympathizers, who took these professions at face value, saw them as granting the people of Russia a degree of religious liberty they had never previously enjoyed.[22] But these were hollow pledges, for the law's operative clauses spelled death for organized religion in the country. Unlike in revolutionary France, where the clergy, after its landed wealth had been nationalized, was placed on government salary, the Soviet edict not only deprived it of state pensions but forbade ecclesiastical and religious bodies to own property of any kind, including houses of worship and objects used in rituals. (Since the government was not yet prepared to shut down all churches, synagogues, and mosques, it authorized local and central state authorities to lease to religious associations "buildings and objects specifi-

---

*A. I. Vvedenskii, *Tserkov' i gosudarstvo* (Moscow, 1923), 114–16. The immediate occasion for this encyclical was the seizure on January 13 of the Aleksandro-Nevskaia Lavra in Petrograd by a detachment of sailors led by Bolsheviks. This was done at the instigation of Alexandra Kollontai. *Ibid.,* 120–23.

†*Dekrety,* I, 371–74. In subsequent publications it was renamed "On the Separation of Church and State," by which title it is has been known ever since.

cally designated for purposes of worship.") Worse still, the decree prohibited the churches from levying dues. The clergy thus was left without any
means of support. In the Soviet Constitution of 1918, under Article 65, it
was deprived of the right to vote and to serve in the soviets.[23] As if these
disabilities were not enough, the Communist authorities subsequently chose
to interpret the principle of separation of church and state to mean that the
clergy could never act in an organized manner, that is, as a single national
church: attempts at coordination among the religious communities or acknowledgment of a hierarchy were viewed as prima facie evidence of counterrevolutionary intent.* Supplementary decrees outlawed the teaching of
religion to persons under 18 years of age.[24] In the Criminal Code of the
Russian Republic of 1922, the teaching of religion to minors in public or
private establishments and schools was designated a crime punishable by
forced labor for up to one year.[25] None of these measures had anything to
do with the principle of separation of church and state.

In its response to the new laws, the Church Council quite correctly stated
that "under the pretext of separating church and state, the Council of
People's Commissars attempts to make impossible the very existence of
churches, church institutions, and the clergy": even the heathen Tatars
when they lorded it over Russia had shown greater respect for Christianity.
The Council warned all who helped implement the decree that they risked
excommunication, and called on the faithful to defend the churches and
monasteries from seizures.[26]

The January 20 decree stimulated throughout Bolshevik-controlled
Russia more raids on churches and monasteries in the course of which
soldiers, sailors, and Red Guards plundered objects of value, often after
overcoming fierce resistance. According to Communist reports, between
February and May 1918, 687 persons died while participating in religious
processions or attempting to protect church properties.[27]

The Orthodox Church and the Communist regime were at war. In
rural Russia, peasants, convinced that Antichrist was abroad and the
Last Judgment near, drank, gambled, and worked themselves into hysterical frenzy.[28] Confronted with this situation, the authorities refrained
from closing the houses of worship: in most localities, the soviets "leased"
back to the communities the expropriated churches, synagogues, and
mosques. For the time being they concentrated on the monastic establishments, which they viewed as centers of religious opposition and which
enjoyed less popular support. In the course of 1918–19 they sacked and
shut down most of the country's monasteries and cloisters: by 1920, 673
monasteries were closed and their assets—not only land, but also factories,
dairies, and hospitals—either handed over to peasants or taken over by

---

*"According to the meaning of the decree separating church and state, the existence of a
'church hierarchy' as such is impossible. The decree envisaged only the existence of separate
religious communities, unconnected by any administrative authority." *Izvestiia*, No. 99/1,538
(May 6, 1922), 1.

state agencies.[29] Private churches and chapels were looted and shut down almost without exception and converted into social clubs or places of amusement.

Tikhon departed from his policy of noninterference in politics in March 1918, after the ratification of the Brest-Litovsk Treaty, to which he took strong exception. "The Holy Orthodox Church," he wrote, "which has since time immemorial helped the Russian people to gather and glorify the Russian state, cannot remain indifferent at the sight of its ruin and decay."[30] It was incontrovertibly a provocative statement on a purely political subject.

The Patriarch directed his boldest protest against the Bolsheviks after they had formally launched in early September 1918 their Red Terror. On October 26, the first anniversary of the Bolshevik coup, he sent a message to the Council of People's Commissars condemning Communist rule for having brought the country nothing but a humiliating peace and a fratricidal war, for spilling rivers of innocent blood, for encouraging robbery and violating freedom. "It is not our task to judge the earthly power," he concluded even as he appealed to the government to:

> celebrate the anniversary of taking power by releasing the imprisoned, by ceasing bloodshed, violence, ruin, constraints on the faith. Turn not to destruction, but establish order and legality. Give the people the respite from the fratricidal strife that they long for and deserve. Otherwise, all the righteous blood you shed will cry out against you (Luke 11:51) and with the sword will perish you who have taken up the sword (Matthew 26:52).[31]

It was the most daring challenge to the new regime that any public figure had had the courage to issue: it recalled the admonition three hundred fifty years earlier by another Metropolitan of Moscow, Philip, to Ivan the Terrible, condemning the tsar's barbarities, for which he paid with his life. It is not quite clear what was on the Patriarch's mind when he spoke out: whether he wanted to arouse the population against the regime or merely to fulfill a moral obligation. Some historians, assuming the former and observing the population's failure to react, conclude that it failed in its purpose.[32] Such judgment ignores not only the atmosphere of unbridled Cheka terror prevailing at the time, but the fact that Tikhon in a subsequent epistle (July 21, 1919) urged Christians under no condition to wreak revenge for the sufferings they had endured at the hands of the regime.[33]

In response, the government placed Tikhon under house arrest. Three months later, in early October, the Soviet press carried a startling message from him: an Epistle instructing the clergy to stay clear of politics, since it was not the Church's mission to incite fratricidal war. In the published version, Christians were enjoined without qualification to obey the Soviet authorities: they were "to do nothing that could justify the suspicion of the Soviet government [and to] submit to its commands."[34] These words evoked great bitterness in the White army, which at this time was approaching Moscow.³⁵ In fact, the text of Tikhon's Epistle had been doctored. The opening of Russian archives makes it possible to ascertain that Tikhon had significantly qualified his call for obedience to the regime by adding that it was due only to the extent that its orders did not "contradict the faith and piety *(vere i blagochest'iu)*."³⁶ Since in the eyes of the Church virtually all of the Communists' actions violated the tenets of Christianity, the injunction—as actually written, not as made public—had a rather hollow ring.

At the same time that it was undermining the economical and juridical position of the Church, the regime also moved against religious faith. Atheist agitation, which blended blasphemy with a carnival atmosphere, was pursued by means of the printed word, caricatures, theatrical performances, and mock religious ceremonies.

On March 1, 1919, Moscow launched a campaign to expose as fraudulent the relics of saints.³⁷ According to the Orthodox faith, the bodies of saints do not decompose after death. Russian churches and monasteries displayed elaborate coffins said to contain perfectly preserved remains of saints: these were popular objects of pilgrimages. When opened on orders of the regime, they turned out to contain either bare skeletons or dummies. Exposure of the relics of St. Sergius of Radonezh, the most revered of national saints, at the St. Sergius Trinity Monastery, created a particular sensation. These disclosures damaged the prestige of the Church among the better-educated. On simple people they seem to have produced the opposite effect, reinforcing their faith by giving rise to tales of wonderful mysteries.³⁸ ("Baryshnia," an old peasant explained to an American visitor, "our holy saints disappeared to heaven and substituted rags and straw for their relics when they found that their tombs were to be desecrated by nonbelievers. It was a great miracle."³⁹)

By the time the Soviet government adopted the New Economic Policy (spring 1921), the Orthodox Church had lost its privileges and properties. Even so, it retained unique status, being the only institution in Soviet Russia (apart from the minuscule Academy of Sciences) outside the Communist Party's control. Strictly speaking, in the eyes of the regime, the "Church" as such did not exist: the state recognized individual religious communities but not a national church hierarchy. For clergymen to assemble for any purpose whatever was seditious. In 1922, referring to one such gathering, *Izvestiia* wrote: "The mere fact of this meeting proves . . . the existence of a special 'church hierarchy' constituting something in the nature of an independent state within Soviet Russia."⁴⁰ It proved nothing of the kind, of course, except to those for whom the state alone had the right to organized activity.

As we will note in the following chapter, for Lenin the relaxation of the state's grip on the economy under the New Economic Policy of 1921 required a corresponding tightening of controls on all other aspects of national life. It is in this context that one has to interpret the offensive he launched against the Orthodox Church in March 1922.

The Church had by then accommodated itself to the new regime and posed to it no threat.[41] But Lenin was an expert at provoking strife, and once he decided to make war on the Church and dismantle what was left of its structure, he had no trouble finding a *casus belli*. He had long perfected the methods of waging civil strife. In this instance, too, he resorted to a coordinated attack from within and without: from within, by exploiting internal dissent in the enemy camp, and from without by producing spurious evidence of "counterrevolutionary" activity. The antichurch campaign of 1922 was meant to destroy, once and for all, what was left of the autonomy of religious bodies—in other words, to carry "October" into the ranks of organized religion, the last relic of the old order. To overcome anticipated resistance, the Fifth Section of the Commissariat of Justice, which was charged with orchestrating the assault, joined forces with the security police.[42]

In 1921, Soviet Russia was struck by famine: according to official figures, by March of 1922, over 30 million people were suffering hunger or actually starving. Various private initiatives were organized to help the famine victims. In July, a group of civic-minded public figures, agrarian experts, physicians, and writers formed, with the government's permission, a committee, popularly known as "Pomgol," to seek foreign assistance that the government found awkward to solicit. Patriarch Tikhon agreed to donate for this purpose church vessels known as "nonconsecrated," most of them made of precious and semiprecious metals. "Consecrated" vessels were not included in the offer because their use for any secular purpose was regarded as sacrilegious.[43] Lenin quickly disposed of such private initiatives, dissolving the committee and arresting its members.[44] He ignored Tikhon's offer, for he had other plans for the Church's assets. Lenin, who even as a youth of 22 had opposed giving humanitarian help to starving peasants in the Volga region during the 1892 famine,[45] had no interest in saving peasants' lives. But he pretended to care in order to force the Church into a position of both un-Christian callousness and defiance of the state by ordering it to do something he knew it could not do, namely turn over consecrated vessels for sale to aid victims of the famine.

The idea seems to have originated with Trotsky, who on January 30, 1922, sent Lenin a proposal to this effect. Trotsky urged that the operation, which was to commence in March, be organized in utmost secrecy.* To lay

---

*TP, II, 670–73. The Communists emulated the French revolutionaries, who in 1791–94 had confiscated the plate of suppressed churches and monasteries and sent it for melting to the mint: J. M. Thompson, *The French Revolution* (Oxford, 1947), 444–45. Trotsky's biographer, Isaac

the foundations for a spurious groundswell of public opinion, the Soviet press began now to carry articles demanding the confiscations of church treasures for the benefit of the hungry.[46] Concurrently, the Party organized mass meetings, which in their resolutions called for the transformation of "gold into bread."[47] On February 23, Trotsky cabled to the provincial authorities a request for no fewer than ten reliable workers and peasants per *guberniia* to be sent to Moscow "who could, in the name of the starving, raise the demand that redundant valuables be converted into help for them."[48] Realizing what lay in store, Tikhon offered to raise money equivalent to the value of the Church's consecrated vessels through voluntary subscriptions and the surrender of additional nonconsecrated vessels, but he was refused.[49] The regime wanted not relief for the hungry but a pretext for breaking the Church.

Throughout February the Communist leaders discussed the strategy and tactics of the coming campaign: apparently, some doubted the wisdom of taking on the Church at a time when Moscow was gaining international recognition.[50] The GPU advised the Central Committee that the confiscation of church valuables might lead to "undesirable disturbances."[51] But Lenin and Trotsky stood their ground: they overcame the opposition and on February 26 an appropriate decree was issued over the signature of Mikhail Kalinin, who occupied the ceremonial post of Chairman of the Central Executive Committee.[52] It instructed local soviets to remove from churches all those objects made of gold, silver, and precious stones the "removal of which cannot substantially affect the interests of the cult," the proceeds to be used to help the starving. The true purpose of the measure was not philanthropic but political; for it was certain to provoke determined resistance from the Church, which Lenin intended to turn against it.[53] The direction of the campaign was entrusted to a commission of the Politburo, chaired by Trotsky.

The timing of this assault was closely calibrated to international events. In October 1921 the Soviet government proposed through Chicherin the convocation of an international conference to resolve the issue of Russia's foreign debts. The Allies accepted the offer, and in February–March 1922 preparations were underway to convene a meeting in Genoa: it was to be the first international gathering to which Soviet Russia was invited. Lenin apparently reasoned that the Allies would not risk jeopardizing repayment of the moneys owed to them for the sake of the Russian Church. If such was his calculation, he turned out to be right.

He was helped by the recklessness of Russian émigré churchmen, headed

---

Deutscher, in *The Prophet Unarmed* (Oxford, 1959), has not a word to say about Trotsky's role in this campaign. Trotsky himself says that among his part-time jobs ("privately and unofficially") was "antireligious propaganda, in which Lenin was very interested." On Stalin's instigation, he was later replaced in this capacity by Iaroslavskii. Lev Trotskii, *Moia zhizn'*, II (Berlin, 1930), 213.

by Antonii Khrapovitskii, who on November 20, 1921, convened a Council in the Yugoslav town of Sremskie Karlovtsy.[54] The most reactionary elements in the Orthodox Church promptly seized control of the Council, politicizing it and calling for the restoration of the monarchy. A resolution addressed to the Allies asked them not to admit Soviet representatives to the Genoa conference and instead to arm Russians to liberate their homeland. Although Tikhon and the hierarchy inside Russia did not approve of these resolutions, they provided a useful tool with which to accuse the entire Orthodox hierarchy, at home and abroad, of counterrevolution.

As expected, Tikhon refused to comply with the decree of February 26. He protested that turning over consecrated vessels to the secular authorities would be sacrilege: he threatened laymen who helped carry it out with excommunication and priests with defrocking.[55] For this act of defiance, he and his followers were charged with being "enemies of the people."[56] In May 1922, Tikhon once again was placed under house arrest.

As forceful seizures got underway, in many localities crowds, some assembled spontaneously, others called out by the priests, offered resistance. In Smolensk, for instance, a multitude filled the cathedral day and night, preventing the removal of valuables.[57] According to a Soviet source, in the first months of the campaign, the Revolutionary Tribunal "reviewed" some 250 cases of defiance.[58] There is a record of 1,414 "bloody excesses" connected with resistance to the removal of church valuables.[59] The GPU and other Soviet sources reported that these incidents were not isolated and spontaneous but directed by a "Black Hundreds counterrevolutionary organization."[60] Disobedience was not confined to the Orthodox Church: in some localities, Catholic and Jewish crowds also fought to prevent the despoiling of their houses of worship.

One incident of such violence occurred in Shuia, a textile town 300 kilometers northeast of Moscow. On Sunday, March 12, worshippers put to flight Communist officials who tried to raid the local church. Three days later, these officials returned in the company of troops equipped with machine guns. An altercation ensued: the soldiers opened fire on a crowd barring their way, killing four or five persons.* These events had a sobering effect on the Communist leadership. A meeting of the Politburo on March 16, in Lenin's and Trotsky's absence, voted to delay further confiscations, and on March 19, instructions were sent to all provincial party organizations to suspend such actions until further notice.[61]

Lenin was ill and resting in the country at this time. He seized on the events in Shuia as justification for an all-out attack on the church hierarchy. In a top secret memorandum dated March 19, dictated over the phone and sent to the Politburo with instructions that no copies be made, he spelled

---

Izvestiia, No. 70/1,509 (March 28, 1922), 1; RTsKhIDNI, F. 5, op. 2, delo 48, list 29. A later internal report stated that no one was killed but that four soldiers and 11 civilians suffered injuries: *ibid.*, list 32.

46. Soldiers removing valuables from Simonov Monastery in Moscow, 1925.

out how the famine and the resistance of the Church to confiscation of vessels could be exploited to serve the government's economic and political ends. This memorandum, first made known from a smuggled version in an émigré publication in 1970 and two decades later reproduced in an official Soviet publication, so well reflects the mentality of the Soviet leader that it deserves to be quoted at length:

> Concerning the events at Shuia, which have already been placed on the Politburo's agenda, it seems to me that it is necessary now to adopt a firm decision in connection with the general plan of the struggle in the given direction. Inasmuch as I doubt that I will be able to attend in person the Politburo meeting of March 20, I shall present my views in writing.

The event in Shuia should be juxtaposed with the information recently sent to the newspapers by Rosta [the Russian Telegraphic Agency] that the Black Hundreds in Petersburg are organizing resistance to the removal of church valuables. Connected with what we know of the illegal appeal of Patriarch Tikhon, it becomes crystal clear that the Black Hundred clergy, headed by its leader, quite deliberately implements a plan to give us decisive battle precisely at this moment.

Apparently at secret consultations of the most influential groups of the Black Hundreds clergy this plan had been thought through and quite firmly adopted. The events in Shuia are but one manifestation of the fulfillment of this plan.

I believe that here our enemy commits a major blunder, trying to engage us in a decisive struggle when it is for him especially hopeless and especially inconvenient. For us, on the contrary, this precise moment is not only uniquely favorable, but offers us a 99 percent chance of shattering the enemy and ensuring for ourselves for many decades the required positions. It is now and only now, when in the regions afflicted by the famine there is cannibalism and the roads are littered with hundreds if not thousands of corpses, that we can (and therefore must) pursue the acquisition of [church] valuables with the most ferocious and merciless energy, stopping at nothing in suppressing all resistance. It is now and only now that the overwhelming majority of the peasantry will either be for us, or, at any rate, not be capable of supporting in any decisive manner that handful of the Black Hundred clergy and reactionary urban burghers who can and wish to test the policy of militant resistance to a Soviet decree.

No matter what, we must accomplish the removal of church valuables in the most decisive and swift manner. In this way we shall assure ourselves of capital worth several hundred million gold rubles (bear in mind the immense wealth of some monasteries). Without such capital it will be utterly unthinkable to carry out governmental work in general [and] in particular to carry out economic construction, and especially to uphold our position at [the] Genoa [conference]. No matter what, we must take into our hands this capital of several hundred million gold rubles (and perhaps even several billion). This can be accomplished successfully only at this time. All considerations indicate that later on we will not succeed, because no other moment except that of desperate hunger will offer us such a mood among the broad peasant masses, which will either assure us of their sympathy, or, at any rate, their neutrality in the sense that victory in the struggle for the removal of the valuables will remain unconditionally and completely on our side. . . .

For this reason I have come to the unequivocal conclusion that we must now give the most decisive and merciless battle to the Black Hundreds clergy and subdue its resistance with such brutality that they will not forget it for decades to come. The campaign for the implementation of this plan I conceive as follows:

Officially, only Comrade Kalinin ought to execute the measures—never, under any circumstances, should Comrade Trotsky appear before the public either in print or in some other manner. . . .

Send to Shuia one of the most energetic, intelligent and efficient members of the All-Russian Central Executive Committee . . . with a verbal instruction conveyed by a member of the Politburo. This instruction ought to call for the arrest in Shuia of as many as possible—no fewer than a few dozen—representatives of the local clergy, local burghers, and local bourgeois on suspicion of direct or indirect involvement in the violent resistance to the decree of the All-Russian Central Executive Committee concerning the removal of church valuables. As soon as this is done, he ought to return to Moscow and make a report to the full Politburo or to two of its authorized members. On the basis of this report, the Politburo will give detailed instructions to the judiciary authorities, also verbal, that the trial of the Shuia rebels who oppose help to the starving should be conducted with maximum swiftness and end with the execution of a very large number of the most influential and dangerous Black Hundreds of Shuia, and, insofar as possible, not only of that city but also of Moscow and several other church centers. . . .

The greater the number of the representatives of the reactionary bourgeoisie and reactionary clergy that we will manage to execute in this affair, the better.[62]

This extraordinary document calls for several comments. Lenin proposes to capitalize on the famine, for which his agrarian policies were largely responsible and which claimed millions of victims, to discredit and break the Church and, along with it, what was left of the "bourgeoisie." Just as in 1918 he had launched a drive against the village under the pretext of feeding the hungry cities,[63] so now the Church was to be crushed under the equally spurious pretext that it refused to aid the hungry village. The wealth extorted from the Church in this manner was to be used not for famine relief, but for the political and economic needs of the regime.* Lenin wanted the courts to be instructed (verbally, so as not to embarrass him and his regime by possible leaks) to sentence many people to death even before they were charged with any crime: it was a precedent and model for the quota system of executions that Stalin would introduce in the late 1930s. Trotsky, whom Lenin placed in charge of the antireligious campaign (he was chairman of the Society of the Godless), because of his Jewish origin was to keep a low profile, lest the government provide ammunition to anti-Semites: the police advised Lenin that workers complained that Jewish houses of worship were exempt from seizures.[64] The official identified with it was to be Kalinin, who looked like a genial rural teacher but was, in fact, a hardened old Bolshevik. Finally, the desperate efforts of the faithful to protect sacred vessels from seizure was depicted as an antistate conspiracy. These beliefs, apparently sincerely held by Lenin, and articulated in a rambling, hysterical

*The American Relief Administration (ARA), which six months later took charge of aid to the starving Russians, contended that there was no need for additional funds to purchase food "since the ARA already had more food and supplies at all ports and on all the lines leading into Russia than the Soviet transportation could handle." Boleslaw Szczesniak, *The Russian Revolution and Religion* (Notre Dame, Ind., 1959), 70.

manner, suggest that by this time his mind was no longer quite balanced.*

The next day the Politburo, composed of Trotsky, Stalin, and Kamenev, along with Molotov, its secretary, resolved to carry out Lenin's instructions:

> Secret supervisory committees are to be set up in the center and the provinces . . . to seize valuables. . . . At the same time, a split should be effected among the clergy, extending state protection to those of the clergy who openly speak in favor of seizures. . . . If possible, well-known priests should not be penalized till the campaign's termination. But they should be officially warned that they will be the first to answer should any excesses occur.[65]

On March 22, the Commission for the Realization of Valuables, meeting under Trotsky's chairmanship, voted to proceed with the requisitions and to dispose of the acquired valuables on foreign markets. The sales were to be arranged by the Soviet delegation to the Genoa Conference, scheduled for April, which enjoyed diplomatic immunity.[66] Krasin had suggested that these valuables not be sold haphazardly but in an organized manner: the confiscated diamonds, he thought, were best marketed though the De Beers Mining company, with whom he had discussed the matter.[67]

The "trials" began almost immediately. On April 13, *Izvestiia* reported that 32 people had been charged with "obstructing" confiscation procedures. In Shuia three defendants were sentenced to death.[68] Elsewhere, the accused were brought before Revolutionary Tribunals on charges of "counterrevolution," attempts to overthrow the Soviet government, which carried a mandatory death sentence.[69] The historian D. A. Volkogonov has seen in Lenin's archive an order from him demanding to be informed on a daily basis of the number of priests who had been shot.[70]

These were the original show trials—carefully staged proceedings in which the verdict was preordained and whose objective it was to humiliate the defendants, and, by their example, to intimidate those who sympathized with their cause. It was a curious instance of life imitating art. In 1919 and the years that followed, Communist propagandists had developed a type of theatrical performance known as *agit-sud,* or "agitational court." At such shows persons and practices odious to the authorities—the "Whites," "kulaks," and "bourgeois," but also Hebrew schools and the Bible—were "tried" and condemned. The proceedings against priests staged in 1922 were such *"agit-sudy"* in all respects but one, namely that the sentences were real. They were rehearsals for Stalin's spectacular mock trials of the 1930s.

---

*Two months later Lenin suffered a stroke, which did not prevent him from carrying out his duties as head of state for another six months, but which seems to have adversely affected his judgment. A doctor who attended him in the later stages of his illness noted that Lenin "frequently displayed signs of strong irritation, which followed a stormy course, accompanied by a sharp influx of blood into the head, dangerous to the patient, the diminution of restraining influences—the natural and unavoidable result of a profound sclerotic lesion of his circulatory system": V. P. Osipov in *KL,* No. 2/23 (1927), 247.

47. Metropolitan Benjamin on trial.

In Moscow there were 54 defendants, both priests and laymen. They were tried between April 26 and May 6, in the theater of the Polytechnic Museum, close to the Lubianka, which accommodated two thousand spectators. Spurious evidence was produced by renegade priests from the so-called "Living Church" (on which more below), that according to canon law under certain conditions the surrender of the consecrated church vessels was not only permitted but mandated. Implementing Lenin's directions, the proceedings were used to demonstrate that the Orthodox Church hierarchy, in conjunction with émigré monarchist circles, had organized a "counter-revolutionary" plot. Since no such plot existed, the defendants had to be punished for efforts to prevent the desecration of religious objects. Eleven of the accused were condemned to death for resisting the government's orders to surrender religious vessels.[71] Six had their death sentences commuted to prison terms: this is said to have been done at the request of Trotskii. The remaining five were executed.[72]

The Moscow trial was followed (June 11–July 5) by similar proceedings in Petrograd: here the defendants numbered 86.* The principal accused was the liberal Metropolitan Benjamin.[73] He was defended by the well-known Jewish attorney Ia. S. Gurovich. The Metropolitan and his codefendants were accused of resisting the decree concerning valuables, permitting "in-

---

*This trial ran concurrently with that of the Socialist-Revolutionary leaders held in Moscow: see below, pp. 403–9.

flammatory" sermons to be preached in the churches of their diocese, and maintaining secret communication with the émigré Church Council at Sremskie Karlovtsy. As star witnesses, the prosecution used two turncoat priests, Vladimir Krasnitskii and Alexander Vvedenskii (later Metropolitan of Moscow), both with close links to the security police. Three witnesses who testified on behalf of the defendants were arrested, following which no more offered to come forward. The trial was staged in what was once the Club of the Nobility in a highly emotional atmosphere. The formal sentences, given the seriousness of the charges, were surprisingly mild: Benjamin was ordered defrocked, as were many of the codefendants. In fact, however, Benjamin and three others were secretly executed.* Reports of the secret executions, which spread quickly, were censored from the press, and foreign correspondents were forbidden to mention them in dispatches.[74]

The charges were devoid of substance and the sentences preordained: as is known from Lenin's memorandum of March 19, party organs instructed the courts what verdicts to render. Soviet judges, operating under the 1922 Criminal Code, could disregard any and all evidence, since the interests of the state were the only criterion of guilt and innocence.[75] The spuriousness of the entire campaign is demonstrated by the fact that Lenin ignored an offer made by the Vatican on May 14, 1922, to redeem for any sum required both Catholic and Orthodox church vessels slated for confiscation.[76] As was also noted at the time, the Communists had in their possession Russian crown jewels, the value of which greatly exceeded that of the church vessels (it was estimated at one billion gold rubles), which could have been sold abroad if aid to the starving had been genuinely intended.†

Most of the violence against the clergy took the form of lynchings and arrests by the security organs, details of which are only sketchily known. There exist harrowing tales of torture and maiming of prominent clerics. Archbishop Andronik of Perm is said to have had his cheeks hollowed, his ears and nose cut off, and his eyes gouged: thus disfigured he was driven through the city and then thrown into the river to drown. Bishop Hermogen of Tobolsk is reported to have been drowned with a rock tied to his neck.[77] Tikhon said in 1920 that to the best of his knowledge, 322 bishops and priests had been executed since 1917.[78] In 1925, shortly before his death, he told an English visitor that about 100 bishops and 10,000

*Regelson, *Tragediia,* 308; Francis McCullagh, *The Bolshevik Persecution of Christianity* (London, 1924), 52; M. Polskii, *Novye mucheniki rossiiskie,* I (Jordanville, N.Y., 1949), 56. The other executed defendants were Archimandrite Sergei (V. P. Shein), a former Duma deputy, and the professors Iu. L. Novitskii and I. M. Kovsharov: Lev Regelson, *Tragediia russkoi tserkvi, 1917–1945* (Paris, 1977), 298–303.

†McCullagh, *Persecution,* 8. In March 1922, Lenin was informed that the authorities had found in the Kremlin Museum *(Oruzheinaia palata)* jewels estimated by experts to be worth at least 300 million gold rubles: RTsKhIDNI, F. 2, op. 2, delo 1165. The Soviet government was prepared in 1923 to sell some of this hoard to pay for German armaments: Rolf-Dieter Müller, *Das Tor zur Weltmacht* (Boppard am Rhein, 1984), 118–19.

priests were in prison or exile.* There exist published lists with the names of 18 murdered or executed bishops. An English journalist learned that the antiChurch campaign cost the lives of 28 bishops and 1,215 priests.[79] Recently released evidence indicates that over 8,000 persons were executed or killed in the course of 1922 in the conflict over church valuables.[80] Among the victims were Jews whom the populace blamed for these outrages and against whom it staged pogroms in Smolensk, Viatka, and several other localities.†

The authorities announced in September 1922 that the drive to collect church valuables had brought in 8 trillion rubles in "money tokens" *(denznaki)* and that the money was used to buy food for the hungry.[81] But the figure was meaningless and the claim a lie. At the end of the year, *Izvestiia* reported and described the loot as "ridiculously small", saying it amounted to 23,997 puds (393 tons) of silver, plus small quantities of gold and pearls: its monetary value was estimated at between 4 and 10 million dollars, the lower figure apparently closer to reality.‡ Very little if any of that money went for famine relief.

The surprising and shocking thing was that these outrages were committed by Russians, who were widely thought to have a deep attachment to their Church, and that the population at large did not rise in protest:

> History must record the fact that, in 1922, Russian Orthodox soldiers plundered churches at the bidding of a Government consisting wholly of atheists and anticlericals. They threw into sacks the chalices to which, ten years ago, they attributed supernatural powers. They tied up priests whom they looked upon, ten years ago, as wonder-workers, able to blast them with a curse. They shot down fellow Christians for attempting to defend their churches; and, lastly, they executed ordained priests of God. It is no use saying that it was Jews, Letts, and Chinamen who did this; the men who did the work were, unfortunately, Russians, and, furthermore, the country as a whole did not express its displeasure by the general insurrection that one would have expected.[82]

*F. A. Mackenzie, *The Russian Crucifixion* (London, n.d.), 84. According to this author, an official list indicated that as of April 1, 1927, 117 metropolitans, archbishops, and bishops were imprisoned or exiled.

†Szczesniak, *Russian Revolution*, 70. The perception of Jewish involvement was exacerbated by the deliberate Bolshevik policy in some instances of sending Jews to despoil churches. "I know of cases," Maxim Gorky wrote to a Jewish publication in New York on May 9, 1922, "of young Jewish Communists being purposely involved in [the persecution of the Church] in order that the philistine and the peasant should see: it is Jews that are ruining monasteries [and] mocking 'holy places.' It seems to me that this was done partly from fear and partly from a clear intent to compromise the Jewish people. It was done by anti-Semites, of whom there are not a few among the Communists": *Novoe russkoe slovo*, No. 15,559 (December 2, 1954), 3.

‡*Izvestiia*, No. 287/1,726 (December 19, 1922), 3, and No. 197/1,636 (September 3, 1922), 4. With silver at the time fetching between 52 and 74 cents an ounce, the loot would have been worth around 8 million dollars. McCullagh (*Persecution*, 8) estimated it at 1,650,000 pounds sterling, which was roughly equivalent. Louis Fischer (*Current History*, July 1923, 594) cited official statistics giving the value at 5 million dollars. According to Walter Duranty (*New York Times*, October 16, 1922, 4) it was "almost impossible" to obtain an accurate figure, but it seemed that "no more than 4 million dollars was realized, probably a good deal less."

48. Inventory of valuables confiscated from churches, 1922.

The campaign against religious organizations was accompanied by a renewed drive against religious belief. In December 1922, using the Komsomol, the government launched an effort to discredit Christmas and the holidays of the other faiths. Mock religious celebrations were hastily staged in the major cities, of which the so-called "Komsomol Christmas" acquired the greatest notoriety. On the eve of Christmas, Komsomol cells received instructions from their central headquarters to "stage mass carnivals" of divinities.[83] During the night of January 6, 1923, and the following day, when the Orthodox celebrated Christmas (according to the old calendar), bands of youths were dispatched into the streets with effigies, to lampoon the religious ceremonies in progress in the churches. The correspondent of *Izvestiia* described the proceedings in Moscow as follows:

God-fearing Moscow philistines saw an unprecedented spectacle. From the Sadovaia to the Square of the Revolution there stretched an unending procession of gods and heathen priests. . . . Here was a yellow Buddha with contorted legs, giving the blessing, exhaustingly cunning and slanted. And the Babylonian Marduk, the Orthodox Virgin, Chinese bonzes, and Catholic priests, the Roman Pope in his yellow tiara blessing the new adepts from his colorful automobile, a Protestant pastor on a high pole. . . . A Russian priest in a typical stole, offering for a small price to remarry anybody. And here is a monk sitting on a black coffin containing a saint's relics: he, too, praises his wares to the undemanding buyer. A Jewish rabbi-cantor with uplifted hands, in an exhausted, mournful voice tells how "the priest had a dog and it ate a piece of meat." The rabbi shows with his hand how large that piece of meat was. "Ah, he killed it. . . ." An orderly column of young girls with flushed faces passes by, fleetingly seen. Frozen steam rises with the sound of the song:

We need no rabbis, we need no priests,
Beat the bourgeois, strangle the kulaks![84]

In the correspondent's judgment, this travesty of one of the holiest days in the Christian calendar was a historic event not only for Moscow, and not only for Soviet Russia, but for mankind.

Similar carnivals were staged in other cities, usually in front of churches during midnight masses. In Gomel, which had a mixed population, a "trial" of Orthodox, Catholic, and Jewish "gods" represented by effigies took place in the theater. The judges, assisted by the audience, condemned them to an auto-da-fé, following which, on Christmas Day, they were ceremoniously burned in the city square.[85]

Measures were taken to discredit in the eyes of Russian children St. Nicholas, the Russian equivalent of Santa Claus, and the angels, the latter accused as symbols used "to enslave the child's mind." To counteract such decadent beliefs, the authorities organized on Christmas Eve theatrical performances that regaled children with "satires on the Lausanne Conference, the Kerensky regime, and bourgeois life abroad."[86]

In the following spring, Easter was subjected to similar treatment. So, later in the year, was Yom Kippur, the most sacred Jewish holiday.[87] Such spectacles, as well as the posters and cartoons that accompanied them, by violating ingrained taboos in a deliberately shocking and vulgar manner, produced an effect not unlike that of pornography.

While the Communist press reported that such productions drew large and enthusiastic crowds, the reality was different. G. P. Fedotoff (Fedotov), a Social-Democrat who later turned to theology, having witnessed the mock Christmas procession in Moscow, wrote that the

> population, and not only the faithful, looked upon this hideous carnival with dumb horror. There were no protests from the silent streets—the years of terror had done their work—but nearly everyone tried to turn off the road when it met this shocking procession. I, personally, as a witness of the Moscow carnival, may certify that there was not a drop of popular pleasure in it. The parade moved along empty streets and its attempts at creating laughter or provocation were met with dull silence on the part of the occasional witnesses.[88]

That this was, indeed, the case is confirmed by the decision of the Party in 1923 to curtail such activities. A resolution adopted by the Twelfth Party Congress held in March of that year demanded that atheists refrain from offending the sensitivities of believers since ridicule only intensified "religious fanaticism."[89] It was a fleeting victory of the Lunacharskii approach over that advocated by Iaroslavskii.

Although the decree on the "Separation of Church and State" granted every citizen the freedom to practice his religion, the holding of religious observances in public places was gradually restricted. It was forbidden even to perform religious rites at funerals. Traditional religious holidays became ordinary working days. They were replaced by secular celebrations, of which there were six: New Year, the anniversaries of Bloody Sunday (January 22) and of the February Revolution (March 12), the day of the Paris Commune (March 10), International Labor Day (May 1), and the anniversary of the October coup (November 7).[90]

1922 saw the appearance of the daily *Bezbozhnik* ("The Godless"), edited by Iaroslavskii, followed in 1923 by a weekly of the same name: the two eventually merged. They published short articles and crude cartoons ridiculing religious beliefs and observances: in the case of Jewish subjects, they resorted to anti-Semitic stereotypes that anticipated the Nazi *Stürmer*. Sympathizers were invited to join the Society of the Godless, formed at the time.

The trials of priests and the antireligious campaigns were only two facets of the atheist drive: they contributed outside pressure. Another aspect of organized atheism was boring from within by pitting the reform-minded Orthodox minority against the conservative establishment and the parish priesthood against the monastic clergy. Such a *divide et impera* strategy, a standard Bolshevik tactic, was mandated by the Politburo's resolution of March 20 calling for "a split [to be] effected among the clergy." In implementing this decision, the authorities relied on elements within the Orthodox Church that for one reason or another opposed its leadership. The Central Committee ordered local party organizations to support the segment of the lower clergy that backed the confiscation of church valuables. "The political task," the message read, "consists in isolating the upper clergy, compromising it on the most concrete issue of help to the starving, and then showing it the stern hand of worker's justice, to the extent that they dare to rise against it."[91]

In line with this directive, the regime created and sponsored a splinter body known as the "Living Church" *(Zhivaia tserkov')*. The idea of splitting the hierarchy seems to have originated with Lunacharskii, who in May 1921 wrote Lenin about Archbishop Vladimir, a renegade priest who had been defrocked for what he called "church Bolshevism." According to Lunacharskii, Vladimir proposed to exploit divisions among the clergy to promote the cause of revolution and reconciliation with the Soviet government.[92] The suggestion was apparently not followed up. Nearly a year later, on March 12, 1922, Trotsky raised the issue once again, proposing to split the Church over the issue of vessels by enrolling pro-Soviet priests to assist in their confiscation. This time the suggestion was accepted by the Politburo the following day.[93] The Living Church was brought into being in late March, first to incriminate the church hierarchy and then to dislodge it from authority.[94] Its composition was diverse. It included bona fide reformers committed to aligning the church with the social changes that had occurred in Russia since 1917. There were also parish clergymen resentful of the monks' exclusive access to higher offices: a central plank in the Living Church's program was allowing married priests to become bishops. And there were ordinary opportunists who accepted bribes from the police for their apostasy.[95] In the latter category were not a few monarchists and adherents of the Black Hundreds: one leader of the Living Church had supported the charge that Jews used Christian blood at the time of the Beilis trial in 1913.[96]

This organization, the clerical equivalent of the Left SRs in 1917–18, was used to carry out a coup in the Church. In mid-May 1922, several priest-collaborators visited Tikhon at the Troitse-Sergeeva Lavra, where he was confined. They demanded that he convoke a Church Council and in the meantime withdraw from all participation in church affairs. This he had to do both because his inflammatory encyclicals were responsible for the death sentences passed on the eleven churchmen tried in Moscow, and because, living under house arrest, he could not fulfill his responsibilities. Tikhon replied that he had never sought the post of Patriarch and would gladly give it up if such was the wish of the Church Council. The same day he wrote Metropolitan Agafangel of Iaroslavl that in view of the prospect of having to stand trial he, Tikhon, could not carry out his obligations and desired him to take charge of the church administration until the Church Council met.[97] The Soviet press falsely reported this action to mean that Tikhon had resigned.[98] When Agafangel made it clear that he would not cooperate with the usurpers, he was prevented from traveling to Moscow to assume his duties; later on, he was arrested and exiled to Siberia. The Patriarch's authority was arrogated by a body calling itself the Higher Church Administration (Vysshee Tserkovnoe Upravlenie), made up of members of the Living Church. On May 20, this organization took over the Patriarch's residence and chancery. It was nothing less than a *coup d'église*. A replica of the defunct Holy Synod of tsarist days, the Higher Church Administration was managed by the Living Church under the nominal authority of the Central Executive Committee of the Soviets, but in fact, under that of the GPU, which established a special department to deal with ecclesiastical matters: church administration thus became a branch of the security police. Objections from abroad against these actions were either ignored or dismissed as impermissible interference in Soviet Russia's internal affairs. Trotsky characterized the protest of the British clergy, headed by the Archbishop of Canterbury, as "having been dictated by narrow caste solidarity, wholly directed against the real interests of the people and the elementary requirements of humanity."[99]

A shrill public campaign was now launched, calling for the abolition of the patriarchate: it sufficiently frightened some bishops that they joined the Living Church. Those who defied the illegitimate hierarchy were arrested and replaced by more compliant clergymen. By August 1922, the Orthodox Church was split: of the 143 bishops, 37 supported the Living Church, 36 opposed it, and the remaining 70 sat on the fence.[100] That month, the Living Church held a congress, one participant in which was V. N. Lvov, the Procurator of the Holy Synod under the Provisional Government and a principal in the Kornilov affair.[101]

Courting martyrdom, Tikhon stood his ground. In December 1922 he anathematized the Higher Church Administration and everyone connected with it as doing the "work of Antichrist" and exhorted Christians to brave death in defense of the true Church.[102] The Patriarchal Church, virtually outlawed, went underground.

The utter subservience of the Living Church to the regime manifested itself in the resolutions of the Second Church Council, which it convened in April 1923 and packed with adherents (of the 430 delegates, 385 represented various branches of the "reforming" movement).[103] The assembly hailed the October 1917 coup as a "Christian creation" for its struggle against capitalism, denied that the Communists persecuted the Church, and voted gratitude to Lenin for his role as "world leader" and "tribune of social truth." The Soviet government, it declared, was the only government in the world that strove to realize "the ideal of the Kingdom of God." Accusing Tikhon of heading a counterrevolutionary plot, it formally deposed him, without granting him a hearing, and abolished the patriarchate. It authorized bishops to marry and widowed priests to remarry.[104]

It was widely expected that in view of the serious charges leveled against him, Tikhon would face trial, and indeed such was the government's intention. But after one month in the GPU prison, he was set free. An internal report by the head of the GPU section charged with overseeing the clergy hints that Tikhon decided to cooperate in order to maintain control over the Church and prevent a disastrous split.[105] Henceforth he was utterly compliant and signed any document placed before him. On June 16, 1923, he addressed a letter to the authorities, almost certainly written by someone else, in which he admitted to charges that had led to his detention and recanted his "anti-Soviet" past. He also withdrew the anathema on the Living Church, pronounced the previous December, claiming it to have been a forgery.[106] As a reward, all charges against him were dropped and the patriarchal churches were allowed to reopen.

Tikhon died in April 1925 of heart failure, leaving a testament in which he praised the Soviet state for ensuring full freedom of religion and urged Christians to support it because it was a "stable and unshakable," "genuinely popular worker-peasant government."[107]

A Russian theologian has suggested that for all its revolutionary posturing, the Living Church really represented "the old, traditional ecclesiastical order,"[108] reviving the tradition of church subservience to the state. Seen in this light, it was the Patriarchal church that stood for innovation in that it wanted a church that was free and self-governing.

The Living Church was brought into being for one purpose only: to divide and subvert the established Church. Once it had accomplished this objective, and this happened following Tikhon's capitulation, it lost its utility. Aware that it enjoyed virtually no favor with the population, the authorities withdrew their support. Soon the Living Church faded from the picture. It disappeared in the early 1930s, when its leaders were arrested.

Of the other members of the Christian community, the Sectarians (members of sects not linked to the Orthodox Church, like the Baptists) enjoyed relatively the most tolerant treatment. This happened because the Bolsheviks believed that having been oppressed by tsarism and the Orthodox establishment, they would be more sympathetic to their regime.[109]

Although many Christians were convinced that their persecution was the work of Jews, and calls for resistance by clergymen were in some localities accompanied by anti-Semitic diatribes, Jewish religious institutions also suffered from Bolshevik antireligious policies. It is impossible, of course, to measure the anguish of adherents of diverse faiths when forbidden to practice their religion. But a case can be made that in some ways Jews suffered more from the Bolshevik policies than Christians, because their religious institutions not only performed rituals and educated youth but served as the center of Jewish life:

> The assault on Jewish religious life was particularly harsh and pervasive because a Jew's religious beliefs and observances infused every aspect of his daily life and were invested with national values and feelings. . . . Family relations, work, prayer, study, recreation, and culture were all part of a seamless web, no element of which could be disturbed without disturbing the whole.[110]

State-sponsored atheism tore the very fabric of social and cultural life of that vast majority of Jews who resided in small towns and led traditional lives. An Orthodox Russian, unable to attend church services, still had his Pushkin, Tolstoy, and Chekhov; an observant Jew cut off from the Torah, the prophets, and the Talmud was left in a cultural no-man's land.

The decree of January 20, 1918, on relations between church and state initially affected Jews less harshly than Orthodox Christians because they never received state subsidies and had no compulsory religious education in schools. Nor did synagogues have many articles of value which the regime could appropriate. Nevertheless, under the terms of this decree, synagogues with their contents were as much subject to confiscation as churches. Under instructions of 1918–19 it was enough for the local soviets to determine that housing for residential, medical, and educational purposes was in short supply or else that the "masses of the people" so desired, for houses of prayer to be converted to secular uses.[111] In practice, as was the case with churches, most synagogues were left intact until 1922.

When in early 1922 the time was judged opportune for a frontal attack on organized religion, the Bolsheviks employed toward the Jewish community the proven *divide et impera* tactics. Whereas in the campaign against the Orthodox Church they exploited the animosity between reform-minded and conservative clerics, as well as between parish priests and monks, in the case of Jews they capitalized on the hostility of Jewish socialists toward rabbis and synagogues. In this they relied mainly on the Bund, the Jewish section of Social-Democracy. After the February Revolution the Bundists found themselves rejected alike by the masses of their people, who followed traditional observances, and by the secularized elements who embraced Zionism. Although they initially opposed the October coup, in their isolation they gravitated toward the Bolsheviks. During the 1920s they were the main agent the regime used to break up the Jewish community. They persecuted their own religion with exceptional zeal in order to prove the anti-Semites wrong. A Bundist convert to Communism argued as follows:

> If the Russian people should once get it into their minds that we are partial to the Jews, it would go hard with Jews. It is for the sake of Jews that we are absolutely objective in our dealings with the clergy—Jewish and non-Jewish alike. The danger is that the masses may think that Judaism is exempt from antireligious propaganda and, therefore, it rests with the Jewish Communists to be even more ruthless with rabbis than non-Jewish Communists are with priests.*

Observing the frenzy with which Jewish Communists profaned their religion, one Jew remarked: "It would be nice to see the Russian Communists tear into the monasteries and the holy days as the Jewish Communists do to Yom Kippur."[112]

As an analogue of the Living Church, the regime created "Jewish Sections" (Evsektsii) of the Russian Communist Party. Overcoming his aversion to Jewish nationalism (for he did not regard Jews as a true nation), Lenin in the fall of 1918 consented, as a matter of propagandistic expediency, to the establishment of special branches of the Russian Communist Party to carry his revolution to the Jewish masses. Their mission has been described as "the destruction of traditional Jewish life, the Zionist movement, and Hebrew culture."[113] They were mostly staffed with ex-members of the Bund, which in 1920 adopted the Communist program and in March 1921 merged with the Communist Party.[114]

---

*Boris D. Bogen, *Born a Jew* (New York, 1930), 329. The speaker, Esther Frumkin, was arrested in 1938 and five years later perished in a Soviet concentration camp: Zvi Gitelman, *A Century of Ambivalence* (New York, 1988), 110.

The Evsektsii opened their offensive in the summer of 1919 following an order of the Central Jewish Commissariat abolishing *kehillas,* the traditional organs of Jewish self-government. The resistance to this decree was fierce and in some cases successful, since here and there *kehillas* survived to the end of the 1920s. In time, every Jewish cultural and social organization came under assault. In 1922, while mounting its offensive against the Orthodox Church, the Party struck at Jewish religious practices. The attack was inspired and carried out by Jews: "the Evsektsiia jealously guarded its monopoly over the persecution of Jewish religion."[115] There were the usual meetings and spectacles, supposedly spontaneous, in fact highly organized, demanding the closing of religious schools; disruptions of services during High Holidays; publications deriding Jewish observances, closely modeled on standard anti-Semitic smut; and mock "trials" of religious schools and practices.

> On Rosh Hashanah, 1921, the Jewish religion was "tried" in Kiev, ironically, in the same auditorium where the Beilis trial had been held. The "judges" saw a strange array of "witnesses": a "rabbi" testified solemnly that he taught religion in order to keep the masses ignorant and subservient; an obese "bourgeois," bedecked in glittering jewelry, testified to the alliance between the exploiters and Judaism. The "prosecutor" . . . demanded a "sentence of death for the Jewish religion." A Hebrew teacher who rose from the audience to defend Judaism was arrested on the spot. The "judges" returned from their chambers and, to no one's surprise, announced a death verdict.[116]

"Red Haggadahs" were published to celebrate the "deliverance" of Jews from capitalism. In Gomel in July 1922, rabbis who resisted the closing of heders (religious schools) were hailed before a court.[117]

The earliest case of a synagogue seizure seems to have occurred in 1921 in Vitebsk, when local authorities, having decided that the city had more than enough synagogues, ordered some closed and turned over to them. Observant Jews surrounded the condemned synagogues, but they were driven off by cavalry, following which the structures were transformed into a Party "university" and club, a kitchen, and a dormitory.[118] Subsequently, large, so-called "choral" synagogues were confiscated in Minsk, Gomel, and Kharkov and converted into Communist centers, clubs, and restaurants.[119]

> The pattern was almost the same everywhere. The Evsektsiia would initiate meetings of "workers," mostly non-Party members of trade unions, at their places of work. Resolutions would be adopted "unanimously," in the name of "all the toilers," they would request the conversion of the synagogue, which was claimed to be empty and of no further use, "serving as a nest of counter-revolution" or "as a speculators' club," into a workers' club or some other institution. The local authorities would, of course, listen to these "wishes of the toilers" and hasten to satisfy them.[120]

Synagogues were robbed of such valuables as they possessed: Torahs, removed from the Holy Arks, were piled up for disposal; in some localities, houses of prayer were vandalized.

The Communists had less success splitting the Jewish religious establishment than the Orthodox. Nothing corresponding to the Living Church emerged in the rabbinate. Of the one thousand rabbis in Soviet Russia, only six expressed sympathy for Communism.[121] Instances of Jewish clergymen incriminating each other, such as occurred in the Orthodox Church, were unknown.

After the resolution of the Twelfth Party Congress demanding greater respect for the sensitivities of believers, the seizures of synagogues, as of churches, stopped. But not for long. The antireligious drive resumed in 1927, and by the end of the 1930s no functioning synagogues remained. Severe punishments awaited Jews who practiced religion in private.

A singular disability imposed on Jews was the prohibition on the use and teaching of Hebrew, the language of religious services but also of the Zionist movement. The Soviet authorities initially saw no harm in the language, but they were persuaded by Evsektsiia Communists that it was the speech of the Jewish "bourgeoisie." In 1919, Hebrew publishing houses were nationalized. Soon all traces of Hebrew publications disappeared. By the mid-1920s, Hebrew was outlawed and taught only in clandestine private schools. Yiddish, which the Bundists of the Evsektsiia regarded as the true speech of the masses, was declared the national language of Jews, a language indeed widely used in everyday conversation but hardly a key to high culture.

The Evsektsii used their newly won power to settle scores with their

49. Antireligious play *Heder*: the letters on the actors' backsides spell "kosher."

50. Torah scrolls from desecrated synagogues.

Zionist rivals. To obtain support of the authorities, who had no views in this matter, they pronounced Jews who wished to emigrate to Palestine to cultivate the soil "bourgeois" and "counterrevolutionary." The zeal with which the Communist authorities persecuted Zionists from 1919 onward was inspired by this internecine Jewish quarrel: for although Lenin rejected the idea of Jewish nationhood and the Zionist ideology based on it, in the first year of his regime he did not bother the Zionists. The persecution began under the influence of Bundists who saw a chance to destroy a competing movement with an incomparably larger following. In September 1919, the Evsektsii shut down the Zionist Central Office and the following year got the Cheka to arrest and exile numerous Zionists. In 1922, the campaign resumed with arrests and trials in Russian and Ukrainian cities. In September 1924, police raids resulted in the detention of several thousand Zionist activists. The movement managed, nevertheless, to survive underground for several years longer, so deep were its roots.

Ultimately, the Evsektsii went the way of the Living Church, being liquidated in December 1929 on the grounds that there was no need to maintain separate organizations for the Jewish "proletariat."[122] Their functionaries were "purged" in 1937 and disappeared from view.[123] The Chairman, Semën Dimanshtein, was shot.

The Catholic Church also did not escape persecution. On March 21, 1923, the authorities opened in Petrograd a trial of Catholic priests, headed by the Polish Archbishop Jan Cieplak, and 15 priests, most of them Poles as well. They were charged with "counterrevolution" and resisting the removal of vessels.[124] This particular show was managed by Nicholas Krylenko, the Deputy Prosecutor of the Russian Republic who had the previous year indicted the Socialists-Revolutionaries. (See below, page 406.) Krylenko accused the defendants of seeking to elevate canon law above the law of the state and providing religious instruction to youth. Archbishop Cieplak and Msgr. Constantin Budkiewicz, the canon of the Church of St. Catherine in Petrograd, were sentenced to death. Bowing to foreign protests, especially strong in Poland, which declared the trial a violation of the Treaty of Riga guaranteeing the religious rights of Poles in Soviet Russia, Moscow relented and commuted the archbishop's sentence to a prison term. It eventually set him free and allowed him to go to Poland. Msgr. Budkiewicz, however, was executed.

Of the three principal religions represented in the Soviet state, the Muslims fared relatively the best. Their comparatively lenient treatment was due entirely to political considerations, namely the fear of alienating the colonial nations whose support was critical to the strategy of the Comintern, since the Middle East Muslims were counted upon to undermine "imperialism." Sultan-Galiev, the leading Communist expert on the subject, cautioned Moscow that antireligious propaganda among Muslims had to be conducted in a very circumspect manner, not only because of their strong attachment to the faith but also because they regarded the Muslim community as an "undivided whole" and perceived an attack on one as an attack on all.[125] There also existed the danger that Russian Muslims might view anti-Islamic propaganda as a revival of Christian missionary activity of prerevolutionary days.[126]

Guided by such considerations, the Communist authorities refrained from directly assaulting Islamic institutions. In the constitutions given the Soviet Muslim republics, Islam was treated much more indulgently than were either Christianity or Judaism in the three Slavic republics. The freedom to propagate atheism was not stipulated and mullahs received full civil rights, including the right to vote. Religious instruction of youth was permitted and religious schools were allowed to keep their properties. Islamic courts retained the authority to judge both civil and criminal suits. These privileges the Muslim clergy retained until the late 1920s.[127]

The effect that persecution had on religious sentiments and practices during the first decade of Communist rule is difficult to assess. There is a great deal of circumstantial evidence, however, that people continued to observe religious rituals and customs, treating the Communists as they would heathen conquerors. Although the observance of religious holidays had been outlawed, the prohibition could not be enforced. As early as 1918 workers received permission to celebrate Easter provided they did not absent themselves from work for more than five days.[128] Later on, the authorities acquiesced in the suspension of work on Christmas under both the old and new calendars.[129] There are reports of religious processions *(krestnye khody)* in the capital as well as in provincial towns. In the rural districts, religious rituals were universally observed. Ignoring Soviet legislation, the peasants insisted on regarding as legitimate only marriages performed by a priest.[130]

Religious fervor, which, along with monarchic sentiments, had perceptibly ebbed in 1917, revived in the spring of 1918, when many Christians courted martyrdom by demonstrating, holding protest meetings, and fasting. The fervor increased with each year: in 1920,

> The churches filled with worshippers: among them there was not that predominance of women that could be noted before the revolution. Confession acquired particular importance. . . . Church holidays attracted immense crowds. Church life in 1920 was fully restored and perhaps even exceeded the old, prerevolutionary one. Without a doubt, the inner growth of church self-consciousness among Russian believers attained a height unknown during the preceding two centuries.[131]

Tikhon confirmed this judgment in an interview with an American journalist the same year, saying that "the influence of the church on the lives of the people was stronger than ever in all its history."[132] Confirming these impressions, one well-informed observer concluded in 1926 that the church had emerged victorious from its conflict with the Communists: "The only thing the Bolsheviks had achieved was to loosen the hierarchy and split the church."[133]

But ahead of it lay trials such as no church had ever endured.

8

NEP: The False Thermidor

Thermidor" was the month of July in the French revolutionary calendar when Jacobin rule came to an abrupt end, yielding to a more moderate regime. To Marxists the term symbolized the triumph of the counterrevolution, which ultimately led to the restoration of the Bourbon monarchy. It was a development they were determined at all costs to prevent. When, in March 1921, confronting economic collapse and massive rebellions, Lenin felt compelled to make a radical turnabout in economic policy resulting in significant concessions to private enterprise, a course that came to be known as the New Economic Policy (NEP), it was widely believed in the country and abroad that the Russian Revolution, too, had run its course and entered its Thermidorian phase.[1]

The historical analogy turned out to be inapplicable. The most conspicuous difference between 1794 and 1921 lay in the fact that whereas in France the Jacobins had been overthrown in the Thermidor and their leaders executed, in Russia it was the Soviet equivalent of the Jacobins who initiated and carried out the new, moderate course. They did so on the understanding that the shift was temporary: "I ask you, comrades, to be clear," said Zinoviev in December 1921, "that the New Economic Policy is only a temporary deviation, a tactical retreat, a clearing of the land for a new and decisive attack of labor against the front of international capitalism."[2]

Lenin liked to compare NEP to the Brest-Litovsk treaty, which in its day had also been mistakenly seen as a surrender to German "imperialism" but was only a step backward: however long it would last, it would not be "forever."[3]

Secondly, unlike the French Thermidor, the NEP limited liberalization to economics: "As the ruling party," Trotsky said in 1922, "we can allow the speculator in the economy, but we do not allow him in the political realm."[4] Indeed, in a deliberate effort to prevent the limited capitalism tolerated under the NEP from sliding into a full-scale capitalist restoration, the regime accompanied it with intensified political repression. It was in 1921–23 that Moscow crushed what remained of rival socialist parties, systematized censorship, extended the competence of the secret police, launched a campaign against the church, and tightened controls over domestic and foreign Communists.

The tactical nature of the retreat was not generally understood at the time. Communist purists were outraged by what they saw as the betrayal of the October Revolution, while opponents of the regime sighed with relief that the dreadful experiment was over. During the last two years of his conscious life, Lenin repeatedly had to defend the NEP and insist that the revolution was on course. Deep in his heart, however, he was haunted by a sense of defeat. The attempt to build Communism in a country as backward as Russia, he realized, had been premature, and had to be postponed until the requisite economic and cultural foundations were in place. Nothing went as planned: "The car is out of control," he let slip once, "a man drives and the car does not go where he steers it, but where it is steered by something illegal, something unlawful, something that comes from God knows where."[5] The internal "enemy," acting in an environment of economic collapse, confronted his regime with a graver danger than the combined armies of the Whites: "On the economic front, with the attempt of transition to Communism, we have suffered by the spring of 1921 a defeat that was more serious than any inflicted on us by Kolchak, Denikin, or Pilsudski, far more serious, far more basic and dangerous."[6] It was an admission that he had been mistaken in insisting as early as the 1890s that Russia was fully capitalist and ready for socialism.[7]

Until March 1921, the Communists tried and in some measure succeeded in placing the national economy under state control. Later this policy came to be known as "War Communism"—Lenin himself first used this term in April 1921 as he was abandoning it.[8] It was a misnomer coined to justify the disastrous consequences of economic experimentation by the alleged exigencies of the Civil War and foreign intervention. Scrutiny of contemporary records, however, leaves no doubt that these policies were, in fact, not so much emergency responses to war conditions as an attempt as

51. Peasant "bag men" peddling grain.

rapidly as possible to construct a Communist society.[9] War Communism involved the nationalization of the means of production and most other economic assets, the abolition of private trade, the elimination of money, the subjection of the national economy to a comprehensive plan, and the introduction of forced labor.[10]

These experiments left Russia's economy in shambles. In 1920–21, compared to 1913, large-scale industrial production fell by 82 percent, worker productivity by 74 percent, and the production of cereals by 40 percent.[11] The cities emptied as their inhabitants fled to the countryside in search of food: Petrograd lost 70 percent of its population, Moscow over 50 percent; the other urban and industrial centers also suffered depletions.[12] The non-agricultural labor force dropped to less than half of what it had been when the Bolsheviks took power: from 3.6 to 1.5 million. Workers' real wages declined to one-third of the level of 1913–14.* A hydralike black market, ineradicable because indispensable, supplied the population with the bulk of consumer goods. Communist policies had succeeded in ruining the world's fifth-largest economy and depleting the wealth accumulated over centuries of "feudalism" and "capitalism." A contemporary Communist economist called the economic collapse a calamity "unparalleled in the history of mankind."[13]

The Civil War ended, for all practical purposes, in the winter of 1919–

---

*E. G. Gimpelson, *Sovetskii rabochii klass, 1918–1920 gg.* (Moscow, 1974), 80; Akademiia Nauk SSSR, Institut Ekonomiki, *Sovetskoe narodnoe khoziaistvo v 1921–1925 gg.* (Moscow, 1960), 531, 536. Closer scrutiny of these statistics reveals that in 1920 the Soviet state had only some 932,000 industrial workers, because more than one-third of the employees counted as workers were in fact artisans working alone or with the help of a single assistant, often a family member: Gimpelson, *loc. cit.,* 82, and *Izmeneniia sotsial'noi struktury sovetskogo obshchestva: Oktiabr' 1917–1920* (Moscow, 1976), 258.

20, and if war needs had been the driving force behind these policies, now would have been the time to give them up. Instead, the year that followed the crushing of the White armies saw the wildest economic experiments, such as the "militarization" of labor and the elimination of money. The government persevered with forcible confiscations of peasant food "surplus." The peasants responded by hoarding, reducing the sown acreage, and selling produce on the black market in defiance of government prohibitions. Since the weather in 1920 happened to be unfavorable, the meager supply of bread dwindled still further. It was now that the Russian countryside, until then relatively well off compared to the cities in terms of food supplies, began to experience the first symptoms of famine.

The repercussions of such mismanagement were not only economic but also social: they eroded still further the thin base of Bolshevik support, turning followers into enemies and enemies into rebels. The "masses," whom Bolshevik propaganda had been telling that the hardships they had endured in 1918–19 were the fault of the "White Guards" and their foreign backers, expected the end of hostilities to bring back normal conditions. The Civil War had to some extent shielded the Communists from the unpopularity of their policies by making it possible to justify them as militarily necessary. This explanation could no longer be invoked once the Civil War was over:

> The people now confidently looked forward to the mitigation of the severe Bolshevik regime. It was expected that with the end of the Civil War the Communists would lighten the burdens, abolish war-time restrictions, introduce some fundamental liberties, and begin the organization of a more normal life. . . . Most unfortunately, these expectations were doomed to disappointment. The Communist state showed no intention of loosening the yoke.[14]

It now began to dawn even on those willing to give the Bolsheviks the benefit of the doubt, that they had been had, that the true objective of the new regime was not improving their lot but holding on to power, and that to this end it was prepared to sacrifice their well-being and even their very lives. This realization produced a national rebellion unprecedented in its dimensions and ferocity. The end of one Civil War led immediately to the outbreak of another: having defeated the White armies, the Red Army now had to battle partisan bands, popularly known as "Greens" but labeled by the authorities "bandits," made up of peasants, deserters, and demobilized soldiers.[15]

In 1920 and 1921, the Russian countryside from the Black Sea to the Pacific was the scene of uprisings that in numbers involved and territory affected greatly eclipsed the famous peasant rebellions of Stenka Razin and Pugachev under tsarism.[16] Its true dimensions cannot even now be established, because the relevant materials have not yet been properly studied.

The Communist authorities have assiduously minimized its scope: thus, according to the Cheka, in February 1921, there occurred 118 peasant risings.[17] In fact, there were hundreds of such uprisings, involving hundreds of thousands of partisans. Lenin was in receipt of regular reports from this front of the Civil War, which included detailed maps covering the entire country, indicating that vast territories were in rebellion.[18] Occasionally, Communist historians give us a glimpse of the dimensions of this other Civil War, conceding that some "bands" of "kulaks" numbered 50,000 and more rebels.[19] An idea of the extent and savagery of the fighting can be obtained from official figures of the losses suffered by the Red Army units engaged against the rebels. According to recent information, the number of Red Army casualties in the campaign of 1921–22, which were waged almost exclusively against peasants and other domestic rebels, came to 237,-908.[20] The losses among the rebels were almost certainly as high and probably much higher.

Russia had known nothing like it, because in the past peasants had traditionally taken up arms against landowners, not against the government. Just as the tsarist authorities had labeled peasant disorders *kramola* (sedition), so the new authorities called them "banditry." But resistance was not confined to peasants. More dangerous still, even if less violent, was the hostility of industrial labor. The Bolsheviks had already lost most of the support they had enjoyed among industrial labor in October 1917 by the spring of 1918.[21] While fighting the Whites they had managed, with the active help of the Mensheviks and SRs, to rally the workers by playing on the fear of a monarchist restoration. Once the Whites had been defeated, however, and the danger of a restoration no longer existed, the workers abandoned the Bolsheviks in droves, shifting to every conceivable alternative, from the extreme left to the extreme right. In March 1921, Zinoviev told the delegates to the Tenth Party Congress that the mass of workers and peasants belonged to no party, and a good portion of those who were politically active favored the Mensheviks or the Black Hundreds.[22] Trotsky was so shocked by the suggestion that, as he interpreted it, "one part of the working class muzzles the remaining 99 percent," that he asked that Zinoviev's remarks be struck from the record.[23] But the facts were irrefutable: in 1920–21, except for its own cadres, the Bolshevik regime had the whole country against it, and even the cadres were rebelling. Had not Lenin himself described the Bolsheviks as but a drop of water in the nation's sea?[24] And the sea was raging.

They survived this national revolt by a combination of repression, enforced with unrestrained brutality, and concessions embodied in the New Economic Policy. But they also benefited from two objective factors. One was the disunity of the enemy: the second Civil War consisted of a multitude of individual uprisings without a common leadership or program.

Flaring up spontaneously, now here, now there, they were no match for the professionally directed and well-equipped Red Army. The other factor was the rebels' inability to conceive of political alternatives, for neither the striking workers nor the mutinous peasants thought in political terms. The same applied to the numerous "Green" movements.[25] A characteristic trait of the peasant mind—an incapacity to conceive government as something capable of being changed—survived the Revolution and all its revolutionary changes.[26] The workers and peasants were very unhappy with what the Soviet government did; that there was a connection between what it did and what it was eluded them, exactly as it had under tsarism, when they had turned a deaf ear to radical and liberal agitation. For this reason, now, as then, they could be appeased by having their immediate grievances satisfied while everything else remained in place. This was the essence of the NEP: to purchase political survival with economic handouts that could be taken back once the population had been pacified. Bukharin put it bluntly: "We are making economic concessions to avoid political concessions."[27] It was a practice learned from the tsarist regime, which had protected its autocratic prerogatives by buying off its main potential challenger, the gentry, with economic favors.[28]

C ommunism affected the rural population in contradictory ways.[29] The distribution to the communes of private land enlarged allotments, and reduced the number of both rich and poor in favor of "middle" peasants, which satisfied the egalitarian propensities of the muzhik. Much of what the peasant had gained, however, he lost to runaway inflation, which robbed him of his savings. He was also subjected to merciless exactions of food "surpluses" and forced to bear numerous labor burdens, of which the duty to cut and cart lumber was the most onerous. Throughout the Civil War, the Bolsheviks waged intermittent warfare on the village, which passively and actively resisted food requisitions.

Culturally, Bolshevism had no influence on the village. The peasants, for whom severity was the hallmark of a true government, respected Communist authority and adapted to it: centuries of serfdom had taught them how to appease and, at the same time, outwit their masters. Angelica Balabanoff noted with surprise "how quickly they had picked up Bolshevik terminology and newly coined phrases and how well they understood the various articles of the new legislation. They seemed to have lived with it all their lives."[30] They adjusted to the new authority as they would to a foreign invader, as their forebears had done under the Tatars. The meaning of the Bolshevik Revolution, the slogans the Bolsheviks propagated, however, remained for them a mystery not worth solving. Investigations by Communist scholars in 1920s found the postrevolutionary village self-contained and closed to outsiders, living, as it always had done, according to its own unwritten rules. Communist presence was hardly visible: such party cells as managed to establish themselves in the countryside were staffed principally with people from the cities. Antonov-Ovseenko, whom Moscow sent in early 1921 to pacify the rebellious Tambov province, in a confidential report to Lenin wrote that the peasants identified Soviet authority with "flying visits by commissars or plenipotentiaries" and food-requisitioning units: they "have become accustomed to viewing the Soviet government as something extraneous, something that does nothing but issue commands, that administers with great zeal but little economic sense."[31]

Literate peasants ignored Communist publications, preferring to read religious and escapist literature.[32] Only the faintest echoes of foreign events reached the village, and those that did were twisted and misunderstood. The muzhiks showed little interest in who governed Russia, although by 1919 observers noted signs of nostalgia for the old regime.[33] Hence it is not surprising that the peasant revolts against the Communists had negative objectives: "[The rebels] aimed not to march on Moscow so much as to cut themselves off from its influence."*

Rural unrest sputtered throughout 1918 and 1919, forcing Moscow to commit major military forces to contain it. At the height of the Civil War, vast areas of the country were under the control of Green bands, which blended anti-Communist, anti-Jewish, and anti-White sentiments with ordinary brigandage. In 1920 these smoldering fires exploded in a conflagration.

The most violent of the anti-Communist jacqueries broke out in Tambov, a relatively prosperous agricultural province with little industry, 350 kilometers southeast of Moscow.[34] Before the Bolshevik coup it had produced up to 60 million puds (one million tons) of grains annually, close to one-third of which was normally shipped abroad. In 1918–1920, Tambov experienced the full brunt of forcible food exactions. This is how Antonov-Ovseenko described the causes behind the outbreak of "banditry" there:

> The requisition assessment for 1920–1921, though reduced by half as against that of the year before, proved to be entirely excessive. With huge areas unsown and an exceedingly poor harvest, a considerable part of the province lacked enough bread to feed itself. According to the data of the commissions of experts of the Guberniia Supply Committee there were 4.2 puds of grain per head (after the deduction of seed grain but with no deduction for fodder). In 1909–1913, consumption had averaged . . . 17.9 puds and, in addition, 7.4 puds of fodder. In other words, in the Tambov province last year the local harvest hardly met one-quarter of the requirements. Under the assessment, the province was to deliver 11 million puds of grain and 11 million puds of potatoes. Had the peasants fulfilled the

---

*Orlando Figes, *Peasant Russia, Civil War* (Oxford, 1989), 322–23. An exception was the leader of the Tambov peasant insurgents, Antonov (see below).

52. Alexander Antonov.

assessment one hundred percent, they would have been left with 1 pud of grain and 1.6 puds of potatoes per person. Even so, the assessment was fulfilled almost fifty percent. Already by January [1921], half the peasantry was starving.[35]

The rebellion broke out spontaneously in August 1920 in a village near the city of Tambov that refused to surrender grain to a requisition team, killed several of its members, and fought off reinforcements.[36] In anticipation of a punitive detachment, the village armed itself with such weapons as it had on hand: some guns, but mainly pitchforks and clubs. Villages nearby joined. The rebels emerged victorious from ensuing encounters with the Red Army. Encouraged by their success, the peasants marched on Tambov, their mass swelling as they neared the provincial capital. The Bolsheviks brought in reinforcements, and in September counterattacked, burning rebellious villages and executing captured partisans. The insurrection might have ended then and there had it not been for the appearance of a charismatic leader in the person of Alexander Antonov.

Antonov was a Socialist-Revolutionary, the son of either an artisan or a metal worker, who in 1905-07 had participated in robberies ("expropriations") organized by his party to replenish its coffers. Caught and convicted, he was sentenced to hard labor in Siberia.[37] In 1917 he returned home and joined the Left SRs. Subsequently he collaborated with the Bolsheviks, but broke with them in the summer of 1918 in protest against their agrarian policies. For the next two years, he staged terrorist acts against Bolshevik functionaries, for which he was sentenced to death in absentia. He managed to elude the authorities and soon became a popular hero. He acted on his own with a small band of followers, under SR slogans, although he no longer maintained a connection with that party.

Antonov reappeared in September 1920 and took charge of the peasants, who had lost heart after failing to capture the city of Tambov. An able organizer, he formed partisan units that carried out hit-and-run attacks on collective farms and railway junctions. The authorities proved unable to cope with such tactics not only because the attacks came at the most unexpected places (sometimes Antonov's men disguised themselves in Red Army uniforms), but because after each such operation the guerrillas returned home and melted into the mass of peasants. Antonov's followers had no formal program: their purpose was to "smoke out" the Communists from the countryside as they once used to "smoke out" landlords. Here and there, as in all opposition movements of the time, anti-Semitic slogans were heard. The Tambov SRs at this time formed a Union of Toiling Peasants, which produced a platform calling for political equality for all citizens, personal economic liberty, and the denationalization of industry. But it is doubtful that this platform meant anything to the peasants, who really wanted two things only: an end to food requisitions and the freedom to dispose of their surplus. Suspicions have been voiced that the platform was tacked on by SR intellectuals who could not conceive of acting without a formal ideology: "Words came as an afterthought" to deeds.[38] Even so, the Union helped the rebels by organizing village committees, which recruited for the partisans.

By the end of 1920, Antonov had up to 8,000 followers, most of them mounted. In early 1921, he went over to conscription, by which means he increased his force to somewhere between 20,000 and 50,000—the number is in dispute. Even at the more modest estimate, it was comparable to the force raised by Russian history's most famous peasant rebels, Razin and Pugachev. Patterned on the Red Army, it was divided into 18 or 20 "regiments."[39] Antonov organized good intelligence and communications networks, assigned political commissars to combat units, and enforced strict discipline. He continued to avoid direct encounters, preferring quick surprise raids. The center of his rebellion was the southeastern part of Tambov province, but it spilled over, without igniting comparable risings, into the adjoining provinces of Voronezh, Saratov, and Penza.[40] Antonov succeeded in cutting the railroad line that carried the confiscated grain to the center; such grain as he did not need, he distributed to peasants.[41] In areas under his control, he abolished Communist institutions and killed captured Communists, often after brutal tortures: the number of his victims is said to have exceeded one thousand. By such methods he managed to sweep from large areas of Tambov province all traces of Communist authority. His ambitions were grander, however, for he issued appeals to the Russian people to join him and march on Moscow to liberate the country from its oppressors.[42]

53. Captured Antonov partisans.

Moscow's initial reaction (August 1920) was to place the province under a state of siege. In public pronouncements, the government described the rebels as "bandits" acting at the behest of the SR Party. It knew better: in internal communications, Communist officials conceded that the uprising was of spontaneous origin and ignited by resistance to requisition teams. Although many local SRs did offer support, the central organs of the party repudiated any connection with the rebellion: the SR Organization Bureau described it as a "semi-bandit movement," and the party's Central Committee forbade its members to have any dealings with it.[43] The Cheka, however, used the Tambov uprising as a pretext for arresting every SR activist it could lay its hands on.

When it became apparent that the regular army could not cope, Moscow delegated Antonov-Ovseenko to Tambov in late February 1921 to head a plenipotentiary commission. Endowed with broad discretionary powers, he was instructed to report directly to Lenin. But success eluded him as well, in good measure because many Red Army soldiers under his command, mostly peasant conscripts, sympathized with the rebels. It became apparent that the only way to quell the disorders was to strike at the rebels' civilian supporters in order to isolate them, and this required resort to unrestricted terror: concentration camps, executions of hostages, mass deportations. Antonov-Ovseenko requested and obtained Moscow's authorization to employ such measures.[44]

During the winter of 1920–21, the food and fuel supply situation in the cities of European Russia recalled that on the eve of the February Revolution. The breakdown of transport and peasant hoarding caused a precipitous fall in deliveries; Petrograd, due to its remoteness from the producing areas, once again suffered the most. Factories closed for lack of fuel; more inhabitants fled the city. Those who stayed headed for the countryside to barter for food manufactured goods issued them gratis by the government or stolen from places of work, only to be stopped on their way back by "barring detachments" *(zagraditel'nye otriady)* that confiscated the produce.

It was against this background that in February 1921 the sailors of Kronshtadt, Trotsky's "beauty and pride of the Revolution," raised the banner of revolt.

The spark that ignited the naval mutiny was a government order of January 22 reducing by one-third the bread ration in a number of cities, including Moscow and Petrograd, for a period of ten days.[45] The measure was necessitated by shortages of fuel, which had shut down several railroad lines.[46] The first protests erupted in Moscow. A conference of partyless metallurgical workers of the Moscow region at the beginning of February heard sweeping denunciations of the economic policy of the regime, demands for the abolition of "privileged" rations for all, including members of the Sovnarkom, and for the replacement of random food exactions with a regular tax in kind. Some speakers called for the convocation of a Constituent Assembly. On February 23–25 many Moscow workers went on strike, demanding that they be allowed to obtain food on their own, outside the official rationing system.[47] These protests were quelled by force.

Disaffection spread to Petrograd, where food rations for industrial workers, the most privileged caste, had been reduced to 1,000 calories a day. In early February 1921, some of the largest enterprises there were forced to shut down for lack of fuel.[48] From February 9, sporadic strikes broke out: the Petrograd Cheka determined that their cause was exclusively economic, there being no evidence of "counterrevolutionary" involvement.[49] From February 23 on, workers held meetings, some of which ended in walkouts. Initially, the Petrograd workers demanded only the right to scour the countryside for food, but before long, probably under Menshevik and SR influence, they added political demands calling for honest elections to the soviets, freedom of speech, and an end to police terror. Here, too, anti-Communist sentiments were occasionally accompanied by anti-Semitic slogans. At the end of February, Petrograd faced the prospect of a general strike. To avert it, the Cheka proceeded to arrest all leading Mensheviks and SRs in the city, a total of 300. Zinoviev's attempt to calm the rebellious workers was unsuccessful: his audiences were hostile and prevented him from speaking.[50]

Confronted with worker defiance, Lenin reacted exactly as had Nicholas II four years earlier: he turned to the military. But whereas the last tsar, weary and unwilling to fight, soon caved in, Lenin was prepared to go to any length to stay in power. On February 24, the Petrograd Committee of the Communist Party formed a "Defense Committee"—"defense" from whom was not specified—that in words reminiscent of General S. S. Khabalov's orders of February 25–26, 1917, proclaimed a state of emergency and prohibited all street gatherings. The committee was chaired by Zinoviev, whom the anarchist Alexander Berkman called "the most hated man in Petrograd." Berkman heard a speech by a member of this group, the Bolshevik M. M. Lashevich, looking "fat, greasy and offensively sensuous," who dismissed the protesting workers as "leeches attempting extortion."[51] The striking workers were locked out, which had the effect of depriving them of food rations. The authorities kept on arresting Mensheviks, SRs, and anarchists in Petrograd and in other parts of the country to keep them away from the rebellious "masses." Whereas in February 1917, the main source of disaffection had been the garrison, now it was the factory. Even so, the Red Army units stationed in Petrograd gave cause for concern, since some of them declared they would not take part in suppressing worker demonstrators. These units were disarmed.

News of labor unrest in Petrograd reached the naval base of Kronshtadt. The 10,000 sailors stationed there had traditionally shown a preference for anarchism of no particular ideological orientation, dominated by hatred of the "bourgeoisie." In 1917, these sentiments had served the Bolsheviks; now they turned against them. Bolshevik support at the naval base began to erode soon after October, and although in 1919 the sailors had fought valiantly for the Reds in the defense of Petrograd, they were far from enthusiastic about the regime, especially after the Civil War was over.[52] In the fall and winter of 1920–21, half the members of the Kronshtadt Party organization, numbering 4,000, turned in their cards.[53] When rumors spread that striking workers in Petrograd had been fired upon, a delegation of sailors was sent to investigate: on its return it reported that workers on the mainland were treated as they once were in tsarist prisons. On February 28, the crew of the battleship *Petropavlovsk,* previously a Bolshevik stronghold, passed an anti-Communist resolution. It called for the reelection of soviets by secret vote, freedom of speech and press (but only "for workers and peasants, anarchists, and left socialist parties"), freedom of assembly and trade unions, and the right of peasants to cultivate their land as they saw fit provided they did not employ hired labor.[54] The following day the resolution was adopted with near-unanimity by an assembly of sailors and soldiers in the presence of Kalinin, who had been sent to pacify the mutineers. Many Communists present at the rally voted for the resolution. On March 2, the sailors formed a Provisional Revolutionary Committee to

54. A typical street scene under War Communism.

55. Muscovites destroying houses for fuel.

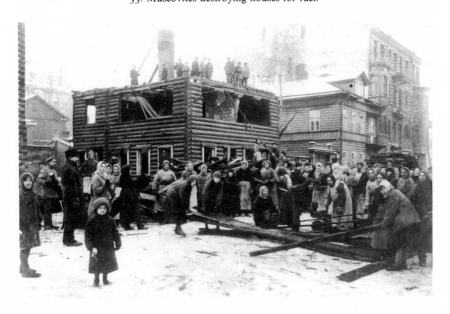

take charge of the island and organize its defense against the anticipated assault from the mainland. The rebels had no illusions about their ability to withstand for long the might of the Red Army, but they counted on rallying the nation and the armed forces to their cause.

In this expectation they were disappointed, for the Bolsheviks took prompt and effective countermeasures to prevent the mutiny's spread: in this respect, the new totalitarian regime proved far more competent than tsarism. The sailors found themselves isolated, and locked in a military struggle they could not possibly win.

It is interesting to observe how quickly the Bolsheviks assimilated the habit of the old regime of attributing any challenge to their authority to dark, foreign forces. Then they had been the Jews; now they were "White Guardists." On March 2, Lenin and Trotsky declared the mutiny to be a plot of "White Guard" generals, behind whom stood the SRs and "French counterintelligence."* To keep the Kronshtadt mutiny from contaminating Petrograd, the Defense Committee ordered troops to disperse crowds and to fire if disobeyed. The repressive measures were coupled with concessions: Zinoviev withdrew the "barring detachments" and dropped hints that the government was about to abandon food requisitioning. The combination of force and concessions mollified the workers, depriving the sailors of vital support.

One week after the outbreak of the Kronshtadt mutiny, the Bolshevik leadership gathered in Moscow for the Tenth Party Congress. Although it was on everyone's mind, the mutiny was not on the agenda. In his address, Lenin made light of it, dismissing it as a counterrevolutionary plot: the involvement of "White generals" had been "fully proven," he declared, and the whole conspiracy had been hatched in Paris.[55] In reality, the leadership took this challenge very seriously.

Trotsky arrived in Petrograd on March 5. He ordered the mutineers to surrender at once and to throw themselves on the mercy of the government; the alternative was military retribution.[56] With minor changes, his ultimatum could have been issued by a tsarist governor-general. One appeal to the rebels threatened that if they continued resistance they would be "shot like partridges."[57] Trotsky ordered the mutineers' wives and children residing in Petrograd to be taken hostage.[58] Annoyed with the insistence of the head of the Petrograd Cheka that the Kronshtadt rebellion was "spontaneous," he asked Moscow to have him dismissed.[59]

Upon learning of Trotsky's actions, the defiant Kronshtadt mutineers recalled the order to the security forces on Bloody Sunday in 1905, attributed to the governor of St. Petersburg, Dmitrii Trepov—"Don't spare bullets." The "toilers' revolution," the rebels vowed, will "sweep from the

---

*Pravda, No. 47 (March 3, 1921), I. Later on, Stalin's propaganda would go further still, claiming that the Kronshtadt rising had been financed by Washington: E. B. Genkina, *Perekhod sovetskogo gosudarstva k Novoi Ekonomicheskoi Politike (1921–1922)* (Moscow, 1954), 39.

face of Soviet Russia, stained by their actions, the vile slanderers and aggressors."[60]

Kronshtadt is an island, which at any other season than winter would have been very difficult to capture by force: but in March, the waters surrounding it were still solidly frozen. This fact facilitated the onslaught, the more so that the rebellious sailors ignored the advice of their officers to break up the ice with artillery. On March 7, Trotsky ordered the assault to begin. The Red forces were under the command of Tukhachevskii. In view of the undependability of the regular troops,[61] Tukhachevskii interspersed in their midst units from special elite divisions formed to combat internal resistance.*

The attack, launched from a base northwest of Petrograd, began in the morning of March 7 with an artillery barrage from mainland batteries. That night, Red troops wrapped in white sheets stepped onto the ice and ran toward the naval base. In their rear were deployed Cheka machine-gun detachments with orders to shoot any soldiers who retreated. The assault turned into a rout as the attackers were cut down by machine-gun fire from the naval base. Some Red soldiers refused to charge; about one thousand went over to the rebels. Trotsky ordered the execution of every fifth soldier who disobeyed orders.

The day after the first shots had been fired, the *Izvestiia* of the Provisional Revolutionary Committee of Kronshtadt published a programmatic statement, "What we are fighting for," calling for a "Third Revolution." The document, anarchist in spirit, bears all the hallmarks of having been written by an intellectual, but that it expressed the sentiments of the defendants is proven by their willingness to fight and die for it.

> In carrying out the October Revolution, the working class hoped to achieve its liberation. The outcome has been even greater enslavement of human beings.
>
> Power has passed from a monarchy based on the police and gendarmerie into the hands of usurpers—Communists—who have given the toilers not freedom but the daily dread of ending up in the torture chambers of the Cheka, the horrors of which exceed many times the rule of tsarism's gendarmerie.
>
> The bayonets, the bullets, the coarse shouts of the *oprichniki*† from the Cheka—this is the fruit of the long struggles and sufferings of Soviet Russia's toilers. The glorious emblem of the toilers' state—the hammer and

---

*In 1919, for the specific purpose of combating counterrevolution, Moscow created an elite army staffed primarily with Communist officers and noncommissioned officers known as "Units of Special Designation" (*Chasti Osobogo Naznacheniia,* or *ChON*). These numbered in December 1921 a cadre of 39,673 and 323,373 conscripts: G. F. Krivosheev, *Grif sekretnosti sniat* (Moscow, 1993), 46n.. In addition, there was an Army of Internal Service (*Voiska Vnutrennei Sluzhby,* or *VNUS*), created in September 1920 for a similar purpose, which had in late 1920 360,000 men under arms. *Ibid.,* 45n.

†Men employed by Ivan IV in the 1560s in the terror campaign *(Oprichnina)* against his presumed enemies.

56. Red Army troops assaulting Kronshtadt.

sickle—Communist authority has in truth replaced with the bayonet and the iron bar, created to protect the tranquil and careless life of the new bureaucracy, the Communist commissars and functionaries.

But basest and most criminal of all is the moral slavery introduced by the Communists: they have also laid their hands on the inner world of the working people, compelling them to think only as they do.

By means of state-run trade unions, the workers have been chained to their machines, so that labor is not a source of joy but a new serfdom. To the protests of peasants, expressed in spontaneous uprisings, and those of the workers, whom the very conditions of life compel to strike, they have responded with mass executions and an appetite for blood that by far exceeds that of tsarist generals.

Toiling Russia, the first to raise the red banner of the liberation of labor, is thoroughly drenched with the blood of the victims of Communist rule. In this sea of blood, the Communists drown all the great and bright pledges and slogans of the toilers' revolution.

It has become ever more clear, and by now it is self-evident, that the Russian Communist Party is not the protector of the working people that it claims to be, that the interests of the working people are foreign to it, and that, having gained power, its only fear is of losing it, and hence that all means [to that end] are permissible: slander, violence, deception, murder, revenge on the families of those who have revolted.

The long suffering of the toilers has drawn to an end.

Here and there the red glow of revolt against oppression and coercion is lighting up the country's sky. . . .

57. After the assault.

> The current revolt finally offers the toilers a chance to have their freely
> elected, functioning soviets, free of violent party pressures, to refashion the
> state-run trade unions into free associations of workers, peasants, and the
> working intelligentsia. At last, the police baton of Communist autocracy is
> smashed.[62]

During the week that followed, Tukhachevskii assembled reinforcements, all the while keeping the defenders off balance with nightly raids.
The morale on the island declined from the lack of mainland support and
the depletion of food supplies. The Red command was apprised of this fact
by Kronshtadt Communists, whom the rebels allowed freedom of movement and access to telephones. To keep up the spirit of their own troops,
reluctant to attack their comrades, the Communists initiated an intense
propaganda effort that depicted the rebels as witless tools of the counterrevolution.

The final assault by 50,000 Red troops began during the night of March
16–17: this time, the main Red force charged from the south, from Oranien-
baum and Peterhof. The defenders numbered 12,000–14,000, of whom
10,000 were sailors, and the rest infantry. The attackers managed to creep
up close to the island before being noticed. Ferocious fighting ensued, much
of it hand to hand. By the morning of March 18, the island was under
Communist control. Several hundred prisoners were slaughtered. Some of
the defeated rebels, leaders included, managed to save themselves by fleeing

across the ice to Finland, where they were interned. It was the intention of the Cheka to distribute the surviving prisoners in the Crimea and the Caucasus, but Lenin told Dzerzhinskii that "it would be more convenient" to have them concentrated "somewhere in the north."[63] This meant isolation in the most savage concentration camps on the White Sea, from which few ever emerged alive.

The crushing of the Kronshtadt uprising was not well received by the population. It did not enhance the reputation of Trotsky: although he loved to dwell on his military and political triumphs, in his memoirs he omitted any mention of his role in this tragic event.

Lenin and Trotsky received regular reports from the field staff of the Revolutionary-Military Council about combat operations against the "bands" operating in Tambov, as if it were a regular war front.[64] Although the staff reported one victory after another, now scattering, now pulverizing the rebels, it was evident that this enemy, waging highly unconventional warfare, could not be defeated by conventional military means. Lenin, therefore, decided to call on Tukhachevskii to mount a decisive campaign.[65] Arriving in Tambov at the beginning of May, Tukhachevskii assembled a force which at the height of the operation numbered over 100,000 men.[66] Assisting the Red Army were "International Units" of Hungarian and Chinese volunteers. Tukhachevskii realized that he confronted not only a military force—thousands of guerrillas—but also a hostile population of millions. Reporting to Lenin after he had broken the back of the insurrection, he explained that the struggle "had to be regarded not as some kind of more or less protracted operation but as an entire campaign and even war."[67] "Our supreme command decided not to be captivated by punitive measures but to conduct a regular campaign," explained another Bolshevik. "It was decided to conduct all operations in a cruel manner so that the very nature of the actions [taken] would command respect."[68] Tukhachevskii's strategy was to conquer the territory methodically, so as to separate the partisans from the civilian population that supplied them with recruits and provided other forms of assistance.[69] Since conquering and occupying a whole province exceeded the capabilities of the force assigned to the mission, Tukhachevskii relied on "cruelty," that is, exemplary terror.

Essential to this strategy was good intelligence. Using paid informers, the Cheka obtained lists of the partisans: a special directive (No. 130), issued by Antonov-Ovseenko's commission, ordered their families to be held as hostages. Using these lists, to which it added the names of peasants designated "kulaks," the Cheka herded thousands of hostages into concentration camps especially built for the purpose. Areas of particularly intensive partisan activity were singled out for what official documents referred to as "massive terror." According to Antonov-Ovseenko's report to Lenin, to break the silence of the inhabitants, Red commanders used the following procedures:

> A special "sentence" is pronounced on these villages which enumerates their crimes against the laboring people. The entire male population is placed under the jurisdiction of the Revolutionary Military Tribunal; all the families of bandits are removed to a concentration camp to serve as *hostages* for the relative belonging to a band; a term of two weeks is given the bandit to give himself up, at the end of which the family is deported from the province and its property (until then sequestered conditionally) is confiscated for good.[70]

Savage as they were, these measures still did not produce the desired results, because the partisans retaliated by taking hostage and executing families of Red Army soldiers and Communist officials, often in a very sadistic manner.[71] Antonov-Ovseenko's commission therefore issued another directive on June 11 (No. 171), which raised still higher the level of terror by ordering the execution without legal formalities of numerous categories of offenders:

> 1. Citizens who refuse to give their name are to be executed on the spot.
> 2. Villages that conceal weapons . . . are sentenced to having hostages taken. These are to be shot if the weapons are not surrendered.
> 3. In the event hidden weapons are found, the eldest worker in the family is to be shot on the spot without a trial.
> 4. A family that has concealed a bandit is to be arrested and exiled from the province. Its property is to be confiscated, and its oldest member to be shot on the spot without a trial.
> 5. A family that gives shelter to members of a bandit's family or hides the property of a bandit is to be treated as bandits; the oldest worker of the family is to be shot on the spot, without a trial.
> 6. In the case of the flight of a bandit's family, its belongings are to be distributed among peasants loyal to Soviet authority and the abandoned dwellings to be burned.
> 7. This order will be carried out strictly and mercilessly. It is to be read to village assemblies.[72]

As a result of these orders, hundreds, if not thousands, of peasants were killed: liable to execution, as later under Nazi rule, were persons whose only crime was giving refuge to the abandoned children of "bandits."[73] In many villages, hostages were executed in batches. According to Antonov-Ovseenko, in "the second most pro-bandit *uezd*," 154 "bandit hostages" were shot, 227 families of "bandits" taken hostage, 17 houses burned, 24 pulled down, and 22 turned over to the "village poor" (a euphemism for collaborators).[74] In instances of particularly stubborn resistance, entire villages were "relocated" to neighboring provinces. Lenin not only approved of these measures but instructed Trotsky to make certain that they were accurately implemented.[75]

Tukhachevskii's campaign got underway in late May 1921. He had been authorized to resort to poison gas against the rebels and lost no time warning them that he meant to use it:

> Members of White Guard bands, partisans, bandits, surrender! Otherwise, you will be mercilessly exterminated. Your families and your belongings have been taken hostage for you. Hide in the village—you will be turned over by your neighbors. If anyone gives shelter to your family, he will be shot and his family arrested. If you hide in the woods—we will smoke you out. The Plenipotentiary Commission has decided to use asphyxiating gas to smoke the bands out of the forests. . . .[76]

Ten days later Antonov's army was surrounded and destroyed, but Antonov himself managed to escape. Another guerrilla army loyal to him held out for a couple of weeks. Eventually, all that remained of his once formidable force were small partisan detachments that carried out desultory raids. The population, terrorized, but also mollified by the abandonment of food exactions in March 1921, withdrew support of the rebels. The next year, 1922, was a good one for Russian peasants: the crops were abundant and the taxes reasonable.

Forsaken by all, Antonov became a hunted quarry. The end came on June 24, 1922: betrayed by his onetime supporters, he was tracked down and killed by the GPU. It is said that the peasants welcomed his death, cursing his body as it was borne through their villages to Tambov and cheering his killers.[77] But then, the entire incident may well have been staged.

The remarkable success of guerrilla leaders like Antonov in standing up to the regular army made a deep impression on the Soviet High Command. M. V. Frunze, the Red Army's Chief of Staff and later Trotsky's successor as Commissar of War, ordered studies to be undertaken of unconventional warfare for future use against a technically superior enemy.[78] On the basis of these investigations, the Red Army would resort to partisan warfare on a large scale against the invading Nazis. And the Nazi command, in turn, would replicate the methods of terror against the civilian population which the Red Army had developed in 1921–22 in its campaign against peasant guerrillas.

The need to pacify the peasantry became apparent to Lenin even before Kronshtadt: the matter was discussed in the Politburo in February 1921. The event that may have prompted these deliberations was the peasant uprising in western Siberia that broke out on February 9.[79] The partisans, numbering in the tens of thousands, occupied several major towns, including Tobolsk, and cut the railroad line linking central Russia with

58. A "food detachment" about to depart for the village.

eastern Siberia. With local forces unable to cope, the Center mobilized 50,000 troops in the area.[80] In intense battles, the regular army eventually succeeded in suppressing the guerrillas. But the two-week disruption of food shipments from Siberia was a calamity that compelled the Soviet leaders, while the uprising was still in progress, to rethink their whole agrarian policy.[81]

The sailors' mutiny finally forced their hand: it was on March 15, as the Red Army stood poised to launch the final assault on the naval base, that Lenin announced what was to become the linchpin of the New Economic Policy, the abandonment of arbitrary food confiscation known as *prodrazvërstka* in favor of a tax in kind. *Prodrazvërstka* had been the most universally despised feature of "War Communism"—despised by peasants, whom it robbed of their produce, but also by the urban population, whom it deprived of food.

Requisitioning had been enforced in an appallingly arbitrary manner. The Commissariat of Supply determined the quantity of foodstuffs it required—a quantity determined by what was needed to feed the consumers in the cities and the armed forces, without regard to what the producers could provide. This figure it broke down, on the basis of inadequate and often outdated information, into quotas for each province, district, and village. The system was as inefficient as it was brutal: in 1920, for example, Moscow set the *prodrazvërstka* at 583 million puds (9.5 million tons) but managed to collect only half that amount.[82]

Collectors acted on the premise that peasants lied when they claimed that the grain they were forced to surrender was not surplus but essential to provide food for their families and seed, and that they could compensate for the loss by digging up their hoard. This the peasants may have been able to do in 1918 and 1919. But by 1920 they had little if anything left to hoard: as a result, as we have seen in the case of Tambov province, *prodrazvërstka*, even if incompletely realized, left them with next to nothing. Nor was this all. Zealous collectors impounded not only "surplus" and food needed for sustenance, but grain set aside for the next season's sowing: one high Communist official admitted that in many areas the authorities appropriated one hundred percent of the harvest.* Refusal to pay resulted in the confiscation of livestock and beatings. In addition, collecting agents and local officials, empowered to label resistance to their demands as "kulak"-inspired or "counterrevolutionary," felt at liberty to appropriate food, cattle, even clothing for their personal use.[83] The peasants resisted fiercely: in the Ukraine alone, they were reported to have killed 1,700 requisition officials.[84]

A more self-defeating policy would be hard to conceive. The system operated on the absurd principle that the more the peasant produced the more would be taken from him; from which it followed with inexorable logic that he would produce little if anything beyond his own needs. The richer a region, the more it was subjected to government plunder, and the more prone it was to curtail production: between 1916–17 and 1920–21, the decline in the sown acreage in the center of the country, an area of grain deficits, was 18 percent, whereas in the main region of grain surpluses it was 33 percent.† And since yields per acre declined from shortage of fertilizer and draft animals as well, grain production, which in 1913 had been 80.1 million tons, dropped in 1920 to 46.1 million-tons.[85] If in 1918 and 1919 it had still been possible to extract a "surplus," by 1920 the peasant had learned his lesson and made sure there was nothing to surrender. It apparently never occurred to him that the regime would take what it wanted even if it meant that he went breadless and seedless.

Prodrazvërstka had to be abandoned for both economic and political reasons. There was nothing left to take from the peasant, who faced starva-

---

*I. I. Skvortsov in *Desiatyi S"ezd*, 69. Instructions exist from Lenin directing the requisitioning even of the grain the peasants needed for their own consumption and seed: Lenin, *PSS*, XLIII, 219. In mid-1921, the Commissariat of Supply ordered half of the seed grain to be shipped out of Tambov province to Samara: *TP*, II, 550–51. On the abuses of *prodrazvërstka*, see *Izvestiia*, No. 42/1,185 (February 25, 1921), 2.

†Frank A. Golder and Lincoln Hutchinson, *On the Trail of the Russian Famine* (Stanford, 1927), 8; *RR*, 697–98. Nationwide, Kamenev estimated that in 1920 the sown acreage diminished by 25 percent: *Pravda*, July 2, 1921, in M. Heller, *Cahiers*, XX, No. 2 (1979), 137. The curtailment of sown acreage was also necessitated by shortages of draft animals caused by requisitions the opposing armies carried out during the Civil War: the number of draft horses and oxen in Russia and the Ukraine in 1920, compared to the immediate prerevolutionary times, declined by 28 and 31 percent, respectively: Genkina, *Perekhod*, 49.

tion; and it fueled nationwide rebellions. The Politburo finally decided to drop *prodrazvërstka* on March 15.* The new policy was made public on March 23.[86] Henceforth, the peasants were required to turn over to government agencies a fixed amount of grain; arbitrary confiscations of "surplus" were terminated.

In announcing the new policy, Lenin emphasized its political significance: in Russia, where the peasantry constituted the vast majority of the population, one could not govern effectively without its support. In an internal communication, Kamenev listed "introducing political tranquillity to the peasantry" as the policy's first objective (followed by encouraging increases in the sown acreage).[87] Previously viewed as a class enemy, the peasant was henceforth to be treated as an ally. Lenin now acknowledged a fact that had eluded him earlier, namely that in Russia, in contrast to much of Western Europe, the majority of rural inhabitants were neither hired hands nor tenants but independent small producers.[88] To be sure, the latter were a "petty bourgeoisie," and concessions to them were a regrettable retreat, but it was temporary: Lenin justified it as an "economic breathing spell," while Bukharin and D. B. Riazanov spoke of a "peasant Brest [-Litovsk]."[89] How long the "breathing spell" would last was left unsaid, but at one point Lenin conceded that "transforming" the peasant could take generations.[90] These and other remarks of Lenin's on the subject suggest that although collectivization remained his ultimate objective, he would not have launched it as early as did Stalin.

As spelled out in April 1921, the new policy imposed on peasant households a standard tax in grain, potatoes, and oil-yielding seeds. Later that year, other agricultural products were added to the list: eggs and dairy products, wool, tobacco, hay, fruits, honey, meat, and raw leather.[91] The size of the grain tax was determined by the minimal requirements of the Red Army, industrial workers, and other nonagricultural groups. Its allocation, left to the discretion of village soviets, was to be commensurate with the ability of a given household to pay, as determined by its size, the quantity of arable land at its disposal, and local grain yields. To encourage the peasants to increase their output, the decree based the amount of land subject to the tax not on that actually under cultivation but on that capable of being cultivated, that is, the total arable. The principle of "collective responsibility" *(krugovaia otvetstvennost')* for meeting state obligations was abandoned.[92]

The first tax in kind was set at 240 million puds, 60 million less than obtained in 1920 and only 41 percent of the *prodrazvërstka* quota previously set for 1921. The government hoped to make up for the shortfall by

---

*Desiatyi S''ezd, 856–57. Trotsky recalled in his autobiography (*Moia zhizn'*, II, Berlin, 1930, 198–99) that he had proposed to the Central Committee that *prodrazvërstka* be abandoned in favor of a tax in kind as early as February 1920, but was outvoted. His proposal is in L. Trotskii, *Sochineniia*, XVII, Pt. 2 (Moscow-Leningrad, 1926), 543–44. It is remarkably prescient.

offering the peasant, on a barter basis, manufactured goods for his surplus grain: this was to bring in an additional 160 million puds.[93] None of these expectations was met because of the severe drought that struck the principal grain-producing areas in the spring of 1921: since the afflicted areas provided next to nothing, instead of 240 million puds, the tax brought in only 128 million.[94] Nor did the proposed exchange bring in any grain, because there were no manufactured goods to barter.

Although the new policy resulted in no immediate improvement—indeed, initially it yielded less food than *prodrazvërstka*—it marked a significant advance in Communist thinking that in the longer run was to prove highly beneficial. For in contrast to past practices that treated peasants as mere objects of exploitation, the tax in kind, or *prodnalog,* also took their interests into account.

While the economic benefits of the new agrarian policy were not immediately apparent, the political rewards were reaped at once. The abandonment of food requisitioning took the wind out of the sails of rebellion. The following year, Lenin could boast that peasant uprisings, which previously had "determined the general picture of Russia," had virtually ceased.*

When they introduced the tax in kind, the Bolsheviks had no idea of its ramifications, for they meant to keep intact the centralized management of the national economy: the last thing they wanted was to abandon the state monopoly on trade and manufacture. They fully expected to absorb the grain surplus by giving the peasant manufactured goods in exchange. It soon became evident, however, that the expectation was unrealistic, in consequence of which, they were compelled, step by step, to carry out ever more ambitious reforms that in the end produced the unique hybrid of socialism and capitalism known as the New Economic Policy. (The term first became current in the winter of 1921–22.)[95] The tax in kind

> necessarily implied the restoration for the peasantry of the right to trade in that part of the surplus produce which remained at their disposal (otherwise the leaving of this surplus at their disposal would have been no more than a nominal concession, possessing very little influence as an incentive to increase peasant production). This in turn implied the revival of a market in agricultural produce, the re-creation of market relations as an essential link between agriculture and industry, and a restored sphere of circulation for money.[96]

Prodnalog thus unavoidably led, in the first place, to the restoration of private trade in grain and other foodstuffs—this barely fifteen months after Lenin had sworn that he would rather have everyone die than relinquish the state monopoly on the grain trade.[97] It further meant a return to conven-

---

*Lenin, *Sochineniia,* XXVII, 347. The text of this passage in the latest edition of Lenin's collected works (*PSS,* XLV, 285) reads differently.

tional monetary practices, with a stable currency backed by objects of acknowledged value. It also implied the abandonment of the state monopoly on industry, since the peasant was likely to part with his surplus only if he could obtain for it manufactured goods: this, in turn, required privatizing a good part of the consumer industry. In this manner, an emergency measure designed to quell a nationwide uprising against them led the Communists into uncharted waters that could end in the restoration of capitalism and its corollary, "bourgeois democracy."*

Between 1922 and 1924, Moscow abandoned the ideal of a moneyless economy and adopted orthodox fiscal practices. The transition to fiscal responsibility was difficult because the government required mountains of paper money to cover budgetary deficits. In the first three years of the NEP, the Soviet Union had, in effect, two currencies circulating side by side: one, the virtually worthless "tokens" known as denznaki or sovznaki; the other, a new gold-based ruble called a chervonets.

Paper rubles were produced as rapidly as the printing presses would allow. In 1921, the issuance was 16 trillion; in 1922, it rose to nearly two quadrillion: "An amount that has sixteen places and that under brighter economic skies is associated with astronomy rather than with finance."[98] The peasants refused paper tokens and used commodities, mainly grain, as a medium of exchange.

While continuing to flood the country with worthless paper, the government took steps to create a new, stable currency. Fiscal reform was entrusted to Nicholas Kutler, a banker and a minister in Sergei Witte's cabinet, and, following his retirement from government service, a Kadet Duma deputy. Kutler was appointed to the board of the State Bank (Gosbank), which was brought into being in October 1921 on his recommendation. It was also on his advice that the regime issued the new currency, and denominated the state budget in tsarist rubles.[99] (Two years later, a similar reform would be carried out in Germany under the aegis of Hjalmar Schacht.) In November 1922, the State Bank was authorized to issue chervontsy, banknotes in five denominations, backed 25 percent by bullion and foreign reserves, and the rest by commodities and short-term obligations: each new ruble represented 7.7 grams of pure gold, the gold equivalent of 10 tsarist rubles.† Chervontsy, intended for large-scale transactions and settlements between state enterprises rather than as legal tender, nevertheless circulated alongside the old tokens, which despite their astronomical denominations were needed for small retail transactions. (Lenin, embarrassed by having to restore gold to its traditional place in monetary policy, promised that as soon as Communism triumphed globally its use would be

---

*Although it is commonly believed that "War Communism" was improvised and NEP planned, in reality it was the other way around.

†In tsarist Russia, "chervonets" was the name given gold coins; although most Soviet chervontsy were paper notes, some were minted.

confined to the building of lavatories.[100]) By February 1924, nine-tenths of all accounts were denominated in chervontsy.[101] In February 1924, token rubles were withdrawn from circulation and replaced with "State Treasury Notes" with the gold content of one tsarist ruble. At this time, peasants were permitted to meet their state obligations partly or wholly in money rather than produce.

The tax system, too, was reformed along traditional lines. The state budget, calculated in gold rubles, was regularized. The deficit, which in 1922 amounted to more than half of the outlays, gradually narrowed. Laws issued in 1924 prohibited the issuance of banknotes as a device for covering deficits.[102]

Despite resistance from managers of the nationalized enterprises, decrees were passed encouraging small-scale private and cooperative industries, which were accorded the status of juridical persons and allowed to employ a limited number of salaried workers. Large enterprises remained in the state's hands and continued to benefit from government subsidies. Well aware that the NEP risked eroding the socialist foundations of the state, and, with it, his power base, Lenin made certain that the government retained control over the "commanding heights" of the economy: banking, heavy industry, and foreign trade,[103] as well as transport. Middle-sized enterprises were ordered to follow sound accounting practices and to become self-supporting, a practice known as khozrazchët. Those that were either idle or unproductive were designated as primary candidates for leasing:[104] over 4,000 such enterprises, a high proportion of them flour mills, were leased either to their previous owners or to cooperatives.[105] These concessions were mainly significant in the principles they established, especially in allowing hired labor, a practice socialists regarded with utmost repugnance. Their effect on production was limited. In 1922, state enterprises accounted for 92.4 percent of the nation's industrial output as measured by value.[106]

The transition to khozrazchët forced the abandonment of the elaborate structure of free services and goods, by virtue of which in the winter of 1920–21 the basic needs of some 38 million citizens had been provided at government expense.[107] Postal services and transportation were to be paid for. Workers received money wages and had to purchase whatever they needed on the open market. Rationing, too, was gradually eliminated. Step by step, retail trade was privatized. Citizens were permitted to deal in urban real estate, to own publishing firms, to manufacture pharmaceuticals and agricultural implements. The right of inheritance, abolished in 1918, was partially restored.[108]

The NEP bred an unattractive type of entrepreneur, very unlike the classic "bourgeois."[109] The environment for private enterprise in the Soviet Union was basically so unfriendly, and its future so uncertain, that those who took advantage of economic liberalization spent their profits without thought for tomorrow. Treated as pariahs by government and society alike,

59. A Moscow produce market under the NEP.

the "nepmen" repaid them in kind. Living lavishly and conspicuously in the midst of poverty, they crowded expensive restaurants and nightclubs, flaunting their fur-wrapped mistresses.

The aggregate results of the measures subsumed under the fully developed New Economic Policy were undoubtedly beneficial, although unevenly so. Just how beneficial it is difficult to determine, for Soviet economic statistics are notoriously unreliable, differing, depending on the source one employs, by as much as several hundred percent.*

The benefits appeared first and foremost in agriculture. In 1922, thanks to donations and purchases of seed grain abroad as well as favorable weather, Russia enjoyed a bumper crop. Encouraged by the new tax policy to increase the cultivated acreage, peasants expanded production: the acreage sown in 1925 equaled that of 1913.[110] Yields, however, remained lower than before the Revolution, and the harvest proportionately smaller: as late as 1928, on the eve of collectivization, it was 10 percent below the 1913 figure.

Industrial production grew more slowly due to shortages of capital,

---

*Thus, at the Tenth Party Congress Zinoviev claimed for the "proletarian" trade unions in 1921 a membership of 4.5 million (*Desiatyi S''ezd,* 343). According to another Communist source, however, Soviet Russia in 1922 had only 1.1 million workers: Akademiia Nauk, Institut Ekonomiki, *Sovetskoe narodnoe khoziaistvo v 1921–1925 gg.* (Moscow, 1960), 531.

60. An open market under NEP.

obsolescence of equipment, and similar causes that defied quick remedies. The foreign concessions on which Lenin had counted to boost production amounted to little because foreigners hesitated to invest in a country that had defaulted on loans and nationalized assets. The Soviet bureaucracy, hostile to foreign capital, did all in its power to obstruct concessions by resort to red tape and other forms of chicanery. And the Cheka, and later the GPU, did their part by treating all foreign economic involvement in Russia as a pretext for espionage. In the final year of NEP (1928) there were only 31 functioning foreign enterprises in the Soviet Union, with a capital (in 1925) of a mere 32 million rubles (16 million dollars). The majority of these enterprises engaged not in manufacturing but the exploitation of Russia's natural resources, especially timber: the latter accounted for 85 percent of the foreign capital invested in concessions.[111]

The NEP precluded comprehensive economic planning, which the Bolsheviks regarded as essential to socialism. The Supreme Council of the National Economy gave up any idea of organizing the economy and concentrated on managing, as best it could, Russia's virtually inoperative industries by means of "trusts." The trusts received from the state financial as well as material subsidies; other materials they were free to purchase on the open market. After their costs were covered, their entire production was turned over to the government. For purposes of economic planning Lenin created in February 1921 a new agency, popularly known as Gosplan, whose immediate task was to carry out a gigantic program of electrification that would provide the basis for future industrial and socialist development. Even before the NEP, in 1920, Lenin had created a State Commission for the Electrification of Russia (GOELRO), which he expected over the next 10 to 15 years vastly to expand the electric power capacity of the country, mainly by developing hydroelectric energy. He entertained fantastic expectations of this project's ability to solve problems that had defied other solutions. The hope found expression in his celebrated slogan, whose precise meaning remains elusive to this day, "The soviets plus electrification equal Communism."[112] In the resolutions of the Twelfth Party Congress (1923), electrification was described as the central focus of economic planning and the "keystone" of the country's economic future. For Lenin its implications were grander still. He genuinely believed that the spread of electric power would destroy the capitalist spirit in its last surviving bastion, the peasant household, and undermine religious belief: Simon Liberman heard him say that for the peasant, electricity will replace God and that he will pray to it.[113]

The entire program was but another utopian scheme that ignored costs and came to naught for lack of money: for it soon became apparent that it required annual outlays of one billion gold rubles (500 million dollars) over a period of 10 to 15 years. "Given the fact that the nation's industry was virtually at a standstill," writes a Russian historian, "and that there were no exports of grain for the purchase abroad of the necessary equipment and technical specifications, the program of electrification in reality resembled 'electro-fiction.' "[114]

In their totality, the economic measures introduced after March 1921 marked a severe setback for the hopes once entertained of introducing Communism into Russia. Triumphant wherever sheer force decided the issue, the Bolsheviks were defeated by the inexorable laws of economic reality. In October 1921 Lenin admitted as much:

> We had counted—or, perhaps it will be more correct to say, we had assumed without adequate calculation—on the [ability] of the proletarian state to organize by direct command state production and state distribution of goods in a Communist manner in a country of small peasants. Life has demonstrated our mistake.[115]

To the Bolsheviks, the loosening of economic controls, which allowed, however conditionally, the reemergence of private enterprise, spelled political danger. They made certain, therefore, to accompany liberalization of the economy with a further tightening of political controls. At the Eleventh Party Congress Lenin explained the reasoning behind these seemingly contradictory policies as follows:

> It is very difficult to retreat after a victorious grand advance. Now the conditions are entirely different. Before, even if you did not enforce discipline, all pushed and rushed forward on their own. Now, discipline has to be more deliberate. It is also a hundred times more necessary, because when the entire army is in retreat, it does not know, it does not see where to stop: all it sees is the retreat. Here a few panicky voices are enough to produce general flight. Now the danger is immense. When such a retreat occurs in a real army, they deploy machine-guns, and when an orderly retreat turns into rout, they order: "Fire." And rightly so.*

The period 1921–28 thus combined economic liberalization with intensified political repression. The latter took the form of persecution of such independent institutions as still survived in Soviet Russia, namely the Orthodox Church and the rival socialist parties; increased repression of the intelligentsia and the universities, accompanied by mass expulsions from the country of intellectuals considered especially dangerous; intensified censorship; and harsher criminal laws. To those who objected that these measures would create a bad impression abroad at the very time when the Soviet state was gaining favor for its economic liberalization, Lenin responded that there was no need to please Europe: Soviet Russia should *"move further* in strengthening the interference of the state in 'private relations' and civil affairs."[116]

The main instrument of such interference was the political police, which under NEP was transformed from an agency of blind terror into an all-pervasive branch of the bureaucracy. According to an internal instruction, its new tasks were to keep close watch on economic conditions, prevent "sabotage" by anti-Soviet parties and foreign capital, and ensure that goods destined for the state were of good quality and delivered on time.[117] The extent to which the security police penetrated every facet of Soviet life is indicated by the positions held by its head, Felix Dzerzhinskii, who served, at one time or another, as Commissar of the Interior, Commissar of Transport, and Chairman of the Supreme Council of the National Economy.

The Cheka was thoroughly hated, and the disrepute it was held in for shedding innocent blood was brought still lower by its venality. In late 1921, Lenin decided to reform it along the lines of the tsarist secret police. The Cheka was now divested of authority over ordinary (other than state) crimes, which were henceforth to be dealt with by the Commissariat of

---

*PSS, XLV, 88–89. Lenin had referred to machine guns as a means of solving political problems at the previous, Tenth Party Congress. When a spokesman for the Workers' Opposition objected to the threat of turning machine guns on dissenters, Lenin, in what must be a unique instance in his career, apologized and promised never again to use such an expression: *Desiatyi S'ezd*, 544. He must have forgotten his pledge, because he did use it again the following year.

61. In the middle, Dzerzhinskii; on his right, Demian Bednyi, 1920.

Justice. In December 1921, while acclaiming the Cheka for its accomplishments, Lenin explained that under NEP new security methods were required and that "revolutionary legality" was the order of the day: the stabilization of the country made it possible to "narrow" the functions of the political police.[118]

The Cheka was abolished on February 6, 1922, and immediately replaced by an organization innocuously named State Political Administration, or GPU *(Gosudarstvennoe politicheskoe upravlenie).* (In 1924, following the creation of the Soviet Union, it was renamed OGPU or "United State Political Administration.") The management remained unchanged, with Dzerzhinskii as head, Ia. Kh. Peters as Deputy, and everyone else in place so that "hardly a Chekist stirred from the Lubianka."[119] Like the tsarist Department of Police, the GPU was made part of the Ministry (Commissariat) of the Interior. It was to suppress "open counterrevolutionary actions, including banditry," combat espionage, protect railroads and waterways, guard Soviet borders, and "carry out special assignments . . . for the defense of the revolutionary order."[120] Other crimes fell within the purview of the courts and Revolutionary Tribunals.

On the face of it, the GPU enjoyed fewer arbitrary powers than the Cheka. But the reality was different. Lenin and his associates believed that problems were caused by people, and that one solved them by getting rid of troublemakers. In March 1922, barely one month after he had brought it into existence, Lenin advised Peters that the GPU "can and must fight bribery" and other economic crimes by shooting the offenders: a directive to this effect was to be sent to the Commissariat of Justice through the Politburo.[121] A decree of August 10 authorized the Commissariat of the Interior by the device of administrative procedure to exile citizens accused of "counterrevolutionary activity" either abroad or to designated localities in Russia for up to three years.[122] An appendix to this decree, issued in November, licensed the GPU to deal with "banditry" as it saw fit, without resort to legal procedures, "up to execution by shooting"; it was further empowered to combine exile with forced labor.[123] In January 1923, the judiciary prerogatives of the GPU were expanded still further, with the authority to exile "persons whose presence in a given locality (and within the borders of the [Russian Republic]) appears, from their activity, their past, [or] their connection with criminal circles, dangerous from the point of view of safeguarding the revolutionary order."[124] As under tsarism, exiles reached their destination guarded by an armed convoy, partly on foot, under harsh conditions. In theory, exile was imposed by the Commissariat of the Interior on the GPU's recommendation, but in practice, a recommendation from the GPU was tantamount to a sentence. On October 16, 1922, the GPU received the power to punish without trial, and even to execute, persons guilty of armed robbery or banditry and caught in the act.[125] Thus, within less than a year of its creation as an organ of "revolutionary legality," the GPU reacquired the arbitrary powers of the Cheka over the lives of Soviet citizens.

The GPU/OGPU evolved a complex structure, with specialized departments responsible for matters not strictly within the purview of the political police, such as economic crimes and sedition in the armed forces. It was compelled to reduce its staff—from 143,000 in December 1921 to 105,000 in May 1922[126]—but even so, it remained a formidable organization. For in addition to its civilian personnel, it disposed of a sizeable military force in the form of an army that in late 1921 numbered in the hundreds of thousands, as well as a separate corps of border guards of 50,000 men.[127] Deployed across the country, these troops performed functions analogous to those of the tsarist Corps of Gendarmes. The GPU established "agencies" *(agentury)* abroad with the twin mission of surveillance and disruption of Russian emigration, and supervision of Comintern personnel. GPU also helped Glavlit implement censorship laws and administered most prisons. There was hardly a sphere of public activity in which it was not involved.

Under the NEP, the network of concentration camps expanded: from 84 in late 1920 to 315 in October 1923.[128] Some were run by the Commissariat of the Interior, others by the GPU. The most notorious of these camps were located in the far north (the "Northern Camps of Special Designation," or SLON), where escape was virtually impossible. Here, along with ordinary criminals, were confined captured officers of the White armies, rebellious peasants from Tambov and other provinces, and Kronshtadt sailors. The death toll among the inmates was high: in one year (1925) SLON recorded 18,350 deaths.[129] When, in the summer of 1923, these camps became overcrowded, the authorities converted into a concentration camp the ancient monastery on Solovetsk Island, which had been used to confine persons accused of antistate or antichurch crimes since the reign of Ivan the Terrible. In 1923, the Solovetskii Monastery camp, the largest operated by the GPU, held 4,000 inmates, including 252 socialists.[130]

The principle of "revolutionary legality" was routinely violated under the NEP, as before, not only because of the extensive extra-judiciary powers given the GPU but also because Lenin regarded law as an arm of politics and courts as agencies of the government. His conception of law became clear in 1922 during the drafting of Soviet Russia's first criminal code. Dissatisfied with the draft submitted by the Commissar of Justice, D. I. Kurskii, Lenin gave precise instructions on how to deal with political crimes. These he defined as "the propaganda and agitation or participation in organizations or assistance to organizations that help (by means of propaganda and agitation)" the international bourgeoisie. Such "crimes" were to be punished by death, or, in the event of extenuating circumstances, by imprisonment or expulsion abroad.[131] Lenin's formulation resembled the equally vague criteria of political crimes given in 1845 in the criminal code of Nicholas I, which mandated severe punishment for persons "guilty of writing or spreading written or printed works or representations intended to arouse disrespect for Sovereign Authority, or for the personal qualities of the Sovereign, or for his government." Under tsarism, however, such actions were not punishable by death.[132] Implementing Lenin's instructions, jurists drew up Articles 57 and 58, omnibus clauses that gave courts arbitrary powers to sentence undesirables for alleged counterrevolutionary activity, which Stalin would later use to give the appearance of legality to his terror. That Lenin realized the implications of his instructions is evident from the guidance he gave Kurskii: the task of the judiciary, he wrote, was to provide "a principled and politically correct (and not merely narrowly juridical) . . . *essence* and *justification* of terror. . . . The court is not to eliminate terror . . . but to substantiate it and legitimize it in principle."[133] For the first time in legal history, the function of legal proceedings was defined to be not dispensing justice but terrorizing the population.

Communist legal historians, discussing the legal practices of the 1920s, defined law as "a disciplining principle that helps strengthen the Soviet state and develop the socialist economy."* This definition justified the repression

---

Sorok let sovetskogo prava, I (Leningrad, 1957), 72. This conception continued, in spirit if not in words, tsarist traditions. According to a leading constitutional authority before the Revolution, in Russia the function of law was not so much to ensure justice as to maintain public order: N. M. Korkunov, *Russkoe gosudarstvennoe pravo*, I (St. Petersburg, 1909), 215–22.

of any individual or group that, in the judgment of the authorities, harmed the interests of the state or inhibited the development of a new economic order. Thus the "liquidation" of "kulaks," carried out by Stalin in 1928–31, in which millions of peasants were dispossessed and deported, mostly to death camps, was carried out strictly within the terms of Leninist jurisprudence.[134] According to Article No. 1 of the first Soviet Civil Code (1923), the civil rights of citizens were protected by law only to the extent that these rights did not "contradict their socioeconomic purpose (naznachenie)."[135]

To make it easier for judges to carry out their new responsibilities, Lenin freed them from customary courtroom procedures. Several innovations were introduced. Crime was determined not by formal criteria—the infraction of a law—but by its perceived potential consequences, that is, by a "material" or "sociological" standard, which defined it as "any action or inaction dangerous to society, which threatens the foundations of the Soviet regime."[136] Guilt could also be established by proving "intent," the object of punishment being "subjective criminal intention."* In 1923, in an appendix to Article 57 of the Criminal Code, "counterrevolutionary" activity was defined in so broad a fashion as to cover any deed of which the authorities disapproved. It stated that in addition to actions committed for the express purpose of overthrowing or weakening the government or rendering assistance to "the international bourgeoisie," "counterrevolutionary" qualified also actions that

> without being directly intended to attain [these] objectives, nevertheless, as far as the person committing the act was concerned, represented a deliberate assault (pokushenie) on the fundamental political and economic conquests of the proletarian revolution.[137]

Under this definition the desire to make a profit, for example, could be interpreted as counterrevolutionary activity and merit capital punishment. Commenting on this revision of Article 57, N. V. Krylenko remarked that such "elasticity" of punitive measures was required to deal with "concealed forms of counterrevolutionary activity," their most prevalent form.[138] The principle of "analogy" made it possible to charge citizens for crimes not directly defined but similar in nature (Article 10 of the Criminal Code.)†

Such standards were infinitely flexible. The Communist jurist A. N. Trai-

---

*Rudolf Schlesinger, Soviet Legal Theory (New York, 1945), 76. Here, too, Muscovite precedent was followed in that according to the Code (Ulozhenie) of 1649, in cases involving crimes against the state, no distinction was drawn between intent and deed: Richard Pipes, Russia under the Old Regime (London–New York, 1974), 109.

†The principle was applied as follows: "[Articles 57 and 74 give] a general definition of counterrevolutionary crimes and crimes against the system of administration. On the basis of Articles 57 and 74, if an act had been committed that falls under the general concept of crime against the state, but is not foreseen specifically, then . . . it is permissible to apply the article of the same chapter that is most approximate." A. N. Trainin, Ugolovnoe pravo R.S.F.S.R.: Chast' Osobennaia (Leningrad, 1925), 7.

nin, pushing the party's legal philosophy to its logical conclusion, argued in 1929, before Stalin's terror got underway, that there are "instances in which criminal repression is applied also in the absence of 'guilt.' "[139] It was hardly possible to go further in the destruction of law and legal process.

The purpose of trials staged on such principles was not to demonstrate the existence or absence of a crime—that was predetermined by the appropriate party authorities—but to provide yet another forum for political agitation and propaganda for the instruction of the citizenry. Defense lawyers, who had to be party members, were required to take their client's guilt for granted and confine themselves to pleading extenuating circumstances. As long as Lenin was alive, full contrition combined with false testimony against other defendants was likely to secure acquittal or, at least, a reduced sentence. Later on, even such actions would prove insufficient.

The principal victims of such a travesty of law were, of course, the defendants whose fate was decided by political and propagandistic considerations. But society at large also paid a heavy price. The mass of Russians had always held justice in low esteem, an attitude the court reform of 1864 had slowly taught them to overcome. This lesson was now quickly unlearned: justice, Bolshevik practices confirmed, was what pleased the strong. And to the extent that respect for law is fundamental to the proper functioning of society, Lenin's formalized lawlessness was antisocial in the fullest sense of the word.

Lenin thrived on combat: political warfare was his true métier. To pursue it, he required enemies. Having been twice defeated—first by failing to spread Communism abroad, and then by failing to construct a socialist economy at home—he now turned his energies to fighting imaginary foes. The enemies he selected for repression were "guilty" not by virtue of anything they had done or even intended to do, but because by the mere fact of their existence they defied the revolutionary order.

The principal victims of his wrath were the clergy and the socialists.

Kronshtadt, Tambov, and the emergence within the Communist Party itself of democratic deviations (see below, pages 448–59) convinced Lenin that the SRs and Mensheviks were at work, exploiting the economic crisis to undermine his regime. He could not admit even to himself that the discontent had valid causes: like a typical tsarist police official he suspected behind all disaffection the handiwork of hostile agitators. In fact, the SRs and Mensheviks had adapted themselves to Lenin's dictatorship, which allowed them to do what they had done under tsarism: grumble and criticize without bearing responsibility. They enrolled in the Communist Party by the thousands. In October 1920, the SR Central Committee ruled out all armed resistance against the Bolsheviks. But in the peculiar world of Bolshevik reasoning, what one wanted "subjectively" and what one was "objectively" were entirely different things. As Dzerzhinskii told an arrested Socialist-Revolutionary: "Subjectively you are a revolutionary such as we would wish to have more of, but objectively you serve the counter-revolution."* In the words of another Chekist, Peters, it was immaterial whether or not the socialists took up arms against the Soviet government: they had to be eliminated.[140]

As long as the Civil War was in progress, the SRs and Mensheviks had been tolerated because they helped Moscow against the Whites. Their persecution began the instant the Civil War was over. Surveillance followed by arrests started in 1920 and intensified in 1921. On June 1, 1920, the Cheka distributed to its agencies a circular outlining how to deal with SRs, Mensheviks, and for good measure, Zionists. They were instructed "to pay particular attention to the destructive activity of Mensheviks working in the trade unions, in cooperative organizations, especially among the printers. Materials for indictment should be painstakingly collected, to bring them to account not as Mensheviks, but as speculators and inciters to strikes, and so forth." In regard to Zionists, the security organs were to register known adherents and subject them to oversight, forbid them to hold meetings and disperse illegal ones, read their mail, refuse them permits for railroad travel, and "gradually, under various pretexts, occupy [Zionist] quarters, justifying this with the needs of the military and other institutions."[141]

But the harassment and arrests of socialists did not solve the problem as long as their ideas appealed to significant segments of the population: Lenin had to discredit the socialists by showing them up as traitors and, at the same time, demonstrating that to criticize his regime from the left no less than from the right was tantamount to counterrevolution. In the words of Zinoviev: "At the present time, all criticism of the party line, even the so-called 'left' kind, is, objectively speaking, Menshevik criticism."[142] To drive this point home, Lenin staged Soviet Russia's first political show trials.

As victims he chose the Socialists-Revolutionaries rather than the Mensheviks, because the former enjoyed almost universal following among the peasantry. Arrests of SRs began during the Tambov rebellion: by the middle of 1921 thousands of them, including all the members of the SR Central Committee, sat in Cheka prisons.

Then, in the summer of 1922, came mock court proceedings.[143] The decision to try the SRs was taken on December 28, 1921, on the recommendation of Dzerzhinskii,[144] but implementation was delayed for half a year to give the Cheka time to fabricate the evidence. Its centerpiece was a book by G. Semenov-Vasilev, an ex-SR terrorist turned Cheka informer, published in Berlin in February 1922.[145] Like any successful deception it was

---

*Marc Jansen, *A Show Trial under Lenin* (The Hague, 1982), 19. By this criterion, of course, "objectively" Lenin in 1917–18 was a German agent.

a compound of truths and lies. Semenov, who had been involved in Fannie Kaplan's attempt on Lenin's life in August 1918, provided some interesting details on this event, but falsely implicated the SR leadership. Later he would stand trial as both defendant and star witness for the prosecution.

On February 20, 1922, one week before the SR trial was announced, Lenin sent an angry letter to the Commissar of Justice complaining that he was too lax in dealing with political and economic crimes. The repression of Mensheviks and SRs was to be intensified by means of Revolutionary Tribunals and People's Courts.* He wanted "exemplary, noisy, *educational* trials":

> the staging [*postanovka*] of a series of *model* trials (in rapidity and vigor of repression, in the *elucidation* to the masses, through the court and the press, of their meaning) in Moscow, Petrograd, Kharkov, and a few other important centers; pressure on the people's judges and members of Revolutionary Tribunals through the party in the sense of improving the activity of the courts and intensifying repression—all this must be done systematically, persistently, with mandatory accounting.[146]

Trotsky supported Lenin's proposal and in a letter to the Politburo called for a trial that would be "a polished political production *(proizvedenie)*."[147] As with the clergy, what followed resembled more *agit-prop* theater than a tribunal: the actors were hand-picked, their roles assigned, the evidence made up, a suitable atmosphere of violence created to justify conviction, the sentences predetermined by party organs, and the "masses" involved as in street theater. The most elementary procedural formalities were set aside, the defendants being accused of crimes that were not crimes when allegedly committed, since the code under which they were tried had been issued only one week before the trial, when they were in prison.

The announcement of February 28 that the leaders of what was called "Right SRs" would be tried by the Supreme Revolutionary Tribunal for counterrevolutionary activities, including terroristic and military actions against the Soviet government,[148] aroused excitement in Western socialist circles, where the Socialists-Revolutionaries had many friends. As will be explained below (p. 422), it so happened that at this time Moscow was interested in pursuing a "united front" with the European socialists. To propitiate them, Radek pledged at the joint conference of the socialist and communist internationals in Berlin in April 1922 that the accused would be free to choose their counsel and that capital punishment would not be applied. Lenin was furious at these concessions ("We paid too much" was the title of an article he wrote on the subject) and reneged on the promise that there would be no death penalty. He did, however, allow the SR

---

*This document, omitted from previous editions of Lenin's works, was first published in full in 1964 in Lenin, *PSS*, XLIV, 396–400. Lenin had prohibited any public mention of its contents because "it is stupid to reveal to enemies our strategy" (*ibid.*, 399).

defendants foreign counsel, making certain that they would be unable to carry out their duties.

The cast of characters was carefully chosen. The accused, of whom there were thirty-four, were divided in two groups. Twenty-four were the true villains: they included twelve members of the SR Central Committee, headed by Abraham Gots and Dmitrii Donskoi. The second category consisted of minor figures: they were "friendly defendants," whose role it was to provide evidence for the prosecution, confess, and repent their "crimes," for which they were to be rewarded with acquittals. The purpose of the spectacle was to persuade the rank-and-file SRs to break all links with their party.[149]

The part of chief prosecutor was assigned to Nicholas Krylenko, who is on record as favoring executing the innocent as a means of impressing the populace.[150] The SR trial would give him experience for Stalin's show trials of the 1930s, in which he would serve as prosecutor. He was assisted by Lunacharskii and the historian M. Pokrovskii. The presiding judge was Grigorii Piatakov, a member of the Communist Central Committee. The accused were defended by three teams of lawyers, one of which, composed of four socialists, came from abroad: its head, the Belgian Emile Vandervelde, was Chairman of the International Bureau of the Second International and a former Minister of Justice of Belgium. On the train journey to Moscow, the foreign lawyers were treated to hostile and at times menacing demonstrations from crowds assembled for the purpose. They were welcomed in Moscow by an organized mob that shouted, "Down with the traitors of the working class!" Dzerzhinskii instructed Cheka personnel to begin a regular "campaign" to discredit Vandervelde by publicizing his habit of manicuring his nails and wearing laced boots.[151] Another team of defense counsel had been appointed by the spectacle's producers: it included Bukharin and Michael Tomskii, both members of the Politburo. Their role was to plead for the "moral rehabilitation" of the friendly defendants.

During the preliminary investigation, which lasted over three months, Krylenko had rounded up many witnesses. Torture was not applied, but the witnesses were pressured in various ways to cooperate. The members of the SR Central Committee refused to comply. Their intention was to emulate political prisoners of the 1870s by using the trial as a forum from which to assail the government. Throughout the proceedings, they behaved with impressive dignity: the SRs always displayed greater courage than wisdom.

The trial opened on June 6, 1922, one month after the conclusion of the proceedings against the Moscow clergy, and four days before similar action was initiated against the Petrograd clergy. The indictment charged the accused in general with waging an armed struggle against the Soviet state as well as with acts of treason and terrorism, and, in particular, with organizing both Fannie Kaplan's attempt on Lenin's life in August 1918

62. The reading of the charges at the SR trial, 1922.

and the Tambov rebellion. Admission to the trial, which took place in the ballroom of what had been the Moscow Club the Nobility, was by tickets, which were issued almost exclusively to reliable party activists. Throughout, the audience acted as it would at the performance of a political play, applauding the prosecution and jeering the defendants and their lawyers. The foreign counsel objected at the outset to several features of the proceedings: to the fact that all the judges belonged to the Communist Party, that many witnesses for the defense were barred from testifying, that admission to the court was denied to all but a few of the defendants' friends. These and other objections the judges brushed aside on the grounds that a Soviet court was not obliged to observe "bourgeois" rules. On the eighth day of the trial, after Radek had withdrawn his promise that no death sentences would be passed, and after their other requests, including the right to have their own stenographer, had been rejected, the four foreign defenders announced they were quitting "the parody of justice." One of them subsequently wrote of the trial, "People's lives [were] dealt with as though they were merchandise."[152]

After two weeks, the proceedings took an even uglier turn. On June 20, the authorities organized a massive demonstration in Moscow's Red Square. The crowd, in the midst of which the presiding judge marched alongside the prosecutor, demanded death sentences for the defendants. Bukharin harangued the crowd. The accused were forced to appear on the balcony and expose themselves to the jeers and threats of the mob. Later, a hand-picked "delegation" was let into the courtroom and screamed "Death to the murderers!" Bukharin, who played a sordid role in this mock trial, which was not very different from the one that sixteen years later would condemn him to death on even more fabricated charges, praised the lynching rabble for articulating the "voice of the workers." Cameras directed by Dziga Vertov, a luminary of Soviet cinema, filmed the incident.[153]

Although they could obtain nothing resembling a fair hearing, the SRs did have the opportunity to subject the Communist regime to uninhibited criticism—the last time this would be possible at a Soviet political trial. In 1931, when it was the Mensheviks' turn to stand in the dock, their testimony would be carefully rehearsed and the lines scripted by the prosecution.[154]

The verdict, announced on August 7, came as no surprise, since Lenin had broadly hinted at what to expect. At the Eleventh Party Congress in March 1922, having ridiculed their views, he had said, addressing the Mensheviks and SRs: "Permit us to put you for this against the wall."[155] Walter Duranty reported to the New York Times on July 23 that the proceedings had demonstrated the "truth" of the charges, that the condemnation of the majority of the defendants was "certain," and that "several death sentences will be carried out."[156] The accused were sentenced under Articles 57 through 60 of the Criminal Code. Fourteen were condemned to death, but three who had collaborated with the prosecution received pardons.* Defendants who had turned state's evidence were also pardoned. Those in the first group admitted to nothing: they refused to stand up when the judges entered to announce the verdict, for which they were expelled (in the words of Duranty) "from their own funeral."[157]

Although Radek's rash Berlin pledge was declared by the court to have no validity and although the SRs refused to petition for pardon, the judges announced a stay of execution. This surprising clemency was due to Lenin's morbid dread of assassination. Trotsky writes in his memoirs that he warned Lenin against proceeding with the executions and suggested instead a compromise: "The death sentence by the tribunal was inevitable [!], but carrying it out meant just as inevitably a retaliatory wave of terrorism. . . . There was no alternative but to make the execution of the sentence dependent on whether or not the party continued the terrorist struggle. In other words, the leaders of the [SR] party must be held as hostages."[158] Trotsky's fertile mind thus came up with another legal innovation: first, to sentence a group of people to death for crimes that they had not committed and that, in any event, were not legally crimes when allegedly committed, and then, to keep their lives hostage to crimes others might commit in the future. Lenin, according to Trotsky, accepted his suggestion "instantly and with relief."

*Bukharin requested clemency for G. Semenov: NYT, August 6, 1922, 16. At Bukharin's show trial sixteen years later, Semenov's name would be invoked to charge Bukharin with terrorist designs against the Soviet leadership: Marc Jansen, Show Trial under Lenin (The Hague, 1982), 183. Semenov, along with Bukharin, perished in the Stalinist purges.

The judges were instructed to announce that the eleven condemned to death would not be executed "if the Social[ist]-Revolutionary Party actually cease[d] all underground and conspiratorial acts of terrorism, espionage and insurrection against the Soviet Government."[159] In January 1924 the death sentences were commuted to five-year prison terms. This the prisoners learned only after a year and a half spent in Lubianka, awaiting execution.

They were executed in any event. In the 1930s and 1940s, when no danger of terror against the Soviet leadership remained, the SRs were systematically killed off. Only two active Socialists-Revolutionaries, both women, are known to have survived Stalin.[160]

Superficially, Russian cultural life under NEP continued to display the comparative diversity of the regime's early years. But processes were at work that paved the way for the stultifying uniformity of the Stalinist era. Once the principle had been established that culture was to serve the Party and that its function was to help create a Communist society, and once the instruments to enforce this principle had been put in place through censorship and the state monopoly on publishing and performing, it was only a matter of time before culture was turned into a handmaiden of politics.

Unusually, the pressure for uniformity in this instance came from below. The Party's leaders faced a difficult choice. They wanted culture to serve them; at the same time, they knew that unlike guns and tractors, art and literature of any quality could not be produced on order. They settled, therefore, on a compromise: silencing overt anti-Communists, but tolerating fellow-travelers. It was spelled out by Trotsky:

> There are realms where the party leads directly and commandingly. There are others where it controls and cooperates. And, finally, there are yet others where it merely keeps itself informed. The realm of art is not one where the party is called upon to command . . . [but] the party must repudiate overtly poisonous, destructive tendencies in art, applying the political criterion.[161]

In practice this precept meant that the authorities would keep a close eye on art and literature but not interfere; in journalism, they would interfere; and in higher education, they would direct.[162] And, indeed, under NEP, when the regime permitted private initiative in manufacture and trade, it could hardly insist on orthodox rigidity in respect to culture.[163] The view was shared by Lenin and Bukharin.

Such tolerance for non-Communist culture came under vigorous assault from self-styled "proletarian" writers.[164] These hacks, whose very names are forgotten, had no audience for their books: according to the director of the State Publishing House, his enterprise received "no requests for a single

proletarian author."[165] Their survival depended entirely on state patronage, preferably of an exclusive sort. To obtain it, they wrapped themselves
in the banners of Communism, attacking politically neutral literature
as counterrevolutionary and demanding that all culture serve party
needs.[166] They enjoyed the support of the semi-educated party cadres,
most of them of nonintelligentsia origin, who took charge of "the cultural front." These apparatchiks had no patience with arguments that
creative intellectuals, and they alone, should be exempt from party controls.[167] Their cause was helped by the fact that in early 1924 Trotsky,
the leading champion of tolerance for fellow-travelers, was falling into
disgrace.

The controversy reached a point where the Party felt it had to take a
stand. This it did, in a somewhat ambivalent fashion, in May 1924, at the
Thirteenth Congress, in a resolution stating that while no one literary
school or "tendency" had the right to speak in the Party's name, something
had to be done to "regulate the question of literary criticism."[168]

> It was the first time that non-political literature had been the subject of
> a resolution at a party congress. It was the last time that the party formal-
> ly reserved its neutrality between different literary "trends, schools
> and groups"; and this neutrality could in the long run scarcely prove com-
> patible with the necessity of scrutinizing literary productions in a party
> light.[169]

Even science was no longer exempt from ideological scrutiny and vilification: by 1922 Communist publications were beginning to assail Einstein
and other "idealistic" scientists.[170]

Russia had experienced periodic crop failures throughout her history: in the years immediately preceding the Revolution, they occurred in
1891–92, 1906, and 1911. Long experience taught the muzhik to cope with
natural disasters by setting aside sufficient reserves to carry him through a
year or even two of bad crops. Normally, crop failures spelled hunger rather
than starvation, although intermittently famine did stalk the land. It took
three years of remorseless, methodical ruination of agriculture by the
Bolsheviks to acquaint Russia with famine in which people died in the
millions.*

The famine was precipitated by a drought that first made itself felt in
1920. Disaster was temporarily averted by the reconquest of the Ukraine

---

*It is understandable why Soviet historians were unable to devote to this subject the attention
it deserves. It is less apparent why Western scholars should have ignored it. E. H. Carr, for
example, in his three-volume *History of the Russian Revolution,* where he finds space for the most
esoteric information, dismisses this calamity in a single paragraph on the specious grounds that
"estimates of those who perished are unreliable." (*The Bolshevik Revolution,* II, 285). Similar
reasoning has been used by neo-Nazi historians as a basis for ignoring the Holocaust. At the time
of writing, there exists not one scholarly monograph on the 1921 famine.

and the Northern Caucasus, which, having escaped Soviet rule, had managed to accumulate large grain reserves: in 1921 half the food obtained by the government under the new tax in kind would come from the Ukraine.[171] However, because in 1920 the food-gathering apparatus in the Ukraine and Siberia had not yet been put fully in place, a heavy burden of requisitioning still fell on the depleted central provinces.[172]

The climatic factors that caused the 1921 famine resembled those of 1891–92. The fall of 1920 was unseasonably dry. In the winter, little snow fell, and that which did, quickly melted. In the spring of 1921, the Volga ran low and did not spill over its banks. Then came scorching heat and drought, which burned the grass and cracked the soil. Vast stretches of the black-earth belt turned into dust bowls.[173] Locusts consumed much of the vegetation that survived.

But the natural disaster only contributed to the tragedy; it did not cause it. The famine of 1921 confirmed the peasant proverb *"Neurozhai, ot Boga; golod, ot liudiei"*—"Bad crops are from God, hunger comes from men." The drought accelerated a catastrophe that was bound to happen sooner or later as a result of Bolshevik agrarian policies: a knowledgeable student of the subject states that the drought would have been of minor consequence were it not for political and economic factors.[174] The mindless confiscations of "surplus" that as often as not was not surplus but grain essential for the peasants' survival, ensured catastrophe. By 1920, in the words of the Commissar of Supply, the peasant harvested just enough to feed himself and provide for seed. There was thus no margin of safety left: no reserves of the kind that in the past had cushioned the peasantry against adverse weather.

The 1921 drought struck approximately half of the food-producing areas; 20 percent of these areas experienced total crop failure. The population afflicted by the famine was recorded in March 1922 in Russia at 26 million and in the Ukraine at 7.5 million, for a total of 33.5 million, more than 7 million of them children. An American expert estimated that some 10 to 15 million of the victims faced either death or permanent physical injury.* Worst affected was the Volga Black Earth region, in normal times a prime supplier of cereals: the provinces of Kazan, Ufa, Orenburg, and Samara, where the 1921 harvest yielded less than 5.5 puds per person—half the quantity required for the peasants' sustenance, with nothing left for seed.† Also affected were the Don basin and the southern Ukraine. In most of the rest of the country, the harvest yielded between 5.5 and 11 puds,

---

Izvestiia, No. 60/1,499 (March 15, 1922), 2; Hutchinson in Golder and Hutchinson, *On the Trail*, 17. Somewhat different figures are given in Pomgol, *Itogi bor'by s golodom v 1921–22 gg.* (Moscow, 1922), 460. The figure for children comes from Roger Pethybridge, *One Step Backwards, Two Steps Forward* (Oxford, 1990), 105.

†Although the figures varied somewhat from region to region, a rough estimate held that the peasant needed annually a *minimum* of 10 puds (163 kilograms) of grain for sustenance and an additional 2.5 to 5 puds (40–80 kilograms) for seed. *RevR*, No. 14–15 (1921), 13. L. Kamenev estimated the *average* grain consumption in Russia per person before 1914 to have been 16.5 puds a year (seed grain included): RTsKhIDNI, F. 5, op. 2, delo 9, list 2.

which was barely enough to feed the local population.[175] Production in the twenty food-growing provinces of European and Asian Russia afflicted by the famine, which before the Revolution had yielded 20 million tons of cereals annually, in 1920 declined to 8.45 million tons, and in 1921 to 2.9 million, or by 85 percent.[176] In 1892, by contrast, when climatic conditions caused the worst crop failure in late tsarist Russia, the harvest was only 13 percent below normal.[177] The difference has to be attributed in large measure to Bolshevik agrarian policies.

The extent to which this catastrophe was due to human actions can be further demonstrated with figures indicating that the areas that had traditionally produced the biggest crops now yielded the smallest. The German Autonomous Republic on the Volga, for instance, usually an oasis of prosperity, was among the worst to suffer, its population declining by over 20 percent: here, in 1920–21, 41.9 percent of the gross grain harvest had been requisitioned.[178]

In the spring of 1921, the peasants in the provinces struck by the drought had to resort to eating grass, tree bark, and rodents. As the hunger persisted, with no relief from the government in sight, enterprising Tatars marketed in the stricken areas a substance advertised as "edible clay," which fetched as much as 500 rubles a pound. With the onset of summer, the peasants, driven mad by hunger, began to abandon their villages and head on foot or by cart for the nearest railroad stations in the hope of making their way to regions where, rumor had it, there was food: first to the Ukraine and, later, Turkestan. Soon millions of wretched human beings congested the railway depots: they were refused transportation because until July 1921 Moscow persisted in denying that any catastrophe had occurred. Here they waited "for trains which never came, or for death, which was inevitable." This is what the Simbirsk railroad station looked liked in the summer of 1921:

> Imagine a compact mass of sordid rags, among which are visible here and there, lean, naked arms, faces already stamped with the seal of death. Above all, one is conscious of a poisonous odor. It is impossible to pass. The waiting room, the corridor, every foot thickly covered with people, sprawling, seated, crouched in every imaginable position. If one looks closely, he sees that these filthy rags are swarming with vermin. The typhus-stricken grovel and shiver in their fever, their babies with them. Nursing babies have lost their voices and are no longer able to cry. Every day more than twenty dead are carried away but it is not possible to remove all of them. Sometimes corpses remain among the living for more than five days. . . .
>
> A woman tries to soothe a small child lying in her lap. The child cries, asking for food. For some time, the mother goes on rocking it in her arms. Then suddenly she strikes it. The child screams anew. This seems to drive the woman mad. She begins to beat it furiously, her face distorted with rage. She rains blows with her fist on its little face, on its head, and at last

she throws it upon the floor and kicks it with her foot. A murmur of horror arises around her. The child is lifted from the ground, curses are hurled at the mother, who, after her furious excitement has subsided, has again become herself, utterly indifferent to everything around her. Her eyes are fixed, but are apparently sightless.[179]

"It is useless to try in a few lines to depict the whole horror of the disaster," wrote an eyewitness from Samara, "nor will one find words able to express it. One has to see with one's own eyes these skeleton-people, these skeleton-children, with their sallow, often swollen faces, with eyes in which burns the fire of hunger, to hear that timid, dying whisper: *'Kusochek'* [a teeny piece]. . . ."[180]

There were numerous reports of the hunger-maddened killing and eating neighbors and even their own. Fridtjof Nansen, the Norwegian philanthropist, who visited Russia at the time, spoke of cannibalism as a phenomenon spreading "to a terrific degree."[181] A professor of Kharkov University who undertook to investigate these reports authenticated 26 cases of cannibalism: in "seven cases . . . murder was committed and the bodies sold for pecuniary gain . . . disguised in sausage form and placed on the open market."[182] Necrophagia—the consumption of corpses—also occurred.

Visitors to the stricken areas passed village after village with no sign of life, the inhabitants either having fled or lying in their cottages, too weak to move. In the cities, corpses littered the streets: they were picked up, loaded on carts—often after having been stripped naked—and dumped into unmarked mass graves.

The famine was accompanied by epidemics, which ravaged bodies weakened by hunger. The main killer was typhus, but hundreds of thousands also fell victim to cholera, typhoid fever, and smallpox.

It is instructive to compare the attitude of the Bolshevik regime to the famine with that of the tsarist government when confronted with a similar tragedy thirty years earlier, when some 12.5 million peasants were afflicted with hunger.[183] Contrary to propaganda spread at the time by radicals and liberals and repeated since then that it did nothing and that such relief as was provided came from private organizations, records show that the tsarist authorities moved quickly and effectively. They arranged food supplies to be delivered to 11 million victims and supplied generous emergency aid to local governments. As a result, the fatalities attributable to the 1891–92 famine are estimated at 375,000 to 400,000—an appalling number, but only one-thirteenth of those suffered by the starving under the Bolsheviks.[184]

The Kremlin watched the spread of the famine as if struck with paralysis. Although reports from the countryside had alerted it to impending disaster, and, after it had occurred, to its dimensions, it did nothing because it could not acknowledge a national calamity that it could not at-

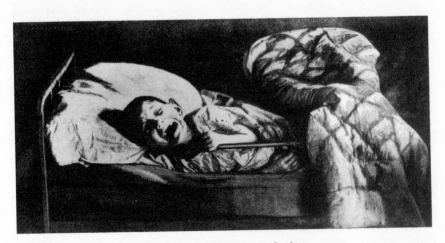

63. One victim of the 1921 famine.

64. Starving mother and child.

tribute to "kulaks," "White Guardists," or "imperialists."* Secondly, it had no obvious remedies: "The Soviet Government was confronted with a problem which, for the first time, it was unable to solve with resort to force."[185] In May and June 1921, Lenin ordered purchases of food abroad, but that was to feed the cities, his principal concern, not the peasantry.[186] The famine troubled him only insofar as it threatened potentially adverse political consequences: in June 1921, for instance, he spoke of a "dangerous situation" developing as a result of the hunger.[187] And he used it, as we have seen, as a pretext for launching an offensive against the Orthodox Church. In July 1921 Dzerzhinskii warned the Cheka of the threat of counterrevolution in areas affected by the famine and ordered harsh preventive measures.[188] The press was forbidden to make any allusion to the crop failure, and even in early July continued to report that all was well in the countryside. The Bolshevik leaders studiously avoided any overt association with the famine: Kalinin, the Kremlin's ambassador to the peasantry, was the only one to visit the affected areas.[189] On August 2, when the famine was at its height, Lenin issued an appeal to the "international proletariat" in which he noted in an offhand manner, "In Russia in a few provinces there is hunger which, apparently, is only slightly less than the misfortune of 1891."[190] In none of Lenin's writings or speeches of that period can one find

65. Corpses of starved children.

*Although on occasion Lenin did try: *e.g., PSS,* XLIV, 75, 312–13.

one word of sympathy for the millions of his subjects who were perishing from hunger. Indeed, it has been suggested that the famine was to him not unwelcome politically because it so weakened the peasantry that it "wiped out any likelihood of peasant resistance" and "pacified" the village even more rapidly than did the repeal of food requisitioning.[191]

In July, the Kremlin finally had to acknowledge what everyone knew, that the country was in the grip of a catastrophic famine. But it did not do so directly, preferring to make the painful admission and plea for help through private channels. On July 13, certainly with Lenin's approval, Gorky issued an appeal "To All Honorable People" soliciting food and medicines. On July 21, the government approved the request of a group of civic leaders to allow the formation of a voluntary, private organization to help the starving. Called the All-Russian Public Committee to Aid the Hungry (*Vserossiiskii Obshchestvennyi Komitet Pomoshchi Golodaiushchim*, or *Pomgol*), it had on its staff 73 members of diverse political affiliations, among them Maxim Gorky, Countess Panina, Vera Figner, S. N. Prokopovich and his wife, Ekaterina Kuskova, along with well-known agronomists, physicians, and writers.[192] The committee replicated the Special Committee for Famine Relief formed in 1891 to assist the tsarist government in a similar predicament, with the difference that on Lenin's orders it had a "cell" of twelve prominent Communists: Kamenev served as chairman and Aleksei Rykov as his deputy. This was to make certain that the first independent organization licensed in Communist Russia did not deviate from the narrow functions assigned to it.

On July 23, Herbert Hoover, the U.S. Secretary of Commerce, responded to Gorky's appeal. Hoover had founded and operated with great success the American Relief Administration (ARA) to supply food and medicines to postwar Europe. Although intensely anti-Communist, he set politics aside and threw himself energetically into famine relief. He posed two conditions: that the American organizations responsible for administering the relief be allowed to operate independently, without interference from Communist personnel, and that American citizens in Soviet prisons be released. The demand that American relief personnel enjoy extraterritoriality infuriated Lenin: "The baseness of America, Hoover, and the League of Nations is rare," he wrote the Politburo. "One must punish Hoover, one must *publicly slap his face*, so that the *whole world* sees; the same goes for the League of Nations." Hoover he described privately as "impudent and a liar," and the Americans as "mercenaries."[193] But he had no choice in the matter and yielded to Hoover's terms.

On July 25, Gorky, on behalf of the Soviet government, accepted Hoover's offer.[194] On August 21, ARA signed with Maxim Litvinov in Riga an accord for American assistance. Hoover started with an 18.6-million-dollar contribution from the U.S. Congress, to which were added private contributions and 11.3 million dollars realized by the Soviet government from the sale of gold. By the time it terminated operations, the ARA had spent 61.6 million dollars (or 123.2 million gold rubles) on Russian relief.*

The instant the accord was reached, Lenin made short shrift of Pomgol: he had used the organization as a go-between to avoid the embarrassment of having to beg help from the "imperialist" enemy. It had served this purpose and now had to bear the brunt of Lenin's wrath. On August 26, Lenin asked Stalin to demand from the Politburo the immediate dissolution of Pomgol and the imprisonment or exile of its leaders, on the ostensible grounds of "unwillingness to work." He further ordered that the press be directed in a "hundred ways" to "ridicule" and "badger" its members at least once a week for two months.[195] At the Politburo meeting at which Lenin's request was discussed, Trotsky, who supported it, pointed out that during negotiations with ARA, the Americans had never alluded to the committee.[196] The following day, as the advance ARA party arrived in Russia and the members of Pomgol assembled to meet with Kamenev, all but two were arrested by the Cheka and incarcerated in Lubianka. (Gorky did not attend, apparently forewarned.)[197] They were subsequently accused in the press of all manner of counterrevolutionary crimes. It was widely expected that they would be executed, but Nansen's intercession saved them; after being released from prison, some were exiled to the interior and others abroad.[198] Pomgol lingered on for another year as a government committee before it was dissolved.[199]

In the summer of 1922, when its activities were at their height, ARA fed up to 11 million persons a day. Other foreign organizations supplied an additional three million. Overall, food imports by the Soviet government and foreign relief agencies during this period amounted to 115–120 million puds, or two million tons.[200] In consequence of these activities, by early summer 1922, "reports of actual death from starvation practically ceased."[201] ARA also provided medicines worth 8 million dollars, which helped contain epidemics. Furthermore, it provided seed grain in 1922 and 1923, which made possible two bumper harvests in succession. Under the arrangement worked out by Hoover, an ARA staff of several hundred Americans supervised the distribution of food and medicines, assisted by thousands of Soviet citizens. Although Communist authorities had agreed not to interfere, ARA's activities were closely watched by the Cheka and its successor, the GPU. Lenin made certain that ARA was thoroughly infiltrated with spies, ordering Molotov to organize a commission to keep an

---

*H. H. Fisher, *The Famine in Soviet Russia* (New York, 1927), 553. The proceeds of Soviet gold sales apparently went to purchase food for the cities exclusively. The earliest instance of foreigners helping to feed Russians during famine occurred in Novgorod in 1231, when the population, decimated by hunger, was saved by a shipment of food from Germany: *Novyi Entsikopedicheskii Slovar'*, XIV (St. Petersburg, n.d.), 40–41.

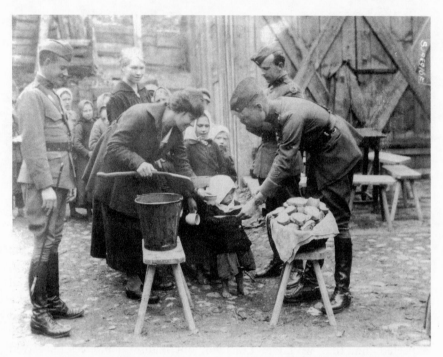

66. American Relief workers feeding Russian children during the 1921–22 famine.

eye on foreigners employed by it and to mobilize "the maximum number of Communists familiar with the English language to introduce them into Hoover's commissions and use for other forms of surveillance and information."[202] Later, after it had been disbanded, Soviet authorities sought to impute to ARA the most sinister motives, including espionage and unloading on Russia goods no one else wanted.[203] Later still, after World War II, apparently to justify Stalin's rejection of Marshall Plan aid, some of the surviving Soviet employees of ARA were made to sign statements incriminating themselves in espionage.

Once the American and other foreign organizations assumed the principal responsibility for feeding starving Soviet citizens, Moscow diverted its resources to other purposes. On August 25—three days after signing an agreement with Hoover—Litvinov informed Moscow that he had sold to an English party jewels worth 20 million gold rubles and that the buyer was prepared to purchase additional jewels for the value of 20 million pounds (100 million dollars)[204]—a sum exceeding the combined U.S. and European donations to starving Russians. In early October 1921, Trotsky instructed the Soviet agent in Germany, Victor Kopp, in strictest secrecy, to place orders for rifles and machine guns worth 10 million gold rubles (5 million dollars).[205] These facts were not known at the time. What became known and caused great consternation in American relief circles was evidence that at the very time the Soviet government was relying on Western charity to feed its people, it was offering foodstuffs for sale abroad.[206] In the fall of 1922 Moscow made it known that it had millions of tons of cereals available for export—this at a time when its own estimates indicated that during the coming winter 8 million Soviet citizens would still require food assistance, only half of which could be met with native resources.[207] When questioned, the Soviet authorities explained that they needed money to purchase industrial and agricultural equipment. The action outraged American relief officials: the Soviet government was "endeavoring to sell part of its food supply in foreign markets, while asking the world to contribute food to replace what had been exported."[208] Hoover protested against "the inhumanity of a government policy of exporting food from starving people in order that through such exports it may secure machinery and raw materials for the economic improvement of the survivors."[209] But with the worst of the famine over, Moscow could defy foreign opinion. Reports of its grain exports made it impossible to raise additional funds for Russian relief and in June 1923 ARA suspended operations in Soviet Russia.

The casualties of the 1921 famine are difficult to ascertain because no one kept track of the victims. The greatest losses occurred in the provinces of Samara and Cheliabinsk and in the German and Bashkir Autonomous Republics, the combined population of which declined by 20.6 percent.[210] In terms of social status, the worst sufferers were the rural poor, especially those lacking a cow, possession of which saved many a family from death.[211] In terms of age, the heaviest losers were the children, many of them abandoned by their starving parents. In 1922, over 1.5 million peasant children were on the loose, begging and stealing; mortality in the asylums for the *besprizornye* attained 50 percent.[212] The Soviet Central Statistical Bureau estimated the population deficit between 1920 and 1922 at 5.1 million.[213] The 1921 famine in Russia was the greatest human disaster in European history until then, other than those caused by war, since the Black Death.

The losses would have been much greater still had it not been for Hoover's philanthropic activities, estimated to have rescued at least 9 million lives.[214] In a letter to Hoover, Gorky hailed his actions as without precedent in human history: "Your help will enter history as a unique, gigantic achievement, worthy of the greatest glory, which will long remain in the memory of the millions of Russians . . . whom you have saved from death."[215]* Many statesmen occupy a prominent place in history for having sent millions to their death; Herbert Hoover, maligned for his performance as president, and soon forgotten in Russia, has the rare distinction of having saved millions.

---

*How curious, therefore, to have an American historian attribute to Hoover the "fantastic belief" that the "federal government should not . . . feed starving people." Arthur M. Schlesinger, Jr., *The Vital Center* (Boston, 1949), 28.

The New Economic Policy affected also Soviet foreign policy, which now, more than ever, operated on two distinct and conflicting levels: the conventional diplomatic-commercial, and the unconventional subversive. Moscow was anxious to enter into regular relations with foreign powers in order to facilitate trade and investments, which formed an integral part of the NEP. Armed action was given up: apart from a hastily improvised and unsuccessful putsch in Germany in 1923, no more attempts were made to stage uprisings in Europe. Instead, the Comintern followed the strategy of gradual penetration of Western institutions.

We have noted that inside Soviet Russia, the corollary of economic liberalization was intensified political repression. The same held true of the international Communist movement. The 21 Points forced on them in 1920 subordinated foreign Communist organizations to Moscow, but preserved the illusion that the Comintern was a federation of equals. This illusion was dispelled in December 1922 at the Fourth Congress of the Comintern. Its resolutions made it explicit that, first, foreign Communist parties had no right to hold independent opinions, and second, whenever the two happened to come in conflict, the interests of the Soviet state took precedence over those of foreign Communist movements.

Paradoxically, the abandonment of the idea of imminent revolution in Europe strengthened Moscow's position vis-à-vis its affiliates abroad:

> Precisely because the world revolution was no longer a current possibility, [foreign] Communists were compelled to pin all their hopes on Soviet Russia. Russia alone had emerged victorious from the class struggles of the revolutionary period, and she had successfully defended herself against innumerable foes. She was a living symbol of the coming world revolution and a powerful bulwark against world capitalism. The more difficult it seemed to Communists abroad to capture power in their own countries, the more firmly they were forced to rally to Soviet Russia. In this depressing world situation nothing was more natural than that Soviet Russia should become a fatherland of Communists throughout the world.[216]

To those for whom, as for the author of these remarks, the stabilization of the postwar world was "depressing" news, Moscow indeed seemed the only hope. And Moscow drew from this reality the appropriate conclusions.

In preparation for its Fourth Congress, Moscow decided to eliminate all remaining traces of federalism from the Comintern's organizational structure. Bukharin, who was placed in charge, interpreted Point 14 of the 21 Points, requiring foreign Communists to help Soviet Russia repel the "counterrevolution," to mean that they were under the obligation at all times to support the foreign policy of the Soviet government.[217] In effect, a Communist was to have only one fatherland, Soviet Russia, and one government, the Soviet government. He had to approve of everything this government did in the conduct of foreign relations, even alliances between the Soviet Union and a "bourgeois country"—including his own—if this served the needs of Soviet Russia as determined by the Russian Politburo. This provision was specifically designed to silence criticism of the Soviet-German treaty concluded at Rapallo in April 1922.

To prevent foreign parties from questioning or interfering with the resolutions of the Comintern's highest nominal authority, its congresses, the Fourth Congress laid it down that henceforth the constituent Communist parties would convene their meetings only after the Comintern Congresses had met. This procedure was to ensure that their delegates would have no authority to move independent resolutions. Delegates to Comintern Congresses were specifically forbidden to bring binding mandates from their parties: such mandates would be null and void because they "contradicted the spirit of an international, centralized, proletarian party." It had been a practice of the Comintern since 1919 to send observers to the meetings of the national Communist parties: this was now formalized in a provision authorizing the Executive "in exceptional circumstances" to send agents to the foreign parties, endowed with "the most comprehensive powers" to oversee their implementation of the 21 Points and the decisions of the Congress, that is, to overrule the national parties and to expel undisciplined members. The national parties were even deprived of the right to send representatives of their choice to the Comintern Executive: these were to be selected by the Congress. No resignations of Comintern officials would be countenanced unless authorized by the International's Executive, on the grounds that "every executive post in a communist party belongs not to the person holding it, but to the Communist International as a whole." Of the 25 members of the new Executive, 15 were required to reside in Moscow.[218]

All of this had been implicit in the practices of the Bolshevik Party since 1903 and in the statutes of the Comintern adopted at the Second Congress. New was the bluntness of the 1922 resolutions, which dropped all pretense of even formal equality between the Russians and their foreign adherents. Hugo Eberlein, the German delegate whom Moscow used as a mouthpiece, brushed aside complaints of Russian high-handedness:

> For us it is self-evident that in the future, too, in the management of the Communist International, in its Presidium and Executive, the Russian comrades must be accorded a stronger, and the strongest, influence, since it is precisely they who in the field of the international class struggle have accumulated the greatest experience. They alone have really carried out a revolution, as a consequence of which background they far surpass in experience all the delegates from the other sections.[219]

The Fourth Congress adopted the new rules unanimously, with one dissent from the delegate from Brazil.

The Communist International had now been transformed into a Bolshevik world party, rigidly centralized and with military-type discipline; ready, as the [Fourth] Congress had demonstrated, to accept Russian orders without question. And the Communist parties all over the world had now, in fact, become sections of the Russian Communist party, ruled by the Politbureau which also ruled the Russian state. They had thus been reduced to agencies of the Russian government.[220]

This transformation, often attributed to Stalin, took place while Lenin was in charge of setting Comintern policy.

The GPU entered now into close working relations with the Comintern Executive, to help oversee its foreign subsidiaries. It opened branches in nine foreign capitals, mostly in Soviet diplomatic missions; each had responsibility for several neighboring countries. Thus, the Paris bureau of the GPU controlled covert operations in seven West European countries besides France, including Great Britain and Italy. Among the functions of the foreign branches of the GPU was supervising Comintern agents.[221] The activities of the Comintern diversified. In 1922–23 it financed 298 publications in 24 languages.[222] It also operated a school to train students from colonial countries in agitational techniques.

European socialists, vexed but not disheartened by these developments, did not give up hope of cooperation with the Comintern. They chose to ignore that the Comintern, treating them as "social fascists," methodically split their ranks, weakening thereby the international socialist movement. They were ever ready for conciliation. For a while, the hope seemed to bear fruit. After the fiasco of the 1921 German revolt, Lenin formulated the tactic of a "united front" with the socialists: because the Communists were too weak in the West to act on their own, he decided, up to a point, on collaboration with the trade unionists and socialists. He presented this idea to the Executive Committee of the Comintern, where it ran into stiff opposition from Zinoviev, Bukharin, and others. With Trotsky's help Lenin managed to overcome the resistance and to present his proposal to the Third Congress of the Comintern (June–July 1921). The idea of cooperation with the "social imperialists" and "social traitors" produced great indignation, but in the end, the Congress approved it.[223] At the same time, Lenin allowed no collaboration with the Russian socialists (Mensheviks and SRs), ostensibly because they were "enemies of Soviet authority," but in reality because, unlike foreign socialists, they were serious contenders for power.[224]

The result of the new tactics was the Comintern's participation in April 1922 at a meeting of the Second (Socialist) International in Berlin for the purpose of formulating a common program of struggle against the growing strength of "capitalism" and for the recognition of Soviet Russia.[225] In May 1923, the European socialist parties gathered separately in Hamburg. The delegates represented 6.3 million members and 25.6 million voters—many times the strength of the parties affiliated with the Comintern.[226] A new organization was formed, called the Labor and Socialist International (LSI). Structurally, it was federated, the member parties being at liberty to decide on internal matters. Menshevik and SR delegates painted for the assembled a devastating picture of conditions in Soviet Russia and the fate of socialists there. They were politely listened to but ignored. An English delegate, to stormy applause, reminded the Congress that "it is the capitalist governments of the West who are chiefly to blame for the victims in Russian prisons, for those who have been executed and for those exiled!"[227] The resolution on Soviet Russia denounced all foreign interference in her internal affairs. While condemning the Soviet government's "terrorist methods," it asserted:

Any intervention [by capitalist governments] would be aimed not at remedying the errors of the current phase of the Russian Revolution, but at destroying the Revolution itself. Far from establishing genuine democracy, it would merely set up a government of bloody counter-revolutionaries, to act as a vehicle for the exploitation of the Russian people by Western Imperialism. [The] Congress, therefore, calls on all socialist parties ... not only to oppose intervention, but to campaign for full diplomatic recognition of the Russian government and rapid restoration of normal diplomatic and trade relations with Russia.[228]

In essence, the European socialist parties and trade unions, while verbally condemning Communist rule in Russia, which they were powerless to do anything about, aligned themselves with Moscow by endorsing policies that they were in a position to influence. This they did by defining Bolshevism as a "phase" in the Russian Revolution, with the implication that its objectionable features were transient; claiming that the only alternative to it was government by "bloody counter-revolutionaries"; and demanding diplomatic recognition of Soviet Russia and the restoration of normal trade relations with it.

The "united front" collapsed almost at once from its inner contradictions—for how was it possible to unite with the socialists whom one was committed to dividing?—and from strong opposition within the ranks of both the Second and Third Internationals. Soon the Comintern resumed treating socialists as "social-fascists."

Soviet foreign policy in the 1920s (and, for that matter, in the 1930s) focused on Germany, which was seen as both the arena of the next revolution and a potential ally against Britain and France, Soviet Russia's principal adversaries. Moscow simultaneously pursued both objectives—subversion and collaboration—even though they were mutually exclusive, thereby clearing the path for Hitler's march to power.

The most consequential event in post-Versailles international relations, second only to America's refusal to join the League of Nations, was the Rapallo Treaty, which Soviet Russia and the Weimar Republic sprang on the unsuspecting world on April 16, 1922, in the course of an international conference at Genoa.

The Genoa Conference was convened for two purposes: to settle the political and economic problems of Eastern and Central Europe left unresolved at Versailles, and to reintegrate Russia and Germany into the international community—the invitations issued to the two countries were the first they had received since the end of World War I. A subsidiary interest of Allied statesmen was forestalling a potential Russo-German rapprochement, of which they had worrisome intimations. As it turned out, the Genoa Conference achieved none of its objectives: its only accomplishment was the very Soviet-German rapprochement it was meant to prevent.

Germany had weighty reasons to come to terms with Soviet Russia. One was the desire for commerce. Germany had traditionally been Russia's leading trade partner. The two economies were well matched in that Russia had an abundance of raw materials and the Germans the high technology and the managerial skills Russia needed. German business circles felt that in the postwar world, certain to be dominated by the "Anglo-Saxon" powers, Germany's only hope of maintaining a viable economy lay in close cooperation with Moscow. The introduction of NEP opened promising perspectives of such cooperation. In 1921–22 German businessmen laid ambitious plans for the development of commercial relations with Soviet Russia, in which that country was treated as something of a potential colony.[229] They were enthusiastic about the prospect of exploiting the vast forests of northern Russia and Siberia, and the Siberian iron and coal mines, which would make up for the loss of Alsace and Lorraine.[230] Grandiose projects were discussed for transforming Petrograd with German technical and financial assistance into a major center of shipping and industry. Trade negotiations between the two countries got underway in early 1921, following Lenin's invitation to foreign firms to invest in Russia.[231] In May, German industrial executives presented Krasin with a proposal calling for large-scale investments to help rebuild the Soviet economy in exchange for control over some of its key sectors.[232]

But commercial interests took second place to geopolitical considerations, namely the conviction that only with the help of Soviet Russia could Germany shake off the shackles imposed on her at Versailles. A large part, perhaps the majority, of Germans considered the terms of the peace treaty so humiliating and so onerous that they were prepared to go to any lengths to be rid of them. Germany's unwillingness (or, as she claimed, inability) to fulfill her obligations under the treaty provoked French retaliations, which undermined the position of pro-Western German politicians still further. Under these circumstances, nationalist circles in Germany looked for an

ally, and who better fitted this role than Communist Russia, another great
nation condemned by the Allies to pariah status?

The Genoa Conference was prompted by a statement of the Soviet Commissar of Foreign Affairs, George Chicherin, on October 28, 1921, that the
Russian government was prepared, under certain conditions, "to recognize
the obligations towards other States and their citizens which arise from
State loans concluded by the Czarist Government before 1914." To this
end, he proposed "an international conference . . . to consider the claims of
the Powers against Russia and of Russia against the Powers, and·to draw
up a definite treaty of peace between them."[233] Lloyd George found this
declaration an irresistible opportunity finally to settle the issues arising
from the Russian Revolution. On January 6, 1922, the Supreme Allied
Council resolved to hold an international conference to consider the economic reconstruction of central and eastern Europe, including the restoration of property rights violated by "confiscation or withholding."

We have noted before (Chapter 4) the role German generals led by Hans
von Seeckt had played in opening in early 1919 backdoor channels to
Communist Russia. The decisive steps leading to Soviet-German military
collaboration were taken in the spring of 1921, following the introduction
of the New Economic Policy and the signing of the Treaty of Riga terminating the war with Poland. Surprised and worried by the dismal showing of
the Red Army against the Poles, Lenin requested Germany's help with the
army's modernization. In this realm, the interests of the two countries
coincided, for Germany was no less eager to enter into military collaboration. By the terms of the Versailles Treaty, she was forbidden to manufacture weapons essential to modern warfare. Soviet Russia, for her part, also
wanted these weapons. On the basis of this common interest, a deal was
eventually struck by virtue of which Soviet Russia provided the German
army with a sanctuary in which to build and test advanced weapons in
exchange for some of this equipment and the training of the Red Army in
their use. This collaboration continued until September 1933, nine months
after Hitler came to power. It greatly benefited both armies. When
the arrangement was finally terminated, Tukhachevskii, then Deputy Commissar for War, told the German chargé d'affaires in Moscow that "in
spite of the regrettable developments" in Germany, "it would never be
forgotten that the Reichswehr had decisively aided the Red Army in its
organization."[234]*

Lenin formally requested the German army to help reorganize the Red
Army in mid-March 1921.[235] In anticipation of such a development, Seeckt

---

*Shortly before, in May 1933, when the possibility of military cooperation with Nazi Ger-
many still seemed realistic, Tukhachevskii told a visiting German delegation: "Always bear
in mind: you and we, Germany and the USSR, can dictate our terms to the whole world if we
stand together.": Iu. L. Diakov and T. S. Bushueva, *Fashistskii mech kovalsia v SSSR* (Moscow, 1992), 25.

had some time earlier organized within the Reichswehr Ministry "Sonder-gruppe R," a clandestine group staffed with officers who had experience dealing with Russians. After Lenin made his request, the negotiations proceeded rapidly. On April 7, Kopp reported to Trotsky from Berlin that the German "Group" had proposed to engage three German arms manufacturers—Blöhm and Voss, Albatrosswerke, and Krupp—to furnish technical personnel and manufacturing facilities for the production, respectively, of submarines, airplanes, and artillery guns and shells. The Germans offered Moscow both credits and technical assistance in building these industries, which were to work concurrently for the Red Army and the Reichswehr. Lenin approved of Kopp's report.[236] Before long, representatives of "Son-dergruppe R" arrived in Moscow to open a branch office. The Germans insisted on strict secrecy. The collaboration was so successfully concealed that for a year and a half Germany's socialist President, Friedrich Ebert, was in the dark: he first learned of it from Seeckt in November 1922, at which time he gave his belated consent.[237]

The decisive turn toward Soviet-German political collaboration occurred in May 1921, after the Allies had rejected a German request for revisions in reparation payments. Gleefully, the most conservative and nationalistic elements in Germany now sought to punish the Allies by making common cause with the Russian Communists.

Soviet interest in such a rapprochement also had obvious motives: in addition to the political and military, they were economic. Lenin believed that the reconstruction of the Soviet economy required massive engagement of Western capital and know-how, and these he could obtain most readily from Germany. The Allies wanted to trade with Soviet Russia but they were unwilling to grant her credits until the debt issue had been satisfactorily resolved. This was not a major obstacle in Russo-German relations, since German losses from Soviet defaults and nationalizations were much lighter and, in any event, substantially made good by the terms of the 1918 treaties between the two countries. Another obstacle to Allied-Soviet trade was Allied insistence that Soviet ministries deal not with individual Western firms but with consortia. This did not suit Moscow at all, for it preferred to pit foreign firms against each other. In contrast to the Allies, the Germans had no objections to letting the Russians deal with their enterprises on a one-on-one basis: Rathenau actually promised Radek that his country would not join any trade consortia without Moscow's approval.[238]

On September 21 and 24, Krasin met with German officers from the General Staff, one of them Seeckt's deputy, to work out the details of Russo-German military cooperation.[239] As he reported to Lenin, he proceeded on the assumption it was pointless to involve German bankers and industrialists who thought only of profits and were easily frightened by the Allies: it was best to deal with those Germans "who thought seriously about revenge." The cooperation was to be kept strictly secret from the German government and remain confined to the military. Germany would provide the financing as well as the technical and managerial personnel to run the projected war industries in Soviet Russia, formal supervision of which would be vested in a Soviet "Trust." The whole undertaking, according to Krasin, was to be disguised as an effort to modernize the Red Army, although its actual immediate purpose was to enable Germany to equip with up-to-date and forbidden weapons an army of hundreds of thousands.

Once he had made up his mind to strike a deal with Germany, Lenin used a ploy that Stalin would replicate in 1939 with even greater success: pretending to seek agreement with the Allies, he pressed the Germans into signing a separate accord. This tactic helped overcome the opposition of pro-Western elements in government and business in Germany which feared antagonizing France and England.

In late January 1922, Radek turned up in Berlin bearing startling news: Moscow was on the verge of concluding an accord with France calling for de jure recognition of Soviet Russia and commercial credits, in return for assurances that Moscow would help enforce the Versailles Treaty. If Russia were willing to do so, France, he claimed, might even cut loose of Poland.* Radek urged Rathenau to forestall such a development by coming to terms with Russia. And this involved a great deal of money. Rathenau offered credits of 5 billion paper marks, protesting that the Russians were "blackmailing" him, but Radek dismissed the figure (50–60 million marks in gold) as too paltry to influence Soviet policy.† Rathenau equivocated, worried about the Allied reaction and skeptical about Russia's ability to pay for imports. The claim of an imminent accord with France had no substance, but it ultimately served Radek and his friends in the German Foreign Office to sway Rathenau: if Germany wanted to avoid a revival of the pre-1914 Franco-Russian alliance, she had to act, and act quickly. To speed up the construction of a modern armament industry in Russia, Radek confided to Seeckt that the Red Army was preparing in the spring to attack Poland: she desperately needed airplanes. The gullible Germans believed these fabrications and hastened in April 1922 to open a Junker air facility at Fili, near Moscow. They also initiated staff discussions with the Red Army on the imaginary invasion of Poland.[240] Radek received support from Chicherin, who arrived in Berlin at the beginning of April en route to Genoa. He

---

*Wipert von Blücher, *Deutschlands Weg nach Rapallo* (Wiesbaden, 1951), 154–55. Gerald Freund, citing this information, calls Radek "irresponsible" (*Unholy Alliance*, New York, 1957, 112–13), intimating that he acted on his own initiative. But, of course, in matters of such gravity nothing was done without the approval of the Politburo and Lenin personally. Proof that this was indeed the case is that the Soviet delegation to Genoa, headed by Chicherin, used the identical tactic two months later to prod the Germans into signing the Rapallo Treaty. Freund, *loc. cit.,* 116–17.

†RTsKhIDNI, F. 2, op. 2, delo 1124. Report from Berlin dated February 14, 1922. In a memorandum to Lenin of February 22, 1922, outlining the strategy for Genoa, Chicherin insisted that without foreign capital there was no hope of reconstructing Soviet transport and industry: *ibid.,* delo 1151.

brought the draft of a proposed Soviet-German accord, which, after being revised with the help of experts from the German Foreign Ministry, would serve as the basic text of the Rapallo Treaty.[241]

The Politburo had approved on February 28 Lenin's agenda for the Genoa Conference as centering on economic accords and encouraging a split in the "bourgeois" camp by separating the "pacifist" wing:

> We should regard and designate "the pacifist part" of the [bourgeois] camp (or use another polite expression especially chosen) the petty bourgeois, pacifist, and semipacifist democracy of the type Second International, Two and a Half International, also of the Keynes type, and so on. One of our principal, if not the principal, political tasks in Genoa is to separate this wing of the bourgeois camp from the camp as a whole, to try to flatter it, to let it know that we find it acceptable and desirable, from our point of view, to conclude with it not only commercial but also political accords (as one of the few chances of the peaceful evolution of capitalism to the new order, about which we, as Communists, are not very optimistic, but are willing to help in the attempt and regard it as our duty, as representatives of one power, in the face of the hostile majority of the others).
>
> Do everything possible and some things which are impossible to strengthen the pacifistic wing of the bourgeoisie and enhance even a little bit its electoral prospects. This is first. Secondly: divide the bourgeois powers that in Genoa will stand united against us. This is our double task in Genoa. Under no circumstances [is it our task] to promote Communist views.[242]

67. Chicherin in Genoa.

When Chicherin protested that pacifism, the linchpin of Lenin's strategy for Genoa, was a "petty bourgeois illusion," Lenin explained with unconcealed irritation that while this was indeed the case, it was no reason not to "utilize the pacifists for the purpose of breaking up the enemy, the bourgeoisie."[243]

The Genoa Conference opened on April 10. The Soviet delegation was headed by Chicherin rather than Lenin: Lenin had intended to go and had actually assumed its chairmanship, but decided to stay home after being warned by Krasin of the danger of assassination. He also refused to allow either Trotsky or Zinoviev to take his place.[244] On the first day, Chicherin announced a comprehensive "pacifist" program of general disarmament. It was a cynical move, given that Soviet Russia had at the time the largest army in the world (over 800,000 men under arms),[245] which it was modernizing with German help. At France's request, the proposal was tabled as irrelevant to the meeting's agenda.

The principal economic Soviet objective in Genoa was securing foreign loans and investments. Count Harry Kessler, a fellow-traveler who in 1918 had served as a liaison between the German Foreign Ministry and the Soviet Ambassador, Adolf Ioffe, was told by the head of the Eastern Department of the German Foreign Office that "all that interests the Russians is money, money, money."[246] Lenin indeed had written in *Pravda* on the eve of the conference that the Russians were going to Genoa "not as Communists but as merchants."[247] Soviet policy at Genoa was to concentrate on the Germans: "An independent German economic policy in Russia," a leading Soviet newspaper argued, "opens the road to a rational employment of German capital, not only in Russia herself, but further to the east, the road whither runs through Russia, and [an area] which Germany is unable to reach by another route."[248]

The Allied proposal called for the Soviet government to acknowledge Russia's foreign debts and compensate foreigners for losses suffered through its "action or negligence." Foreign claims were to be met by the emission abroad of Soviet bonds.[249] Chicherin expressed a willingness, couched in highly conditional terms, to compensate foreigners for their losses, provided his country received diplomatic recognition as well as loans needed for reconstruction.[250] While pretending to negotiate on these terms, the Russian delegation was quietly working toward a separate treaty with Germany.

In this endeavor they were helped by Lloyd George's diplomatic ineptitude. To establish himself as *primus inter pares,* the Prime Minister held in Genoa lunches with the various delegations, including the Soviet. His private encounters with the Russians unwittingly confirmed Radek's and Chicherin's warnings to the Germans of an impending Allied-Russian accord.[251] Convinced by advisers that something untoward was about to happen, Rathenau overcame his misgivings and on April 16, at the Hotel

St. Margherita in nearby Rapallo, placed his signature to a Soviet-German accord, essentially as drafted in Moscow.* Subsequently, to counter charges of duplicity, the Germans justified their action with the argument that the Allies, too, were working for a separate treaty with Moscow.[252]

By the terms of the accord, the signatories granted each other diplomatic recognition and most-favored-nation status.[253] They renounced mutual claims arising from the war and pledged to promote friendly economic relations. Germany further relinquished claims for losses suffered by her government and citizens from Soviet nationalization measures. Rapallo marked the third occasion since the Armistice that Germany had acted in foreign policy independently of the Allies and contrary to their wishes: in each case she did so in favor of Russia—first by refusing in 1919 to join the blockade, and then by denying France in 1920 permission to ship war matériel across her territory to Poland.

Caught by surprise, the Allies sent the Germans a collective protest accusing them of a unilateral initiative on issues subject to international negotiations: Germany had been invited as an equal partner and had responded by violating the spirit of unity. By this action, she excluded herself from further joint discussions with Soviet Russia.[254] The Genoa Conference broke up. The West was probably less alarmed by the provisions of the Rapallo Treaty than by its implications, namely a looming "union of an angry Germany and a hungry Russia."[255]

Rapallo was the first international treaty signed by Germany after Versailles. Most German politicians supported it on the grounds that it opened up Russia to German economic and political penetration. The Social Democrats dissented, warning that Russia was using Germany for purposes of world revolution.[256]

The Treaty did enhance Soviet-German trade, at the expense of Russia's trade with Britain. In 1922 and 1923, one-third of Soviet imports came from Germany. In 1932, this figure rose to 47 percent.[257]

For Moscow, it was essential to keep the Allies and Germany at daggers drawn, and to this end it found in the Versailles Treaty a perfect vehicle. And inasmuch as the SPD, Germany's leading socialist party, sought to work within the Treaty's terms and to keep on friendly terms with the Allies, the Communists turned to the most reactionary, nationalistic elements in Germany. In December 1920 Lenin declared that the German "bourgeoisie" was being driven toward an alliance with Soviet Russia:

[Germany], constrained by the Versailles Treaty, finds herself in conditions that make existence impossible. And in this situation Germany naturally

*Two months later he paid with his life for the Rapallo Treaty, murdered by nationalist assassins as a "pro-Communist Jew."

68. Germany and Russia reemerging united after Rapallo:
a contemporary German magazine cartoon.

pushes for an alliance with Russia. . . . An alliance with Russia of that
suffocating country . . . has produced in Germany political confusion: the
German Black Hundreds have been moving with sympathy toward the
Russian Bolsheviks and Spartacists.[258]

In truth, it was not the German "Black Hundreds" who courted the Communists but the Communists who fawned on the Black Hundreds, that is,
on the Nazis and their kindred souls. Communist-"Fascist" collaboration
came to a climax after January 1923, when the French and Belgians,
declaring Germany in default on reparation payments, occupied the Ruhr.
The Comintern Executive at once backed Germany in her confrontation

with France, and Moscow promised help should the Poles attack at France's behest.[259] In May 1923, the Communist Party of Germany (KPD) adopted a resolution that acknowledged the feasibility of recruiting the nationalist masses.[260]

Lenin's main agent in dealing with Germany's conservative and radical right circles was Karl Radek. Radek felt that the only way open to the German Communists to break out of their isolation was the formation of alliances with nationalistic elements. Such a turnabout he justified with the argument (which Zinoviev echoed) that in the case of "oppressed nations," nationalism was a "revolutionary" phenomenon.[261] To the despondent Germans he proposed a united front against the Allies. He advised the German government that in the event of a war with France, Soviet Russia would pursue a policy of "benevolent neutrality" and the German Communist Party would offer active support.[262] In June 1923, in a speech to the Executive of the Communist International, he lavished praise on Albert Schlageter, a Nazi thug shot by the French for sabotaging transport in the Ruhr: he was the "martyr of German nationalism," a "brave soldier of the counterrevolution" who had earned "the sincere respect of the soldiers of the revolution." "If the patriotic circles in Germany," he declared, "do not resolve to make the cause of the majority of the people their own and in this manner form a front against the Allied capitalists and German capital, then Schlageter's journey will have been a journey into a void."[263] Radek later revealed that the text of this sensational speech had the approval of both the Politburo and the Comintern Executive.[264] The organ of the German Communists (KPD), *Die Rote Fahne*, now opened its pages to Nationalists; Nazis spoke at Communist rallies and Communists at Nazi ones. The KPD put out posters that blended the swastika with the red star.[265] The Spartacist Ruth Fischer, herself Jewish, exhorted German students to "trample" and "hang" Jewish capitalists.[266] This collaboration ended in August 1923, when the Nazis pulled out.

To confuse the situation still further, Moscow accompanied two aspects of its German policy—alliance with the government and cooperation with its right-wing enemies—with a third, social revolution. To prevent the new Prime Minister, Gustav Stresemann, from realizing his policy of negotiating with the Allied powers for financial assistance and for an easing of the Versailles terms, which would place Germany firmly in the Western camp, the Politburo decided on August 23, 1923, to overthrow his government.[267] Hoping to take advantage of a wave of strikes that broke out at the time in Germany, Trotsky dispatched there a military mission headed by General Alexis Skoblevskii to organize the coup.[268] One million tons of grain were stockpiled in Petrograd and at frontier points to help the Germans withstand an anticipated Allied blockade; a relief fund of 200 million gold rubles was also set aside.[269] Trotsky discussed the revolutionary tactics with German Communists, on whose advice it was decided to begin the coup in Saxony and Thuringia. But German workers failed to respond to revolutionary appeals and the coup, which was concurrent with the right-wing Kapp putsch, failed miserably. From November 1923 to March 1924 the German Communist Party was outlawed.

Rapallo accelerated military cooperation between the two countries. On July 29, 1922, an agreement was concluded between A. P. Rozengolts, a member of the Soviet Military-Revolutionary Council, and representatives of General Seeckt. (The document has not been located so far.*) A Soviet mission, headed by E. M. Sklianskii, Trotsky's deputy during the Civil War, arrived in Berlin in January 1923. It offered to purchase weapons for 300 million gold marks, to be paid for by German credits, but the Germans rejected the proposal on the grounds that their manufacturing facilities were unable to meet their own needs.[270] Soviet Russia then agreed to let Germany produce weapons prohibited by the Versailles Treaty on Russian territory in facilities financed and managed by Germany. She further consented to have German military personnel trained there in their use.[271] In return, the Germans undertook to instruct Soviet officers.[272] The following year, the Reichswehr allocated 75 million gold marks for this purpose and opened a branch office in Moscow.[273] Representatives of the two countries discussed in confidence joint military operations against Poland and even against the Allies.[274]

The production of weapons proved something of a disappointment to the Germans because of the primitiveness and inefficiency of the Soviet economy. The principal benefit to both parties from this military collaboration derived from the testing of and training in advanced weapons designed for the next world war.

By 1924, several leading German armament manufacturers had concessions in the Soviet Union. Three German military facilities in Soviet Russia have been identified: the one in Fili to manufacture Junker airplanes, another in Samara province to produce mustard gas and phosgene, and a third in Kazan to build tanks.[275] German officers, disguised as civilians, traveled to Russia for combat practice.[276] From early 1924 on, German pilots received training at Lipetsk, flying Fokker fighters secretly purchased in Holland: ultimately, 120 pilots and 450 flight personnel underwent instruction there. They constituted the core of Hitler's air force.[277] According to General Helm Speidel, a member of "Sondergruppe R," the training at Lipetsk laid the "spiritual foundation of a future Luftwaffe."[278] The experi-

*Rolf-Dieter Müller, *Das Tor zur Weltmacht* (Boppard am Rhein, 1984), 100. It is referred to in a document ("Aus Tagebuch Hasse") in the archive of von Rabenau, N 62/39, H. 5, Bl. 60, on the basis of information from Seeckt: Bundesarchiv-Militärarchiv Freiburg, Nachlass von Rabenau, 62/39, Bd. 2 (1938), Heft 5. Cf. Freund, *Unholy Alliance,* 124. On Rozengolts, who perished in 1938 in Stalin's purges, see P. V. Volobuev in *Revvoensovet* (Moscow, 1991), 318–25.

ence gained in Russia is said to have given the German air force a ten-year advantage over the Allies.[279] Russian pilots and ground personnel, too, received training at the Lipetsk base.

German officers also practiced tank and chemical warfare at Kazan and Samara. An unknown quantity of the weapons produced in Soviet Russia was surreptitiously shipped to Germany. In 1926, German pacifists would discover three Soviet ships in the port of Stettin loaded with 300,000 artillery shells produced in Soviet Russia. The discovery enabled the socialist leader Philipp Scheidemann to reveal the military collaboration between the two countries and to accuse the government of using Soviet ammunition against German workers.* But the German hopes of developing large-scale manufacture of forbidden equipment in Russia were disappointed. The production of poison gas ran into difficulties. Even more problems afflicted the airplane plant at Fili: the failure of the Russians to place orders caused the Reichswehr in 1925 to shut it down.[280] The submarine project apparently never left the drawing table.

Beginning in 1925, Soviet officers, variously disguised, some posing as Bulgarians, observed Reichswehr exercises. Others were detailed to Germany to attend secret courses taught at the General Staff by Hitler's future generals, including Field Marshal Werner von Blomberg, the first Nazi Defense Minister, as well as generals Model, Brauchitsch, Keitel, and Guderian; among the students are said to have been Tukhachevskii and Iakir. "During these courses the Russians were able to see and study all directives, tactical and operational studies, methods of recruitment and training, and even the organizational plans of the illegal rearmament itself. Nothing seems to have been withheld from them."[281]

Obviously, collaboration on such a scale could not go unnoticed. In fact, Polish and French intelligence had gotten wind of it and it became public knowledge after Scheidemann's revelations. But the Allies for some reason were not alarmed. They did nothing to stop it, and in the years that followed, technical cooperation between the two countries continued without interruption.

In this manner, Soviet Russia helped lay the foundations of a revived German army, which Hitler would put to his own uses. The tactics of dive bombing, of motorized warfare, and of combined air and land operations, which formed the basis of Hitler's *Blitzkrieg*, were first tested on Soviet soil. The Red Army, for its part, owing to this collaboration proved better prepared for the German assault during World War II than the Allied forces.

The German generals who engaged in collaboration with the Soviet

*F. L. Carsten in *Survey*, No. 44–45 (1962), 121; Freund, *Unholy Alliance*, 211; Müller, *Das Tor*, 146. Apparently forewarned, the Soviet press on the same day—December 16—admitted the existence of German installations in the U.S.S.R., but depicted them as defensive: *Pravda*, No. 291/3,520 (December 16, 1926), 1. Cf. Karl Radek in *Izvestiia*, No. 291–92 (December 16, 1926), 2. These seem to have been the only references in the Soviet press to military collaboration with Weimar Germany.

Union were preparing for a World War II that would abrogate the Versailles Treaty and win for Germany the continental hegemony that had eluded her in World War I. Obviously, they would not have initiated the Russians into their military secrets unless they expected them to be on their side in future hostilities. Thus the outlines of the Nazi-Soviet Pact of 1939, which unleashed World War II, and in which Germany, with Moscow's benevolent neutrality, conquered most of Europe, took shape in the early 1920s, when Lenin was alive and in charge.

9

The Crisis of
the New Regime

> How do you solve the following problem: if the peasantry is not with us, if the working class falls under the influence of various anarchist elements and also tends to abandon us—on what can the Communist Party now base itself?
>
> *Iurii Milonov at the Tenth Congress of the Communist Party (March 1921)*[1]

> Nothing has been left that could obstruct the central government, but, by the same token, nothing could shore it up.
>
> *Alexis de Tocqueville*[2]

The political crisis that shook the Communist Party in 1921–23 was due to the fact that the suppression of rival parties did not eliminate dissent, but merely shifted it from the public arena into the inner ranks of the party. This development violated the cardinal tenet of Bolshevism, disciplined unity. The resolutions of the Eleventh Party Congress obliquely acknowledged what was occurring:

> In order to consolidate the victory of the proletariat and to maintain its dictatorship under conditions of an exceedingly stressful civil war, the proletarian vanguard had to deprive all political groupings hostile to Soviet authority of the freedom to organize. The Russian Communist Party was left the country's only legal political party. This circumstance, of course, gave the working class and its party many advantages. But, on the other hand, it also produced phenomena that have extremely complicated the party's work. Inevitably, into the ranks of the only legal political party streamed, seeking to exert their influence, groups and strata that under different conditions would be found not in the ranks of the Communist Party but those of Social-Democracy or another variant of petty-bourgeois socialism.[3]

As Trotsky put it: "Our party is now the only one in the country; all discontent goes only through our party."[4] The leadership thus confronted a painful choice: whether to sacrifice unity and all the advantages that flowed from it by tolerating dissent within party ranks, or to outlaw dissent and maintain unity even at the risk of both the ossification of the party's leading apparatus and its estrangement from the rank and file. Lenin unhesitatingly opted for the second alternative: by this decision, he laid the groundwork for Stalin's personal dictatorship.

The Bolshevik leaders, and no one more than Lenin, fretted about the progressive bureaucratization of their regime. They had the feeling—and statistical evidence to support it—that both the party and the state were being weighed down by a parasitic class of functionaries who used their offices to promote personal interests. To make matters worse, the more the bureaucracy expanded, the more of the budget it absorbed, the less got done. This held true even of the Cheka: in September 1922 Dzerzhinskii demanded a thorough accounting of what Cheka personnel were doing, adding that he believed such a survey would yield "deadly" *(ubiistvennye)* results.[5] For Lenin in the last period of his life the bureaucracy became an obsessive concern.

That they should have been surprised by this phenomenon only provides further evidence that under the hard-bitten realism of the Bolsheviks lurked a remarkable naïveté.* It should have been apparent to them that the nationalization of the country's entire organized life, economic activity included, was bound to expand the number of white-collar workers. It apparently never occurred to them that "power" *(vlast')*, of which they never had enough, meant not only opportunity but also responsibility; that the fulfillment of that responsibility was a full-time occupation calling for correspondingly large cadres of professionals; and that these professionals were unlikely to be concerned exclusively or even primarily with public welfare but would also attend to their own needs. The bureaucratization of life that accompanied Communist rule opened unprecedented opportunities for clerical careers to lower-middle-class elements previously barred from them: they were its principal beneficiaries.[6] And even workers, once they left the factory floor for the office, ceased to be workers, merging with the bureaucratic caste, although in party censuses they often continued to be listed as workers: in a private letter to Lenin, Kalinin urged that only persons engaged in manual labor be listed as workers, whereas "foremen, markers, watchmen" should be classified as office personnel *(sluzhashchie)*.[7] This is how the Menshevik émigré organ analyzed the phenomenon on the eve of NEP:

*In April 1921, Lenin admitted that in the first year and a half of the regime he had not been aware of the dangers of bureaucratization. He publicly acknowledged it in only in 1919 at the Eighth Party Congress, which adopted a new party program. The program noted with regret the "partial reemergence of bureaucratism inside the soviet system." Lenin, *PSS*, XLIII, 229. But even then Lenin blamed this phenomenon on the methods of primitive production and trade operations necessitated by the Civil War: *ibid.*, 230.

The Bolshevik dictatorship . . . has ejected from all spheres of governmental and public administration not only the tsarist bureaucracy, but also the intelligentsia from bourgeois circles, with their diplomas, and in this manner opened the "path upward" to that countless offspring of the petty bourgeoisie, the peasantry, the working class, the armed forces, and so forth, who previously, by virtue of the privileged status of wealth and education, had been attached to the lower classes and who now make up the huge "soviet bureaucracy"—this new urban stratum, in its essence and ambitions a petty bourgeoisie, all of whose interests bind it to the Revolution, because it alone enabled them to climb to where they are, freed of hard productive labor and involved in the mechanism of state administration, rising *above* the nation's masses.[8]

The Bolsheviks failed to anticipate this development because their philosophy of history taught them to regard politics exclusively as a by-product of class conflicts, and governments as nothing but instruments of the ruling class: a view that precluded the state and its corps of civil servants having interests distinct from those of the class they were said to serve. The same philosophy prevented them from understanding the nature of the problem once they had become aware of it. Like any tsarist conservative, Lenin could think of no better device to curb the abuses of the bureaucracy than piling one "control" commission on top of another, sending out inspectors, and insisting there was no abuse that "good men" could not correct. The systemic sources of the problem eluded him to the end.

Bureaucratization occurred in the apparatus of the party as well as of the state.

Although structured in a highly centralized fashion, the Bolshevik party traditionally cultivated within its ranks a certain degree of informal democracy.[9] Under the principle of "democratic centralism," decisions taken by the directing departments had to be carried out by the lower organs with no questions asked. But the decisions were reached by majority vote—first of the Central Committee, and then of the Politburo—after thorough debate in which everyone had a chance to have his say. Provincial party cells were routinely consulted. Even as dictator of the country, within the party Lenin was only *primus inter pares:* neither the Politburo nor the Central Committee had a formal chairman. Delegates to the party's congresses, its highest organs, were elected by local organizations. Local party officials were chosen by fellow members. In fact, Lenin almost always prevailed by the force of his personality and stature as the party's founder: but victory was not assured and on occasion eluded even him.

As the party assumed ever greater responsibilities for managing the country, its membership expanded and so did its administrative apparatus. Until March 1919, a single person, Iakov Sverdlov, carried in his head all the details of party organization and personnel. He ran the party from day to day, freeing Lenin and his associates to make the political and military decisions.[10] Such a system could not last for long in any event, given that by March 1919 the party had 314,000 members. Sverdlov's sudden death at this time made it imperative to place the party's management on a more formal basis. To this end the Eighth Party Congress in March 1919 created two new organs of the Central Committee: the Politburo, initially of five members (Lenin, Trotsky, Stalin, Kamenev, Nikolai Krestinskii), to decide swiftly on urgent issues, without resort to the entire Central Committee; and the Orgburo, also of five members, to attend to organizational matters, which in practice meant personnel appointments. The third institution, the Secretariat, established in March 1917, until Stalin's appointment as its chairman in April 1922, seems to have occupied itself mainly with shuffling papers. Its head, the Secretary, was required to be a member of the Orgburo. Judging by the agenda of the Orgburo and the Secretariat after Stalin had taken over, there was no strict division of responsibilities between them, both dealing with personnel matters, although the Orgburo seems to have been more directly responsible for monitoring the performance of the cadres.[11] The creation of these organs began the process of concentrating authority in party affairs at the top, in Moscow.

By the time the Civil War ended, the Communist Party had a sizeable staff occupied exclusively with paperwork. A census conducted toward the end of 1920 revealed interesting facts about its composition. Only 21 percent of the members engaged in physical labor in industry or agriculture; the remaining 79 percent held various white-collar positions.* The members' educational level was exceedingly low and not commensurate with their responsibilities and authority: in 1922, only 0.6 percent (2,316) had completed higher education, and 6.4 percent (24,318) had secondary school diplomas. On the basis of this evidence, one Russian historian has concluded that at that time 92.7 percent of party members were functionally semiliterate (18,000, or 4.7 percent, were completely illiterate).[12] From the body of white-collar personnel emerged an elite of functionaries employed in Moscow by the central organs of the Communist Party. In the summer of 1922, this group numbered over 15,000 persons.[13]

> The bureaucratization of party life had inevitable consequences. . . . The Party official engaged exclusively on Party business was at an obvious advantage compared with the rank-and-file Party member who had a full-time job in a factory or in a government office. The sheer force of professional preoccupation with Party management rendered the officialdom the center of initiative, direction, and control. At every level of the Party hierarchy, a transfer of authority became visible, first from the congresses

---

*N. Solovev in *Pravda*, No. 190 (August 28, 1921), 3–4. Although not complete—the census covered only two-thirds of the Russian Republic—it was assumed to be representative of the Party as a whole. The figures also do not include the capital city, Moscow, the statistics for which were declared "unreliable": if these were counted, the proportion of Communists holding white-collar jobs would have been considerably higher, since the capital was the hub of the bureaucratic empire.

or conferences to the committees which they nominally elected, and then from the committees to the Party secretaries who ostensibly executed their will.[14]

The Central Committee apparatus, gradually, naturally, and almost imperceptibly, supplanted the local organs of the Party not only in making most of the decisions but also in selecting executive personnel at all levels. The process of centralization did not stop there, progressing with an inexorable logic: first the Communist Party took over all organized political life; then the Central Committee assumed direction of the Party, stifling initiative and silencing criticism; next, the Politburo began to make all the decisions for the Central Committee; then three men—Stalin, Kamenev, and Zinoviev—came to control the Politburo; until finally one man alone, Stalin, decided for the Politburo. Once the process culminated in a one-man dictatorship, it had nowhere further to go, with the result that Stalin's death led to the gradual disintegration of the Party and its authority over the country.

Already in 1920 it was common for the Orgburo to designate provincial Party officials without consulting the organizations they were selected to manage[15]: a practice which came to be known as *naznachenstvo*, or "appointmentitis." In a country accustomed for centuries to bureaucratic rule and the flow of directives from above, such procedures seemed normal, and opposition to it was confined to a small and ineffective minority.

Although there undoubtedly were Communists who joined the Party for idealistic reasons, the majority did so for the advantages membership bestowed. Members enjoyed privileges that in the nineteenth century had been associated with gentry *(dvorianstvo)* status, namely, assured access to executive ("responsible") positions in government. Trotsky labeled them "radishes" (red outside, white inside). Those sufficiently high in the Communist hierarchy received additional food rations and access to exclusive shops, as well as cash allowances. They had virtual immunity from arrest and prosecution, which in the lawless Soviet society was no mean privilege. Emulating tsarist practices, the Soviet government established as early as 1918 the principle that its officials could not be brought to justice for actions committed in the performance of duties.[16] Whereas under tsarism, an official could be tried only with the concurrence of his immediate superiors, a Communist functionary could be arrested "only with the knowledge and approval of the Party organization corresponding to the rank he held in the Party."[17] Lenin strenuously objected to this practice, demanding that Communists be punished for wrongdoing more severely than others, but he was powerless to change custom.[18] From the beginning of its reign, the Communist Party's status as an entity above the law transferred also to its membership.

Such power, combined with legal immunity, inevitably led to abuses.

Beginning with the Eighth Party Congress (1919), complaints were heard of the corruptibility of party personnel and their estrangement from the masses.[19] The pages of the Communist press were filled with accounts of violations of the most elementary norms of decency by party officials: judging by some, Communist bosses behaved like eighteenth-century owners of serfs. Thus, in January 1919 the Astrakhan organ of the Communist Party reported on the visit of Kliment Voroshilov, Stalin's comrade-in-arms and commander of the Tenth Army at Tsaritsyn. Voroshilov made his appearance in a luxurious *shestërka,* a coach pulled by six horses, followed by ten carriages with attendants, and some fifty carts piled high with trunks, casks, and other wares. On such forays, the local inhabitants were required to render the visiting dignitaries all manner of personal services and were threatened with revolvers if they refused.[20]

To end such scandalous behavior, the Party carried out a purge in late 1921 and early 1922. Although ostensibly directed at careerists who had enrolled under the relaxed admission procedures in force during the Civil War, its true targets were persons who had transferred from the other socialist parties, notably Mensheviks, whom Lenin blamed for injecting democratic and other heretical ideas into Communist ranks.[21] Many were expelled; and with voluntary resignations, especially by disgruntled workers, the membership declined from 659,000 to 500,000, and then sank still lower, below 400,000.* The practice was instituted at this time of appointing "candidate members," who had to undergo a period of apprenticeship before qualifying for admission. In subsequent purges (1922–23) more were expelled or resigned, until nearly half of the party turned over.[22] These procedures may have rid the party of Mensheviks and other "petty-bourgeois socialists" but not of corrupt Communists. Abuses continued because they inhered in the privileged status of the Communist Party and its complete freedom from accountability. If the citizen had no means of redress against those administering him either as voter or as the owner of property, and if, moreover, party members were exempt from legal responsibility, then it was inevitable that the administrative corps would turn into a self-contained, self-perpetuating, and self-gratifying body. The Control Commission established in 1920 to oversee the ethics of the Party reported that party officials felt they were accountable for the performance of their duties only to those who had appointed them, not to the "party masses,"[23] let alone to the population at large. It was a carryover of attitudes prevalent among officials under tsarism.[24]

To make matters worse still, the Party itself began to corrupt the bureaucracy. In July 1922, the Orgburo passed an innocuous-sounding ruling,

*A report to Stalin by the Party's Organizational Department (Orgotdel) in September 1922 stated that in 1921–22, depending on the province, resignations from the Party ranged from 6.8 to 9.2 percent: RTsKhIDNI, F. 558, op. 1, delo 2429. According to Kalinin, the majority of those quitting the Party were peasants and workers: RTsKhIDNI, F. 5, op. 2, delo 27, list 9.

"On the improvement of the living conditions of active party workers," originally published in a truncated version.[25] It established a salary scale for party functionaries: they were to receive several hundred (new) rubles, with additional allowances for families and overtime, which in their totality could double their basic pay—this at a time when the average industrial worker earned 10 rubles. High party bureaucrats were further entitled, free of charge, to extra food rations, as well as housing, clothing, and medical care, and, in some instances, chauffeured cars. In the summer of 1922 "responsible workers" employed in the central organs of the Party were issued supplementary food rations entitling them to 26 pounds of meat and 2.6 pounds of butter a month. They traveled in special train coaches, upholstered and lit by candles, while ordinary mortals, fortunate enough to obtain tickets, had to squeeze into crowded third-class compartments or freight cars.[26] The very highest officials had the right to vacations and rest cures of one to three months in foreign sanitoria, for which the Party paid in gold rubles. In November 1921, no fewer than six top-level Communists were receiving medical care in Germany: one of them (Lev Karakhan) went there for hemorrhoid surgery.[27] Allocations of such benefits were made by Stalin's Secretariat, the staff of which, on his assumption of office, numbered 600.[28] In the summer of 1922, the number of persons entitled to special benefits exceeded 17,000; in September of that year, the Orgburo raised it to 60,000.

The Party's leaders qualified for dachas. The first to acquire a country house was Lenin, who in October 1918 took over an estate at Gorki, 35 kilometers southwest of Moscow, the property of a tsarist general. Others followed suit: Trotsky took over one of the most luxurious landed estates in Russia, Arkhangelskoe, the property of the princes Iusupov, while Stalin made himself at home in the country house of an oil magnate at Zubalovo.[29] At Gorki, Lenin had at his disposal a fleet of six limousines operated by the GPU.[30] Although he rarely asked favors for himself, he was not averse to requesting them for members of his family and friends, as, for instance, directing that the private coach in which his sister and the Bukharins were traveling to the Crimea, almost certainly on vacation, be attached to military trains to speed up their journey.[31] When attending the theater or opera, the new leaders occupied as a matter of course the imperial loges.

Imperceptibly, the new rulers slipped into the habits of the old. Adolf Ioffe complained to Trotsky in 1920 of the spreading rot:

> From top to bottom and from bottom to top, it is everywhere the same. On the lowest level, it is a pair of shoes and a soldier's shirt [gimnasterka]; higher up, an automobile, a railroad car, the Sovnarkom dining room, quarters in the Kremlin or the "National" hotel; and on the highest rungs, where all this is available, it is prestige, prominent status, and fame.[32]

According to Ioffe it was becoming psychologically acceptable to believe that "the leaders can do anything." None of these patrician habits of public

69. A new elite in the making: a party functionary
(extreme right) reads while workers labor.

servants had anything to do with Marxism, but they did have a great deal
to do with the political traditions of Russia.

The key territorial administrators under the new regime were the chairmen
of the provincial *(guberniia)* committees of the Party, popularly known as
gubkomy. Since Peter the Great, the *guberniia* had been the basic administrative unit of Russia, and its chief, the governor, enjoying broad executive and
police powers, represented imperial authority. The Bolshevik regime followed this tradition: secretaries of the *gubkomy* became, in effect, successors
to imperial governors. The authority to designate them, therefore, was a
source of considerable patronage. Before the Revolution, governors had
been appointed by the tsar on the recommendation of the Minister of the
Interior; now they were appointed by Lenin at the recommendation of the
Orgburo and the Secretariat. A special department of the latter, called
Uchraspred (Uchetno-Raspredetil'nyi Otdel), established in 1920, selected
and transferred party personnel. In December 1921, it was ruled that to
qualify as *gubkom* secretary one had to have joined the Party before October
1917; secretaries of district *(uezd)* party committees *(ukomy)* had to have
belonged for a minimum of three years. All such appointments were to be
approved by a higher party authority.[33] These provisions may have helped
safeguard discipline and orthodoxy, but at the price of depriving party cells
of the right to choose their own officers. Although little noticed at the time,
they vastly enhanced the powers of the central apparatus: "The right of
confirmation by the Orgburo or Secretariat . . . became in practice tantamount to a right of 'recommendation' or 'nomination.' "[34] All this had

occurred before Stalin assumed the post of General Secretary in April 1922.

As a result of these practices, appointments to key Party posts in the provinces increasingly were made not by the members but by the "Center." During 1922, thirty-seven *gubkom* secretaries were removed or transferred by Moscow, and forty-two appointed on its "recommendation."* Now, as under tsarism, loyalty was the supreme qualification for appointment: in a circular sent out by the Central Committee, "the loyalty of a given comrade to the Party" was listed as the very first criterion for office.[35] In the course of 1922, the Secretariat and Orgburo made over 10,000 assignments.[36] Since the Politburo was overburdened with work, many of these assignments were made at the discretion of the General Secretary and the Orgburo. Frequently, inspection teams were sent to the provinces to report on the performance of *gubkomy*—an echo of the "revisions" of Imperial Russia. At the Tenth Party Conference held in May 1921, it was resolved that *gubkom* secretaries were to come to Moscow every three months to report to the Secretariat.[37] Viacheslav Molotov, who worked for the Secretariat, justified these practices with the argument that left to themselves the *gubkomy* attended mostly to their own, local affairs and ignored national party concerns.[38] In effect, the *gubkomy* turned into "conveyor belts for Moscow directives."[39]

The Secretariat acquired the additional authority to select delegates to party congresses, nominally the party's highest authority. By 1923, most delegates were appointed on the recommendation of *gubkom* secretaries, who themselves were in good measure appointees of the Secretariat.[40] This authority enabled the Secretariat to muzzle opposition from the rank and file. Thus at the Tenth Party Congress (1921), which witnessed acrimonious debates pitting the so-called "Workers' Opposition" and "Democratic Centralists" against the Central Committee, 85 percent of the delegates fell in line with the Central Committee's resolutions condemning the dissenters: a vote which, judging by the available evidence, hardly reflected the sentiments of the membership at large.[41] Two years later, at the Twelfth Congress, the opposition was reduced to an impotent fringe. At the next Congress, there no longer was an opposition.

Thus an aristocracy emerged in the Communist service class. The practices adopted five years after the power seizure were a far cry from the early days of the regime, when the Party insisted on its members' receiving lower salaries than the average worker and confining their living quarters to one room per person.[42] They also meant the abandonment of regulations that denied Communists employed in factories special privileges, while imposing on them heavier obligations.[43]

*Merle Fainsod, *How Russia Is Ruled*, revised ed. (Cambridge, Mass., 1963), 633, note 10. In 1923, E. A. Preobrazhenskii said that 30 percent of *gubkom* secretaries were "recommended" by the Central Committee, which he called a "state within the state" (*Dvenadtsatyi S"ezd RKP(b)*, Moscow, 1968, 146).

So much for the Party bureaucracy.

The state bureaucracy expanded at an even more spectacular rate. The structure of nationwide soviets rapidly lost the little influence they had had on Bolshevik policies, and by 1919–20 turned into rubber stamps for party decisions transmitted through the Council of People's Commissars and its branches. Their "elections" turned into ceremonies to approve nominees picked by the Party: fewer than one in four eligible citizens bothered to vote.[44] The soviets were supplanted by bureaucratic state institutions, behind which stood the all-powerful Party. In 1920, the last year that the soviets were allowed to hold open discussions, it was common to hear complaints about the spread of the bureaucracy.[45] In February 1920, the office of Worker-Peasant Inspection (Rabkrin) was created, with Stalin as chairman, to oversee abuses in state institutions; but as Lenin conceded two years later, it did not meet his expectations.[46]

The expansion of the governmental bureaucracy is explainable first and foremost by the fact of the government taking over the management of institutions that before October 1917 had been in private hands. By eliminating private enterprise in banking and industry, by abolishing zemstvos and city councils, by dissolving all private associations, the government assumed liability for their functions, which, in turn, demanded a proportionate expansion of officialdom. One example will suffice. Before the Revolution, the nation's schools were partly supervised by the Ministry of Public Instruction, partly by the Orthodox Church, and partly by private bodies. When, in 1918, the government nationalized all schools under the Commissariat of Enlightenment, it had to create a staff to replace the clerical and private personnel previously in charge of nongovernmental schools. In time, the Commissariat of Enlightenment was also given responsibility for directing the country's cultural life, previously almost entirely in private hands, and for enforcing censorship. As a consequence, as early as May 1919 it had on its payroll 3,000 employees—ten times the number employed by the corresponding tsarist ministry.[47]

But enhanced administrative responsibilities were not the sole reason for the increase in the Soviet bureaucracy. An employee even on the lowest rungs of the civil service ladder acquired precious advantages of survival under the harsh conditions of Soviet life: access to goods not available to ordinary citizens, as well as opportunities to obtain bribes and tips.

The result was massive featherbedding. White-collar jobs multiplied in the various bureaus directing the Soviet economy at the very time that production was declining. While the number of workers employed in Russian industry dropped from 856,000 in 1913 to 807,000 in 1918, the number of white-collar employees rose from 58,000 to 78,000. Thus, already in the first year of the Communist regime, the ratio of white- to blue-collar industrial employees grew by one-third, compared to 1913.[48] In the next three years, this ratio rose even more dramatically: whereas in 1913, for every 100 factory workers there were 6.2 white-collar employees, in the summer of 1921 their proportion rose to 15.0 per hundred.[49] In transport, with railroad traffic declining by 80 percent and the number of workers remaining stationary, bureaucratic personnel increased by 75 percent. Whereas in 1913 there were 12.8 employees, both blue- and white-collar, per one kilometer (five-eighths of a mile) of railroad track, in 1921 20.7 were required to perform the same tasks.[50] An inquiry into one rural district of Kursk province, carried out in 1922–23, showed that the local agriculture department, which under tsarism had 16 employees, now had 79—and this while food output had dropped. The police chancery in the same district had doubled its personnel compared to prerevolutionary days.[51] Most monstrous was the expansion of the bureaucracy charged with managing the economy: in the spring of 1921, the Supreme Council of the National Economy (VSNKh) employed 224,305 functionaries, of whom 24,728 worked in Moscow, 93,593 in its provincial agencies, and 105,984 in the districts *(uezdy)*—this at a time when the industrial productivity of which it was in charge had dropped to below one-fifth of what it had been in 1913.[52] In 1920, to Lenin's astonishment and anger, Moscow housed 231,000 full-time functionaries, and Petrograd, 185,000.[53] Overall, between 1917 and the middle of 1921, the number of government employees increased nearly fivefold, from 576,000 to 2.4 million. By then, the country had over twice as many bureaucrats as workers.[54]

Given the immense need for officials and the low educational level of its own cadres, the new regime had no choice but to hire large numbers of ex-tsarist officials, especially personnel qualified to run ministerial bureaus. The following table indicates the percentages of such officials in the commissariats as of 1918:[55]

Commissariat of the Interior	48.3%
Supreme Council of National Economy	50.3%
Commissariat of War	55.2%
Commissariat of State Control	80.9%
Commissariat of Transport	88.1%
Commissariat of Finance	97.5%

"Indications are that over half the officials in the central offices of the commisariats, and perhaps ninety percent of upper echelon officials, had worked in some kind of administrative position before October 1917."[56] Only the Cheka, with 16.1 percent ex-tsarist officials, and the Commissariat of Foreign Affairs, with 22.9 percent (both figures are for 1918), were staffed primarily with new personnel.[57] On the basis of this evidence, one Western scholar has reached the startling conclusion that the changes in government personnel made by the Bolsheviks in the first five years "could perhaps be compared with those occurring in Washington in the heyday of the 'spoils system.' "[58]

The new bureaucracy modeled itself on the tsarist. As before 1917, officials served the state, not the nation, which they viewed as a hostile force. The anarchist Alexander Berkman, who visited Russia in 1920, thus depicted the typical government office under the new regime:

> The Soviet institutions [in the Ukraine] present the familiar picture of the Moscow pattern: gatherings of worn, tired people, looking hungry and apathetic. Typical and sad. The corridors and offices are crowded with applicants seeking permission to do or to be exempt from doing this or that. The labyrinth of new decrees is so intricate, the officials prefer the easier way of solving perplexing problems by "revolutionary method," on their "conscience," generally to the dissatisfaction of the petitioners.
>
> Long lines are everywhere, and much writing and handling of "papers," and documents by *baryshni* (young ladies) in high heeled shoes, that swarm in every office. They puff at cigarettes and animatedly discuss the advantages of certain bureaus as measured by the quantity of the *paëk* [ration] issued, the symbol of Soviet existence. Workers and peasants, their heads bared, approach the long tables. Respectfully, even servilely, they seek information, plead for an "order" for clothing, or a "ticket" for boots. "I don't know," "In the next office," "Come tomorrow," is the usual reply. There are protests and lamentations, and begging for attention and advice.[59]

As in the days of tsarism, Soviet officialdom was elaborately stratified. In March 1919, the authorities divided the civil service into 27 categories, each minutely defined. Salary differentials were relatively modest: thus employees in the lowest rank *(razriad)*, made up of junior doormen, charwomen, and the like, received 600 (old) rubles a month, those in the 27th rank (heads of commissariat departments, and such like) were paid 2,200 rubles.[60] But wages counted for little, because of hyperinflation: the meaningful salary took the form of perquisites, of which food rations were the most important. Thus Lenin in 1920 obviously did not live on his monthly salary of 6,500 rubles, which would have bought him thirty cucumbers on the black market, the only place where they were available to ordinary citizens.[61] In addition to the *paëk,* even the lowest officials had ways of supplementing their wages by means of bribery, which was rampant, notwithstanding severe laws against it.[62]

Lenin liked to ascribe the unsatisfactory state of the Soviet apparatus to the large number of ex-tsarist bureaucrats in its employ: "With the exception of the Commissariat of Foreign Affairs," he wrote, "our state apparatus, most of all, represents a survival of the old apparatus, least of all subjected to the smallest changes. It is only slightly adorned at the top; in other respects, it is the most typically old of our old state apparatus."[63] But as his disjointed and confused remarks on the subject indicate, he had not the slightest idea what had gone wrong and why. The size of the bureaucracy was determined by the scope of his government's ambitions, while its corruptibility was assured by freedom from public controls.

In the summer of 1920 the Communist Party was shaken by a heresy the party establishment designated the "Workers' Opposition." It reflected the dissatisfaction of Bolshevik industrial workers with the manner in which intellectuals had taken control of the country, and, more specifically, with the bureaucratization of industry and the concurrent decline in the authority and autonomy of trade unions. Although its spokesmen were veteran Communists, the movement also expressed the sentiments of that majority of workers who either belonged to no party or inclined toward Menshevism. Its main bases of support were Samara, where the Workers' Opposition took over the *gubkom,* the Donbass region, and the Urals. Its adherents were very influential in the metallurgical, mining, and textile industries.[64] Alexander Shliapnikov, its head, ran the Metal Workers' Union, the strongest union in the country and the one traditionally most friendly to the Bolsheviks. The highest Bolshevik functionary of worker background, during World War I Shliapnikov had directed the party's underground in Petrograd, and in October 1917 took over the Commissariat of Labor. Alexandra Kollontai, his mistress, was the movement's most articulate theorist. Alongside the Workers' Opposition emerged a second heresy known as "Democratic Centralism." Composed of well-known Communist intellectuals, it objected to the bureaucratization of the party and the employment in industry of "bourgeois specialists." Its adherents wanted greater power for the soviets, while opposing trade union demands for a dominant role in economic management. One of their leaders, T. V. Sapronov, an old Bolshevik, also of worker origin, had the temerity at a party congress to call Lenin an "ignoramus" *(nevezhda)* and an "oligarch."*

The Workers' Oppositionists were stalwart Bolsheviks. They accepted the dictatorship of the Party and its "leading role" in the trade unions; they approved of the abolition of "bourgeois" freedoms and the suppression of political parties. They found nothing wrong with the party's treatment of the peasantry. When Kronshtadt rebelled in 1921 they were among the first to volunteer for the Red Army units formed to suppress the mutiny. In Shliapnikov's words, their differences with Lenin were not over objectives,

---

*Struck from the record, these epithets were first made public by Stalin in 1924: I. Stalin, *Ob oppozitsii* (Moscow-Leningrad, 1928), 73.

70. Shliapnikov.

but over means. They found it unacceptable that the intelligentsia, formed into a new bureaucracy, was displacing labor as the country's ruling class. For indeed, the country's "worker" government had not a single worker in a position of authority: most of its leading officials had not only never worked in a factory or on a farm, but had never even held a steady job.[65]

Lenin took this challenge extremely seriously: he was not inclined to ignore "worker spontaneity," which he had fought ever since founding the Bolshevik party. Denouncing the Workers' Opposition as a species of Menshevism and syndicalism, he counterattacked and crushed it in no time. But in so doing he had recourse to procedures that destroyed, once and for all, what was left of democracy in Communist ranks. To maintain the fiction that the Bolshevik dictatorship was a government of workers while ignoring the workers' wishes, he ensured the government's isolation even from its own supporters.

The Workers' Opposition emerged into the open at the Ninth Party Congress (March 1920) in connection with Moscow's decision to introduce into industry the principle of one-man management. Until then, Soviet Russia's nationalized enterprises had been administered by boards, on which sat, alongside technical specialists and party officials, representatives of trade unions and factory committees. This arrangement proved inefficient and was blamed for the collapse of industrial production. The party leadership had determined already in 1918 to shift to personal management, but the decision was difficult to implement because of labor resistance. Now that the Civil War was over, the Ninth Party Congress resolved to put into effect, "from top to bottom, the frequently stated principle of express responsibility of a given person for the given work. *Collegiality,* to the extent that it has a place in the process of deliberation or decision-making, must unconditionally yield to *individualism* in the process of execution."[66] In anticipation of this resolution, the Central Council of Soviet Trade Unions had voted in January 1920 against one-man management. Lenin disregarded its wishes. He similarly ignored the preference of the workers of Donbass, whose delegates voted 21 to 3 in favor of retaining the collegial system of industrial management.[67]

Under the new arrangement, introduced nationwide in 1920 and 1921, trade unions and factory committees no longer participated in decision-making, but only in the implementation of decisions made by professional managers. Lenin had the Ninth Party Congress pass a resolution forbidding trade unions to interfere with management. He justified such procedures with the argument that under Communism, which had eliminated the exploiting classes, trade unions no longer had to defend the interests of the workers since this was done for them by the government. Their proper function was to act as government agents in improving production and maintaining labor discipline:

> Under the dictatorship of the proletariat, trade unions transform themselves from organs of struggle of the vendors of labor against the ruling class of capitalists, into instruments of the ruling working class. The tasks of trade unions lie, mainly, in the areas of organization and education. These tasks the trade unions must fulfill not as a self-sufficient, organizationally isolated force, but as one of the basic instruments of the Soviet state, led by the Communist Party.[68]

In other words, Soviet trade unions henceforth were to represent not the workers but the government. Trotsky fully subscribed to this view, arguing that in a "workers' state" the trade unions had to rid themselves of the habit of viewing the employer as an adversary, and turn into factors of productivity under the party's guidance.[69] This view of their function meant in practice that trade union officials would not be elected by their members but appointed by the party. As had so often happened in the course of Russian history, an institution created by a social group to defend its interests was taken over by the state for its own purposes.

Russia's trade union leaders took seriously the claim that their country was a "dictatorship of the proletariat": strangers to the subtleties of dialectic, they failed to understand how the party leadership, composed of intellectuals, could know better what was good for labor than labor itself. They objected to the dismissal of worker representatives from industrial management and the return to positions of authority, in the guise of "specialists," of former captains of industry. These people, they complained, treated them exactly as they had done under the old regime. What, then, had changed? and what had the revolution been for? They further objected to the introduction into the Red Army of a command hierarchy and to the restoration in it of ranks. They criticized the bureaucratization of the Party and the accumulation of power in the hands of its Central Committee. They denounced the practice of having provincial party officials appointed by the Center. To bring the Party into direct contact with the laboring masses, they proposed that its directing organs be subjected to frequent personnel turnovers, which would open access to true workers.[70]

The emergence of the Workers' Opposition brought into the open a smoldering antagonism that went back to the late nineteenth century, between a minority of politically active workers and the intellectuals who claimed to represent them and speak in their behalf.[71] Radical workers, usually more inclined to syndicalism than Marxism, cooperated with the socialist intelligentsia and allowed themselves to be guided by them because they knew they were short of political experience. But they never ceased to be aware of a gulf between themselves and their partners: and once a "workers' state" had come into being, they saw no reason for submitting to the authority of the "white hands."*

The concerns expressed by the Workers' Opposition stood at the center of the deliberations of the Tenth Party Congress in March 1921. Shortly before it convened, Kollontai released for internal party use a brochure in which she assailed the regime's bureaucratization.[72] (Party rules prohibited venting party disputes in public.) The Workers' Opposition, she argued, made up exclusively of laboring men and women, felt that the Party's leadership had lost touch with labor: the higher up the ladder of authority one ascended, the less support there was for the Workers' Opposition. This happened because the Soviet apparatus had been taken over by class enemies who despised Communism: the petty bourgeoisie had seized control of the bureaucracy, while the "grand bourgeoisie," in the guise of "specialists," had taken over industrial management and the military command.

The Workers' Opposition submitted to the Tenth Congress two resolutions, one dealing with party organization, the other with the role of trade unions. It was the last time that independent resolutions—that is, resolutions not originating with the Central Committee—would be discussed at a party congress. The first document spoke of a crisis in the party caused by the perpetuation of habits of military command acquired during the Civil War, and the alienation of the leadership from the laboring masses. Party affairs were conducted without either *glasnost'* or democracy, in a bureaucratic style, by elements mistrustful of workers, causing them to lose confidence in the party and to leave it in droves. To remedy this situation, the party should carry out a thorough purge to rid itself of opportunistic elements and increase worker involvement. Every Communist should be required to spend at least three months a year doing physical labor. All

---

*In 1925, Krupskaia wrote Clara Zetkin that "the broad layers of peasants and workers identify the intelligentsia with large landowners and the bourgeoisie. The hatred of the intelligentsia among the people is strong" (*IzvTsK*, No. 2/289, February 1989, 204).

functionaries should be elected by and accountable to their members; appointments from the Center should be made only in exceptional cases. The personnel of the central organs should be regularly turned over: the majority of the posts should be reserved for workers. The focus of party work should shift from the Center to the cells.[73]

The resolution on trade unions was no less radical.[74] It protested the degradation of unions, to the point where their status was reduced to "virtual zero." The rehabilitation of the country's economy required the maximum involvement of the masses: "The systems and methods of construction based on a cumbersome bureaucratic machine stifle all creative initiative and independence" of the producers. The party must demonstrate trust in the workers and their organizations. The national economy ought to be reorganized from the bottom up by the producers themselves. In time, as the masses gain experience, management of the economy should be transferred to a new body, an All-Russian Congress of Producers, not appointed by the Communist Party, but elected by the trade unions and "productive" associations. (In the discussion of this resolution, Shliapnikov denied that the term "producers" included peasants.)[75] Under this arrangement, the Party would confine itself to politics, leaving the direction of the economy to labor.

These proposals by veteran Communists from labor ranks revealed a remarkable ignorance of Bolshevik theory and practice. Lenin, in his opening address, minced no words in denouncing them as representing a "clear syndicalist deviation." Such a deviation, he went on, would not be dangerous were it not for the the economic crisis and the prevalence in the country of armed banditry (by which he meant peasant rebellions). The perils of "petty bourgeois spontaneity" exceeded even those posed by the Whites: they required greater party unity than ever.[76] As for Kollontai, he dismissed her with what apparently was intended as a humorous aside, a reference to her personal relations with the leader of the Workers' Opposition ("Thank God, we know well that Comrade Kollontai and Comrade Shliapnikov are 'bound by class ties [and] class consciousness' ").*

Worker defections confronted Lenin and his associates with a problem: how to govern in the name of the "proletariat" when the "proletariat" turned its back on them. One solution was to denigrate Russia's working class. It was now often heard that the "true" workers had given their lives in the Civil War and that their place had been taken by social dregs. Bukharin claimed that Soviet Russia's working class had been "peasantified" and that, "objectively speaking," the Workers' Opposition was a Peasant Opposition, while a Chekist told the Menshevik Dan that the

*Lenin, *PSS*, XLIII, 41. Cf. Angelica Balabanoff, *My Life as a Rebel* (Bloomington, Ind., and London, 1973), 252. Lenin was so furious at Kollontai for joining the Workers' Opposition that he refused to talk to her or even about her: Angelica Balabanoff, *Impressions of Lenin* (Ann Arbor, Mich., 1964), 97–98.

Petrograd workers were "scum" *(svoloch)* left over after all the true proletarians had gone to the front.[77] Lenin, at the Eleventh Party Congress, denied that Soviet Russia even had a "proletariat" in Marx's sense, since the ranks of industrial labor had been filled with malingerers and "all kinds of casual elements."[78] Rebutting such charges, Shliapnikov noted that 16 of the 41 delegates to the Tenth Congress supportive of the Workers' Opposition had joined the Bolshevik party before 1905 and all had done so before 1914.[79]

Another way of dealing with the challenge was to interpret the "proletariat" as an abstraction: in this view, the party was by definition the "people" and acted on their behalf no matter what the living people thought they wanted.[80] This was the approach taken by Trotsky:

> One must have the consciousness, so to speak, of the revolutionary historic primacy of the party, which is obligated to assert its dictatorship notwithstanding the transient hesitations of the elemental forces *(stikhiia)*, notwithstanding the transient wavering even among the workers. . . . Without this consciousness the party may perish to no purpose at one of the turning points, of which there are many. . . . The party as a whole is held together by the unity of understanding that over and above the formal factor stands the dictatorship of the party, which upholds the basic interests of the working class even when the latter's mood is wavering.[81]

In other words, the Party existed in and of itself and by the very fact of its existence reflected the interests of the working class. The living will of living people—*stikhiia*—was merely a "formal factor." Trotsky criticized Shliapnikov for making a "fetish of democracy": "The principle of elections within the labor movement is, as it were, placed above the Party, as if the Party did not have the right to assert its dictatorship even in the event that this dictatorship temporarily clashed with the transient mood within the worker democracy."[82] It was not possible to entrust the management of the economy to workers, if only because there were hardly any Communists among them: in this connection, Trotsky cited Zinoviev to the effect that in Petrograd, the country's largest industrial center, 99 percent of the workers either had no party preference, or, to the extent that they did, sympathized with the Mensheviks or even the Black Hundreds.[83] In other words, one could have either Communism ("the dictatorship of the proletariat") or worker rule, but not both: democracy spelled the doom of Communism. There is nothing to indicate that Trotsky or any other leading Communist saw the absurdity of this position. Bukharin, for example, explicitly acknowledged that Communism could not be reconciled with democracy. In 1924, at the closed Plenum of the Central Committee, he said:

> Our task is to acknowledge two dangers. In the first place, the danger that emanates from the centralization of our apparatus. In the second, the danger of political democracy, which may occur if democracy goes

over the edge. The opposition sees only one danger—bureaucracy. Behind the bureaucratic danger it *does not see the danger of political democracy.* . . . To maintain the dictatorship of the proletariat, we must support the dictatorship of the party.*

Shliapnikov conceded that "unity" was indeed the supreme objective, but, he argued, the party lost the unity it had enjoyed in the past, before taking power, from lack of communication with its rank and file.[84] This rupture accounted for the wave of strikes in Petrograd and the Kronshtadt mutiny. The problem was not the Workers' Opposition: "The causes of the discontent that we see in Moscow and other worker cities lead us not to the 'Workers' Opposition' but to the Kremlin." The workers felt completely estranged from the party. Among Petrograd metal workers, a traditional bastion of Bolshevism, fewer than 2 percent were members; in Moscow, the proportion of metallurgists belonging to the party fell to a mere 4 percent.† Shliapnikov rejected the argument of the Central Committee that the economic disasters resulted from "objective" factors, notably the Civil War: "That which we presently observe in our economy is the result not only of objective causes, independent of us. In the breakdown which we see, a share of responsibility falls also on the system we have adopted."[85]

The motions of the Workers' Opposition were not submitted to a vote but the delegates could register their preferences by casting ballots for or against two resolutions introduced by Lenin: "On the unity of the party," and "On the syndicalist and anarchist deviations in our party," which repudiated the platform of the Workers' Opposition and condemned its sponsors. The first collected 413 votes against 25, with 2 abstentions; the second, 375 against 30, with 3 abstentions and one invalid vote.[86]

The Workers' Opposition suffered a decisive defeat and was ordered to dissolve. It was doomed from the outset not only because it challenged powerful vested interests of the central apparatus, but because it accepted the undemocratic premises of Communism, including the idea of a one-party state. It championed democratic procedures in a party that was by its ideology and, increasingly, by its structure committed to ignoring the popular will. Once the Opposition conceded that the unity of the party was the supreme good, it could not carry on without opening itself to charges of subversion.

We have spent much time on what turned out to be an episode in the history of the Communist Party because the Workers' Opposition, for the first and, as it turned out, the last time, confronted the Party with a funda-

---

*Dmitrii Volkogonov, *Triumf i tragediia,* I/1 (Moscow, 1989), 197. Emphasis added. Bukharin was addressing himself to Trotsky, who by 1924, for reasons that will be spelled out below, had reversed himself and become a champion of the ideas espoused earlier by the Workers' Opposition.

†A confidential report to Lenin's Secretariat from Petrograd in early 1922 confirmed Shliapnikov's assessment, stating that in that city only 2 to 3 percent of the factory workers belonged to the Communist Party: RTsKhIDNI, F. 5, op. 2, delo 27, list 11.

mental choice. The Party, whose base of support among the population at large had dwindled to a wafer-thin layer, now faced rebellion in its own ranks from workers, its putative masters. It could either acknowledge this fact and retire, or else ignore it and stay in power. In the latter event, it would have no choice but to introduce into the party the same dictatorial methods it employed in running the country. Lenin chose the second alternative, and he did so with the hearty support of his associates, including Trotsky and Bukharin, who later, when these methods were turned against them, would pose as tribunes of the people and champions of democracy. In taking this fateful step, he ensured the hegemony of the central apparatus over the rank and file; and since Stalin was about to become the unchallenged master of the central apparatus, he ensured Stalin's ascendancy.

To make impossible further dissent in the party, Lenin had the Tenth Congress adopt a new and fateful rule that outlawed the formation of "factions": these were defined as organized groupings with their own platforms. The key, concluding article of the resolution "On the unity of the party," kept secret at the time, provided severe penalties for violators:

> In order to maintain strict discipline within the party and in all soviet activities, [in order] to attain the greatest unity by eliminating all factionalism, the Congress authorizes the Central Committee in instances of violations of discipline, or the revival or tolerance of factionalism, to apply all measures of party accounting up to exclusion from the party.*

Exclusion required a two-thirds vote of the members and candidate members of the Central Committee and the Control Commission.

Although Lenin and the majority that voted for his resolution seem to have been unaware of its potential implications, it was destined to have the gravest consequences: Leonard Schapiro regards it as the decisive event in the history of the Communist Party.[87] Simply put, in Trotsky's words, the ruling transferred "the political regime prevailing in the state to the inner life of the ruling party."[88] Henceforth, the party, too, was to be run as a dictatorship. Dissent would be tolerated only as long as it was individual, that is, unorganized. The resolution deprived party members of the right to challenge the majority controlled by the Central Committee, since individual dissent could always be brushed aside as unrepresentative, while organized dissent was illegal.

> The ban on inner-party groupings was self-perpetuating and irreversible: under it no movement for its revision could be set afoot. It established within the party that barrack discipline which may be meat for an army but is poison for a political organization—the discipline which allows a single man to vent a grievance but treats the joint expression of the same grievance by several men as mutiny.[89]

*Desiatyi S"ezd RkP(b): Stenograficheskii otchet (Moscow, 1963), 573. The clause was first made public by Stalin in January 1924 at the Thirteenth Party Conference, to condemn Trotsky: I. V. Stalin, Sochineniia, VI (Moscow, 1947), 15.

Nothing was better calculated to ensure the bureaucratic rigidity that ultimately stifled everything that was alive in the Communist movement. For it was mainly to enforce the ban on factions that Lenin created in 1922 the post of General Secretary and agreed to Stalin being the first holder of that office.

The consequences of the ban on factions became visible in the representation of the Eleventh Party Congress the following year. Of the 30 delegates who had the courage at the Tenth Congress to vote against Lenin's resolution condemning the Workers' Opposition as an "anarcho-syndicalist deviation" (the voting was open), all but six had been purged and replaced with more compliant delegates. Molotov could now boast that all party factions had been eliminated.[90] By the time the Twelfth Congress convened in 1923, three of the surviving six were gone as well, Shliapnikov among them.[91] Such silent purges ensured the unchallenged domination of the Central Committee, which packed party congresses with delegates supportive of its position and interests: suffice it to say that 55.1 percent of the delegates to the Twelfth Congress (1923) were fully occupied with party work, and an additional 30.0 percent were so part-time.[92] Not surprisingly, at the Twelfth Congress and subsequently, all resolutions were adopted unanimously. Like the "Land Assemblies" of Muscovite Russia, these gatherings were (in the words of the historian Vasilii Kliuchevskii) "consultations of the government with its own agents."

Even in the face of such formidable obstacles, the Workers' Opposition tried to persevere. Ignoring party resolutions, in May 1921, the Communist Party faction of the Metal Workers' Union rejected by a vote of 120 to 40 the list of officers submitted to it by the Center. The Central Committee disqualified this vote, and proceeded to take over the direction of this and the other trade unions. Union membership became compulsory, and virtually the entire financing of unions henceforth came from the state.[93]

The anti-faction resolution made the Workers' Opposition an illegal body and provided grounds for its prosecution. Lenin harried its leaders with a vengeance. In August 1921, he asked the Central Committee Plenum to have them expelled, but his motion fell one vote short of the required two-thirds majority.* Even so, they were subjected to harassment and removed, under one pretext or another, from party posts.[94] Unable to get a hearing, the Workers' Opposition unwisely took its case to the Executive Committee of the Comintern, without securing prior approval of either the party or the Russian delegation to that body. The Executive, by now a section of the Russian Communist Party, rejected the appeal. In September

---

*Lenin, *PSS*, XLV, 526–27; *Odinadtsatyi S"ezd*, 748. Lenin's actions on this occasion contradict the frequently heard claim by his admirers that as long as he was in charge no leading party figure or party grouping was expelled or threatened with expulsion (*e.g.*, Vadim Rogovin, *Byla li al'ternativa?*, Moscow, 1992, 25). The author committed the same mistake in his *Russian Revolution* (p. 511).

1923, following a wave of strikes, many adherents of the Workers' Opposition were arrested.[95] Stalin would make certain all were killed. Kollontai was the one exception: in 1923 she was sent to Norway, then to Mexico, and ultimately to Sweden to serve as ambassador—the first woman in history, it was said, to head a diplomatic mission. It seems to have gratified Stalin's ribald sense of humor to have the apostle of free love represent him in the country of free love. Shliapnikov he had shot in 1937.

The first symptoms of Lenin's illness appeared in February 1921, when he began to complain of headaches and insomnia. They were not entirely physical in origin. Lenin had suffered a succession of humiliating defeats, including the military debacle in Poland, which ended the hope of spreading the revolution to Europe, and the economic disasters that necessitated a humiliating capitulation to market forces. The physical symptoms resembled those he had suffered in 1900, at another critical moment in the history of the party, when the Social-Democratic movement seemed about to collapse from internal divisions.* In the course of the summer of 1921 the headaches gradually eased, but he continued to suffer from sleeplessness.† In the fall, the Politburo, concerned that Lenin was overworking, requested that he lighten his schedule. On December 31, still unhappy over his condition, it ordered him to take a six-week vacation: he was not to return to his office without the permission of the Secretariat.[96] Strange as such orders may appear, they were routinely issued by the highest party organs to Communist personnel: as E. D. Stasova, Lenin's principal secretary, told General S. S. Kamenev, Bolsheviks were to regard their health as "a treasury asset."[97]

Lenin's condition showed no improvement. He grumbled that he, who in the past had been able to work for two, now could hardly do the work of one. He spent most of March 1922 resting in the country, where he closely followed the course of events and drafted speeches for the Eleventh Party Congress. He was gruff and irritable, and the physicians treating him misdiagnosed his problem as "neurasthenia induced by exhaustion."[98] At this time his habitual truculence assumed ever more extreme and even abnormal forms: it was while in this state that he ordered the arrest, trial, and execution of the SRs and clergymen.

Lenin's physical deterioration became apparent at the Eleventh Party Congress, held in March 1922, the last he would attend. He delivered two rambling speeches, defensive in character and replete with ad hominem

---

*N. K. Krupskaia, *Vospominaniia o Lenine,* 2nd ed. (Moscow, 1933), 35. This time he was further shaken by the sudden death (September 1920) from typhus of his beloved Inessa Armand.

†Lenin would order sedatives for himself (Sumnacetin and Veronal) from the Kremlin pharmacy: RTsKhIDNI, F. 2, op. 1, delo 23036.

71. Inessa Armand.

attacks on anyone who disagreed with him, subjecting some of his closest associates to ridicule. Observing his erratic motions, lapses of memory, and occasional speech difficulties, some doctors now concluded that he was suffering from a more serious malady, namely progressive paralysis, for which there was no cure and which was bound to end before long in total incapacitation and death. Lenin, who as recently as February had denied in a private letter to Kamenev and Stalin that his illness showed any "objective symptoms,"[99] apparently accepted this diagnosis, because he began to make preparations for an orderly transfer of authority. This was for him a very painful task, not only because he loved power above all else, but also because, as he would make clear in his so-called "Testament" of December 1922, he thought no one was truly qualified to inherit his mantle.* He further worried that his withdrawal from active politics would set off destructive personal rivalries among his associates.

At the time, Trotsky seemed the natural heir to Lenin: who but the "organizer of victory," as Radek called him,[100] had a better right to be his successor? But Trotsky's claim had more appearance than substance, for he had much going against him. He had joined the Bolshevik Party late, on the eve of the October coup, after subjecting Lenin and his followers for years to ridicule and criticism. The Old Guard never forgave him for his past: no

---

*There is a curious note from him dated March 21, 1922, requesting the Central Committee's approval to have a visiting German specialist on "nervous diseases" examine Chicherin, Trotsky, Kamenev, Stalin, and some other high Soviet officials: RTsKhIDNI, F. 2, op. 1, delo 22960.

72. Trotsky, 1918.

matter what his accomplishments since 1917, he remained an outsider to the party's inner circle. Although a member of the Politburo, unlike Zinoviev, Stalin, and Kamenev, his principal rivals, he held no executive post in the party and hence lacked a base of support in its cadre, not to speak of the power of patronage. In elections to the Central Committee at the Tenth Party Congress (1921), he came in tenth, behind Stalin and even the relatively unknown Viacheslav Molotov.[101] At the next Congress a young Armenian Communist, Anastas Mikoyan, disparagingly referred to him as "a military man" ignorant of the way the party operated in the provinces.[102] Nor was Trotsky's personality an asset. He was widely disliked for arrogance and lack of tact: as he himself admitted, he had a reputation for "unsociability, individualism, aristocratism."[103] Even his admiring biographer concedes he "could rarely withstand the temptation to remind others of their errors and to insist on his superiority and insight."[104] Scorning the collegiate style of Lenin and the other Bolshevik leaders, he demanded, as commander of the country's armed forces, unquestioned obedience to himself, giving rise to talk of "Bonapartist" ambitions. Thus in November 1920, angered by reports of insubordination among Red Army troops facing Wrangel, he issued an order that contained the following passage: "I, your Red leader, appointed by the government and invested with the confidence of the people, demand complete faith in myself." All attempts to question his orders were to be dealt with by summary execution.[105] His high-handed administrative style attracted the attention of the Central Committee, which in July 1919 subjected them to severe criticism.[106] His ill-considered attempt to militarize labor in 1920, not only cast doubts on his judgment, but reinforced suspicions of Bonapartism.[107] In March 1922 he addressed a long statement to the Politburo, urging that the party withdraw from direct involvement in managing the economy. The Politburo rejected his proposals and Lenin, as was his wont with Trotsky's epistles, scribbled on it, "Into the Archive," but his opponents used it as evidence that Trotsky wanted to "liquidate the leading role of the Party." [108] Refusing to involve himself in the routine of day-to-day politics, frequently absent from cabinet meetings and other administrative deliberations, Trotsky assumed the pose of a statesman above the fray. "For Trotsky, the main things were the slogan, the speaker's platform, the striking gesture, but not routine work."[109] His administrative talents were, indeed, of a low order. The hoard of documents in the Trotsky archive at Harvard University, with numerous communications to Lenin, indicate a congenital incapacity for formulating succinct, practical solutions: as a rule, Lenin neither commented nor acted on them.

For all these reasons, when in 1922 Lenin made arrangements to distribute his responsibilities, he passed over Trotsky. He was much concerned that his successors govern in a collegial manner: Trotsky, never a "team player," simply did not fit. We have the testimony of Lenin's sister, Maria Ulianova, who was with him during the last period of his life, that while Lenin valued Trotsky's talents and industry, and for their sake kept his feelings to himself, "he did not feel sympathy for Trotsky": Trotsky "had too many qualities that made it extraordinarily difficult to work collectively with him."* Stalin suited Lenin's needs better. Hence, Lenin assigned to Stalin ever greater responsibilities, with the result that as he faded from the scene, Stalin assumed the role of his surrogate, and thus in fact, if not in name, became his heir.

---

*IzvTsK, No. 12/299 (December 1989), 197. According to her, Trotsky, in contrast to Lenin, could not control his temper, and at one meeting of the Politburo called her brother a "hooligan." Lenin turned white as chalk but made no reply: ibid.

In April 1922, Stalin was appointed General Secretary, that is, head of the Secretariat: this was formalized at the Party Plenum on April 3, apparently on Kamenev's recommendation.* It has been asserted, by contemporaries in a position to know, that Lenin took this step because Stalin was continuously warning him of the danger of splits in the party and assuring him that he, Stalin, alone was capable of averting them.[110] But the circumstances of this event remain obscure, and it has also been suggested that Lenin had no idea of the importance of Stalin's promotion to a post that until then had been of very minor significance.[111]

The Secretariat under Stalin's direction had two responsibilities: to monitor the flow of paperwork to and from the Politburo, and to prevent deviations in the party.

In his report on organizational matters to the Eleventh Party Congress, Molotov complained that the Central Committee was swamped with paperwork, much of it trivial: in the preceding year, it had received 120,000 reports from the local branches of the party, and the number of questions it had to take up increased by almost 50 percent.[112] At the same Congress, Lenin ridiculed the fact that the Politburo had to deal with such weighty issues as imports of meat conserves from France.[113] He thought it absurd to have him sign every directive issued by the government.[114] One of the tasks of the General Secretary was to ensure that the Politburo received only important papers and that its decisions were properly implemented.[115] In this capacity, the Secretary was responsible for preparing the Politburo agenda, supplying it with pertinent materials, and then relaying its decisions to the lower party echelons. These functions made the Secretariat a two-way conveyor belt. But because it was not, strictly speaking, a policy-making post, few realized the potential power that it gave the General Secretary:

> Lenin, Kamenev, Zinoviev, and to a lesser extent, Trotsky, were Stalin's sponsors to all the offices he held. His jobs were of the kind which would scarcely attract the bright intellectuals of the Politburo. All their brilliance in matters of doctrine, all their powers of political analysis would have found little application either at the Workers' and Peasants' Inspectorate or at the . . . Secretariat. What was needed there was an enormous capacity for hard and uninspiring toil and patient and sustained interest in every detail of organization. None of his colleagues grudged Stalin his assignments.[116]

The key to Stalin's rising power was the combination of functions vested in him as member of the Orgburo and chairman of the Secretariat. At his command, officials could be promoted, relocated, or dismissed. This power Stalin used not only to eliminate anyone who challenged the judgment of the Central Committee, as Lenin wanted, but to appoint functionaries

---

*Volkogonov, *Triumf,* I/1, 132–36. Trotskii (*Moia zhizn',* II, Berlin, 1930, 202–3 and *The Suppressed Testament of Lenin,* New York, 1935, 22) claims, without providing any evidence, that the appointment was made against Lenin's wishes; he further muddles matters by asserting that Stalin was appointed at the Tenth Party Congress and on Zinoviev's initiative.

personally loyal to him. Lenin's intention was to have the General Secretary ensure ideological orthodoxy by keeping close watch on party personnel and rejecting or expelling divisive elements. Stalin promptly realized that he could use these powers to enhance his personal authority in the party by appointing to responsible posts, in the guise of safeguarding ideological purity, individuals beholden to him. He drew up registers *(nomenklatury)* of party officials qualified for executive positions, and selected for appointment only those listed on them. In 1922, Molotov reported that the Central Committee kept files on 26,000 party functionaries (or "party workers," as they were euphemistically called) subject to close scrutiny; in the course of 1920, 22,500 of them had received assignments.[117] To make certain nothing escaped his attention, Stalin required provincial party secretaries to report to him personally once a month.[118] He also made an arrangement with Dzerzhinskii to have the GPU send his Secretariat on the seventh day of every month its regular summaries.[119] In this manner Stalin acquired unrivaled knowledge of party affairs down to their lowest levels, knowledge that, together with the power to make appointments, gave him effective control of the party machine. By ruling that a high proportion of party documents, including protocols of plenums, were secret, he withheld this information from his potential rivals.[120]

Stalin's self-aggrandizement did not go unnoticed: at the Eleventh Congress an associate of Trotsky's complained he had taken on too many responsibilities. Lenin impatiently brushed such objections aside.[121] Stalin got things done, he understood the supreme need to preserve party unity, he was modest in his behavior and personal needs. Later, in the fall of 1923, Stalin's associates, led by Zinoviev, who in a private letter to Kamenev referred to "Stalin's dictatorship," held a secret conclave to curb his powers. It failed because Stalin cleverly outmaneuvered his rivals.[122] In his eagerness to stir the cumbersome machine of state and to prevent splits, Lenin endowed Stalin with powers that he himself six months later would characterize as "boundless." By then it would be too late to curb them.

Lenin did not anticipate that as a result of the regime he had introduced, Russia would come under one-man rule. He thought that impossible. In January 1919, in a personal exchange with the Menshevik historian N. A. Rozhkov, who had expressed such fears, he wrote:

> As concerns "personal dictatorship," if you pardon the expression, it is utter nonsense. The apparatus has grown altogether gigantic—in some respects [excessive]. And under these conditions, a "personal dictatorship" is (in general) unrealizable.[123]

In fact, he had little idea how gigantic the apparatus had grown and how much money it cost. He reacted with disbelief to information supplied by

Trotsky in February 1922 that in the preceding nine months the party's budget absorbed 40 million gold rubles.*

He was worried about something different: he dreaded the prospect of the party being torn apart by rivalries at the top and paralyzed by the bureaucracy from below. He had not expected either to be a threat. Communists treated everything that happened as inevitable and scientifically explicable except their own failures: here they became extreme voluntarists, blaming whatever went wrong on human error. To a detached observer the problems that troubled Lenin and jeopardized his revolution appear embedded in the premises of his regime. One need not share Isaac Deutscher's romantic view of the Bolsheviks' aspirations to accept his analysis of the contradictions they had created for themselves:

> In its dream the Bolshevik party saw itself as a disciplined yet inwardly free and dedicated body of revolutionaries, immune from corruption by power. It saw itself committed to observe proletarian democracy and to respect the freedom of the small nations, for without this there could be no genuine advance to socialism. In pursuit of their dream the Bolsheviks had built up an immense and centralized machine of power to which they then gradually surrendered more and more of their dream: proletarian democracy, the rights of small nations, and finally their own freedom. They could not dispense with power if they were to strive for the fulfillment of their ideals; but now their power came to oppress and overshadow their ideals. The gravest dilemmas arose; and also a deep cleavage between those who clung to the dream and those who clung to the power.[124]

This link between premise and effect escaped Lenin. In the last months of his active life, he could think of nothing better to safeguard his regime than restructuring institutions and reassigning personnel.

He reluctantly concluded that the fusion of party and state organs that he had enforced since taking power could not be permanently institutionalized because it depended on one person, himself, directing both in his double capacity as Chairman of the Sovnarkom and titular leader of the Politburo. The arrangement, in any event, was becoming unworkable because the policy-making organs of the party were becoming clogged from the multitude of affairs, important and petty, mostly petty, that the state apparatus forwarded to them for decision. After Lenin's partial withdrawal, the old arrangement had to be altered. In March 1922, Lenin protested that "everything gets dragged from the Sovnarkom to the Politburo," and conceded that he bore blame for the resulting disarray, "because much that concerned links between the Sovnarkom and the Politburo was done personally by me. And when I had to leave, it transpired that the two wheels did not work in a coordinated manner."[125]

In April 1922, at the same time that Stalin assumed the post of General

---

*RTsKhIDNI, F. 2, op. 1, delo 22737. The sum was nearly equivalent to the credit which Germany had offered Soviet Russia at this time (above, p. 427).

Secretary, Lenin came up with the idea of naming two trusted associates to act as watchdogs over the state apparatus. He suggested to the Politburo the creation of two deputies (*zamestiteli,* or *zamy* for short), one to run the Sovnarkom, the other the Council of Labor and Defense (Sovet Truda i Oborony, or STO).* Lenin, who chaired both institutions, suggested the agrarian specialist Alexander Tsiurupa for the Sovnarkom and Rykov for the STO, each to oversee a number of commissariats.† Trotsky, who was given no voice in economic management, subjected this proposal to harsh criticism, arguing that the *zamy*'s responsibilities were so broad as to be meaningless. He believed that the economy would continue to perform unsatisfactorily unless subjected to authoritarian methods of management from the Center, without Party interference[126]—an argument widely interpreted to mean that he aspired to become "dictator" of the economy. Lenin called Trotsky "fundamentally wrong" and accused him of passing ill-formed judgments.[127]

On May 25–27, 1922, Lenin suffered his first stroke, which resulted in a paralysis of the right arm and leg and deprived him temporarily of the ability to speak or write. For the next two months he was out of commission, most of the time resting at Gorki. Physicians now altered their diagnosis to read arteriosclerosis of the brain, possibly of hereditary origin (two of Lenin's sisters and his brother would die in a similar manner). During this period of forced absence, his most important posts—the rotating chairmanships of the Politburo and of the Sovnarkom—were assumed by Kamenev, who also headed the Moscow Party organization. Stalin chaired the Secretariat and the Orgburo, in which capacities he directed the day-to-day business of the party apparatus. Zinoviev was chief of the Petrograd Party organization and the Comintern. The three formed a "troika," a directory that dominated the Politburo and, through it, the party and state machines. Each, even Kamenev, who was Trotsky's brother-in-law, had reasons for joining forces against Trotsky, their common rival. They did not even bother to inform Trotsky, who was vacationing at the time, of Lenin's stroke.[128] They were in constant communication with Lenin. The log of Lenin's activities during this time (May 25–October 2, 1922) indicates

---

*Lenin, *PSS,* XLV, 152–59. The Council was the most important commission of the Sovnarkom. It occupied itself mainly with economic questions, and constituted something of an "economic cabinet" (Alex Nove, *An Economic History of the USSR,* Hammondsworth, 1982, 70). Cf. E. B. Genkina, *Perekhod sovetskogo gosudarstva k Novoi Ekonomicheskoi Politike* (Moscow, 1954), 362. On the background of this proposal see T. H. Rigby, *Lenin's Government: Sovnarkom, 1917–1922* (Cambridge, 1979), Chapter 13.

†Isaac Deutscher (*The Prophet Unarmed,* London, 1959, 35–36), with general reference to the Trotsky Archive, claims that on April 11, 1922, at a meeting of the Politburo, Lenin offered Trotsky the post of third Deputy. However, there is no record of a Politburo meeting on that day and there is no document in the Trotsky Archive confirming this statement. Nor is there any evidence for Deutscher's claim that Trotsky justified the rejection of the alleged offer on the grounds that it "would have effaced him politically": Deutscher, *ibid.,* 87. See further, Rigby, *Lenin's Government,* 292–93.

73. The "troika," from left to right: Stalin, (Rykov), Kamenev, Zinoviev.

Stalin to have been the most frequent visitor to Gorki, meeting with Lenin twelve times; according to Bukharin, Stalin was the only member of the Central Committee whom Lenin asked to see during the most serious stages of his illness.* According to Maria Ulianova, these were very affectionate encounters: "V. I. Lenin met [Stalin] in a friendly manner, he joked, laughed, asked that I entertain him, offer him wine, and so on. During this and further visits, they also discussed Trotsky in my presence, and it was apparent that here Lenin sided with Stalin against Trotsky."[129] Lenin also frequently communicated with Stalin in writing. His archive contains many notes to Stalin requesting his advice on every conceivable issue, including questions of foreign policy. Worried lest Stalin overwork himself, he asked that the Politburo instruct him to take two days' rest in the country every week.[130] After learning from Lunacharskii that Stalin lived in shabby quarters, he saw to it that something better was found for him.[131] There is no record of similar intimacy between Lenin and any other member of the Politburo.

After obtaining Lenin's consent and then settling matters among themselves, the triumvirate would present to the Politburo and the Sovnarkom

---

*IzvTsk, No. 12/299 (December 1989), 200, note 19. Later, however, Bukharin confided to the Menshevik historian Boris Nicolaevsky that he had frequently visited Lenin in late 1922 and had serious conversations with him: Boris I. Nicolaevsky, *Power and the Soviet Elite* (New York, 1965), 12–13.

resolutions that these bodies approved as a matter of course. Trotsky either voted with the majority or abstained. By virtue of their collaboration in a Politburo that at the time had only seven members (in addition to them and the absent Lenin, Trotsky, Tomskii, and Bukharin), the troika could have its way on all issues and isolate Trotsky, who had not a single supporter in that body.

Stalin played a brilliant game that deceived everyone, from Lenin down. He would take on himself essential jobs that no one else wanted: drudgeries involving the flow of paper from the party cells to the Politburo and from the Politburo to the party cells, along with countless personnel assignments. No one seemed aware that they formed the basis of patronage, which enabled him to fashion an invincible political machine. He always claimed to have the good of the party uppermost in mind. He seemed devoid of personal ambitions and vanity, quite content to let Trotsky, Kamenev, and Zinoviev bask in the public limelight. He did this so skillfully that in 1923 it was widely thought that the battle for Lenin's succession pitted Trotsky against Zinoviev.[132] Sometimes Stalin would insist that the unity of the party was the supreme good and that for its sake even principles had to be sacrificed. At other times he would argue that if necessary to uphold principles a split should not be avoided. He would resort now to this, now to that argument, depending on which happened to suit him at a given moment. In disputes his was always the voice of reason, striving to reconcile lofty standards with expediency, a model of moderation and a threat to no one. He had no enemies, except possibly Trotsky, and even him he sought to befriend until rebuffed: Trotsky dismissed him as the party's "outstanding mediocrity" (*vydaiushchaiasia posredstvennost'*), too insignificant to bother with. At his country dacha, Stalin would gather the party's leaders, sometimes with their wives and children, to discuss matters of substance but also to reminisce, sing, and dance.[133] Nothing he did or said suggested that underneath his amiable exterior lurked murder. Like a predator mimicking harmless insects, he insinuated himself into the midst of his unsuspecting prey.

On September 11, 1922, Lenin addressed to Stalin a note for the Politburo in which he suggested that in view of Rykov's imminent departure for a vacation and Tsiurupa's inability to handle the whole load by himself, two new deputy chairmen be appointed, one to help oversee the Council of People's Commissars, the other, the Council of Labor and Defense (STO): both were to work under close supervision of the Politburo and himself. For the posts he suggested Trotsky and Kamenev. A great deal has been made by Trotsky's friends and enemies alike of this bid: some of the former went so far as to claim that Lenin chose him as his successor. (Max Eastman, for example, wrote not long afterward that Lenin had asked Trotsky to "become the head of the Soviet Government, and thus of the revolutionary movement of the world.")[134] The reality was more prosaic. According to

Lenin's sister, the offer was made for "diplomatic reasons," that is, to smooth Trotsky's ruffled feathers[135]; in fact, it was because it was so insignificant that Trotsky would have none of it. When the Politburo voted on Lenin's motion, Stalin and Rykov wrote down "Yes," Kamenev and Tomskii abstained, Kalinin stated "No objections," while Trotsky wrote "Categorically refuse."* Trotsky explained to Stalin why he could not accept the offer. He had previously criticized the institution of *zamy* on grounds of substance. Now he raised additional objections on grounds of procedure: the offer had not been discussed either at the Politburo or at the Plenum, and, in any event, he was about to leave on a four-week vacation.[136] But his true reason very likely was the demeaning nature of the proposal: he was to be one of four deputies—one of them not even a Politburo member—without clearly defined responsibilities: a meaningless "deputy as such." Acceptance would have humiliated him; refusal, however, handed his enemies deadly ammunition. For it was quite unprecedented for a high Soviet official "categorically" to refuse an assignment.

Stalin returned to Gorki the next day. What he discussed with Lenin during their two-hour encounter is not known. But it is not unreasonable to assume that Trotsky's rejection of Lenin's offer was one of the topics; nor, in view of what followed, is there reason to doubt that Lenin agreed to Trotsky's being formally reprimanded. The Politburo, meeting on September 14, in Trotsky's absence, expressed "regrets" that he had not seen fit to accept the proffered post. It was the first shot in a campaign of discreditation. Not long afterwards, Kamenev, acting on behalf of the triumvirate, in a personal communication to Lenin suggested expelling Trotsky. Lenin reacted furiously: "To throw Trotsky overboard—this is what you are hinting at. It cannot be interpreted otherwise—the height of absurdity. Unless you think me hopelessly deceived, how can you think so???? 'Bloodied children before the eyes' . . .†

The political constellation, however, suddenly changed in Trotsky's favor. In September, physicians permitted Lenin to resume work. On October 2, over the protests of Stalin and Kamenev, who pleaded concern with his health, he reappeared at the Kremlin and adopted a grueling schedule, which kept him busy between ten and twelve hours a day. Closer acquaintance with the activities of the troika during his absence aroused his suspicions: "He seemed to sense," writes Trotsky, presuming a nonexistent partnership with Lenin, "the almost imperceptible threads of conspiracy being woven behind our backs in connection with his illness."[137] Lenin

---

*RTsKhIDNI, F. 2, op. 1, delo 26002; Stalin in *Dvenadtsatyi S'ezd*, 198n. Stalin's recollection of this episode was omitted from the original edition of the protocols of the Twelfth Congress at his request: *ibid.*, 199n.

†RTsKhIDNI, F. 2, op. 2, delo 1239. The document is dated by the archivist as "after July 12, 1922": October 1922 seems a more likely date, as argued by V. Naumov in *Kommunist*, No. 5 (1991), 36. It was almost certainly connected with Kamenev's and Zinoviev's proposal—vetoed by Stalin—to remove Trotsky from the party. See below, p. 485.

indeed discerned a cabal whose purpose was to isolate him. He had the sense, soon to turn into conviction, that while treating him with outward deference, his colleagues were assiduously at work to eliminate him from the conduct of affairs. One item of evidence was the procedures followed at Politburo meetings. Because he was easily exhausted, Lenin often had to leave these meetings early. The next day he would learn of critical decisions that had been made in his absence.[138] To put a stop to such practices, he ruled on December 8 that Politburo meetings were to last no longer than three hours (from eleven A.M. to two P.M.): all unresolved questions were to be deferred to the next meeting. The agenda was to be distributed at least 24 hours in advance.[139]

Lenin's late rapprochement with Trotsky began over a minor issue, the monopoly of foreign trade; it was cemented by disagreement with Stalin over the "Georgian question," which broke out at the same time. (See below.) During Lenin's absence, the Central Committee had voted to grant Soviet entrepreneurs and firms greater latitude in their dealings with foreign countries. Krasin, who saw in this measure a breach in the state monopoly on foreign trade, objected on the grounds that the monopoly placed Soviet Russia at a great advantage in dealing with competing foreign countries and enterprises.[140] For Lenin, the monopoly on foreign trade was one of the "commanding heights" reserved by the state under the New Economic Policy. His anger against this measure stemmed from the feeling that his associates were taking advantage of his absence to dismantle the safeguards he had built against the restoration of capitalism. Having learned that Trotsky shared his view, he dictated notes to him on December 13 and 15, requesting that at the next session of the Central Committee Plenum he defend their common stand.[141] Trotsky did so, and on December 18 managed without great difficulty to persuade the Plenum to adopt Lenin's position.

This minor bureaucratic defeat, and the specter of a Lenin-Trotsky alliance, alarmed the triumvirate: their political survival demanded Lenin's complete insulation from government affairs. On December 18, the day that Trotsky won his victory, Stalin and Kamenev obtained from the Plenum a mandate giving Stalin authority over Lenin's health regimen. The critical clause of the resolution, as communicated by Stalin to Lenin's secretary, Lydia Fotieva, read:

> To place on Comrade Stalin personal responsibility for the isolation *(izo-liatsiiu)* of Vladimir Ilich both in respect to personal contacts with [Communist] workers and correspondence.[142]

According to Stalin's instructions, Lenin was to work only at brief intervals, to dictate to secretaries, one of whom was N. I. Allulieva, Stalin's wife. It was an astonishing measure, which treated Lenin and his wife as mentally incompetent. Lenin came immediately to suspect that the Central Committee was not acting on the advice of physicians, but, on the contrary, was telling the physicians what to say.[143]

Feeling ensnared by a web of intrigue, at the heart of which he came increasingly to suspect Stalin, Lenin turned for help to Trotsky, who was in a similar predicament. According to Trotsky, and we only have his word for it, in a private conversation sometime in the first half of December—it was to be the last direct contact between the two men—Lenin urged him once again to accept the post of Deputy Chairman of Sovnarkom. But on this occasion, Trotsky claims, Lenin went further, offering to join him in a "bloc" against the bureaucracy in general and the Orgburo in particular. Trotsky understood it to mean a coalition against Stalin.[144]

During the night of December 15–16 Lenin suffered another stroke, following which physicians ordered forced rest and abstention from all political activity. Lenin refused to obey.[145] He felt on the brink of complete physical incapacitation, possibly death, and wanted to make certain he left everything in good order. On December 22, he requested Fotieva to provide him with cyanide in the event he lost the capacity to speak.[146] He had made a similar request of Stalin as early as May, a fact in which Maria Ulianova saw proof of Lenin's special confidence in Stalin.*

On December 21, apparently distrusting his secretaries, Lenin dictated to Krupskaia a warm note to Trotsky, congratulating him on winning the battle over the foreign trade monopoly "without a single shot being fired, simply by a tactical maneuver." He urged him to press the attack.[147] The contents of this note were at once communicated to Stalin, who now had confirmation of his suspicion that Lenin and Trotsky were joining forces against him. The next day he telephoned Krupskaia, berating her crudely for having transcribed her husband's dictation in violation of the regimen he had established under the party's authority, and threatening her with an investigation by the Central Control Commission. After hanging up, Krupskaia fell into hysterics, crying and rolling on the floor.[148] That night, before she could tell Lenin of the incident, he suffered yet another stroke. Krupskaia wrote Kamenev that in all her years as party member no one had spoken to her as Stalin had done. Who cared more for the health of her husband than she, and who knew better what was good for him?[149] Ap-

---

*IzvTsK, No. 12/299 (December 1989), 198. Her statement was written at the request of Bukharin, acting at Stalin's behest, and it is preserved in Bukharin's handwriting, which raises some questions about its reliability: Rogovin, *Byla li,* 71. In 1939, shortly before he was murdered, Trotsky recalled an incident at a Politburo meeting in February 1923, at which Stalin, with a sinister leer, reported that Lenin had asked him for poison to end his hopeless condition. L. D. Trotskii, *Portrety* (Benson, Vt., 1984), 45–49. Trotsky to the end of his life believed it likely that Lenin died from toxin supplied by the General Secretary: Houghton Library, Harvard University, Trotsky Archive, bMS Russian 13 T-4636, T-4637, and T-4638. There was something disingenuous about Trotsky's claim, because he was in possession of a cable from Dzerzhinskii, dated February 1, 1924, that advised him that the autopsy had revealed no traces of poison in Lenin's blood: RTsKhIDNI, F. 76, op. 3, delo 322. According to Fotieva, Stalin never supplied Lenin with poison: *MN,* No. 17 (April 23, 1989), 8.

prised of the letter, Stalin thought it prudent to call her to apologize; but, acting in concert with Kamenev, he also took further precautions to enforce Lenin's quarantine. On December 24, following instructions of the Politburo (Bukharin, Kamenev, and Stalin), the doctors ordered Lenin to confine his dictation to 5 to 10 minutes a day. His dictations were to be regarded as personal notes rather than as communications requiring an answer: it was a subtle way of prohibiting him from intervening in affairs of state and corresponding with Trotsky. "Neither friends, nor domestics," the instruction read, were "to inform Vladimir Ilich of anything about political life, so as not to give him material for reflections and excitement."[150] Thus, under the pretense of safeguarding his health, Stalin and his associates in effect placed Lenin under house arrest.*

Lenin was paying dearly for his political habits. For twenty years he had dominated his associates; but now they had tasted power, and were burning with impatience to be on their own. They justified what amounted to a quiet coup d'état in a whispered campaign within party circles that the "old man" was out of touch and even something of a "mental invalid."[151] Trotsky disloyally joined in this campaign. In January 1923, Lenin wrote for *Pravda* an article intended for the forthcoming Party Congress, in which he voiced anxiety over the possibility of a split in the party and suggested ways of averting it.[152] The Politburo and Orgburo, meeting in joint session, debated at length whether to publish an essay likely to cause consternation in party ranks, which were never told of any disgreements in the leadership. Since Lenin demanded to see the issue of *Pravda* with his article, V. V. Kuibyshev proposed printing a single issue for his eyes only. In the end it was decided to publish the article, minus one passage urging that meetings of the Politburo be attended by representatives of the Central Control Commission (TsKK), who were under no condition to be influenced by any "personalities," the General Secretary specifically included.[153] At the same time, the leadership sent a confidential circular to the provincial and district party organizations intended to neutralize the article's potentially harmful effect. The letter, dated January 27, drafted by Trotsky and signed by all the members of the Politburo and Orgburo on hand, including Stalin, advised that Lenin was unwell and unable to participate in Politburo meetings. This explained why he did not realize that, in fact, there was not the slightest risk of a split in the party.[154] Had he known of this document, Lenin might well have echoed the words Nicholas II had written in his diary after being forced to abdicate: "All around treason and cowardice and deception!"

As a reward for Trotsky's collaboration, Stalin in January once again offered him the post of a *zam* in charge of either the VSNKh or the Gosplan. Trotsky again refused.[155]

---

*These measures had a curious echo thirty years later. In the fall of 1952 Stalin's physician found him unwell and urged that he immediately cease all work. Stalin, probably mindful of precedent, ordered him arrested: Egor Iakovlev in *MN*, No. 4/446 (January 22, 1989), 9.

Lenin fought back like a cornered animal. In lucid moments between strokes he informed himself of what the triumvirate was doing and prepared against it a major campaign. Although obviously in no condition to do so, he planned to intervene with Trotsky's help at the Twelfth Party Congress scheduled for March, to force through drastic changes in the country's political and economic management. Trotsky was his natural ally in this endeavor, for he, too, was politically isolated. Had Lenin succeeded, Stalin's career would have been seriously set back, if not ruined.

Lenin's hostility toward Stalin, which was assuming obsessive forms, was aggravated by Stalin's high-handed methods in dealing with ethnic minorities. Lenin attached immense importance to the proper treatment of Russia's minorities, not only because he felt it essential for the cohesion of the Soviet state, but also because of the repercussions it was likely to have on colonial nations. On matters of substance, he had no quarrel with Stalin: nationalism was a "bourgeois" relic that had no place in the "dictatorship of the proletariat." The Soviet state had to be centralized and decisions made without regard to national preferences. His differences with Stalin were over manners. Lenin believed that the ethnic minorities had justified grievances against Russians because of their past maltreatment. These grievances he meant to assuage by essentially formal concessions such as granting them the appearance of federal status along with limited cultural autonomy, and, above all, by treating them with utmost tact. A person totally devoid of national sentiments, he despised and feared Great Russian chauvinism as a threat to the global interests of Communism.

Stalin, a Georgian who spoke Russian with a comic foreign accent, viewed the matter differently. He realized early that the power base of Communism lay among the Great Russian population. Of the 376,000 party members registered in 1922, fully 270,000, or 72 percent, were Russian, and of the remainder, a high proportion was Russified: of the Ukrainian members, one-half, and of the Jewish, two-thirds.[156] Moreover, in the course of the Civil War, and even more so during the war with Poland, a subtle fusion occurred between Communism and Russian nationalism. Its clearest manifestation was the so-called "Smena Vekh," or "Change of Landmarks," movement, which gained popularity among conservative émigrés by acclaiming the Soviet state as the champion of Russian national greatness and urged all émigrés to return home. At the Tenth Party Congress (1921) a delegate remarked that the achievements of the Soviet state "have filled with pride the hearts of those who had been connected with the Russian Revolution and engendered a peculiar Red Russian patriotism."[157] To an ambitious politician like Stalin, more interested in acquiring power at home than in overturning the world, this development spelled not danger but opportunity. From the beginning of his career, and more overtly with each year of his dictatorship, he identified himself with Great Russian nationalism at the expense of the ethnic minorities.

By 1922, the Communists had reconquered most of the borderlands populated by non-Russians. The decisive factor in this imperial expansion had been the Red Army. But native Communists had also contributed, with their propaganda and subversion, and once the new regime was installed, they wanted a voice in local affairs. To this demand the center paid scant attention: in the capacity of Commissar of Nationalities and General Secretary, Stalin treated each so-called Soviet republic as an intrinsic part of Russia, much as had been the case under tsarism. The result was resentment and conflicts between local Communists and the Moscow apparatus, which came to Lenin's attention in late 1922.

The most violent confrontation of this kind occurred in Georgia. Stalin regarded the subjugated Menshevik stronghold as his personal bailiwick, and after Georgia had been occupied, he ran roughshod over the local Communists with the help of a fellow Georgian, Sergo Ordzhonikidze, the head of the Caucasian Bureau of the Communist Party. Implementing Lenin's instructions to integrate the economy of Transcaucasia, Ordzhonikidze merged Georgia with Armenia and Azerbaijan into a single federation, preliminary to the area's incorporation into Soviet Russia. Local Communists, led by Budu Mdivani and Philip Makharadze, resisted and complained to Moscow of Ordzhonikidze's high-handed behavior.[158] Yielding to their protests, Lenin temporarily postponed the political and economic integration of Transcaucasia: then, in March 1922, he ordered the merger to proceed. At that time Ordzhonikidze announced the establishment of the Federal Union of the Soviet Socialist Republics of Transcaucasia: most of the powers exercised by the governments of the three republics were to be transferred to the new federal entity. Protests from Tiflis had no effect on Lenin, who in such matters relied on Stalin's counsel.

In the summer of 1922, the Communist realm consisted of four republics: Russia (RSFSR), the Ukraine, Belorussia, and Transcaucasia. Formal relations among them were regulated by bilateral treaties; in reality, all four were administered by the Russian Communist Party. It was now decided that the time had come to place relations between these republics on a more orderly basis. The task of working out the principles of a federal union Lenin entrusted in August 1922 to a commission headed by Stalin.[159] Stalin came up with a solution of striking simplicity: the three non-Russian republics would enter the RSFSR as autonomous entities, and the central state organs of the Russian Republic would assume federal functions. Under this arrangement, no constitutional distinction would be drawn between the Ukraine or Georgia on the one hand, and the autonomous republics of the RSFSR, such as Iakutiia or Bashkiriia, on the other. It was an exceedingly centralistic arrangement that assigned all essential state functions to the government of the Russian Republic.[160] In effect, it reverted to the "Russia one and indivisible" principle of tsarist times.

This was not at all what Lenin had in mind. As early as 1920 he had conceived two kinds of Soviet entities, "union" republics, endowed with formal sovereignty, for the major ethnic groups, and "autonomous" republics for the smaller ones. Stalin thought the distinction scholastic, inasmuch as in terms of administrative practice Moscow drew no distinction between large and small national minorities.[161] With Lenin's mandate, he now proceeded to design a new state structure according to his own conceptions.

The draft of Stalin's proposal, based on the concept of "autonomization," was sent to the republics for approval. It ran into a hostile reception. Most displeased were the Georgian Communists, who on September 15, 1922, declared the proposal "premature."[162] Ordzhonikidze overruled them and advised Stalin on behalf of the Transcaucasian Federation that his draft had been approved. The Ukraine withheld judgment, while Belorussia hedged, declaring it would be guided by the Ukraine's decision. Stalin's commission adopted his plan with virtual unanimity.

Lenin acquainted himself with Stalin's draft on September 25. He also read the resolutions of the Central Committee of the Georgian Communist Party, to which Stalin appended an explanatory letter of unusual (for him) length. Stalin justified his plan on the grounds that there really was no middle ground between genuine independence of each republic and complete unity. Regrettably, Stalin wrote, during the years of the Civil War when "we had to demonstrate Moscow's liberalism in the nationality question, we managed to produce among Communists, against our wishes, genuine and consequential social-independists *(sotsial-nezavisimtsy)*, who demand genuine independence."[163]

Lenin was very unhappy with the contents as well as the tone of what he read. Stalin had not only ignored the objections of the non-Russian Communists, but treated them rudely. He summoned Stalin for a conversation (September 26) which lasted two hours and forty minutes, following which he sent the Politburo a note in which he subjected Stalin's draft to scathing criticism.[164] Instead of the three non-Russian republics being incorporated into the Russian Republic, he proposed that they join with the RSFSR to form a new supranational entity tentatively called "The Union of Soviet Republics of Europe and Asia." By omitting "Russia" from the name of the new state, Lenin wished both to stress the equality of its constituent entities (in his words, so as not to "give food to the 'separatists' ") and to create a nucleus around which would consolidate countries that went Communist in the future.* Lenin further proposed that instead of having the Russian Central Executive Committee assume all-Union functions, as Stalin had envisaged, a new Central Executive Committee be formed for the federal entity.

In his response to Lenin's criticism, Stalin displayed none of the custom-

---

*As Stalin noted at the time, the new Union marked a "decisive step on the road toward uniting the toilers of the world into a World Soviet Socialist Republic": I. V. Stalin, *Sochineniia,* V (Moscow, 1947), 155.

ary deference due the Party's leader. While bowing to Lenin's wishes on the structure of the new state, and submitting to his commission a revised plan, he persisted in demanding that the Central Executive Committee of the RSFSR turn into the federal CEC. Lenin's other objections he dismissed as trivial. At one point he accused Lenin of "national liberalism."[165] In the end, however, he was forced to accede to all of Lenin's wishes and revised his proposal accordingly.[166] In this form, it became the charter of the Union of Soviet Socialist Republics, which would be formally proclaimed on December 30, 1922, at the Tenth Congress of Soviets of the RSFSR. Augmented by representatives of the three non-Russian republics, the Congress proclaimed itself the First All-Union Congress of Soviets.

The Georgians stood their ground: they found it intolerable that whereas the Ukraine and Belorussia entered the Union directly, as formally sovereign republics, they had to do so through the Transcaucasian Federation, that is, as autonomous entities. Bypassing Stalin's Secretariat, they informed the Kremlin that if the proposal went through they would resign in a body.[167] In his response Stalin advised them that the Central Committee had unanimously rejected their objections. On October 21 a cable came from Lenin in which he, too, rebuffed the Georgians for the substance of their protest as well as for the manner in which it had been presented.[168] On its receipt, on October 22, the entire Central Committee of the Georgian Communist Party tendered its resignation; it was an unprecedented event in the history of the Communist Party.[169] Ordzhonikidze took advantage of this gesture to replace the Central Committee with a new body staffed with young converts to Communism, pliable to his and Stalin's wishes. On October 24, Stalin cabled him the Central Committee's approval.[170]

Up to this point Lenin had agreed with Stalin in the matter of Georgia. But in late November, already in an anti-Stalin mood, studying materials sent him from Tiflis, he concluded that there could be more to the Georgian case. He requested a fact-finding commission to be sent to Georgia. Stalin appointed Dzerzhinskii to head it. Distrustful of the General Secretary's machinations and wishing to establish his own channel to Tiflis, Lenin asked Rykov to go to Georgia as well. One of Lenin's secretaries noted that he awaited the results of the investigations with burning impatience.[171]

Dzerzhinskii returned from his mission on December 12. Lenin at once left Gorki for Moscow to meet with him. Dzerzhinskii completely exonerated Ordzhonikidze and Stalin, but Lenin was not persuaded. He was especially upset to learn that in the course of a political argument Ordzhonikidze had struck a Georgian comrade. (He had called Ordzhonikidze a "Stalinist ass.")[172] Lenin ordered Dzerzhinskii to return to Georgia to gather more evidence. The next day (December 13) he saw Stalin for two hours: it was to be their last encounter. Following the talk, Lenin intended to write Kamenev a substantial memorandum on the whole nationality question, but before he could do so, on December 15 he was laid low by another stroke.

Lenin felt so betrayed by his associates that during the thirteen months he had left to live he categorically refused to see any of them, communicating only indirectly, through his secretarial staff. The chronicle of his activities indicates that during 1923 he saw neither Trotsky, nor Stalin; not Zinoviev, Kamenev, Bukharin, or Rykov. All were kept away on his explicit orders.[173] This separation from his closest associates resembled the decision of Nicholas II, in the last months of his reign, to break off relations with the Grand Dukes.

Lenin returned to work later that month, and in the two months of lucidity left to him, in the brief intervals when permitted to work, dictated short essays in which he gave expression to a desperate concern over the direction Soviet policy had taken during his illness and charted the course of reforms. These essays are distinguished by lack of cohesion, a digressive style, and repetitiveness, all symptoms of a deteriorating mind. The most damaging of them remained unpublished in the Soviet Union until after Stalin's death. Initially used by Stalin's successors to discredit him, later, in the 1980s, they served to legitimize Mikhail Gorbachev's *perestroika*. The writings dealt with economic planning, cooperatives, the reorganization of Worker-Peasant Inspection, and the relationship between the party and the state. Through all his late writings and speeches runs, as a common theme, the sense of despair over Russia's cultural backwardness: he now came to regard its low level of culture as the principal obstacle to the construction of socialism in Russia. "Previously we placed and had to place the center of gravity on the political struggle, on the revolution, on conquest of power, and so on. Now, however, that center of gravity changes to that extent, that it shifts to peaceful 'cultural' work."[174] With these words Lenin tacitly acknowledged that he had been wrong thirty years earlier in rejecting as "bourgeois" the arguments of Peter Struve that before Russia could attain socialism she had to admit her want of culture and graduate from the school of capitalism.[175]

The most important of Lenin's late writings dealt with the issues of succession and the nationalities. Between December 23 and 26, with an addendum on January 4, Lenin dictated, in brief bursts, a series of personal comments on his associates—subsequently known as his "Testament"—for distribution to the forthcoming, Twelfth Party Congress.* Worried about

---

*Lenin, *PSS*, XLV, 343–48. In the spring of 1924, Krupskaia, in accord with Lenin's wishes, turned Lenin's last writings over to his associates. Kamenev read the "Testament" to the Council of Seniors at the Thirteenth Party Congress in 1924. Stalin was rescued from the acute embarrassment it might have caused him, had it been distributed to the delegates, by Zinoviev's suggestion to let bygones be bygones. Over Krupskaia's objections, but with Trotsky's concurrence, it was agreed that it would be made known to the delegates but not published: Egor Iakovlev in *MN*, No. 4/446 (January 22, 1989), 8–9. Its contents first became public knowledge from an article by Max Eastman in the *New York Times*, October 18, 1926, 1, 5. Trotsky, who in 1925 had categorically denied that Lenin left a "testament" (*Bolshevik*, No. 16, 1925, 68), ten years later published it in *The Suppressed Testament of Lenin*. Here he recalled that when the

the rivalry between Stalin and Trotsky, he proposed to enlarge the Central Committee from twenty-seven to as many as one hundred members, the newcomers to be drawn from the peasantry and working class. This would have the double effect of closing the gap between the party and the "masses" and diluting the power of the party's directing organs, now firmly in the hands of Stalin.

Lenin wanted this and other, related documents to be kept in strictest secrecy, ordering that they be placed in sealed envelopes to be opened either by him or by Krupskaia. M. A. Volodicheva, the secretary who took the dictation on December 23, however, troubled by the responsibility that knowledge of such an important document placed on her, consulted Fotieva, who advised her to show it to the General Secretary. Having read it in the presence of Bukharin and Ordzhonikidze, Stalin asked Volodicheva to burn it, which she did, without betraying that four more copies were deposited in a safe at Gorki.[176]

Unaware of her indiscretion, the following day Lenin dictated to Volodicheva still more explosive lines on the leading figures of the party.[177] Stalin, having become General Secretary, had accumulated "unbounded [*neob'iatnaia*] power": "I am not convinced that he will always know how to use this power with sufficient circumspection." On January 4 he dictated to Fotieva the following addendum:

> Stalin is too coarse [*grub*], and this shortcoming, fully tolerable within our midst and in our relations, as Communists, becomes intolerable in the post of General Secretary. For this reason I suggest that the comrades consider how to transfer Stalin from this post and replace him with someone who in all other respects enjoys over Comrade Stalin only one advantage, namely greater patience, greater loyalty, greater courtesy and attentiveness to comrades, less capriciousness, etc.[178]

Lenin thus fathomed only Stalin's minor vices, flaws of conduct and temperament: his sadistic cruelty, his megalomania, his hatred of anyone superior, eluded him to the end.

Trotsky he characterized as the "most capable person in the current Central Committee," but also someone "overly prone to self-confidence and overly attracted to the purely administrative aspect of work." By the latter he meant addiction not to paperwork but to a noncollegial command style of management. He recalled the shameful behavior of Kamenev and Zinoviev in October 1917, when they had opposed the power seizure, but he had some nice, if qualified, things to say about Bukharin and Piatakov— the former he characterized as the most outstanding theoretician in the party and the party's favorite, yet not quite a Marxist and something of a

---

"Testament" was read to the party leaders, on hearing Lenin's remarks about him Stalin blurted out a "phrase" expressive of his true feelings about Lenin: what it was he did not say (*Suppressed Testament*, 16). The "Testament" was first published in the U.S.S.R. in 1956.

scholastic.* There was no indication whom he wanted as General Secretary, but he left no doubt that Stalin had to go. The impression one gains from reading these rambling comments is that he considered no one fit to inherit his mantle. Fotieva promptly communicated these remarks to Stalin.[179]

Next Lenin addressed himself to the nationality question, on which subject he dictated on December 30–31 three memoranda. Here, he severely criticized the manner in which the Communist apparatus dealt with the minorities.† The thrust of his comments was that Stalin's proposal of "autonomization"—now abandoned—had been entirely inopportune and that its purpose was to enable the Soviet bureaucracy, mostly holdovers from tsarism, to lord it over the country. He accused Stalin and Dzerzhinskii, assimilated non-Russians, of chauvinism: Stalin he called "not only a genuine and veritable 'social-nationalist,' but also a crude Great Russian Dzerzhimorda" (a policeman in Gogol's *Inspector General,* whose name means "Snout-Muzzler"). Stalin and Dzerzhinskii were to be held personally accountable for "this truly Great Russian nationalistic campaign" against the Georgians. In his practical conclusions, Lenin demanded that the Union be strengthened, but, at the same time, that the minority peoples be given the maximum of rights compatible with national unity: any attempts at independence on the part of the republican ministries, he noted, could be "adequately paralyzed by the authority of the Party." It was a typically Leninist solution, in which a democratic facade was to conceal the totalitarian substance.

Whether or not Stalin knew of Lenin's essay on the nationalities is not clear: in any event, he could have no doubt now that Lenin was readying an all-out campaign against him, likely to result in his losing most of if not all his posts. (To Trotsky, Lenin confided he was "preparing a bomb" against Stalin at the Twelfth Party Congress.) Stalin was fighting for his political life: powerfully positioned though he was, once Lenin personally took the field, he stood no chance. His one hope was that Lenin would be fully incapacitated before he could bring him down.

Dzerzhinskii returned from his second mission to Georgia at the end of January 1923. To Lenin's request for the materials he had brought with him, he responded evasively that he had turned them over to Stalin. Stalin could not be found for two days; when finally located, he told Fotieva that he could grant Lenin's request only if authorized by the Politburo. In an aside he asked whether "she was not telling Lenin something unnecessary," and "how was it that he was abreast of current business?" Fotieva denied telling Lenin anything; in fact, she was telling everything to Stalin. Lenin

---

*A year earlier, Lenin had jotted down four adjectives to describe Kamenev: "Poor chap" *(bednenkii),* weak, cheerful, well-informed": RTsKhIDNI, F. 2. op. 2, delo 22300.

†First published in *SV,* No. 23–24/69–70 (December 17, 1923), 13–15, for reasons stated below, the essays were not released in the Soviet Union until the Twentieth Party Congress in 1956: *PSS,* XLV, 356–62. My translation, published two years earlier, in 1954 (*Formation of the Soviet Union,* 273–77), was based on the copy in the Trotsky Archive at Harvard.

later said to her face that he suspected her of disloyalty.[180] He was right. It has been subsequently established from archival sources that Fotieva, ignoring Lenin's orders that his dictations be kept "absolutely" and "categorically secret," routinely passed on their contents to Stalin and several other members of the Politburo.*

On February 1, the Politburo at last acceded to Lenin's request and delivered to his secretaries the materials collected by Dzerzhinskii on his second mission. In no condition to read them, Lenin distributed the papers among his secretarial staff with exact instructions as to what information to locate. They were to report to him as soon as they finished. Building a case for the Party Congress against Stalin, Dzerzhinskii, and Ordzhonikidze, he followed the progress of his staff with keen interest: according to Fotieva, during February 1923 the Georgian question was uppermost on his mind.[181] The report was delivered to him on March 3. Once he familiarized himself with it, Lenin threw his full support behind the Georgian opposition. On March 5, he forwarded to Trotsky his memoir on the nationality question with a request that he take charge of the defense of the Georgian Communists in the Central Committee. "The matter is being 'prosecuted' by Stalin and Dzerzhinskii, on whose objectivity I cannot rely. Quite the contrary."[182]

It so happened that on that very day, March 5, after Lenin questioned her about a telephone conversation he had overheard, Krupskaia told him of the incident with Stalin the previous December.[183] Lenin immediately dictated the following letter to Stalin:

> Respected Comrade Stalin!
> You had the rudeness to telephone my wife and abuse her. Although she has told you of her willingness to forget what you have said, this fact came to be known, through her, also to Zinoviev and Kamenev. I have no intention of forgetting so easily what is done against me, and, needless to say, I consider whatever is done against my wife to be directed also against myself. For this reason I request you to inform me whether you agree to retract what you have said and apologize, or prefer a breach of relations between us.†

Krupskaia vainly tried to stop Lenin from dispatching this letter: it was personally delivered to Stalin by Volodicheva on March 7, with copies to Kamenev and Zinoviev.[184]

Stalin calmly read it and then wrote a response, first published in 1989, which can only be described as a very qualified apology. Insisting that he

---

*Volkogonov, *Triumf*, I/1, 153. As a reward, Stalin spared Fotieva's life during the purges of the 1930s. She outlived him and died in 1975.

†Lenin, *PSS*, LIV, 329–30. Lenin did not address colleagues with the adjective "Respected" (*Uvazhaemyi*): the use of this form suggests that he no longer considered Stalin a colleague. The text of the letter makes it clear that Lenin did not "break all personal and comradely relations" with Stalin, as Trotsky subsequently claimed (*e.g.*, *Portrety*, 42), but only threatened to do so if Stalin did not apologize—which Stalin did.

had meant no offense and was merely reminding Krupskaia of her responsibility for Lenin's health, he concluded: "If you feel that for the preservation of 'relations' I should 'retract' the above words, I can take them back, failing, however, to understand what it is all about, wherein lies my 'fault,' and what, really, is wanted of me."*

The following day, Lenin dictated another note—it was to be the very last communication of his life—to the leaders of the Georgian opposition, with copies to Trotsky and Kamenev, informing them that he was following their case "with all my heart," that he was appalled by the "connivances" of Stalin and Dzerzhinskii, and that he was preparing a speech on the subject.[185]

Stalin faced the prospect of political annihilation. With Lenin offering to break relations and Trotsky in charge of the prosecution, his chances of staying on as General Secretary were close to nil. But the news was not all bad, for Lenin's physicians, with whom he was in constant communication, advised him that the patient's health was growing worse. So he decided to play for time. On March 9, *Pravda* carried a terse, one-sentence announcement from him, without explanation, that the forthcoming Party Congress, which was scheduled for mid-March, was deferred to April 15.[186]

The gamble paid off. Three days later (March 10), Lenin suffered a massive stroke, which robbed him of the power of speech: until his death ten months later, he could utter only such monosyllables as *"vot-vot"* ("here-here") and *"s"ezd-s"ezd"* ("congress-congress").[187] Physicians attending him—there were forty of them, including several specialists from Germany—concluded that he would never again be able to play an active role in politics. In May, he was moved permanently to Gorki, where on fine days he sat in a wheelchair in the park. For all practical purposes he was a living corpse: for although he seemed to understand what was said to him and was able to read, he could not communicate. In August, Krupskaia tried to teach him to write with his left hand, but the results were not encouraging and she gave up.[188]

In this, the last period of his life, he seems to have been overwhelmed by a sense of failure. It was evidenced by an uncharacteristic craving for praise, for reassurance that whatever the outcome, he had made history. In 1923 and early 1924, Lenin, who in the past had paid no attention to the opinions of others, whether favorable or hostile, craved panegyrics. He read with visible pleasure Trotsky's article comparing him to Marx, Gorky's assertion that without him the Russian Revolution would not have triumphed, and the encomiums of such foreign admirers as Henri Guilbeaux and Arthur Rhys Williams.[189]

---

*IzvTsK, No. 12 (December 1989), 193. According to Maria Ulianova, Lenin's health deteriorated so rapidly that he never had a chance to read Stalin's "apology": ibid., 199.

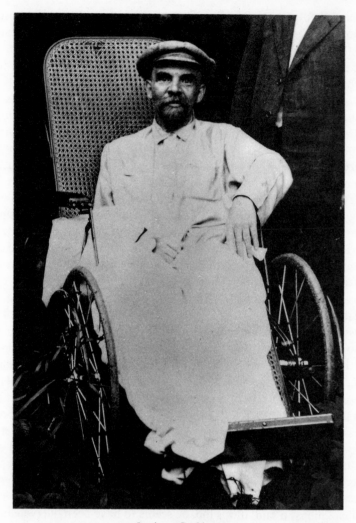

74. Lenin at Gorki, 1923.

With Lenin out of the picture, Stalin still had to neutralize Trotsky, who had Lenin's mandate to discredit him for his handling of the Georgian question. The task proved unexpectedly easy, because Trotsky evaded the responsibility that Lenin had entrusted to him. Instead of executing Lenin's commission, he abandoned the Georgians to their fate: when a secretary read to him over the telephone Lenin's letter of March 5, Trotsky flatly refused to speak for the Georgians at the Plenum, on grounds of ill health: he claimed to be nearly paralyzed. But, he added, after earlier hesitations he had now come fully to side with the Georgian opposition.[190] Even so, he fell in line with Stalin's self-serving decision to defer the opening of the

Twelfth Congress.[191] On the eve of the Congress, he assured Kamenev that he would support Stalin's reappointment as General Secretary and oppose the expulsion of Dzerzhinskii and Ordzhonikidze.[192] He turned down Stalin's offer, made in an effort to coopt him, to deliver to the Congress the report of the Central Committee, traditionally given by Lenin. He thought Stalin, as General Secretary, was better qualified. Stalin modestly declined and the honor went to Zinoviev, who was heedlessly elbowing his way to the front, convinced Lenin's mantle was his for the asking.[193]

Trotsky's behavior at this critical juncture in his and Stalin's careers has mystified both contemporaries and historians. He himself never provided a satisfactory explanation. Various interpretations have been advanced: that he underestimated Stalin; or that, on the contrary, he thought the General Secretary too solidly entrenched to be successfully challenged; that he had no stomach for a conflict certain to divide the Party.[194] Some of his acolytes claim that he considered political infighting below his dignity, having "no idea whatever of personal political maneuvering."[195] His biographer, Issac Deutscher, attributes Trotsky's passivity to his "magnanimity" and "heroic character," in which respect, he claims, he had "only very few equals in history."[196]

Trotsky's behavior seems to have been caused by a number of disparate factors that are difficult to disentangle. He undoubtedly considered himself best qualified to take over Lenin's leadership. Yet he was well aware of the formidable obstacles facing him. He had no following in the party leadership, which clustered around Stalin, Zinoviev, and Kamenev. He was unpopular in party ranks for his non-Bolshevik past as well as his aloof personality. Another factor inhibiting him—imponderable by its very nature but certainly weighty—was his Jewishness. This came to light with the publication in 1990 of the minutes of a Central Committee Plenum of October 1923, at which Trotsky defended himself from criticism for having refused Lenin's offer of deputyship. Although his Jewish origins held for him no meaning, he said, it was politically significant. By assuming the high post Lenin offered him, he would "give enemies grounds for claiming that the country was ruled by a Jew." Lenin had dismissed the argument as "nonsense" but "deep in his heart he agreed with me."[197]

Such considerations moved Trotsky in 1922–23 to behave in a very contradictory fashion, as he strove to act independently of the majority and, at the same time, cooperated with it to avoid the fatal stigma of "factionalism." In the end he not only lost the political battle, but forfeited the moral esteem that a more courageous stand would have earned him.

With Trotsky's connivance, the Twelfth Party Congress, which could have been the scene of Stalin's ruin, witnessed his triumph. On March 16, exuding confidence, Stalin cabled Ordzhonikidze in Tiflis that "despite everything," the Congress would approve the conduct of the Transcaucasian Committee.[198] He proved right. At the Congress, he patiently explained why introducing more democratic procedures into a party of 400,000 would transform it into a "discussion club" incapable of action, at a time when the country was under continuous threat from the "wolves of imperialism."[199] He agreed with Lenin on the utility of enlarging the Central Committee with fresh elements, while ignoring his proposals for structural and personnel changes. Lenin's notes on the nationality question were distributed to the delegates but not made public.* In the report he delivered on this subject, Stalin cleverly steered a middle course, neutralizing Lenin's arguments on behalf of the Georgian opposition and a looser Union: he even had the temerity to condemn "Great Russian chauvinism," with which Lenin had charged him.[200] The minutes record that on the completion of his organizational report on behalf of the Central Committee, the delegates rewarded Stalin with "loud, protracted applause."† (Lenin's speeches at Party Congresses normally rated only "loud applause.") Trotsky confined himself to an address on the future of Soviet industry—it was his only intervention at the Congress and he received bare "applause." Stalin was readily reconfirmed as General Secretary.

Trotsky's appeasement availed him little. In his memoirs he writes that during Lenin's incapacitation, Stalin's associates formed a conspiracy involving all the members of the Politburo except for himself, which caucused before any decisions were to be taken and then acted in unison. To qualify for appointments, party members had to meet only one criterion: enmity to Trotsky.[201] In the new Central Committee of forty members he could count on no more than three supporters.[202]

Aware that the odds were overwhelmingly against him and that he had nothing to lose, Trotsky gave up currying favor with his enemies and went on the offensive. To restore his faltering fortunes, he assumed the pose of spokesman for the party masses: if the entrenched Old Guard insisted on treating him as an outsider, he would become the champion of the outsiders. The latter were the vast majority of the Party's membership: according to the census of 1922, only 2.7 percent of the 376,000 members had joined before 1917 and thus qualified for the Old Guard.[203] But that 2.7 percent

---

*On April 16, Fotieva, on her own authority, sent Stalin a copy of Lenin's essay on the nationalities. Stalin refused to accept it on the grounds that he did not want to "involve himself" (*vmeshivatsia*) in this matter. Copies then went to the Central Committee. That evening, Stalin secured from Fotieva a letter in which she cited Lenin's sister to the effect that Lenin did not give instructions to have it published, adding on her own that he did not consider it ready for publication. On receipt of Fotieva's letter, Stalin wrote the Central Committee a complaint against Trotsky for keeping secret so important a statement by Lenin, ending: "I believe that the articles of Comrade Lenin [on the nationality question] should be published in the press. One can only regret that as it transpires from Comr. Fotieva's letter, they cannot be published inasmuch as Comrade Lenin has not yet looked them over." Instead, copies of Lenin's essay on the nationalities were distributed "for their information" to the delegates. The relevant documents on this matter, deposited in RTsKhIDNI, F. 5, op. 2, delo 34, have been reproduced in *IzvTsK*, No. 9 (September 1990), 153–61.

†*Dvenadtsatyi S"ezd RKP(b)*, 62. The only other speaker to receive this kind of accolade was Zinoviev (*ibid.*, 47)—further evidence that he was being touted as Lenin's successor.

monopolized the Party's directing organs and, through them, the apparatus of the state.* Friends assured Trotsky that he was an influential Communist leader and that his name was inseparably bound to Lenin's.[204] Why not, then, rally the Communist rank-and-file to his side? Although couched in moral terms, Trotsky's counteroffensive, launched in October 1923, was little more than a desperate gamble. Since October 1917 no one had insisted more resolutely on the supreme importance of party unity and rejected more derisively the calls for greater party democracy voiced by the Workers' Opposition and the Democratic Centralists. His sudden conversion to party democracy could not have been motivated by fundamental changes in the way the Party was run, since no such changes had occurred. What had shifted was his standing in the Party: once an insider, he had become an outcast.

On October 8, 1923, Trotsky addressed to the Central Committee an Open Letter charging the leadership with abandoning democratic procedures in the Party.[205] (In the Party only—as he reminded the Plenum that met to discuss his letter: "You, comrades, know very well that I was never a 'democrat.' "†) The event that precipitated the move was Dzerzhinskii's demand that Communists who had knowledge of factional activity be required to inform the GPU and other appropriate Party organs.[206] Well aware that this provision was directed against him and his followers, he interpreted it as symptomatic of the Party's bureaucratization. What has happened, he demanded to know, that a special instruction had to be issued requiring Communists to do that which it was their duty to do in any event? He aimed his fire against the concentration of power at the top of the hierarchy, singling out the practice of *naznachenstvo,* the appointment of secretaries of provincial party organizations by the Center:

> The bureaucratization of the Party has developed to unheard-of proportions as a result of the procedure of secretarial selection. . . . There has been created a very broad stratum of party workers, in the apparatus of the government and the Party, who completely renounce their own party opinion, at least in its open expression, as if assuming that the secretarial hierarchy represents the apparatus that creates party opinion and makes party decisions. Beneath the stratum of those who abstain from [expressing] their own opinions, lies the broad mass of the Party, for whom every decision comes in the form of a ready summons or command.[207]

While conceding that "old Bolsheviks" had a right to special status, he reminded them that they constituted but a minuscule minority. He con-

---

*According to Leonard Schapiro, the vast majority of persons in key party positions in the early 1920s had been Leninists before the Revolution. "The organizational structure after the revolution was therefore in this respect very close to the pre-revolutionary underground structure" (*The Communist Party of the Soviet Union,* London, 1960, 236–37).

†Nikolai Vasetskii, *Likvidatsiia* (Moscow, 1989), 22. As late as May 1922, he had opposed legalizing the Menshevik and SR parties: *Pravda,* No. 102 (May 10, 1922), 1.

cluded: "There must be an end to secretarial bureaucratism. Party democracy—at any rate, within such limits without which the party is threatened with ossification and degeneration—must acquire its rights."[208]

All of which was true enough: yet only three years earlier Trotsky himself had dismissed identical complaints as "formalism" and "fetishism." On his new platform he acquired some support, especially from the so-called "Group of 46," members who shared his views and sent a letter to this effect to the Central Committee.[209] The directing organs of the Party, however, had a ready answer: the letter constituted a "platform" that could lead to the creation of an illegal faction.[210] In a lengthy rebuttal, it took Trotsky to task:

Two or three years ago, when Comrade Trotsky began his "economic" pronouncements against the majority of the Central Committee, Lenin himself explained to him dozens of times that economic questions belong to a category that precludes quick successes, that requires years and years of patient and persistent work to achieve serious results. . . . To secure correct leadership of the country's economic life from a single center and to introduce into it the maximum of planning, the Central Committee in the summer of 1923 reorganized the STO, introducing into it personally a number of the leading economic workers of the republic. In that number, the Central Committee elected also Comrade Trotsky. But Comrade Trotsky did not consider making an appearance at meetings of the STO, just as for many years he had failed to attend meetings of the Sovnarkom and rejected the proposal of Comrade Lenin to be one of the deputies of the Sovnarkom Chairman. . . . At the basis of Comrade Trotsky's discontent, of his whole irritation, of all his assaults over the years against the Central Committee, of his decision to rock the party, lies the circumstance that Comrade Trotsky wants the Central Committee to have him and Comrade [A. L.] Kolegaev take charge of our economic life. Comrade Lenin had long fought against such an appointment, and we believe he was entirely correct. . . . Comrade Trotsky is a member of the Sovnarkom and of the reorganized STO. He has been offered by Comrade Lenin the post of deputy of Sovnarkom chairman. Had he wanted, in all these positions Comrade Trotsky could have demonstrated to the entire party in fact, in deed, that he can be entrusted with that de facto unlimited authority in the field of economic and military affairs for which he strives. But Comrade Trotsky preferred a different method of action, one which, in our opinion, is incompatible with the duties of a Party member. He has attended not a single meeting of the Sovnarkom either under Comrade Lenin or after Comrade Lenin's retirement from work. He has attended not a single meeting of the STO, whether old or reorganized. He has not moved once either in the Sovnarkom, or in the STO, or in the Gosplan any proposals concerning economic, financial, budgetary, and so forth, questions. He has categorically refused to be Comrade Lenin's deputy: this he apparently considers below his dignity. He acts according to the formula "All or Nothing." In fact, Comrade Trotsky has assumed toward the Party the attitude that it either must grant him dictatorial powers in the economic and military spheres, or else he will, in effect, refuse to work in the economic realm, reserving himself only the right to engage in systematic disorganization of the Central Committee in its difficult day-to-day work.[211]

The response did not answer the political questions raised by Trotsky's letter: instead, following the principle that Lenin and Trotsky had long established in political controversies, it assailed him personally. The assault was powerful and must have discredited Trotsky still further in the eyes of the Communist cadres.

Defiant, on October 23, in a letter to the Plenum of the Central Committee, Trotsky expanded on the themes he had raised and denied charges he was promoting divisiveness in party ranks.[212] Taking note of his refusal to fall in step, the Plenum voted 102 against 2 (with 10 abstentions) to reprimand him for engaging in "factionalism." It also "completely approved" the conduct of the Party's leadership.[213] Kamenev and Zinoviev wanted Trotsky expelled from the Party, but Stalin thought this not prudent: on his urging, the motion was rejected. The Politburo published in *Pravda* a resolution stating that notwithstanding Trotsky's improper behavior, it was inconceivable to carry on work without him: his continued collaboration in the highest party organs was "absolutely indispensable."* Realizing that the regime of the "troika" was coming under increasing criticism, Stalin thought it advisable to pretend that he wished to retain Trotsky as a valued if errant associate. As he would later explain:

> We did not agree with comrades Zinoviev and Kamenev because we knew that the policy of severance is fraught with dangers for the party, that the method of severance is the method of blood-letting. It is dangerous, contagious: today they will cut off one, tomorrow another, the day after, a third, and then there will be no one left in the Party.[214]

As always, Stalin's was the voice of reason and compromise.

In December 1923, Trotsky finally broke ranks and took his case to the public with an article in *Pravda* called "The New Course." Here he contrasted the Party's youth, fired with democratic ideals, with the entrenched Old Guard. His operative conclusion was "The party must subordinate to itself its apparatus."[215] To which Stalin replied: "Bolshevism cannot accept pitting the party against the party apparatus."[216]

Now according to the party rules adopted at the Tenth Congress, with Trotsky's approval, the actions in which he engaged, in particular consultations with the Group of 46, indisputably constituted "factionalism." The crime was compounded by the leakage of his two letters—accidental or deliberate, no one could tell—to the public. The Party Conference that convened in January 1924, therefore, was entirely within its rights in con-

---

**Pravda, No. 287 (December 18, 1923), 4. Bukharin later reminded Zinoviev that in 1923 he, Zinoviev, had wanted Trotsky arrested: *Pravda*, No. 251/3,783 (November 2, 1927), 3. On Lenin's reaction, see above, p. 467.

demning Trotsky and "Trotskyism" as a "petty-bourgeois" deviation.[217]

The game was up for Trotsky: the rest was anticlimactic. He had no defense against the party majority for, as he would himself concede in 1924: "None of us wants to be and none of us can be right against the Party. In the final analysis, our party is always right."[218] In January 1925, he would be forced to resign as Commissar of War. There followed expulsion from the Party and exile, first to Central Asia and then abroad; and, finally, assassination. The moves to oust him, masterminded by Stalin, with the connivance of Zinoviev, Kamenev, Bukharin, and the others, were carried out with the backing of the party cadres, who believed they served to safeguard party unity from a selfish schemer.

There are many instances in history when the loser earns posterity's sympathy because he is seen as morally superior to the victors. It is difficult to muster such sympathy for Trotsky. Admittedly he was more cultured than Stalin and his confederates, intellectually more interesting, personally more courageous, and, in dealings with fellow Communists, more honorable. But as in the case of Lenin, such virtues as he possessed manifested themselves exclusively within the Party. In relations with outsiders as well as those insiders who strove for greater democracy, Trotsky was at one with Lenin and Stalin. He helped forge the weapons that destroyed him. He suffered the same fate that was meted out, with his wholehearted consent, to the opponents of Lenin's dictatorship: the Kadets, the Socialists-Revolutionaries, the Mensheviks; ex-tsarist officers who would not fight in the Red Army; the Workers' Opposition; the Kronshtadt sailors, and the Tambov peasants; the priesthood. He awoke to the dangers of totalitarianism only when it threatened him personally: his sudden conversion to party democracy was a means of self-defense, not the championship of principle.

Trotsky liked to depict himself as a proud lion brought down by a pack of jackals; and the more monstrous Stalin revealed himself to be, the more persuasive this image appeared to those in Russia and abroad who wanted to salvage an idealized vision of Lenin's Bolshevism. But the record indicates that in his day Trotsky, too, was one of the pack. His defeat had nothing ennobling about it. He lost because he was outsmarted in a sordid struggle for political power.

Lenin died in the evening of Monday, January 21, 1924. Apart from the family and attending physicians, the only witness to his last moments was Bukharin.* As soon as they heard the news, Zinoviev, Stalin, Kamenev, and Kalinin rushed to Gorki on motorized sleds; the rest of the leadership followed by train. Stalin, who led the procession to the

---

*Bukharin in *Pravda*, No. 17/2,948 (January 21, 1925), 2. In a letter to Stalin from prison in February 1937, pleading for his life, he wrote that Lenin had "died in his arms": *NYT*, June 15, 1992, p. A 11.

dead leader's bedside, raised his head, pressed it to his heart, and kissed it.[219] The next day, Dzerzhinskii drafted a brief note on Lenin's death, warning the population not to "panic" so as not to compel the GPU to carry out mass arrests.[220]

On the day of Lenin's death, Trotsky arrived in Tiflis en route to the resort city of Sukhumi. He learned of it the next day from a coded telegram signed by Stalin.[221] In response to a cabled query, Stalin advised him that the funeral would take place on Saturday (January 26), and added that since there was not enough time for him to return for the funeral, the Politburo thought it best that he proceed to Sukhumi as planned.[222] As it turned out, the funeral took place on Sunday. Trotsky subsequently accused Stalin of deliberately misinforming him in order to have him miss the funeral. The charge does not stand up to scrutiny. Lenin died on Monday and Trotsky had the information on Tuesday morning. It had taken him three days to travel from Moscow to Tiflis. Had he immediately turned around, he could have reached Moscow by Friday at the latest, in good time to attend the funeral even if it had been held on Saturday.* Instead, for reasons he never satisfactorily explained, he followed Stalin's advice and went on to Sukhumi. There he basked in the Black Sea sun while Lenin's body lay in state in wintry Moscow attended by the Old Guard. His absence caused widespread surprise and dismay.

What was to be done with Lenin's remains?[223] In his will, which has not been published so far, Lenin had expressed the wish to be buried by the side of his mother in Petrograd. This was also what Krupskaia wanted: in a letter to *Pravda,* she spoke strongly against a cult of Lenin—she wanted no monuments, no celebrations, and, implicitly, no mausoleum.[224] But the Party's masters had other ideas. The Politburo had discussed embalming Lenin's body months before his death: this course was especially favored by Stalin and Kalinin, who wanted the dead leader buried in "a Russian manner." They needed the physical Lenin on permanent exhibit to cater to the popular belief, rooted in Orthodox religion, that the remains of saints were immune to decay. None of them, except their common enemy, Trotsky, was widely known: Stalin, who by this time had acquired, by virtue of bureaucratic infighting, nearly dictatorial powers, was hardly a household name. A dead, and therefore mute but corporeal, Lenin, suitably preserved, would provide validation of the faith he had founded and provide continuity between the October Revolution and the rule of his successors. The decision to embalm Lenin's remains and display them in a

---

*The decision to postpone Lenin's funeral to Sunday was announced only on Friday, January 25 (Lenin, *Khronika,* XII, 673), so that it is by no means apparent that in cabling on January 22 that it would take place on Saturday, Stalin was deliberately deceiving him, as Trotsky later claimed. (*Moia zhizn',* II, 249–50). Deutscher, in a not uncharacteristic instance of carelessness favorable to his hero, claims that Stalin advised Trotsky the funeral would be "the next day" (*Prophet Unarmed,* 133). Stalin's second cable stated that the funeral would be on Saturday, *i.e.,* not the "next" day but in four days.

75. Stalin viewing Lenin's body.

mausoleum on Red Square was taken over the objections of Bukharin and Kamenev.

Lenin's body lay in state in the Hall of Columns of the Dom Soiuzov, where it was seen by tens of thousands. On January 26, Stalin delivered a funeral speech with a "pledge" in which, using religious cadences he had learned in the seminary, he vowed in the name of the Party faithfully to carry out Lenin's commands.[225] On Sunday, January 27, the body was borne to a temporary wooden mausoleum.* Unfortunately, by March, with the advent of spring, the corpse began to decompose.[226] What was to be done? Krasin, placed in charge of the funeral arrangements, believed in resurrection and suggested that the corpse be frozen: special apparatus for this purpose was imported from Germany, but the idea had to be dropped as impractical. Then Dzerzhinskii, whose job it was to know everything, learned that a Kharkov anatomist by the name of V. P. Vorobev had developed new methods of preserving live tissue. After lengthy discussions, the leadership decided to entrust Vorobev with the task of embalming Lenin. The group he headed was named the Immortalization Commission.

Helped by an assistant, Vorobev worked for three months on replacing the water in the cells and tissues with a chemical fluid of his own invention.

*Lenin's brain was removed and transferred to the V. I. Lenin Institute, where scientists were assigned to discover the secret of his "genius" and to prove that it represented a "higher stage in the evolution of mankind." Later on, the brains of Stalin and some other Communist luminaries were added to the collection. Lenin's heart was deposited in the V. I. Lenin Museum. *AiF*, No. 43/576 (November 1991), 1.

This compound was said not to evaporate at normal temperatures and humidity, to destroy bacteria and fungi, and to neutralize fermentation. Embalming was completed in late July, and the following month the body was exposed to view in a new wooden mausoleum. In 1930 this was replaced with a mausoleum of stone that Stalin unveiled and that subsequently became the object of state-sponsored veneration. In 1939, Stalin assigned 22 scientists to a laboratory to oversee the mummy, which, despite precautions, did not remain stable. The most advanced scientific methods were applied to prevent further decay or changes in appearance.

Thus, the Bolsheviks who five years earlier in a noisy campaign of blasphemy and ridicule exposed as sham the relics of Orthodox saints, created a holy relic of their own. Unlike the church's saints, whose remains were revealed to be nothing but rags and bones, their god, as befitted the age of science, was composed of alcohol, glycerin, and formalin.

Reflections on the
Russian Revolution

The Russian Revolution of 1917 was not an event or even a process, but a sequence of disruptive and violent acts that occurred more or less concurrently but involved actors with differing and in some measure contradictory objectives. It began as a revolt of the most conservative elements in Russian society, disgusted by the Crown's familiarity with Rasputin and the mismanagement of the war effort. From the conservatives the revolt spread to the liberals, who challenged the monarchy from fear that if it remained in office, revolution would become inevitable. Initially, the assault on the monarchy was undertaken not, as widely believed, from fatigue with the war but from a desire to pursue the war more effectively: not to make revolution but to avert one. In February 1917, when the Petrograd garrison refused to fire on civilian crowds, the generals, in agreement with parliamentary politicians, hoping to prevent the mutiny from spreading to the front, convinced Tsar Nicholas II to abdicate. The abdication, made for the sake of military victory, brought down the whole edifice of Russian statehood.

Although initially neither social discontent nor the agitation of the radical intelligentsia played any significant role in these events, both moved to the forefront the instant imperial authority collapsed. In the spring and summer of 1917, peasants began to seize and distribute among themselves noncommunal properties. Next, the rebellion spread to frontline troops, who deserted in droves to share in the spoils; to workers, who took control of industrial enterprises; and to ethnic minorities, who wanted greater self-rule. Each group pursued its own objectives, but the cumulative effect of their assault on the country's social and economic structure by the autumn of 1917 created in Russia a state of anarchy.

The events of 1917 demonstrated that for all its immense territory and claim to great power status, the Russian Empire was a fragile, artificial structure, held together not by organic bonds connecting rulers and ruled, but by mechanical links provided by the bureaucracy, police, and army. Its 150 million inhabitants were bound neither by strong economic interests nor by a sense of national identity. Centuries of autocratic rule in a country with a predominantly natural economy had prevented the formation of strong lateral ties: Imperial Russia was mostly warp with little woof. This fact was noted at the time by one of Russia's leading historians and political figures, Paul Miliukov:

> To make you understand [the] special character of the Russian Revolution, I must draw your attention to [the] peculiar features, made our own by the whole process of Russia's history. To my mind, all these features converge into one. The fundamental difference which distinguishes Russia's social structure from that of other civilized countries, can be characterized as a certain weakness or lack of a strong cohesion or cementation of elements which form a social compound. You can observe that lack of consolidation in the Russian social aggregate in every aspect of civilized life: political, social, mental and national.
>
> From the political point of view, the Russian State institutions lacked cohesion and amalgamation with the popular masses over which they ruled. . . . As a consequence of their later appearance, the State institutions in Eastern Europe necessarily assumed certain forms which were different from those in the West. The State in the East had no time to originate from within, in a process of organic evolution. It was brought to the East from outside.[1]

Once these factors are taken into consideration, it becomes apparent that the Marxist notion that revolution always results from social ("class") discontent cannot be sustained. Although such discontent did exist in Imperial Russia, as it does everywhere, the decisive and immediate factors making for the regime's fall and the resultant turmoil were overwhelmingly political.

Was the Revolution inevitable? It is natural to believe that whatever happens has to happen, and there are historians who rationalize this primitive faith with pseudoscientific arguments: they would be more convincing if they could predict the future as unerringly as they claim to predict the past. Paraphrasing a familiar legal maxim, one might say that psychologically speaking, occurrence provides nine-tenths of historical justification.

Edmund Burke was in his day widely regarded as a madman for questioning the French Revolution: seventy years later, according to Matthew Arnold, his ideas were still considered "superannuated and conquered by events"— so ingrained is the belief in the rationality, and therefore the inevitability, of historical events. The grander they are and the more weighty their consequences the more they appear part of the natural order of things which it is quixotic to question.

The most that one can say is that a revolution in Russia was more likely than not, and this for several reasons. Of these, perhaps the most weighty was the steady decline of the prestige of tsardom in the eyes of a population accustomed to being ruled by an invincible authority—indeed, seeing in invincibility the criterion of legitimacy. After a century and a half of military victories and expansion, from the middle of the nineteenth century until 1917, Russia suffered one humiliation after another at the hands of foreigners: the defeat, on her own soil, in the Crimean War; the loss at the Congress of Berlin of the fruits of victory over the Turks; the debacle in the war with Japan; and the drubbing at the hands of the Germans in World War I.[2] Such a succession of reverses would have damaged the reputation of any government: in Russia it proved fatal. Tsarism's disgrace was compounded by the concurrent rise of a revolutionary movement which it was unable to quell despite resort to harsh repression. The half-hearted concessions made in 1905 to share power with society neither made tsarism more popular with the opposition nor raised its prestige in the eyes of the people at large, who simply could not understand how a ruler would allow himself to be abused from the forum of a government institution. The Confucian principle of T'ien-ming, or Mandate of Heaven, which in its original meaning linked the ruler's authority to righteous conduct, in Russia derived from forceful conduct: a weak ruler, a "loser," forfeited it. Nothing could be more misleading than to judge a Russian head of state by the standard of either morality or popularity: what mattered was that he inspire fear in friend and foe—that, like Ivan IV, he deserve the sobriquet of "Awesome." Nicholas II fell not because he was hated but because he was held in contempt.

Among the other factors making for revolution was the mentality of the Russian peasantry, a class never integrated into the political structure. Peasants made up 80 percent of Russia's population; and although they took hardly any active part in the conduct of state affairs, in a passive capacity, as an obstacle to change and, at the same time, a permanent threat to the status quo, they were a very unsettling element. It is commonplace to hear that under the old regime the Russian peasant was "oppressed," but it is far from clear just who was oppressing him. On the eve of the Revolution, he enjoyed full civil and legal rights; he also owned, either outright or communally, nine-tenths of the country's agricultural land and the same proportion of livestock. Poor by Western European or American standards, he was better off than his father, and freer than his grandfather, who more likely than not had been a serf. Cultivating allotments assigned to him by fellow peasants, he certainly enjoyed greater security than tenant farmers of Ireland, Spain, or Italy.

The problem with Russian peasants was not oppression, but isolation. They were isolated from the country's political, economic, and cultural life, and therefore unaffected by the changes that had occurred since the time that Peter the Great had set Russia on the course of Westernization. Many contemporaries observed that the peasantry remained steeped in Muscovite culture: culturally it had no more in common with the ruling elite or the intelligentsia than the native population of Britain's African colonies had with Victorian England. The majority of Russia's peasants descended from serfs, who were not even subjects, since the monarchy abandoned them to the whim of the landlord and bureaucrat. As a result, for Russia's rural population the state remained even after emancipation an alien and malevolent force that took taxes and recruits but gave nothing in return. The peasant knew no loyalty outside his household and commune. He felt no patriotism and no attachment to the government save for a vague devotion to the distant tsar from whom he expected to receive the land he coveted. An instinctive anarchist, he was never integrated into national life and felt as much estranged from the conservative establishment as from the radical opposition. He looked down on the city and on men without beards: Marquis de Custine heard it said as early as 1839 that someday Russia would see a revolt of the bearded against the shaven.[3] The existence of this mass of alienated and potentially explosive peasants immobilized the government, which believed that it was docile only from fear and would interpret any political concessions as weakness and rebel.

The traditions of serfdom and the social institutions of rural Russia—the joint family household and the almost universal system of communal landholding—prevented the peasantry from developing qualities required for modern citizenship. While serfdom was not slavery, the two institutions had this in common that like slaves, serfs had no legal rights and hence no sense of law. Michael Rostovtseff, Russia's leading historian of classical antiquity and an eyewitness of 1917, concluded that serfdom may have been worse than slavery in that a serf had never known freedom, which prevented him from acquiring the qualities of a true citizen: in his opinion, it was a principal cause of Bolshevism.[4] To serfs, authority was by its very nature arbitrary: and to defend themselves from it they relied not on appeals to legal or moral rights, but on cunning. They could not conceive of government based on principle: life to them was a Hobbesian war of all against all. This attitude fostered despotism: for the absence of inner discipline and respect for law required order to be imposed from the outside. When despotism ceased to be viable, anarchy ensued; and once anarchy had run its course, it inevitably gave rise to a new despotism.

The peasant was revolutionary in one respect only: he did not acknowledge private ownership of land. Although on the eve of the Revolution he owned nine-tenths of the country's arable, he craved for the remaining 10 percent held by landlords, merchants, and noncommunal peasants. No economic or legal arguments could change his mind: he felt he had a God-given right to that land and that someday it would be his. And by his he meant the commune's, which would allocate it justly to its members. The prevalence of communal landholding in European Russia was, along with the legacy of serfdom, a fundamental fact of Russian social history. It meant that along with a poorly developed sense for law, the peasant also had little respect for private property. Both tendencies were exploited and exacerbated by radical intellectuals for their own ends to incite the peasantry against the status quo.*

Russia's industrial workers were potentially destabilizing not because they assimilated revolutionary ideologies—very few of them did and even they were excluded from leadership positions in the revolutionary parties. Rather, since most of them were one or at most two generations removed from the village and only superficially urbanized, they carried with them to the factory rural attitudes only slightly adjusted to industrial conditions. They were not socialists but syndicalists, believing that as their village relatives were entitled to all the land, so they had a right to the factories. Politics interested them no more than it did the peasants: in this sense, too, they were under the influence of primitive, nonideological anarchism. Furthermore, industrial labor in Russia was numerically too insignificant to play a major role in revolution: with at most 3 million workers (a high proportion of them peasants seasonally employed), they represented a mere 2 percent of the population. Hordes of graduate students, steered by their professors, in the Soviet Union as well as the West, especially the United States, have assiduously combed historical sources in the hope of unearthing evidence of worker radicalism in prerevolutionary Russia. The results are weighty tomes, filled with mostly meaningless events and statistics, that prove only that while history is always interesting, history books can be both vacuous and dull.

A major and arguably decisive factor making for revolution was the intelligentsia, which in Russia attained greater influence than anywhere else. The peculiar "ranking" system of the tsarist civil service excluded outsiders from the administration, estranging the best-educated elements and making them susceptible to fantastic schemes of social reform, conceived but never tried in Western Europe. The absence until 1906 of representative institutions and a free press, combined with the spread of education, enabled the

---

*Vera Zasulich, who had begun her revolutionary career in the 1870s and lived to witness Lenin's dictatorship, acknowledged in 1918 the responsibility of socialists for Bolshevism in that they had goaded workers—and, one could add, peasants—to seize property, but taught them nothing of citizens' obligations: *NV*, No. 74/98 (April 16, 1918), 3.

cultural elite to claim the right to speak on behalf of a mute people. There exists no evidence that the intelligentsia actually reflected the opinion of the "masses": on the contrary, the evidence indicates that both before and after the Revolution peasants and workers deeply mistrusted intellectuals. This became apparent in 1917 and the years that followed. But since the true will of the people had no channels of expression, at any rate, until the short-lived constitutional order introduced in 1906, the intelligentsia was able with some success to pose as its spokesman.

As in other countries where it lacked legitimate political outlets, the intelligentsia in Russia constituted itself into a caste: and since ideas were what gave it identity and cohesion, it developed extreme intellectual intolerance. Adopting the Enlightenment view of man as nothing but material substance shaped by the environment, and its corollary, that changes in the environment inevitably change human nature, it saw "revolution" not as the replacement of one government by another, but as something incomparably more ambitious: a total transformation of the human environment for the purpose of creating a new breed of human beings—in Russia, of course, but also everywhere else. Its stress on the inequities of the status quo was merely a device for gaining popular support: no rectification of these inequities would have persuaded radical intellectuals to give up their revolutionary aspirations. Such beliefs linked members of various left-wing parties: anarchists, Socialists-Revolutionaries, Mensheviks, and Bolsheviks. Although couched in scientific terms, their views were immune to contrary evidence, and hence more akin to religious faith.

The intelligentsia, which we have defined as intellectuals craving power, stood in total and uncompromising hostility to the existing order: nothing the tsarist regime could do short of committing suicide would have satisfied it. They were revolutionaries not for the sake of improving the condition of the people but for the sake of gaining domination over the people and remaking them in their own image. They confronted the Imperial regime with a challenge that it had no way of repulsing short of employing the kind of methods introduced later by Lenin. Reforms, whether those of the 1860s, or those of 1905–06, only whetted the appetite of the radicals and spurred them to still greater revolutionary excesses.

Buffeted by peasant demands and under direct assault from the radical intelligentsia, the monarchy had only one means of averting collapse, and that was to broaden the base of its authority by sharing power with conservative elements of society. Historic precedent indicates that successful democracies have initially limited power-sharing to the upper orders; these eventually came under pressure from the rest of the population, with the result that their privileges turned into common rights. Involving conservatives, who were far more numerous than the radicals, in both decision-making and administration would have forged something of an organic bond between the government and society, assuring the crown of support in the event of upheavals, and, at the same time, isolating the radicals. Such a course was urged on the monarchy by some far-sighted officials and private individuals. It should have been adopted in the 1860s, at the time of the Great Reforms, but it was not. When finally compelled in 1905 by a nationwide rebellion to concede a parliament, the monarchy no longer had this option available, for the combined liberal and radical opposition forced it to concede something close to a democratic franchise. This resulted in the conservatives in the Duma being submerged by militant intellectuals and anarchist peasants.

World War I subjected every belligerent country to immense strains, which could be overcome only by close collaboration between government and citizenry in the name of patriotism. In Russia such collaboration never materialized. As soon as military reverses dissipated the initial patriotic enthusiasm and the country had to brace for a war of attrition, the tsarist regime found itself unable to mobilize public support. Even its admirers agree that at the time of its collapse the monarchy was hanging in the air.

The motivation of the tsarist regime in refusing to share political power with its supporters, and when finally forced to do so, sharing it grudgingly and deceitfully, was complex. Deep in their hearts, the Court, the bureaucracy, and the professional officer corps were permeated with a patrimonial spirit that viewed Russia as the tsar's private domain. Although in the course of the eighteenth and nineteenth centuries Muscovite patrimonial institutions were gradually dismantled, the mentality survived. And not only in official circles: the peasantry, too, thought in patrimonial terms, believing in strong, undivided authority and regarding the land as tsarist property. Nicholas II took it for granted that he had to keep autocracy in trust for his heir: unlimited authority was to him the equivalent of a property title, which, in his capacity of trustee, he had no right to dilute. He never rid himself of the feeling of guilt that to save the throne in 1905 he had agreed to divide ownership with the nation's elected representatives.

The tsar and his advisers also feared that sharing authority with even a small part of society would disorganize the bureaucratic mechanism and open the door to still greater demands for popular participation. In the latter event, the main beneficiary would be the intelligentsia, which he and his advisers considered utterly incompetent. There was the additional concern that the peasants would misinterpret such concessions and go on a rampage. And finally, there was the opposition to reforms of the bureaucracy, which, accountable only to the tsar, administered the country at its discretion, deriving from this fact numerous benefits.

Such factors explain but do not justify the monarchy's refusal to give conservatives a voice in the government, the more so that the variety and complexity of issues facing it deprived the bureaucracy of much effective authority in any event. The emergence in the second half of the nineteenth century of capitalist institutions shifted much of the control over the country's resources into private hands, undermining what was left of patrimonialism.

In sum, while the collapse of tsarism was not inevitable, it was made likely by deep-seated cultural and political flaws that prevented the tsarist regime from adjusting to the economic and cultural growth of the country, flaws that proved fatal under the pressures generated by World War I. If the possibility of such adjustment existed, it was aborted by the activities of a belligerent intelligentsia bent on toppling the government and using Russia as a springboard for world revolution. It was cultural and political shortcomings of this nature that brought about the collapse of tsarism, not "oppression" or "misery." We are dealing here with a national tragedy whose causes recede deep into the country's past. Economic and social difficulties did not contribute significantly to the revolutionary threat that hung over Russia before 1917. Whatever grievances they may have harbored—real and fancied—the "masses" neither needed nor desired a revolution: the only group interested in it was the intelligentsia. Stress on alleged popular discontent and class conflict derives more from ideological preconceptions than from the facts at hand, namely from the discredited idea that political developments are always and everywhere driven by socioeconomic conflicts, that they are mere "foam" on the surface of currents that really guide human destiny.

The relatively minor role played by social and economic factors in the Russian Revolution becomes apparent when one scrutinizes the events of February 1917. February was not a "workers' revolution": industrial labor played in it the role of a chorus that reacted to and amplified the actions of the true protagonist, the army. The mutiny of the Petrograd garrison stimulated disorders among the civilian population unhappy over inflation and shortages. The mutiny could have been contained had Nicholas chosen to quell it with the same brutality Lenin and Trotsky employed four years later when faced with the Kronshtadt rising and nationwide peasant rebellions. But Lenin's and Trotsky's sole concern was holding on to power, whereas Nicholas cared for Russia. When the generals and Duma politicians persuaded him that he had to go to save the army and avert a humiliating capitulation, he acquiesced. Had staying in power been his supreme objective, he could easily have concluded peace with Germany and turned the army loose against the mutineers. The record leaves no doubt that the myth of the tsar being forced from the throne by the rebellious workers and peasants is just that. The tsar yielded not to a rebellious populace but to generals and politicians, and he did so from a sense of patriotic duty.

The social revolution followed rather than preceded the act of abdication. The garrison soldiers, peasants, workers, and ethnic minorities, each group pursuing its own aims, made the country ungovernable: what chance there was of restoring order was frustrated by the insistence of the intelligentsia running the soviets that they and not the Provisional Government were the true source of legitimate authority. Kerensky's inept intrigues, coupled with his insistence that democracy had no enemies on the left, accelerated the Government's downfall. The country at large—its political entities as well as its resources—became the subject of *duvan*, the division of loot, which no one was strong enough to stop until it had run its course.

Lenin rode to power on that anarchy, which he did much to promote. He promised every discontented group what it wanted. He took over the Socialist-Revolutionary program of "land socialization" to win over the peasants. Among the workers, he encouraged syndicalist trends of "worker control" of factories. To the men in uniform, he held out the prospect of peace. The ethnic minorities he offered national self-determination. In fact, all these pledges ran contrary to his program and all were violated soon after they had served their purpose, which was to undermine the Provisional Government's efforts to stabilize the country.

Similar deception was applied to divest the Provisional Government of authority. Lenin and Trotsky concealed their bid for one-party dictatorship with slogans calling for the transfer of power to the soviets and the Constituent Assembly, and they formalized it by a fraudulently convened Congress of Soviets. No one but a handful of the leading figures in the Bolshevik party knew the truth behind these promises and slogans: few, therefore, realized what had happened in Petrograd on the night of October 25, 1917. The so-called "October Revolution" was a classic coup d'état. The preparations for it were so clandestine that when Kamenev disclosed in a newspaper interview a week before the event was to take place, that the party intended to seize power, Lenin declared him a traitor and demanded his expulsion.[5] Genuine revolutions, of course, are not scheduled and cannot be betrayed.

The ease with which the Bolsheviks toppled the Provisional Government—in Lenin's words, it was like "lifting a feather"—has persuaded many historians that the October coup was "inevitable." But it can appear as such only in retrospect. Lenin himself thought it an extremely chancy undertaking. In urgent letters to the Central Committee in September and October 1917 from his hideaway, he insisted that success depended entirely on the speed and resoluteness with which the armed insurrection was carried out: "To delay the uprising is death," he wrote on October 24, "everything hangs on a hair."[6] These were not the sentiments of a person prepared to trust the forces of history. Trotsky later asserted—and who was in a better position to know?—that if "neither Lenin nor [he himself] had been in Petersburg, there would have been no October Revolution."[7] Can one conceive of an "inevitable" historical event dependent on two individuals?

And if this evidence still fails to convince, one only has to look closely at the events of October 1917 in Petrograd to find the "masses" acting as spectators, ignoring Bolshevik appeals to storm the Winter Palace, where sat elderly ministers of the Provisional Government clad in overcoats, defended by youthful cadets, a battalion of women, and a platoon of invalids. We have it on the authority of Trotsky himself that the October "revolution" in Petrograd was accomplished by "at most" 25,000–30,000 persons[8]—this in a country of 150 million and a city with 400,000 workers and a garrison of over 200,000 soldiers.

From the instant he seized dictatorial power Lenin proceeded to uproot all existing institutions so as to clear the ground for a regime subsequently labeled "totalitarian." This term has fallen out of favor with Western sociologists and political scientists determined to avoid what they consider the language of the Cold War. It deserves note, however, how quickly it found favor in the Soviet Union the instant the censor's prohibitions against its use had been lifted. This kind of regime, unknown to previous history, imposed the authority of a private but omnipotent "party" on the state, claiming the right to subject to itself all organized life without exception, and enforcing its will by means of unbounded terror.

Seen in perspective, Lenin owes his historical prominence not to his statesmanship, which was of a very inferior order, but to his generalship. He was one of history's great conquerors: a distinction not vitiated by the fact that the country he conquered was his own.* His innovation, the reason for his success, was militarizing politics. He was the first head of state to treat politics, domestic as well as foreign, as warfare in the literal sense of the word, the objective of which was not to compel the enemy to submit but to annihilate him. This innovation gave Lenin significant advantages over his opponents, for whom warfare was either the antithesis of politics or else politics pursued by other means. Militarizing politics and, as a corollary, politicizing warfare enabled him first to seize power and then to hold on to it. It did not help him build a viable social and political order. He grew so accustomed to storming on all "fronts" that even after asserting undisputed authority over Soviet Russia and her dependencies, he had to invent ever new enemies to fight and destroy: now the church, now the Socialists-Revolutionaries, now the intelligentsia. This belligerence became a fixed feature of the Communist regime, culminating in Stalin's notorious "theory" that the closer Communism approached final victory the more intense grew social conflicts—a notion that justified a bloodbath of unprecedented ferocity. It caused the Soviet Union in the sixty years that followed Lenin's death to exhaust itself in entirely unnecessary domestic and foreign conflicts that eviscerated her both physically and spiritually.

*Clausewitz had noted already in the early 1800s that it had become "impossible to obtain possession of a great country with a European civilization otherwise than by internal division": Carl von Clausewitz, *The Campaign of 1812 in Russia* (London, 1843), 184.

The failure of Communism, which since 1991 is no longer in dispute, having been conceded even by the leaders of the former Soviet Union, is often blamed on human beings' falling short of its allegedly lofty ideals. Even if the endeavor failed, apologists say, its aspirations were noble and the attempt worthwhile: in support of which claim they could cite the Roman poet Propertius, "In magnis et voluisse sat est"—"In great endeavors, even to want is enough." But how great was an endeavor so at odds with ordinary human desires that to pursue it, recourse had to be had to the most inhuman methods?

The Communist experiment is often labeled "utopian." Thus a recent history of the Soviet Union, far from sympathetic, bears the title *Utopia in Power.* The term, however, is applicable only in that limited sense in which Engels used it to criticize socialists who did not accept his and Marx's "scientific" doctrines, by making in their visions no allowance for historic and social realities. Lenin himself was forced to admit toward the end of his life that the Bolsheviks, too, were guilty of ignoring the cultural realities of Russia and its unpreparedness for the economic and social order that they tried to impose on it. The Bolsheviks ceased to be utopians when, once it had become obvious the ideal was unattainable, they persisted in the attempt with resort to unrestrained violence. Utopian communities always postulated the concurrence of their members in the task of creating a "cooperative commonwealth." The Bolsheviks, by contrast, not only did not care to obtain such concurrence, but dismissed as "counterrevolutionary" every manifestation of individual or group initiative. They also displayed a constitutional inability to deal with opinions different from their own except by abuse and repression. For these reasons they should be regarded not as utopians but as fanatics: since they refused to admit defeat even after it stared them in the face, they satisfied Santayana's definition of fanaticism as redoubling one's efforts after forgetting one's aim.

Marxism and Bolshevism, its offspring, were products of an era in European intellectual life that was obsessed with violence. The Darwinian theory of natural selection was promptly translated into a social philosophy in which uncompromising conflict occupied a central place. "No one who has not waded through some sizeable part of the literature of the period 1870–1914 writes Jacques Barzun, "has any conception of the extent to which it is one long call for blood, nor of the variety of parties, classes, nations, and races whose blood was separately and contradictorily clamored for by the enlightened citizens of the ancient civilization of Europe."[9] No one embraced this philosophy more enthusiastically than the Bolsheviks: "merciless" violence, violence that strove for the destruction of every actual and potential opponent, was for Lenin not only the most effective, but the only way of dealing with problems. And even if some of his associates shrank from such inhumanity, they could not escape the corrupting influence of their leader.

Russian nationalists depict Communism as alien to Russian culture and tradition, as a kind of plague imported from the West. The notion of Communism as a virus cannot withstand the slightest examination since, although an intellectual movement international in scope, it first took hold in Russia and among Russians: the Bolshevik party both before and after the Revolution was overwhelmingly Russian in composition, acquiring its earliest base in European Russia and among Russian migrants in the borderlands. Undeniably, the *theories* underpinning Bolshevism, notably those of Karl Marx, were of Western origin. But it is equally undeniable that Bolshevik *practices* were indigenous, for nowhere in the West has Marxism led to the totalitarian excesses of Leninism-Stalinism. In Russia, and subsequently in Third World countries with similar traditions, Marxism fell on a soil devoid of traditions of self-rule, observance of law, and respect for private property. A cause that yields different results in different circumstances can hardly serve as a sufficient explanation.

Marxism had libertarian as well as authoritarian strains, and which of the two prevailed depended on a country's political culture. In Russia, those elements in the Marxist doctrine gained ascendancy that fitted her patrimonial heritage. The Russian political tradition since the Middle Ages was for the government—or, more precisely, the ruler—to be the subject and "the land" the object. This tradition fused readily with the Marxist concept of the "dictatorship of the proletariat," under which the ruling party claimed undivided control over the country's inhabitants and resources. Marx's notion of such a "dictatorship" was sufficiently vague for it to be filled with the content nearest at hand, which in Russia was the historic legacy of patrimonialism. It was the grafting of Marxist ideology onto the sturdy stem of Russia's patrimonial heritage that produced totalitarianism. Totalitarianism cannot be explained solely with reference either to Marxist doctrine or to Russian history: it was the fruit of their union.

Important as ideology was, however, its role in the shaping of Communist Russia must not be exaggerated. If an individual or a group profess certain beliefs and refer to them to guide their conduct, they may be said to act under the influence of ideas. When, however, ideas are used not so much to direct one's personal conduct as to justify one's domination over others, whether by persuasion or force, the issue becomes confused, because it is not possible to determine whether such persuasion or force serves ideas or, on the contrary, ideas serve to secure or legitimize such domination. In the case of the Bolsheviks, there are strong grounds for maintaining the latter to be the case, because they distorted Marxism in every conceivable way, first to gain political power and then to hold on to it. If Marxism means anything it means two propositions: that as capitalist society matures it is doomed to collapse from inner contradictions, and that this collapse ("revolution") is effected by industrial labor ("the proletariat"). A regime motivated by Marxist theory would at a minimum adhere to these two principles. What do we see in Soviet Russia? A "socialist revolution" carried out in an economically underdeveloped country in which capitalism was still in its infancy, and power taken by a party committed to the view that the working class left to its own devices is unrevolutionary. Subsequently, at every stage of its history, the Communist regime in Russia did whatever it had to do to beat off challengers, without regard to Marxist doctrine, even as it cloaked its actions with Marxist slogans. Lenin succeeded precisely because he was free of the Marxist scruples that inhibited the Mensheviks. In view of these facts, ideology has to be treated as a subsidiary factor: an inspiration and a mode of thinking of the new ruling class, perhaps, but not a set of principles that either determined its actions or explains them to posterity. As a rule, the less one knows about the actual course of the Russian Revolution the more inclined one is to attribute a dominant influence to Marxist ideas.*

For all their disagreements, contemporary Russian nationalists and many liberals are at one in denying links between tsarist and Communist Russia. The former refuse to acknowledge the connection because it would make Russia responsible for her own misfortunes, which they prefer to blame on foreigners, especially Jews. In this they resemble German conservatives who depict Nazism as a general European phenomenon in order to deny that it had any antecedents in Germany's past, or that Germany bears any particular blame for it. Such an approach finds a ready audience among the peoples affected, since it shifts the responsibility for whatever went wrong onto others.

Liberal and radical intellectuals—not so much in Russia as abroad—similarly deny affinities between Communism and tsarism because that would make the whole Revolution a costly and meaningless blunder. They prefer to focus on the declared objectives of the Communists and compare them with the realities of tsarism. This procedure does produce a glaring contrast. The picture, of course, changes substantially as soon as one compares Communist and tsarist realities.

The affinities between the regime of Lenin and traditional Russia were noticed by more than one contemporary, among them the historian Paul

---

*The debate over the role of ideas in history is not confined to Russian historiography. In both Great Britain and the United States, sharp battles have been fought over this issue. The proponents of the ideological school suffered notable defeats, especially at the hands of Louis Namier, who demonstrated that in eighteenth-century England ideas, as a rule, served to rationalize actions inspired by personal and group interests.

Miliukov, the philosopher Nicholas Berdiaev, the veteran socialist Paul Akselrod,[10] and the novelist Boris Pilniak. According to Miliukov, Bolshevism had two aspects:

> One is international; the other is genuinely Russian. The international aspect of Bolshevism is due to its origin in a very advanced European theory. Its purely Russian aspect is chiefly concerned with its practice, which is deeply rooted in Russian reality and, far from breaking with the "ancien regime," reasserts Russia's past in the present. As geological upheavals bring the lower strata of the earth to the surface as evidence of the early ages of our planet, so Russian Bolshevism, by discarding the thin upper social layer, has laid bare the uncultured and unorganized substratum of Russian historical life.[11]

Berdiaev, who viewed the Revolution primarily in spiritual terms, denied that Russia even had a Revolution: "All of the past is repeating itself and acts only behind new masks."[12]

Even someone entirely ignorant of Russia should find it inconceivable that on a single day, October 25, 1917, in consequence of an armed putsch, the course of a thousand-year-old history of a vast and populous country could undergo complete transformation. The same people, inhabiting the same territory, speaking the same language, heirs to a common past, could hardly have been fashioned into different creatures by a sudden change of government. It takes great faith in the power of decrees, even decrees backed by physical force, to believe in the possibility of such drastic mutation, unknown to nature. Only by viewing human beings as inert matter entirely molded by the environment could such an absurdity even be entertained.

To analyze the continuities between the two systems we shall have reference to the concept of patrimonialism, which underpinned the Muscovite government and in many ways survived in the institutions and political culture of Russia to the end of the old regime.[13] Tsarist patrimonialism rested on four pillars: one, autocracy, that is, personal rule unconstrained by either constitution or representative bodies; two, the autocrat's ownership of the country's resources, which is to say, the virtual absence of private property; three, the autocrat's right to demand unlimited services from his subjects, resulting in the lack of either collective or individual rights; and four, state control of information. A comparison of tsarist rule at its zenith with the Communist regime as it looked by the time of Lenin's death reveals unmistakable affinities.

To begin with, the autocracy. Traditionally, the Russian monarch concentrated in his hands full legislative and executive powers, and exercised them without interference from external bodies. He administered with the help of a service nobility and a bureaucracy that owed allegiance to his person rather than to the nation or the state. Lenin from the first day in office instinctively followed this model. Although as a concession to the ideal of democracy he gave the country a constitution and representative bodies, they performed purely ceremonial functions, since the constitution was not binding on the Communist Party, the country's true ruler, and the parliament was not elected but hand-picked by the same party. In the performance of his duties, Lenin resembled the most autocratic of the tsars, Peter I and Nicholas I, in that he insisted on personally attending to the most trifling details of state affairs, as if the country were his private domain.

As had been the case with his Muscovite forerunners, the Soviet ruler claimed title to the country's productive and income-producing wealth. Beginning with decrees nationalizing land and industries, the government took over all assets except for articles of purely personal use; and since the government was in the hands of one party, and that party, in turn, obeyed the will of its leader, Lenin was de facto owner of the country's material resources. (De jure ownership lay with the "people," defined as synonymous with the Communist Party.) Industries were run for the state by state-appointed managers. Their output, and, until March 1921, the production of the land, were disposed of as the Kremlin saw fit. Urban real estate was nationalized. With private commerce outlawed (until 1921 and again after 1928), the Soviet regime controlled all legitimate wholesale and retail trade. These measures went beyond the practices of Muscovy, but they perpetuated its principle that Russia's sovereign not only ruled the country but owned it.

He also owned its people. The Bolsheviks reinstituted obligatory state service, one of the distinguishing features of Muscovite absolutism. In Muscovy, the subjects of the tsar, with minor exceptions, had to work for him either directly, in the armed forces or the bureaucracy, or indirectly, by cultivating his land or that conditionally leased to his servitors. As a result, the entire population was bonded to the Crown. Its manumission began in 1762, when the gentry were given the right to retire into private life, and concluded ninety-nine years later with the liberation of the serfs. The Bolsheviks promptly revived the Muscovite practice, unknown in any other country, of requiring every citizen to work for the state: the so-called "universal labor obligation" introduced in January 1918 and enforced, according to Lenin's instructions, by the threat of execution, would have been perfectly understandable to a seventeenth-century Russian. In regard to peasants, the Bolsheviks revived also the practice of *tiaglo,* or forced labor, such as lumbering and carting, for which they received no compensation. As in seventeenth-century Russia, no inhabitant was allowed to leave the country without permission.

The Communist bureaucracy, both that employed by the party and that by the state, quite naturally slipped into the ways of its tsarist predecessor. A service class with duties and privileges but no inherent rights, it constituted a closed and minutely graded caste accountable exclusively to its superiors. Like the tsarist bureaucracy, it stood above the law. It also operated without *glasnost'*, that is, outside public scrutiny, administering much of the time by means of secret circulars. Under tsarism, advancement to the topmost ranks of the bureaucratic hierarchy bestowed hereditary nobility. For Communist officials, advancement to the highest ranks was rewarded with inclusion in the rolls of the *nomenklatura,* which carried entitlements beyond the reach of ordinary servitors, not to speak of the common people—the Communist equivalent of a service nobility. The Soviet bureaucracy, like the tsarist, did not tolerate administrative bodies outside its control, and made certain they were promptly "statified," that is, integrated into its chain of command. This it did to the soviets, the new regime's putative legislative organs, and to the trade unions, agencies of its equally putative "ruling class."

That the Communist bureaucracy should so quickly adapt old ways is not surprising, given that the new regime in so many respects continued old habits. Continuity was facilitated by the fact that a high percentage of Soviet administrative posts was staffed by ex-tsarist functionaries, who brought with them and communicated to Communist newcomers habits acquired in the tsarist service.

The security police was another important organization that the Bolsheviks adopted from tsarism, since they had no other prototype for what became a central institution of totalitarianism. Tsarist Russia was unique in that she alone had two police formations, one to defend the state from its citizens, the other to protect citizens from each other.* State crimes were very loosely defined, little distinction being drawn between intention and deed.[14] The tsarist state police developed sophisticated methods of surveillance, infiltrating society through a network of paid informers and opposition parties with the help of professional agents. The tsarist Department of Police had the unique authority to impose administrative exile for crimes that were not crimes in any other European country, such as expressing a desire for change in the political system. Through a variety of prerogatives granted it in the aftermath of the assassination of Alexander II, the tsarist police between 1881 and 1905 virtually ruled Russia.[15] Its methods were all too familiar to Russian revolutionaries who, on coming to power, adopted them and turned them against their enemies. The Cheka and its successors assimilated the practices of the tsarist state police to such an extent that as late as the 1980s, the KGB distributed to its staff manuals prepared by the Okhrana nearly a century earlier.[16]

Finally, as concerns censorship. In the first half of the nineteenth century Russia was the only European country to enforce preventive censorship. In

---

*Many European countries had political police departments, but their functions were to investigate and turn suspects over to the judiciary. Only in tsarist Russia did the political police have judiciary authority, which allowed it to arrest and exile suspects without recourse to courts.

the 1860s censorship was eased and in 1906 it was abolished. The Bolsheviks reinstituted the most oppressive tsarist practices, shutting down every publication that did not support their regime, and subjecting all forms of intellectual and artistic expression to preventive censorship. They also nationalized all publishing enterprises. These procedures went back to the practices of Muscovy: they had no European equivalent.*

In all these instances the Bolsheviks found models not in the writings of Marx, Engels, or other Western socialists, but in their own history: not so much the history described in books but that which they had experienced in their own persons fighting tsarism under the regime of Reinforced and Extraordinary Safeguard instituted in the 1880s to deter the revolutionary intelligentsia.[17] These practices they justified with arguments borrowed from socialist literature that gave them a mandate to behave with a brutality and ruthlessness that far exceeded anything known under tsarism, for tsarism was inhibited by the desire to be viewed favorably by Europe, whereas the Bolsheviks treated Europe as an enemy.

It is not that the Bolsheviks wanted to copy tsarist practices: on the contrary, they wanted to have nothing in common with them, to do the very opposite. They emulated them by force of circumstance. Once they rejected democracy—and this they did conclusively in January 1918 by dispersing the Constituent Assembly—they had no choice but to govern autocratically. And to rule autocratically meant ruling the people in a manner to which they had been accustomed. The regime introduced by Lenin on coming to power had its immediate antecedents in the most reactionary reign of Imperial Russia, that of Alexander III, under which Lenin had grown up. It is uncanny how many of his measures replicated the "counterreforms" of the 1880s and 1890s, even if under different labels.

Nor is it surprising that the Russian Revolution should have ended up where it did. Revolutionaries may have the most radical ideas of remaking man and society, but they must build the new order with human material molded by the past. For that reason, sooner or later, they succumb to the past themselves. "Revolution" derives from the Latin *revolvere*, "to revolve," a concept originally applied to the motions of the planets, and used by medieval astrologers to explain sudden and unexpected turns in human events. And objects that revolve do return to their starting point.

O ne of the most controversial issues arising from the Russian Revolution is the relationship of Leninism to Stalinism—in other words, Lenin's responsibility for Stalin. Western Communists, fellow-travelers, and sym-

---

*"In contrast to Western countries where, from the moment of the emergence of book-printing, typographies were in private hands and the publication of books was a matter of private initiative, in Russia the printing of books was from the beginning a monopoly of the state, which determined the direction of publishing activity . . ." C. P. Luppov, *Kniga v Rossii v XVII veke* (Leningrad, 1970), 28.

pathizers deny any link between the two Communist leaders, insisting that Stalin not only did not continue Lenin's work but subverted it. This view became mandatory in Soviet historiography after 1956 when Nikita Khrushchev delivered his secret address to the Twentieth Party Congress: it has served the purpose of disassociating the post-Stalinist regime from its despised predecessor. Curiously, the same people who depict Lenin's rise to power as inevitable abandon their philosophy of history when they came to Stalin, whom they represent as a historic aberration. They have been unable to explain how and why history should have taken a thirty-year detour from its allegedly predetermined course.

An examination of Stalin's career reveals that he did not seize power after Lenin's death but ascended to it, step by step, initially under Lenin's sponsorship. Lenin came to rely on Stalin in managing the party apparatus, especially after 1920, when the party was torn by democratic heresies. The sources indicate that contrary to Trotsky's retrospective claims, Lenin depended not on him but on his rival to carry on much of the day-to-day business of government and to advise him on a great variety of issues of domestic and foreign policy. Thanks to this patronage, by 1922, when illness forced Lenin increasingly to withdraw from affairs of state, Stalin was the only person to belong to all three of the ruling organs of the Central Committee: the Politburo, Orgburo, and Secretariat. In these capacities, he supervised the appointment of executive personnel to virtually all branches of the party and state administration. Owing to the rules established by Lenin to forestall the rise of an organized opposition ("factionalism"), Stalin could repress criticism of his stewardship on the grounds that it was directed not at him but at the party and therefore, by definition, served the cause of the counterrevolution. The fact that in the last months of his active life Lenin developed doubts about Stalin and came close to breaking off personal relations with him, should not obscure the fact that until that moment he had done everything in his power to promote Stalin's ascendancy. And even when Lenin became disappointed with his protégé, the shortcomings he attributed to him were not very serious—mainly rudeness and impatience—and related more to his managerial qualifications than his personality. There is no indication that he ever saw Stalin as a traitor to his brand of Communism.

But even the one difference separating the two men—that Lenin did not kill fellow-Communists and Stalin did so on a massive scale—is not as significant as may appear at first sight. Toward outsiders, people not belonging to his order of the elect—and that included 99.7 percent of his compatriots—Lenin showed no human feelings whatever, sending them to their death by the tens of thousands, often to serve as an example to others. A high Cheka official, I. S. Unshlikht, in his tender recollections of Lenin written in 1934, stressed with unconcealed pride how Lenin "mercilessly made short shrift of philistine party members who complained of the mercilessness of the Cheka, how he laughed at and mocked the 'humanness' of the capitalist world."[18] The difference between the two men lay in the conception of the "outsider." Lenin's insiders were to Stalin outsiders, people who owed loyalty not to him but to the Party's founder and who competed with him for power; and toward them, he showed the same inhuman cruelty that Lenin had employed against his enemies.

Beyond the strong personal links binding the two men, Stalin was a true Leninist in that he faithfully followed his patron's political philosophy and practices. Every ingredient of what has come to be known as Stalinism save one—murdering fellow Communists—he had learned from Lenin, and that includes the two actions for which he is most severely condemned: collectivization and mass terror. Stalin's megalomania, his vindictiveness, his morbid paranoia, and other odious personal qualities should not obscure the fact that his ideology and modus operandi were Lenin's. A man of meager education, he had no other source of ideas.

In theory, one can conceive a Trotsky, Bukharin, or Zinoviev grasping the torch from the dying Lenin and leading the Soviet Union in a different direction than Stalin.* What one cannot conceive is *how* they could have been in a position to do so, given the realities of the power structure at the time of Lenin's illness. By throttling democratic impulses in the Party in order to protect his dictatorship, and by imposing on the Party a top-heavy command structure, Lenin ensured that the man who controlled the central party apparatus controlled the Party and through it, the state. And that man was Stalin.

The revolution inflicted on Russia staggering human losses. The statistics are so shocking that they inevitably give rise to doubts. But unless someone can come up with alternate numbers, the historian is compelled to accept them, the more so that they are shared alike by Communist and non-Communist demographers.

The following table indicates the population of the Soviet Union within the borders of 1926 (in millions):

Fall 1917:   147.6

Early 1920: 140.6

Early 1921: 136.8

Early 1922: 134.9[19]

---

*Although even this proposition has been questioned: see, for example, Aleksandr Tsipko's impassioned argument that Lenin's associates would have acted no differently from Stalin: *Nasilie Izhi* (Moscow, 1990).

The decrease—12.7 million—was due to deaths from combat and epidemics (approximately 2 million each); emigration (about 2 million); and famine (over 5 million).

But these figures tell only half the story, since obviously, under normal conditions, the population would not have remained stationary but grown. Projections by Russian statisticians indicate that in 1922 the population should have numbered more than 160 million rather than 135 million. If this figure is taken into account, and the number of émigrés is deducted, the human casualties of the Revolution in Russia—actual and due to the deficit in births—rise to over 23 million*—two and a half times the fatalities suffered by all the belligerent countries in World War I combined, and a loss nearly equal to the combined populations at the time of the four Scandinavian countries plus Belgium and the Netherlands. The actual losses were heaviest in the age group 16-49, particularly in its male contingent, of which it had eradicated by August 1920—that is, before the famine had done its work—29 percent.[20]

Can one—should one—view such an unprecedented calamity with dispassion? So great is the prestige of science in our time that not a few contemporary scholars have adopted, along with scientific methods of investigation, the scientists' habit of moral and emotional detachment, the habit of treating all phenomena as "natural" and therefore ethically neutral. They are loath to allow for human volition in historical events because free will, being unpredictable, eludes scientific analysis. Historical "inevitability" is for them what the laws of nature are to the scientist. But it has long been known that the objects of science and the object of history are vastly different. We properly expect physicians to diagnose diseases and suggest remedies in a cool and dispassionate manner. An accountant analyzing the finances of a company, an engineer investigating the safety of equipment, an intelligence officer estimating enemy capabilities obviously must remain emotionally uninvolved. This is so because their investigations have as their objective making it possible to arrive at sound decisions. But for the historian the decisions have already been made by others, and detachment adds nothing to understanding. Indeed, it detracts from it: for how can one comprehend dispassionately events that have been produced in the heat of passion? "Historiam puto scribendam esse et cum ira et cum studio"—"I maintain that history should be written with anger and enthusiasm," wrote a nineteenth-century German historian. Aristotle, who in all matters preached moderation, said that there were situations in which "inirascibil-

---

*S. G. Strumilin (*Problemy ekonomiki truda,* Moscow, 1957, 39) estimates the losses until late 1920—*i.e.,* before the 1921 famine—at 21 million. With the famine victims added, the figure would rise to 26 million. Iu. A. Poliakov (*Sovetskaia strana posle okonchaniia grazhdanskoi voiny,* Moscow, 1986, 128) speaks of over 25 million. The American demographer Frank Lorimer sets the number of deaths between 1914 and 1926 at 26 million (exclusive of emigration). Lorimer, however, overstates the number of Russian fatalities in World War I (2 million instead of 1.1 million): Frank Lorimer, *The Population of the Soviet Union* (Geneva, 1946), 41.

ity" was unacceptable: "For those who are not angry at things they should be angry at are deemed fools."[21] The assembling of the relevant facts must certainly be carried out dispassionately, without either anger or enthusiasm: this aspect of the historian's craft is no different from the scientist's. But this is only the beginning of the historian's task, because the sorting of these facts—the decision as to which are "relevant"—requires judgment, and judgment rests on values. Facts as such are meaningless, since they furnish no guide to their selection, ordering, and emphasis: to "make sense" of the past, the historian must follow some principle. He usually does have it: even the most "scientific" historians, consciously or not, operate from preconceptions. As a rule, these are rooted in economic determinism because economic and social data lend themselves to statistical demonstration, which creates the illusion of impartiality. The refusal to pass judgment on historical events rests on moral values, too, namely the silent premise that whatever occurs is natural and therefore right: it amounts to an apology of those who happen to win out.

J udged in terms of its own aspirations, the Communist regime was a monumental failure: it succeeded in one thing only—staying in power. But since for Bolsheviks power was not an end in itself but means to an end, its mere retention does not qualify the experiment as a success. The Bolsheviks made no secret of their aims: toppling everywhere regimes based on private property and replacing them with a worldwide union of socialist societies. They succeeded nowhere outside the boundaries of what had been the Russian Empire in spreading their regime until the end of World War II, when the Red Army stepped into the vacuum created in Eastern Europe by the surrender of Germany, the Chinese Communists seized control of their country from the Japanese, and Communist dictatorships, aided by Moscow, established themselves in a number of recently emancipated colonial areas.

Once it had proven impossible to export Communism, the Bolsheviks in the 1920s dedicated themselves to constructing a socialist society at home. This endeavor failed as well. Lenin had expected through a combination of expropriations and terror to transform his country in a matter of months into the world's leading economic power: instead, he ruined the economy he had inherited. He had expected the Communist Party to provide disciplined leadership to the nation: instead, he saw political dissent, which he had muzzled in the country at large, resurface within his own party. As the workers turned their backs on the Communists and the peasants rebelled, staying in power required unremitting resort to police measures. The regime's freedom of action was increasingly impeded by a bloated and corrupt bureaucracy. The voluntary union of nations turned into an oppressive empire. Lenin's speeches and writings of the last two years reveal, besides a striking paucity of constructive ideas, barely controlled rage at his political and economic impotence: even terror proved useless in overcoming the ingrained habits of an ancient nation. Mussolini, whose early political career closely resembled Lenin's and who even as Fascist dictator observed the Communist regime with sympathy, concluded already in July 1920 that Bolshevism, a "vast, terrible experiment," had miscarried:

> Lenin is an artist who worked on humans as other artists work on marble or metal. But human beings are harder than granite and less malleable than iron. No masterwork has emerged. The artist has failed. The task has proven beyond his powers.[22]

Seventy years and tens of millions of victims later, Lenin's and Stalin's successor as head of Russia, Boris Yeltsin, conceded as much in an address to the American Congress:

> The world can sigh in relief. The idol of Communism which spread everywhere social strife, animosity, and unparalleled brutality, which instilled fear in humanity, has collapsed. It has collapsed, never to rise again.[23]

Failure was inevitable and imbedded in the very premises of the Communist regime. Bolshevism was the most audacious attempt in history to subject the entire life of a country to a master plan, to rationalize everybody and everything. It sought to sweep aside as useless rubbish the wisdom that mankind had accumulated over millennia. In that sense, it was a unique effort to apply science to human affairs: and it was pursued with the zeal characteristic of that breed of intellectuals who regard resistance to their ideas as proof that they are sound. Communism failed because it proceeded from the erroneous doctrine of the Enlightenment, perhaps the most pernicious idea in the history of thought, that man is merely a material compound, devoid of either soul or innate ideas, and as such a passive product of an infinitely malleable social environment. This doctrine made it possible for people with personal frustrations to project them onto society and attempt to resolve them there rather than in themselves. As experience has confirmed time and again, man is not an inanimate object but a creature with his own aspirations and will—not a mechanical but a biological entity. Even if subjected to the fiercest dressage, he cannot pass on the lessons he has been forced to learn to his children, who come into this world ever fresh, asking questions that are supposed to have been settled once and for all. To demonstrate this commonsensical truth required tens of millions of dead, incalculable suffering for the survivors, and the ruin of a great nation.

The question of how such a flawed regime succeeded in maintaining itself in power for so long certainly cannot be met with the answer that, whatever we may think of it, it had the support of its own people. Anyone who explains the durability of a government not based on an explicit mandate of its citizens by its alleged popularity must apply the same rationale to every other enduring authoritarian regime, including tsarism—which survived not seven decades but seven centuries—and then still face the unenviable task of having to explain how tsarism, presumably so popular, collapsed in a matter of days.

In addition to demonstrating the inapplicability of scientific methods to the conduct of human affairs, the Russian Revolution has raised the profoundest moral questions about the nature of politics, namely the right of governments to try to remake human beings and refashion society without their mandate and even against their will: the legitimacy of the early Communist slogan, "We will drive mankind to happiness by force!" Gorky, who knew Lenin intimately, agreed with Mussolini that he regarded human beings as a metalworker regards ore.[24] His was but an extreme expression of an attitude common to radical intellectuals everywhere. It runs contrary to the morally superior as well as more realistic principle of Kant's that man must never be used as merely means for the ends of others, but must always be regarded also as an end in himself. Seen from this vantage point, the excesses of the Bolsheviks, their readiness to sacrifice countless lives for their own purposes, were a monstrous violation of both ethics and common sense. They ignored that the means—the well-being and even the lives of people—are very real, whereas the ends are always nebulous and often unattainable. The moral principle that applies in this case has been formulated by Karl Popper: "Everyone has the right to sacrifice himself for a cause he deems deserving. No one has the right to sacrifice others or to incite others to sacrifice themselves for an ideal."[25]

Hippolyte Taine drew from his monumental study of the French Revolution a lesson that he himself described as "puerile," namely that "human society, especially a modern society, is a vast and complicated thing."[26] One is tempted to supplement this observation with a corollary, that precisely because modern society is so "vast and complicated" and therefore so difficult to grasp, it is neither proper nor feasible to impose on it patterns of conduct, let alone try to remake it. What cannot be comprehended cannot be controlled. The tragic and sordid history of the Russian Revolution—such as it really was, not as it appears to the imagination of those foreign intellectuals for whom it was a noble attempt to elevate mankind—teaches that political authority must never be employed for ideological ends. It is best to let people be. In the words attributed by Oscar Wilde to a Chinese sage: There is such a thing as leaving mankind alone—but there never was such a thing as governing mankind.

GLOSSARY

NOTE: The accent of a Russian letter indicates the stress. The letter ë is pronounced "yo" and stressed.

agit-prop	agitation and propaganda
agit-sud/y	agitational trial/s
agitka/i	short agitational performance/s
ataman	Ukrainian and Cossack headman or warlord
Basmachis	Central Asian anti-Communist partisans
besprizornyi/e	abandoned children
burzhui	"bourgeois" (in the pejorative sense)
Cheka	Political police, 1917–1922
chervonets/y	gold-based currency introduced in 1922
dacha	country retreat
denznak/i	"money token"/s
duvan	Turkish word signifying division of loot
Evsektsiia/ii	Jewish section/s of the Communist Party
Glavlit	Central Censorship Bureau created in 1922
Gosizdat	State Publishing House
Gosplan	State Planning Committee
GPU	Successor to Cheka
guberniia/ii	Province/s
gubkom/y	Provincial Committee/s of Communist Party
inogorodnyi/e	"outlander/s" in Cossack regions
jadidism	Muslim reform movement
Kavbiuro	Caucasian Bureau of Communist Party
khozrazchët	self-supporting enterprise
Komsomol	Communist Youth League
Komuch	Committee of the Constituent Assembly (1918)
kulak	well-to-do peasant or peasant hostile to the Communists
meshchanin/ne	burgher/s
muzhik	familiar term for peasant

Narkompros	Commissariat of Enlightenment
nomenklatura/y	person/s qualified for high positions in the Communist Party
OGPU	successor to GPU
paëk	ration
pogrom	beating and looting, usually of Jews
Polrevkom	Polish Committee of Communist Party (1920)
Pomgol	Committee to aid victims of 1921 famine
prodnalog	food tax in kind introduced in 1921
prodrazvërstka	food extraction
Proletkul't	"Proletarian Culture" movement
Rabfak/i	"Worker Faculty/ies"
Rabkrin	"Worker and Peasant Inspection"
razgrom	assault on property
Revvoensovet	Revolutionary Military Council
Sovnarkom	Council of People's Commissars
STO	Council of Labor and Defense
uchraspred/y	Communist Party personnel bureaus
uezd	lowest administrative entity
vlast'	power, authority, government
vozhd'	leader
zam/y	deputy chairman/men of Sovnarkom
zemstvo/a	organs of local self-rule in late tsarist Russia

CHRONOLOGY*

1917

March 4: Ukrainian Rada formed
May 1: All-Russian Muslim Congress held in Moscow
June 10: Ukrainian Rada's "Universal"
August 15: Council of Orthodox Church opens in the Moscow Kremlin
October: Tikhon elected Patriarch
November: Congress of Soviets of Turkestan bars Muslims from participation in government; Kokand government formed
December 6 (NS): Finland proclaims independence
December 11 (NS): Lithuania proclaims independence
December: Volunteer Army formed in the Don region

1918

January 12 (NS): Latvia proclaims independence
January 18: Soviet government repudiates all Russian debts
January 20: Communist decree on state-church relations
January 27 (February 9, NS): Tomsk Regional Council proclaims independence of Siberia
February 21: Volunteer Army begins "Ice March"
April 13: Kornilov killed, Denikin assumes command of Volunteer Army
April: National Center and Union for the Regeneration of Russia formed in Moscow
May: Volunteer Army recaptures Rostov and Novocherkassk; Communists begin partial conscription
May 30: Russia's schools nationalized
June 8: Czech Legion captures Samara; Komuch formed
June 23: Volunteer Army begins Second Kuban campaign
July: Soviet government begins to draft ex-tsarist officers
July: non-Bolshevik newspapers and periodicals shut down
August 7: Czechs capture Kazan
September: formation of Directory; creation of Revvoensovet under Trotsky's chairmanship
September 10: Latvians in Red service capture Kazan
October 8: Alekseev dies

*Dates are given "Old Style" for events before February 1918, which in the twentieth century was thirteen days behind the Western calendar, and subsequently, "New Style," which corresponds to the calendar in use in the West.

October 24: SRs adopt "Chernov Manifesto"
October 26: Tikhon's encyclical condemning Communist terror
November 17–18: Directory overthrown in Omsk; Kolchak proclaimed "Supreme Ruler"
November 23: first French and British landings in Novorossiisk
December: French landings in Odessa; Kolchak's troops capture Perm

1919

January 3: Red Army takes Riga
January 5: Communist putsch in Germany
January–February: Mensheviks and SRs back Soviet regime against Whites and are readmitted to soviets
February 6: Red Army takes Kiev
March: beginning of Kolchak's offensive; Bullitt mission
March 2–7: Communist International founded in Moscow
March: 9th Congress of Bolshevik party renamed (in 1918) Communist Party; creation of Politburo, Orgburo, and Secretariat
March 21: Communist regime installed in Hungary
April: French troops evacuate Russia; Kolchak's troops approach Volga
April 28: beginning of Red counteroffensive against Kolchak
Spring: Volunteer Army occupies eastern Ukraine; first Iudenich offensive against Petrograd
June: Tukhachevskii's Fifth Army penetrates Urals
June 12: Denikin recognizes Kolchak as Supreme Ruler
June 30: Wrangel captures Tsaritsyn
July: S. S. Kamenev appointed Commander of Red Army
July 3: Denikin's "Moscow Directive"
July 24–25: Red Army takes Cheliabinsk
August: British cabinet reassesses aid to Whites
August 1: Communist regime in Hungary overthrown
August 31: Whites capture Kiev
August–September: Mamontov's raid behind Red lines
August–September: worst anti-Jewish pogroms in the right-bank Ukraine
August–September: arrests and mass executions of National Center members
September 20: Whites capture Kursk
September–October: most Allied troops evacuate Murmansk and Archangel
October 7: "Final packet" of British aid to Denikin
October 11: Iudenich launches second offensive against Petrograd
October 13–14: Volunteer Army captures Orel
October 18–19: Red "Striking Force" attacks and mauls Volunteer divisions
October 20: Whites abandon Orel
October 21: Red counteroffensive against Iudenich begins
October 24: Budennyi's cavalry captures Voronezh
November 8: Lloyd George's Guildhall speech
November 14: Red Army enters Omsk; Kolchak departs for Irkutsk
November 15: Red cavalry captures Kastornoe
November 17: Whites abandon Kursk, begin disorganized retreat
November 26: decree on the "liquidation of illiteracy"

1920

Early January: socialists take over Irkutsk, declare Kolchak deposed, later that
     month turn city over to Bolsheviks
February 7: Kolchak executed
April 2: Denikin resigns, Wrangel takes command of southern White Army
April 6: Far Eastern Republic proclaimed
April 20: Kavbiuro formed
April 25: Polish invasion of the Ukraine
April 27: Communist coup in Baku: Azerbaijan sovietized
Spring: beginning of year-long, nationwide peasant rebellions
May: Krasin in London to open commercial negotiations
May 7: Poles take Kiev; Soviet government signs treaty with Georgia
June: Poles expelled from the Ukraine; Wrangel effects landings on the mainland
July 19: Second Congress of Comintern opens in Petrograd, then moves to
     Moscow
August: outbreak of anti-Communist rebellion in Tambov under Antonov
mid-August: Red Army defeated at gates of Warsaw
September: Congress of the Peoples of the East in Baku
October: autonomy of Proletkult abrogated
October 18: armistice with Poland
October 20: Red Army begins assault on the Crimea
November 14: Wrangel's army evacuates to Constantinople
November 18: abortion legalized
December: Sovietization of Armenia

1921

February 9: outbreak of anti-Communist peasant rebellion in western Siberia
February 21: invasion of Georgia by Eleventh Red Army
late February: mass strikes in Petrograd
February 28: mutiny at Kronshtadt
March: Tenth Congress of Communist Party; "factionalism" outlawed
March 15: abolition of *prodrazvërstka*
March 17: Kronshtadt captured by Red Army
Spring: beginning of secret collaboration between Red Army and the German
     Wehrmacht
May: Tukhachevskii pacifies Tambov
Summer–Fall: height of famine
August: Moscow requests foreign food aid; ARA begins relief

1922

February 6: Cheka renamed GPU
February 26: Moscow orders church to surrender consecrated vessels
March: Lenin orders all-out assault on church; Living Church created
April 3: Stalin appointed General Secretary of Communist Party
April–July: show "trials" of clergy in Moscow and Petrograd
April 16: Rapallo Treaty between Soviet Russia and Germany
May: Tikhon compelled to relinquish duties

May 25: Lenin suffers stroke
June 6: creation of central censorship bureau (Glavlit)
June 6–August 7: show trial of Socialists-Revolutionaries in Moscow
August 10: administrative exile reintroduced
August–September: hundreds of intellectuals exiled abroad
September 14: Politburo reprimands Trotsky
November: emission of gold-based chervonets
December: Fourth Congress of Comintern
December 15: Lenin suffers another stroke
Late December–early January: Lenin dictates "Testament" and "Notes on the
    Nationality Question"

1923

January–March: Lenin preoccupied with Georgia
March: trial of Catholic clergy in Petrograd
March 10: Lenin paralyzed
October 23: Trotsky reprimanded by Plenum of Party
December: Trotsky's "New Course"

1924

January 21: Lenin's death

NOTES

1. The Civil War: The First Battles (1918)

1. Lenin, *PSS*, XLIX, 15.
2. N. Bukharin and E. Preobrazhenskii, *Azbuka kommunizma* (Moscow, 1920), 105.
3. Cited by N. Sukhanov in *NZh*, No. 113/328 (June 11, 1918), 1.
4. Lenin, *PSS*, XXXVI, 233–34.
5. N. Kakurin, *Kak srazhalas' revoliutsiia*, II (Moscow, 1925), 135; *TP*, I, 241.
6. N. N. Golovin, *Rossiiskaia kontr-revoliutsiia v 1917–1918 gg.* (Tallinn, 1935), Vol. 2, Book 5, 65.
7. Norman Stone, *The Eastern Front, 1914–1917* (New York, 1975), 21; *RR*, 309–13.
8. Kakurin, *Kak srazhalas'*, II, 133.
9. *Ibid.*, II, 132.
10. S. P. Melgunov, *Tragediia Admirala Kolchaka*, III, Part 1 (Belgrade, 1931), 69–70.
11. Winston S. Churchill, *The World Crisis: The Aftermath* (London, 1929), 232–33.
12. Evan Mawdsley, *The Russian Civil War* (Boston, 1987), 181.
13. W. H. Chamberlin, *The Russian Revolution* (New York, 1935), II, 275.
14. D. A. Kovalenko, *Oboronnaia promyshlennost' Sovetskoi Rossii v 1918–1920 gg.* (Moscow, 1970), 27–28.
15. A. Volpe in A. S. Bubnov, S. S. Kamenev, and R. P. Eidenman, *Grazhdanskaia voina, 1918–1921*, II (Moscow, 1928), 390–92.
16. Volpe in *Ibid.*, 373. See further, Kakurin, *Kak srazhalas'*, I, 147–48, and M. N. Tukhachevskii, *Izbrannye sochineniia*, II (Moscow, 1964), 26–27.
17. Kovalenko, *Oboronnaia promyshlennost'*, 117, citing A. A. Manikovskii, *Boevoe snabzhenie russkoi armii v mirovoiu voinu*, II (Moscow, 1930), 332–33, 335.
18. Tukhachevskii, *Izbrannye sochineniia*, II, 27.
19. Iu. Larin in *EZh*, No. 14 (January 22, 1920), 1; Kakurin, *Kak srazhalas'*, II, 12.
20. Kakurin, *Kak srazhalas'*, II, 13.
21. Denikin, *Ocherki*, III, 129.
22. *RM* (Sofia), May–July, 1921, 214.
23. General B. Kazanovich in *ARR*, VII (1922), 192.
24. Denikin, *Ocherki*, II, 198–99; *Vospominaniia Generala A. S. Lukomskogo*, I (Berlin, 1922), 286.
25. *Vospominaniia Generala Lukomskogo*, I, 289.
26. *RR*, 439–67.
27. *Vospominaniia Generala Lukomskogo*, I, 287.
28. *Bol'shaia sovetskaia entsiklopediia*, 1972 ed., Vol. 8, 451–52.
29. Denikin, *Ocherki*, III, 61.
30. L. Trotskii, *Moia zhizn'*, II (Berlin, 1930), 187–88.
31. K. N. Sokolov, *Pravlenie Generala Denikina* (Sofia, 1921), 33–39.
32. Ludovic-H. Grondijs, *La Guerre en Russie et en Sibérie* (Paris, 1922), 227n.
33. Kakurin, *Kak srazhalas'*, I, 117.
34. Kazanovich in *ARR*, VII (1922), 196, 198.

35. Denikin, *Ocherki*, II, 192.
36. *Vospominaniia Generala Lukomskogo*, I, 289; Kazanovich in *ARR*, VII (1922), 185.
37. Golovin, *Kontr-revoliutsiia*, Vol. 5, Book 10, 32.
38. N. Kakurin, *Strategicheskii ocherk grazhdanskoi voiny* (Moscow-Leningrad, 1926), 31–32.
39. Denikin, *Ocherki*, II, 229.
40. George Stewart, *The White Armies of Russia* (New York, 1933), 40.
41. Khan Khadzhiev, *Velikii Boiar* (Belgrade, 1929), 369, 396.
42. Denikin, *Ocherki*, II, 300–1.
43. On him, see Dimitry V. Lehovich, *White against Red: The Life of General Anton Denikin* (New York, 1974).
44. Sokolov, *Pravlenie*, 81.
45. D. Kin, *Denikinshchina* (Leningrad, 1926), 52.
46. See his *Put' russkogo ofitsera* (New York, 1953).
47. *RR*, 624–35.
48. V. Maksakov and A. Turunov, *Khronika grazhdanskoi voiny v Sibiri (1917–1918)* (Moscow-Leningrad, 1926), 143–44.
49. *Ibid.*, 76.
50. *RR*, 539–58.
51. G. Lelevich, *V dni samarskoi uchredilki* (Moscow, 1921), 6.
52. *RR*, 627–35.
53. G. Gins, *Sibir', Soiuzniki i Kolchak*, I/1 (Peking, 1921), 132.
54. Lelevich, *V dni*, 9–10.
55. *Vechernaia Zaria*, No. 151, July 25, 1918, cited in Piontkovskii, *Grazhdanskaia voina*, 219–20.
56. I. M. Maiskii, *Demokraticheskaia kontr-revoliutsiia* (Moscow, 1923), 145; Gins, *Sibir'*, Vol. II, Pt.2, 170.
57. A. Argunov, *Mezhdu dvumia Bol'shevizmami* [Paris, 1919], 11; Maiskii, *Demokraticheskaia kontr-revoliutsiia*, 161–62.
58. I. I. Vatsetis in *Volia Rossii*, VIII–IX (1928), 161.
59. A. M. Gak et al. in *ISSSR*, No. 1 (1960), 137–43.
60. Gins, *Sibir'*, I/1, 143–44. On their powers: Maiskii, *Demokraticheskaia kontr-revoliutsiia*, 60–62.
61. Melgunov, *Tragediia*, I, 137; Maiskii, *Demokraticheskaia kontr-revoliutsiia*, 175–87.
62. *RR*, 609–12.
63. John Erickson in Richard Pipes, ed., *Revolutionary Russia* (Cambridge, Mass., 1968), 224–56.
64. V. I. Gurko in *ARR*, XV (1924), 8–9.
65. *RR*, Chapter 14.
66. V. Miakotin in *Na chuzhoi storone*, II (1923), 181.
67. Bogdan Pavlu in *Dnevnik* of September 18, 1918, cited in Argunov, *Mezhdu*, 11–12.
68. The full protocols are in *Russkii Istoricheskii Arkhiv*, I (Prague, 1929), 57–280. See further Maiskii, *Demokraticheskaia kontr-revoliutsiia*, 214–55; Gins, *Sibir'*, I/1, 207–55; and Argunov, *Mezhdu*, 16–20.
69. Maiskii, *Demokraticheskaia kontr-revoliutsiia*, 218–19.
70. Sokolov, *Pravlenie*, 70.
71. Gins, *Sibir'*, I/1, 259.
72. Colonel John Ward, *With the "Die-Hards" in Siberia* (London, 1920), 114.
73. *ARR*, XII (1923), 189–93.
74. Churchill, *The Aftermath*, 247.
75. Peter Fleming, *The Fate of Admiral Kolchak* (New York, 1963), 99–103; William S. Graves, *America's Siberian Adventure, 1918–1920* (New York, 1931), 116.
76. Aleksei Budberg, *Dnevnik belogvardeitsa* (Leningrad, 1929), 108.
77. V. G. Boldyrev, *Direktoriia, Kolchak, interventy* (Novonikolaevsk, 1925), 74.

78. Maiskii, *Demokraticheskaia kontr-revoliutsiia*, 308.
79. Gins, *Sibir'*, I/1, 263.
80. Boldyrev, *Direktoriia*, 54.
81. Ward, *With the "Die-Hards,"* 112.
82. Maiskii, *Demokraticheskaia kontr-revoliutsiia*, 65.
83. Gins, *Sibir'*, I/1, 311.
84. Melgunov, *Tragediia*, I, 231–33; Golovin, *Kontr-revoliutsiia*, Book 9, 25, 57.
85. Denikin, *Ocherki*, III, 154–56.
86. On him in 1917, see *RR*, 660–61.
87. P. N. Miliukov in *PN*, No. 1, 697 (November 4, 1925), 3; Golovin, *Kontr-revoliutsiia*, Book 6, 75.
88. *Vospominaniia Generala Lukomskogo*, II, 116n.
89. Kakurin, *Strategicheskii ocherk*, 23–24.
90. Denikin, *Ocherki*, III, 149.
91. *Ibid.*, III, 179.
92. *Ibid.*, III, 210; Golovin, *Rossiiskaia kontr-revoliutsiia*, Book 11, 41.
93. *RR*, 662–66.
94. Denikin, *Ocherki*, III, 180.
95. *Ibid.*, III, 182.
96. Sokolov, *Pravlenie*, 30–31, 81–82.
97. *Ibid.*, 81.
98. *Ibid.*, 83.
99. *Ibid.*, 44, 85–86.
100. I. B. Shekhtman, *Pogromy Dobrovol'cheskoi Armii na Ukraine* (Berlin, 1932), 291.
101. Sokolov, *Pravlenie*, 41, 43.
102. *Ibid.*, 65.
103. *Ibid.*, 66.
104. E. Varneck and H. H. Fisher, eds., *The Testimony of Kolchak and Other Siberian Materials* (Stanford, 1935), 157.
105. Fleming, *Kolchak*, 108.
106. Gins, *Sibir'*, I, 284. See also Golovin, *Rossiiskaia kontr-revoliutsiia*, Book 9, 23.
107. *SZ* No. 45 (1931), 348–52. English translation in James Bunyan, *Intervention, Civil War, and Communism in Russia* (Baltimore, 1936), 362–65. See also Varneck and Fisher, *Testimony of Kolchak*, 160–61, 246–47.
108. Boldyrev, *Direktoriia*, 93–94.
109. *Ibid.*, 93.
110. V. Zenzinov, *Gosudarstvennyi perevorot admirala Kolchaka* (Paris, 1919), 192.
111. Varneck and Fisher, *Testimony of Kolchak*, 168–69.
112. Gins, *Sibir'*, I/1, 307; Varneck and Fisher, *Testimony of Kolchak*, 170.
113. Fleming, *Kolchak*, 112.
114. Général Maurice Janin in *Le Monde Slave* (December 1924), 238; General J. Rouquerol, *L'Aventure de l'Amiral Koltchak* (Paris, 1929), 44. See further, Fleming, *Kolchak*, 113.
115. *The Slavonic Review*, III (1924–25), 724; Ullman, *Intervention*, 280–81.
116. Fleming, *Kolchak*, 113.
117. Zenzinov, *Gosudarstvennyi perevorot*, 9.
118. Boldyrev, *Direktoriia*, 111–13.
119. Gins, *Sibir'*, I/1, 308.
120. [Argunov], *Mezhdu*, 39.
121. Maiskii, *Demokraticheskaia kontr-revoliutsiia*, 335–37.
122. Gins, *Sibir'*, I/1, 309.
123. Ward, *With the "Die-Hards,"* 132–38.
124. Mikhail Lindgren, *Nevedomaia stranitsa* (Chita, 1921).
125. Piontkovskii, *Grazhdanskaia voina*, 300–1.
126. Melgunov, *Tragediia*, III, 36–41.

127. Vladimir N. Brovkin, *The Mensheviks after October* (Ithaca, 1987), 292–93.

128. Partiia Sotsialistov-Revoliutsionerov, *Deviatyi Sovet partii i ego rezoliutsii* (Paris 1920), 15.

129. *Izvestiia*, No. 186 (August 30, 1918), 2.

130. I. Vardin [Mgeladze], *O melkoburzhuaznoi kontrrevoliutsii i restavratsii kapitalizma* (Moscow, 1922) 39–40, cited in Helena Zand, *Z dziejow wojny domowej w Rosji* (Warsaw, 1973), 116.

131. *Vechernye Izvestiia Moskovskogo Soveta R. i Kr. Deputatov*, No. 105, November 22, 1918, cited in Lenin, *Sochineniia*, XXIV, 760.

132. Cited in Abraham Ascher, *The Mensheviks and the Russian Revolution* (Ithaca, 1976), 118.

133. L. M. Spirin, *Klassy i partii v grazhdanskoi voine v Rossii (1917–1918 gg.)* (Moscow, 1968), 311–12.

134. *RR*, 563; *Izvestiia*, No. 263/527 (December 1, 1918), 2.

135. Spirin, *Klassy i partii*, 300. On these negotiations see K. Burevoi, *Raspad, 1918–1922* (Moscow, 1923); and V. Volskii in *K prekrashcheniiu voiny vnutri demokratii* (Moscow, 1919), 38–51.

136. Zand, *Z dziejow*, 105. See further, Golovin, *Rossiiskaia kontr-revoliutsiia*, Book 9, 96.

137. Zand, *Z dziejow*, 106.

138. E. Roubanovitch, V. Soukhomline, and V. Zenzinof, eds., *Le Parti Socialiste Révolutionnaire et la situation actuelle en Russie* (Paris, 1919), 12–13, 15.

139. Zand, *Z dziejow*, 109.

140. *Izvestiia*, No. 45/597 (February 27, 1919), 4.

141. Partiia Sotsialistov-Revoliutsionerov, *Deviatyi Sovet Partii*, 15.

142. Melgunov, *Tragediia*, III, 219–20; K. A. Popov, ed., *Dopros Kolchaka* (Leningrad, 1925), 222.

143. Varneck and Fisher, *Testimony of Kolchak, passim*.

144. Fleming, *Kolchak*, 122–23.

145. Rouquerol, *L'aventure*, 53–54; A. M. Spirin, *Razgrom armii Kolchaka* (Moscow, 1957), 23; Graves, *America's Siberian Adventure*, 124.

146. *Armiia i narod* (Ufa), November 23, 1918, cited in Chamberlin, *Russian Revolution*, II, 182.

147. Graves, *Adventure*, 108. See further, Stewart, *White Armies*, 268–69.

148. Graves, *Adventure*, 7–8.

149. *Ibid.*, 55–56, 101.

150. *Ibid.*, 175, 186.

151. *Ibid.*, 165.

152. Piontkovskii, *Grazhdanskaia voina*, 299.

153. Varneck and Fisher, *Testimony of Kolchak*, 187.

154. Maiskii, *Demokraticheskaia kontr-revoliutsiia*, 331–32.

155. Richard H. Ullman, *Britain and the Russian Civil War* (Princeton, 1968), 169n.

156. E. L. Woodward and Rohan Butler, eds., *Documents on British Foreign Policy, 1919–1939*, First Series, III (London, 1949), 362–64.

157. Piontkovskii, *Grazhdanskaia voina*, 299.

158. See his autobiographical remarks in Varneck and Fisher, *Testimony of Kolchak*, 1–37.

159. Ullman, *Britain*, 43.

160. Varneck and Fisher, *Testimony of Kolchak*, 38, 162.

161. Fleming, *Kolchak*, 111.

162. Ward, *With the "Die-Hards,"* 111.

163. Aleksei Budberg in *ARR*, XV (1924), 331–32.

164. Gins, *Sibir'*, II, 367.

2. The Civil War: The Climax (1919–1920)

1. A. G. Kavtaradze, *Voennye spetsialisty na sluzhbe Respubliki Sovetov, 1917–1920 gg.* (Moscow, 1988), 69–70.

2. N. N. Golovin, *Rossiiskaia kontr-revoliutsiia* (Paris, 1937), Book 6, 7.

3. *Dekrety*, III, 111–13.
4. Lev Trotskii, *Kak vooruzhalas' revoliutsiia*, I (Moscow, 1923), 151.
5. Kavtaradze, *Voennye spetsialisty*, 110–11.
6. Francesco Benvenuti, *The Bolsheviks and the Red Army, 1918–1922* (Cambridge, 1988), 65–87.
7. Kavtaradze, *Voennye spetsialisty*, 25–27.
8. Golovin, *Rossiiskaia kontr-revoliutsiia*, Book 1, 84.
9. Kavtaradze, *Voennye spetsialisty*, 96, 98, 100–6.
10. *RR*, 646–52.
11. Iu. I. Korablev in *Revvoensovet Respubliki* (Moscow, 1991), 36.
12. *Pravda*, No. 188 (September 4, 1918), 3.
13. Shatagin, *Organizatsiia*, 96–97.
14. Kavtaradze, *Voennye spetsialisty*, 199.
15. John Erickson in Richard Pipes, ed., *Revolutionary Russia* (Cambridge, Mass., 1968), 245.
16. Kavtaradze, *Voennye spetsialisty*, 175–78.
17. *Ibid.*, 210.
18. *TP*, I, 715.
19. Isaac Deutscher, *The Prophet Armed* (New York and London, 1954), 446.
20. Dmitrii Volkogonov, *Trotskii*, I (Moscow, 1992), 254.
21. L. Trotskii, *Moia zhizn'*, II (Berlin, 1930), 143–50.
22. Leon Trotsky, *How the Revolution Armed*, II (London, 1979), *passim*.
23. Trotskii, *Moia zhizn'*, II (Berlin, 1930), 141.
24. Lenin, *PSS*, LI, 33.
25. *Ibid.*, LI, 33–34.
26. *TP*, II, 272–73.
27. *Ibid.*, II, 80–81.
28. S. V. Lipitskii in *Revvoensovet Respubliki* (Moscow, 1991), 373.
29. Trotskii, *Moia zhizn'*, II, 184–85.
30. S. Olikov, *Dezertirstvo v krasnoi armii i bor'ba s nim* (Leningrad, 1926).
31. V. Antonov-Ovseenko, *Zapiski o grazhdanskoi voine*, IV (Moscow-Leningrad, 1933), 133.
32. Olikov, *Dezertirstvo*, 30–31; cf. Figes in *Past and Present*, No. 129 (November 1990), 200, where somewhat different figures are given.
33. Figes, *Ibid.*, 204–5.
34. *Direktivy komandovaiia frontov krasnoi armii* (Moscow, 1971), II, 400.
35. Olikov, *Dezertirstvo*, 33.
36. A. M. Selishchev, *Iazyk revoliutsionnoi epokhi*, 2nd ed. (Moscow, 1928), 211.
37. I. V. Stalin, *Sochineniia*, IV (Moscow, 1951), 197–224.
38. *TP*, I, 343.
39. *Ibid.*, I, 359.
40. *Ibid.*, I, 651.
41. Trotsky's order of December 28, 1918, in *ARR*, XVIII (1926), 270–71.
42. Lev Trotskii, *Sochineniia*, XVII, Pt. 1 (Moscow-Leningrad, 1926), 509–10.
43. Trotskii, *Kak vooruzhalas' revoliutsiia*, I, 235.
44. *ARR*, XVIII (1926), 272.
45. Iu. I. Korablev in *Revvoensovet*, 48–49.
46. *TP*, I, 116–17; cf. Vladimir Eremenko in *LR*, No. 50/1454 (December 14, 1990), 17.
47. *ARR*, XVIII (1926), 272–77.
48. Volkogonov, *Trotskii*, I, 295.
49. Evan Mawdsley, *The Russian Civil War* (Boston, 1987), 181.
50. *IA*, No. 1 (1958), 55; report of February 1919.
51. V. M. Shcherbak, *Bol'shevistskaia agitatsiia i propaganda, 1918–1919* (Moscow, 1969).
52. David Lloyd George, *The Truth about the Peace Treaties*, I (London, 1938), 316.
53. *Ibid.*, 331.
54. John M. Thompson, *Russia, Bolshevism, and the Versailles Peace* (Princeton, N. J., 1966), 4.
55. Speech of November 8, 1919: *The Times* (London), November 10, 1919, 9.

56. Department of State, *Papers Relating to the Foreign Relations of the United States: 1919, Russia* (Washington, D.C., 1937), 15–18.
57. Lloyd George, *The Truth*, I, 353–54.
58. Official Soviet translation in *The Nation*, January 17, 1920, 88–89.
59. V. P. Potëmkin, ed., *Istoriia Diplomatii*, III (Moscow-Leningrad, 1945), 61.
60. Winston Churchill, *The World Crisis: The Aftermath* (London, 1929), 173.
61. G. Gins, *Sibir', soiuzniki i Kolchak* (Peking, 1921), II, 88–90.
62. Thompson, *Russia*, 119.
63. *Ibid.*, 119.
64. Lloyd George, *The Truth*, I, 331.
65. Thompson, *Russia*, 132; Churchill, *The Aftermath*, 172.
66. Thompson, *loc.cit.*, 152–53.
67. *Ibid.*, 167–77.
68. Department of State, *1919, Russia*, 77–80.
69. Cited in Beatrice Farnsworth, *William C. Bullitt and the Soviet Union* (Bloomington, Ind., 1967), 42.
70. Thompson, *Russia*, 236.
71. *RR*, 633–34, 661.
72. Martin Gilbert, *Winston S. Churchill* (Boston, 1975), IV, 318.
73. Lloyd George, *The Truth*, I, 327.
74. Gilbert, *Churchill*, IV, 305–6.
75. Churchill, *The Aftermath*, 259.
76. Ullman, *Britain*, 11.
77. Gilbert, *Churchill*, IV, 426–27.
78. *Ibid.*, 314.
79. *Ibid.*, 277.
80. Ullman, *Britain*, 13–15.
81. Lloyd George, *The Truth*, I, 382–83.
82. Thompson, *Russia*, 200–3.
83. *Ibid.*, 46.
84. Ullman, *Britain*, 165; Thompson, *Russia*, 204.
85. Thompson, *Russia*, 46.
86. E. L. Woodward and Rohan Butler, eds., *Documents on British Foreign Policy, 1919–1939*, First Series, III (London, 1949), 369–70.
87. Anne Hogenhuis-Seliverstoff, *Les Relations Franco-Soviétiques, 1917–1924* (Paris, 1981), 109–10.
88. N. Kakurin, *Kak srazhalas' revoliutsiia*, II (Moscow-Leningrad, 1925), 135.
89. Ullman, *Britain*, 15.
90. Kakurin, *Kak srazhalas'*, II, 88.
91. A. I. Gukovskii, *Frantsuzskaia interventsiia* (Moscow-Leningrad, 1928), 122–23.
92. George Brinkley, *The Volunteer Army and Allied Intervention in South Russia, 1917–1921* (Notre Dame, 1966), 134.
93. *Direktivy glavnogo komandovaniia krasnoi armii* (Moscow, 1969), 307.
94. Stewart, *White Armies*, 171–72.
95. Brinkley, *The Volunteer Army*, 134.
96. Kakurin, *Kak srazhalas'*, II, 124–25.
97. Bernard Pares, *My Russian Memoirs* (London, 1931), 525.
98. Mawdsley, *Civil War*, 145; Fleming, *Kolchak*, 136.
99. Richard Luckett, *The White Generals* (London, 1971), 262–63.
100. William S. Graves, *America's Siberian Adventure* (New York, 1931), 200–1.
101. Fleming, *Kolchak*, 148–49.
102. Aleksei Budberg, *Dnevnik belogvardeitsa* (Leningrad, 1929), 175.
103. Gins, *Sibir'*, II, 346.
104. *IA*, No. 1 (1958), 43.

105. *Direktivy glavnogo komandovaniia*, 561.
106. A. M. Spirin, *Razgrom armii Kolchaka* (Moscow, 1957), 247.
107. Vatsetis in *IA*, No. 2 (1958), 37–38.
108. Spirin, *Razgrom*, 114, 118.
109. Lenin, *PSS*, XXXVIII, 271.
110. Spirin, *Razgrom*, 114, 118.
111. *Direktivy glavnogo komandovaniia*, 577.
112. Stewart, *White Armies*, 273.
113. Gins, *Sibir'*, II, 389–90.
114. Olikov, *Dezertirstvo*, 13.
115. Woodward and Butler, *Documents*, III, 317–19.
116. Ullman, *Britain*, 161.
117. Mawdsley, *Civil War*, 143–44; Churchill, *The Aftermath*, 246.
118. Woodward and Butler, *Documents*, III, 362–64; Ullman, *Britain*, 169.
119. Luckett, *White Generals*, 273.
120. Department of State, *1919, Russia*, 337–38; Thompson, *Russia*, 291–92.
121. Department of State, *1919, Russia*, 337.
122. Denikin, *Ocherki*, V, 72.
123. *Ibid.*, V, 72–73; Lenin, *PSS*, L, 326.
124. Volkogonov, *Trotskii*, I, 255.
125. *Ibid.*, 256.
126. *IA*, No. 1 (1958), 43.
127. Denikin, *Ocherki*, V, 73.
128. *BD*, V (1928), 119.
129. Denikin, *Ocherki*, V, 79–80.
130. A. I. Egorov, *Razgrom Denikina, 1919* (Moscow, 1931), 91.
131. *Sobranie Uzakonenii i Rasporiazhenii izdannye Osobym Soveshchaniem pri Glavnokoman-duiushchim Vooruzhennymi Silami na Iuge Rossii*, No. 18 (August 27, 1919), Decree No. 96, pp. 246–47.
132. Denikin, *Ocherki*, IV, 210–15; Chamberlin, *Russian Revolution*, II, 254–55.
133. Denikin, *Ocherki*, IV, 201, 211.
134. *Direktivy komandovaniia frontov*, 241–43, 252–54, 257–58; Lenin, *PSS*, L, 306, 341.
135. *The Memoirs of General Wrangel* (London, 1929), 84–88; Denikin, *Ocherki*, V, 107.
136. *Direktivy glavnogo komandovaniia*, 557.
137. *Direktivy komandovaniia frontov*, II, 710.
138. *Ibid.*, II, 712: status as of June 22, 1919.
139. Churchill, *The Aftermath*, 245.
140. Spirin, *Razgrom*, 221–39.
141. *Ibid.*, 239.
142. *Ibid.*, 252.
143. Denikin, *Ocherki*, V, 108.
144. S. Piontkovskii, *Grazhdanskaia voina v Rossii* (Moscow, 1925), 515–16.
145. *The Memoirs of General Wrangel*, 89.
146. *Ibid.*, 89.
147. Denikin, *Ocherki*, V, 117–18.
148. Kakurin, *Kak srazhalas'*, II, 242–45, 306.
149. *Direktivy komandovaniia frontov*, II, 311.
150. M. Kritskii in *ARR*, XVIII (1926), 277.
151. *TP*, I, 663; Lenin, *PSS*, XXXIX, 172.
152. G. N. Rakovskii, *V Stane Belykh* (Constantinople, 1920), 25.
153. *Direktivy komandovaniia frontov*, II, 337.
154. *The Memoirs of General Wrangel*, 87.
155. Kakurin, *Kak srazhalas'*, II, 306.
156. Stewart, *White Armies*, 182.

157. N. I. Shtif, *Pogromy na Ukraine* (Berlin, 1922), 8–9.
158. Kakurin, *Kak srazhalas'*, II, 308.
159. Denikin, *Ocherki*, IV, 245.
160. Chamberlin, *Russian Revolution*, II, 301; see further, M. K. Dziewanowski, *Joseph Pilsudski: A European Federalist, 1918–1922* (Stanford, 1969), 193.
161. Piotr S. Wandycz, *Soviet-Polish Relations, 1917–1921* (Cambridge, Mass., 1969), 133; Kutrzeba, *Wyprawa*, 24; Brinkley, *Volunteer Army*, 205.
162. Kutrzeba, *Wyprawa*, 24–25.
163. Dziewanowski, *Pilsudski*, 184–857; Karnicki in *Torpeda*, October 4, 1936, cited in Titus Komarnicki, *Rebirth of the Polish Republic* (London, 1957), 468–69.
164. PAN, *Dokumenty*, II, 424–25.
165. *Ibid.*, II, 388.
166. Wandycz, *Soviet-Polish Relations*, 133–34.
167. Julian Marchlewski, *Pisma wybrane*, II (Warsaw, 1956), 755. See also Vatsetis in *TP*, I, 355.
168. Denikin, *Ocherki*, V, 175.
169. Wandycz, *Soviet-Polish Relations*, 128–29.
170. *Ibid.*, 128.
171. PAN, *Dokumenty*, II, 313n.; Piotr Wandycz in *SR*, XXIV, No. 3 (September 1965), 425–49; Fischer, *Soviets in World Affairs*, I, 239.
172. Wandycz, *Soviet-Polish Relations*, 138.
173. PAN, *Dokumenty*, II, 408–13, 439.
174. RTsKhIDNI, F. 2, op. 2, ed. khr. 206.
175. Denikin, *Ocherki*, V, 178–79; Kutrzeba, *Wyprawa*, 27.
176. *TP*, I, 758–59; PAN, *Dokumenty*, II, 477.
177. Kutrzeba, *Wyprawa*, 32.
178. *Ibid.*, 27.
179. A. I. Denikin, *Pol'sha i Dobrovol'cheskaia Armiia* (Paris, 1926); E. G. f.-Val, *Kak Pilsudski pogubil Denikina* (Tallin, 1938); the Polish counterargument: Komarnicki, *Rebirth*, 478.
180. A. Juzwenko in H. Zielinski, ed., *Z badan na wplywem i znaczeniem rewolucji rosyjskich 1917 roku dla ziem polskich* (Wroclaw, 1968), 85.
181. *Ibid.*, 84–85.
182. *The Memoirs of Marshal Mannerheim* (London, 1953), 221; Mawdsley, *Civil War*, 197.
183. *KA*, No. 2/33 (1929), 128.
184. Woodward and Butler, *Documents*, III, 429.
185. Hubert Gough, *Soldiering On* (New York, n.d.), 191.
186. *Ibid.*, 190–91.
187. C. Jay Smith, *Finland and the Russian Revolution* (Atlanta, 1958), 168; Churchill, *The Aftermath*, 266–67.
188. Ullman, *Britain*, II, 258.
189. Mawdsley, *Civil War*, 198.
190. *KA*, No. 2/33 (1929), 129, 140–42; Woodward and Butler, *Documents*, III, 430.
191. *Ibid.*, 133.
192. Woodward and Butler, *Documents*, III, 394n–395n; *KA*, No. 2/33 (1929), 131; Smith, *Finland*, 151–52.
193. *KA*, No. 2/33 (1929), 138; Denikin's concurrence: *ibid.*, 144.
194. *Ibid.*, 136–37; Mannerheim, *Memoirs*, 221.
195. Mawdsley, *Civil War*, 198.
196. Ullman, *Britain*, 266–67.
197. *Ibid.*, 274.
198. Woodward and Butler, *Documents*, III, 553–54.
199. Ullman, *Britain*, 281.

200. *Ibid.*, 279–80.
201. On him, see his memoirs: *Russkaia revoliutsiia: Zapiski v trekh knigakh*, 3 vols. (Paris, 1929–1937); P.Arshinov,*Istoriiamakhnovskogodvizheniia,1918–1921gg.*(Berlin,1923); and David Footman in *Soviet Affairs*, No. 2 (New York, 1959), 77–127.
202. Makhno, *Russkaia Revoliutsiia*, II, 119–35.
203. Luckett, *White Generals*, 326.
204. Denikin, *Ocherki*, V, 130–34, 234–35; Kritskii in *ARR*, XVIII, 269.
205. Kakurin, *Kak srazhalas'*, II, 287–88.
206. *Ibid.*, II, 281–82.
207. Luckett, *White Generals*, 298.
208. Woodward and Butler, *Documents*, III, 460–64; see further, *ibid.*, 464n.
209. *Ibid.*, III, 464.
210. Ullman, *Britain*, 209.
211. *Ibid.*, 366.
212. Woodward and Butler, *Documents*, III, 525.
213. Churchill, *The Aftermath*, 275.
214. Ullman, *Britain*, 211–12.
215. Brinkley, *Volunteer Army*, 216–19.
216. Churchill, *The Aftermath*, 240–41.
217. *Ibid.*, 242.
218. *Ibid.*, 244; George F. Kennan, *Russia and the West under Lenin and Stalin* (Boston-Toronto, 1960–61), 90.
219. Ullman, *Britain*, 212n.
220. Tu. I. Korablev, *Revvoensovet* (Moscow, 1991), 51.
221. RTsKhIDNI, F. 2, op. 1, delo 27501.
222. *RR*, 177–78, 184.
223. Denikin, *Ocherki*, V, 145.
224. Iurii Larin, *Evrei i antisemitizm v SSSR* (Moscow-Leningrad, 1929), 58, 49–50.
225. I. M. Bikerman in *Rossiia i Evrei*, Sbornik I (Berlin, 1924), 22–23.
226. I. B. Shekhtman, *Pogromy Dobrovol'cheskoi Armii na Ukraine* (Berlin, 1932), 81.
227. Bikerman in *Rossiia i Evrei*, I, 62–63.
228. Nora Levin, *The Jews in the Soviet Union since 1917*, I (New York and London, 1988), 49.
229. I. Iu. Levin in *Rossiia i Evrei*, I, 131.
230. G. A. Ziv, *Trotskii: kharakteristika* (New York, 1921), 46n.
231. Shekhtman, *Pogromy*, 295.
232. Joseph Nedava, *Trotsky and the Jews* (Philadelphia, 1972), 116.
233. Baruch Knei-Paz, *The Social and Political Thought of Leon Trotsky* (Oxford, 1978), 546, 547.
234. Orlando Figes in *Past and Present*, No. 129 (November 1990), 196.
235. *TP*, I, *passim;* Trotsky, *Revolution Armed*, II, *passim.*
236. RTsKhIDNI, F. 17, op. 3, ed. khr. 2.
237. See below, pp. 110–11.
238. Shekhtman, *Pogromy*, 54; Denikin, *Ocherki*, V, 145.
239. Shekhtman, *ibid.*, 54–55.
240. Denikin, *Ocherki*, V, 146.
241. *Ibid.*, V, 145.
242. Shekhtman, *Pogromy*, 65–67.
243. Denikin, *Ocherki*, V, 150n.
244. Peter Kenez in *The Wiener Library Bulletin*, XXX, New Series, Nos. 41/42 (1977), 7.
245. Bikerman in *Rossiia i Evrei*, I, 61.
246. I. Cherikover, *Antisemitizm i pogromy na Ukraine 1917–1918 gg.* (Berlin, 1923).
247. Shekhtman, *Pogromy*, 129.
248. *Ibid.*, 295.

249. Elias Heifetz, *The Slaughter of the Jews in the Ukraine in* 1919 (New York, 1921), 185-200; Chamberlin, *The Russian Revolution,* II, 229.
250. Heifetz, *Slaughter,* 202-27.
251. Arnold Margolin, *Ukraina i politika Antanty* (Berlin, 1921), 334.
252. V. A. Antonov-Ovseenko, *Zapiski o grazhdanskoi voine,* IV (Moscow-Leningrad, 1933), 153.
253. Cable from Kh. Rakovskii of May 12, 1919, in *Direktivy glavnogo komandovaniia,* 234.
254. Heifetz, *Slaughter,* 243-48.
255. Chamberlin, *Russian Revolution,* II, 217.
256. *TP,* I, 427.
257. Chamberlin, *Russian Revolution,* II, 234.
258. N. Gergel in *YIVO Annual of Jewish Social Science,* VI (1951), 240-41.
259. Shekhtman, *Pogromy,* 101.
260. *Kievlianin,* No. 37 (October 8/21, 1919), cited in Shekhtman, *Pogromy,* 368.
261. Shekhtman, *Pogromy,* 343-44.
262. Gergel in *YIVO Annual,* VI, 238-39.
263. Shekhtman, *Pogromy,* 190.
264. Kenez in *Wiener Library Bulletin,* XXX, New Series, No.41/42 (1977), 5.
265. Shtif, *Pogromy,* 76-85.
266. Shekhtman, *Pogromy,* 187, 303-4. Other examples, 187-88, 304-7; Shtif, *Pogromy,* 87.
267. Shekhtman, *loc. cit.,* 216.
268. Shtif, *Pogromy,* 88-89; Shekhtman, *Pogromy,* 195, 203, 291.
269. *TP,* I, 364.
270. Lenin, *PSS,* XXXVIII, 242-43.
271. *Dekrety,* V, 525.
272. Shtif, *Pogromy,* 7.
273. Kenez in *Wiener Library,* XXX, New Series, No. 41/42 (1977), 3.
274. RTsKhIDNI, F.5, op. 1, delo 120, listy 6-8.
275. Gergel in *YIVO Annual,* VI (1951), 249.
276. See below, Chapter 5.
277. Shekhtman, *Pogromy,* 298-99.
278. I. Iu. Levin in *Rossiia i Evrei,* I, 126.
279. Domenico Settembrini in George R. Urban, ed., *Eurocommunism* (London, 1978), 159; Hermann Rauschning, *Hitler Speaks* (London, 1939), 234.
280. Lenin, *PSS,* XLV, 98.
281. Knei-Paz, *Leon Trotsky,* 546n.
282. Shtif, *Pogromy,* 5-6.
283. Stewart, *White Armies,* 294-95.
284. Mawdsley, *Civil War,* 154-55.
285. *TP,* I, 768-71.
286. Francis McCullagh, *A Prisoner of the Reds* (London, 1921), 28-29.
287. *Ibid.,* 32-33.
288. Fleming, *Kolchak,* 175.
289. Piontkovskii, *Grazhdanskaia voina,* 314-15.
290. S. P. Melgunov, *Tragediia Admirala Kolchaka,* III/ 2 (Belgrade, 1930), 137.
291. K. A. Popov, ed., *Dopros Kolchaka* (Leningrad, 1925). In English: Varneck and Fisher, eds., *The Testimony of Admiral Kolchak.*
292. *Pravda,* No.51 (March 6, 1920), 2; [S. Chudnovskii in] *PN,* No.1477 (February 17, 1925), 2.
293. Trotsky Archive, Harvard University, bMs Russ 13, T-416. Emphasis added.
294. *TP,* II, 32-33.
295. Spirin, *Razgrom,* 279.
296. [Chudnovskii in] *PN,* No. 1477 (February 17, 1925), 2.
297. *Izvestiia,* No. 51/898 (March 6, 1920), 2.

298. *TP*, II, 40–41; *Direktivy Glavnogo komandovaniia*, 600; Spirin, *Razgrom*, 281–82.

299. *Pravda*, No. 151 (July 12, 1919), 1; N. A. Kornatovskii, *Razgrom kontrevoliutsionnykh zagovorov v Petrograde v 1918–1919 gg.* (Leningrad, 1972), 48–50.

300. L. Kamenev in *Izvestiia*, No. 225/777 (October 9, 1919), 2.

301. *Petrogradskaia Pravda*, No. 218 (September 27, 1919), 1; Kamenev in *Izvestiia*, No. 255/777 (October 9, 1919), 2.

302. *Izvestiia*, No. 213/763 (September 25, 1919), 2; Kornatovskii, *Razgrom*, 54–58.

303. Kamenev in *Izvestiia*, No. 225/777 (October 9, 1919), 2.

304. Bakhmeteff Archive, Rare Book and Manuscript Library, Columbia University, Panina Papers, Pack. 3, Folder 16.

305. P. E. Melgunova-Stepanova in *Pamiati pogibshikh* (Paris, 1919), 81.

306. Private communication on March 6, 1962, of P. E. Melgunova (Stepanova).

307. L. Kamenev in *Izvestiia*, No. 228/780 (October 12, 1919), 3, cited in Melgunova-Stepanova, *Pamiati*, 80.

308. Message dated August 22, 1919, in *Izvestiia*, No. 228/780 (October 12, 1919), 2.

309. Kakurin, *Kak srazhalas'*, II, 308.

310. *Direktivy glavnogo komandovaniia*, 473.

311. Simon Liberman, *Building Lenin's Russia* (Chicago, 1945), 36–37; *RR*, 823.

312. N. I. Shatagin, *Organizatsiia i stroitel'stvo Sovetskoi Armii* (Moscow, 1954), 132–33.

313. K. V. Agureev, *Razgrom Belogvardeiskikh voisk Denikina* (Moscow, 1961), 82.

314. A. P. Rodzianko, *Vospominaniia o Severo-Zapadnoi Armii* (Berlin, 1921), 95–97.

315. Stewart, *White Armies*, 229–30.

316. Kakurin, *Kak srazhalas'*, II, 333.

317. *TP*, I, 694–97.

318. Trotskii, *Kak vooruzhalas'*, II/1, 400–2.

319. *Ibid.*, II/1, 400–16. On tanks: 411.

320. *TP*, I, 718–19.

321. Mawdsley, *Civil War*, 200–1; Rodzianko, *Vospominaniia*, 115.

322. Trotskii, *Moia zhizn'*, II, 156–61.

323. V. M. Primakov in *Latyshskie strelki v bor'be za sovetskuiu vlast'* (Riga, 1962), 338; Kakurin, *Kak srazhalas'*, II, 321.

324. *Direktivy komandovaniia frontov*, II, 349; Egorov, *Razgrom Denikina*, 147–48.

325. Primakov, *Latyshskie strelki*, 338; Kakurin, *Kak srazhalas'*, II, 312; *Direktivy glavnogo komandovaniia*, 472, 474, 478.

326. Denikin, *Ocherki*, V, 230.

327. Egorov, *Razgrom Denikina*, 144.

328. RTsKhIDNI, F.2, op. 1, ed. khr. 24348.

329. Kakurin, *Kak srazhalas'*, II, 311–12; Luckett, *White Generals*, 329; *Direktivy komandovaniia frontov*, II, 354.

330. Egorov, *Razgrom Denikina*, 146.

331. Primakov in *Latyshskie strelki*, 342.

332. Denikin, *Ocherki*, V, 235–36.

333. Luckett, *White Generals*, 333.

334. *The Times*, November 10, 1919, 9.

335. Ullman, *Britain*, 306.

336. Denikin, *Ocherki*, V, 172.

337. C. E. Bechhofer, *In Denikin's Russia and the Caucasus* (London, 1921), 121.

338. Stewart, *White Armies*, 338.

339. Bechhofer, *In Denikin's Russia*, 100–1.

340. Stewart, *White Armies*, 346–47.

341. A. P. Ermolin, *Revoliutsiia i kazachestvo* (Moscow, 1982), 170–72.

342. On his rule, see Nikolai Ross, *Vrangel' v Krymu* (Frankfurt a/M., 1982).

343. *The Memoirs of General Wrangel*, 131–32; Ullman, *Anglo-Soviet Accord*, 71.

344. Denikin, *Ocherki*, V, 363.

345. Stewart, *White Armies,* 358–59; Ullman, *Anglo-Soviet Accord,* 73–75; *The Memoirs of General Wrangel,* 147–48.
346. V. Obolenskii, *Krim pri Vrangele* (Moscow-Leningrad, 1927), 25.
347. Chamberlin, *Russian Revolution,* II, 320.
348. Wrangel in *Beloe Delo,* VI, (n.d.) 58–65.
349. Kakurin, *Kak srazhalas',* II, 385.
350. Iu. I. Korablev in *Revvoensovet,* 49.
351. RTsKhIDNI, F. 2, op. 2, ed. khr. 463.
352. RTsKhIDNI, F. 5, op. 1, delo 2103, list 82, and delo 368.
353. Denikin, *Ocherki,* III, 10, 263; Kolchak in Melgunov, *Tragediia,* I, p. ix.
354. Ward, *With the "Die Hards,"* p. xi.
355. *RM,* May–July 1921, 211.
356. Denikin, *Ocherki,* II, 237.
357. Iu. Martov, ed., *Oborona revoliutsii* (Moscow, 1919), cited in S. Volin, *Deiatel'nost menshevikov v profsoiuzakh pri sovetskoi vlasti* (New York, Inter-University Project on the History of the Menshevik Movement, 1962), 82.
358. Churchill, *The Aftermath,* 233–34.
359. Cited in Orlando Figes, *Peasant Russia, Civil War* (Oxford, 1989), 175.
360. G. Krivosheev, ed., *Grif sekretnosti sniat* (Moscow, 1993), 54.
361. B. Ts. Urlanis, *Voina i narodonaselenie Evropy* (Moscow, 1960), 185, 188.
362. Iu. A. Poliakov, *Sovetskaia strana posle okonchaniia grazhdanskoi voiny* (Moscow, 1986), 113.
363. Orlando Figes in *Past and Present,* No. 129 (November 1990), 172.
364. Poliakov, *Sovetskaia strana,* 119–22.
365. Hans von Rimscha, *Russland jenseits der Grenzen* (Jena, 1927), p. x. On this subject see further Marc Raeff, *Russia Abroad* (New York, 1990).
366. Donald Greer, *The Incidents of the Emigration During the French Revolution* (Cambridge, Mass., 1951), 112.
367. Peter Struve, *Itogi i sushchestvo kommunisticheskogo khoziaistva* (Berlin, 1921), 30; (reprinted in Richard Pipes, ed., Peter Struve, *Collected Works in Fifteen Volumes,* XII (Ann Arbor, Mich., 1970). See further, Richard Pipes, *Struve: Liberal on the Right* (Cambridge, Mass., 1980), 318–19.
368. Gleb Struve, *Russkaia literatura v izgnanii,* 2nd ed. (Paris, 1984), 21.
369. "Sirin" [Vladimir Nabokov], *Rul',* No. 2,120 (November 18, 1927), 2.

3. The Red Empire

1. Martha Brill Olcott, *The Kazakhs* (Stanford, 1987), 118–26.
2. On this, see also *RR,* 368–69.
3. Above, p. 24.
4. Richard Pipes, *The Formation of the Soviet Union,* rev. ed. (Cambridge, Mass., 1964), 137.
5. L. N. Maimeskulov *et al., Vseukraininskaia Chrezvychainaia Komissiia (1918–1922)* (Kharkov, 1990).
6. V. I. Masalskii, *Turkestanskii krai* (St. Petersburg, 1913), 354.
7. *Nasha gazeta* (Tashkent), November 23, 1917, cited in G. Safarov, *Kolonial'naia revoliutsiia (Opyt Turkestana)* ([Moscow], 1921), 70.
8. Safarov, *Kolonial'naia revoliutsiia,* 86.
9. RTsKhIDNI, F. 2, op. 2, ed. khr. 395.
10. On him, Pipes, *Formation,* 168–70, 260–63, and Alexandre Bennigsen and Chantal Lemercier-Quelquejay, *Sultan-Galiev, le père de la révolution tiers-mondiste* (Paris, 1986).
11. Bennigsen and Lemercier-Quelquejay, *Sultan-Galiev.*

12. Vadim Rogovin, *Byla li al'ternativa?* (Moscow, 1992), 92–93.
13. Winfried Baumgart, *Deutsche Ost-Politik 1918* (Vienna and Munich, 1966), 185–90.
14. Lenin, *PSS,* LI, 163–64.
15. RTsKhIDNI, F. 64, op. 2, ed. khr. 21, cited in G. Zhvaniia, *Bol'sheviki i pobeda sovetskoi vlasti v Gruzii* (Tiflis, 1981), 254–60.
16. RTsKhIDNI, F. 85, op. 15, ed. khr. 2.
17. Lenin, *PSS,* LI, 191.
18. Pipes, *Formation,* 227.
19. S. I. Iakubovskaia, *Ob"edinitel'noe dvizhenie za obrazovanie SSSR* ([Moscow], 1947), 99.
20. F. Makharadze, *Sovety i bor'ba za sovetskuiu vlast' v Gruzii* (Tiflis, 1928), 223.
21. Georgian Archive, Houghton Library, Harvard University, bMS Georgian 2, Box 37.
22. RTsKhIDNI, F. 5, op. 1, delo 2104, list 18.
23. République de Géorgie, *Documents relatifs à la question de la Géorgie devant la Société des Nations* (Paris, 1925), 67–68.
24. RTsKhIDNI, F. 2, op. 2, ed. khr. 520.
25. Zhvaniia, *Bol'sheviki,* 311; Lenin, *PSS,* XLII, 367; Serge Afanasyan, *L'Arménie, l'Azerbaidjan et la Géorgie* (Paris, 1981), 188n–189n.
26. John Donald Rose, "British Foreign Policy in Relation to Transcaucasia, 1918–1921," Ph.D. Dissertation, University of Toronto, 1985, 246–47.
27. RTsKhIDNI, F. 76, op. 3, delo 153.
28. Zhvaniia, *Bol'sheviki,* 319–23.
29. G. Chicherin in *Zaria Vostoka* (Tiflis), March 5, 1925, cited by Irakli Tsereteli in *Prométhée* (Warsaw), June 1928, 11.
30. RTsKhIDNI, F. 17, op. 2, ed. khr. 56, list 2, in Zhvaniia, *Bol'sheviki,* 323.
31. Trotsky Archive, Houghton Library, Harvard University, T-632.
32. *Ibid.,* T-637.
33. RTsKhIDNI, F. 85, op. 15, ed. khr. 80, list 1.
34. Lenin, *PSS,* XLII, 356–57.
35. *Ibid.,* 367.

4. Communism for Export

1. Lenin, *PSS,* XXXVI, 341–42.
2. Ossip K. Flechtheim, *Die Kommunistische Partei Deutschlands in der Weimarer Republik* (Offenbach a.M., 1948), 35; Arthur Rosenberg, *Geschichte der Deutschen Republik* (Karlsbad, 1935), 22–23.
3. *RR,* 619–23, 667–68.
4. Radek's recollections of his German mission are in *KN,* No. 10 (October 1926), 139–75; there exists a German translation, with additional materials, by O.-E. Schüddekopf in *AfS,* II (1962), 87–166.
5. Julius Braunthal, *History of the International,* II (New York-Washington, 1967), 127–28; Gerald Freund, *Unholy Alliance* (New York, 1957), 36.
6. Schüddekopf in *AfS,* II (1962), 95.
7. Eduard Bernstein, *Die deutsche Revolution,* I (Berlin, 1921), 188.
8. Flechtheim, *Kommunistische Partei,* 54.
9. *Ibid.,* 55.
10. Radek in *KN,* No. 10 (October 1926), 152.
11. Branko Lazitch and Milorad M. Drachkovitch, *Lenin and the Comintern,* I (Stanford, 1972), 104–5.
12. Lenin, *PSS,* XXXVIII, 321–22.
13. *Sovetsko-Germanskie Otnosheniia ot peregovorov v Brest-Litovske do podpisaniia Rapall'skogo dogovora,* II (Moscow, 1971), 43, 44, 49, 68, 94.
14. Bennett Kovrig, *Communism in Hungary* (Stanford, 1979), 21–31.
15. Braunthal, *History,* II, 136.

16. *Ibid.*, II, 137.
17. Alfred L. P. Dennis, *The Foreign Policies of Soviet Russia* (New York, 1924), 348.
18. Franz Borkenau, *World Communism: A History of the Communist International* (Ann Arbor, Mich., 1962), 121.
19. Braunthal, *History*, II, 148.
20. Neil McInnes in *The Impact of the Russian Revolution, 1917–1967* (London, 1967), 122.
21. *Protokoll des Zweiten Welt-Kongresses der Kommunistischen Internationale* (Hamburg, 1921), 601.
22. Simon Liberman, *Building Lenin's Russia* (Chicago, 1945), 71.
23. *RR*, 382–84.
24. Angelica Balabanoff, *My Life as a Rebel* (New York and London, 1938), 210.
25. Lazitch and Drachkovitch, *Lenin*, I, 39.
26. *S"ezdy Sovetov v Postanovleniiakh* (Moscow, 1935), 116.
27. *Die Kommunistische Internationale*, No. 1 (August, 1919), xii.
28. *Petrogradskaia Pravda*, No. 255 (November 7, 1919), 1.
29. *Protokoll des Zweiten Welt-Kongresses*, 237; *Desiatyi S"ezd RKP(b): Stenograficheskii Otchet* (Moscow, 1963), 514.
30. Lazitch and Drachkovitch, *Lenin*, I, 132; Braunthal, *History*, II, 144n.
31. *Protokoll des Zweiten Welt-Kongresses*, I, 123.
32. Dennis, *Foreign Policies*, 352; Jane Degras, ed., *The Communist International, 1919–1943: Documents*, I (London, 1956) 453.
33. RTsKhIDNI, F. 2, op. 2, ed. khr. 348. See also Lenin's remarks in L.-O. Frossard, *De Jaurès a Lénine* (Paris, 1930), 137, and Radek's in Lazitch and Drachkovitch, *Lenin*, I, 535.
34. *TP*, II, 20–21.
35. N. E. Kakurin and V. A. Melikov, *Voina s Belopolakami* (Moscow, 1925), 67–70; *Direktivy glavnogo komandovaniia*, 673–78. On the intended Soviet attack on Poland in early 1920, see also A. S. Bubnov, S. S. Kamenev, and R. P. Eidenman, eds., *Grazhdanskaia voina, 1918–1921*, III (Moscow, 1928), 309–10, 317–18; and Mawdsley, *Civil War*, 250–51.
36. Kakurin and Melikov, *Voina*, 73.
37. RTsKhIDNI, F. 2, op. 1, ed. khr. 24364.
38. PAN, *Dokumenty*, II, 749–53.
39. Norman Davies, *White Eagle, Red Star* (London, 1972), 84–85, 92.
40. Ivan Stepanov, *S krasnoi armiei na panskuiu Pol'shu* (Moscow, 1920), 78.
41. P. Wandycz, *Soviet-Polish Relations, 1917–1921* (Cambridge, Mass., 1969), 211–12.
42. Kakurin and Melikov, *Voina*, 206.
43. L. Trotskii, *Moia zhizn'*, II, (Berlin, 1930), 192–95; *Direktivy glavnogo komandovaniia*, 641–42.
44. Wandycz, *Soviet-Polish Relations*, 215; Kakurin and Melikov, *Voina*, 475–76.
45. L. L. Lorwin, *Labor and Internationalism* (London, 1929), 207.
46. Degras, *Communist International*, I, 133–34.
47. Zinoviev in *Protokoll des Zweiten Welt-Kongresses*, 111; Degras, *Communist International*, I, 127.
48. *Protokoll des Zweiten Welt-Kongresses*, 119, 124; Lenin, *PSS*, XLI, 191.
49. Degras, *Communist International*, I, 131.
50. Lenin, *PSS*, XLI, 54–55.
51. Degras, *Communist International*, I, 150–55.
52. *Protokoll des Zweiten Welt-Kongresses*, 470; see *RR*, 179.
53. *Ibid.*, II, 477–78.
54. Lazitch and Drachkovitch, *Lenin*, 346–47, 349.
55. *Ibid.*, 53–54.
56. *Protokoll des zweiten Welt-Kongresses*, 583.
57. Braunthal, *History*, II, 182.

58. Jozef Pilsudski, "Rok 1920," in *Pisma zbiorowe*, VII (Warsaw, 1937), 20.
59. Davies, *White Eagle*, 34.
60. *Ibid.*, 153.
61. Lenin, *PSS*, LI, 264–66.
62. *TP*, II, 278–79.
63. *Ibid.*, II, 176–77.
64. S. Budennyi, *Proidennyi Put'*, II (Moscow, 1965), 304.
65. *Direktivy glavnogo komandovaniia*, 709.
66. Dmitrii Volkogonov, *Triumf i tragediia*, I, Pt. 1 (Moscow, 1989), 103.
67. Leon Trotsky, *Stalin* (London, 1947), 328–32.
68. *LS*, XXXIV, 345.
69. Titus Komarnicki, *Rebirth of the Polish Republic* (London, 1957), 683.
70. Piotr Wandycz in *JCEA*, XIX, No. 4 (1960), 357–65.
71. *L'Information*, August 21, 1920, cited by Wandycz, *ibid.*, 363.
72. Mawdsley, *Civil War*, 254.
73. Viscount d'Abernon, *The Eighteenth Decisive Battle of the World: Warsaw, 1920* (London, 1931), 49.
74. Pilsudski, *Pisma*, VII, 119.
75. Davies, *White Eagle*, 197–98.
76. F. A. Arciszewski, *Cud nad Wisla* (London [1958]), 119; D'Abernon, *Eighteenth Decisive Battle*, 77, 107–08; G. F. Krivosheev, ed., *Grif sekretnosti sniat* (Moscow, 1993), 28–29.
77. Davies, *White Eagle*, 207.
78. RTsKhIDNI, F. 2, op. 2, ed. khr. 454; also *ibid.*, ed. khr. 717.
79. Trotskii, *Moia zhizn'*, II, 193–94.
80. RTsKhIDNI, F. 5, op. 1, delo 2103, list 42.
81. Chiang Chung-cheng [Chiang Kai-shek], *Soviet Russia in China* (New York, 1957), 22.
82. Angelica Balabanoff, *Impressions of Lenin* (Ann Arbor, Mich., 1964), 87–88, and *My Life*, 276–77.
83. Godfrey Scheele, *The Weimar Republic* (London, 1946), 149.
84. Braunthal, *History*, II, 224; Flechtheim, *Kommunistische Partei*, 70–71.
85. Flechtheim, *Kommunistische Partei*, 73–75; Braunthal, *History*, II, 226–28.
86. Degras, *Communist International*, I, 216.
87. Braunthal, *History*, II, 189.
88. Stephen Graubard, *British Labour and the Russian Revolution, 1917–1924* (Cambridge, Mass., 1956), 147–48, 151–52.
89. Lenin, *PSS*, XLI, 38.
90. Lorwin, *Labor and Internationalism*, 202.
91. Lazitch and Drachkovitch, *Lenin*, 216–23.
92. Neil McInnes in *The Impact of the Russian Revolution, 1917–1967* (London, 1967), 65.
93. Borkenau, *World Communism*, 192. Cf. McInnes in *The Impact*, 106.
94. Borkenau, *ibid.*, 210.
95. *Ibid.*, 205.
96. Balabanoff, *Impressions*, 29.
97. Walter Kendall, *The Revolutionary Movement in Britain, 1900–1921* (London, 1969), 245–46.
98. L.-O. Frossard, *De Jaurès à Léon Blum* (Paris, 1943), 140.
99. Max Shachtman in Preface to Leon Trotsky, *Terrorism and Communism* (Ann Arbor, Mich., 1961), p. x.
100. Angelica Balabanoff, *Errinnerungen und Erlebnisse* (Berlin, 1927), 257.
101. F. I. Firsov in *VIKPSS*, No. 10 (1987), 117.
102. *ZhN*, No. 3 (November 24, 1918), 2.
103. *Protokoll des Zweiten Welt-Kongresses*, 137–232. See also Carr, *The Bolshevik Revolution, 1917–1923*, III (New York, 1953), 251–59.

104. Lenin, *PSS*, XLI, 167.
105. Degras, *Communist International*, I, 138–44.
106. Pervyi S"ezd Narodov Vostoka. Baku, 1–8 sentiabria 1920 g., *Stenograficheskii otchet* (Petrograd, 1920).
107. Carr, *Bolshevik Revolution*, III, 248.
108. Leonard Shapiro, ed., *Soviet Treaty Series*, I (Washington, D.C., 1950), 100–2.
109. Xenia Joukoff Eudin and Robert C. North, *Soviet Russia and the East, 1920–1927* (Stanford, 1957), 113–16.
110. Richard Lowenthal in *The Impact of the Russian Revolution*, 292.
111. Eudin and North, *Soviet Russia and the East*, 95–103; Carr, *Bolshevik Revolution*, III, 242–44, 470.
112. RTsKhIDNI, F. 2, op. 2, delo 451.
113. *Izvestiia*, No. 251 (November 9, 1920), 1–2.
114. *Ibid.*, No. 255 (November 11, 1922), 1.
115. *RR*, 128.
116. Braunthal, *History*, II, 269.
117. Eugene Lyons, *Assignment in Utopia* (New York, 1937), 70, 94–95.
118. RTsKhIDNI, F. 2, op. 2, ed. khr. 270.
119. Mrs. Philip Snowden, *Through Bolshevik Russia* (London, 1920).
120. *Ibid.*, 114.
121. *Ibid.*, 188.
122. British Labour Delegation to Russia 1920, *Report* (London, [1920]), 27.
123. H. G. Wells, *Russia in the Shadows* (London [1920 or 1921]), 11.
124. *Ibid.*, 55, 63.
125. *Ibid.*, 90.
126. The Bullitt Mission to Russia: Testimony before the Committee on Foreign Relations, U.S. Senate by William C. Bullitt (New York, 1919). On him see: Beatrice Farnsworth, *William C. Bullitt and the Soviet Union* (Bloomington, Ind., 1967).
127. *The Bullitt Mission*, 50.
128. Karl Kautsky, *Die Diktatur des Proletariats*, 4th ed. (Vienna, 1919), 3.
129. Otto Bauer, *Bolschewismus oder Sozialdemokratie?* (Vienna, 1921), 69.
130. Graubard, *British Labour*, 81.
131. *Ibid.*, 242–43.
132. Peter G. Filene, *Americans and the Soviet Experiment, 1917–1933* (Cambridge, Mass., 1967), 53–54.
133. *Ibid.*, 36.
134. Wells, *Russia in the Shadows*, 117.
135. George Lansbury, *What I Saw in Russia* (London 1920), xiv.
136. James Crowl, *Angels in Stalin's Paradise* (Lanham, Md., 1982), 41.
137. Lyons, *Assignment*, 101.
138. Balabanoff, *Impressions*, 105.
139. Lyons, *Assignment*, 67.
140. Alfred Sherman in *Survey*, No. 41 (April 1962), 83.
141. Arthur Koestler, *The Invisible Writing* (New York, 1954), 402.
142. Malcolm Muggeridge, *Chronicles of Wasted Time: The Green Stick* (New York, 1973), 272.
143. Koestler, *Invisible Writing*, 53.
144. Anna Strong, *I Change Worlds* (New York, 1937), 90.
145. David Caute, *Fellow-travellers*, rev. ed. (New Haven and London, 1988), 97.
146. Robert A. Rosenstone, *Romantic Revolutionary: A Biography of John Reed* (New York, 1981), 11–13.
147. *Ibid.*, 4.
148. Robert Hallowell in *The New Republic*, November 17, 1920, 298.
149. See A. Startsev, *Russkie bloknoty Dzhona Rida* (Moscow, 1977), 25 and *passim.*

150. *The Modern Monthly*, X, No. 3 (January 1937), 3.
151. Louise Bryant, *Mirrors of Moscow* (New York, 1937), 48–49.
152. Lincoln Steffens, *Letters*, II (Westport, Conn., 1974), 759.
153. Simon I. Liberman, *Building Lenin's Russia* (Chicago, 1945), 127.
154. Cited in Jordan A. Schwarz, *The Speculator: Bernard M. Baruch in Washington, 1917–1925* (Chapel Hill, N.C., 1981), 485.
155. *The Times*, February 11, 1920, 9.
156. Cited in Filene, *Americans*, 121, 123.
157. *RR*, 622–23.
158. Note to British, French, and Italian governments of March 1922 in Jane Degras, ed., *Soviet Documents on Foreign Policy*, I (London, 1951), 295.
159. Walter Duranty in *NYT*, October 7, 1921, 1.
160. Filene, *Americans*, 106; Dennis, *Foreign Policies*, 379.
161. Richard Pipes, *Struve: Liberal on the Right* (Cambridge, Mass., 1980), 273.
162. G. G. Shvittau, *Revoliutsiia i narodnoe khoziaistvo v Rossii (1917–1921)* (Leipzig, 1922), 337.
163. Carr, *Bolshevik Revolution*, III, 163.
164. RTsKhIDNI, F. 2, op. 2, delo 969.
165. *Ibid.*, delo 1026.
166. *Ibid.*, delo 1105.
167. E. L. Woodward and Rohan Butler, eds., *Documents on British Foreign Policy, 1919–1939*, First Series, II (London, 1948), 874.
168. Memo by E. F. Wise, in *ibid.*, 867n–70n.
169. John M. Thompson, *Russia, Bolshevism, and the Versailles Peace* (Princeton, 1966), 346–47.
170. Lenin, *PSS*, XL, 377, note 33.
171. *Izvestiia*, No. 149 (July 9, 1920), 1.
172. The Department of State, *Papers Relating to the Foreign Relations of the United States, 1920*, III (Washington, D.C., 1936), 466–68.
173. *House of Commons*, Fifth Series, CXIV (April 16, 1919), 2943.
174. Martin Gilbert, *Winston S. Churchill*, IV (Boston, 1975), 331, 349.
175. *Ibid.*, IV, 379–80.
176. Ullman, *Anglo-Soviet Accord*, 94.
177. *Ibid.*, 92.
178. Gilbert, *Churchill*, IV, 416. Dated July 23, 1920.
179. Ullman, *Anglo-Soviet Accord*, 96.
180. *Ibid.*, 104. Cf. I. Maiskii, *Vneshniaia politika RSFSR, 1917–1922* (Moscow, 1923), 96.
181. Gilbert, *Churchill*, IV, 416.
182. Kautsky, *Die Diktatur*, 3.
183. *Terrorismus und Kommunismus: Ein Beitrag zur Naturgeschichte der Revolution* (Berlin, 1919).
184. Lenin, *PSS*, XXXVII, 105, 107.
185. Trotsky, *Terrorism and Communism*, 168–70.
186. Borkenau, *World Communism*, 87.
187. Paul Levi, ed., *Die Russische Revolution: Eine kritische Würdigung; Aus dem Nachlass von Rosa Luxemburg* ([Berlin], 1922), 65–120. Additional passages can be found in Felix Weil, ed., in *Archiv für die Geschichte des Sozialismus und der Arbeiterbewegung*, XIII (1928), 285–98.
188. Levi, ed., *Die Russische Revolution*, 107–8.
189. *Ibid.*, 109.
190. *Ibid.*, 110–11.
191. *Ibid.*, 113.
192. *Ibid.*, 116.
193. Cited in Braunthal, *History*, II, 127. See also Flechtheim, *Kommunistische Partei*, 41.

194. Braunthal, *History,* II, 131.

195. Trotsky, *Terrorism and Communism,* 58.

196. *Pravda,* No. 266 (November 23, 1923), 1.

197. Leonid Luks, *Enstehung der kommunistischen Faschismustheorie* (Stuttgart, 1984), 84.

198. On this, see Rudolf-Dieter Müller, *Das Tor zur Weltmacht* (Boppard am Rhein, 1984).

199. Thompson, *Russia, Bolshevism,* 319; Dennis, *Foreign Policies,* 92.

200. Flechtheim, *Kommunistische Partei,* 55.

201. On this subject, see O.-E. Schüddekopf, *Linke Leute von Rechts* (Stuttgart, 1960).

202. Cited in Freund, *Unholy Alliance,* 129. See further Müller, *Das Tor,* 23–24.

203. Paul Eltzbacher, *Der Bolshewismus und die deutsche Zukunft* (Jena, 1919).

204. Radek in *KN,* No. 10 (October 1926), 155–66.

205. Ruth Fischer, *Stalin and German Communism* (Cambridge, Mass., 1948), 206–7.

206. Walther Rathenau, *Briefe,* II (Dresden, 1926), 220, 229–30, 233.

207. *Sovetsko-Germanskie Otnosheniia,* II, 138–40. Chicherin's warning to Germany: *ibid.,* 137–38.

208. *Ibid.,* 222–23.

209. Gustav Hilger and Alfred G. Meyer, *The Incompatible Allies* (New York, 1953), 17–26.

210. Hans von Seeckt, *Gedanken eines Soldaten,* 2nd ed. (Leipzig, 1935), 92.

211. Further on him: G.F.W. Hallgarten in *JMH,* vol. 21, No. 1 (March 1949), 28–34, and Lionel Kochan in *Contemporary Review,* No. 1015 (July 1950), 37–40. Seeckt was a prolific writer; his books include *The Future of the German Empire* (London, 1930) and *Wege deutscher Aussenpolitik* (Leipzig, 1931).

212. Hans von Seeckt, *Aus seinem Leben, 1918–1936* (Leipzig, 1940), 474–81.

213. Helm Speidel in *VfZ,* I, No. 1 (1953), 9; Hans W. Gatzke in *AHR,* Vol. 63, No. 3 (1958), 566.

214. See Freund, *Unholy Alliance,* 201–12; F. L. Carsten in *Survey,* No. 44–45 (October 1962), 114–32; Hans W. Gatzke in *AHR,* Vol. 63, No. 3 (April 1958), 565–97; and Walter Laqueur, *Russia and Germany* (London, 1965), 130–31. Very important archival materials on Soviet-German military collaboration from 1919 to 1933 are reproduced in Iu. L. Diakov and T. S. Busheva, *Fashistskii mech kovalsia v SSSR* (Moscow, 1992).

215. Müller, *Das Tor,* 34.

216. Cited by Carsten in *Survey,* October 1962, 115–16. See further Komarnicki, *Rebirth,* 643.

217. RTsKhIDNI, F. 2, op. 2 delo 1132; letter dated February 11, 1922.

218. Müller, *Das Tor,* 31–32.

219. Freund, *Unholy Alliance,* 70.

220. Otto Gessler, *Reichswehrpolitik in der Weimarer Zeit* (Stuttgart, 1958), 185–88.

221. *Sovetsko-Germanskie Otnosheniia,* II, 119–20. Letter dated June 4, 1919.

222. *Ibid.,* 153.

223. *Ibid.,* 122–23.

224. *Ibid.,* 163–64.

225. *Ibid.,* 248–50.

226. Cited in Freund, *Unholy Alliance,* 84.

227. RTsKhIDNI, F. 5, op. 1, delo 2137; F. 2, op. 2, 781 and 1328.

228. Wipert von Blücher, *Deutschlands Weg nach Rapallo* (Wiesbaden, 1951), 151.

229. Bertrand Russell, *Bolshevism* (New York, 1920), 40.

230. See Chapter 6.

231. *BSE,* 3rd ed., XXII (Moscow, 1975), 309.

232. Fred Kupferman, *Au pays des Soviets: Le voyage français en Union soviétique, 1917–1939* (Paris, 1979), 173–75.

233. Ordinance of December 21, 1917, in *SUiR,* No. 12 (December 30, 1917), 183–84. See further, Iurii Felshtinskii, *K istorii nashei zakrytosti* (London, 1988).

234. Muggeridge, *Chronicles,* 223.

235. *The History of the Times,* IV (London, 1952), Pt. 1, 465–66, and Pt. 2, 911–12.

236. Ullman, *Anglo-Soviet Accord,* 272.

237. *The Times*, No. 42,493 (August 19, 1920), 10.
238. Ullman, *Anglo-Soviet Accord*, 270–73, 283–84; Kendall, *The Revolutionary Movement*, 253–54; and Christopher Andrew, *Her Majesty's Secret Service* (New York, 1986), 262–64.
239. *The New Republic*, Supplement, August 4, 1920, 10.
240. Crowl, *Angels*, 12–13.
241. This information and that which follows on Duranty is based on Crowl's *Angels, passim.* See also S. J. Taylor, *Stalin's Apologist* (Oxford, 1990).
242. *NYT*, August 13, 1921, 1.
243. *Ibid.*, September 28, 1921, 21.
244. Crowl, *Angels*, 35.
245. *Ibid.*, 34–35; Joseph Finder, *Red Carpet* (New York, 1983), 67.
246. Lyons, *Assignment*, 67.
247. Walter Duranty, *I write as I please* (New York, 1935), 200.
248. *NYT*, May 3, 1932, 6.
249. *Ibid.*, September 28, 1932, 5.
250. Crowl, *Angels*, 24, and *passim.*
251. Paul Miliukov, *Bolshevism: An International Danger* (London, 1920).
252. Borkenau, *World Communism*, 413.
253. See, *e.g.*, Snowden, *Through Bolshevik Russia*, 32.
254. *Protokoly zasedanii VTsIKa 4-go sozyva* (Moscow, 1920), 231, 235.
255. RTsKhIDNI, F. 2, op. 1, ed. khr. 24694. Document dated September 8, 1921.
256. Kendall, *The Revolutionary Movement*, 229.
257. John S. Clarke in *The Communist*, I, No. 8 (September 23, 1920), 2; Graubard, *British Labour*, 136–37.
258. Balabanoff, *My Life*, 220.
259. Balabanoff, *Impressions*, 103, 28–30.
260. Boris Sokolov, *Bol'sheviki o Bol'shevikakh* (Paris, 1919), 91–92.

5. Communism, Fascism, and National Socialism

1. Jean Touchard, *Histoire des idées politiques*, II (Paris, 1959), 696.
2. *E.g.*, Carl J. Friedrich, *Totalitarianism* (Cambridge, Mass., 1954); Ernst Nolte, ed., *Theorien über den Faschismus* (Koln-Berlin, 1967); Renzo de Felice, *Le interpretazioni del Fascismo* (Bari, 1972); Bruno Seidel and Siegfried Jenkner, eds., *Wege der Totalitarismus-Forschung* (Darmstadt, 1968); and Ernest A. Menze, ed., *Totalitarianism Reconsidered* (Port Washington, N.Y., and London, 1981).
3. Karl Bracher, *Die deutsche Diktatur*, 2nd ed. (Cologne-Berlin, 1969).
4. *RR*, Chapter 12.
5. Hans Buchheim, *Totalitarian Rule* (Middletown, Conn., 1968), 25.
6. Hannah Arendt, *The Origins of Totalitarianism* (New York, 1958), 319.
7. Peter Christian Ludz in Seidel and Jenkner, *Wege*, 536. See the pioneering works of Ernst Fraenkel, *The Dual State* (New York, 1941); Sigmund Neumann, *Permanent Revolution* (New York and London, 1942); and Franz Naumann, *Behemoth* (London, 1943). In the first postwar decade, the major studies of totalitarianism were also written by German émigrés, notably Arendt, *Origins*, and Friedrich, *Totalitarianism*.
8. Carl J. Friedrich and Zbigniew K. Brzezinski, *Totalitarian Dictatorship and Autocracy* (Cambridge, Mass., 1956).
9. Leonid Luks, *Entstehung der kommunistischen Faschismustheorie* (Stuttgart, 1984), 177.
10. Axel Kuhn, *Das faschistische Herrschaftssystem und die moderne Gesellschaft* (Hamburg, 1973), 22.
11. Seidel and Jenkner in *Wege*, 26. The same objection is raised by Kuhn in *Das faschistische Herrschaftssystem*, 87.
12. Buchheim, *Totalitarian Rule*, 38–39.

13. Friedrich, *Totalitarianism,* 49.

14. Among the works that deal seriously with Mussolini's early socialism and its affinities to Lenin's Bolshevism are Renzo de Felice's *Mussolini il rivoluzionario, 1883-1920* (Turin, 1965); Gaudens Megaro's *Mussolini in the Making* (Boston and New York, 1938); two studies by A. James Gregor, *Young Mussolini and the Intellectual Origins of Fascism* (Berkeley, 1979) and *The Fascist Persuasion in Politics* (Princeton, 1974); and essays by Domenico Settembrini, "Mussolini and Lenin," in George R. Urban, ed., *Euro-communism* (New York, 1978), 146-78, and "Mussolini and the Legacy of Revolutionary Socialism," in George L. Mosse, ed., *International Fascism* (London and Beverly Hills, 1979), 91-123.

15. Benito Mussolini, *Opera Omnia,* III (Florence, 1952), 137.

16. Angelica Balabanoff, *My Life as a Rebel* (New York, 1938), 44-52.

17. Mussolini, *Opera Omnia,* II (Florence, 1951), 31, and IV (Florence, 1952), 153.

18. *Ibid.,* IV, 156.

19. A. Rossi, *The Rise of Italian Fascism, 1918-1922* (London, 1938), 134.

20. Carl J. Friedrich, *The New Image of the Common Man* (Boston, 1950), 246.

21. De Felice, *Mussolini,* 122-23.

22. Gregor, *The Fascist Persuasion,* 145.

23. Editorial of January 9, 1910, in Mussolini's *Opera Omnia,* III, 5-7.

24. Gregor, *Young Mussolini,* 135.

25. Lenin, *PSS,* XXI, 409.

26. *La Lotta di Classe,* August 5, 1911, cited in De Felice, *Mussolini,* 104.

27. Mussolini, *Opera Omnia,* VI (Florence, 1953), 311.

28. Ernst Nolte, *Three Faces of Fascism* (London, 1965), 168.

29. Mussolini, *Opera Omnia,* VII (Florence, 1951), 101. See also Gregor, *The Fascist Persuasion,* 171.

30. Mussolini, *loc.cit.*; Gregor, *The Fascist Persuasion,* 168-71.

31. Lenin, *PSS,* XLVIII, 155.

32. Rossi, *The Rise,* 19.

33. De Felice, *Mussolini,* 742-45.

34. *Ibid.,* 730.

35. Rossi, *The Rise,* 39.

36. *Ibid.,* 163.

37. Nolte, *Theorien,* 231.

38. Rossi, *The Rise,* 134-35.

39. *Ibid.,* 138.

40. Erwin von Beckerath, *Wesen und Werden des faschistischen Staates* (Berlin, 1927), 109-10.

41. Yvon de Begnac, *Palazzo Venezia: Storia di un Regime* (Rome, [1950]), 361.

42. Hermann Rauschning, *Hitler Speaks* (London, 1939), 134.

43. Mussolini, *Opera Omnia,* XXIX (Florence, 1959), 63-64; *cf.* Gregor, *The Fascist Persuasion,* 184-85.

44. Norman Cohn, *Warrant for Genocide* (London, 1967).

45. *Ibid.,* 90-98.

46. *RR,* 586.

47. Erich Ludendorff, *Kriegsführung und Politik* (Berlin, 1922), 51.

48. On him, see Walter Laqueur, *Russia and Germany* (London, 1965), 114-18.

49. F. Vinberg, *Krestnyi put',* I, 2nd ed. (Munich, 1922), 359-72.

50. Cohn, *Warrant,* 293.

51. Laqueur, *Russia and Germany,* 55.

52. Rauschning, *Hitler Speaks,* 235.

53. *Ibid.,* 235-36.

54. Alexander Stein, *Adolf Hitler, Schüler der "Weisen von Zion"* (Karlsbad, 1936).

55. Cohn, *Warrant,* 194-95.

56. Eberhard Jäckel, *Hitlers Weltanschauung* (Tübingen, 1969), cited in Kuhn, *Das faschistische Herrschaftssystem*, 80.

57. Laqueur, *Russia and Germany*, 115.

58. Rauschning, *Hitler Speaks*, 185.

59. Cited in Max H. Kele, *Nazis and Workers* (Chapel Hill, N.C., 1972), 93.

60. David Schoenbaum, *Hitler's Social Revolution* (New York and London, 1980), 25.

61. *Ibid.*, 17.

62. Bracher, *Die deutsche Diktatur*, 59.

63. Schoenbaum, *Hitler's Social Revolution*, 48.

64. Alan Bullock, *Hitler: A Study in Tyranny*, rev. ed. (New York, 1962), 157.

65. *The Impact of the Russian Revolution, 1917–1967* (London, 1967), 340.

66. Rauschning, *Hitler Speaks*, 48–49.

67. *Ibid.*, 242.

68. Schoenbaum, *Hitler's Social Revolution*, xiv.

69. Rauschning, *Hitler Speaks*, 187.

70. Hermann Rauschning, *The Revolution of Nihilism* (New York, 1939), 55, 74–75, 105.

71. *Ibid.*, 19.

72. Pierre Gaxotte, *The French Revolution* (London and New York, 1932), Chapter 12.

73. Anatole Leroy-Beaulieu, *Les Doctrines de Haine* (Paris [1902]). Cf. *RR*, 136–37.

74. Gottfried Feder, *Der deutsche Staat auf nationaler und sozialer Grundlage*, 11th ed. (Munich, 1933).

75. Carl Schmitt in *Archiv für Sozialwissenschaft und Sozialpolitik*, Vol. 58, Pt. 1 (1927), 4–5.

76. Rauschning, *Hitler Speaks*, 134.

77. Angelica Balabanoff, *Errinerungen und Erlebnisse* (Berlin, 1927), 260.

78. *RR*, 510n.

79. Sergio Panunzio, cited in Neumann, *Permanent Revolution*, 130.

80. Aryeh L. Unger, *The Totalitarian Party* (Cambridge, 1974), 85n.

81. Giselher Schmidt, *Falscher Propheten Wahn* (Mainz, 1970), 111.

82. See below, p. 455.

83. Beckerath, *Wesen und Werden*, 112–14.

84. The Communist and Nazi parties are compared in Unger's *Totalitarian Party*. On Hitler's control of the NSDAP before 1933, see Bracher, *Die deutsche Diktatur*, 108, 143.

85. M. Manoilescu, *Die Einzige Partei* (Berlin, [1941]), 93.

86. Buchheim, *Totalitarian Rule*, 93. The subject is the theme of Fraenkel's *Dual State*.

87. Beckerath, *Wesen und Werden*, 141.

88. *RR*, Chapter 12.

89. Bracher, *Die deutsche Diktatur*, 251, 232.

90. Friedrich and Brzezinski, *Totalitarian Dictatorship*, 145.

91. De Felice in Urban, *Euro-communism*, 107.

92. Rossi, *The Rise*, 347–48; emphasis added.

93. Buchheim, *Totalitarian Rule*, 96.

94. George Mosse in *Journal of Contemporary History*, Vol. 14, No. 1 (1989), 15. See further, George Mosse, *Masses and Man* (New York, 1980), 87–103.

95. Carl Landauer and Hans Honegger, eds., *Internationaler faschismus* (Karlsruhe, 1928), 112.

96. H. O. Ziegler, *Autoritäter oder totaler Staat?* (Tübingen, 1932).

97. Unger, *Totalitarian Party*, 71–79.

98. Schoenbaum, *Hitler's Social Revolution*, 82–85.

99. *Ibid.*, 79.

100. Unger, *Totalitarian Party*, 78.

101. Angelica Balabanoff, *Impressions of Lenin* (Ann Arbor, Mich., 1964), 7.

102. Bracher, *Die deutsche Diktatur*, 395.

103. *Strany mira: Ezhegodnyi Spravochnik* (Moscow, 1946), 129.

104. A. James Gregor, *Ideology of Fascism* (New York, 1969), 304–6.
105. Beckrath, *Wesen und Werden*, 143–44.
106. Theodor Maunz in Schoenbaum, *Hitler's Social Revolution*, 146–47. See also Feder, *Der deutsche Staat*, 22.
107. Schoenbaum, *loc. cit.*, 147.
108. Bracher, *Die deutsche Diktatur*, 247.
109. Schoenbaum, *Hitler's Social Revolution*, 114, 116.
110. Neumann, *Permanent Revolution*, 169–70.
111. *Revolution of Nihilism*, 56.
112. Henry A. Turner, Jr., *German Big Business and the Rise of Hitler* (New York, 1985), 340–1.
113. Neumann, *Permanent Revolution*, 170.
114. *RR*, 193, 369–72, 410–12.
115. *Ibid.*, 676–79.
116. Mussolini, *Opera Omnia*, XVII (Florence, 1955), 295.
117. Kele, *Nazis and Workers*, 92.
118. Schoenbaum, *Hitler's Social Revolution*, 3.
119. Gregor, *Fascist Persuasion*, 176–77.
120. Rauschning, *Hitler Speaks*, 113, 229–30.
121. Henry Picker, ed., *Hitlers Tischgespräche im Führerhauptquartier, 1941–1942* (Bonn, 1951), 133.
122. *NYT*, August 31, 1990, A2.
123. Gregor, *Fascist Persuasion*, 148–49.

6. Culture as Propaganda

1. Joseph Brodsky, *Less than One* (New York, 1986), 270–71.
2. This is the theme of Christopher Read's *Culture and Power in Revolutionary Russia* (London, 1990).
3. L. Trotskii, *Literatura i revoliutsiia* (Moscow, 1924), 140.
4. Lenin, *PSS*, XII, 102–3.
5. *Ibid.*, 100.
6. Oskar Anweiler and Karl-Heinz Ruffman, eds., *Kulturpolitik der Sowjetunion* (Stuttgart, 1973), 19.
7. Trotskii, *Literatura i revoliutsiia*, 11, 141–42.
8. V. I. Charnoluskii, *Shkol'noe zakonodatel'stvo v RSFSR* (Moscow, 1927), 13.
9. Sheila Fitzpatrick, *The Commissariat of Enlightenment* (Cambridge, 1970), 19.
10. Richard Pipes, *Russia under the Old Regime* (London and New York, 1974), 254.
11. V. Sirin [V. Nabokov], *Rul'*, No. 2, 120 (November 18, 1927), 2.
12. Marc Slonim, *Russian Theater* (Cleveland and New York, 1961), 229; Alexander Blok, *Sobranie sochinenii v vos'mi tomakh*, I (Moscow-Leningrad, 1960), pp. l–li.
13. *NZh*, No. 183/177 (November 17, 1917), 4.
14. Trotskii, *Literatura i revoliutsiia*, 17, 19.
15. Vera Alexandrova, *A History of Soviet Literature* (New York, 1963), 19.
16. N. Bychkova and A. Lebedev, *Pervyi narkom prosveshcheniia* (Moscow, 1960), 23.
17. *Lunacharskii o narodnom obrazovanii* (Moscow, 1958), 117.
18. *PiR*, No. 1 (May–July 1921), 3–9.
19. *E.g.*, Bogdanov, *Iz psikhologii obshchestva* (St. Petersburg, 1904), and *Kul'turnye zadachi nashego vremeni* (Moscow, 1911).
20. *PK*, No. 15–16 (April–July 1920), 50.
21. *Ibid.*, 50–52.
22. Jutta Scherrer in *Cahiers*, No. 19 (1978), 259–84.
23. Lenin, *PSS*, XLI, 304–5.
24. *Ibid.*, XII, 99–100.

25. Decree of November 9, 1917, in *Dekrety*, I, 61.

26. V. Kerzhentsev in *PK*, No. 5 (November 1918), 24.

27. *Tvori!*, No. 2 (1921), 17.

28. *Pervaia Moskovskaia Obshchegorodskaia Konferentsiia Proletarskikh Kul'turno-Pros-vetitel'nykh Organizatsii* (Moscow, [1918]), 39; Wladimir Berelowitch, *La Soviétisation de l'école russe, 1917–1931* (Lausanne, 1990), 52.

29. *PK*, No. 9/10 (1919), 44.

30. Richard Stites, *Revolutionary Dreams* (New York, 1989), 155.

31. Anweiler and Ruffman, *Kulturpolitik*, 196.

32. *Pervaia Moskovskaia Obshchegorodskaia Konferentsiia*, 61.

33. P. I. Lebedev-Polianskii (Valerian Polianskii) in *PK*, No. 1 (July 1918), 6.

34. V. V. Gorbunov in *VIKPSS*, No. 1 (1958), 24–39.

35. A. F. Kerensky and R. P. Browder, *The Russian Provisional Government, 1917* (Stanford, 1961), I, 228; II, 977–79.

36. *RR*, 521–22.

37. Lenin, *PSS*, XLIV, 79.

38. *Znamia truda*, No. 134 (February 17, 1918), 1.

39. There exists no authoritative history of Communist censorship. For legislative materials, see L. G. Fogelevich, ed., *Deistvuiushchee zakonodatel'stvo o pechati*, 2nd ed. (Moscow, 1929).

40. A. Z. Okorokov, *Oktiabr' i krakh russkoi burzhuaznoi pressy* (Moscow, 1970), 168n–70n.

41. *Gazeta Vremennogo Rabochego i Krest'ianskogo Pravitel'stva*, December 24, 1917, cited in Okorokov, *Oktiabr'*, 203.

42. *Dekrety*, I, 432–34. See also M. Shchelkunov in *PiR*, No. 7 (1922), 180.

43. Okorokov, *Oktiabr'*, 203–4, 343–76.

44. Shchelkunov in *PiR*, No. 7 (1922), 179–80.

45. *Dekrety*, I, 54–56.

46. I. S. Smirnov, *Lenin i russkaia kul'tura* (Moscow, 1960), 110.

47. Lenin, *PSS*, XXXVI, 100.

48. *NZh*, No. 90/305 (May 15, 1918), 3.

49. Shchelkunov in *PiR*, No. 7 (1922), 180.

50. *Novyi vechernyi chas*, No. 108 (July 8, 1918), 1.

51. *Pravda*, No. 140 (July 9, 1918), 2.

52. *Ibid.*, No. 155 (July 26, 1918), 3.

53. *Dekrety*, II, 553.

54. Smirnov, *Lenin*, 110.

55. Pipes, *Russia under the Old Regime*, 129, 255–56.

56. *Dekrety*, V, 243–44.

57. A. I. Nazarov, *Oktiabr' i kniga* (Moscow, 1968), 137.

58. *Knizhnyi ugol* (Petrograd), No. 8 (1922), 60.

59. RTsKhIDNI, F. 2, op. 2, ed. khr. 940.

60. *Izvestiia*, No. 137 (June 23, 1922), 5.

61. S. A. Fediukin, *Bor'ba kommunisticheskoi partii s burzhuaznoi ideologiei v pervye gody NEP'a* (Moscow, 1977), 171–72; dated February 10, 1922.

62. *Literaturnaia Entsiklopediia*, II (1929), 543–46.

63. Panteleimon Romanov, *Pravo na zhizn'* (Letchworth, England, 1970), 24–25.

64. *Dekrety*, I, 296–98; IV, 68–70; V, 412.

65. Nazarov, *Oktiabr' i kniga*, 136.

66. "*Ia boius'* " in E. Zamiatin, *Litsa* (New York, 1955), 190.

67. Cited in Trotskii's *Literatura i revoliutsiia*, 45. See further Blok's "O naznachenii poeta," in his *Sobranie sochinenii v vos'mi tomakh*, VI (Moscow-Leningrad, 1963), 160–68.

68. Walter L. Adamson in *AHR*, No. 2 (1990), 359–90; Vladimir Markov, *Russian Futurism: A History* (Berkeley and Los Angeles, 1968).

69. Joshua C. Taylor, *Futurism* (New York, 1961), 124–25.

70. Alexandrova, Soviet Literature, 60.
71. Edward J. Brown, Russian Literature Since the Revolution, rev. ed. (New York, 1969), 37.
72. LN, Vol. 65 (1958), 210.
73. Bengt Jangfeldt in Scando-Slavica, Vol. 33 (1987), 129–39.
74. Fediukin, Bor'ba, 223–24.
75. Demian Bednyi, Sobranie sochinenii v vos'mi tomakh, III (Moscow, 1964), 185.
76. Trotskii, Literatura i revoliutsiia, 162.
77. F. I. Shaliapin, Maska i dusha (Paris, 1932), 276.
78. Blok, Sobranie sochinenii, VII, 356–57.
79. Ibid., VII, 365.
80. Vassily Aksyonov in Partisan Review, No. 2 (1992), 182.
81. Dekrety, VI, 69–73.
82. Le Théâtre d'Agit-Prop de 1917 à 1932, 4 vols. (Lausanne, 1977–78), and René Fülöp-Miller, Geist und Gesicht des Bolschewismus (Zürich, 1926), 157–206.
83. Izvestiia, No. 240 (October 27, 1920), 2.
84. V. V. Maiakovskii, Polnoe sobranie sochinenii v dvenadtsati tomakh, III (Moscow, 1930), 59, 86.
85. Fülöp-Miller, Geist und Gesicht, 187–88.
86. Peter Gorsen and Eberhard Knödler-Bunte, Proletkult, II (Stuttgart, 1975), 127–28.
87. Lef, No. 4 (August–December 1924), 218.
88. A. Ia. Altshuller, et al., eds., Teatr i dramaturgiia (Leningrad, 1967), 143–44.
89. Frantisek Deak in The Drama Review, Vol. 19, No. 2 (T-66, June 1975), 7–22.
90. Richard Taylor and Ian Christie, The Film Factory (Cambridge, Mass., 1988), 57. On this subject see further Jay Leyda, Kino (London, 1960), 111–69; Richard Taylor, The Politics of the Soviet Cinema, 1917–1929 (Cambridge, 1979), 26–86; and Denise J. Youngblood, Soviet Cinema in the Silent Era, 1918–1935 (Ann Arbor, Mich., 1985), 1–38.
91. Cited in Taylor and Christie, The Film Factory, 47.
92. Taylor, Politics, 56.
93. Decree of August 27, 1919, in Dekrety, VI, 75–76.
94. Luda and Jean Schnitzer et al., eds., Cinema in Revolution (London, 1973), 71.
95. Dekrety, II, 94–95.
96. Fülöp-Miller, Geist und Gesicht, 150.
97. Aleksei Gan, Konstruktivizm (Tver, 1922), 3, 18, 48.
98. Christina Loder, Russian Constructivism (New Haven and London, 1983), 2–3.
99. The Henry Art Gallery, Art into Life: Russian Constructivism, 1914–1932 (Seattle, Wash., 1990), 47.
100. John E. Bowlt in Abbot Gleason, et al., eds., Bolshevik Culture (Bloomington, Ind., 1985), 203.
101. Anweiler and Ruffman, Kulturpolitik, 260–62. On Chagall's relations with the Communists, see Read, Culture and Power, 89–91.
102. Fülöp-Miller, Geist und Gesicht, 139.
103. Boris Schwarz, Music and Musical Life in Soviet Russia (Bloomington, Ind., 1972), 18–19.
104. Ibid., 19–20.
105. Ibid., 61, 63.
106. Fülöp-Miller, Geist und Gesicht, 245.
107. Jeffrey Brooks in William M. Todd III, ed., Literature and Society in Imperial Russia (Stanford, 1978), 97–150; Ia. Iakovlev, Derevnia kak ona est' (Moscow, 1923), 86.
108. A. V. Lunacharskii in Literaturnaia gazeta, No. 4–5/232–33 (January 29, 1933), 1; Dekrety, II, 95–96, 644, and III, 47–48, 118–19; Lenin, PSS, L, 182; Smirnov, Lenin, 347–69.
109. Izvestiia, No. 155/419 (July 24, 1918), 4–5.
110. Berelowitch, La Soviétisation, 10.

111. *RR*, 125–28.

112. Lenin, *PSS*, XXXVII, 76–77.

113. Institut IMELS, *Kommunisticheskaia Partiia Sovetskogo Soiuza v rezoliutsiiakh i resheniiakh S"ezdov, Konferentsii i Plenumov TsK*, I (Moscow, 1953), 419.

114. *Ot doshkol'nogo otdela Narodnogo Komissariata po Prosveshcheniiu: Direktivy i postanovleniia*, II (December 1917), 254, cited in Oskar Anweiler, *Geschichte der Schule und Pedagogik in Russland vom Ende des Zarenreiches bis zum Beginn der Stalin Ära* (Heidelberg, 1964), 150.

115. E. A. Preobrazhenskii, *O morali i klassovykh normakh* (Moscow-Leningrad, 1923), 101.

116. *Dekrety*, II, 358–59.

117. Edward Thaden, *Conservative Nationalism in Nineteenth-Century Russia* (Seattle, 1964), 190.

118. Decree of September 30, 1918, in *Dekrety*, III, 374–80; *Narodnoe obrazovanie v SSSR: Sbornik dokumentov, 1917–1973 g.g.* (Moscow, 1974), 137–45.

119. Anweiler, *Geschichte der Schule*, 190n.

120. Berelowitch, *La Soviétisation*, 65–66.

121. N. K. Krupskaia, *Pedagogicheskie sochineniia v desiati tomakh*, XI (Moscow, 1963), 192.

122. A. V. Lunacharskii, *O narodnom obrazovanii* (Moscow, 1958), 128, 237. See further Anweiler, *Geschichte der Schule*, 123–45.

123. *Direktivy i dokumenty po voprosam pionerskogo dvizheniia* (Moscow, 1959), 72.

124. Ralph T. Fisher, Jr., *Pattern for Soviet Youth* (New York, 1959).

125. Anweiler, *Geschichte der Schule*, 155.

126. F. F. Korolev, *Ocherki po istorii sovetskoi shkoly i pedagogiki, 1917–1920* (Moscow, 1959), 277.

127. N. Ognev [M. G. Rozanov] *Dnevnik Kosti Riabtseva* (Moscow, 1966), 19–20. The book has been translated into English as *The Diary of a Communist Schoolboy* (New York, n.d.).

128. *Kul'turnoe stroitel'stvo SSSR* (Moscow, 1956), 80.

129. Lunacharskii in *Izvestiia*, No. 214 (September 25, 1921), 1.

130. Fitzpatrick, *Commissariat*, 286–88.

131. *Lunacharskii o narodnom obrazovanii*, 245, in Anweiler, *Geschichte der Schule*, 193. See also Anweiler and Ruffman, *Kulturpolitik*, 28–29.

132. Anweiler, *Geschichte der Schule*, 241–42. The results of the survey come from V. N. Shulgin, ed., *Deti i Oktiabr'skaia revoliutsiia: ideologiia sovetskogo shkol'nika* (1928).

133. *NP*, No. 89/90 (1921), 1 ff.

134. The best study of this subject remains Vladimir Zenzinov's *Besprizornye* (Paris, 1929). It has been translated into German and French.

135. *Ibid.*, 99.

136. Lunacharskii in *Izvestiia*, No. 49 (February 26, 1928), 5. Krupskaia in *Pravda*, No. 51 (March 7, 1923), 1.

137. M. Boguslavskii in *KN*, No. 8 (1927), 140–41.

138. Malcolm Muggeridge, *Chronicles of Wasted Time: Chronicle I: The Green Stick* (New York, 1973), 219.

139. Alan Ball in *Jahrbücher*, XXXIX, No. 1 (1991), 40–41.

140. Zenzinov, *Besprizornye*, 96n.

141. *Pravda*, No. 275 (December 2, 1925), 1.

142. See Sh. Kh. Chanbarisov, *Formirovanie sovetskoi universitetskoi sistemy* (Ufa, 1973); James T. McClelland, "Bolsheviks, Professors and the Reform of Higher Education in Soviet Russia, 1917–1921," Ph.D. dissertation, Princeton University, 1970; and *Narodnoe obrazovanie v SSSR: Sbornik Dokumentov, 1917–1973* (Moscow, 1974).

143. McClelland, "Bolsheviks," 105.

144. Cited in V. A. Ulianovskaia, *Formirovanie nauchnoi intelligentsii v SSSR, 1917–1937 gg.* (Moscow, 1966), 54.

145. G. D. Alekseeva, *Oktiabr'skaia revoliutsiia i istoricheskaia nauka, 1917-1923 gg.* (Moscow, 1968), 263-64.

146. Alexander Vucinich, *Empire of Knowledge* (Berkeley, 1984), 91-122; Fitzpatrick, *Commissariat*, 68-73; Smirnov, *Lenin*, 236-97.

147. *Dekrety*, III, 381-82.

148. Terence Emmons, Introduction to *Time of Troubles: The Diary of Iurii Vladimirovich Got'e* (Princeton, 1988), 20; M. Novikov in *Moskovskii Universitet, 1755-1930: Iubileinyi Sbornik* (Paris, 1930), 159.

149. *Dekrety*, IV, 311-12.

150. *Izvestiia*, No. 145 (July 12, 1918), 4; Read, *Culture and Power*, 133-41.

151. McClelland, "Bolsheviks," 219-20.

152. Anweiler, *Geschichte der Schule*, 240-41.

153. See Zev Katz in *SS*, VII, No. 3 (January 1956), 237-47, on these Party-run schools.

154. A. S. Butiagin and Iu. A. Saltanov, *Universitetskoe obrazovanie v SSSR* (Moscow, 1957), 52.

155. *KPSS v rezoliutsiiakh i resheniiakh*, I (Moscow, 1953), 892.

156. *SUiR*, No. 65 (November 9, 1921), Decree No. 486, pp. 593-98. See *RR*, 4.

157. Sergei Zhaba, *Petrogradskoe studenchestvo* (Paris, 1922), 46, and V. Stratonov in *Moskovskii Universitet*, 219-26.

158. Read, *Culture and Power*, 181.

159. Fediukin, *Bor'ba*, 249.

160. Stratonov in *Moskovskii Universitet*, 239-42. See also *Rul'*, No. 535 (September 2, 1922), 4; No. 536 (September 3, 1922), 3; No. 555 (September 26, 1922), 3. More on this, see Chapter 8 below.

161. *Dekrety*, III, 138-41.

162. Novikov and Stratonov in *Moskovskii Universitet*, 158, 201-2.

163. *NP*, No. 6-7 (1919), 142. Cf. Fitzpatrick, *Commissariat*, 77.

164. James C. McClelland in *Past and Present*, No. 80 (August 1978), 123n.

165. *NP*, No. 82 (May 20, 1921), 6.

166. Read, *Culture and Power*, 228.

167. Mervyn Matthews, *Class and Society in Soviet Russia* (New York, 1972), 294.

168. Clara Zetkin, *Errinerungen an Lenin* (Berlin, 1957), 19.

169. *Dekrety*, VII, 50-51.

170. Helen Sullivan in the *Encyclopaedia of the Social Sciences*, IX (New York, 1933), 521.

171. I. M. Bogdanov in *NP*, No. 5 (1928), 113-14.

172. Fülöp-Miller, *Geist und Gesicht*, 402.

173. *Narodnoe khoziaistvo Soiuza SSR v tsifrakh* (Moscow, 1925), 22-23.

174. B. N. Mironov in *ISSSR*, No. 4 (1985), 137-53.

175. I. M. Bogdanov in *NP*, No. 5 (1928), 114.

176. *Ibid.*, 118.

177. Krupskaia, *Pedagogicheskie sochineniia*, IX (Moscow, 1957), 404-8.

178. *Ibid.*, 289.

179. The examples that follow are from André Mazon, *Lexique de la guerre et de la révolution en Russie* (Paris, 1920), and A. M. Selishchev, *Iazyk revoliutsionnoi epokhi*, 2nd ed. (Moscow, 1928).

180. *SUiR*, No. 12 (December 30, 1917), Decree No. 176, pp. 185-86.

181. Preobrazhenskii, *O morali*, 101-2.

182. N. Bukharin, *Teoriia istoricheskogo materializma* (Moscow, 1921), 278-79.

183. Frederick Engels, *The Origin of the Family, Private Property and the State* (New York, 1972), 128, 137-38.

184. *Ibid.*, 139. See further August Bebel's *Woman and Socialism* (New York, 1910).

185. *Dekrety*, I, 237-39.

186. N. A. Semashko, *Health Protection in the USSR* (London, 1934), 82-84.

187. Zlata Lilina, *Sotsial'no-trudovoe vospitanie* (Moscow, 1921), 24, 29.

188. Anweiler, *Geschichte der Schule*, 151–52.

189. Zenzinov, *Besprizornye*, 107.

190. See Alexandra Kollontai, *The Autobiography of a Sexually Emancipated Communist Woman* (New York, 1971). Also Beatrice Farnsworth, *Alexandra Kollontai* (Stanford, 1980).

191. Alexandra Kollontai, *Novaia moral' i rabochii klass* (Moscow, 1919).

192. Clara Zetkin, *Reminiscences of Lenin* (London, 1929), 51–59.

193. I. Gelman, *Polovaia zhizn' sovremennoi molodezhy* (Moscow-Petrograd, 1923), 95.

194. *Ibid.*, 94–95.

195. Sheila Fitzpatrick in *JMH*, No. 2 (1978), 268.

196. *Ibid.*, 269.

197. Gelman, *Polovaia zhizn'*, 79; Fitzpatrick, *loc. cit.*, 265.

198. Gelman, *ibid.*, 80.

199. V. E. Kliachkin in *Sotsial'naia gigiena*, No. 6 (1925), 130, cited in Fitzpatrick, *JMH*, No. 2 (1978), 269.

200. Rudolf Schlesinger, ed., *The Family in the U.S.S.R.* (London, 1949), 271–72.

201. *Ibid.*, 251–54.

202. Lenin, *PSS*, XLV, 23–33; Michel Heller in *Cahiers*, XX, No. 2 (1979), 155.

203. Lenin, *PSS*, LIV, 198. First published in 1959.

204. *Ibid.*, 265–66.

205. RTsKhIDNI, F. 2, op. 1, delo 1338.

206. *SUiR*, No. 51 (September 5, 1922), Decree No. 646, pp. 813–14. Cf. A. P. Kositsyn, ed., *Istoriia sovetskogo gosudarstva i prava*, II (Moscow, 1968), 580.

207. RTsKhIDNI, F. 2, op. 2, delo 1245. Further on this, see Michel Heller in *Cahiers*, XX, No. 2 (1979), 131–72, especially 163–64; and Fediukin, *Bor'ba*, 177. Also Fediukin, *Velikii Oktiabr' i intelligentsiia* (Moscow, 1972), 287.

7. The Assault on Religion

1. Christopher Read, *Religion, Revolution and the Russian Intelligentsia, 1900–1912* (London, 1979), 13.

2. Cited in F. O. Oleshchuk, ed., *Pochemu nelzia verit' v Boga* (Moscow, 1965), 221–22.

3. Cited in Oskar Anweiler, *Geschichte der Schule und Pädagogik in Russland* (Berlin, 1964), 236.

4. Lenin, *PSS*, XI, 142–47; XVIII, 230–33; XLVIII, 226.

5. Cited in A. A. Valentinov, *Chërnaia kniga* (Paris, 1925), 19.

6. René Fülöp-Miller, *Geist und Gesicht des Bolshewismus* (Zurich, 1926), 356.

7. *Izvestiia*, No. 5/1,742 (January 10, 1923), 4.

8. John S. Curtiss, *The Russian Church and the Soviet State* (Boston, 1953), 10.

9. B. V. Titlinov, *Tserkov' vo vremia revoliutsii* (Petrograd, 1924), 56–58.

10. Alexander Kerensky and Robert Paul Browder, eds., *The Russian Provisional Government: Documents*, II (Stanford, Calif., 1961), 813–14, 818–19; Matthew Spinka, *The Church and the Russian Revolution* (New York, 1927), 115; William C. Emhardt, *Religion in Soviet Russia* (Milwaukee, Wis., and London, 1929), 4.

11. Curtiss, *Russian Church*, 20–21; Bohdan R. Bociurkiw in Taras Hunchak, ed., *The Ukraine, 1917–1921* (Cambridge, Mass., 1977), 221.

12. Archbishop Ioann Shakhovskoi, *Vera i dostovernost'* (Paris, 1982), 27.

13. Irinarkh Stratonov, *Russkaia tserkovnaia smuta, 1921–1931 gg.* (Berlin, 1932), 12–13.

14. *Tserkovnye vedomosti*, No. 36–37 (1917), 311–13, cited in Lev Regelson, *Tragediia russkoi tserkvi, 1917–1945* (Paris, 1977), 209–10.

15. Francis McCullagh, *The Bolshevik Persecution of Christianity* (London, 1924), 14, 77.

16. Emhardt, *Religion*, 7–8.

17. Valentinov, *Chërnaia kniga*, 160–61; *Rul'*, No. 791 (July 8, 1923), 3; and Grigorii Trubetskoi in *Rul'*, No. 798 (July 17, 1923), 2.

18. A. N. Anfimov and I. F. Makarov in *ISSSR*, No.1 (1974), 85.
19. *Dekrety*, I, 247–49.
20. Emhardt, *Religion*, 19.
21. *Dekrety*, I, 374; *NZh*, No. 3 (January 5, 1918), 2; *NZh*, No. 18 (January 25, 1918), 4; *Izvestiia*, No.8/272 (January 12, 1918), 1; Titlinov, *Tserkov'*, 106.
22. See, for example, John Haynes Holmes in *The Nation*, No. 3,018 (May 9, 1923), 542.
23. *Dekrety*, II, 561; P. V. Gidulianov, *Tserkov' i gosudarstvo po zakonodatel'stvu RSFSR* (Moscow, 1923), 53–60.
24. Circular of March 3, 1919, in Gidulianov, *Tserkov'*, 27.
25. *Sobranie kodeksov R.S.F.S.R.*, 3rd ed. (Moscow, 1925), 549.
26. Titlinov, *Tserkov'*, 119–20.
27. Curtiss, *Russian Church*, 57.
28. *RR*, 725.
29. *RiTs*, No. 9–12 (1920), 83.
30. *Tserkovnye vedomosti*, No. 9–10 (1918), cited in Regelson, *Tragediia*, 234–35.
31. Regelson, *Tragediia*, 251–55.
32. Curtiss, *Russian Church*, 90–91.
33. Regelson, *Tragediia*, 259–62.
34. *Ibid.*, 262–64.
35. Grigorii Trubetskoi in *Rul'*, No. 798 (July 17, 1923), 2.
36. RTsKhIDNI, F. 5, op. 1, delo 120, list 8.
37. D. M. Pospielovsky, *Soviet Antireligious Campaigns and Persecutions*, II (Houndmills and London, 1988), 19; Gidulianov, *Tserkov'*, 9.
38. G. P. Fedotoff, *The Russian Church since the Revolution* (London, 1928), 42–44; Pospielovsky, *Soviet Antireligious Campaigns*, II, 19–23.
39. Marguerite E. Harrison, *Marooned in Moscow* (New York, 1921), 134.
40. *Izvestiia*, No. 99/1,538 (May 6, 1922), 1.
41. Stratonov, *Tserkovnaia smuta*, 13–14.
42. Fedotoff, *Russian Church*, 53.
43. Boleslaw Szczesniak, ed., *The Russian Revolution and Religion* (Notre Dame, Ind., 1959), 67.
44. See below, p. 417.
45. *RR*, 350–51.
46. See *e.g.*, *Izvestiia*, No.32/1,471 (February 10, 1922), 1; Spinka, *The Church*, 172; McCullagh, *Persecution*, 5; Fedotoff, *Russian Church*, 55.
47. *E.g.*, *Izvestiia*, No. 31/1,470 (February 9, 1922), 2; and No. 32/1,471 (February 10, 1922) 1.
48. RTsKhIDNI, F. 5, op. 2, delo 48, list 76.
49. Szczesniak, *Russian Revolution*, 69.
50. Stratonov, *Tserkovnaia smuta*, 45; *Izvestiia*, No. 32/1471 (February 10, 1922), 1.
51. RTsKhIDNI, F. 5, op. 2, delo 48, list 1; dated March 2, 1922.
52. *Izvestiia*, No. 46/1,485 (February 26, 1922), 3.
53. I. Trifonov, *Ocherki istorii klassovoi bor'by v SSSR v gody Nepa (1921–27)* (Moscow, 1960), 21–35.
54. Emhardt, *Religion*, 241–60.
55. Valentinov, *Chërnaia kniga*, 253–54.
56. *Izvestiia*, No. 70/1,509 (March 28, 1922), 2.
57. RTsKhIDNI, F. 5, op. 2, delo 48, list 34.
58. Trifonov, *Ocherki*, 34.
59. *Izvestiia*, No. 82/1,819 (April 15, 1923), 6.
60. *RiTs*, No. 1–3 (1923), 65. GPU report to Lenin and other members of the Politburo dated March 20–21, 1922, in RTsKhIDNI, F. 5, op. 2, delo 48, lists 35 and 36.
61. RTsKhIDNI, F. 5, op. 2, delo 48, lists 15 and 81–82.
62. *IzvTsK*, No. 4/303 (April 1990), 190–93.
63. *RR*, 722.
64. RTsKhIDNI, F. 5, op. 2, delo 48, list 44.

65. *IzvTsK*, No. 4/303 (April 1990), 194-95.

66. RTsKhIDNI, F. 5, op. 2, delo 48, list 21.

67. *Ibid.*, F. 2, op. 2, delo 1166; dispatch to Lenin dated March 10, 1922.

68. *Izvestiia*, No. 89/1,528 (April 23, 1922), 3; Curtiss, *Russian Church*, 118.

69. See, for instance, *Izvestiia*, No. 102/1,541 (May 10, 1922), 3; *Pravda*, No. 101 (May 9, 1922), 1.

70. *Literator* (Leningrad), No. 32/37 (August 31, 1990), 4.

71. *Izvestiia*, No. 101/1,540 (May 9, 1922), 3; *Pravda*, No. 101 (May 9, 1922), 1.

72. D. A. Volkogonov, *Trotskii*, I (Moscow, 1992), 367; McCullagh, *Persecution*, 26.

73. An official account of the trial: *RiTs*, No. 1-3 (1923), 65-102.

74. McCullagh, *Persecution*, 52.

75. *Ibid.*, 353-58.

76. *Ibid.*, XVII-XVIII, 368-69.

77. On Andronik, see Valentinov, *Chërnaia kniga*, 36. On Hermogen, see Regelson, *Tragediia*, 242; *RiTs*, No. 3-5 (1919), 48.

78. Harrison, *Marooned*, 132.

79. A. I. Vvedenskii, *Tserkov' i gosudarstvo* (Moscow, 1923), 230; Szczesniak, *Russian Revolution*, 156-57; McCullagh, *Persecution*, p. ix.

80. Sergei Bychkov in *Moscow News*, No. 32 (August 19-26, 1990), 8-9; Vladimir Eremenko in *LR*, No. 50/1,454 (December 14, 1990), 16-18.

81. *Izvestiia*, No. 208/1,647 (September 16, 1922), 1.

82. McCullagh, *Persecution*, 27; also Denikin, *Ocherki*, IV, 236.

83. A. Vakurova in M. Enisherlov, *et al.*, eds., *Voinstvuiushchee bezbozh'e v SSSR za 15 let* (Moscow, 1932), 305.

84. Mark Krinitskii in *Izvestiia*, No. 5/1,742 (January 10, 1923), 4.

85. Pospielovsky, *Soviet Antireligious Campaigns*, II, 44, citing *Bezbozhnik*, No. 8 (February 1923), 2.

86. *NYT*, December 15, 1922, 4.

87. *Ibid.*

88. Fedotoff, *Russian Church*, 47-48.

89. *Kommunisticheskaia Partiia Sovetskogo Soiuza v Rezoliutsiiakh i Resheniiakh S"ezdov, Konferentsii i Plenumov TsK*, 7th ed., I (Moscow, 1953), 744.

90. Gidulianov, *Tserkov'*, 11-13.

91. Trifonov, *Ocherki*, 33-34.

92. RTsKhIDNI, F. 5, op. 1, delo 120, listy 12-13.

93. *Ibid.*, op. 2, delo 48, listy 10 and 13.

94. See its founding manifesto, "The Letter of a Group of Clergymen," published in *Krasnaia Gazeta* on March 25, and reprinted in *Izvestiia*, No. 71/1,510 (March 29, 1922), 2.

95. Pierre Pascal, *The Religion of the Russian People* (London and Oxford, 1976), 94; Sergei Bychkov in *MN*, No. 32 (August 19-26, 1990), 8-9.

96. Fedotoff, *Russian Church*, 67.

97. *Zhivaia tserkov'*, No. 2 (May 23, 1922), 1; Emhardt, *Religion*, 61.

98. Regelson, *Tragediia*, 286; *Izvestiia*, No. 108/1,547 (May 17, 1922), 1.

99. *TP*, II, 740-43.

100. Curtiss, *Russian Church*, 139.

101. *RR*, 451-56. See his article endorsing the confiscation of church valuables in *Izvestiia*, No. 102/1,541 (May 10, 1922), 3.

102. Regelson, *Tragediia*, 313.

103. Emhardt, *Religion*, 59-123.

104. McCullagh, *Persecution*, 68-78; Regelson, *Tragediia*, 327-29.

105. RTsKhIDNI, F. 89, op. 4, delo 118, list 5.

106. *Izvestiia*, No. 141/1,878 (June 27, 1923), 1. See further *ibid.*, No. 149/1,886 (July 6, 1923), 6, and *Ibid.*, No. 153/1,890 (July 11, 1923), 5.

107. *Ibid.*, No. 86/2,419 (April 15, 1925), 1; V. A. Kuroedov, *Religiia i tserkov' v sovetskom gosudarstve* (Moscow, 1981), 75-76.

108. Fedotoff, *Russian Church*, 68.

109. *KPSS v Rezoliutsiiakh*, I, 858.
110. Nora Levin, *The Jews in the Soviet Union since 1917*, I (New York and London, 1988), 70–71.
111. Aryeh Y. Yodfat in *Soviet Jewish Affairs*, III/1 (1973), 49.
112. Cited in Zvi Gitelman, *Jewish Nationality and Soviet Politics* (Princeton, 1972), 304.
113. Levin, *Jews*, I, 57.
114. *Ibid.*, I, 64–65; *Desiatyi S"ezd RKP(b): Stenograficheskii Otchet* (Moscow, 1963), 446–47.
115. Gitelman, *Jewish Nationality*, 298–99.
116. Zvi Gitelman, *A Century of Ambivalence* (New York, 1988), 118.
117. Regelson, *Tragediia*, 310.
118. Yodfat in *Soviet Jewish Affairs*, III/1 (1973), 49.
119. *NYT*, April 10, 1923, 3.
120. Yodfat in *Soviet Jewish Affairs*, III/1 (1973), 51.
121. Gitelman, *Jewish Nationality*, 306.
122. *Ibid.*, 477.
123. Levin, *Jews*, I, 325–28.
124. *RiTs*, No. 1–3 (1923), 102–16.
125. *Metody antireligioznoi propagandy sredi Musulman* (Moscow, 1922), 4–5.
126. Alexandre Bennigsen and Chantal Lemercier-Quelquejay, *Islam in the Soviet Union* (New York and Washington, 1967), 141.
127. *Ibid.*, 144–49.
128. *NZh*, No. 83/298 (May 4, 1918), 3.
129. Louis Fischer in *Current History*, July 1923, 597.
130. Judith Stora-Sandor, *Alexandra Kollontai: Marxisme et la révolution sexuelle* (Paris, 1973), 32–33.
131. Stratonov, *Tserkovnaia smuta*, 14. See also Michel d'Herbigny, "L'aspect religieux de Moscou en octobre 1925," *Orientalia Christiana*, No. 20 (1926), 189, 192; and Harrison, *Marooned*, 130, 133–34.
132. Harrison, *Marooned*, 132–33.
133. Fülöp-Miller, *Geist und Gesicht*, 356–57.

8. NEP: The False Thermidor

1. See Tamara Kondratieva, *Bolcheviks et Jacobins* (Paris, 1989).
2. A.L.P. Dennis, *The Foreign Policies of Soviet Russia* (New York, 1924), 418, citing *Ost-Information*, No. 191, January 11, 1922.
3. Lenin, *PSS*, XLIII, 61; XLIV, 310–11.
4. *Odinadsatyi S"ezd RKP(b): Stenograficheskii Otchet* (Moscow, 1961), 137.
5. Lenin, *PSS*, XLV, 86.
6. *Ibid.*, XLIII, 18, 24; XLIV, 159.
7. Richard Pipes, *Struve: Liberal on the Left* (Cambridge, Mass., 1970), *passim*.
8. Lenin, *PSS*, XLIII, 205–45.
9. *RR*, 671–72.
10. *Ibid.*, 673.
11. *Ibid.*, 696. Further on this subject: V. Sarabianov, *Ekonomika i ekonomicheskaia politika SSSR*, 2nd ed., (Moscow, 1926), especially pp. 204–47.
12. *Desiatyi S"ezd RKP(b): Stenograficheskii Otchet* (Moscow, 1963), 290. See further Paul Avrich, *Kronstadt 1921* (New York, 1970), 24, citing *Krasnaia gazeta*, February 9, 1921; and League of Nations, *Report on Economic Conditions in Russia* (n.p. [1922]), 16n.
13. L. N. Kritsman, *Geroicheskii period velikoi russkoi revoliutsii*, 2nd ed. (Moscow, 1926), 166.
14. Alexander Berkman, *The Kronstadt Rebellion* (Berlin, 1922), 5.
15. Oliver H. Radkey, *The Unknown Civil War in Soviet Russia* (Stanford, 1976), 32–33.
16. See the forthcoming book by Vladimir Brovkin, *Behind the Front Lines of the Civil War*.
17. Seth Singleton in *SR*, No. 3 (September 1966), 498–99.

18. RTsKhIDNI, F. 5, op. 1, delo 3055, 2475, and 2476, for May 1919, the second half of 1920, and all of 1921, respectively; *Ibid.*, F. 2, op. 2, delo 303, for the first half of May 1920.

19. I. Ia. Trifonov, *Klassy i klassovaia bor'ba v SSSR v nachale NEPa*, I (Leningrad, 1964), 4.

20. G. F. Krivosheev, ed., *Grif sekretnosti sniat* (Moscow, 1993), 54.

21. *RR*, 558–65.

22. *Desiatyi S"ezd*, 347.

23. *Ibid.*, 350.

24. See above, p. 113.

25. Radkey, *Unknown Civil War*, 69.

26. See Richard Pipes, *Russia under the Old Regime* (London, 1974), 157–58; and *RR*, 114, 118–19.

27. Bukharin at the Third Congress of the Comintern, July 8, 1921, in *The New Economic Policies of Soviet Russia* (Chicago, [1921]), 58.

28. Pipes, *Old Regime*, 114.

29. *RR*, Chapter 16.

30. Angelica Balabanoff, *Impressions of Lenin* (Ann Arbor, Mich., 1964), 54–55.

31. *TP*, II, 494–97.

32. Ia. Iakovlev, *Derevnia kak ona est'* (Moscow, 1923), 86, 96–98.

33. A. Okninskii, *Dva goda sredi krest'ian* (Riga, 1936), 290–92.

34. Radkey, *Unknown Civil War, passim;* Mikhail Frenkin, *Tragediia krest'ianskikh vosstanii v Rossii, 1918–1921 gg.* ([Jerusalem, 1988]), Chapter V; and Orlando Figes, *Peasant Russia Civil War* (Oxford, 1989), Chapter 7. For Communist views, see Trifonov, *Klassy*, I, 245–59. New materials from military archives were recently published in P. A. Aptekar, in *Voenno-istoricheskii zhurnal*, No. 1 (1993), 50–55, and No. 2 (1993), 66–70. My attention was drawn to this source by Mr. Robert E. Tarleton.

35. *TP*, II, 492–95.

36. Iu[rii] P[odbelskii], in *RevR*, No. 6 (April 1921), 23–24.

37. Radkey, *Unknown Civil War*, 48–58.

38. *Ibid.*, 75.

39. *IA*, No. 4 (1962), 203.

40. On Saratov, see Figes, *Peasant Russia*, Chapter 7.

41. *TP*, II, 424–25.

42. *Rodina*, No. 10 (1990), 25.

43. Marc Jansen, *Show Trial under Lenin* (The Hague, 1982), 15; *IA*, No. 4 (1962), 207–8; *TP*, II, 498, 554; Frenkin, *Tragediia*, 128–29, 132–33; Singleton in *SR*, No. 3 (September 1966), 501.

44. *TP*, II, 510–13.

45. *Pravda*, No. 14 (January 22, 1921), 3.

46. *EZh*, No. 14 (January 22, 1921), 2.

47. Lenin, *Sochineniia*, XXVI, 640; *Pravda*, No. 27 (February 8, 1921), 1; *Desiatyi S"ezd*, 861–62; RTsKhIDNI, F. 76, op. 3, delo 166.

48. *Pravda*, No. 32 (February 13, 1921), 4.

49. RTsKhIDNI, F. 76, op. 3, delo 167.

50. *Ibid.*

51. Alexander Berkman, *Kronstadt*, 6, and *The Bolshevik Myth* (London, 1925), 292.

52. Avrich, *Kronstadt*, 62–71.

53. *Ibid.*, 69.

54. *Pravda o Kronshtadte* (Prague, 1921), 8–10.

55. Lenin, *PSS*, XLIII, 23–24.

56. Berkman, *Kronstadt*, 31–32; L. Trotskii, *Kak vooruzhalas' revoliutsiia*, III/1 (Moscow, 1924), 202.

57. *Petrogradskaia pravda*, No. 48 (March 4, 1921), cited in N. Kornatovskii, ed., *Kronshtadskii miatezh* (Leningrad, 1931), 188–89.

58. Berkman, *Kronstadt*, 14–15, 18, 29.

59. RTsKhIDNI, F. 76, op. 3, delo 167.
60. *Pravda o Kronshtadte,* 68.
61. RTsKhIDNI, F. 76, op. 3, delo 167: Cheka report.
62. *Pravda o Kronshtadte,* 82-84.
63. RTsKhIDNI, F. 76, op. 3, delo 167.
64. *Ibid.,* F. 5, op. 1, delo 2477, for the period January 31-June 21, 1921.
65. *Ibid.,* F. 2, op. 1, ed. khr. 24558.
66. S. A. Esikov and L. G. Protasov in *VI,* No. 6-7 (1992), 52.
67. *TP,* II, 480-81.
68. *IA,* No. 4 (1962), 204.
69. *TP,* II, 480-81.
70. *Ibid.,* II, 532-34.
71. Pitirim A. Sorokin, *Leaves from a Russian Diary* (Boston, 1950), 254-56.
72. "Moskvich" in *Volia Rossiii,* No. 264 (July 27, 1921), 2.
73. Radkey, *Unknown Civil War,* 324.
74. *TP,* II, 536-37, 544-45.
75. *Ibid.,* II, 562-63.
76. Aptekar, in *Voenno-istorichesf kis zhurnal,* No. 1 (1993), 53.
77. Radkey, *Unknown Civil War,* 372-76.
78. Trifonov, *Klassy,* I, 6.
79. *Ibid.,* I, 265-70.
80. *Desiatyi S"ezd,* 430.
81. *Pravda,* No. 51 (March 8, 1921), 1; Radkey, *Unknown Civil War,* 229.
82. *Desiatyi S"ezd,* 415, 418.
83. Radkey, *Unknown Civil War,* 31.
84. Tsiurupa in *Desiatyi S"ezd,* 422.
85. Alec Nove, *An Economic History of the USSR* (Hammondsworth, England, 1982), 94.
86. *Izvestiia,* No. 62/1,205 (March 23, 1921), 2.
87. RTsKhIDNI, F. 5, op. 2, delo 9.
88. Lenin, *PSS,* XLIII, 57-58.
89. *Ibid.,* XLIII, 69-70; *Desiatyi S"ezd,* 224, 468.
90. Lenin, *PSS,* XLIII, 60-61.
91. Decree of April 21, 1921, *SUiR,* No. 38 (May 11, 1921), 205-8; E. B. Genkina, *Perekhod sovetskogo gosudarstva k Novoi Ekonomicheskoi Politike (1921-1922)* (Moscow, 1954), 123-24.
92. *SUiR,* No. 26 (April 11, 1921), Article 147, p. 153.
93. E. H. Carr, *The Bolshevik Revolution,* II (New York, 1952), 283-84.
94. Genkina, *Perekhod,* 302.
95. Iu. Poliakov in Akademiia Nauk SSSR, Institut Istorii SSSR, *Novaia Ekonomicheskaia Politika* (Moscow, 1974), 5.
96. Maurice Dobb, *Soviet Economic Development Since 1917* (London, 1948), 131.
97. *PSS,* XXXIX, 407. See, Iu. Poliakov, *Perekhod k nepu i sovetskoe krest'ianstvo* (Moscow, 1967).
98. Arthur Z. Arnold, *Banks, Credit and Money in Soviet Russia* (New York, 1937), 126.
99. Carr, *Bolshevik Revolution,* II, 350-52.
100. Lenin, *PSS,* XLIV, 225.
101. N. D. Mets, *Nash rubl'* (Moscow, 1960), 68.
102. *Sovetskoe narodnoe khoziaistvo v 1921-1925 gg.,* 495-96, 498.
103. Lenin, *PSS,* XLV, 289-90.
104. RTsKhIDNI, F. 5, op. 2, delo 27, list 34.
105. Genkina, *Perekhod,* 232-33.
106. Carr, *Bolshevik Revolution,* II, 302-3.
107. *RR,* 700.
108. Alan M. Ball, *Russia's Last Capitalists* (Berkeley, 1987), 21-22.

109. *Ibid., passim.*
110. *Sovetskoe narodnoe khoziaistvo v 1921–1925 gg.*, 73, 343.
111. A. A. Kiselev in *Novaia Ekonomicheskaia Politika*, 113.
112. Lenin, *PSS*, XLII, 159.
113. Simon Liberman, *Building Lenin's Russia* (Chicago, 1945), 60.
114. N. S. Simonovin *ISSSR*, No. 1 (1992), 52.
115. Lenin, *PSS*, XLIV, 151.
116. *Ibid.*, 412.
117. RTsKhIDNI, F. 2, op. 2, delo 1154, draft by I. S. Unshlikht dated February 27, 1922.
118. Lenin, *PSS*, XLIV, 327–29.
119. Lennard G. Gerson, *The Secret Police in Lenin's Russia* (Philadelphia, 1976), 222.
120. *Izvestiia*, No. 30/1,469 (February 8, 1922), 3.
121. Lenin, *PSS*, LIV, 196.
122. See above, p. 335.
123. *SUiR*, No. 65 (November 6, 1922), Decree No. 844, p. 1053.
124. *Ibid.*, No. 8 (March 10, 1923), Resolution No. 108, dated January 3, 1923, p. 185; Gerson, *Secret Police*, 249–50.
125. *Izvestiia*, No. 236/1,675 (October 19, 1922), 3.
126. Gerson, *Secret Police*, 228.
127. See below, p. 383n.
128. Andrzej Kaminski, *Konzentransionlager 1896 bis heute: eine Analyse* (Stuttgart, 1982), 87. Cf. Gerson, *Secret Police*, 256–57.
129. Sergei Masaiov in *Rul'*, No. 3,283 (September 13, 1931), 5. Cf. Gerson, *Secret Police*, 314.
130. David J. Dallin and Boris I. Nicolaevsky, *Forced Labor in Soviet Russia* (New Haven, 1947), 173; *SV*, No. 9/79 (April 17, 1924), 14.
131. Lenin, *PSS*, XLV, 190.
132. Pipes, *Old Regime*, 294–95.
133. Lenin, *PSS*, XLV, 190.
134. *Sorok let sovetskogo prava*, I (Leningrad, 1957), 74–75.
135. *Grazhdanskii Kodeks R.S.F.S.R.* (Moscow, 1923), 5; Harold Berman, *Justice in Russia* (Cambridge, Mass., 1950), 27.
136. *Ugolovnyi Kodeks R.S.F.S.R.*, 2nd ed. (Moscow, 1922), Article 6, p. 3.
137. *SUiR*, No. 48 (July 25, 1923), Decree No. 479, p. 877.
138. A. N. Trainin, *Ugolovnoe pravo R.S.F.S.R.: Chast' Osobennaia* (Leningrad, 1925), 30n.
139. A. N. Trainin, *Ugolovnoe pravo: Obshchaia Chast'* (Moscow, 1929), 260–61.
140. M. I. Latsis, *Chrezvychainye komissii po bor'be s kontr-revoliutsiei* (Moscow, 1921), 16–17.
141. *SV*, No. 5 (1921), 12–14.
142. *Dvenadtsatyi S"ezd RKP(b)* (Moscow, 1968), 52.
143. The following account is based largely on Marc Jansen's *Show Trial.*
144. *V. I. Lenin i VChK* (Moscow, 1987), 518.
145. *Voennaia i boevaia rabota Partii Sotsialistov-Revoliutsionerov za 1917–1918 gg.*
146. Lenin, *PSS*, XLIV, 396–97.
147. *TP*, II, 708–9.
148. Lenin, *Sochineniia*, XXVII, 537–38.
149. Jansen, *Show Trial*, 29.
150. *RR*, 822.
151. RTsKhIDNI, F. 76, op. 3, delo 252.
152. Jansen, *Show Trial*, 66.
153. Roger Pethybridge, *One Step Backwards, Two Steps Forward* (Oxford, 1990), 206.
154. *Protsess kontrrevoliutsionnoi organizatsii Menshevikov* (Moscow, 1931).
155. Lenin, *PSS*, XLV, 90.

156. NYT, July 27, 1922, 19.
157. Ibid., August 10, 1922, 4.
158. L. Trotskii, Moia zhizn', II (Berlin, 1930), 211–12. Cf. L. A. Fotieva, Iz zhizni V. I. Lenina (Moscow, 1967), 183–84.
159. NYT, August 10, 1922, 4.
160. Jansen, Show Trial, 178.
161. L. Trotskii, Literatura i revoliutsiia, 2nd ed. (Moscow, 1924), 165.
162. Pethybridge, One Step, 223.
163. E. H. Carr, Socialism in One Country, 1924–1926, II (New York, 1960), 78.
164. On these controversies, ibid., II, 76–87.
165. N. Meshcheriakov on May 9, 1924, in Voprosy kul'tury pri diktature proletariata (Moscow, 1925), 120.
166. Pravda, No. 40 (February 19, 1924), 6.
167. Christopher Read, Culture and Power in Revolutionary Russia (London, 1990), 203.
168. Trinadtsatyi S"ezd RKP(b): Stenograficheskii Otchet (Moscow, 1963), 653–54.
169. Carr, Socialism in One Country, II, 82–83.
170. Pethybridge, One Step, 213.
171. Lenin, PSS, XLIV, 667; LIII, 391.
172. Ibid., XLIII, 13–14.
173. RevR, No. 14/15 (November–December 1921), 14–15.
174. L. Hutchinson in F. A. Golder and Lincoln Hutchinson, On the Trail of the Russian Famine (Stanford, 1927), 14.
175. H. H. Fisher, The Famine in Soviet Russia (New York, 1927), 50.
176. Jean M. Ingersoll, Historical Examples of Ecological Disasters (Harmon-on-Hudson, N.Y., 1965), 20.
177. V. I. Pokrovskii in A. I. Chuprov and A. S. Posnikov, eds., Vliianie urozhaev i khlebnykh tsen na nekotorye storony russkogo narodnogo khoziaistva, II (St. Petersburg, 1897), 202.
178. V. E. Den, Kurs ekonomicheskoi geografii (Leningrad, 1924), 209; Figes, Peasant Russia, 272.
179. Cited in Fisher, Famine, 90.
180. RevR, No. 14/15 (November–December 1921), 15.
181. Fisher, Famine, 300.
182. Ibid., 436n.
183. Richard G. Robbins, Jr., Famine in Russia, 1891–1892 (New York and London, 1975).
184. Ibid., 171.
185. Michel Heller in Cahiers, XX, No. 2 (1979), 137.
186. Lenin, PSS, LII, 184–85, 290, 441–42; LIII, 105.
187. Ibid., XLIII, 350.
188. G. A. Belov, et al., eds., Iz istorii Vserossiiskoi Chrezvychainoi komissii (Moscow, 1958), 443–44.
189. Pethybridge, One Step, 117.
190. Lenin, PSS, XLIV, 75.
191. Pethybridge, One Step, 119.
192. Izvestiia, No. 159/1,302 (July 22, 1922), 2; Heller in Cahiers, XX, No. 2 (1979), 131–72; Fisher, Famine, 51.
193. Lenin, PSS, LIII, 110–11, 115.
194. Fisher, Famine, 52–53.
195. First published in 1965 in PSS, LIII, 141–42.
196. B. M. Weissman, Herbert Hoover and Famine Relief to Soviet Russia (Stanford, 1974), 76.
197. M. Heller, Introduction to Pomoshch (London, 1991), 2.
198. Report of Unshlikht to Lenin, November 21, 1921, in RTsKhIDNI, F. 2, op. 2, delo 1023.
199. Heller in Cahiers, XX, No. 2 (1979), 152–53; Izvestiia, No. 206/1,645 (September 14, 1922), 4.
200. Fisher, Famine, 298n.

201. Hutchinson in Golder and Hutchinson, *On the Trail*, 18.
202. RTsKhIDNI, F. 2, op. 2, ed. khr. 830; dated August 23, 1921.
203. See, *e.g.*, Lenin, *Sochineniia*, XXVII, 514.
204. RTsKhIDNI, F. 2, op. 2, ed. khr. 837.
205. *TP*, II, 596–99; RTsKhIDNI, F. 2, op. 2, delo 914.
206. Fisher, *Famine*, Chapter 14.
207. *Ibid.*, 315, 321; *NYT*, October 16, 1922, 4.
208. Fisher, *Famine*, 321.
209. *Ibid.*, 321–22.
210. Den, *Kurs*, 209.
211. *EZh*, No. 292 (December 24, 1922), 5; Figes, *Peasant Russia*, 271.
212. Ingersoll, *Historical Examples*, 36; Peter Scheibert, *Lenin an der Macht* (Weinheim, 1984), 166.
213. Den, *Kurs*, 210.
214. Ingersoll, *Historical Examples*, 27.
215. Cited by H. Johnson in *Strana i mir*, No. 2/68 (1992), 21.
216. Julius Braunthal, *History of the International*, II (New York and Washington, 1967), 258.
217. Bukharin in *Izvestiia*, No. 6/1,743 (January 11, 1923), 3.
218. *Protokoll des vierten Kongresses der Kommunistichen Internationale* (Hamburg, 1923), 994–97.
219. *Ibid.*, 807.
220. Braunthal, *History*, II, 263.
221. Dennis, *Foreign Policies*, 366.
222. *Ibid.*, 369.
223. Isaac Deutscher, *The Prophet Unarmed* (Widner, 1959), 61–65.
224. Lenin, *PSS*, XLV, 131.
225. Braunthal, *History*, II, 245–50; *TP*, II, 704–5.
226. Braunthal, *History*, II, 264.
227. *Ibid.*, II, 269, citing *Protokoll des Internationalen Sozialistischen Arbeiterkongressen in Hamburg* (Berlin, 1923), 80.
228. Braunthal, *History*, II, 270, citing *ibid.*, 105, 107.
229. Rolf-Dieter Müller, *Das Tor zur Weltmacht* (Boppard am Rhein, 1984), 50–65.
230. *Ibid.*, 46–47.
231. Lenin, *PSS*, XLII, 55–83; first published in 1963.
232. R. G. Himmer in *Central European History*, Vol. 9, No. 2 (1976), 155.
233. *Correspondence with Mr. Krassin Respecting Russia's Foreign Indebtedness, Parliamentary Papers*, Russia, No. 3, Cmd. 1546 (London, 1921), 4–5.
234. Dispatch of November 6, 1933, in Department of State *Documents on German Foreign Policy*, Series C, Vol. II (Washington, D.C., 1959), 81.
235. Gerald Freund, *Unholy Alliance* (New York, 1957), 92n. See further, E. H. Carr, *The Bolshevik Revolution*, III (New York, 1953), 361–64; and Deutscher, *Prophet Unarmed*, 57–58.
236. *TP*, II, 440–43.
237. Freund, *Unholy Alliance*, 149.
238. RTsKhIDNI, F. 5, op. 1, delo 2103, list 84, and F. 2, op. 2, delo 1124.
239. *Ibid.*, F. 2, op. 2, delo 897, 933, and 939.
240. Freund, *Unholy Alliance*, 99; F. L. Carsten in *Survey*, No. 44–45, (October 1962), 119.
241. Herbert Helbig, *Die Träger der Rapallo-Politik* (Göttingen, 1958), 79–81.
242. Lenin, *PSS*, XLIV, 407–8.
243. First published in *Literaturnaia gazeta*, No. 45 (November 5, 1972), 11.
244. *TP*, II, 656–59; RTsKhIDNI, F. 2, op. 1, delo 27069.
245. RTsKhIDNI, F. 5, op. 2, delo 27, list 74.
246. Harry Kessler, *In the Twenties* (New York, [1971]), 176.
247. Lenin, *PSS*, XLV, 70.
248. *EZh*, No. 71 (March 29, 1922), 1.

249. Dennis, *Foreign Policies*, 427.
250. *Ibid.*, 431–32.
251. Freund, *Unholy Alliance*, 116–17.
252. *Sovetsko-Germanskie otnosheniia ot peregovorov v Brest-Litovske do podpisaniia Rapall'-skogo dogovora*, II (Moscow, 1971), 485–86.
253. Text in *NYT*, April 18, 1922, 1.
254. *Sovetsko-Germanskie otnosheniia*, II, 486–87.
255. Dennis, *Foreign Policies*, 430.
256. Freund, *Unholy Alliance*, 148.
257. Müller, *Das Tor*, 84. Walter Laqueur, *Russia and Germany* (London, 1965), 132.
258. Lenin, *PSS*, XLII, 104–5. Cf. *Ost-Information* (Berlin), No. 81, December 4, 1920, cited in Dennis, *Foreign Policies*, 155.
259. Freund, *Unholy Alliance*, 153; Louis Fischer, *The Soviets in World Affairs*, I (London, 1930), 451; Gustav Hilger, *The Incompatible Allies* (New York, 1953), 120.
260. Arthur Spencer in *Survey*, No. 44–45 (1962), 139.
261. Leonid Luks, *Entstehung der kommunistischen Faschismustheorie* (Stuttgart, 1984), 62.
262. Ruth Fischer, *Stalin and German Communism* (London, 1948), 265.
263. Karl Mielcke, *Dokumente zur Geschichte der Weimarer Republik* (Braunschweig, 1951), 46, 48.
264. *Protokoll: Fünfter Kongress der Kommunistischen Internationale*, II (Hamburg, [1925]), 713; *Die Lehren der deutschen Ereignisse: Das Präsidium des Exekutivkomitees der Kommunistischen Internationale zur deutschen Frage* (Hamburg, 1924), 18; Braunthal, *History*, II, 277.
265. Braunthal, *History*, II, 277.
266. Ossip K. Flechtheim, *Die Kommunistische Partei Deutschlands in der Weimarer Republik* (Offenbach a.M., 1948), 89.
267. Braunthal, *History*, II, 278–79; Freund, *Unholy Alliance*, 172.
268. E. H. Carr, *The Interregnum, 1923–1924* (New York, 1954), 209–12.
269. *Ibid.*, 218; G. Z. Besedovskii, *Na putiakh k Termidoru*, I (Paris, 1930), 123.
270. Müller, *Das Tor*, 105–6.
271. Kochan, *Russia and the Weimar Republic*, 60–61; Fischer, *Stalin*, 515–36; Raphael R. Abramovitch, *The Soviet Revolution* (New York, 1962), 247–58.
272. Freund, *Unholy Alliance*, 125.
273. Hans W. Gatzke in *AHR*, Vol. 63, No. 3 (April 1958), 573–76.
274. Müller, *Das Tor*, 113–14.
275. Gatzke in *AHR*, Vol. 63, No. 3 (April 1958), 578; Müller, *Das Tor*, 144–45.
276. Freund, *Unholy Alliance*, 207–8.
277. *Ibid.*, 209.
278. Helm Speidel in *VfZ*, I, 1 (January 1953), 28.
279. Freund, *Unholy Alliance*, 209.
280. Iu. L. Diakov and T. S. Bushueva, *Fashistskii mech kovalsia v SSSR* (Moscow, 1992), 20–23.
281. Freund, *Unholy Alliance*, 210; Helm Speidel in *VfZ*, I, 1 (1953), 35.

9. The Crisis of the New Regime

1. *Desiatyi S"ezd RKP (b): Stenograficheskii Otchet* (Moscow, 1963), 84.
2. Alexis de Tocqueville, *The Ancient Regime and the French Revolution*, Chapter 12.
3. *Odinadtsatyi S"ezd RKP (b): Stenograficheskii Otchet* (Moscow, 1961), 545.
4. *Ibid.*, 352. See also Bukharin's remarks: *ibid.*, 322.
5. RTsKhIDNI, F. 76, delo 265.
6. Daniel Orlovsky in Diane P. Koenker, *et al.*, eds., *Party, State and Society in the Russian Civil War* (Bloomington, Ind., 1989), 180–209.
7. RTsKhIDNI, F. 5, op. 2, delo 27, list 9.

8. *SV*, No. 2 (February 16, 1921), 1.

9. The best discussions of the centralization and bureaucratization of the Communist Party can be found in Merle Fainsod's *How Russia Is Ruled*, revised ed. (Cambridge, Mass., 1963), Chapter 6, and Leonard Schapiro's *The Origin of the Communist Autocracy* (Cambridge, Mass., 1977), Part III.

10. Krestinskii in *Desiatyi S"ezd*, 499.

11. RTsKhIDNI, F. 17, op. 112.

12. *Pravda*, No. 17 (January 26, 1923), 3; A. V. Pantsov in *VI*, No. 5 (1990), 80.

13. Fainsod, *How Russia Is Ruled*, 181.

14. *Ibid.*, 181.

15. Rafail [R. B. Farbman] in *Desiatyi S"ezd*, 97.

16. I. Zaitsev in *Novyi den'*, No. 16 (April 12, 1918), 1; *RR*, 63.

17. Konstantin Shteppa in Simon Wolin and Robert M. Slusser, *The Soviet Secret Police* (New York, 1957), 86–87.

18. Lenin, *PSS*, XLIV, 398; XLV, 53.

19. *E.g.*, N. Osinskii in *Vos'moi S"ezd RKP(b): Protokoly* (Moscow, 1959), 27–28 and 164–67; and A. A. Solts in *Desiatyi S"ezd*, 57–58.

20. *Kommunist* (Astrakhan), No. 6 (January 11, 1919), cited in *Izvestiia*, No.12/564 (January 18, 1919), 4.

21. Lenin, *PSS*, XLIV, 122–24.

22. "Aleksandrov," *Kto upravlaet Rossiei?* (Berlin, [1933]), 28.

23. Solts in *Desiatyi S"ezd*, 60.

24. *RR*, 61–75.

25. A. Podshchekoldin in *AiF*, No. 27/508 (July 7–13, 1990), 2.

26. Alexander Berkman, *The Bolshevik Myth* (London, 1925), 43.

27. RTsKhIDNI, F. 2, op. 2, delo 1005.

28. S. K. Minin in *Desiatyi S"ezd*, 92.

29. Svetlana Alliluyeva, *Twenty Letters to a Friend* (New York, 1967), 26–27; Dmitrii Volkogonov, *Triumf i tragediia*, I/1 (Moscow, 1989), 190; Dmitrii Volkogonov, *Trotskii*, I (Moscow, 1992), 345.

30. Lenin, *PSS*, LIV, 649, 266.

31. *TP*, II, 444–47.

32. Volkogonov, *Trotskii*, I, 379–80.

33. E. H. Carr, *The Interregnum, 1923–1924* (New York, 1954), 277*n*–278*n*; *Odinadtsatyi S"ezd*, 555.

34. Carr, *Interregnum*, 278*n*.

35. *Pravda*, No. 64 (March 25, 1921), 1.

36. Fainsod, *How Russia Is Ruled*, 182.

37. *Kommunisticheskaia Partiia Sovetskogo Soiuza v Rezoliutsiiakh i Resheniiakh*, I (Moscow, 1953), 576.

38. *Odinadtsatyi S"ezd*, 156–57.

39. Roger Pethybridge, *One Step Backwards, Two Steps Forward* (Oxford, 1990), 154.

40. Aleksandrov, *Kto upravliaet*, 22–23.

41. *Desiatyi S"ezd*, 137.

42. M. Dewar, *Labour Policy in the USSR, 1917–1928* (New York, 1956), 162–63.

43. *Desiatyi S"ezd*, 881.

44. Pethybridge, *One Step*, 158.

45. V. P. Antonov-Saratovskii, *Sovety v epokhu voennogo kommunizma*, Pt. 2 (Moscow, 1929), 57, 68, 97–100.

46. Pethybridge, *One Step*, 161–68; Lenin, *PSS*, XLV, 383–88.

47. Sheila Fitzpatrick, *The Commissariat of Enlightenment* (Cambridge, Mass., 1970), 24.

48. L. N. Kritsman, *Geroicheskii period Velikoi Russkoi Revoliutsii* (Moscow-Leningrad, 1926), 197.

49. E. G. Gimpelson, *Sovetskii rabochii klass, 1918–1920 gg.* (Moscow, 1974), 122.

50. Gimpelson, *Ibid.,* 81; Kritsman, *Geroicheskii period,* 198.
51. Ia. Iakovlev, *Derevnia kak ona est'* (Moscow, 1923), 121.
52. V. P. Diachenko, *Istoriia finansov SSSR* (Moscow, 1978), 87.
53. *SV,* No. 1 (February 1, 1921), 1. Cf. Alfons Goldschmidt, *Die Wirtschaftsorganisation Sowjet-Russlands* (Berlin, 1920), 141; Lenin, *PSS,* LII, 65.
54. *Izmeneniia sotsial'noi struktury sovetskogo obshchestva: Oktiabr' 1917-1920* (Moscow, 1976), 268; Kritsman, *Geroicheskii period,* 198; *EZh,* No. 101 (May 9, 1922), 2.
55. M. P. Iroshnikov in *Problemy gosudarstvennogo stroitel'stva v pervye gody sovetskoi vlasti: Sbornik Statei* (Leningrad, 1973), 54.
56. T. H. Rigby, *Lenin's Government: Sovnarkom, 1917-1922* (Cambridge, 1979), 62.
57. Iroshnikov in *Problemy gosudarstvennogo stroitel'stva,* 55.
58. Rigby, *Lenin's Government,* 51.
59. Berkman, *Bolshevik Myth,* 219-20.
60. Dewar, *Labour Policy,* 179-80.
61. Alfons Goldschmidt, *Moskau 1920* (Berlin, 1920), 62, 88.
62. *SUiR, 1917-1918,* No. 35 (May 18, 1918), Decree No. 467, pp. 436-37.
63. Lenin, *PSS,* XLV, 383.
64. Shliapnikov to Lenin, August 21, 1921, RTsKhIDNI, F. 2, op. 1, delo 24625.
65. Rigby, *Lenin's Government,* 149-56.
66. *Deviatyi S"ezd RKP(b): Protokoly* (Moscow, 1960), 411.
67. *Ibid.,* 177.
68. *Ibid.,* 417.
69. *Desiatyi S"ezd,* 813-15.
70. *Ibid.,* 240.
71. On this, see my *Social Democracy and the St. Petersburg Labor Movement, 1885-1897* (Cambridge, Mass., 1963).
72. *Rabochaia oppozitsiia* (limited, private edition). In English: *The Workers' Opposition in Russia* (London, n.d.).
73. *Desiatyi S"ezd,* 651-56.
74. *Ibid.,* 685-91.
75. *Ibid.,* 359-60, 362, 530.
76. *Ibid.,* 27-29.
77. *Ibid.,* 223-24; F. Dan, *Dva goda skitanii* (Berlin, 1922), 122.
78. *Odinadtsatyi S"ezd,* 37-38.
79. *Desiatyi S"ezd,* 530.
80. Cf. *RR,* 131-32.
81. *Desiatyi S"ezd,* 351-52.
82. *Ibid.,* 350.
83. See above, p. 373.
84. *Desiatyi S"ezd,* 71-76.
85. *Ibid.,* 361.
86. *Ibid.,* 571-76, 769.
87. Schapiro, *Origin of the Communist Autocracy,* 319-20.
88. Leon Trotsky, *The Revolution Betrayed* (New York, 1937), 96.
89. Isaac Deutscher, *The Prophet Unarmed: Trotsky, 1921-1929* (London, 1959), 115-16.
90. *Odinadtsatyi S"ezd,* 583-602, 46.
91. *Desiatyi S"ezd,* 778; *Odinadtsatyi S"ezd,* 583-97; *Dvenadtsatyi S"ezd RKP(b)* (Moscow, 1968), 729-59.
92. Vadim Rogovin, *Byla li al'ternativa?* (Moscow, 1992), 89.
93. S. Volin, *Deiatel'nost' Menshevikov v profsoiuzakh pri sovetskoi vlasti* (Inter-university Project on the History of the Menshevik Movement, No. 13, New York, 1982), 87.
94. V. V. Kosior in *Odinadtsatyi S"ezd,* 127; also Molotov, *ibid.,* 54-55.
95. Carr, *Interregnum,* 292-93; Isaac Deutscher, *Stalin* (New York, 1967), 258.
96. RTsKhIDNI, F. 558, op. 1, ed. khr. 4376.

97. G. A. Kamenev in *Revvoensovet Respubliki* (Moscow, 1991), 115. Cf. *IzvTsK*, No. 4/291 (April 1989), 161–68.
98. N. Petrenko, in *Minuvshee* (Paris), No. 2, 1986, 198.
99. RTsKhIDNI, F. 2, op. 1, ed. khr. 24760.
100. *Pravda*, No. 56 (March 14, 1923), 4.
101. *Desiatyi S"ezd*, 402.
102. *Odinadtsatyi S"ezd*, 430.
103. L. Trotskii, *Moia zhizn'*, II, (Berlin, 1930), 246.
104. Deutscher, *Prophet Unarmed*, 34.
105. *RevR*, No. 3 (February 1921), 7.
106. Iu. I. Korablev in *Revvoensovet* (Moscow, 1991), 51.
107. *RR*, 707–8.
108. RTsKhIDNI, F. 2, op. 2, delo 1164; *Dvenadtsatyi S"ezd*, 817.
109. Volkogonov, *Triumf*, I/1, 116.
110. N. Shteinberger in *VI*, No. 9 (1989), 175–76.
111. *Ibid.*
112. *Odinadtsatyi S"ezd*, 53, 59.
113. Lenin, *PSS*, XLV, 100–3, 114.
114. *LS*, XXIII, 228.
115. Volkogonov, *Triumf*, I/1, 136.
116. Deutscher, *Stalin*, 234. Cf.
117. *Odinadtsatyi S"ezd*, 49, 56.
118. Pethybridge, *One Step*, 155.
119. RTsKhIDNI, F. 76, op. 3, delo 253; dispatch dated July 6, 1922.
120. *Ibid.*, delo 270.
121. E. Preobrazhenskii in *Odinadtsatyi S"ezd*, 84–85; Lenin, *PSS*, XLV, 122.
122. *IzvTsK*, No. 4/315 (April 1991), 198; Carr, *Interregnum*, 290–91; Fainsod, *How Russia Is Ruled*, 186; Nikolai Vasetskii, *Likvidatsiia* (Moscow, 1989), 33.
123. RTsKhIDNI, F. 2, op. 1, delo 8492.
124. Deutscher, *Prophet Unarmed*, 73.
125. Lenin, *PSS*, XLV, 113–14.
126. Trotsky Archive, Houghton Library, Harvard University, T-746 and T-747, documents dated April 18 and 19, 1922, respectively; above, note 108.
127. Lenin, *PSS*, XLV, 180–82.
128. Trotskii, *Moia zhizn'*, II, 207–8.
129. *IzvTsK*, No. 12/299 (December 1989), 198.
130. *Ibid.*, No. 4/291 (1989), 185.
131. RTsKhIDNI, F. 2, op. 1, delo 24699.
132. Carr, *Interregnum*, 270.
133. Alliluyeva, *Twenty Letters*, 29–31; Volkogonov, *Triumf*, I/1, 191.
134. Max Eastman, *Since Lenin Died* (London, 1925), 18.
135. *IzvTsK*, No. 12/299 (December 1989), 198.
136. *TP*, II, 831.
137. Trotskii, *Moia zhizn'*, II, 212.
138. V. Naumov in *Kommunist*, No. 5 (1991), 36.
139. Lenin, *PSS*, XLV, 327.
140. Boris Souvarine, *Staline* (Paris, 1977), 269–70; L. B. Krasin in *Vospominaniia o V. I. Lenine*, II (Moscow, 1957), 570–75.
141. Lenin, *PSS*, LIV, 324, 325–26.
142. RTsKhIDNI, F. 5, op. 2, delo 27, list 88.
143. Lenin, *PSS*, XLV, 485.
144. L. Trotsky, *The Real Situation in Russia* (New York, 1928), 304–5; and *Moia zhizn'*, II, 215–17.
145. *Khronika*, XII, 542–43.

146. Maria Ulianova in *IzvTsK*, No. 6/317 (June 1991), 190.
147. Lenin, *PSS*, LIV, 327–28.
148. Ulianova in *IzvTsK*, No. 12/299 (December 1989), 198.
149. Lenin, *PSS*, LIV, 674–75.
150. *Ibid.*, XLV, 710.
151. Leon Trotskii in *Biulleten Oppozitsii*, No. 46 (December 1935), 4.
152. Lenin, *PSS*, XLV, 383–88.
153. *Pravda*, No. 16 (January 25, 1923), 1. Cf. Lenin, *PSS*, XLV, 387.
154. First published in *IzvTsK*, No. 11/298 (November 1989), 179–80.
155. *Dvenadtsatyi S"ezd*, 198n–199n.
156. Richard Pipes, *Formation of the Soviet Union*, revised ed. (Cambridge, Mass., 1964), 278.
157. V. P. Zatonskii in *Desiatyi S"ezd*, 203.
158. Pipes, *Formation*, 266–69.
159. *Ibid.*, 270; *IzvTsK*, No. 9/296 (September 1989), 191.
160. Stalin's proposal was first published in 1964: Lenin, *PSS*, XLV, 557–58. Further archival materials on the dispute over his "autonomization" proposal are in *IzvTsK*, No. 9/296 (September 1989), 191–218.
161. Lenin, *Sochineniia*, XXV, 624.
162. *IzvTsK*, No. 9/296 (September 1989), 196.
163. *Ibid.*, 199.
164. Lenin, *PSS*, XLV, 211–13. First published in 1959.
165. *Ibid.*, XLV, 558. Stalin's response: *TP*, II, 752–55.
166. Lenin, *PSS*, XLV, 559.
167. *Pravda*, No. 225/25,777 (August 12, 1988), 3.
168. Lenin, *PSS*, LIV, 299–300.
169. Pipes, *Formation*, 274–75.
170. RTsKhIDNI, F. 558, op. 1, ed. khr. 2446.
171. *VIKPSS*, No. 2 (1963), 74.
172. *Pravda*, No. 225/25,557 (August 12, 1988), 3.
173. V. P. Osipov in *KL*, No. 2/23 (1927), 243; Petrenko in *Minuvshee*, No. 2, 259–60.
174. Lenin, *PSS*, XLV, 376.
175. P. B. Struve, *Kriticheskie zametki k voprosu ob ekonomicheskom razvitii Rossii*, I (St. Petersburg, 1894), 288; Richard Pipes, *Struve: Liberal on the Left* (Cambridge, Mass., 1970), Chapter 6.
176. Egor Iakovlev in *MN*, No. 4/446 (January 22, 1989), 8; Genrikh Volkov in *Sovetskaia kul'tura*, No. 9/6,577 (January 21, 1989), 3.
177. Lenin, *PSS*, XLV, 344–46.
178. *Ibid.*, 346.
179. Egor Iakovlev in *MN*, No. 4/446 (January 22, 1989), 8–9.
180. Lenin, *PSS*, XLV, 477.
181. L. A. Fotieva in *VIKPSS*, No. 4 (1957), 162–63.
182. Lenin, *PSS*, LIV, 329.
183. Rogovin, *Byla li*, 75.
184. *IzvTsK*, No. 9/308 (September 1990), 151.
185. Lenin, *PSS*, LIV, 330.
186. *Pravda*, No. 53 (March 9, 1923), 1; Naumov in *Kommunist*, No. 5 (1991), 39; *IzvTsK*, No. 9 (September 1990), 152.
187. V. P. Osipov in *KL*, No. 2/23 (1927), 236–47; Petrenko, in *Minuvshee*, No. 2 (1986), 146; Naumov in *Kommunist*, No. 5 (1991), 39.
188. RTsKhIDNI, F. 2, op. 2, delo 1289 and 1290.
189. Petrenko in *Minuvshee*, No. 2, 279–84; Trotskii, *Moia zhizn'*, II, 251–52.
190. *IzvTsK*, No. 9 (September 1990), 149; *Pravda*, No. 225/25,577 (August 12, 1988), 3.
191. Naumov in *Kommunist*, No. 5 (1991), 39.
192. Trotskii, *Moia zhizn'*, II, 224–25.
193. *Ibid.*, II, 228–29.

194. *E.g., ibid.,* II, 217–18; and Deutscher, *Prophet Unarmed,* 93.
195. Max Eastman, *Since Lenin Died* (London, 1925), 17.
196. Deutscher, *Prophet Unarmed,* ix. See also *ibid.,* 91.
197. V. P. Danilov in *Ekonomika i Organizatsiia Promyshlennogo Proizvodstva (EKO)* (Novosibirsk), No. 1/187 (1990), 60.
198. RTsKhIDNI, F. 558, op. 1, ed. khr. 2518.
199. *Dvenadtsatyi S''ezd,* 181–82.
200. *Ibid.,* 479–95; Pipes, *Formation,* 289–93.
201. Trotskii, *Moia zhizn',* II, 241.
202. Deutscher, *Prophet Unarmed,* 106.
203. I. P. Trainin, *SSSR i natsional'naia problema* (Moscow, 1924), 27.
204. Trotskii, *Moia zhizn',* II, 230.
205. *IzvTsK,* No. 5/304 (May 1990), 165–73.
206. *Ibid.,* 165.
207. *Ibid.,* 170.
208. *Ibid.,* 173.
209. *Ibid.,* No. 6/305 (June 1990), 189–91.
210. *Ibid.,* No. 5/304 (May 1990), 178–79 and No. 7/306 (July 1990), 176–89.
211. *Ibid.,* No. 7/306 (July 1990), 177–79.
212. *Ibid.,* No. 10/309 (October 1990), 167–81.
213. *Ibid.,* 188–89.
214. Cited in Vasetskii, *Likvidatsiia,* 37.
215. *Pravda,* No. 281 (December 11, 1923), 4.
216. I. V. Stalin, *Sochineniia,* VI (Moscow, 1947), 16.
217. *Kommunisticheskaia Partiia Sovetskogo Soiuza v Rezoliutsiiakh i Resheniiakh . . .* 7th ed., I (Moscow, 1953), 778–85.
218. *Trinadtsatyi S''ezd RKP (b)* (Moscow, 1963), 158.
219. V. Bonch-Bruevich in *KN,* No. 1 (1925), 186–91.
220. RTsKhIDNI, F. 76, op. 3, delo 287.
221. Text in Volkogonov, *Trotskii,* II, 42.
222. Trotsky, *Stalin,* 381–82.
223. On this see Nina Tumarkin, *Lenin Lives!* (Cambridge, Mass., 1983), Chapter 6.
224. *Pravda,* No. 23 (January 30, 1924), 1.
225. Stalin, *Sochineniia,* VI, 46–51; originally in *Pravda,* No. 23 (January 30, 1924), 6.
226. The account that follows is based on Iurii Lopukhin in *Glasnost'* (Moscow), October 18, 1990, 6; and Tumarkin in *Lenin Lives!,* 182–89.

Reflections on the Russian Revolution

1. Paul Miliukov, *Russia To-day and To-morrow* (New York, 1922), 8–9.
2. On this, see William C. Fuller, Jr., *Strategy and Power in Russia, 1600–1914* (New York, 1992).
3. Marquis [A. de] Custine, *Russia* (London, 1854), 455.
4. Michael Rostovtseff in *NV,* No. 109/133 (July 5, 1918), 2.
5. *RR,* 484–85.
6. Lenin, *PSS,* XXXIV, 435–36.
7. Lev Trotskii, *Dnevniki i pis'ma* (Tenafly, N. J., 1986), 84.
8. L. Trotskii, *Istoriia russkoi revoliutsii,* II, Pt. 2 (Berlin, 1933), 319.
9. Jacques Barzun, *Darwin, Marx, Wagner: Critique of a Heritage* (Boston, 1941), 100–1.
10. *SV,* No. 6 (April 20, 1921), 6.
11. Paul Miliukov, *Bolshevism: An International Danger* (London, 1920), 5.
12. Cited in Jane Burbank, *Intelligentsia and Revolution* (New York and Oxford, 1986), 194.
13. On this subject, see my *Russia under the Old Regime* (London and New York, 1974).
14. *Ibid.,* 109.
15. *Ibid.,* Chapter 11.

16. Oleg Kalugin, *Vid s Liubianki* (Moscow, 1990), 35.
17. Pipes, *Russia under the Old Regime,* 305–10.
18. RTsKhIDNI, Fond 2, op. 1, delo 25609, list 9.
19. Iu. A. Poliakov, *Sovetskaia strana posle okonchaniia grazhdanskoi voiny* (Moscow, 1986), 94.
20. S. G. Strumilin, *Problemy ekonomiki truda* (Moscow, 1957), 39.
21. Aristotle, *Nicomachaean Ethics,* IV, 5.
22. Benito Mussolini, *Opera Omnia,* XV (Florence, 1954), 93.
23. *NYT,* June 18, 1992, p. A18.
24. *NZh,* No. 177/171 (November 10, 1917), in H. Ermolaev, ed., Maxim Gorky, *Untimely Thoughts* (New York, 1968), 89.
25. Cited in *Frankfurter Allgemeine Zeitung,* No. 291 (December 24, 1976), Section VI, 1.
26. Hippolyte Taine, *The French Revolution,* II (New York, 1881), Preface, p. v.

SELECTED BIBLIOGRAPHY

The literature on Russia in 1919–1924 is rich and often of high quality, although with the opening of Russian archives much of it may have to be revised. Below is a selection of secondary works that I have found particularly instructive in my work.

The Civil War

While a definitive history of the Russian Civil War remains to be written, the following impressed me as informative: Volume 2 of W. H. Chamberlin's *The Russian Revolution* (New York and London, 1935) and Evan Mawdsley's *The Russian Civil War* (London and Boston, 1987). N. Kakurin, *Kak srazhalas' revoliutsiia*, 2 vols., (Moscow, 1925), is a narrowly military account based on Red Army archives. Lev Trotskii, *Kak vooruzhalas' revoliutsiia*, 3 vols. (Moscow, 1923–25), is a collection of Trotsky's wartime directives.

On the anti-Bolshevik forces, George Stewart's *The White Armies of Russia* (New York, 1933) does a creditable job. Indispensable are the memoirs of General A. Denikin, *Ocherki russkoi smuty*, Vols. 3–5 (Berlin, 1924–1925). The story of Kolchak is told by S. P. Melgunov, *Tragediia Admirala Kolchaka* (Belgrade, 1930–31; repr. New York, 1963) and Peter Fleming, *The Fate of Admiral Kolchak* (New York, 1963).

On the Ukrainian pogroms in 1918–20, there is I. B. Shekhtman, *Pogromy Dobrovol'cheskoi Armii na Ukraine* (Berlin, 1932).

For particulars of the complex diplomatic relations involving Russia, Red and White, and the foreign powers during and after the Civil War (other than Germany) the reader can consult John M. Thompson, *Russia, Bolshevism, and the Versailles Peace* (Princeton, N. J., 1966), Richard H. Ullman, *Britain and the Russian Civil War* (Princeton, 1968), and Piotr S. Wandycz, *Soviet-Polish Relations, 1917–1920* (Cambridge, Mass., 1969).

The repercussions of the Civil War in the rural areas is the subject of Orlando Figes's *Peasant Russia, Civil War* (Oxford, 1989). Iu. A. Poliakov, *Sovetskaia strana posle okonchaniia grazhdanskoi voiny* (Moscow, 1986) is a Communist account of the effects of the Civil War on Russia and her inhabitants.

The Red Empire

A general history of the disintegration of the Russian Empire and its reconquest and reintegration by the Communists is Richard Pipes, *The Formation of the Soviet Union*, rev. ed. (Cambridge, Mass., 1964).

Communism for Export

A good account of the Comintern is by an ex-member, Franz Borkenau, *World Communism: A History of the Communist International* (Ann Arbor, Mich., 1962). Julius Braunthal, *History of the International*, II (London, New York, and Washington, 1967), is written from a socialist perspective. Angelica Balabanoff's *Impressions of Lenin* (Ann Arbor, Mich., 1964) are by an admiring but not uncritical Secretary of the Comintern.

Soviet Russia's external relations during this period are described by Alfred L. P. Dennis, *The Foreign Policies of Soviet Russia* (London and New York, 1924). Her relations with Germany are treated in Gerald Freund, *Unholy Alliance* (New York, 1957), and Rolf-Dieter Müller, *Das Tor zur Weltmacht* (Boppard am Rhein, 1984). Russo-British relations in 1920 and after are dealt with in Richard Ullman's *The Anglo-Soviet Accord* (Princeton, N.J., 1972).

Norman Davies deals with the Russo-Polish war of 1920 in *White Eagle, Red Star* (London, 1972).

Pro-Communist foreign intellectuals are dissected in David Caute's *The Fellow-travellers*, rev. ed. (New Haven and London, 1988).

Communism, Fascism, National Socialism

There is no book that deals specifically with the influence of Bolshevism on right-wing movements. Of the extensive literature on totalitarianism, I found the following particularly informative: Carl J. Friedrich, *Totalitarianism* (Cambridge, Mass., 1954), and, with Zbigniew K. Brzezinski, *Totalitarian Dictatorship and Autocracy* (Cambridge, Mass., 1956). Hans Buchheim, *Totalitarian Rule* (Middletown, Conn., 1968); a brilliant, succinct analysis. Hermann Rausch-ning, *Germany's Revolution of Destruction* (London, 1939), also published as *The Revolution of Nihilism* (New York, 1939), is by an early Hitler confidant.

Culture as Propaganda

The single most illuminating insight into early Communist cultural policies is René Fülöp-Miller's *Geist und Gesicht des Bolschewismus* (Zurich, 1926). The English condensation, *Mind and Face of Bolshevism* (London and New York, 1927) conveys little of the original's richness.

A good account of every aspect of Soviet cultural policies can be found in Oskar Anweiler and Karl-Heinz Ruffmann, eds., *Kulturpolitik der Sowjetunion* (Stuttgart, 1973). The central administrative entity directing cultural life is described in Sheila Fitzpatrick's *The Commissariat of Enlightenment* (London and Cambridge, Mass., 1970).

The best history of Soviet educational policies is Oskar Anweiler's *Geschichte der Schule und Pädagogik in Russland vom Ende des Zarenreiches bis zum Beginn der Stalin Ära* (Heidelberg, 1964).

The Assault on the Church

Lev Regelson, *Tragediia russkoi tserkvi, 1917–1945* (Paris, 1977), is a collection of documents. Relations between the new regime and Orthodoxy are treated by John S. Curtiss in *The Russian Church and the Soviet State* (Boston, 1953). B. V. Titlinov, *Tserkov' vo vremia revoliutsii* (Petrograd, 1924), is a Communist account.

Nora Levin, *The Jews in the Soviet Union since 1917*, 2 vols. (New York and London, 1988), is well-informed and intelligent. Zvi Gitelman, *Jewish Nationality and Soviet Politics* (Princeton, 1972), is a basic study.

On Communist policies toward the Muslims, see Alexandre Bennigsen and Chantal Lemercier-Quelquejay, *Islam in the Soviet Union* (London, New York, and Washington, 1967).

NEP: The False Thermidor

No authoritative history of the New Economic Policy exists. Much information can be found in Volume 2 of E. H. Carr's *The Bolshevik Revolution* (London and New York, 1952). Roger Pethybridge, *One Step Backwards, Two Steps Forward* (Oxford, 1990), studies its im-plementation on the local level. Simon Liberman, *Building Lenin's Russia* (Chicago, 1945), recounts fascinating experiences of a Menshevik expert in Communist service.

On the peasant revolt against Communist rule in 1920–21, the literature is still limited by the paucity of archival sources. Oliver H. Radkey, *The Unknown Civil War in Soviet Russia* (Stanford, 1976), and Mikhail Frenkin, *Tragediia krest'ianskikh vosstanii v Rossii, 1918–1921 gg.* ([Jerusalem], 1987), give the fullest accounts. I. Ia. Trifonov, *Klassy i klassovaia bor'ba v*

SSR v nachale NEPa, 2 vols. (Leningrad, 1964), is the only Communist work with serious information on the subject. A. Okninskii, *Dva goda sredi krest'ian* (Riga, 1936), is unique in providing a firsthand account of peasant reactions.

On the sailor mutiny, there is Paul Avrich, *Kronstadt, 1921* (New York and London, 1970).

The Volga famine of 1921 also awaits its historian. For the time being, the best is the account of a member of Hoover's Relief Administration, H. H. Fisher, *The Famine in Soviet Russia* (New York, 1927).

The Crisis of the New Regime

As documents are released from Russian archives, most of the secondary literature on Soviet politics of 1921–24 must be regarded as obsolete. A large number of previously unpublished documents appeared in *Izvestiia TsK* when it resumed publication in the late 1980s.

The internal conflicts are described in Merle Fainsod, *How Russia Is Ruled,* rev. ed. (London and Cambridge, Mass., 1963); Leonard Schapiro, *The Origin of the Communist Autocracy* (London and Cambridge, Mass., 1977); E. H. Carr, *The Interregnum, 1923–1924* (London and New York, 1954); and Vadim Rogovin, *Byla li al'ternativa?* (Moscow, 1992). Robert Daniels, *The Conscience of the Revolution* (London and Cambridge, Mass., 1960), discusses the opposition groups within the Party. T. H. Rigby, *Lenin's Government: Sovnarkom, 1917–1922* (Cambridge, 1979), traces the evolution of state institutions. Soviet treatment of workers and trade unions is the subject of Margaret Dewar's *Labour Policy in the USSR, 1917–1928* (London and New York, 1956).

In addition, much on intraparty conflicts is to be found in the biographies of the chief protagonists. Isaac Deutscher's *The Prophet Unarmed: Trotsky, 1921–1929* (London, 1959), although very readable, is marred by uncritical adulation of its protagonist and careless use of sources. It is somewhat balanced by Dmitrii Volkogonov's *Trotskii,* 2 vols. (Moscow, 1992). Trotsky's autobiography, *My Life,* 2 vols. (London and New York, 1930), is full of interest.

On Stalin's rise to power there are Boris Souvarine's *Staline* (Paris, rev. ed., 1985) and Dmitrii Volkogonov's *Stalin* (London and New York, 1991), the latter the first to draw on archival sources.

ARCHIVAL SOURCES

Russkii Tsentr Khraneniia i Izucheniia Dokumentov Noveishei Istorii (RTsKhIDNI), Moscow (previously: Central Party Archive)
Fond 2
opis 1: Lenin's published and recently declassified documents
opis 2: Lenin's unpublished documents
Fond 5: Lenin's Secretariat
Fond 17: The Central Committee of the Communist Party
Fond 64: The Caucasian Bureau of the Central Committee
Fond 76: F. E. Dzerzhinskii
Fond 85: G. K. Ordzhonikidze
Fond 89: E. M. Iaroslavskii
Fond 489: Second Congress of the Comintern
Fond 495: The Executive Committee of the Comintern (IKKI)
Fond 558: I. V. Stalin
Harvard University, Houghton Library
Trotsky Archive (bMS Russian 13)
Georgian Archive (bMS Georgian 2)
Bakhmeteff Archive, Rare Book and Manuscript Library, Columbia University
Denikin Papers
Aleksei Brusilov Collection
Panina Papers

In the text of the book, many Russian names have been Anglicized. Here, save for a few (e.g., Tolstoy and Trotsky) that have entered the English vocabulary, they are given in their original spelling. Since Russian stressing practices follow no obvious rules, proper names frequently referred to in the book are provided with a stress; thus, "Kérensky" should be accented on the first syllable, Alekséev on the third syllable. The letter "ë" is pronounced "yo" and stressed.

Page numbers in italics indicate illustrations.

A Note About the Author

Richard Pipes, Baird Professor of History at Harvard University, is the author of numerous books and essays on Russia, past and present. His most recent book is *The Russian Revolution* (1991). In 1981–82 he served as President Reagan's National Security Council adviser on Soviet and East European affairs. He lives in Cambridge, Massachusetts.